A SHORT HISTORY

OF

EDUCATIONAL IDEAS

A SHORT HISTORY

OF

EDUCATIONAL IDEAS

BY

S. J. CURTIS, M.A., Ph.D.

LATE READER IN EDUCATION IN THE UNIVERSITY OF LEEDS

AND

M. E. A. BOULTWOOD, M.A.

SENIOR LECTURER IN EDUCATION IN THE UNIVERSITY OF LEEDS

With a Foreword by SIR CHARLES MORRIS, M.A., LL.D., D.LITT.
Formerly Vice-Chancellor of the University of Leeds

UNIVERSITY TUTORIAL PRESS LTD

9-10 GREAT SUTTON STREET, LONDON, E.C.1

Published 1953
Reprinted 1954
Second Edition 1956, *reprinted* 1958
Third Edition 1961, *reprinted* 1963
Reprinted with minor alterations 1964
Fourth Edition 1965, *reprinted* 1966, 1970

A/370.1

ISBN: 0 7231 0467 0

PRINTED IN GREAT BRITAIN BY UNIVERSITY TUTORIAL PRESS LTD, FOXTON
NEAR CAMBRIDGE

FOREWORD

By Sir CHARLES MORRIS, M.A., LL.D., D.Litt., Formerly Vice-Chancellor of the University of Leeds

A BOOK about the educational ideas of the past is timely. We suffer, I think, in our day from not giving enough attention to ideas, and actions tend to spring from tactical considerations rather than to be based upon fundamental thinking.

We suffered perhaps, or at least we tend now to think we suffered, from too much thinking and too little willing and doing between the wars. We saw the good in all things and in all men and we were too mellow in our judgments, and also perhaps too nostalgic for perfection, to take upon ourselves any pregnant decisions. We allowed the obvious next step to wait upon prolonged consideration of whether there might not be something better, something free from all possible objection. Now we seem driven, not altogether deliberately or consciously perhaps, not to make that particular mistake again.

We constantly remind ourselves of "facts" conscientiously established by "science". Politics is concerned with the possible and not with what we should like in heaven. The moral progress of the individual must take account of human nature; and advance at one front will be offset, we may rely upon it, by a retreat or even a catastrophe at another. Education must carefully appreciate the situation, before it plans an action; the forces of social background have their own ineluctable laws which cannot be cheated, and even for the individual at the ultimate level there is always Freud in the background. We tend therefore to think only of techniques and to hand over the command to the technician.

All this has its very good points. We have gained greatly from the triumphs of technique in the past generation or two. We have learned much about working with the nature of the child rather than against it; and many benefits and conveniences have come to us from the skill and energy which have been devoted to subject analysis. But it has its faults also. Experience seems to suggest that really vigorous study of techniques does not go well with a really active care for first principles and fundamental aims. At a time when there is so much which needs doing we tend to tell ourselves that basic questions of philosophy are very difficult and would take a long time to answer; and that *whatever* the answer to them may ultimately prove to be, the next few steps are obvious enough in any case and the immediate task is to see that they are well and truly taken. Real thinking can be put off to another day—some day.

I sometimes think that in our generation we have swallowed this faith hook, line, and sinker. It may be that there comes a point for every generation, as for every man, when it is determined whether for the rest of its time it will be practically minded or whether it will really think. No doubt the practical man sometimes has a thought or a fancy or two in a casual hour; and the philosopher occasionally takes a decision and performs an action. But in the last resort, it may be, the man and the generation find themselves each committed to the one habit of mind or to the other; and the way of life will bear the marks of this commitment right through.

So it seems to me that this book is timely. The writers are forcing no doctrine upon us, explicit or implied. They are giving us a generous opportunity to remind ourselves, or to learn for the first time, about the ideas of the great thinkers of the past, and of some not so great but still for various reasons worthy of consideration in our day. They show wide learning, and great imagination and sympathy in making the stranger ideas intelligible to us. Their task has involved much labour and patience, but they can have the satisfaction of knowing that it was very well chosen.

PREFACE TO THE SECOND EDITION

EDUCATION has its phases and fashions. During the past few decades, teaching methods and child study have almost kept pace with the dramatic expansion of psychology, but in this post-war period there are indications of a reversion of interest towards the theory and philosophy of education, the study of which engaged the attention of many educators during the early years of the century.

The new spate of argument on the content of teacher training courses is but a symptom of the change of attitude. There is a growing realisation of the need for a fresh examination and assessment of the aims of education—a task which can only be fruitful if it be attempted in the light of the experience and ideas inherited from the past. At the same time, our thinking should take into account the present as well as the past, the new as well as the old.

In this volume we have presented the creative ideas, which from the earliest times to the present day, have shaped men's conceptions of the aims and meaning of the educational process. The biographical approach was deliberately selected to make the reader aware of the dangers of over-generalisation in educational thinking, and the mis-application of past ideas to present circumstances. Every educational thinker is to a great extent a creature of his age and environment. In addition, his own individual personality and attitude have to be considered. All our thinkers developed ideas which were related to transitory conditions alone but, on the other hand, all formulated certain ideas which appear to us as timeless and universal.

We have made no attempt to formulate a set of conclusions which conform to a particular school of philosophical thought. We are two individuals who view problems from different standpoints and our contributions are made in the light of our own preferences. It is for the reader himself to form his own conclusions, and the Suggestions for Further Reading have been drawn up with this end in view.

It was inevitable that a number of philosophers and educationalists should either have been omitted or given brief attention in the original edition of this book. Experience in using it with post-graduate students has shown the need for the inclusion of other thinkers, and in some cases a rearrangement of the text in regard to those already mentioned. As a consequence the following amendments and additions have been made.

A fuller treatment has been accorded to French Renaissance writers, Rabelais, and Montaigne, and more attention has been given to eighteenth-century educational thinkers in Britain. In Chapter XV the treatment of the Utilitarian contribution has been revised to remove certain ambiguities. Chapter XVII now consists of the original section on John Dewey, slightly amplified. The section on Montessori and other European experiments is now augmented and forms an additional chapter. The account of educational writers of the present century has been enlarged by the addition of the views of Gentile, Croce, and Bergson. Finally, minor corrections and additions have been made throughout.

The authors hope that the new edition will meet the needs which have been expressed by different readers.

NOTE TO THE FOURTH EDITION

This edition has been enlarged by a chapter which deals with those Existentialists and Personalists who have contributed to the theory of education. A short account of Logical Positivism is included and is followed by a brief account of education in the U.S.S.R., together with suggestions for further reading in these topics. Readers have kindly pointed out a few minor printing errors in the text and index of the previous edition and these have been corrected.

S. J. C.
M. E. A. B.

CONTENTS

ix

A SHORT HISTORY OF EDUCATIONAL IDEAS

CHAPTER I

GREEK IDEAS ABOUT EDUCATION—PLATO

Chronologically, no doubt, one should commence the study of educational ideas with an account of the views professed and taught by Socrates and Plato, but the pursuit of this method raises a considerable number of problems. Plato's educational theory emerges from his philosophical thinking. It is intimately connected with his views about the nature of the state and the end which the citizen should strive to attain. Moreover, the state in question was the Greek city state and the citizens members of that small group of freemen in whose hands the conduct of civic policy rested. Thus to estimate rightly the full significance of Plato's educational theory, one should first study the development of his philosophical doctrines so that what he has to say on the subject of education will be revealed in its natural setting. Every thinker is to a certain extent conditioned by the age in which he lives and this is true of even the greatest. In numerous ways the educational theory of Plato soars beyond the narrow limits set by the educational practice of his day, but one must always keep in mind that the principles he enunciated took their point of departure from what was actually being carried out in such states as Athens and Sparta during his own lifetime. Hence one should view Plato's contributions to educational theory in the light of the Greek way of life, of the institutions developed by the Greek peoples, and of the outlook and methods of the Hellenic schools.

Such a programme is obviously impossible within one short chapter of a work of this type and therefore the only practicable course is to survey Plato's educational theory, detached as far as it may be, from the main current of his philosophy. In defence of this plan it may perhaps be urged that there are many excellent works dealing with different aspects of the philosophy of Plato, or with the Greek view of life, which are accessible to the student and some of the most useful of these are indicated in the bibliography. Even more essential is the study of Plato's own writings and the student is advised at every turn to consult such a translation of the *Dialogues* as that of Jowett.

Socrates, so far, has not been considered. It is well known that he never put his thoughts into writing. He appears as a major character in most of the Platonic Dialogues but one is naturally prompted to ask how far the opinions attributed to him are those of the historic Socrates. On the whole, writers of the nineteenth century in stressing Plato's excellence as a dramatic artist, took the view that the character of Socrates served merely as a convenient mouthpiece for the expression of Plato's own beliefs. More recently, such scholars as J. Burnet and A. E. Taylor have developed the theory that the Socrates of the earlier dialogues is the historic Socrates. Eventually Plato's thought outstripped anything that can justifiably be attributed to Socrates, and in the later dialogues, Socrates either takes a more subordinate position or does not appear at all. The dividing line is assumed to be that of the middle books of the *Republic* in which Plato begins to develop a line of thought which passes beyond anything that may be attributed to Socrates. There is no space to consider the arguments for and against this theory but it may be stated, that without committing themselves to a belief in it, the writers have adopted as a working hypothesis the point of view held by Burnet and Taylor. One advantage of this arrangement is that the separate consideration of Socrates can be eliminated.

It is difficult to say which personal experiences of Plato had most to do with the shaping of his outlook on life but one may hazard that prominent amongst them must have been the trial and death of Socrates, the founding of the Academy, and the unsuccessful attempt of Plato to realise his ideals in the person of Dionysius II of Syracuse. The first was still the most influential when Plato was writing the earlier portion of the *Republic* in which the preliminary education of the guardians is discussed. As his thoughts turned more and more to the foundation of the Academy and his projected programme of studies, Plato's plan for the higher education of the guardians as described in the latter part of the *Republic* took shape. Finally, when his experience of Dionysius convinced him, that at any rate for the present, his ideals could not be realised amongst men, Plato set out in the *Laws* to draw a picture of a less perfect state and the type of education which was suited to it.

One striking feature about the writings of Plato is that they present no finished cut and dried system of philosophy or education. You may look for one but you will not find it. Plato was not a system maker. He was convinced that the truth about the things which really matter cannot be obtained ready made. It comes as a result of thought and discussion. One starts with opinions that seem to be acceptable but when they are submitted to criticism by one's fellow searchers after truth, the inadequacy of them becomes apparent and it is necessary to modify, supplement, or restate them. Unsatisfactory ideas are rejected and as a result of discussion and criticism, the mind gradually moves forward in its quest for truth. Each new idea must be thoroughly tested and hammered out, as it were, before it can be accepted and when it has been justified, it is no longer an opinion taken over from others but a conviction which has become part and parcel of the thinker's own self.

This explains why the dialogue form commended itself to Plato. It was not only in line with the traditions of the schools but it could lay before us the actual progress of thought, a forward movement activated in part by the thinker himself, in part through the impact of other minds upon him. All through his life Plato evinced a decided mistrust of the written word, especially of the formal philosophical treatise. His own teaching in the Academy was purely oral. Aristotle speaks of his "unwritten dogmas" and this phrase has generally been taken to mean that Plato never wrote his lectures. Some of his hearers took notes of them and even published accounts of his most famous lecture on the Good. This was entirely foreign to Plato's mind and in the Seventh *Epistle*, which is now generally recognised as genuine, he set forth his own view in most unmistakable terms. He wrote, "There exists no writing of mine on this subject, nor ever shall. It is not capable of expression like the other sciences. It is only after long intercourse and a common life devoted to the subject, that a light is suddenly kindled, as though by a leaping flame, and reaching the soul, it thereafter feeds itself". (*Ep.* vii, 341c.)

In the *Phaedrus* (274b—278e), Plato asserts that discussion is the only sure way of attaining truth. Socrates introduces a myth, which Phaedrus claims has been invented for the occasion, to illustrate how writing was introduced. In ancient Egypt there was a god named Theuth who invented the art of writing and recommended it to Ammon who was king in the city of Thebes. Theuth tried to persuade the king to adopt the art of letters on the ground that it would improve the memories of the Egyptians and make them wiser. Ammon was not convinced and retorted that Theuth was claiming for his invention a quality that it did not possess. Instead of improving the memories of men, written records tend to make them forget. They trust to the written characters and neglect the use of memory. They think that they know a great many things but in reality they have learnt nothing. The book is like a picture. The artist's figures may seem to be alive, but if they are questioned, they cannot answer. In a similar way, if you question a book about its meaning, you will obtain no reply. It is only the living voice of the author that can explain his meaning. Once a thing has been written down, it is liable to get into the hands of unintelligent folk who are likely to misunderstand it.

Although in many of his dialogues, Plato makes numerous references to education, the most complete expression of his views is to be found in the *Republic* and the *Laws*. The opening book of the *Republic* creates the impression that it has little to do with the subject. It professes to seek the answer to the question, What is Justice ? Cephalus, the old man who has held a reputation for goodness and justice throughout his life is unable to answer. His son, Polemarchus, a well-meaning young man but who has little experience of life and has therefore taken his opinions at second hand from the poets, follows Simonides by defining justice as giving each man what is due to him. Socrates has no difficulty in showing the unsatisfactory nature of this statement, but in the midst of the argument he is interrupted by the Sophist, Thrasymachus, who loudly asserts that justice is the interest of the stronger.[1] Thrasy-

---

[1] The early philosophers of the Ionian school in seeking φύσις, the fundamental reality of the universe had given answers in terms of materialism. Even their successors could not free themselves from this taint and although Anaxagoras had introduced the idea of mind (νοῦς) and seemed, as Aristotle remarked, "like a sober man in contrast with the random talk of his predecessors" (*Metaphysics*, 984b), he made little use of the conception. For Plato's criticism of Anaxagoras see *Phaedo* (98b). By the middle of the fifth century B.C. the attempts of a materialistic science to explain the world had broken down and men's interests turned to what one may call human problems, in particular, the problem of knowledge and conduct. This was the period when the Sophists arose.

The Sophists were professional teachers who claimed that they were able to teach goodness (ἀρετή), by which they meant the power to direct families and states aright. They demanded fees for their tuition and this savoured of professionalism to which the aristocratic Athenian at once took objection. Athens at this time was a democracy and the Sophists claimed that they could instruct the wealthy young man who came from an aristocratic family

machus, blusteringly overstates his case and falls an easy prey to Socrates. He is silenced for a time and then opens up a new line of argument by appealing to the facts of contemporary Greek city life. Certainly, injustice when committed by the petty sneak-thief does not pay; he is quickly discovered and punished. Injustice, however, when practised on the grand scale is altogether another matter. It not only succeeds but brings ample profit to the Napoleon or Hitler of crime; in fact, what is usually considered as injustice becomes justice if carried out on a sufficiently large scale. The just man is the weak man who is the victim of the stronger and utterly unscrupulous personality.

Once again, Socrates is able to refute Thrasymachus who departs discomforted, but there are two characters of the dialogue who are not at all satisfied with the conclusions reached by the discussion. They are Plato's brothers, Glaucon and Adeimantus, who would like to believe that the practice of justice is the right rule in life but feel that they are unable to produce adequate answers to the contrary assertions which they hear at every hand on every day of their lives.

Book I of the *Republic* is the classical example of the methods of the historic Socrates. Aristotle tells us that "two things may be fairly ascribed to Socrates—inductive arguments and universal definition, both of which are concerned with the starting-point of science".[1] Dr Boyd describes the procedure of Socrates as follows: "Socrates sought to make men define to themselves what they meant in common life when they spoke of actions as just or unjust, etc. First of all, he would get the inquirer to attempt a definition. What is justice? The answer probably takes the form of a list of just acts. But Socrates wants more than this. What is it that makes an act just? Then under the guidance of leading questions, another attempt is made at definition. Socrates shows its inadequacy. Another definition is constructed to meet the objections, again to be criticised, and again reconstructed. So the process goes on till both

---

how to succeed in a democratic state. In particular, how he could get off when he was brought before the law-courts. In practice their instruction emphasised the arts of rhetoric and disputation. This explains why Plato termed them paid huntsmen of rich young men and Aristotle defined them as men who made a fortune out of apparent wisdom. (See Plato-*Soph.* 223b and Aristotle-*Soph. El.* 165a.) Plato did not intend to attack the more prominent Sophists; in fact he held such men as Protagoras in great respect.

[1] *Metaphysics,* 1078b. 28-31.

Socrates and the learner are satisfied, and the definition is pronounced complete".[1]

To return to Glaucon and Adeimantus. The brothers make the following request to Socrates. Supposing they state in another form and as convincingly as possible the arguments of the Sophists, can Socrates lead them to a decisive answer ? Glaucon and Adeimantus represent the intelligent, thoughtful, and earnest seekers after truth. They are disciples of Socrates who not only understand what he has to say but they can materially contribute to the course of the argument by advancing pertinent criticisms of his statements. When they argue that it is more important to acquire a reputation for justice than actually to be just, Socrates introduces a new factor into the discussion by relegating for the time being the discussion of the problem of justice as it concerns the individual. Justice is most clearly seen in the social and political relations of men; writ small in the individual, it is writ large in the state. It may be an easier task to discover the meaning of justice in the community at large and when this has been accomplished, it may be that what justice in the individual involves will stand out all the more clearly.

Socrates begins this new line of thought by tracing the origin and development of the community. One can fairly ascribe the beginnings of organised society to the need for providing shelter, food, and clothing, in fact, to the satisfaction of men's material needs. At this level the community will consist of a band of mutually helpful husbandmen, artisans, and merchants. Glaucon objects that a state of this kind will be a community of swine rather than of human beings. Socrates admits the justice of this contention and proceeds to sketch a more complex type of community, in which the luxuries, and refinements necessary to a highly civilised life, have been added. There will not only be those whose job it is to supply the material necessities and luxuries of civilisation but the citizens of a more highly developed state need recreation, and amusement, and therefore it will be necessary to cater for their minds as well as for their bodies. There will be a corresponding development in the arts and now our city will include artists, poets, musicians, actors, and dancers. A more luxurious standard of living will have an effect upon the health of the community. Hence

---

[1] W. Boyd, *An Introduction to the Republic of Plato*, p. 14, George Allen and Unwin, reprint, 1922.

there will be a demand for doctors. The net result of this development will be that the territories of the original city will become insufficient to support the increased number of inhabitants and the state will be forced to expand and, in so doing, will come into collision with its neighbours. This calls attention to a new element in the community. Socrates envisages the formation of a standing army. It will be no mere citizen militia but a highly trained body of men and, to show what he has in mind, he deliberately chooses the name auxiliaries (ἐπίκουροι), the technical term which was used to describe the professional soldiers who formed the personal guard of monarchs.

So far, two classes of people have been discovered within the state—the ordinary citizens who are concerned with supplying the needs of a civilised life, and a military class from whom the actual rulers or guardians will be selected. In the *Republic*, Plato has nothing to say about the education of the "lower orders", though in the *Laws*, he makes some attempt to supply the omission. It was not merely that Plato as a member of a noble family was biased in favour of an aristocracy, but also, like all free-born Greeks, he tended to take the view that manual labour, trade, and even *professionalism* rendered the individual unsuited to take his part in war or politics. It is essential to realise that Plato is not suggesting a system of castes. The division into classes rests upon merit and ability, not upon the accident of birth. Those who show themselves unfitted to continue in the class in which they were born, will be degraded to a lower class and members of the latter may likewise be raised to higher estate. In fact, he denies any suggestion of a caste system in his famous myth (*Republic*, 415). Some are born with gold in their composition; others are made of silver, and again, others of brass and iron. They are destined to become respectively, the rulers, auxiliaries, and the ordinary citizens of the state. The hereditary principle is by no means absolute. Parents who are guardians or auxiliaries may produce offspring with a mixture of brass and iron and vice versa. In short, Plato recognised that heredity is not the only factor which counts; the other is what the child actually becomes and this is determined very largely by environment of which education must be regarded as the most important part. Special attention, therefore, must be given to the early education of those from whom the guardians will be chosen. Plato, therefore, describes at some length, a programme of training which is designed to develop the latent talents of the possible rulers.

Before considering the early education of the guardians, it will be necessary to clear up one important point. Some commentators have identified the lowest class in the state with the "working class" of a modern industrial community. Plato's division of the state into classes is designed to emphasise that there are different kinds of social service which the citizens perform. Since the activity of ruling is distinct from that of fighting, the guardians are divided into the older and more experienced men who have proved themselves fit to bear rule, the guardians proper, and the younger men whose duty it is to ward off enemy attacks and maintain law and order in the community. The lowest class in the state undoubtedly includes wage earners but it also contains shopkeepers, merchants, employers of labour, professional men, and what we should now call men of independent means. In fact it is composed of all those who are not actually engaged in ruling or defending the state.

The temptation to discuss the specific virtues of the three classes of the community, temperance, courage, and wisdom, and to show how the fourth cardinal virtue, that of justice, emerges from the harmonious relations between the classes, would, if indulged, carry us beyond the limits imposed by one short chapter. In the same way, justice in the individual, consisting in the unity and harmony of the rational, spirited, and the appetitive elements of the soul, cannot be discussed here. This extremely sketchy summary of the early part of the *Republic* is only intended to serve as an introduction to Plato's theory of education.

Plato is quite definite in his view about the aim of education. He believes that education means a great deal more than merely imparting information. It involves the redirection of the whole personality; in modern terms, education is equivalent to conversion, the turning of the eyes of the soul towards the light which hitherto has been unperceived. This is stated emphatically: "Our present argument shews us that there is a faculty residing in the soul of each person, and an instrument enabling each of us to learn; and that, just as we might suppose it to be impossible to turn the eye round from darkness to light without turning the whole body, so must this faculty or this instrument, be wheeled round, in company from the perishing world, until it be enabled to endure the contemplation of the real world, and the brightest part thereof, which, according to us, is the Form of the Good. Hence, this very process of revolution must give rise to an art, teaching in what way the change will most easily and most effectually be brought about. Its object will not be to generate in the person the power of seeing. On the contrary, it assumes that he possesses it, though he is turned in a wrong direction, and does not look towards the right quarter; and its aim is to remedy this defect".[1]

This redirection of the soul must be achieved by turning it towards the right objects, and this can be accomplished because there is something in the nature of soul to assist our efforts. It is of the very essence of the soul to be imitative. Surround it with the right kind of environment and it will begin to assimilate itself. The main problem of education is to discover how to provide the individual with the most suitable kind of environment. Hence, in Plato's programme for the elementary education of the guardians, one will look in vain for an account of teaching methods. The emphasis is upon placing the individual in the midst of those things which are like what we desire him to become. The first step will be to see that the individual has the right ideas about the gods whom he worships and the great men whom he should reverence and admire. Later, we shall see that the same thought occupies Plato's mind when he speaks about the effects upon the soul which are the consequence of the contemplation of beauty and of education in the sciences.

The content of the early training given to the guardians is based upon Plato's conception of the nature of the soul. Since it is a living, developing entity, at one stage of its growth it will be more susceptible to certain agencies and media than at others. In the early stage it is reached through the imagination and the emotions and therefore the aim of education during this period will be to stimulate the love of the beautiful in all its varied appearances. At a later stage, when the reasoning powers have developed, education will have as its object the love and acquisition of truth, and at the highest stage, the purpose of the educator will be to bring the soul to a knowledge of the Good.

The instruments by which the early training is to be effected are music ($\mu o \upsilon \sigma \iota \kappa \acute{\eta}$) and gymnastic ($\gamma \upsilon \mu \nu \alpha \sigma \tau \iota \kappa \acute{\eta}$). Plato accepted these from the practice current in the schools of his age but he also was aware of the common faults of his countrymen. In Sparta,

---

[1] *Republic,* 518b.

where the emphasis was upon military training, the young men tended to grow up strong and hardy but rough and uncultured. In contrast, the Athenians concentrated upon intellectual and cultural activities with the result that they neglected self-discipline and stability of character. Hence there is much justice in the comment of some writers that the ideal state pictured in the *Republic* is a combination of all the most worthy features of Spartan discipline and Athenian culture.

Plato believed that one can hardly make too early a start in the business of education. He realised that in childhood, first impressions occupy a privileged place. Hence Socrates says, "In every work the beginning is the most important part, especially in dealing with anything young and tender; for that is the time when any impression which one may desire to communicate, is most easily stamped and taken".[1] Elementary education begins with a training in music, but as the time draws near when the youth will have to take his place as a member of the armed forces of his city, it will be supplemented by gymnastic. It should not be assumed that these two kinds of training are meant to be mutually exclusive. Plato presumes that even in the early years the child will receive some training in gymnastic and be given instruction in the elements of number and calculation.

The term μουσική has a much wider significance than the English word "music". Its connotation includes what we should now call a training in literature, music, and the arts. Thus we should not be surprised to find that education in μουσική will begin with the myths and fables the child learns at his mother's knee and then extends to poetry, music in the narrower sense, and to a variety of plastic arts. In *Republic*, Book II, Socrates states that the object of education in music is to train the soul; that of gymnastic the body, but later he informs Glaucon that the teachers of both arts have principally in mind the improvement of the soul.[2]

It will be necessary to exercise a strict superintendence over the stories which young children are told to prevent them from gaining false impressions about the things which really matter in life. After saying this, one is for a moment astonished to find that Socrates advocates introducing to the children narratives which are false. A narrative may be false in two ways: as regards fact and in the moral and spiritual lesson it conveys. Plato has in mind the myth

[1] *Republic*, 377.   [2] *ibid.*, 410.

in which the truth of fact is subsidiary to the inner truth that is represented by the story. Few men have been more skilful than Plato in the use of myth and allegory as a means of instruction and in his hands they played a part somewhat similar to the Parables of the New Testament.

Why does Socrates insist upon a close censorship of the stories which are told to children ? The answer to this question arises from the position which the poets of Greece held as teachers of moral and religious truth. One might almost say that for the Greeks the poets took the place which the Old Testament stories held in the estimation of an earlier generation of Englishmen. It has been suggested that Plato's criticism was aimed at the Homeric conceptions about gods and heroes. This is only partially true. His chief objection was directed to the new religious attitude represented by Hesiod and other poets of his age which in reality was a religious revolution and which was typified in the Orphic mysteries. It was not that Plato failed to see the aesthetic merits of their work; indeed, on this account they were all the more dangerous. The picture they presented was untrue. Hence all accounts which depicted the gods as intriguing, fighting, lying, practising fraud and deceit, and committing the foulest of crimes, were unfit for the young listener. In a similar way, later in Book II, when the dramatists are severely criticised, it is Aeschylus rather than Sophocles who is the main target.

The prime essential in educating young children is to foster a right attitude towards religion and for this reason, Socrates deals first with the stories about the gods. Children must start with a worthy conception of God. Since the ultimate aim of education is knowledge of the Good, in these early years, the Good will be presented in the form of a Being Who is supremely good and true. Unlike the gods in the *Theogony* of Hesiod, the true God is incapable of change or deceit. Neither can He lie. Plato was well aware that telling the truth was not a virtue for which the Greeks were distinguished. He puts into the mouth of Socrates the distinction between the verbal lie and the lie in the soul of which the former is a pale imitation. The lie in the soul is described as "lying with the highest part of oneself, and concerning the highest subjects". The lie in the soul is a state rather than an act; its essence is that the whole personality is turned in the wrong direction. It stands for a life in which the person who lives it has deceived himself and whilst accepting evil as his goal in place of good, is under the delusion that what he does is entirely justified.   One of the chief aims of education is to turn the soul in the right direction and save it from a life of self-deceit and delusion.[1]

The next step is to consider the stories concerning the heroes and the souls of the departed.   The characters of great men should always be presented to children as worthy of imitation and any of their actions which suggest cowardly, undisciplined, or immoral behaviour should never be mentioned.   Nor is it desirable to picture the life beyond the grave as a gloomy existence and one to be feared, a course which would bring up young people to fear death.   Our aim is to train them to be truthful and temperate and the latter virtue will comprise obedience to persons in authority, control of the bodily appetites, and avoidance of pride and insolence.

So far only the content of literature has been discussed.   The next problem is concerned with its form.   Plato has now in mind older children in whom the artistic sense has begun to develop.   He divides literary form into three types: that which consists wholly in imitation, *i.e.* where the author employs direct speech as represented by the drama; that which uses indirect speech, the poet himself telling the story, *i.e.* the narrative and lyric; and that which is a combination of both these types, *i.e.* the epic.   He is not concerned with the respective merits of these forms considered purely as works of art.   He believes that literature is a most potent factor in the formation of character because the individual will always tend to imitate the actions of the characters he admires.   He is not interested in deciding which is the highest form of the literary art; the main object in his thoughts is to emphasise that whatever is placed before the young upon which their imitative powers may work, must be the most worthy in the spiritual and moral sense.   His criterion is ethical rather than aesthetic.

The treatment of music taken in the narrower sense is similar. He attaches considerable importance to the influence for good or for ill that music exercises upon the emotions.   Therefore he would exclude from the community all songs and melodies that are sensuous and effeminate.   Likewise, many-stringed instruments

---

[1] The lie in the soul may be compared to the meaning attached by some commentators to the New Testament phrase, "sin against the Holy Spirit". To understand fully what Plato meant by this term, the reader should study two *Sermons* of Bishop Butler: no. vii, *Upon the Character of Balaam*, and no. x, *Upon Self-Deceit.*

would be banned and the only type of music to be encouraged is the stirring martial rhythm. A similar censorship would apply to the arts and crafts. So strongly does Plato feel on this matter, that he suggests government supervision of all craftsmen and artists. Speaking of education in μουσική Socrates declares: "Is it then, Glaucon, on these accounts that we attach such supreme importance to a musical education, because rhythm and harmony sink most deeply into the recesses of the soul, and take most powerful hold of it, bringing gracefulness in their train, and making a man graceful if he be rightly nurtured, but if not, the reverse ? and also because he that has been duly nurtured therein will have the keenest eye for defects, whether in the failures of art, or the misgrowths of nature; and feeling a most just disdain for them, will commend beautiful objects, and gladly receive them into his soul, and feed upon them, and grow to be noble and good; whereas he will rightly censure and hate all repulsive objects, even in his childhood, before he is able to be reasoned with; and when reason comes, he will welcome her most cordially who can recognise her by the instinct of relationship, and because he has been thus nurtured".[1]

Although a training in what we should now call physical education will begin in childhood, Plato reserves the more systematic instruction in gymnastic until the last two or three years of adolescence when the youth is looking ahead to the time he will enter upon his full-time military service. Like music, gymnastic is valuable because of its influence upon the soul, the part it plays in the building of character. Without doubt it will promote bodily health and develop physical skill, strength, and hardiness, but these qualities, desirable as they are, should not be regarded as the chief aim of physical education. The mental qualities which will be encouraged by a right training in gymnastic are of supreme importance and foremost are spirit and courage. Education in μουσική has been a training in culture but gymnastic prevents the development of a one-sided personality. "Those who have devoted themselves to gymnastic exclusively, become ruder than they ought to be; while those who have devoted themselves to music are made softer than is good for them."[2] The blending of the two kinds of training will produce a well-balanced and harmonious character.

Plato does not enter into the details of training in gymnastic but he criticises severely the Greek system which was designed to produce

[1] *Republic*, 402. [2] *ibid.*, 410.

athletes to compete in the games. From the practical point of view, gymnastic should prepare men for their military duties and make them "wakeful like watch-dogs, and possess the utmost quickness both of eye and ear". They must be able to withstand changes of climate, privation of food and drink; in short, they should be fitted to endure the hardships of a military campaign. Their training must be of the type undergone by the commandos of the late war. The professional training of the athlete will not do this. The athlete submits himself to short periods of intensive preparation but in the intervals, he sleeps away his time and indulges freely in the good things of the table. The key-note to gymnastic training is simplicity both in diet and exercise. Hence the condemnation of the Syracusan table, the Sicilian variety of dishes, and the Athenian confectionery. The sure sign of intemperance and dissoluteness in the state is the readiness to have recourse to the law-court and the doctor. Plato knew the disease that was consuming the Athens of his day. The Athenian was really uneducated because he did not know how to plan his life morally and physically.

The next problem is the choice of the future rulers of the state. The elementary education, so far discussed, is not sufficient of itself to produce the perfect guardian who must combine philosophic insight and practical experience. Hence from about the age of twenty to thirty, the auxiliaries will receive a secondary education which will be predominantly scientific in character. A period of higher education in dialectic will follow and then, for about fifteen years, those who have successfully completed those courses will gain practical experience through dealing with the day to day problems of administration. Only then will it be possible to choose the rulers. Meanwhile, the young auxiliaries will be subjected to a close scrutiny. Examinations and tests are by no means new. It is true that intelligence and vocational tests were unknown but Plato insists that the auxiliaries ought to be given rigorous tests to discover any defects of character or intelligence which will unfit them for the work of a guardian. It is essential that the would-be guardian should not only know what is good for the community but he should love it and strive for it with all his powers of body and mind. Public interests must come before private and therefore, in Book V, Socrates outlines what has often been called a socialistic or communist state.

Much nonsense has been written about Plato's so-called communism because the fundamental difference between his view of the individual and that of modern socialism has been ignored. Modern socialism advocates increased state control in the supposed interests of the individual, *e.g.* state control of food and other necessaries of life, subsidies to keep down the costs of living, state insurance and medical services, state education, etc. Plato views the situation from the angle of the state and therein lies the weakness which Aristotle was not slow to perceive. Plato would encourage men to follow the good life by taking away, as far as possible, the inducements to evil, just as the mediaeval monastic saw in seclusion from the world the removal of temptations which might keep the individual from all that would impair his service to God. The view which is more popular in modern times asserts that strength and goodness of character are more manifest when a man attempts to serve God amidst the distractions of the world, the flesh, and the devil.

Again, the suggested abolition of the family and the alleged communism of women also form points for misunderstanding. As A. E. Taylor remarks: "The overwhelming probability is that if any society should attempt to enforce on any part of itself regulations of the kind proposed in the *Republic*, the attempt would fail just because of their intolerable severity. No actual ruling class would be likely to consent to the absolute elimination of the affections of the family circle from its own life, even if it were prepared to reduce the gratification of the physical impulse of sex to the contemplated minimum. The true criticism on the whole treatment of sex in the *Republic* is that, like all non-Christian moralists, rigorist or relaxed, Socrates very much underestimates the significance of sex for the whole of the spiritual life".[1]

One important educational principle, however, emerges from this section of the *Republic*. Are women to receive the same educational opportunities as men, and are they also to be eligible to rule the state ? It would be wrong to assume that Plato was a champion of feminist rights. He settles the whole matter on principle. The interests of the state are paramount and the kind of education which will produce good men will also produce good women. He believes that the differences between the sexes are not vital in considering this problem. Although on the whole men are more suitable than

[1] A. E. Taylor, *Plato—The Man and his Work*, p. 278, Methuen, 1926.

women for war and government, they have no special talent which marks them out alone for these functions. Women will therefore receive the same kind of training as men and the same opportunities will be open to them. Aristotle did not agree and held that the differences between men and women are sufficient to affect the social functions of the sexes. Plato would urge co-operation between the sexes; Aristotle made the point that men and women are complementary to each other. Hence such a statement as Sir Richard Livingstone's must be read with the above reservation in mind. He says, "Plato held that women and men were to receive the same education; it is an amazing notion for a society where women were inferior beings confined to the home, and one that had to wait for the late nineteenth century before slowly and painfully it won acceptance".[1]

One may now proceed to consider the scientific education of the guardians. Certain preliminary remarks seem necessary at this point. In the first place, although in the dialogue Socrates still holds the stage, a point has been reached where the historic character is no longer dominant and Socrates is used to express views that more properly represent Plato's own contribution to thought. The historic Socrates was chiefly concerned with problems of knowledge and conduct. He was neither mathematician nor scientist. Plato was both and in the curriculum he sets forth, he is really describing that which formed the course of study in the early days of the Academy. In later years many important modifications were introduced.

It is also well known that Plato was profoundly influenced by the doctrines of the Pythagoreans and this is evident in two ways. The conception of education as the conversion of the soul, the turning from pre-occupation with the visible world to the contemplation of the realities which give it significance, is characteristically Pythagorean. In addition, the division of the sciences into the four studies of arithmetic, geometry, astronomy, and music, was not only Pythagorean but it is interesting to note that these same studies formed the Quadrivium, the second group of studies of the Seven Liberal Arts of mediaeval times.

Finally, all these studies are basically mathematical. This is accounted for by the fact that in the Greek world the only science which had been developed to any great extent was mathematics,

[1] *Plato and Modern Education*, p. 6, C.U.P., 1944.

and a good deal of the advance sprang from the work of Plato and the Academy. Aristotle was in future years to add to the mathematical sciences the biological. This is not, however, a complete explanation of the special significance which mathematical training possessed for Plato. One thing we can be certain about. Although he recognised the value of mathematics in everyday life, it was not the utilitarian value of the study which impressed him. He says, "Therefore, Glaucon, it will be proper to enforce the study by legislative enactment, and to persuade those who are destined to take part in the weightiest affairs of state, to study calculation and devote themselves to it, not like amateurs, but perseveringly, until, by the aid of pure reason, they have attained to the contemplation of the nature of numbers—not cultivating it with a view to buying and selling, as merchants or shopkeepers, but for purposes of war, and to facilitate the conversion of the soul itself from the changeable to the true and real".[1]

One may summarise Plato's belief as follows. By nature and training the ruler must be a philosopher. "Unless it happen either that philosophers acquire the kingly power in states, or that those who are now called kings and potentates, be imbued with a sufficient measure of genuine philosophy, that is to say, unless political power and philosophy be united in the same person—there will be no deliverance, my dear Glaucon, for cities, nor yet, I believe, for the human race."[2] The true philosopher does not conduct his life by expediency, by a superficial species of knowledge which Plato terms "opinion". He lives and acts on principles; he seeks the realities and is not guided by surface appearances, even though they may constitute what he calls "true opinion". His proud boast is that the philosopher is "privileged to contemplate all time, and all existence". The ability to frame principles and to apply them to particular cases involves the capacity of being able to handle abstract ideas and in the time of Plato, mathematics was the one study which dealt with universal and abstract conceptions to any adequate extent. When, in modern times, the aspect of the practical application of mathematics in relation to business and civic life, engineering, and science, tends to be emphasised in schools, it is salutary to remember that the utilitarian value of mathematics is not the only one.

[1] *Republic*, 425.   [2] *ibid.*, 473.

Plato enlarges the original sciences of the Pythagorean school by dividing the study of geometry into plane and solid. Glaucon replies that the latter branch has not so far been developed.[1] It is now known that solid geometry was one of the special studies of Plato's pupil, Theaetetus, the brilliant mathematician of the Academy. It should be noted, that while the study of music in the early education of the guardians was undertaken because of its influence upon the soul by means of the emotions, it is at this stage more properly a discipline in the principles of harmonics, the determination of the harmonic intervals and their reduction to numerical ratios, a study which operates on the soul which has now become susceptible to reason.

Plato has been charged with teaching a faculty psychology and with upholding the doctrine of the transfer of training.[2] It is quite true that Plato and Aristotle also frequently make use of the term δύναμις which is often translated as faculty, but to suggest that they supported a faculty psychology in the sense in which the term is employed by twentieth-century psychologists, is to misread them entirely. When Plato, for instance, tells us "that those who have a turn for arithmetic are, with scarcely an exception, naturally quick at all sciences; and that men of slow intellect, if they be trained and exercised in this study, even supposing they derive no other benefit from it, at any rate progress so far as to become invariably quicker than they were before", he is really pointing out that the study of mathematics gives an insight into certain principles of the intelligible world, furnishing the students, as it were, with a pattern of thinking, which is by no means the only one, but a pattern which is to be found in other departments of life.[3]

In other contexts, Plato emphatically denies the theory of formal discipline and its corollary, the transfer of training. Thus when Socrates asserts that the scientific studies serve as a prelude to dialectic, he puts the query, "But you surely would not regard the skilled mathematician as a dialectician?" Glaucon replies, "Assuredly not, I have hardly ever known a mathematician who was

[1] *Republic*, 528.
[2] See R. R. Rusk, *The Doctrines of the Great Educators*, pp. 22-4, reprint, 1948, Macmillan.
[3] Plato's view bears a similarity to modern doctrines such as those expressed by Professor P. Meredith when he deals with the function of relational structures and inferential skills in learning. See *Transfer of Training through the Application of Topic Analysis*, Researches and Studies, no. 2, University of Leeds Institute of Education, May 1950.

capable of reasoning".[1] In the *Theaetetus*, Socrates asks whether colours and sounds are perceived with or by means of the eyes and ears and his reply leaves no room for doubt. He says, "No one can suppose that in each of us, as in a sort of Trojan horse, there are perched a number of unconnected senses, which do not at all meet in some one nature, the mind, or whatever we please to call it, of which they are the instruments, and with which through them we perceive objects of sense".[2] In other words he is maintaining the position that seeing, and hearing, and the other so-called faculties are but powers and functions of a unitary consciousness.

Plato's conception of education as the turning of the whole personality in the direction of the light is admirably illustrated by the famous allegory of the prisoners in the cave. This is so familiar that it is not necessary to repeat it and the reader who is not familiar with it should read the opening paragraphs of *Republic*, Book VII. As already mentioned, education in the sciences is a prelude to the study of dialectic which Plato describes as the coping-stone of all the sciences. He believes that scientific knowledge is all very well as far as it goes but the scientist has not arrived at the truth of things. One restriction of mathematics lies in the fact that the mathematician cannot prove the first principles upon which his science is based. He is forced to assume them. He adopts certain hypotheses or postulates about the nature of number, space, a straight line, etc. Therefore, mathematical science rests upon certain assumptions which the mathematician takes for granted and having done so, he then proceeds to show what conclusions logically follow from his premises. It is the business of dialectic to examine the nature and validity of these postulates.

Again, although the sciences are not primarily concerned with the individual and concrete objects of sense but rather with the laws or principles which they exemplify, the scientist cannot avoid an appeal to the sensible. The mathematician, for instance, draws a square and its diagonal. When he is demonstrating the relations which hold between the diagonal and the sides of the square, he is not arguing about the particular square and its diagonal but about the absolute square and diagonal which can only be perceived with the eye of the mind. The postulate of the three kinds of angles, right angle, acute angle, and obtuse angle, is an example of what

---

[1] *Republic*, 531.   [2] *Theaetetus*, 184.

Plato does not hesitate to say it is the business of dialectic to destroy. "The view of science taken in the *Republic* really does demand the destruction of the hypotheses of the special sciences. The hypothesis of three kinds of angles has a spatial character, and that is just why the geometer is forced to use sensible diagrams. The ideal is that arithmetic, geometry, and the rest should all be reduced to one science, and this cannot be done so long as their special hypotheses remain. It is only when these have been removed that we can ascend to a first principle which is no longer a postulate, namely, the Form of the Good. Then, and not till then, can we descend once more without making use of sensible diagrams of any kind. The whole of science would thus be reduced to a sort of teleological algebra."[1]

The higher education of the guardians will consist in the study of dialectic which leads to an understanding of the Form of the Good. Plato deprecates beginning the study of dialectic at too early an age. He says, "Whenever boys taste dialectic for the first time, they pervert it into an amusement, and always employ it for purposes of contradiction, and imitate in their own persons the artifices of those who study refutation—delighting, like puppies, in pulling and tearing to pieces with logic anyone who comes near them".[2] With a similar thought in his mind, Aristotle remarks at the beginning of the *Ethics* that a young man does not make a suitable student of politics.

It is essential to grasp what Plato understood by dialectic. For Socrates, it meant the art of discussion which involved the asking of questions and the giving of answers. He believed that it was equally important to know the kind of questions to ask as to be able to supply the answers. Plato widened and deepened the connotation of the term. In his hands it came to mean two things; firstly and more commonly, a right method of reasoning which could be employed either for the discovery, the communication, or the demonstration of truth. The term is also used in quite a different sense, especially in the *Republic*, to denote what completed knowledge would be if the dialectic method had been carried out in each of the several branches of knowledge. It is in the latter sense that the term is frequently employed in the later books of the *Republic* and it corresponds to what Aristotle had in mind when he referred to First Philosophy or metaphysics.

[1] J. Burnet, *Thales to Plato*, pp. 229-30, Macmillan, 1914.   [2] *Republic*, 539.

If the ideal of dialectic in this sense were attained, the seeker after truth would grasp in its entirety the efficient principle of the whole universe, or to use Plato's terminology, he would understand the Form of the Good. The doctrine of the Forms has usually been ascribed to Plato and with many writers goes by the name of the Theory of Ideas. The choice of the latter phrase is unfortunate, because, although Plato sometimes uses the word idea, it suggests the modern usage of idea as being equivalent to a thought or even to any mental content.

According to Burnet and Taylor, the doctrine of the Forms taught in the *Phaedo* is that of Socrates who developed it from the Pythagoreans. It can be expressed briefly as follows. Our experience of sensible things causes our minds to envisage certain standards. Thus we speak of two sticks as being equal in length although we know that they are not exactly equal. The approximately equal is given through sense perception but the perfectly equal is only to be found in the realm of thought, the intelligible world. The same line of reasoning holds good of moral and aesthetic qualities. When Cebes discusses with Socrates the evidence for the immortality of the soul, he receives the answer that "if there be anything beautiful other than absolute beauty—it can be beautiful only in so far as it partakes of absolute beauty".[1] Socrates means that an object is called beautiful because of its participation in the form of beauty.

Another way of expressing the same thought is that the objects of the sense world are real only in so far as they partake of or share in the nature of the ideal. This leads to the contrast between the world of sense experience as one of change, becoming, approximation, and the intelligible world which is the real and the eternal. In later life, Plato was not satisfied with the solution offered by Socrates and criticised it severely. In the *Phaedo*, there is nothing to suggest that Socrates had worked out a hierarchy of Forms with the Form of the Good at its apex. In the central books of the *Republic*, however, Plato definitely asserts this view. He compares the Form of the Good in the intelligible world to the sun in the sensible. It stands to the objects of knowledge as the sun does to the objects of vision. The sun is responsible for visual colours and also enables the eye to see, but it is neither the things which are seen nor the eye which perceives them. In a similar way, the Good confers on the objects of scientific knowledge both their being

[1] *Phaedo,* 100.

and the means by which they are known. Plato uses the above analogy because he admits that he is unable to give any more adequate explanation of the nature of the Good.

Is it correct to assume that the Form of the Good is equivalent to what the Christian understands by God? The answer is definitely negative. The Good is a Form but in the *Timaeus*, which is probably the latest of Plato's dialogues, we are introduced to the Demiurge, the Creator of the visible universe and the best soul who fashions all things after the pattern of mathematical forms. The Demiurge approximates to the Christian conception of God, but one should remember that Plato considered the Form of the Good to be the superior. On the other hand, it must be admitted that many of the qualities attributed by Plato and his successors in the Academy to the Good are those which the Christian believes belong to God.

It is perhaps in some ways a misfortune that educationists have studied the *Republic* to a far greater extent than the *Laws*. The latter is Plato's longest work and was written in his old age when he had become disillusioned by the failure of his attempts to develop in Dionysius the qualities of the philosopher king. It was not that he abandoned his ideals but that he realised that contemporary circumstances prevented the establishment of the ideal state. Hence he set himself to contemplate the second-best, the best possible state. The result was that the treatment given in the *Laws* as regards education is more concrete and practical than the account of the *Republic*. It is significant that Socrates ceases to be a character of the dialogue. His place is taken by the Athenian stranger who is in reality Plato himself. This suggests that Plato had developed his own thought to a stage at which it would seem unnatural and untrue to put it into the mouth of Socrates. Moreover, although the *Laws* keeps to the dialogue form, it is really a treatise. One misses the dramatic appeal of the *Republic* and this is why the latter has more strongly attracted English readers. The speakers of the *Laws* do little more than register assent to the statements made; in fact, one might look upon this dialogue as a halfway house towards the systematic philosophical exposition which appears in the writings of Aristotle.

The *Laws* was intended to be a practical work. Each of the Greek cities and colonies had its own written constitution and code of laws, and the work of framing or modifying them fell either to some individual or to a small committee. No doubt, many cities who wished to redraft their constitutions applied to the Academy for the services of a trained and expert legislator. Hence it is not surprising that when the Romans came into contact with the Greek colonies in Sicily and southern Italy, they were influenced by Greek ideas about law. It has been claimed that the legal aspect of Greek philosophical speculation was responsible for the development of the *jus gentium*, the common principles of law which applied equally to native and foreigner.

Plato finds it difficult to repress the thoughts which were uppermost in his mind and quite early in the *Laws* the problems of choosing the best ruler for the state and the type of education needed to produce him are introduced. Plato clings to his belief that the process of education should start as soon as possible. He even suggests pre-natal care as necessary for the production of healthy offspring. He realises that the young baby is an active creature and he appeals to the practice of nurses who calm disturbed and restless infants by rocking them or by taking them into their arms and walking about with them. "Nursing and moving about by day and night," he says, "is good for them all, and that the younger they are, the more they will need it; infants should live, if that were possible, as if they were always rocking at sea. This is the lesson which we may gather from the experience of nurses, and likewise from the use of the remedy of motion in the rites of the Corybantes."[1]

The newly born baby can only express his wants by crying and this stage lasts until about three years of age. It is, however, a very important period as far as education is concerned. Although it is true that the behaviour of the baby is governed by his feelings of pleasure and pain, it would be a grave error to suppose that all his wants should be immediately gratified. The aim should be to produce in him a state of calm which lies between the extremes of pleasure and pain. Even the youngest infant is amenable to discipline. His random kicks and screams can be subjected to rhythm, for all infants find pleasure in melody and well marked rhythm. This result can be accomplished through music and dance. At three, the child is old enough to be punished when he

---

[1] *Laws*, 790. The Corybantic priests believed in the purgative value of music and physical activity. Hysterics were subjected to the music of the pipe, which after exciting them to violent physical activity, produced exhaustion and sleep from which the patients arose calmed in body and mind.

does wrong but care should be exercised lest punishment results in sullenness and resentment.

Plato more than anticipates later thinkers in his insistence upon play as the natural activity of childhood. Leave young children to themselves and you will discover that they soon find plenty of activities which delight them; they will, in fact, invent their own games. Play should be regarded not only as a means of producing healthy bodies; it also accustoms children to co-operate with one another and is a good antidote to the growth of selfishness. It is not wise for adults to interfere too freely with children's play. Nevertheless, nurses should be appointed to give adequate supervision to see that they play in an orderly fashion and do not harm one another. Moreover, a special place should be selected for their play. One might with considerable justice suggest that here we have the idea of the nursery school.

There would be a good deal of truth in ascribing to Plato the origin of the Play Way in education. Not only did he teach that the child expresses himself freely and naturally in play but he realised the importance of imitative play. The individual activities of young children soon begin to take definite patterns through association with rhythmic chants. Children delight in copying the actions of other children, and of adults, and this leads to the growth of traditional forms of play. Plato attached much importance to the established forms and ritual of play. Innovations disturb the young and lead to undesirable effects in later years. Moreover, in his play, the child represents through his imagination the kind of person he would like to be when he has grown up. Plato tells us, "People are apt to fancy—that when the plays of children are altered they are merely plays, not seeing that the most serious and detrimental consequences arise out of the change—not considering that these children who make innovations in their games, when they grow up to be men, will be different from the last generation of children, and, being different, will desire a different sort of life, and under the influence of this desire will want other institutions and laws". It is in this way that revolutionaries are produced.

As children grow older and receive more formal instruction, the play approach to learning should not be neglected. Plato commends the methods of teaching practised by the Egyptians. "In that country arithmetical games have been invented for the use

¹ *Laws*, 798.

of mere children, which they learn as a pleasure and amusement. They have to distribute apples and garlands, using the same number sometimes for a larger and sometimes for a lesser number of persons. They adapt to their amusement the numbers in common use, and in this way make more intelligible to their pupils the arrangements and movements of armies and expeditions—and again in measurements of things which have length, and breadth, and depth, they free us from that natural ignorance of all these things which is so ludicrous and disgraceful."[1]

Boys and girls should play together until they are six years of age and then should be separated. "Let boys live with boys, and girls in like manner with girls."[2] The boys will be taught horsemanship and the use of warlike weapons. The training of the girls should be on similar lines. Both sexes should be ambidextrous; use of the right hand alone means that the whole of the body is not being employed, a factor which may be disadvantageous to the soldier in battle.

The musical and gymnastic training of the *Republic* is retained. Although both sexes will receive similar instruction, the spirit in which it is given will be different. The boys are destined to be soldiers and should be trained with that end in view. The girls will become mothers of families and only in later life, when they have passed the age of childbearing, will they be called upon in an emergency to defend the state. In other words, the nature of the training given to boys and girls will be affected by the respective demands made upon them in later life. Moreover, the education provided is not, as in the *Republic*, limited to a small section of the community; it will be universal and compulsory for the children of all free citizens. Education should aim at producing the best type of citizen both for war and peace. In fact, the latter has the precedence and since the training of the young is for the direct benefit of the state, the control of education should be in the hands of a government department. Thus we see that the social implications of education and the idea of a planned education for a planned society are not inventions of the twentieth century.

Plato attached a high value to state supervision and control. The most important official in the state should be the Minister of Education. He should be at least fifty years old, a married man with children of his own. He should be elected by the magistrates

[1] *Laws*, 819.   [2] *ibid.*, 794.

to hold office for five years.[1]   He would decide exactly what should
be taught and who would teach it, and a small committee of experts
would be constituted to give him advice on technical matters.   For
example, he would decide whether children should be set to learn
by heart the works of entire poets or be asked to memorise books
of extracts.

The periods for primary and secondary education are prescribed
in the *Laws*.   "A fair time for a boy of ten years old to spend in
letters is three years; the age of thirteen is the proper time for him
to begin to handle the lyre, and he may continue at this for another
three years, neither more nor less, and whether his father or himself
like or dislike the study, he is not to be allowed to spend more or
less time in learning music than the law allows."[2]

But what of the dull and backward child ?   Plato has an answer
ready.   Such pupils must keep at their learning until they can read
and write, but if by nature they are not able to attain the finer
points of these arts within a prescribed period, they should be let
alone.   Plato was worried about the use of prose literature.   He
believed that it is dangerous for young boys and girls to read the
works of philosophers and scientists.   They are not ripe for such
studies, but he was prepared to allow treatises on the laws and the
principles of legislation to be read.   Space will not permit discussion
of the training in gymnastic about which in the *Laws*, Plato has
more detail to give than in the *Republic*.

Plato distinguishes between two forms of secondary education.
He says, "There still remain three studies suitable for free men.
Arithmetic is one of them; the measurement of length, surface, and
depth is the second; and the third has to do with the revolutions of
the stars in relation to one another.   Not everyone has need to toil
through all these things in a strictly scientific manner, but only a
few—not to know what is necessary for mankind in general, and
what is the truth, is disgraceful to every one : and yet to enter into
these matters minutely is neither easy, nor at all possible for every
one; but there is something in them which is necessary and cannot be
set aside".[3]   The few who will enter upon a thoroughly systematic
study of the mathematical sciences are those who show by character
and intelligence that they are fitted to be members of the ruling
class.   Thus he envisages two kinds of secondary education: one
is almost tempted to suggest that he is feeling his way towards the

[1] *Laws*, 765-6.   [2] *ibid.*, 810.   [3] *ibid.*, 818.

distinction which at the present time marks the difference in aims of the grammar and the secondary modern schools.

How far does Plato supply the omission of technical and vocational education to which attention was drawn in discussing the range of studies outlined in the *Republic* ? Although he has not abandoned the views about the nature of education which he expressed in the earlier dialogue, he now realises more clearly the importance of training for the work of adult life. He says, "According to my view, anyone who would be good at anything must practise that thing from his youth upwards, both in sport and earnest, in its several branches; for example, he who is to be a good builder, should play at building children's houses; he who is to be a good husbandman, at tilling the ground; and those who have the care of their education should provide them when young with mimic tools. They should learn beforehand the knowledge which they will afterwards require for their art. For example, the future carpenter should learn to measure or apply the line in play; and the future warrior should learn riding, or some other exercise, for amusement, and the teacher should endeavour to direct the children's inclination and pleasures, by the help of amusements, to their final aim in life. The most important part of education is right training in the nursery. The soul of the child in his play should be guided to the love of that sort of excellence in which when he grows up to manhood he will have to be perfected".[1] The reader should notice the emphasis upon approaching practical activities in the spirit of play.

Higher education in dialectic is not discussed in the *Laws*, though in the *Epinomis*, which A. E. Taylor regards as a genuine work of Plato and as a "thirteenth" book of the *Laws*, more is said about advanced studies in the sciences. As in the *Republic*, the aim in educating the select few is stated as the acquisition of wisdom (σοφία) and Plato once more expresses his opinion that the subject most fitted for this purpose is pure mathematics. The treatise ends by reasserting that the attainment of wisdom is only possible for the few and that the state should insist that the guardians devote themselves entirely to its quest.

Finally, the *Laws* presents a picture of a carefully planned system of schools staffed with trained teachers who are paid salaries for their work. The latter savoured of professionalism which was

[1] *Laws*, 643.

anathema to the Greek mind; hence Plato is careful to add that of course the teachers will be foreigners. The practical proposals of the *Laws* are admirably summarised by Burnet in the following words: "We may easily miss the significance of Plato's proposals as to the education of boys and girls from the age of ten onwards. We must remember that in his day there were no regular schools for young people of that age. They were taken to one teacher for music-lessons and to another to be taught Homer, and there was no idea of co-ordinating all these things in a single building under a single direction with a regular staff of teachers. By founding the Academy Plato had invented the university, and now he has invented the secondary school. In consequence we find such schools everywhere in the Hellenistic period, and the Romans adopted it with other things, quaintly translating the Greek term by *ludus*. That is the origin of the mediaeval grammar school and of all that has come out of it since. It will be seen that the *Laws* is not a work we can afford to despise if we wish to understand Plato's influence".[1]

SUGGESTIONS FOR FURTHER READING

In this chapter, quotations from the dialogue are taken from the version of Davis and Vaughan (Golden Treasury Series, Macmillan) in the case of the *Republic*; otherwise, from Jowett's translation of the *Dialogues of Plato* (O.U.P.).

For those who wish to make a further study of Plato, Dr Boyd's *Introduction to the Republic of Plato* (Geo. Allen and Unwin, reprint, 1922) is the simplest approach. R. L. Nettleship, *Lectures on the Republic of Plato* (Macmillan, reprint, 1922) is the classic for the study of the *Republic* and gives the student an insight into some of the most important philosophical ideas of Plato and Aristotle. Nettleship's essay on Plato's educational theory was published in *Hellenica* in 1880. It has been republished under the title of *The Theory of Education in Plato's Republic* (O.U.P., 1935, reprint, 1947). This is an excellent book and should be read by all those who are beginning a study of the educational ideas of Plato. For more advanced students, especially those who wish to view Plato's educational theory in its philosophical setting, the following are recommended: —

[1] J. Burnet, *Thales to Plato*, p. 311, Macmillan, 1914.

A. E. Taylor, *Plato—The Man and his Work*, Methuen, 1926 (Chapter XI on the *Republic*, and XVIII on the *Laws and Epinomis*).

J. Burnet, *Greek Philosophy—Thales to Plato*, Macmillan, 1914 (Books II and III deal with Socrates and Plato).

Another useful work is R. C. Lodge, *Plato's Theory of Education* (Kegan Paul, Trench, Trubner, 1947). An interesting feature of this book is the comparison between the teaching of Plato and modern educational theory and practice. The best account of the theory and practice of education in the Greek states in the days of Socrates and Plato is that given by K. J. Freeman, *Schools of Hellas* (Macmillan, 1932).

CHAPTER II

ARISTOTLE AND EDUCATION

The transition from the study of Plato to that of Aristotle appears at first sight like travelling from one country to another where the climate and the conditions of life are entirely different. This has led some to refer to Plato and Aristotle as if they were distinct types after one or the other of which each of us is fashioned so that the well-known lines of W. S. Gilbert could be applied to assert that everybody is born either a little Platonist or a little Aristotelian. It is as fallacious to exaggerate the differences between the two thinkers as it is to underestimate certain fundamental similarities which become apparent after further reflection upon their works. There is indeed much truth in the assertion that Aristotle was the first Platonist, and that in some respects he was even more Platonic than his master.

Certain differences between the two admit of quite a simple historical explanation. It is a matter of fact that while we possess all the written works of Plato, our knowledge of his oral teaching in the Academy is mainly derived from the criticisms of Aristotle. With the exception of the fragment on the *Constitution of Athens*, discovered in the late nineteenth century, all Aristotle's dialogues and treatises have been lost. Both Cicero and Quintilian praised his "golden eloquence", and it is more than likely that if the Aristotelian dialogues were discovered, they would resemble those of Plato. The present Aristotelian corpus consists either of the draft of his lectures, written out before they were delivered, or summaries of his lectures by his students. The former is the more probable. It is also possible that if we possessed the text of Plato's lectures, we should find that they had a greater affinity to the extant works of Aristotle than to the Platonic dialogues.

There is another factor which should be considered. At the time when Socrates was cross-examining the adherents of views current in his day, there was no technical language of philosophy, as distinct from that of everyday speech. He used terms taken from the ordinary vocabulary of his fellows but the very act of defining accurately their meaning would tend to earmark them for the purposes of philosophical thought. This process was adopted by Plato and in the dialogues there is already an indication that a technical philosophical vocabulary was in the making. If we possessed an account of Plato's lectures, we should probably find that the growth of a technical philosophical language had proceeded much further than in the dialogues. In Aristotle, words and phrases, which a century before his time, had been indistinguishable from those used in everyday speech, had now become highly technical and constituted a specialised philosophical language. One has only to recall such frequently used phrases as form ($\epsilon \tilde{\iota} \delta o s$), matter ($\tilde{\upsilon} \lambda \eta$), actuality ($\dot{\epsilon} \nu \dot{\epsilon} \rho \gamma \epsilon \iota a$), potentiality ($\delta \dot{\upsilon} \nu a \mu \iota s$), and cause ($a \dot{\iota} \tau \iota a$), to realise that such a development had taken place. Thus Book Δ of the *Metaphysics* supplied a very real need of the student of philosophy. It served as a short philosophical dictionary intended to give the meaning of terms now used for the distinctive purposes of philosophy.

The above remarks, however, should not be taken as minimising certain very important differences between the two thinkers. Plato was essentially a mathematician; Aristotle a physician and a biologist. His knowledge of mathematics was but slight. It was limited to arithmetic and the collection and use of simple statistics. He never really understood the deeper implications of Plato's fully developed thought as expounded in the oral teaching of the Academy. From the little we know of it, we can be sure that Plato not only turned to the different branches of mathematics as illustrations of his principles but that the latter were mathematical in form. Such a conception as that of the one and the indeterminate dyad would have little meaning for Aristotle.

Perhaps the most important event in Aristotle's life was his appointment as tutor to the young Alexander. His teaching does not seem to have created in Alexander the power of self-control but there was one permanent effect of his contact with Aristotle. Alexander, when he started on his career of conquest did not forget his old tutor whom he always regarded with admiration and respect. He arranged that all the information available about the government and constitutions of the states he invaded, details concerning the life, customs, and traditions of the people, accurate knowledge about the flora and fauna of these regions and many other facts, should be transmitted to Aristotle without delay. Thus Aristotle was the fortunate possessor of an accumulation of detailed facts such as has never until recent times been at the disposal of any one man or group of men. Something of the same kind occurred at the end of the last war when the armies of the victorious allies overran the territories of Germany and Italy and an immense collection of scientific and other facts became available to the United Nations.

An example of the wealth of information in the hands of Aristotle is the fact that when he compiled the *Politics*, he had before him the details of 158 different constitutions. Aristotle attached great importance to the possession of the relevant facts. Plato believed that if one was confronted with a problem and thought sufficiently hard and deeply about it and discussed it with other people who were both experienced and intelligent, sooner or later, one would arrive at a solution. Aristotle's reaction was to make sure that one had all the relevant facts. Then, if one thought about them deeply enough and on logical lines, something of value would emerge. This attitude was bound up with his own experience of medicine and biology. At this time, neither of these studies had arrived at the stage where they could formulate general principles of the type common to the mathematical sciences. They were still in the factual and descriptive stage of development. Some cynics may remark, that even at the present time, medicine does not seem to have passed much beyond this stage.

Two consequences of Aristotle's study of biology should be noted. He was not only the founder of scientific zoology, but Theophrastus, his immediate successor in the Lyceum, initiated the scientific study of botany. Plato's successors in the Academy were responsible for important contributions to mathematical knowledge. Aristotle also developed a dynamic conception of the universe. He regarded it as a realm of purposes working themselves out to their fulfilment. He takes his start from the concrete individual things of our experience, statues, houses, trees, horses, and men and he asks into what they can be analysed by means of thought.

If any natural or artificial object is considered, thought can distinguish two different aspects or moments in its being. Thus the statue has a definite shape given to it by the sculptor, a Form which marks it out as a statue of Hercules and not of Apollo. The statue, however, was carved from a certain kind of material, marble, bronze, or wood. Before it received its completed form at the hands of the sculptor, it was a piece of rough unshapen material. If, however, the analysis is carried a stage further, it will be discovered that the material used by the artist for his sculpture is raw material in a relative sense only. It possesses a definite form of its own which constitutes it marble and not bronze or wood, and in virtue of which it exhibits physical and chemical properties quite different from these other kinds of raw material. Ultimately the analysis would lead to the idea of a raw material which is the underlying substratum of all that exists, the "stuff" from which everything is constituted. This First or Primary Matter, devoid of all properties and which cannot be described or defined, since all attempts at definition or description must be through the Form, has no real independent existence apart from this Form. The individual objects of the sense world are thus composite in character; their existence is derived from the imposition of Form on Matter or the development of Form within the Matter. First Matter, therefore, is the fundamental basis of all concrete individual existence, the indeterminate "somewhat" common to all beings. Apart from the substratum is the Form, the definite structural organisation which makes any individual thing exactly what it is and constitutes all those complex properties which distinguish the object from an individual in another species.

All change in nature, all coming into being or passing out of being are brought about by Matter receiving or losing Form or one Form being replaced by another. One can stress the purposive, dynamic aspect of nature by using another pair of concepts closely related to Matter and Form, namely, actuality and potentiality. It will be seen that First Matter is a sheer potentiality whilst Form is a principle of actuality. The seed develops under favourable conditions to a fully mature plant of a certain species; the child grows into a man; the raw material of bronze is shaped by the craftsman into a bowl or a candlestick. Two seeds may look so exactly similar that it is difficult to distinguish them. Allow them to germinate, and one grows into a stock and the other into a wallflower. The process of growth could not have been reversed. The acorn can produce an oak but it cannot grow into an elm or a sycamore. The seed seems to contain within itself the lines of its future development, the laws which determine its growth into a fully developed member of its species. This idea can be expressed by saying that the acorn is potentially the oak and unless circumstances prevent, it will in due time become the fully fledged oak tree. The individual oak is the realisation or actualisation of the potentialities contained within the seed. In the same way, it will be seen that the process of education seeks to develop the child's potentialities so that he may become a good and efficient citizen of the Greek city state. Each potential object will develop towards its appointed end or Entelechy (ἐντελέχεια). All such development, it should be noted, is a development within the species. Aristotle was a firm believer in the fixity of species and any idea of evolution as understood by modern biologists, was quite foreign to his thought. The idea of an appointed end which each individual strives to attain is fundamental to Aristotle's thought and plays an important part in his theory of education.

Sufficient has been said about the differences between Plato and Aristotle; now a few words about their similarities. Several important features in the Aristotelian philosophy, *e.g.* the doctrine of God and the nature of Active Intellect, are not only Platonic but represent a development of Plato's thought to an extent which he never contemplated. In the same way, much of Aristotle's theory of education is derived directly from Plato. Neither thinker produced a treatise entirely devoted to the study of education. Both treat the subject as part of the study of politics. It is only in recent times that thinkers have returned to this point of view and have considered education primarily from the political, social, and economic standpoint. In the *Republic* and the *Laws*, Plato gave a fairly full exposition of his views about the nature of education besides which that of Aristotle appears fragmentary. This is indeed the case, for at the end of the *Politics*, Aristotle abruptly breaks off the discussion without giving any hint of a plan of higher education comparable to that of the Academy. In fact he did not complete his account of the education of the adolescent.

Aristotle's views about education are contained in his *Ethics* and *Politics*. A beginning may be made with the more theoretical discussion of the *Ethics*. Aristotle looked upon ethics as a practical science. Some sciences such as geometry achieve their end through the simple activity of knowing. The learner attacks a proposition in geometry with the purpose of understanding and mastering it. Once this has been accomplished, his activity ceases for the time being. He does not, or at least he did not, in the time of Aristotle, study the theorem with any other end but knowledge in view. Such sciences are termed theoretical or speculative. At the opposite extreme are those sciences in which the main object is to make something, a house or a temple. These are the productive sciences. A practical science lies between the two. It is not completed when the intellectual activity has ceased; it aims at something over and above the activity of knowing. Ethics is a practical science, because like the master science of politics and the subsidiary science of education, it aims not only at the discovery of the chief good for man but also at devising a practical scheme of achieving goodness. It endeavours to formulate principles and rules which will enable man to attain his good. In the *Ethics*, Aristotle has mainly in view the good of man as an individual, whilst in the *Politics* he is more concerned with the practical problem of how the state can be organised to realise that good. Naturally the two aspects cannot be completely isolated and one would expect both of them entering into the discussion of each treatise.

Men have a great many ends or purposes in life but they are not all equal in value. Some are subordinate to others. For instance, the aim of the armourer is to fashion weapons. The soldier who uses them in battle regards them as merely means to his end, the defeat of the enemy. Ability to use his weapons effectively is the end of the soldier but his training and skill serve as means to the statesman. The soldier, because he has to use weapons, gives the armourer instructions about their manufacture. The statesman orders the soldier when and with what purpose in view he is to employ his weapons. Aristotle regarded that art which uses things supplied by another art as the superior and directing art. The supreme art is politics because it makes use of all the other arts. The supreme end of the statesman is the well-being of the community, and he gives instructions how all should practise their respective arts in order to realise that object.

Education is the most important of the subordinate arts. The statesman needs certain qualities of mind and certain types of character amongst the members of the state. The educator aims at producing men and women who have the right kind of intelligence and ability and the right type of character. This suggests that the study of ethics will be a necessary introduction to politics. It will give guidance with regard to the kind of mental and moral qualities which the educator aims at developing in the younger members of the community. This is essential for the well-being of the state, for a good moral tone in each individual member will result in a good moral tone in the community. It should be noted that Aristotle has constantly in mind the individual as a member of the community, not as an isolated unit. He believes that the moral life only has meaning when the different relations in which the individual stands to his fellow men are considered. In other words, on Aristotelian principles, one could hardly speak of Robinson Crusoe living a moral life on his desert island; it was only when Man Friday appeared that morality became possible. Hence Aristotle's idea of the good life is one which is lived amongst our fellow men. Bearing this in mind, our problem becomes one of discovering which is the best life for a member of society.

Aristotle is in complete agreement with Plato that the best kind of life is the happy life. As against Plato, he insists that happiness is not a state or a possession but should be regarded as essentially an activity. This statement, however, does not take us much further, for nearly everyone has his own ideas about what constitutes happiness. Ideas about the happy life can be grouped into three classes. Firstly, there is the lowest type, the man who puts pleasure as his chief aim in life. Such a life only differs from that of the animal in being more refined and fastidious. Higher on the scale are those who choose the active life. They aim at achieving honour and reputation. This is the life pursued by those who take an active part in the government of the community. Honour is certainly a superior object of desire but a closer scrutiny reveals that there is something superficial about it. Honour and reputation seem to depend on the giver rather than the receiver and it should be a characteristic of the Good that it is something which is a man's very own and which cannot be easily taken away from him. Moreover, those who pursue this kind of life always desire to be honoured by the good and the wise. This suggests that goodness and wisdom are superior to honour. Nor can the pursuit of wealth bring the happy life. Men seek wealth because of those things which it brings in its train, but the good is desirable for its own sake.

Later in the *Ethics*, Aristotle teaches that the ideal life is one which is devoted to the disinterested pursuit of knowledge and wisdom, but this is only possible for the few. At this stage he is concerned with the majority. In order to discover the essential character of the good life, he utilises a Platonic principle by asking, "What is the function of man?" In the community, each artisan and tradesman has his own special function or task. The parts of the human body, the eye, the hand, and the foot, have each their respective functions. Is it reasonable to suppose that man as man possesses no function which is peculiar to him ? The function of the eye is to see and the good eye sees well. Therein lies its special virtue or goodness. What is the special virtue of man ? It cannot be life, for that is shared with the plants and animals. For the same reason, life on the level of sense perception is excluded. Man's special virtue must lie in the activity of the highest part of himself, namely, the rational part for it is the possession of reason which differentiates men from brutes. This, however, is only part of the answer. The function of a harp player is to play the harp and the good harp player plays his instrument well. Hence the function of man will consist in an activity of the rational part of his nature, and the good man will be he who performs this function wisely and well. The good life and the happy life, then, will be a life lived in accordance with reason. The good for man is defined as "an activity of the soul in accordance with goodness or virtue, and, if there are more kinds of goodness or virtue than one, in accordance with that which is best and most complete". But, as one swallow or one fine day does not make a spring, the words "in a complete life" must be added.

The above definition has raised the problem whether there is more than one kind of goodness. To answer this question, it will be necessary to know something about the nature of the soul. Aristotle is not concerned in the *Ethics* with an intensive analysis of the nature of the soul and its operations; he had already carried this out in the *De Anima*. He agrees with the Platonic division of the soul into a rational and an irrational part. Whether this refers to different faculties or to different aspects of the one soul is here beside the point. The irrational part of the soul is subdivided. One part which is responsible for nutrition and growth is not peculiar to man but is shared with all other living creatures. The other element is still irrational but has a certain share in rationality by reason of its obedience to the rational. Aristotle is thinking of the appetitive powers of the soul which include the bodily appetites, instincts, and passions. The significant point in this distinction is that there are two elements in the soul, the rational and that which is not truly rational but which can be governed by reason.

It follows from the existence of these two elements in the soul that there will be two forms of goodness or virtue. "Now goodness will also be divided in accordance with this difference. We speak of some forms of goodness as goodness of character and of some as goodness of intellect; wisdom, intelligence, and prudence being intellectual, while liberality and temperance are moral."[1] Another line of thought will lead to the same conclusion. The essence of the good life lies in following the right rule. It is, of course, necessary to know the right rule before it can be followed. The wicked follow a wrong rule of life; the morally weak know the right rule but passion and self-interest prevent them from observing it. Mankind can be classified into those who are able to discover the right rule for themselves, and those who are unable to do this but can recognise the right rule when it is presented to them by the teacher or the law giver. In addition, each individual must be able to discipline his feelings and desires so as to obey the rule. Thus there are two forms of goodness; goodness of intellect which one might term practical wisdom, and goodness of character, that is, moral goodness. Only the few can attain intellectual goodness but moral goodness is within reach of all. Intellectual goodness is produced and developed through instruction which aims at the acquisition of the insight necessary for the discovery of the right rule. Moral goodness is dependent upon the formation of good habits.

Aristotle is at pains to emphasise that goodness of character is not a natural gift. Natural capacities result in one kind of activity only; they cannot be habituated to function in a different way. "For example, a stone, which naturally tends to fall downwards, cannot be habituated to rise upwards, not even if we try to train it by throwing it up an indefinite number of times, nor can anything else that acts in one way by nature be habituated to act in another way."[2] It is otherwise with a rational capacity. It has a two-fold potentiality. The child can develop into a morally good or a morally bad adult. Good character is the result of training and the inculcation of the right habits. There is, however, a further difference between a natural and a rational capacity. We possess natural capacities before we begin to use them. It is not by seeing or hearing frequently that we obtain the senses of sight or hearing. We have the senses to start with and then we begin to exercise them. It is quite the contrary with the different kinds of goodness; they

[1] *Ethics*. 1103a.   [2] *ibid.*, 1103a.

are produced by what one might call a process of learning by doing. The analogy of the arts provides an apt illustration of this principle. "We become good builders by building and good harp players by playing the harp. In the same way it is by doing just acts that we become just, by doing temperate acts that we become temperate, and by doing brave deeds that we become brave."[1] The production of a bad character is based on exactly the same principle. An individual develops a character for cowardice by constantly acting as a coward in the presence of danger. In other words, both the capacities and the matter of goodness, and badness, are the same. Our feelings and actions are the raw material from which goodness, and badness, of character are formed. Hence one of the prime tasks of the educator is to train the young to perform the right kind of actions. Children should be trained to speak the truth before they understand why it is right to speak the truth. Unless the young learn to control themselves and to form the right habits, they will never reach the stage at which they can discover for themselves the right rule.

Aristotle realised that his doctrine was open to the objection that if the individual is able to perform a just or a temperate act he must already be just or temperate. It might be said that in the sphere of the arts, those who can spell correctly or play the right notes are constituted scholars or musicians by this fact. This is not strictly true, for a person may spell correctly by accident, *i.e.* not knowing the rule, or at another's suggestion. There is, however, an essential difference between moral and productive activity. All that is demanded of the craftsman is that he should produce an article which conforms to the required standard. The carpenter is judged to be a good or a bad workman in the light of the articles he makes. He is assessed in terms of his knowledge and skill; it matters not that he is a brave man or a coward. In the moral sphere, knowledge and skill play a much less important part. The external action which is visible to the eyes of men is only part of the activity. Much depends upon the internal condition of the agent. "Actions in conformity with goodness—are not justly or temperately performed if they are merely of a certain character looked at in themselves, but only if the agent is in a certain condition when he performs them, in the first place if he acts with knowledge, in the second, if he wills them and wills them for their own sake, and

[1] *Ethics*, 1103b.

thirdly, if they proceed from a fixed and unalterable condition of the soul."[1] In other words, the moral judgment on the goodness or badness of an action has to take into account the motives of the agent and the spirit in which the act is performed. We judge not an isolated part but the whole of the action, the man performing the act. He concludes, "We say, then, that deeds are just and temperate when they are such as a just or temperate man would perform, but that a just or temperate man is not merely the man who does those deeds, but the man who does them as just and temperate people do them".[2]

Aristotle reminds us that the study of ethics is not purely speculative. "The object of our inquiry is not to know what goodness is, but to become good ourselves. Otherwise it would be of no use whatever." It is, therefore, necessary to know why one kind of activity is morally good and another morally bad. Aristotle begins by saying that goodness consists in a condition of the soul. How is it, then, that one condition of the soul is considered good and another the reverse ? Aristotle answers by the famous doctrine of the mean. Goodness consists in choosing the mean between excess and defect. The idea of the mean originated with the Pythagoreans and was associated with the tuning of the lyre. All the strings of this instrument were of equal length and tuning was effected by tightening or relaxing the string. When Aristotle speaks of the mean he frequently has this illustration in mind. The right pitch of a string is that which is neither too high nor too low and the correct tuning is judged by the ear. It is important to realise that Aristotle is not thinking of the arithmetical mean. He says distinctly that the mean in conduct is always relative to the individual. "It does not follow, if ten pounds of meat are much and two are little for a man to eat, that the trainer will prescribe six pounds: that would be too little for Milo (the professional athlete), but too much for a beginner in gymnastics."[3] The rule consists of regulating one's actions by the mean relative to oneself. Those who are capable of intellectual goodness have the insight necessary to choose the mean suited to them, but for the majority, the law giver or educator, who knows what the mean should be, will be called upon to say what is right for particular individuals in particular circumstances.

[1] *Ethics*, 1105b.   [2] *ibid.*, 1105b.   [3] *ibid.*, 1106b.

A considerable section of the *Ethics* is taken up in showing how the mean can be ascertained with regard to particular virtues and vices. This account need not detain us; one illustration will suffice. "With regard to feelings of fear and boldness, the mean state is Courage. Of those who exceed—he who exceeds in boldness is called rash. On the other hand, he who exceeds in fearing and is deficient in boldness is called a coward."[1] Aristotle acknowledges that in practice it is not an easy matter to hit the mean. One cannot formulate rules of conduct that are universally applicable since every action is a particular action carried out in particular circumstances. The individual has to judge whether in a particular instance his conduct deflects from the mean. The person who is in good general health has little difficulty in feeling whether his bath water is too hot or too cold. In the same way, the person who is in a state of good moral health, that is, one who has through training acquired the right habits, will at once perceive if an action errs by excess or defect in a particular case. This emphasises the importance of moral education since it is only the man who has formed the right habits who can perceive the right amount of indignation he ought to show on a given occasion.

So far, Aristotle has been dealing with producing in the individual the kind of character required for the good citizen. That, however, is only one essential aspect of the work of the educator; it is not the sole nor even the highest aim of education. It is at this point that he makes a noteworthy contribution to the theory of education. To the ideas of education for citizenship and for one's future life, must be added the conception of an education for leisure. Aristotle differentiates between the aims of education in the following passage of the *Politics*. He says, "The whole of life is divided into two parts, business and leisure, war and peace, and all actions into those which are necessary and useful, and those which are honourable. And the preference given to one or the other class of actions must necessarily be like the preference given to one or other part of the soul and its actions over the other; there must be war for the sake of peace, business for the sake of leisure, things useful and necessary for the sake of things honourable. All these points the statesman should keep in view when he frames his laws; he should consider the parts of the soul and their functions, and above

[1] *Ethics,* 1107b

all the better and the end; he should also remember the diversities of human lives and actions. For men must engage in business and go to war, but leisure and peace are better; they must do what is necessary and useful, but what is honourable is better. In such principles children and persons of every age which requires education should be trained".[1] The same thought is expressed in the *Ethics*. "Happiness is believed to depend on leisure; for the aim of all our business is leisure just as the aim of war is peace. Now the activities of the practical forms of goodness are displayed in politics and war, and occupations of this kind clearly do not admit of leisure. This is altogether true of warlike activities; for no one chooses war for war's sake or tries to produce war. But political activity, too, is incompatible with leisure. Over and above the activity it has to produce reputation and power, or again the happiness of the statesman himself and his fellow citizens, which is different from the political activity, and which we are looking for as something different."[2]

Aristotle does not confuse leisure with amusement or relaxation. Amusement is a form of relaxation; it is only because of the frailty of human nature that we require relaxation to fit us once more for serious activity. Man's chief good is happiness and this must lie in the activity of the highest part of his nature, the rational. Moral goodness is only a means to this end. All work and business, the activities of war and of public life are pursued for one object, namely, to enable man to live in his leisure the highest kind of life that is possible for him. This consists in purely intellectual activity ($\theta\epsilon\omega\rho\iota\alpha$) It is difficult to find an English translation which exactly fits this word. We may call it the Contemplative Life so long as we do not thereby confuse it with the "Contemplative Life" of the mediaeval mystic who allows himself to be the passive recipient of Divine illumination. $\theta\epsilon\omega\rho\iota\alpha$ is essentially an activity and perhaps the most apt description of it is the disinterested pursuit of wisdom and knowledge. When engaged in this activity, man for a few brief hours enjoys that bliss which is God's eternally. It includes not only study and research, but all creative efforts in the arts and in literature, and furthermore, the enjoyment which follows from the appreciation of that which is perfect and beautiful. Aristotle has indeed raised the oft discussed question whether the aim of education should be culture or that of fitting a young person to

[1] *Politics*, 1333.   [2] *Ethics*, 1177b.

pursue his work or profession in adult life. He has no doubt how the problem should be answered. The educator should take both aims into account, but he should realise that the practical things of life, essential as they are, must be subordinate to the right enjoyment of leisure. It may be necessary to be skilled in the craft by which one earns a living, but he is exceptionally fortunate who is able to express the highest part of himself in his work or profession. In a great many cases, the pursuit of a humdrum occupation is a pre-requisite to having leisure to enjoy. The Greeks did not live in a mechanical age and Aristotle was speaking to those who because of the abundance of slave labour, had no need to worry about earning a livelihood. Nevertheless, his view is still of value. The fallacy of many moderns is to think of these two aims of education as being incompatible. In a world which is becoming more and more materialistic in outlook, the vocational and technical tends to exclude the cultural. The individual has not been taught how to employ his leisure to gain satisfaction through creative activities and through appreciation and as a consequence turns to others to provide him with amusement.

The discussion of education in the *Politics* is largely concerned with the practical measures the state should take to make the good life possible for the citizen. Aristotle believed that education should be under the control of the state and not in private hands. As regards the early years, he is in agreement with Plato in insisting that we should aim at promoting physical health through exercise and at ennobling the mind through literature, art, and music. Until five years of age, children should receive no set lessons but should be fully occupied with healthy play. Then, until seven, there is a transition period during which they may look on at the older children who are busy with their lessons so that they may have some idea of what they are to do later on. It is important that young children should not consort with slaves and servants, from whom they may pick up low tastes and vulgar habits. The state inspectors of education should maintain a careful watch over them to see that this does not happen and that they are preserved from seeing and hearing things which are vulgar or improper. They should also exercise a strict supervision over the stories which are told to children. At seven years of age the child will begin his elementary education.

Speaking of his own time, Aristotle makes some remarks which are unfortunately still true. He says, "No one knows on what principle we should proceed—should the useful in life, or should virtue, or should the higher knowledge, be the aim of our training; all three opinions have been entertained. Again, about the means there is no agreement; for different persons, starting with different ideas about the nature of virtue, naturally disagree about the practice of it. There can be no doubt that children should be taught those useful things which are really necessary, but not all things".[1]

Although Aristotle would see that children learn "useful things" such as reading and writing, the Greek attitude towards professionalism is very apparent. He draws a distinction between liberal subjects, that is, studies suitable for the free citizen, and illiberal subjects, that is, the arts and crafts practised by slaves, and he would exclude from the curriculum of the free man's children, everything which would make the individual "mechanical" and all wage-earning occupations. "They absorb and degrade the mind." No subject, therefore, should be included in the curriculum solely because of its value for a particular trade or profession. The same idea is applied to the study of music. The teacher should not aim at producing the professional musician. The chief object in teaching music should be to develop the power of appreciation and to influence the formation of character. The former will provide an admirable means by which the individual can employ his leisure. He considers that in order to foster appreciation, the pupil should have some training in the playing of an instrument. Like Plato, he believes that music, art, and literature are powerful influences in the building of character.

Once more, he agrees with Plato that music is the most imitative of all the arts for it can imitate different emotional dispositions. If the young are brought up to take pleasure in the imitation of the virile, the orderly, and the noble, that training will have a marked effect upon their characters. At this point, however, he diverges widely from the views expressed in the *Republic*. Plato believed that voluptuous and ornate melodies should be banned from the ideal state. The same kind of censorship would apply to poetry and the drama. Aristotle would retain these arts because they fulfil a very important function to which he gives the name of

[1] *Politics,* 1337.

purgation (κάθαρσις). The meaning of the term is given in the *Politics* and more fully elaborated in the *Poetics*. It should be remembered that Aristotle was a physician and the term was primarily associated in his mind with medical practice. He was familiar with the custom of the Corybantic priests who employed the music of the flute to cure persons suffering from acute emotional tension. His view is that music and other arts assist the individual in freeing himself of his pent up feelings which he cannot discharge in the ordinary natural course. If he cannot rid himself of the excess of his emotions, they will remain as a source of hindrance and weakness. It is not so much that Aristotle believes it to be a bad thing to feel pity or fear, but that it is essential to purge away excessive accumulations of these feelings which may have a bad effect upon our mental health. The spectator of a great tragedy, such as Sophocles has given the world, discharges his accumulated emotions by identifying himself with the feelings of the outstanding personality of the drama, and he leaves the theatre calmed and pleasantly relieved of his pent up feelings. The process which Aristotle describes is akin to abreaction, the working off of a strong emotion, a procedure which occupies a prominent place in the practice of psycho-analysis. Aristotle, then, would permit the use of sensational and exciting music and drama for its cathartic value but he would not recommend more than its occasional employment.

The full curriculum for the adolescent would contain the following subjects: (1) Reading and writing, (2) Gymnastic, (3) Music, and (4) Drawing. Unfortunately the *Politics* breaks off without concluding the discussion on music, and we are given no details about the training in gymnastic nor any hint about the higher education of young men. As regards the earlier training in gymnastic, Aristotle insists that it should not aim at producing the professional athlete nor should it be so strenuous as to impair the natural growth of the child's body. We are told that at about the age of nineteen, the adolescent should begin a course "devoted to hard exercise and strict regimen" but nothing is said about its length. Probably it consisted of exercises and drills preliminary to military training. He records his view that "Men ought not to labour at the same time with their minds and with their bodies; for the two kinds of labour are opposed to one another—the labour of the body impedes the mind, and the labour of the mind the body".[1]

[1] *Politics*, 1339.

From the general trend of Aristotle's writing we can form some idea of the course of higher education in the Lyceum. It would most certainly have reflected his interests in medical and biological studies. Physics and ethics would have occupied an honoured place, and the study of logic would have made an introduction to First Philosophy and Theology (Metaphysics) and Ethics.

SUGGESTIONS FOR FURTHER READING

A translation of the *Ethics* is available in the Everyman Series. The most accessible translation of the *Politics* is that of Jowett (Clarendon Press, 1908). J. Burnett, *Aristotle on Education*, includes the sections of the *Ethics* and *Politics* concerned with education and is furnished with an introduction and notes (C.U.P., 1926). A simple introduction to the philosophy of Aristotle will be found in A. E. Taylor, *Aristotle*, Discussion Book Series (Nelson). For an advanced study of Aristotle, W. D. Ross, *Aristotle* (Methuen, 2nd edition, 1930), is recommended. J. L. Stocks, *Our Debt to Greece and Rome—Aristotelianism* (Harrap), gives an outline of his philosophy and traces its influence.

CHAPTER III

ROMAN EDUCATION—QUINTILIAN

The Roman civilisation, although it did not produce any thinker comparable with Plato or Aristotle, nevertheless exercised considerable influence upon the theory and practice of after ages, especially through the writings of Cicero and Quintilian. Roman education falls naturally into four well marked periods each of which possesses certain important characteristics. The legendary period of the monarchy is completely outside this classification since we have no certain knowledge about educational ideas in that early age.

(1) For nearly five centuries, the Roman Republic developed an entirely national scheme which was practically unaffected by external influences. There is no contemporary written account of Roman education during the early years of the Republic so that one has to depend upon statements made by later writers who cannot be reckoned as fully trustworthy. Many of them, looking backwards from the time of the later Republic and the early Empire were inclined to regard this period as a golden age and to attribute to it virtues which only existed in their imagination. Thus when Livy speaks of the existence of schools at quite an early date, his evidence should be received with considerable reserve.

There is no doubt that during the early days of the Republic the main educational agency was the home, and the younger Pliny is not far from the truth when he writes: "It was the ancient custom that we should learn from our elders, not only through the ear but also through the eye, those things that we should soon have to do, and in our turn hand them down to our successors. Each one was instructed by his own father, and to the person who had no father, the oldest and most distinguished citizens stood in place of one".[1] The intellectual training of the home did not pass beyond reading and writing and the earliest stages of number, but the merits of this home education lay in the physical and moral lessons it provided. It was the custom for the Roman boy to accompany his father in his daily routine and he learned from what his father did how he would have to conduct himself when he became an adult. Boys

[1] *Letters,* viii, 1, 4-6.

received practical training in farming and in military life and girls learned the arts of home management from their mothers.

The poorer citizens would not be able to provide so effective training for their children as was given in the homes of the wealthy. When, as the result of successful military campaigns, the Roman state began to expand, the household depended more and more upon the services of slaves and it became the custom to employ them as teachers of the children. The boy still obtained from his father the lessons of piety; he accompanied him when he offered sacrifices to the gods; he listened to the accounts told by his father and his acquaintances of the great deeds of the heroes of the past, and if his father was a senator, he would go with him to meetings of the senate. He also learned the laws of the Twelve Tables which were memorised by chanting, somewhat like the method adopted in many schools of the present in regard to multiplication tables. The important characteristic of Roman education in the olden days of Rome was its practical and vocational aim. There was little in the training of the Roman boy comparable with the education in music to which both Plato and Aristotle attached so much value.

(2) A great change occurred in the character of Roman education about the middle of the third century B.C. and which coincided with the conclusion of the first Punic War. Military operations and the growth of commerce had brought the Romans into contact with the Greek colonies in Sicily and southern Italy. The immediate result was that Roman traders and officials found it an advantage to learn the Greek language. This was intensified by the introduction into Roman households of increasing numbers of Greek slaves who had been captured during the war. Hence the practical interests in the Greek tongue very quickly developed into a desire to acquire a knowledge of Greek thought and literature. It is true that the Romans only came into contact with Greek civilisation when its decadence was well advanced but in some respects this was an advantage. The practical Roman would not have understood the refinements of Greek philosophical thought of the best period but he was able to absorb the somewhat diluted culture which came from southern Italy.

Towards the close of the earlier period there had grown up at Rome a class of teachers known as writing masters (*litteratores*). They were often slaves or freedmen. Quite soon the language teachers (*grammatici*) who taught the Roman children to read, write, and speak Greek, appeared on the scene. Though the learning of Greek was at first due to practical interests, it soon developed into a study of Greek literature. One can scarcely overestimate the consequences of this development. One might almost say that Greek was to the Roman as Latin to the nations of Europe in the Middle Ages. It represented the language of civilisation and culture and as soon as Greek thought began to permeate Rome, a movement began which has still its influence at the present day.

The Greek teachers brought with them as a textbook the works of Homer. Livius Andronicus, a Greek of Tarentum, was brought to Rome about 250 B.C. He translated the *Odyssey* into Latin and this has generally been considered as the commencement of Latin literature. Livius had been a slave but when he gained his freedom he still continued to teach. His work was continued by Q. Ennius, who although half a Greek himself, is considered as the founder of Roman poetry. The Roman historian, Suetonius, ascribed the introduction of the study of grammar to Crates of Mellos who came to Rome as ambassador in 169 B.C. and was detained there by a broken leg. He began to lecture in Rome and provided a model which the Romans were not slow to imitate. As a result of his example, teachers of grammar and literature began to appear in the capital. The movement was warmly supported by Aemilius Paullus who brought a number of Greek manuscripts to Rome, and by his son, Scipio Africanus the younger. It is not known when the earliest Roman grammar schools were opened. On the authority of Plutarch, Spurius Carvilius is recorded as the first Roman teacher to open a school and to charge fees for tuition. No doubt schools existed before this time but Carvilius broke with the accepted tradition. The Romans shared to a certain extent the Greek feeling that receiving a salary for instruction was, at the least, something unworthy. There seems, however, no reluctance on the part of teachers to accept good-will gifts. Carvilius also achieved the notoriety of being the first man in Rome to divorce his wife. There is no evidence to show that the school taught by him was a grammar school though shortly after his time grammar schools became established institutions (*c.* 230 B.C.). Later still, schools in which rhetoric and philosophy were studied became recognised, possibly as early as 160 B.C.

The infiltration of the Greek language and literature, and the ideas which accompanied them, did not go unchallenged. A definite reaction set in which was supported by representatives of some of the noblest families of Rome. Two Epicurean philosophers were banished, and even as late as 92 B.C., schools which taught rhetoric in Latin were closed on the plea that the instruction given in them was not in accordance with ancient custom (*mos maiorum*). One of the most powerful opponents of Greek influence was Cato the Elder. He undertook the education of his son in the good old-fashioned way, but even the strong personality of a man like Cato, the very embodiment of the old Roman virtue, could not for long stem the rising tide of Greek culture. By the beginning of the last century of the Republic, Greek influence had triumphed. This does not mean, however, that Greek culture had entirely supplanted the Roman traditions.[1] The latter still lived on and their influence was a tempering factor in the change that took place. The practical outlook of the Roman decided the content of education. There was always a certain amount of mutual suspicion between the two races. The Roman regarded the Greek as effeminate and in turn the latter thought of the Roman as little removed from the barbarian.

(3) The period of the later Republic and the early Empire exhibited two significant developments. The adoption of Greek ideas was now complete and one of the consequences of the change was the increasing interest in education shown by the State. So long as education was primarily an affair of the home there was no occasion for State intervention, but as the Roman dominions extended there arose the need for a more elaborate organisation of the Empire. The troubled years of the later Republic were in part a consequence of running a vastly extended commonwealth with ideas and institutions that had suited a city state but which had long been out-dated. Although the early Emperors did not attempt to establish a State controlled system of education, they showed

[1] Adams emphasised this when he wrote: "There is a general impression that Roman education follows naturally from Greek education, this view being strengthened by, if not indeed founded on, the time-honoured epigram: 'Captive Greece took captive her proud conqueror'. There is, however, no direct evolution from Greek education to Roman. The two ran a similar course at their earlier stages, and at the end Roman education appropriated some of the later and less desirable elements of the Greek".—*Evolution of Educational Theory*, p. 141, Macmillan, 1912.

considerable interest in educational institutions, especially those concerned with higher education, and exercised what amounted to a patronage of learning. The commencement of this policy was the action of Julius Caesar in extending the franchise to all foreign teachers of the liberal arts who were resident at Rome. Augustus continued this policy by founding public libraries at Rome, and when he issued a decree banishing all foreigners from the city, he made an exception in the case of teachers. The next step was the endowment of education. According to Suetonius, Vespasian was the first to bring Latin and Greek teachers of rhetoric into the service of the State by endowing chairs of rhetoric at Rome with a salary of 100,000 sesterces (approximately £800 a year). Quintilian was the first holder of the chair of Latin rhetoric.

The second important development of this period was also closely connected with the growth of organised education. In the early days of the Republic, before Greek influence became predominant, education was distinctly practical in its aim and there was little need for theorising. By the time that Rome had been transformed by Greek culture, the ideas of Plato and Aristotle which connected education closely with the state and the training of worthy citizens, had largely lost their force. The growing complexity of administration under the later Republic and early Empire had resulted in the formation of what may be termed a class of professional civil servants and a demand arose for a type of education which would fit young men for specific professional posts. Hence the increasing attention paid not only to the study of language and literature but in particular to the practice of oratory. One can see this influence in the writings of Cicero. He regarded rhetoric as a study necessary for those who aspired to public office. Cicero was a man of wide general culture; hence he did not disparage the study of philosophy but insisted that the skilled rhetorician should also be somewhat of a philosopher. The result of these changes was that an interest in the theory of education began to develop although it was a rather narrowed and restricted theory.

(4) Education during the later Empire displayed certain new features which were a logical consequence of the developments of the previous period. State intervention passed beyond the stage of patronage and the Emperors began to work out a definite educational policy which eventually led to State control of the schools.

The new tendencies began with Hadrian who showed great admiration for all aspects of Greek culture. He extended his patronage to all teachers of philosophy and rhetoric and built the Athenaeum at Rome to serve as a centre for literary studies. He confirmed the privileges given to teachers by his predecessors and tried to restore the ascendancy of Athens as a seat of learning. Hadrian's policy was continued and extended by the Antonines; Trajan, Antoninus Pius, and Marcus Aurelius. Trajan, for example, made grants for the education of 5,000 orphans and poor children (*alimentarii pueri et puellae*). Alexander Severus extended the "scholarship" system and Marcus Aurelius completed the work of Hadrian by making Athens the chief seat of culture in the Roman world. Sometimes, private individuals followed the same policy; thus the younger Pliny founded and endowed a school for the citizens of his own city of Comum. More and more, education came to be assisted from the public funds and there soon followed the demand of the State for direct control of the schools.

Antoninus Pius extended the educational privileges of Rome to the whole Empire. Some years earlier, indeed, Agricola had established schools in Britain and was evidently carrying out the Imperial policy. Municipalities were required to maintain an establishment of professional teachers which varied according to the size and status of the city. The municipal councils appointed the teachers, and the Imperial treasury gave financial assistance to poor municipalities who were unable to meet the cost. The usual practice was for the salaries of the teachers to be supplemented by charging fees. When the Imperial administration was overhauled by Diocletian, the State took over the control of all secondary and higher education. A definite scale of teachers' salaries was introduced which was based upon the nature of the instruction given. Thus teachers of rhetoric received five times and teachers of grammar four times the stipend of those who taught reading. Constantine continued this policy and granted teachers exemption from military service. Julian issued a decree in 362 which declared the right of the Emperor to supervise nominations to chairs and, if he considered it necessary, to make the appointment himself.[1] Gratian in 376 ordered municipalities to pay the salaries of teachers of grammar and rhetoric from the rates. The control of the State was

[1] This was in support of Julian's policy of restoring paganism. His Christian successors, however, maintained the decree.

completed by an edict of Theodosius in 425 which placed all education under the supervision of the Imperial government and forbad unauthorised persons to teach. It is worthwhile noticing that centralised control and rate assistance for education were by no means inventions of the nineteenth century.

The despotic rule of the later Emperors extinguished the last vestiges of freedom enjoyed under the Republic to which lip-service had been paid by Augustus and his immediate successors. This had a two-fold effect. The studies of the school, especially rhetoric, tended to become unreal and artificial. At the same time, the content and the methods of education became more highly organised. The schools were regarded as "technical" institutions which provided specific training for the law, the army, or for service in the State. The practical outlook and the Roman genius for organisation and system prevailed until the closing days of the Empire and the spirit of formalism and artificiality which had developed passed on to the Middle Ages. The Imperial grammar schools, already in decline in the fifth century, were unable to withstand the shock of the barbarian invasions, and except in Italy, they gradually disappeared. In that country, the grammar schools and schools of rhetoric continued to exist and were able to contribute scholars for the Carolingian revival of learning in the eighth century. When the Church converted the barbarian kingdoms, the grammar schools of the Empire furnished one of the models for the new Christian schools.

The most influential educational thinker produced by Rome was Quintilian. Although by birth he was a Spaniard he should be regarded as a typical cultured citizen of the Empire. He was born about A.D. 35, and it has been stated that his father who was himself a teacher of rhetoric, brought the youth to Rome. However this may be, Quintilian first came to notice as a student and later as a "junior" of the famous lawyer Domitius Afer. After the death of his patron, Quintilian returned to Spain to practise as a teacher of rhetoric. In A.D. 68 the Emperor Galba brought him back to Rome and he was appointed by Vespasian, A.D. 79, to the first chair of rhetoric at Rome. His salary was about £800 per annum and this was supplemented by good-will gifts from his pupils amongst whom was Pliny the Younger. Quintilian was not only a teacher but an advocate and in this capacity he undertook the defence of the Jewish queen, Berenice. He retired from his official post about A.D. 90 and commenced the composition of his famous *Instituto Oratoria*. This work contained the knowledge and experience he had accumulated in over twenty years as a teacher and pleader in the law-courts and is the most important treatise on education produced by the Empire. In addition to embodying the very best of Roman educational theory, the *Instituto* gives a full account of secondary and higher education in the greatest days of the Empire.

Our knowledge of elementary education under the Empire is very fragmentary. As one writer has remarked, "Elementary education in Rome presumably served its purpose, but we know little of it with certainty. Lack of precision in the picture is reflected in the rather vague and even contradictory accounts which modern writers base on their reading of the classical authors".[1] The extant accounts including that of Quintilian are concerned with the education of the wealthier section of the community, so that there is no opportunity of ascertaining how widespread were the facilities for elementary education. The elementary stage lasted for about five years and was under the supervision of the *literator* or *ludi magister* who taught his pupils reading, writing with the stilus on a wax tablet, and simple arithmetic using the abacus. At some time between twelve and fourteen years of age, the boy passed to the grammar school (school of the *grammaticus*). As the name indicates, grammar was the main study. One should bear in mind, however, that the term "grammar" included much more than it does in modern times, and was roughly equivalent to the study of language and literature. Grammar introduced the pupil to the study of the great poets, historians, and orators of the past, but even in Quintilian's day it was becoming more restricted in scope and eventually became practically synonymous with the meaning attached to grammatical studies at the present day.

Composition in prose and poetry was closely associated with instruction in grammar. All the other studies of the grammar school were strictly subsidiary. Music and dancing were traditionally part of the curriculum but little attention was given to them in Roman schools. The Romans thought it unseemly for citizens to dance. Mathematics, including arithmetic, geometry, and astronomy appealed to the practical sense of the Romans. The

[1] T. L. Jarman, *Landmarks in the History of Education*, p. 30, Cresset Press, 1951.

Roman notation was ill-suited to arithmetical computation and at a later age St Augustine confessed that he was able to understand how to add and subtract, but when he came to multiplication, he found the process so difficult that he lost heart. Very little progress could be made with arithmetic until the Arabic numerals came into general use towards the close of the Middle Ages. Roman boys were driven to use the fingers for calculation and mechanical apparatus such as the abacus served for more complicated computations. Instruction was also given in physical training and in speech, but the Romans differed widely from the Greeks in their outlook upon this training. They considered that the main value in the instruction consisted in its influence upon the bearing and speech of the youth.

When the boy reached the age of sixteen or seventeen he assumed the *toga virilis* and could commence the study of rhetoric. Sometimes the elements of rhetoric were taught in the grammar school but more often the study was reserved for the school of the rhetor. Quintilian as a teacher of rhetoric has a good deal to tell us about the training given by the rhetor and the methods employed in the schools. It is essential to note that the curriculum in all types of Roman school was not the result of a careful study of the aims of education. It developed in response to practical needs and to the pressure of public opinion, and in this respect it offers a parallel to the growth of the English elementary school curriculum in the nineteenth century. Quintilian accepted the curriculum as it stood and his main object was to show how each of the studies contributed towards producing the perfect orator. As Dr Boyd writes, the real interest of the *Institutio* "is not in the information it provides, valuable as that is, but in the fact that it is a description and discussion of the educational practice of Rome from within by the most successful teacher of the time. Considered in this way, the most striking feature of the book is the view it gives of the educational process as it concerns the pupil".[1]

Much of the *Institutio* is concerned with technical affairs pertaining to the practice of rhetoric. Book I, the early part of Book II, and certain chapters of Book III, are the portions of the work which are of most interest to the student of the history of educational ideas. In the system expounded by Quintilian the orator

---

[1] W. Boyd, *History of Western Education*, p. 75, 1st edition, A. C. Black, 1921.

takes the place occupied by the philosopher in the Platonic dialogues. It is not that Quintilian despises philosophy. He thought that the good orator was equivalent to the good man and that the teacher of rhetoric should know the ancient philosophers so thoroughly that the whole of his instruction would be permeated by philosophic principles. He deprecated attachment to a particular school of philosophy. It is impossible to discover how far he was sincere in this respect. No doubt his political principles were influential in adopting this attitude. The two most popular schools of philosophy in his day were those of the Stoics and Cynics and both advocated the withdrawal of the individual from public life and were opposed to the principle of hereditary succession in the Imperial line. Hence in his introduction to the *Institutio*, he wrote, "It is the perfect orator that we are training and he cannot even exist unless he is a good man. We therefore demand in him not only exceptional powers of eloquence but also every mental excellence".[1] To the view that it is the business of the philosopher to discover and apply the principles which produce an upright and honourable life, he replied, "For the ideal citizen, fitted to take his share in the management of public and private affairs, able to govern cities by his wise counsels, to establish them upon a sure foundation of good laws, and to improve them by the administration of impartial justice, is undoubtedly none other than the orator".[2]

What has Quintilian to say about the early stages of education ? He believed that training cannot begin too soon. It starts from the cradle and this means that careful thought must be expended upon the choice of the infant's nurses. They should be folk who speak correctly, and naturally, and should have an unblemished character. When the child begins to talk, the speech of his nurses will serve as a model for his imitation. Philip of Macedon chose Aristotle as tutor for his son Alexander. It is impossible for the father to exercise too much care in the selection of the child's nurses.

The parents also carry a grave responsibility. It is well if both father and mother have themselves been well educated. If this is not so, then parents, aware of their own deficiencies, should exercise all the greater care in the early upbringing of their children. The same principles should apply to the slaves with whom the child will have contact. This is especially true of the *paedagogi*; if they

---

[1] *Institutio*, Book I, Introduction, para. 9.   [2] *ibid.*, para. 10.

are not themselves well educated, the next best thing is that they should be aware of their shortcomings.[1] Those who have a little knowledge are prone to form false ideas about what they actually know and in turn, they may influence their young charges to the detriment of their morals.

Quintilian preferred a boy to start by learning the Greek tongue. His argument for this course is interesting. Latin, he asserted, will be picked up as a result of his day by day experience without much effort on the part of the teacher. Also, because Roman culture has largely been derived from the Greek, it is logical to begin with the study of the Greek language. This does not mean that for a long period the pupil should only speak and study Greek. Such a method would lead to endless faults in pronunciation. The pupil should spend a short time on Greek and then commence the study of Latin so that the two languages would then be studied together.

Quintilian proposes a problem which is much discussed at the present day. Should children begin their letters before the age of seven ? Some of his contemporaries replied in the negative but Quintilian agrees with Chrysippus that an even earlier start than this might be made with some children. The essential point to observe is to avoid overburdening the child's mind and so cause him to dislike his studies. Therefore, he writes, "Let this first instruction be in the form of play; let the pupil be asked questions and praised for his answers; let him never rejoice in ignorance of anything. Sometimes when he is unwilling to learn, let another be taught of whom he may be jealous: let him compete sometimes with others and quite often think himself victorious: let him also be spurred on by rewards, which at that age are eagerly sought after".[2] Quintilian offers some practical hints which probably represent the methods adopted by contemporary teachers of young children. He advocates giving the child ivory letters to play with and he should be encouraged to handle, observe, and then name them. When he begins to write, his early efforts should be assisted by making use of a board in which the forms of the letters are cut and his hand can then be guided along the grooves as though they were furrows. This will set up the motor habits required and there

[1] *Paedagogi* were slaves who accompanied the children to school, waited while they received instruction and brought them home again. *Paedagogi* were a common institution in Greece and were adopted by the Romans when they came under the influence of Greek culture.
[2] *Institutio*, Book I, c. 1.

will be no need for the teacher to guide his hand when forming the
letters. He also stresses the value of neat and rapid writing. "For
since writing itself is the most essential thing in our studies and the
one thing from which alone springs true and deeply rooted proficiency, a slow pen hinders thought and a badly formed and careless hand is difficult to read."[1]

Quintilian was an opponent of soft pedagogy. He believed in
building a firm foundation at the elementary stages. For example,
he insisted that spellings should be learnt by heart but he added
that this should not prove too difficult a task for the young child.
During childhood, the pupil's memory is extremely retentive and
advantage should be taken of this fact. In all learning, the key-
note should be thoroughness and to achieve effective memorising
constant repetition is necessary. This part of the discussion is
concluded by a remark which calls to mind the practice of the
nineteenth-century schools. "I would urge that lines which are set
as models for copying should not be such as express idle sentiments
but which convey some useful instruction."

He then turns to consider a problem which was destined to be
reopened in later ages. Many wealthy Roman parents preferred
to engage a private tutor for the education of their children rather
than send them to school. Does this practice represent the ideal
or are there certain benefits which the school alone can confer?
We shall see that Locke and Rousseau were convinced of the
advantages of private tuition. Quintilian, however, decided in
favour of the school. When one reads his argument, it is difficult
to realise that nearly two thousand years separate his age from ours.
The case for the private tutor follows the lines that have become
familiar to us through Locke. The tutor can give his pupil his sole
and undivided attention so that his progress is both thorough and
rapid. The schools have a demoralising effect upon many young
boys. They often form undesirable companionships which counteract the influence of a cultured home. In other words, the school
tends to corrupt the manners and morals of its pupils.

Quintilian concedes that there is something to be said for this
point of view but when the whole question is carefully examined,
the school has certain advantages which out-weigh those of any
kind of private tuition. The school is a society in miniature and
when the pupil becomes a member of the school community, he

[1] *Institutio*, Book I, c. 1.

experiences the bracing influence of healthy competition. The "sympathy of numbers" has its effect upon the teacher as well as the pupil. Quintilian was sufficient of a realist to entertain no illusions about the atmosphere of the average Roman family in the wealthier section of the community. He knew that the claims made for the superiority of the family influence were often more sentimental than real. In the homes of well-to-do Romans, ambition, greed for money, and desire of advancement and love of pleasure, did not provide an environment which favoured the growth of morality, culture, and refinement. The actual facts were that children brought up at home were often spoiled by softness and indulgence and tended to follow the practice rather than the precepts of their parents. One of Quintilian's greatest merits was that he was able to consider the process of education from the child's point of view.

It is true he observes that the tutor can devote himself entirely to the care of his pupil but attention to individuals is also possible under the conditions of class teaching. The teacher himself gains inspiration from dealing with pupils in a group and it is only the third-rate practitioner who really prefers to teach the individual. The skilled teacher can handle his class as a group and at the same time give individual attention to those who need it. Pupils who can go ahead of their own accord may be safely left to do so and the teacher has opportunities of attending to the difficulties of individuals. Not only does the presence of an audience bring forth the best qualities of a teacher but, in turn, he becomes a source of inspiration to his pupils just as the sun sheds its light upon all things that are fortunate enough to receive its rays. The good teacher soon discerns the child of outstanding ability and contrives that he shall receive the right amount of encouragement at the appropriate time. It is also essential to remember that our future orator will exercise his art in public and it is therefore good that he should be accustomed to speak and act in the presence of others from a very early age.

Certain modern writers have deprecated the use of rivalry and competition within the school. Not so Quintilian. He believed that healthy competition is a spur to progress and he would have heartily commended the Scottish practice of the early nineteenth century whereby pupils took their place in class according to their efforts and abilities. He wrote, "There is one useful method known to me, which was employed by my own teachers. They arranged us in classes, determining the order of speaking according to the ability of the pupils. Thus as each boy appeared to excel in proficiency he stood highest in the order of declamation. Tests of progress were held from time to time, and to earn promotion was a great prize with us, whilst to be head of the class was by far the most coveted honour".[1]

In still another way, Quintilian anticipated modern ideas about education. When a teacher meets a new pupil, his first business should be to discover the boy's abilities and natural aptitudes. Nowadays one would say, "Set him an intelligence and an attainment test". Quintilian would have phrased it, "Make a study of him to discover his abilities, the standard of his attainments and any particular mental characteristics that he possesses". He was intensely distrustful of the precocious youth. His promise frequently disappeared within a short space of time. The most important task that faces the teacher when he meets a new class is that of getting to know and understand his pupils.

A very pertinent question now arises. What place, if any, should corporal punishment hold in the school ? Quintilian is quite decided in his answer. "As for corporal punishment, though it is a recognised practice . . . I am completely opposed to it, first because it is disgusting, fit only for slaves and undoubtedly an insult . . . in the next place, because a pupil whose mind so ill befits a free man's son as not to be corrected by reproof, will remain obdurate even in face of blows—like the vilest of slaves: and finally because there will be no need of such chastisement if there is always somebody present to diligently supervise the pupil's studies . . . If you coerce the child when he is young by means of blows, what will you do when he is a young man who cannot be compelled through fear and has many more important things to learn?"[2]

The teacher should remember that each pupil has his own individual characteristics and should be dealt with along lines best suited to him. Quintilian is quite optimistic about the attitude of the average pupil. He is not at all averse to learning; in fact he delights in acquiring knowledge and really wants to make progress. If this quality appears to be lacking in him, more often than not, the fault is the teacher's and not the child's.

From the elementary school the pupil passes to the grammar school and Quintilian, having in mind the wider conception of grammar, declared that it is the foundation on which all further

[1] *Institutio*, Book I, c. 2.   [2] *ibid*., c. 3.

progress must be built. The idea of grammar as the basis of all learning was attractive to the thinkers of the Middle Ages and Renaissance who frequently emphasised that grammar is the gateway to all higher studies. Their notion of grammar, however, was much narrower than Quintilian's. He divided grammatical studies into the art of correct speaking and the interpretation of the poets. (*recte loquendi scientiam et poetarum enarrationem.*) His liberal views on the curriculum of the grammar school appear in the following remarks: "In its recesses, the subject comprises much more than superficially appears. For with speaking is joined the theory of writing, and the interpretation of the poets is preceded by correct reading, and criticism is connected with both of these . . . In addition, it is not sufficient to have read the poets. All types of writings must be examined not only for their content but also for words which frequently derive their authority from the writers who use them. Further, grammar cannot be complete without a study of music, because it has to give a decision about questions of metre and rhythm. Nor is it able to make the poets intelligible without a knowledge of the movements of the heavenly bodies. For example, the poets in order to indicate the seasons of the year, nearly always refer to the rising and setting of constellations. Nor can grammar dispense with a knowledge of philosophy".[1]

The Renaissance thinkers echoed Quintilian's view of grammar, but it was not long before the curriculum of the grammar school became so narrow and restricted that Huxley was, with considerable justification, able to describe it as "gerund grinding". For Quintilian, the grammar master was *par excellence* a teacher of literature. When he undertook a study of a literary extract in class, his aim should be to draw from it everything possible in the way of thought and style. Quintilian's idea was analogous to the French method of "texte expliqué", or "texte commenté".

Even in the grammar school, the pupils should receive some training for their further work in the school of rhetoric. Quintilian advised: "Our pupils should therefore learn to recite such fables as those of Aesop, which immediately follow the stories told them by their nurses, and then to attain to the same grace of style in writing them. They must begin by learning how to break up lines of poetry and then how to put the sense into different words, and after this, to paraphrase more boldly, with freedom to abbreviate

[1] *Institutio*, Book I, c. 4.

or to adorn, except that they do not alter the meaning of the poet. Such a task is not an easy one even for the experienced teacher and he who has accomplished this in a competent fashion will be ready to learn anything".[1]

Other arts and sciences should find a place in the grammar school curriculum. Thus the pupil will study music, arithmetic, and geometry. Attention will also be given to gymnastics and training in speech. It should not be our aim to produce actors and professional athletes. Quintilian speaks most disparagingly about those "who devote part of their lives to anointing themselves with oil for wrestling, part to over-indulgence in wine—men who bring about the destruction of the mind by excessive care of the body (such men I would keep as far away as possible from those we teach)".[2]

In an important chapter, Quintilian discusses a topic which constitutes a serious problem at the present day, namely, the overcrowding of the school curriculum. He asks: "Granting that all these things should be learned, can they be all taught and acquired at one and the same time ? Some deny this because they believe that the mind is confused and fatigued by so many diverse studies, for which there is neither mental nor bodily strength nor enough time; believing, too, that however true it may be that pupils who are more mature can stand up to the toil, the years of childhood should not be burdened".[3] Quintilian does not altogether agree with this view. He states that he believes it to be a bad practice to learn subjects in succession because this hinders concentration upon any one subject for a length of time. A change of diet benefits the digestion and in a similar way, a change of occupation is good for the mind. Variety in study is as necessary as in other aspects of life. "Thus reading affords a respite from writing and the monotony of reading is relieved by a change of subject." Childhood is a period when learning comes easy. The boy can learn Latin in about two years, but the adult slave, whose mind is fixed and less flexible than the child's, "wrestles for many years with the Latin tongue". Quintilian's reasoning might be challenged by modern psychologists on the ground that young children quickly become fatigued and this is counteracted by a change of occupation.

The object of the grammar school is to provide a general education; that of the school of rhetoric to give a more specialised training.

---

[1] *Institutio*, Book I, c. 9.   [2] *ibid.*, c. 11.   [3] *ibid.*, c 12.

In fact, the school of rhetoric in Quintilian's day, was a technical institution because it aimed at producing the skilled orator just as the technical college of to-day has for its object the production of the trained engineer or craftsman. The age of transition from the grammar school to the school of rhetoric was not fixed. Much depended upon the individual pupil. He should enter the school of rhetoric when he showed himself fit for it, which might be at the age of thirteen or fourteen or even later. The moral character of the teacher of rhetoric should weigh considerably when it comes to a decision about which school the boy should enter. In his description of the good teacher of rhetoric, Quintilian's practical experience in handling youths is easily apparent. Speaking of the teacher, he declares: "It is not sufficient that he should himself manifest severe self-control, he must also by the strictness of his discipline control the behaviour of those who gather round him. Let him, then, above all, adopt the attitude of a parent towards his pupils and consider that he is taking the place of those who entrust their children to him. He should be free from vice himself and must tolerate none in his pupils. Let him be stern but not melancholy, friendly but not familiar, lest in the one case he incur dislike, in the other contempt. He must constantly discourse on the honourable and good for the more he admonishes his pupils the less he will need to punish them. He must never lose his temper, yet he will not ignore faults which deserve correction. He must be simple in his teaching, able to endure hard toil, assiduous rather than exacting.

"He must freely answer questions and put questions himself to those who do not ask them. In praising the recitations of his pupils he must neither be niggardly nor extravagant, for in the former case he will create a dislike for work, in the latter a spirit of self-complacency. When he corrects faults he will not be harsh and never abusive; for many are turned away from the studies they have entered upon because some teachers find fault as though they hated the offender.

"He must recite something every day, nay, many things, so that his audience have something to carry away. Though he may supply them with copious examples for imitation from the works they are reading, yet what is called the living voice gives fuller nourishment, especially if it be the voice of a teacher whom pupils, if they are rightly trained, both love and respect. It is a very difficult matter to assess how much more readily we imitate those whom we like".[1] In this quotation one should note Quintilian's insistence upon the friendly and sympathetic relationship that ought to exist between teacher and pupils.

Quintilian's account of the curriculum of the school of rhetoric is valuable because it describes the content of the higher education of the Empire as set forth by the most accomplished teacher of that time. The studies of the young orator may be divided into: (1) a more advanced training in composition and style both written and oral, which leads to practice in the art of declamation; (2) a study of prose writers with special attention to the principles of literary criticism; and (3) the formal instruction in rhetoric which is dealt with in Books III to XII and which is of a highly technical character. In addition to attending lecture classes, the pupil was expected to do a good deal of private reading and to work exercises. The latter included exercises in composition, the translation of Greek authors and the paraphrase of Latin writers. Quintilian believed that a boy of fifteen and upwards is capable of private study and that he should be encouraged by his tutor to undertake it. Much of the work of the school was concerned with practice in themes, the kind of argument and advocacy which later the pupil would use in the law-court. In the later books of the *Institutio*, Quintilian gives numerous examples of such themes.

Quintilian is an important figure in the history of educational ideas not only because of the information about Roman education which he gives but also because of his influence upon subsequent generations of teachers. In the Middle Ages his works were only known through a mutilated text, but even so, their influence can be traced in Cassiodorus and in Isidore of Seville. The complete text of the *Institutio* was discovered in 1416 and had a striking effect upon Renaissance thinkers who steeped themselves in it. In particular, Vittorino da Feltre, Vives, and Erasmus, were profoundly influenced by his teaching. English educational thinkers were not so strongly influenced by Quintilian but Sir Thomas Elyot and Roger Ascham had studied him and some eighteenth-century writers such as Vicesimus Knox quote freely from the *Institutio*. Brinsley knew and appreciated Quintilian and Charles Hoole used his declamations in the Grammar School at Rotherham.

[1] *Institutio, Book II, c. 2.*

SUGGESTIONS FOR FURTHER READING

The Latin text with English translation of the *Institutio* is accessible in the Loeb edition. W. M. Smail, *Quintilian on Education* (O.U.P., 1938), contains a translation of selected passages from the *Institutio*. The introduction to this book is most useful and includes an account of the environment of Quintilian and a summary of his educational theory. R. R. Rusk, *The Doctrines of the Great Educators* (Macmillan, reprinted 1948), includes a chapter on Quintilian. A. Wilkins, *Roman Education* (C.U.P., reprint, 1921), gives a useful summary of education under both the Republic and the Empire. Aubrey Gwynn, S.J., *Roman Education from Cicero to Quintilian* (O.U.P., 1926), is also recommended.

CHAPTER IV

ST AUGUSTINE (354-430)

The eminence of St Augustine as a theologian and philosopher has tended to conceal that he was also one of the greatest educational thinkers. If Locke and Rousseau be considered as typical representatives of one particular school of thought, then St Augustine must be counted as the most outstanding example of the opposite point of view. His doctrine of interior illumination marks him off entirely from all thinkers who believe that knowledge takes its beginning from sense experience.

St Augustine's life is so well known from his *Confessions* that there is no need to repeat here what may easily be read elsewhere. There are, however, certain events in his life which had such a profound influence upon the direction of his thought with regard to education, that they should receive particular attention. His father, Patricius, though by no means a wealthy man, was exceedingly ambitious for his son and did his utmost to provide the boy with the best education that he could afford and in this he was supported by his wife, Monnica. The young Augustine followed a course of studies similar to those described by Quintilian in the *Institutio*. He started in the school of the *ludi magister* where he received elementary instruction in reading, writing, and counting. His memories of his early school days were not happy ones. He recorded: "I loved not study, and hated to be forced to it. Yet I was forced, and this was well done towards me, but I did not well; for, unless forced, I had not learnt".[1] From the elementary school he passed to the school of the *grammaticus* and even here it was some time before he began to take an interest in his studies. Life at the grammar school at Tagaste, which was near his home, was harsh. The master had not the kindly regard for his pupils which Quintilian displayed and Augustine frequently suffered under the rod of the master. This left bitter memories not so much because of the physical pain he endured but more because he felt the punishment he received was unjust. He had started to read Greek at the school of the *ludi magister* and he disliked it intensely. It was for

[1] *Confessions*, translation of Dr Pusey, Everyman Series, J. M. Dent, I, 12.

him a foreign language and even when at the grammar school he began the study of Homer, the story held no attraction for him. Looking back upon his experiences, he wrote: "But why did I so much hate the Greek, which I studied as a boy ? I do not yet fully know. For the Latin I loved; not what my first masters, but what the so-called grammarians taught me. For these first lessons, reading, writing, and arithmetic, I thought as great a burden and penalty as any Greek".[1] This antipathy towards Greek remained with him all his life so that although he knew a certain amount of the language, he never became a Greek scholar.

As he grew older, Augustine became more interested in his studies and began to develop the habit of wide reading. Virgil made a great appeal and later, he declared that if he were deprived of the works of that poet, he would weep unceasingly. Arithmetic bored him. " 'One and one, two; two and two, four'; this was to me a hateful sing-song: 'the wooden horse lined with armed men', and 'the burning of Troy', and 'Creusa's shade and sad similitude', were the choice spectacle of my vanity."[2] Augustine's own comment on his love of Virgil is worth recording. "No doubt then, that a free curiosity has more force in our learning these things, than a frightful enforcement."

From the grammar school at Tagaste, Augustine was sent to the school at Madaura, the birthplace of Apuleius, the author of the *Golden Ass*. Augustine read this work and admired it to the end of his life. From Madaura he went to the school of rhetoric at Carthage which was taught by a certain Democrates. Augustine soon showed a flair for higher studies, and became head of the class in rhetoric. It was at this time that his first conversion took place. Many readers of the *Confessions* think of Augustine's conversion as a sudden momentary experience which took place later in his life. A more careful study would seem to show that his conversion was a process extending over a number of years and punctuated by three definite stages which themselves merit the name of conversion because of the emotional and intellectual effect they had upon him. The first conversion was to the study of philosophy. Let him tell the story in his own words: "In the ordinary course of study, I fell upon a certain book of Cicero, whose speech almost

[1] *Confessions*, I, 13.
[2] *ibid.*, I, 14. The text of the *Hortensius* has been lost and only a few fragments have been preserved.

all admired, not so his heart. This book of his contains an exhortation to philosophy, and is called the *Hortensius*. But this book altered my affections, and turned my prayers to Thyself, O Lord; and made me have other purposes and desires. Every vain hope at once, became worthless to me; and I longed with an incredible burning desire for an immortality of wisdom . . . For with Thee is wisdom. But the love of wisdom is in Greek called 'philosophy', with which that book inflamed me . . . I was delighted with that exhortation, so far only, that I was thereby strongly roused, and kindled, and inflamed to love, and seek, and obtain, and hold, and embrace not this or that sect but wisdom itself whatever it were; and this alone checked me thus enkindled, that the name of Christ was not in it".[1]

It was shortly after this that Augustine was attracted to the Manichean heresy and was for nine years a member of that sect. At the age of twenty-one, he returned to Tagaste as a teacher of rhetoric. He did not remain long there for we soon find him teaching rhetoric in a school at Carthage. He was not happy there for he was seriously disturbed by the wild behaviour of the students. "At Carthage, there reigns among the scholars a most disgraceful and unruly licence. They burst in audaciously, and with gestures almost frantic, disturb all order which any one hath established for the good of his scholars."[2] Augustine's disciplinary troubles so weighed upon his mind that he was not sorry to leave Carthage to teach at Rome where he had been told the students were not so difficult to manage. Whilst he was at Carthage, he first became acquainted with the logic of Aristotle. He began to read the treatise on the Categories after a warning that it was so difficult a work that nobody could understand it. Much to his surprise, he was able to say, "I read and understood it unaided". Augustine knew nothing of the philosophical works of Aristotle. He looked upon Aristotle as a logician whose method was useful in expounding the Scriptures.

After recovering from a severe attack of malaria, Augustine opened his own rhetoric school in Rome. He soon had plenty of pupils but he found things were not so pleasant as he had been led to believe. If the students at Carthage were hooligans, those at Rome were thieves. When the time came for the payment of fees, they deserted in a body to attend the school of another master.

[1] *Confessions*, III, 4.   [2] *ibid.*, V, 8.

Augustine's next move was to Milan where he came to know St Ambrose. Under the influence of the latter, Augustine relinquished his membership of the Manicheans and offered himself for instruction in the Christian faith. His second conversion took place at Milan. One of his acquaintances, "a huge mountain of a man" introduced him to the works of the Neo-Platonist, Marius Victorinus. They were translations of part of the *Enneads* of Plotinus. The study of these books produced a lasting change in his thought and even after his final conversion, Augustine, as far as his philosophy was concerned, remained a Platonist. Victorinus later became a Christian and his example had an effect upon Augustine. It should be noted that Augustine knew very little of Plato himself. He may have read a fragment of a Latin translation of the *Timaeus* which was easily accessible but he never drew the distinction between the teaching of Plato and that of Plotinus and the Neo-Platonists.

Augustine's final conversion took place in July, A.D. 386, and the account of it is so well known that it need not be repeated here. He, with his natural son, Adeodatus, received Baptism at the hands of St Ambrose and shortly afterwards he resigned his post as teacher of rhetoric. He was ordained a priest in 391 and was consecrated Bishop of Hippo, near Carthage, in 396, where he remained until his death which took place in 430 when the city was besieged by the Vandals.

Augustine's experience as a teacher exercised three most important influences upon his life and thought. In the first place, his knowledge of teaching method proved to be of great assistance in his work as a bishop. The policy of the Church, which was intensified when the barbarian invaders of the Empire were converted to Christianity, was to recruit the clergy from the native population of each region.[1] One of Augustine's problems was that of instructing native Numidian priests in the Latin necessary for the services and teaching them the rudiments of Church music. This task, coupled with his previous experience as a teacher, was a factor which induced him to reflect seriously about the principles of teaching method, especially in regard to the teaching of language and music.

More important still was the effect which his school training and his experience as a teacher of rhetoric exercised upon his whole

---

[1] It was this which led Augustine of Canterbury to found the first English school as part of the establishment of his cathedral.

outlook as regards education. He was thoroughly versed in the poetry and philosophy of the pagan world. This was responsible for the significant difference in standpoint between himself and many of his contemporaries. Augustine, more than any thinker of his period, brought about the fusion of the ancient culture with the Christian religion. The Christians of the second and third centuries had been faced by a formidable dilemma. They had no special antagonism towards the Empire as such. Had not Christ recognised the authority of the Emperor by saying: "Render unto Caesar the things which are Caesar's, and unto God the things which are God's?"

The clash came when the authorities demanded that, as a demonstration of their loyalty to the Empire, Christians should burn incense before the statue of the Emperor and offer sacrifice to the pagan gods of Rome. A faithful Christian could not obey such a command for it amounted to a betrayal of his faith and a fall into the hated sin of idolatry. Hence the authorities came to regard Christians as traitors to the Empire and inflicted death, torture, and imprisonment upon them. Persecution convinced Christians that they were aliens dwelling in the land of Babylon who could have no part in a system steeped in idolatry. Hence their avoidance of all things pagan. This included the literature of Greece and Rome. How could they send their children to the schools where the whole atmosphere was laden with pagan beliefs and practices? Still less could a Christian become a teacher in the Roman schools. The Church Fathers of the second and third centuries put this view in unmistakable terms. Tertullian typified the Christian attitude towards pagan literature and philosophy. Secular learning, he declared, was not only superfluous; it was mere folly. What bond existed between the Christian and the pagan world? His true citizenship was in the Church of Christ. There could be no mingling between the heathen world and the heavenly Jerusalem. The Christian's hope of salvation lay in Christ and for this, the Sacred Scriptures contained all that was necessary for him to know.

The Fathers of the Eastern Church were not so uncompromising in their condemnation of pagan culture. Clement of Alexandria, and Origen, had studied in the schools before their conversion and realised that pagan learning contained in itself much that was useful and true. They regarded certain aspects of it as a suitable preparation for Christianity and in the Catechetical School of

Alexandria, both religious and secular knowledge was taught. St Basil expressed the same view when he stressed that the Christian should regard the present life as a prelude to the true life of the world to come, and that it was quite legitimate for the Christian to make use of poets, historians, philosophers, and rhetoricians, for his mental cultivation. He believed that much written by pagans was good and true and noble, and that some of the teaching of Plato resembled that of St Paul. The more tolerant attitude towards pagan learning was slow in spreading in the west, but in the third century some of the Christian leaders were less uncompromising. Education was a necessity and they reluctantly agreed that Christians were obliged to send their children to the schools.

They consoled themselves with the thought that by using what was necessary and true in pagan literature they were taking what really belonged to them. St Ambrose, for instance, declared that all the good and noble thoughts of pagan literature were derived from the Old Testament and hence Christians need not scruple about using them. He himself was well read in the classical authors and quoted quite freely from the poets and philosophers of Greece and Rome. In spite of this, many Christians were not at all happy about the use of pagan learning. St Jerome was an example of a classical scholar and an earnest Christian whose conscience was sorely troubled about this problem. He was an enthusiastic admirer of Cicero and he suffered from a severe mental conflict between his love of classical literature and his duty as a Christian. When in late middle life he retired to live a hermit's existence in the desert, he took his books with him. The inner struggle did not cease. "Wretched man that I was," he cried, "in the midst of my fasts I read Cicero. After passing sleepless nights and weeping bitterly at the thought of my sins, I read Plautus. When at times I came back to myself and tried to read the Prophets, the crude and careless style of their writings at once repelled me." His *Epistles* give a clear picture of his uncertainty of mind, and even when he was close on seventy, he had not come to a decision. He was not sure whether he should be proud or ashamed of his love for the classics.

"The debate which St Jerome could only close by leaving it open was closed for ever by St Augustine . . . Augustine was an African, born and bred on the shores of the Mediterranean facing Europe. From his childhood all the influences that have gone to the making of our civilisation were focused upon him: Semitic influences transmitted through the society, perhaps through the blood, of the Phoenicians whose language and traditions were still alive and familiar to him; Persian influences, brought to bear upon him by the Manichaeism in which he became involved; Latin and Greek influences, infused into him by way of education by his father, his nurses, and his schoolmasters; Christian influences, urged upon him gently but persistently by his mother from his infancy, and at last by the overwhelming force with which it recommended itself to his great heart and his great mind."[1]   Thus when Augustine and other like-minded Fathers of the Church brought classical learning into the service of Christianity, they accepted the tradition of the liberal arts.   Augustine's part in handing on this tradition will be considered later in this chapter.

As mentioned above, Augustine never entirely abandoned the Platonism which he discovered in the translations of Victorinus.   He rejected those doctrines which he found were contrary to Christian belief such as the Platonic teaching about the pre-existence of the human soul and reincarnation.   Other doctrines he transformed so as to assimilate them with Christianity.   For example, the Platonic forms which dwelt in the intelligible world, became for him, the ideas or exemplars of the Divine mind after the pattern of which God created heaven and earth.   Even with these modifications, one can justly claim that Augustine's psychology and philosophy remained a Christian Platonism and when he considered some of the fundamental problems of education he regarded them through the eyes of Plato.   His influence in this respect had immense repercussions on the thought of the Middle Ages.   Until St Thomas Aquinas in the thirteenth century produced his great synthesis of Christianity and Aristotelian philosophy, Augustine was the greatest authority in theology and philosophy.   Even when the Aristotelian influence was at its height, Augustine still retained that position in theological studies.

Augustine's educational ideas, with one exception, are scattered throughout the many volumes of his works.   The treatise, *On the Teacher* (*De Magistro*), is devoted entirely to the discussion of some of the basic problems of educational theory and the solutions at which he arrives are the very antithesis of the doctrines of Locke

[1] From the essay entitled *St Augustine and Humanism* by Fr John-Baptist Reeves, O.P., in *A Monument to St Augustine*, p. 137, Sheed and Ward, 1934.

and Rousseau. It is strange that of all the writings of Augustine this particular one has received the least attention from English students. This neglect is unfortunate since in the *De Magistro*, Augustine expounds most fully his theory about the origin of ideas and raises a number of important points concerning the relation between our ideas and their verbal expression.

The treatise is cast into dialogue form, the speakers being St Augustine himself and his son, Adeodatus. The dialogue was based on an actual discussion that took place between them. Adeodatus was a natural son of Augustine, born in the period before his final conversion and Baptism. In the *Confessions* (IV, 2), he wrote: "In those years (from nineteen to twenty-eight) I had one—not in that which is called lawful marriage, but whom I had found out in a wayward passion, void of understanding; yet, but one, remaining faithful even to her".

Monnica was deeply grieved about her son's liason and constantly besought him to put away his mistress and marry into a good family. Eventually he acceded to her wishes and was betrothed to a maiden under age for whom he had to wait two years. This was not satisfactory for Augustine. "Meanwhile my sins were being multiplied, and my concubine being torn from my side as a hindrance to my marriage, my heart which clave unto her was torn and wounded and bleeding. And she returned to Africa, vowing unto Thee never to know any other man, leaving with me my son (Adeodatus) by her. But unhappy I, who could not imitate a very woman, impatient of delay, inasmuch as not till after two years was I to obtain her I sought, not being so much a lover of marriage, as a slave to lust, procured another, though no wife, that so by the servitude of an enduring custom, the disease of my soul might be kept up and carried on in its vigour or even augmented, into the dominion of marriage." (*Confessions*, VI, 15.)

In another passage of the *Confessions* there is a reference to the composition of the *De Magistro* (IV, 6). Speaking of his Baptism, Augustine wrote: "We joined with us (*i.e.* to his friend Alypius) the boy Adeodatus born after the flesh, of my sin. Excellently hadst Thou made him. He was not quite fifteen, and in wit surpassed many grave and learned men . . . There is a book of ours entitled *The Master*; it is a dialogue between him and me. Thou knowest, that all there ascribed to the person conversing with me, were his ideas, in his sixteenth year. Much besides, and yet more admirable,

I found in him. That talent struck awe into me. And Who but Thou could be the workmaster of such wonders ? Soon didst Thou take his life from the earth; and I now remember him without anxiety, fearing nothing for his childhood or youth, or his whole self".

This passage fixes the date of the *De Magistro* as 389. The treatise is again mentioned in the *Retractions* (I, 12). "At the same time I wrote a book entitled *De Magistro*. In it is disputed and sought and found that there is no master who teaches man knowledge, save God, according to that which is written in the Gospel, 'One is your Master, Christ'. This book begins, What do we seem to you to seek to do when we speak ?" Adeodatus is mentioned on two other occasions. "There was also with us, in age the youngest of all, but whose talents, if affection deceives me not, promise something great, my son Adeodatus." (*Vita Beata*, § 6.) In the *Confessions* (IX, 12) we are told that he was present at the deathbed of Monnica. "But when she breathed her last, the boy Adeodatus burst out into a loud lament; then checked by us all, held his peace."

The *De Magistro* is an inquiry into the origin of our ideas, a problem which no system of philosophy, ancient or modern, is able to ignore. Is the source of our ideas to be found in the mind itself, *i.e.* are they innate, or do they come as the result of some external agency such as sense experience or the communication of ideas from one person to another through the medium of language ? Popular thought does not doubt the possibility of the transference of ideas and points to teaching and learning as instances which show quite clearly that there is an interchange of ideas. The pupil is thought to receive his ideas from the teacher and learning thus becomes nothing more than the process by which the mind of the learner assimilates the ideas put before him by the schoolmaster using the medium of speech. The role of the pupil becomes one of passivity and receptivity. The teacher is active in teaching which is the imparting of knowledge, and his pupils, when they learn, passively absorb what is presented to them. This does not mean that the teacher needs no skill. There are good teachers and bad teachers and the former are recognised by the skilful way in which they adjust their exposition to the receptive capacity of the minds of their pupils. Hence, as the result of communication, ideas are transferred from one mind to another and so the ideas of one person are not peculiar to himself but can be shared by many. Is this the correct account of teaching and learning ? Augustine thinks not. For such a view to be true, one must suppose a constant and unfailing correspondence between language and thought and Augustine proceeds to examine the alleged correspondence to see if he can detect any flaws in it.

Language, spoken or written, is the normal medium for the expression of thought. Whether we express the contents of our mind to another or are engaged in soliloquy as in silent prayer, we make use of words. What is the nature of the spoken word? It is essentially a sound produced by vibrations in the air which impinge upon the ear. If I am ignorant of Latin and I hear the word *lapis* uttered, it will have no meaning for me; it is a sound and nothing more. My previous experience of language will enable me to realise that the speaker is referring to something which has a meaning for him, but what it is, I cannot even guess. Unless I have some experience or idea which has become associated with the particular sound, hearing the word will convey nothing to me. In uttering the sound, the speaker wishes to convey what he is experiencing or thinking at that moment. We may say, then, that the word is a sign of something in the speaker's mind. To every sign, however, there corresponds that which is signified (*significabilia*) and in the case of the spoken word, the *significabilia* is the meaning carried by the word. The written word is merely a symbol to recall to the mind the spoken word and its meaning.

We have grown so accustomed to spoken and written language that we are apt to think of words as the only possible signs that can be used for communication. In many instances, however, gesture, facial expression or action can indicate my meaning as clearly as the spoken word. If someone asks me what a wall (*paries*) is, I may simply point to a wall with my finger and that is equivalent to saying, "That is a wall". This applies to most concrete objects and their sensible qualities. Primitive peoples employ a language which consists largely of gestures and the deaf mute conveys his meaning to another by this means. Consider a child learning his mother tongue or beginning the study of a foreign language. The teacher has little difficulty in causing him to learn the names of objects and those qualities belonging to them which are immediately apparent to the senses. He shows the object to the pupil and pointing to it, utters its name. The same applies to actions. The name of the action can often be taught by performing the action. If the teacher wants the pupil to know the meaning of *ambulo*, he walks and as he walks, he says, *ambulo*. To understand the meaning of bird snaring, *i.e.* the art of catching a bird by imitating its song, the learner could be shown the bird snarer at work. This method may not always be the quickest and most effective, and may even give rise to misconceptions, but as a rule, in those cases where the object is at hand, it is the natural way of teaching its name. It is obvious that Augustine was a believer in the direct method of teaching a language.

The following passage from the dialogue will show how carefully each point in the argument is considered:

Aug. If I ask what the three syllables mean when the word *paries* is uttered, can you not point to it with your finger so that I can see the object whose sign is this three syllable word, thus showing it to you without uttering any word?

Ad. I agree this can be done only in the case of those names which signify bodies and only if they are present.

Aug. Do we call colour a body or rather a quality of a body ?

Ad. The latter is true.

Aug. Cannot colour be shown by pointing ? If in addition to bodies you consider the qualities of bodies, so long as these are present to the senses, cannot they be taught without words ?

Ad. When I say bodies, I ought to say all corporeal things, *i.e.* everything belonging to bodies which is perceived by sense.

Aug. Think now at this point whether you should make some exceptions.

Ad. That is useful advice, for I should have said, not all corporeal but all visible things. I agree that sound, smell, taste, weight, heat, and other qualities which are perceived by the other senses, although they cannot be experienced in the absence of bodies and are therefore corporeal, yet they cannot be shown by pointing.

Aug. Have you never seen men conversing with deaf people by gestures, and also that deaf mutes ask and reply, teach or indicate, all or nearly all they want by means of gestures ? The fact that this happens proves that not only visible things but sounds, smells and other like things can be indicated without using words. Thus actors in the theatre can relate and illustrate whole stories without words and this is chiefly done by dancing.

Ad. I can say nothing to contradict you . . .

Aug. If I ask you what *ambulare* and *surgere* mean, what would you do ? Would you not perform the action rather than teach me by words or other signs ?

Ad. I agree that I would and I am shamed that I was so slow in seeing this. From this example thousands of things occur to me which can be explained through actions and not through signs, as *edere, bibere, sedere, stare, clamare,* and many others.

Aug. Now, tell me, if I was totally ignorant of the meaning of *ambulare,* and I asked you as you were walking alone, how would you teach me ?

Ad. I would do it by moving more quickly so that after your question you would learn by the change in my action and yet nothing else would be done save that action which needed showing.

Aug. But do you not know that walking is one thing and hurrying another ? He who walks does not necessarily hurry and he who hurries does not necessarily walk. Also we speak of haste in regard to writing and reading and many other things. If in reply to my question you did more quickly what you were already doing, I might think that walking was the same as hurrying. The latter is something new that you added and because of this I would be mistaken.

Ad. I agree that the action cannot be explained without a sign, if we are asked when we are doing it. If we add nothing, the questioner will think that we do not wish to show him and that we ignore him because we continue in what we were doing. If, however, he asks about those actions we can do when we are not doing them, we can reply to his question and answer him by an action instead of a sign.

To return to the main problem. What is the function of a word or a gesture ? It should be realised that the link between ideas and language is not as close as popular thought imagines. It is a commonplace of experience that a thinker who tries to convey his ideas by means of language may completely fail in doing so and may even convey a meaning which he does not intend.

St Augustine quotes the example of an Epicurean who believes that the soul is mortal. In his lectures he presents to his students the arguments of more enlightened philosophers than Epicurus to the effect that the soul is immortal. The lecturer is convinced that the view he presents is a false one. His attitude of mind, however, does not prevent certain of his hearers from understanding that these proofs are true. This is an example of a teacher who does not know that the soul is immortal but uses in his teaching the same words he would use if he did know and believe it. On the other hand, the pupil knows that the soul is immortal because he hears the arguments of a teacher who does not believe it. Is this not a case of a teacher who teaches what he does not know? The teacher does not convey to his pupils his real opinions. Thus in two minds, the same words need not have the same value as truth. A similar distinction between the sign and the idea signified is seen in the examples of telling a lie and in slips of the tongue. He wrote: "Consider in addition, lying and deceit, through which you easily understand that the real thought of the mind is not only not revealed but is actually concealed by the words that are used . . . Again, we have often experienced both in ourselves and others that words reveal what we do not intend. This can happen in two ways. Firstly, when we make a speech from memory, we often in the course of it, use words other than those we wish to say. This frequently occurs in singing a hymn. Secondly, words we do not mean to use escape us through a slip of the tongue. In such a case, it is not the signs of what we intend that are heard, but those who tell a lie do intend what they say, and even if we do not know whether they are telling the truth, we do know that what they say is intentional".

We often find two people arguing about the same term because each attaches a different meaning to it. This could not happen if words always convey the same meaning. Thus my opponent declares that animals are superior to men. I do not agree with his statement because I understand the word "superior" in a different sense. He is thinking of certain physical superiorities such as strength and agility, acuteness in hearing and keen sight. I am thinking of man's intellectual superiority, and I argue with him because his words have not conveyed what he intended. Can we then hold the view that words convey ideas from one person to another, when the same words can be understood by two people in quite different senses ? Words have not the same meaning for all who hear them.

We think that an interchange of ideas takes place between the teacher and the pupil but we are mistaken. There is only an interchange of words. The true function of language is not to bring ideas into our minds but to stimulate and awaken those that are already there. How this can be we have yet to determine. One may object that too much stress has been placed on misunderstandings, slips of the tongue, and such occasional happenings, and that in normal conversation, when we grasp the words that are used, we understand the thoughts of the speaker. We have already seen some instances of a dissociation between language and thought. Perhaps in normal cases the correspondence is not as close as generally supposed. Let us take an instance where the same words are used and have the same meaning for speaker and listener. When a teacher is instructing his class, does he introduce into the minds of his pupils his own ideas through the words he uses ? To answer this one must consider different types of teaching. When the teacher is dealing with material objects and their properties, the problem is simple. Let us suppose that the pupil is reading the account of the three young men who were cast into the fiery furnace. He is told in the *Vulgate* that by the intervention of God, they are preserved from death and walk about unhurt in the flames. He then comes to the line, *Et saraballae eorum non sunt immutatae.* (*Daniel,* iii, 27.) He asks his teacher what a *saraballa* is and receives the answer that it is a head-covering. The pupil can understand this explanation because he has had previous experience of people and knows the meaning of head and a covering for the head. The *saraballa* is a special type of headcovering which is unfamiliar to the pupil because it is obsolete and peculiar to Eastern peoples. Without further explanation he will naturally think of headcovering in terms of the head dresses with which he is familiar, and the idea he forms will be inaccurate. His teacher might illustrate the meaning of *saraballa* through verbal description, taking care to use words and gestures which would recall to the pupil familiar experiences, or he might draw a *saraballa*. If by teaching we mean the transference of the teacher's ideas to the pupil, then no teaching has taken place. In reality, the teacher has stimulated the pupil to employ experiences and ideas which were already in his mind to form a new idea through the reflection on experiences he had previously had.

In another type of teaching the master is concerned to illustrate the meaning of an idea. What will be his procedure? He will explain or define the idea in words that his pupils understand because they recall what is already familiar and so they build up the meaning of the new idea in terms of old experiences and ideas. But the teacher has not transferred his ideas to the pupil's mind. In fact, the very opposite has taken place. When words present a meaning to the minds of those who hear them, this meaning is necessarily already present in their own thought and it is this meaning with which their intelligence clothes the words addressed to them. The classic instance of this is that described by Socrates in the *Meno* (82-86). Socrates questions an ignorant slave about geometry and proves that this slave is capable of discovering truth for himself. When questioned by Socrates, the slave was able to reply. Did he not implicitly possess this knowledge before? It is absurd to suppose that his questioner transferred his own ideas through his questions. It is true that the slave came eventually to affirm as true certain things that he had previously denied as false. This, however, was because of the frailty and slowness of his mental vision which hindered him from grasping the steps of the problem as a whole. Socrates asked him a series of questions to stimulate him to do this. These questions, however, although they guided his thought from stage to stage, did not teach him truths of which he had been ignorant. Their function was to turn to knowledge that which had formerly been implicit in his experience. Augustine's conclusion is *numquam discere* but he does not mean by this that teaching is impossible, only that it cannot take place on the hypothesis of a transference of ideas. He now turns to investigate the true meaning of the activities of teaching and learning.

Teaching, then, is the activity of causing pupils to learn.

When the pupil learns he does not receive ideas from the teacher. The process of learning is an active not a passive one. Ideas and experiences which were dormant become aroused and the pupil reacts to an external stimulus or understands something, as the case may be. "Words, then," comments Fr D'Arcy, "though they are the vehicles of communication, cannot cause ideas. If the subject matter be sensible, explanation is useless without some personal experience; if the subject matter be ideas, then the teacher suggests something to the pupil's mind.   The former's task, however little he may know it, is to direct the pupil to foregather with himself and, in the chambers of his mind, find the truth which is there".[1] The pupil does not find out the thoughts of the teacher nor, when he learns, does he seek to do so.   No parent would be so foolish as to send his child to school to learn the thoughts of the master. He is sent to school to learn the truth about things and in relation to truth, the master is in the same position as the pupil.   The truth belongs neither to the master nor to the pupil; it is common to both. The master learnt the truth through its presence in his own soul and he stimulates the pupil to do the same.   The following extracts from the *De Magistro* illustrate this conclusion.   (The references are to the numbered columns in Migne's *Latin Patrology*.)

(*a*) "Concerning all which is the object of our intellectual activity, the master we consult is not the person who speaks to us externally; the master is within, the truth which dwells in the soul itself.   The words of the teacher have only stimulated us to consult the inner master." (1216)

(*b*) "What I say to a pupil is understood by means of his own reflections not through my words." (1217)

(*c*) "Whosoever can understand intellectually is inwardly the disciple of truth and externally the judge of him who speaks, yea, even of the discourse itself." (1218)

The last quotation makes it clear that the pupil does not necessarily take for granted what has been told him by his teacher. He may think about the conclusions reached by the teacher and decide that he does not accept them.   Naturally, only a few brilliant pupils will have the ability to do this and only when they have reached a fairly advanced stage in their studies.

Whence comes this truth which dwells in the soul ?   It is a light which proceeds from God Who is very Truth.   The Divine Word is the true teacher of the soul Who illumines the mind from within, for He is the True Light which lighteth every man coming into the world.   Such a conclusion may at first seem fantastic to modern minds, though one might hazard a guess that Augustine is speaking

[1] Fr M. C. D'Arcy, S.J., in the essay, *The Philosophy of St Augustine, A Monument to St Augustine*, p. 178, Sheed and Ward, 1934.

metaphorically. Hence it is necessary to ask what he really means when he describes Christ as the Secret Teacher of the Soul or when he speaks in other of his works, of Divine Illumination. Divergent views have been held about the meaning of this phrase and this makes it all the more difficult to disentangle the truth. Unfortunately, the *De Magistro* has little to say about the nature of Divine Illumination and it is necessary to turn to other writings of Augustine for elucidation.

Some thinkers have taken Augustine literally. Neo-Platonic influences acting through the Arabians, especially Avicenna, led to the interpretation that the human mind sees all things in God as in a book. Such was the teaching of William of Auvergne in the thirteenth century. This doctrine appeared again in the seventeenth century, in particular, in Malebranche, who was influenced by the Cartesian idealism. Others have affirmed that at root there is little real difference between the teaching of St Augustine and St Thomas Aquinas and that the role of Divine Illumination is the same as that of Active Intellect. Both interpretations are in contradiction to the facts. Divine Illumination is not to be identified with God any more than the sun which enables us to see is the same as the eye. "The nature of the soul is so made," says Augustine in the *De Trinitate* (IX, xv, 24), "that by the disposition of its Creator it is naturally united to intelligible things; hence it is that it sees them in a kind of incorporeal light of a special sort (*in quadam luce sui generis incorporea*), just as the bodily eye sees the things which surround it in this corporeal light, for which it was created and disposed". To attempt to assimilate the teaching of Augustine to that of Aquinas is a serious historical blunder. It ignores the influence of Platonism on the thought of Augustine and it is the strong current of Platonism running through his thought which provides the clue to the sense in which Divine Illumination should be understood.

Augustine makes it quite clear that Divine Illumination is a metaphor. He frequently compares the activity of the mind in thinking to that of the eye in vision. Corporeal things must be rendered visible by the light of the sun before they can be seen. In a similar manner, scientific truths must be made intelligible by a kind of light before they can be grasped. As the sun is the source of light in sense vision, so God is the means of spiritual illumination which enables us to understand universal and necessary truths.

God stands related to our thought as the sun does to our light. What does this metaphor mean ?

In all discussions about the origin of our ideas, three problems have to be solved.

(a) How is the content of our ideas derived ?

(b) Whence do they obtain their character of universality and necessity ?

(c) What is the guarantee of the truth of our ideas ?

(a) Augustine answers the first by his analysis of sense experience. The latter provides us with the content of our ideas. Like Dewey at a later period, Augustine strongly protests against the view that sense experience is wholly passive. It is essentially an activity and its essence lies not so much in the impression upon the sense organs made by contact with an external object as in the total reaction of the individual to the sense impression. In estimating the individual's experience not only the actual sense impression and his feelings of pleasure or the reverse, but his volitions and his actions have to be taken into account. His experience consists not only of the cognition of something external but also the meaning that he attaches to the situation and his reaction to it in the light of that meaning. It is incorrect to say that external objects impress themselves upon the mind. This would be impossible because the inferior cannot impress or react directly upon a superior. "The thought cannot be entertained," wrote Augustine, "that a body can cause anything in a spirit, as though the spirit, like matter, were subject to the action of a body". (*De Genesi ad litteram,* XII. 14.) Augustine's account of sense experience contains certain interesting features. His definition of sense perception indicates the direction his doctrine is going to take. "Every sense perception is an affection of the body which is not concealed from the mind." (*Omnis sensus passio corporis non latens animam.*) Suppose a person sees a column of smoke in the distance. This is perceived through an affection of a bodily organ, namely, the eye. As we should say at the present time, certain light waves set up physical and chemical changes in the eye. This is on the physiological level and at this stage there is no perception. Then occurs the mysterious part of the process. The mind which is closely connected with the body, perceives the modifications produced in the nervous system and raises to its own level the response which is to be given. If the impact on the sense organ passes unnoticed, the response will be unconscious. It is the act of attention or consciousness which constitutes the essential nature of sense perception. Hence, *sensum puto esse non latere animam quod patitur corpus*—sense perception belongs not to the body but to the mind through the body.

We may proceed to a further stage and make a statement that beneath the smoke there is a fire, although at the moment we cannot actually see it. This must be distinguished from sense perception. It is really an act of judgment, an inference from what is perceived. It belongs to the class which Bradley called a Synthetic Judgment of Sense. It goes beyond the immediate given in perception. In true sense perception it is the mind which senses and forms an image of the body and its affections. "It is the act of attention or consciousness which is sensation. The explanation is obviously based upon Augustine's theory of the interrelation of body and soul. The soul ensconced within its own spirituality lives in conjunction with a body of its own. When something happens to that body, it listens and raises to its own level the response to be given."[1] It is through this active process of experience that we receive the content of our ideas. "Whatever is known to us is known through the senses of the body and the experience of life." Experience is therefore a necessary condition of knowledge but it is not of itself knowledge. Its function is to supply the raw material from which knowledge grows. Unfortunately, Augustine shows more interest in investigating the nature of our knowledge of truth than in the stages in the formation of ideas. He does indeed speak of the mind as actively working upon experience and through comparison and analogy, perceiving likenesses and differences but he has not left us any detailed account.

(*b*) The second problem is concerned with the characteristics of universality and necessity in our ideas. How is it, for example, that we see the fundamental truths of mathematics as universal and necessary ? The answer is given through the metaphor of Divine Illumination. There is nothing mystical about this conception. Divine Illumination is part of the ordinary scheme of nature and Augustine is at pains to emphasise this by the frequent use of such terms as *natura* and *naturalis ordo*. God does not take the place

[1] Fr M. C. D'Arcy, S.J., in the essay, *The Philosophy of St Augustine*, *A Monument to St Augustine*, p. 176, Sheed and Ward, 1934.

of man's intellect and do his thinking for him. Each man possesses his own individual intelligence which he uses according to his natural capacity to develop his own knowledge. Just as the eye needs the light of the sun to be able to see, so in the mental sphere, the intelligence requires the Divine Light for its activity of thought which is really a mental vision. The human mind is naturally constituted to receive this illumination which is direct. Augustine stresses this by the phrase *nulla natura interposita*—there is no intermediary.

The universal truths which are grasped by the mind are the Divine ideas. One should note Augustine's adaptation of Platonism to bring it into line with the Christian religion. The Divine ideas are described by a variety of terms—ideas, forms, species, thoughts, and laws. They exist in a two-fold manner. Primarily and originally they are the ideas in the mind of God, the patterns or exemplars which He used when He created the universe. They then came into the world of sense experience as the principles or laws which govern the physical world, and which confer on it the reality it possesses. The physical world is permeated by the Divine ideas so that St Paul could describe God as "the God in whom we live and move and have our being". The world is, therefore, an orderly, systematic world, not a mere jumble of conflicting principles. Our minds constitute the instruments by which we know and understand the world. We have the power of penetrating the conflicting masses of detail and grasping the underlying laws and principles which account for the behaviour of things. In other words, the mind sees the Divine ideas as they are exemplified in the physical world but at first it does not grasp the laws and various interrelations between things.

The child adds together three sticks and five sticks and by counting them, finds that he has now eight sticks. He does the same with beads, counters, and other material objects. Then, at some stage which depends upon the grade of his intelligence, there comes the flash of illumination and he realises that three added to five make eight. Moreover, this truth is recognised as universal and necessary. It does not matter whether the units added are sticks or stones, sheep or cows; he has discovered a universal principle. As soon as the child begins to use words and is able to count and measure, he has grasped a certain number of simple abstract ideas. It is a matter of common experience that some children do this earlier and with greater ease than others. Everything depends upon the nature and complexity of the ideas, the quality of the individual's intelligence and the wealth of sense experience available to him.

(c) It is through Divine Illumination, understood in this way, that the validity and truth of our knowledge is guaranteed. God is ultimately the source of all our knowledge and Augustine speaks of Him as the Teacher of the Soul, the Father of Intellectual Light, and the Father Who illumines our minds.

The lesson which Augustine teaches is an extremely important one for the educator. In no sense is it the role of the teacher to impart knowledge; in fact this is impossible. Ideas are not introduced into the mind through communication. The latter may serve as a stimulus for thought, but ideas are the result of the activity of the mind itself which by reflection upon what is given in experience or by communication, grasps the truth by a flash of intellectual insight and realises its universality and necessity. The teacher, in modern terms, has the function of so arranging the environment of learning, that the flash of illumination comes sooner rather than later. The art of teaching is the art of stimulating pupils to think and to learn. Both Plato and St Augustine are in agreement on this fundamental point. Education does not consist in the accumulation of facts. It is an illumination of the soul, a turning of the eyes of the mind towards the light.

We can now return to the part played by Augustine in bringing about the fusion of classical culture with the Christian religion. His point of view is explained fully in the *De Doctrina Christiana*. This treatise expresses his conception of the methods and aims of Christian education and its influence was widespread in the early Middle Ages, especially in the twelfth century, the period when the universities of mediaeval Europe began to take shape. The keynote of Augustine's conception of Christian education is to be found in Book II, chapter 17. "Let every good and faithful Christian understand that truth, wherever it may be found, is the truth of his Lord and Master." (*Quisquis bonus verusque Christianus est, Domini sui esse intelligat, ubicumque invenerit veritatem.*) Hence it is the truth that matters whether it comes from a Christian or a pagan source.

The treatise opens by drawing a distinction between things which are enjoyed as an end in themselves and those which are means to an end. God is the perfect example of the first. Things used for an end are of two kinds; those which are useful because of what they are in themselves and those which serve to make known something other than themselves. The latter are signs. Natural signs are related to the thing signified as smoke is a natural sign of fire, being its effect. Conventional signs have been produced by the wit of man in order to communicate his feelings, perceptions, and thoughts to others. Words, writing, and books, are such conventional signs. The most important words are those which compose the books of Holy Scripture, which declare the will of God unto men. Scripture, however, must be read and interpreted. For this task, men must acquire the knowledge of written signs so that they can understand what is signified by each letter and word. The meaning of the signs has been handed down by tradition and is embodied in what are called the liberal arts. In reality, we must be instructed in two distinct traditions. It is necessary to know the tradition of the Apostles which they received from Christ, *i.e.* the meaning of the signs established by God, and also the tradition of men which consists of the liberal arts.

The Christian should utilise every assistance available even if it comes from a pagan source. Augustine compares the Christian emerging from the spiritual bondage of paganism with the exodus of the Children of Israel from Egypt. Although Egypt was a land of idols and the temples of false gods, the Israelites on their journey were commanded by God to take with them gifts made by the Egyptians, vessels and ornaments of gold and silver which were for their own use. The Israelites put to a good use the very things which the Egyptians had employed for evil purposes. In a similar way, the writings of the pagans contain much that is idolatrous and evil, but Divine Providence has so ordered things that they also include gold and silver, things which are useful and moral, and which lead to the worship of the true God. Hence the Christian would do wrong to despise what is valuable in pagan learning. His policy should be that of spoiling the Egyptians, *i.e.* making use of what is true in pagan literature for the service of Christ. He should select the very best in secular culture for his own use.

What is the content of the liberal arts which have been handed down to us? The first is grammar, which deals with the use of words as signs. The next is dialectic, which is the science and art of reasoning and helps us to understand the meaning of signs even when no teacher is present to instruct us. It is not man-made but exists eternally in the reason of things and it originates from God. Rhetoric is a means of moving the hearts and minds of men and is of value in setting forth the truth. The other arts study the signs which nature presents. The first is the science of number, arithmetic. Music is concerned with the numbers or metres employed by the poets. The earth, solid and immovable, is the sign of all that is constant and has figure and proportion and so gives rise to the science of geometry. Finally, we should use all things that have been said aright by the philosophers, especially the Platonists, and make them our own. It will be noticed that Augustine has enumerated seven liberal arts, but there is no evidence that he attached any significance to the number seven. Thus in the *De Ordine*, six arts are listed. Arithmetic is included in geometry, and astronomy is substituted for philosophy. Evidently, Augustine had not definitely fixed the number of the liberal arts, and he had certain qualms about the inclusion of astronomy which was closely bound up with heathen astrology. Nevertheless, astronomy was a means of determining the date of Easter and other Church festivals and so could be of use to Christians.

There are two features about Augustine's teaching on the liberal arts. In the first place, the idea was not new, but in adopting it, he entirely transformed earlier views about the content of Christian education and established a tradition which was to govern the curriculum of the schools, and later, the universities, for many centuries to come. Secondly, later thinkers developed the idea of the liberal arts with greater precision. Each of these features should be examined in turn.

The idea of the liberal arts can be traced back, at least, as far as Plato. Aristotle, as was seen earlier in this book, had regarded a liberal education as one suitable for a freeman who was not concerned with the practical application of what he learnt, but rather with the effects the study had in producing moral and intellectual excellence. When Greek culture passed over to Rome, the idea of the liberal arts accompanied it. Neither the Greeks nor the Romans specified any fixed number for the arts. Thus, Varro (116-27 B.C.), a contemporary of Cicero, listed nine arts or disciplines which included the seven listed by Augustine (astrology taking the place of philosophy) and the addition of medicine and architecture. Both the Younger Seneca and Quintilian were familiar with the writing of Varro, and if one examines the curriculum of secondary and higher education as described by Quintilian, it will be seen that the subjects of instruction consisted of the liberal arts.

Another writer whose compilation was studied by after ages more thoroughly than it deserved, was Martianus Capella, who may have been contemporary with Augustine, though some authorities claim that he wrote early in the fourth century. If so, Augustine had probably read his work. It was entitled, *The Marriage of Philology and Mercury (De nuptiis Philologiae et Mecurii)*, and was an allegory spread over nine books.[1] The treatise describes how Mercury presents his bride with seven bridesmaids who symbolise the liberal arts, grammar, rhetoric, dialectic, arithmetic, geometry, astronomy, and music. The first two books are taken up with the description of the marriage ceremony. In the remaining seven, each bridesmaid in turn expounds in dull and wearisome fashion, the particular art of discipline she represents. It should be noted that Capella rejected Varro's addition of medicine and architecture. His reason was that they were concerned with perishable earthly things and could not be considered liberal studies. Capella's book eventually found its way into the schools, and boys read it after they had mastered the elements of Latin grammar in Donatus. This accounts for Capella's influence in the early Middle Ages.

Augustine had read the treatise of Varro and he relates that when he was at Milan, he wrote a book on grammar and part of another on music. After his Baptism, he finished his treatise on music and claimed to have written on the five other arts. Of these only the *De Musica* is extant. The others that are published in Migne's *Patrology* are probably not by Augustine.

[1] H. O. Taylor in *The Mediaeval Mind*, vol. 1, p. 71, Macmillan, 1919, has a very low opinion of Capella's work. He writes: "Possibly some good Christian of the time could have composed a worse book, or at least one somewhat more deflected from the natural objects of primary education. But the *De nuptiis* is astonishingly poor and dry. The writer was an unintelligent compiler, who took his matter not from original sources, but from compilers before him, Varro above all. Capella talks of Eratosthenes, Hipparchus, Euclid, Ptolemy; but if he had ever read them, it was to little profit".

The work of Capella is a sad commentary on the state of classical learning in the fourth and fifth centuries.

The next steps consisted of fixing the number of the arts at seven and dividing them into the Trivium and the Quadrivium. Three names are associated with this development. The first is that of Boethius (*c.* 470—*c.* 525), the author of the famous *Consolation of Philosophy.* Boethius came of a noble Roman family and became the friend and chief minister of Theodoric, King of Italy. He was a man of upright and austere character whose intense dislike of fraud and deceit made him many enemies among the corrupt officials employed by the king. Theodoric in later life developed into a moody and suspicious tyrant who believed that his Roman officials were conspiring to bring Italy under the rule of the Emperor at Constantinople. The enemies of Boethius brought a charge of treason against him, and he was cast into prison and eventually executed. The great ambition of Boethius was to make the works of the Greek philosophers accessible to the Romans of his day. He began by making a Latin translation of the logical works of Aristotle and of the *Isagoge* of Porphyry. It was his comments on the latter treatise that gave rise to the controversy about the nature of universal ideas which occupied so important a position in early mediaeval thought. In addition, he wrote treatises on arithmetic and music which became textbooks for after generations. The treatise on arithmetic is the important one for the present topic. It opens by defining the scope of arithmetic and its relation to other studies. Arithmetic deals with number or multitude as it exists in itself. Some numbers are relative, such as double, half, next but one, etc. Relative numbers belong to the science of music. Geometry studies immovable magnitude, but the knowledge of the heavenly bodies which are movable magnitudes belongs to astronomy. Boethius then remarks: "This, then, is that quadrivium in which those must travel whose mind being raised above the senses, is brought to the heights of intelligence". So far as is known, Boethius was the first to employ the term quadrivium, and the context makes it clear that he thought of these studies as leading to the higher discipline of philosophy. He did not use the term trivium, although the idea of it was latent in his thought.

The number of the liberal arts was fixed at seven by Cassiodorus 477-570) who also gave his reasons for taking this step. Cassiodorus was the friend and contemporary of Boethius. He served under Theodoric for forty years and eventually became praefect of the praetorian guard. After the death of Theodoric he retired to the monastery he had founded in Calabria where he devoted himself to study and the copying of manuscripts. It was his example which to a great extent made the copying of manuscripts one of the important tasks undertaken by the monasteries. He was also the author of a number of treatises among which was the *Institutiones divinarum et saecularium litterarum*. This was a guide to the monks for their religious and secular studies. The first book of the treatise is concerned with Scripture, but the second is a summary of the seven liberal arts of which dialectic is accorded the fullest treatment.[1] Cassiodorus, like many early Christians, attached great importance to numbers. In keeping with Jewish and Christian tradition, he regarded seven as the sacred number. Thus he opens the second book with the paragraph: "Now is the time that we should run through the text of the present book under the seven other titles of secular letters. It should be clearly understood that whenever the Holy Scriptures wish to set forth anything as complete and lasting, as they frequently do, it is comprehended under that number, for as David says; 'Seven times in the day have I spoken praises unto Thee', and Solomon, 'Wisdom hath builded her house, she hath hewn out her seven pillars'". (*Proverbs*, ix, 1.) Thus the number of the arts was fixed at seven, the mystical number which signified the perfect and complete, and the authority of Scripture was found to support this step. It should be noted that Cassiodorus calls the subjects of the Trivium, arts; those of the Quadrivium are termed disciplines.

The final development of the idea was the work of Isidore, Bishop of Seville (d. 636). He is mainly known for his encyclopaedic work in twenty books, the *Etymologiae*.[2] It was so called because Isidore attempted to give the derivation of each thing that he described or defined. Needless to say, his derivations are not by any means accurate and when definite knowledge was lacking, he drew freely upon his imagination. The idea of the *Etymologiae* was to present the whole of sacred and secular knowledge which was current at that time. The first three books are entitled, *De grammatica, De rhetorica et dialectica*, and *De quatuor disciplinis mathematicis*. Isidore completed the development by regarding the Trivium (grammar, rhetoric, and dialectic) as a preliminary to the Quadrivium (arithmetic, geometry, music, and astronomy) which in turn served as an introduction to the higher studies of philosophy

---

[1] The text is given in Migne, vol. 70.   [2] *ibid.*, vol. 82.

and theology. The seven liberal arts comprised the curriculum of secondary and higher education throughout the mediaeval period and for long after. It is possible to trace these subjects in the curriculum of the school of York under Albert and Alcuin and in the studies of the school of Chartres. When the mediaeval universities developed, the subjects of the Trivium were relegated to the grammar school. The studies of the university included the Quadrivium (medicine was added later as an additional subject) which were the prelude to the higher studies of philosophy and theology, the queen of the sciences.

SUGGESTIONS FOR FURTHER READING

The life of St Augustine is treated in detail in *St Augustine*, Giovanni Papini, translated by Mary Prichard Agnetti (Hodder and Stoughton, 1930). *A Monument to St Augustine* (Sheed and Ward, 1930, cheaper edition, 1934), consists of a series of essays by eminent scholars on the different aspects of Augustine's teaching. The *Confessions* is available in the Everyman series, J. M. Dent (Dr Pusey's translation). The Loeb series contains the Latin text and English translation of the *Confessions*. The Latin text of Augustine's works has been published in numerous editions, that in Migne's *Latin Patrology* is probably the most easily accessible. Recently, an English translation of the *De Magistro* has been published and will be found in *Basic Writings of Saint Augustine*, edited, Whitney J. Oates, vol. 1 (Random Publishing House, New York, 1947).

CHAPTER V

THE SCHOLASTIC METHOD—ST THOMAS AQUINAS

The mediaeval period added practically nothing to educational ideas so far as the schools were concerned. The curriculum of the grammar schools was based upon the Trivium, and of these subjects, Latin grammar held the prime place. In the early mediaeval period, the schools had attempted to teach the whole of the liberal arts, but when the universities began to develop in the latter part of the twelfth century, the recognised theory was that the studies of the Quadrivium were the proper subjects for scholars of the university. In practice, things turned out quite differently. Although the Trivium was supposed to have been taught in the grammar school, the standard reached by many university entrants was extremely low. One has to bear in mind that the youth entered the university at a very early age, at fourteen years or even earlier in some cases. He was supposed to be able to read and write and to possess a working knowledge of the Latin tongue. A great many candidates did not reach this modest standard with the result that the first two years of the university course had to be devoted to perfecting the students' knowledge of the subjects of the Trivium. As one might expect university studies in the twelfth century were unorganised, but when, at the beginning of the following century, the system of academic degrees began to take shape, the curriculum of the university began to develop a definite pattern.

The curricula of the European universities differed in minor details but the statutes imposed upon the University of Paris by the English cardinal legate, Robert Curzon, in 1215, furnish a fairly clear picture of the course in the Faculty of Arts at this period. Latin grammar was taught but there seems to have been no study of the classical authors. The textbook used was the *Institutio de Arte Grammatica* of Priscian (sixth century) and in some instances, the *Ars Maior* of Donatus, the teacher of St Jerome. After 1366, the new grammar in doggerel verse, the *Doctrinale* of Alexander of Villa Dei had largely replaced Priscian.

The most important study for the licence to teach was logic which was represented by the *Organon* of Aristotle[1] and the *Isagoge*

---

[1] Aristotle did not regard logic as a separate subject but rather as an instrument of general culture which was a necessary introduction to the study of the other sciences. Hence the collection of his logical treatises was

of Porphyry which its writer had intended as an introduction to Aristotle's treatise on the Categories. Rhetoric and philosophy seem to have been generally neglected and could only be read on feast days. The usual textbooks in rhetoric were the *Barbarismus* (the third book of the *Ars Maior* of Donatus) and the *Topics* of Aristotle which was a part of the "new" logic. Philosophy consisted of a hotch-potch of the first three books of Aristotle's *Ethics* and the subjects of the Quadrivium. As there were no specified books for the latter, one can well imagine that these four subjects received scant attention. The study of the remaining philosophical works of Aristotle, for reasons which will presently be discussed, was forbidden. Oxford appears to have given rather more attention to the Quadrivium than Paris and eventually became famous for the teaching of mathematics and natural science.

The main contribution to educational ideas in the Middle Ages was in regard to university studies and the method of university teaching and it was closely connected with two important developments which occurred during the first half of the thirteenth century. These were the introduction of the complete works of Aristotle to Western Europe and the entry of the Mendicant Orders into the universities. The development of the universities, the organisation of the system of academic degrees, the growth of the collegiate system, and the two features mentioned above have been dealt with in the companion book to this. (S. J. Curtis, *History of Education in Great Britain*, chapter 2, "The Mediaeval Universities", University Tutorial Press.) The gradual infiltration of the works of Aristotle, however, is a topic which needs a somewhat fuller treatment if one is to understand the educational ideas which shaped the curriculum and the teaching methods of the mediaeval university.

The entrance of Aristotle's works into the Latin world falls into two well marked periods. The first begins with the translations of Boethius and ends about the middle of the twelfth century. During this period, only the logical works of Aristotle were known. Even as late as 1120, Abelard recorded that he only possessed two of

known as the *Organon* or instrument. The early Middle Ages did not possess the whole of the *Organon*, but during the first half of the twelfth century, Aristotle's logical treatises gradually became available either in new translations or in the rediscovered versions of Boethius. The freshly discovered treatises were known as the "new" logic as distinct from those which had been accessible to earlier scholars, the "old" logic.

the logical treatises, but by the middle of the century, John of Salisbury had access to the whole of the *Organon*. The second stage began in 1162 with the translations of Henry of Brabant and lasted until William of Moerbeke had completed his work of translation in 1267. It was in this period that the philosophical writings of Aristotle became available. Earlier ages had known him only as a logician, but in the thirteenth century he became the Philosopher, spelt with a capital.

The philosophical works of Aristotle had a history which is a romance in itself. The crucial date is 750. By that time the works of Aristotle had been translated into Syriac, and that year is notable because of the invitation of the Caliph of Bagdad issued to Syrian scholars to take up their residence in the capital and begin the task of rendering their Syriac versions of Aristotle into Arabic. In 832, the Caliph, Al Mamoun, set up a school of translators at Bagdad where most of the works of Aristotle were translated into Arabic. At the same time, commentaries on Aristotle by Alexander of Aphrodisias (flourished 198-214), and Themistius (317-387) were also translated. Plato was not well known to the Arabs, but they received a flood of works imbued with the doctrines of the Neo-Platonists which influenced their thought to a considerable extent.

Once the Arabs came into possession of these translations, they began to interpret and comment upon them. Two Arabian thinkers, Avicenna (980-1037) and Averroes (1126-1198), were much more than mere commentators. They were both original thinkers who attempted to combine philosophy with their own religious views. Avicenna was the more faithful commentator but his attempt to synthesise philosophy and religion roused the wrath of orthodox Mohammedans with the result that the philosophers were expelled from the Eastern Caliphate. They were forced to find a new home in Spain. Averroes gathered together all the threads of previous Arabian speculation. From Spain the works of Aristotle with many which were falsely attributed to him, together with the Arabian commentaries, passed into France. Amongst these was a treatise known as the *De Causis* which was attributed to Aristotle. Aquinas pointed out that the book was really a compilation from Proclus, one of the most influential of the Neo-Platonists. It was translated into Latin and was at first accepted in Western Europe as a genuine work of Aristotle. The Jews also acted as transmitters of this ill-assorted mixture of Aristotelianism and Neo-Platonism. The most distinguished Jewish philosopher was Moses Maimonides (1135-1204). Somewhat late in life he became acquainted with the writings of Averroes and expressed great admiration for them. His *Guide for the Perplexed* inspired later mediaeval Jewish thinkers and had a considerable influence upon the West.

Towards the middle of the twelfth century, the work of translating Aristotle's writings into Latin was undertaken by Raymund, Archbishop of Toledo, who established a school of translators in that city. It has been claimed that the first works bearing the name of Aristotle to reach Paris came from that school. Not only was there a complete absence of discrimination between the genuine works of Aristotle and Neo-Platonic treatises falsely ascribed to him, but Raymund's translators who were by no means expert linguists, relied to a great extent upon Arabian or Jewish versions of Syriac translations of the original. In the three-fold and sometimes four-fold process of translation the meaning of the original text was obscured. In later years, Roger Bacon caustically criticised the reliance placed upon these faulty translations and emphasised the necessity of a thorough knowledge of Greek so that scholars could go straight to the original text. Accompanying these translations came the commentaries of Avicenna, Averroes, Maimonides, and many other Arabian and Jewish thinkers.

Rashdall put the situation very clearly when he wrote: "Aristotle thus came to Paris in an orientalised dress; and that was not all. He was accompanied or followed by Arabic commentators and by independent works of Arabian philosophers, some of which at first claimed the sanction of Aristotle's name. Now the Arabic interpretation of Aristotle as exhibited by Avicenna and more decidedly by Averroes . . . emphasised and developed precisely the most anti-Christian elements in the teaching of the philosopher—the eternity of matter, the unity of the 'active intellect', the negation of individual immortality".[1]

It was, therefore, not surprising that at the beginning of the thirteenth century, the study of the "new" Aristotle was roundly condemned by the Church. Mandonnet in his work, *Siger de Brabant* (Louvain, 1911), gave several instances. It seems that the

[1] Hastings Rashdall, *The Universities of Europe in the Middle Ages*, vol. 1, p. 353, new edition, reprinted, O.U.P., 1942.

first condemnation was at the ecclesiastical Council of Sens held at Paris in 1210. "Under pain of excommunication, we forbid Parisian masters to lecture on Aristotle's books of natural philosophy and the commentaries upon them, either privately or publicly." The word used in this inhibition was *legere* which was the technical term for lecturing, *i.e.* the reading and explanation of a text. This suggests that certain masters had already been studying and giving lectures upon the new books. In 1215, Robert Curzon renewed the prohibition in the decree he imposed upon the University of Paris. "The books of Aristotle on metaphysics and natural philosophy and summaries of them shall not be read, nor the teaching of David of Dinant, the heretic Amalric of Chartres and Maurice of Spain." The latter person, who is here classed with the two heretics already condemned by the Church, is supposed to have been Averroes himself. In spite of these decrees, it was still permissible to read and lecture upon the logical and ethical treatises of Aristotle, and we have seen that these formed a regular part of the course in the Faculty of Arts.

The Dispersion of the University of Paris in 1229 brought about the intervention of Pope Gregory IX. The Pope maintained the prohibition as a temporary measure until the different treatises could be examined and a faithful translation made. In 1231, he charged three masters of Paris, William of Auxerre, Simon of Anthie, and Etienne of Provence, to make the translation, but because of the difficulty of reconciling the teaching of Aristotle with dogma, the revision was never carried out. The most effective way of securing that a book will be read is to prohibit its circulation. It was so in this case. In defiance of the prohibition, the works of Aristotle were read with avidity. In 1255, however, a statute of the University of Paris marked the entrance of Aristotle into the Faculty of Arts, and in 1265, Urban IV officially recognised the Aristotelian philosophy and allowed it to be studied in the schools.

All this concern about the translation of Aristotle may seem to the modern reader a great deal of fuss and bother about something very insignificant. In actual fact, the Church at the beginning of the thirteenth century was facing a crisis of the first magnitude. The doctrines which had come in from Spain were already producing a crop of heresies and in particular, the Albigensian heresy in Southern France was showing tendencies which if not checked would have threatened the religious, moral, and political set-up of

Western Europe with disintegration. The danger becomes apparent if one manufactures a modern analogy. Let us imagine that for the last two thousand years America and Western Europe had access only to a small fragment of the New Testament. Suddenly, the remainder of the New Testament became available but a great deal of the teaching of the Gospels had been replaced by the doctrines of Russian Communism. Such teaching backed by the recognised prestige of the New Testament would have disastrous effects upon every part of the life of the Western nations. The danger which threatened in the thirteenth century was comparable to that of our fictitious illustration. The Church met it by the condemnation of heresies, the institution of the Inquisition and by military force. Such measures never in the end succeed and the real victory was the result of the work of two scholars, Albert the Great and St Thomas Aquinas.

These two thinkers were largely instrumental in bringing about the change in the policy of the authorities with regard to the University of Paris. Before this time, Augustinian theology and philosophy had dominated in the schools. Albert and Aquinas adopted the bold idea of making Aristotle respectable in the eyes of the Church and the university. It was Albert who conceived the idea of popularising Aristotle with the Latins and with this object in view, he organised a scheme of incorporating Aristotle and his commentators and adding his own observations. Aquinas adopted a new plan which represented a veritable revolution in the view of many thirteenth-century scholars who held resolutely to the teaching of St Augustine. His idea was nothing less than that of bringing about a synthesis of Aristotelian philosophy and the Christian religion. Before he could undertake this he knew that two other essential tasks would have to be undertaken. An accurate translation of Aristotle and a literal and critical commentary on his works were needed. The former was carried out by William of Moerbeke, probably at the request of St Thomas and with the sanction of the Pope. William was a Dominican who became Archbishop of Corinth. He was a competent Greek scholar and his translation which was completed in 1267, although by no means perfect, provided a satisfactory Latin version which was recognised as a standard until after the Renaissance. A chronicler of the period informs us: "William of Brabant (Moerbeke), Bishop of Corinth, of the Order of Preachers, a man who excelled in humanistic studies, translated all the books of Aristotle on natural and moral philosophy and metaphysics, from Greek into Latin. It was a word for word translation and we now use it in the schools. In the days of Master Albert, everyone as a rule used the old translations". The second need, for literal and critical commentaries on Aristotle was met by Albert, but more especially by the commentaries of Aquinas himself.

The introduction of Aristotelian philosophy resulted in a widening and an enrichment of university studies. Thus the statutes of 1366 show a considerable change when compared with those of 1215. They give a list of the books read by students in the Faculty of Arts. The *Grecismus* of Eberhard of Béthune and the *Doctrinale* of Alexander of Villa Dei had taken the place of Priscian. The whole of the logical works of Aristotle and the *Topica* of Boethius, and in addition, the *De Anima* of Aristotle were studied. These were the textbooks for the Bachelor's course. The degree of B.A. had come into existence after the time of Robert Curzon. For the Chancellor's Licence, the student was required to read the *Physics*, the *Metaphysics*, and a number of the minor treatises of Aristotle, together with certain unspecified books on mathematics. Amongst the latter was probably the *De Sphaera* of John of Sacrobosco (John of Halifax in Yorkshire). In the period between the granting of the Licence and the Inception when the new Master in Arts was received as a member of the masters' gild, the *Ethics* and part of the *Meteorics* were studied.

At Oxford, the curriculum was rather more elastic than that of Paris. Aristotle did not dominate to the same degree and the theory that the university curriculum should comprise the whole of the liberal arts was more successfully maintained. Thus the *Arithmetic* and *Music* of Boethius were studied, a small amount of Euclid and the theory of the planets according to Ptolemy. Under the heading of rhetoric certain works of Cicero, Ovid, and Virgil were included. These items were in addition to logic and the three philosophies, *i.e.* natural, moral, and metaphysical philosophy. The examples of Grosseteste and Roger Bacon encouraged the study of mathematics at Oxford. Towards the end of the Middle Ages, degrees in music were given and there were possibly chairs in Greek and Hebrew. One striking feature at Oxford was the teaching of the French language, an item which appeared in the course of no other university. It was regarded strictly as an extra and had a definite utilitarian purpose; until the later Middle Ages, the business of the law-courts was conducted in French and most charters and official documents were written in that language.

On the other hand, the introduction of Aristotelian studies was not an undiluted gain. It was unfortunate that mediaeval scholars came face to face with the completed system of Aristotelian logic and philosophy before they had to any great extent been able to develop their own lines of thought. The result was, that with the exception of a few of the greatest mediaeval thinkers, they were content to accept the opinions of Aristotle without question to the consequent detriment of original and constructive thinking. If the Dialogues of Plato had become accessible at the same time they would have had a rival system of thought as an alternative and they would not have been dazzled by the achievements of Aristotle. Bertrand Russell puts this in his usual vigorous manner. "He came at the end of the creative period in Greek thought, and after his death it was two thousand years before the world produced any philosopher who could be regarded as approximately his equal. Towards the end of this long period his authority had become almost as unquestioned as that of the Church, and in science, as well as in philosophy, had become a serious obstacle to progress. Ever since the beginning of the seventeenth century, almost every serious intellectual advance has had to begin with an attack on some Aristotelian doctrine; in logic, this is still true at the present day."[1]

The synthesis between Aristotelian thought and the Catholic Faith, which originated in the twelfth century and received its most complete form at the hand of St Thomas Aquinas, is usually known as the Scholastic philosophy. In this book, we are not concerned with the content of Scholastic philosophy but it is most important to realise that the term Scholasticism can be used in a secondary sense to denote a method of exposition. This method of teaching or lecturing also originated in the twelfth century and was perfected by Aquinas. The genesis of the Scholastic method of exposition is generally attributed to Peter Abelard (1079-1142) who applied dialectic to theological dogma in his famous treatise, *Sic et Non* (*Yes and No*). The idea did not originate with Abelard. For nearly two centuries before his time, the canon lawyers had been engaged

---

[1] B. Russell, *History of Western Philosophy*, p. 182, George Allen and Unwin, 1946.

upon the task of collecting and arranging the various decisions of Church Councils and the decrees of Popes. They found much conflicting material and they endeavoured to find some means of reconciling apparently contradictory statements. One of the best known of the early Canonists was Ivo of Chartres, the pupil of Lanfranc. The example of the canon lawyers was copied by the theologians. Thus Anselm of Laon (d. 1117) and William of Champeaux (d. 1121), extracted certain sayings from the Scriptures, the Church Fathers, and Doctors and collected from them into a composition generally known as *Sentences* (*Liber Sententiarum*). It should be noted that Abelard had studied for some time under both these masters.

In the Prologue to the *Sic et Non*, Abelard described the method and purpose of the compilation. He stated that the opinions of the Fathers seemed to be not only diverse but often contradictory. One could not charge them with being really at variance for they were guided by the Holy Spirit. "Wherefore," he continued, "We thought it good to collect the diverse statements of the Holy Fathers, as they have come to our memory, containing some problem which they seem to raise because of their lack of agreement, so that it may stimulate youthful readers to greater energy in the inquiry after truth and make them more acute in the pursuit of it. For the first key to wisdom is called questioning, diligent and unceasing . . . By doubting we are led to inquiry; by inquiry we perceive the truth." The *Sic et Non* assembled 158 such questions or problems. Unfortunately Abelard did not take the further step of attempting solutions himself but preferred to leave his readers to puzzle out the answers for themselves. There is good reason to think that Abelard's intention was not to discredit the teaching of the Church as some of his contemporaries asserted. He believed that the apparent contradictions could be reconciled and that his treatise would help the young student to gain a fuller understanding of the points involved by studying the pros and cons and coming to a reasoned decision instead of accepting dogmas on authority. The Prologue really contains an important educational principle, namely, that every weighty question has two sides and that a rational decision can only be reached by a careful study of both of them, a principle which is of immense importance in our present propaganda ridden world.

The *Sic et Non* was fiercely attacked by Abelard's opponents. Its influence, however, was far reaching. In the first place it affected the methods of the canon lawyers. The study of Canon Law had been enriched and stimulated by the work of Gratian at Bologna. He wrote the famous *Decretum* about 1140, or to give its more significant title, the *Concordantia discordantium Canonum*. In it the influence of the *Sic et Non* is unmistakable. Gratian handled his citations from lawyers and writers on Canon Law in a similar way to Abelard's use of quotations from the Fathers, except that in his case, he drew principles from the reconciliation of his discordant authorities. The *Decretum* quickly became the recognised textbook in the law schools of the universities.

Abelard's example was also followed by Peter the Lombard who was one of his pupils and who became Bishop of Paris (1159-1164). Peter was one of those writers whose fame rests upon one work only. His treatises on the Psalms and other books of Scripture were neglected and his work entitled *The Sentences* (*Quatuor libri sententiarum*) became the most important textbook in the theological faculties of the universities. It is no exaggeration to say that it ranked, according to mediaeval opinion, next to the Bible and the logic of Aristotle. Like the *Sic et Non*, it was a compilation of passages from Church Fathers and theologians, but Peter attempted to rationalise their differences and by means of subtle distinctions and a nice balancing of authorities, he brought them into line with orthodox doctrine. Although the *Sentences* were attacked by certain theologians such as John of Cornwall, who scented heresy in some of the Lombard's statements, the work became exceedingly popular. In the theological faculties it was the work of the Bachelor in Theology to expound the *Sentences* and the lectures of some of the more famous masters such as St Thomas Aquinas, Duns Scotus, and William of Ockham are still accessible.

The Lombard's work was responsible for a whole crop of books of *Sentences*. As time progressed, theologians aimed at more concise and systematic expositions which should cover the whole ground of theology. Such treatises were known as *Summae*. Mgr. Grabmann defines the *Summa* as "a more original systematic abridgment of the subject-matter of a given science". *Summae* were written not only in regard to theological studies but also dealing with philosophy, law, logic, and grammar. The *Summae* of the thirteenth century were comprehensive textbooks which possessed a logical structure and an organic unity which were not to be found in the books of *Sentences*; *e.g.* the *Summa Universae*

Theologiae of Alexander of Hales (1180-1245), the *Summa Theologica* of Albert the Great (1193-1280), and the *Summa Theologica* of St Thomas Aquinas (*c.* 1225-1274). The last named work represented a great advance on its predecessors. This was largely because of a thorough application of the principles of the "new Logic" especially the *Topics* of Aristotle. Its importance in the history of educational ideas lies in the close connection of the exposition of the *Summa Theologica* with the procedure adopted in the discussions or disputations that developed in the schools of Paris.

St Thomas wrote the *Summa* as a textbook for the use of young students in the Faculty of Theology and accordingly he sought to develop a method which would be suitable for beginners. This aim explains why the *Summa* adopts a method of exposition very different from that found in modern textbooks. As it was intended for theological students it was cast into a form which would be familiar to them, that of a discussion or disputation. In accordance with his object, St Thomas tried to avoid the multiplication of useless problems, and arguments, and to make his own exposition as clear and as simple as the subject-matter would permit. He states his aim in the Prologue: "We have considered that students in this science have frequently been frustrated by what they found written by other authors, partly because of the multiplication of useless questions, articles, and arguments; partly also because those things that are necessary for them to know are not taught according to the order of the subject-matter, but according as the plan of the book might require, or the occasion of the argument offer; partly, too, because frequent repetition generated weariness and confusion in the minds of the readers. We shall, therefore, try to avoid these and other similar faults, and shall endeavour by the help of God, to set forth whatever is relevant to this sacred science as briefly and clearly as the subject-matter itself will permit".

There were two main methods of teaching in the mediaeval university, the *lectio* and the *disputatio*. To understand why these methods were developed it is necessary to realise the conditions under which teaching in a mediaeval university was carried on. Books were both costly and rare. Each book had to be written by hand on expensive parchment, a process which was extremely tedious and slow. A poor student would not be able to own a book and even the more wealthy members of the university could only afford to buy a few of the more important books such as the Bible or the *Sentences* of Peter the Lombard. In the later mediaeval period, the copying and selling of books became a regular industry in university cities. Texts were copied by the stationers (*stationarii*) and sold or hired out to students by the booksellers (*librarii*). In the thirteenth century, the master would probably be the only person in the class who possessed the text, so that he had to rely upon oral methods of teaching. In the *lectio*, which was perhaps more akin to the modern lesson than the formal university lecture, the master read and explained the text to his students. When he was a Bachelor of Theology at Paris, St Thomas dealt with the *Sentences* in this way and afterwards committed his lessons to writing in his *Commentary on the Sentences*.

The nature of the *lectio* can best be understood if one examines an actual example. The following is taken from the *Commentary on the three books of Aristotle's De Anima* by St Thomas Aquinas. The particular illustration is the study of chapter 6 of Book II. The text is as follows: "In considering each separate sense we must first treat of their objects. By the sensible object may be meant any one of three things, two of which we say are perceived in themselves, or directly, while the third is perceived *per accidens* or indirectly. Of the first two the one is the special object of a particular sense, the other an object common to all the senses. By a special object of a particular sense I mean that which cannot be perceived by any other sense and in respect to which deception is impossible; for example, sight is of colour, hearing of sound, and taste of flavour, while touch no doubt has for its object several varieties. But at any rate each single sense judges of its proper objects and is not deceived as to the fact that there is a colour or a sound; though as to what or where the coloured object is or what or where the object is which produces the sound, mistake is possible. Such then, are the special objects of the several senses. By common sensibles are meant motion, rest, number, figure, size: for such qualities are not the special objects of any single sense, but are common to all. For example, a particular motion can be perceived by touch as well as sight. What is meant by the indirect object of sense may be illustrated if we suppose that the white thing before you is Diares' son. You perceive Diares' son, but indirectly, for that which you perceive is accessory to the whiteness. Hence you are not affected by the indirect sensible as such. Of the two classes of sensibles directly perceived it is the objects special to the different senses which are properly perceptible: and it is to these that the essential character of each sense is naturally adapted". (From the translation of the *De Anima*, by R. D. Hicks, C.U.P., 1907.) The commentary of St Thomas is numbered 13 in the series which deal with the Second Book (*lectio XIII*). It proceeds as follows:

"After the Philosopher has shown the relation which exists between sense and the objects of sense, he begins by an exposition of sense and the objects of sense considered as independent of their relationships. This exposition is divided into two parts: the first is concerned with the objects of sense, the second with the activity of sensation. The first problem is dealt with in two stages. First he distinguishes the proper objects of the senses from other objects. Then he presents his theory of the proper objects of the senses showing how each sense object is related to its particular sense. In regard to the first stage, Aristotle does two things. He begins by showing what are the different kinds of sense objects and then he deals with each kind. He points out that before one can formulate a theory of sense perception it is necessary to say what are the objects perceived by each particular sense and what are the objects proper to that sense. He shows that there are three kinds of sensible object. Of these, the first two are perceived in themselves and the third, indirectly or *per accidens*. The two former kinds divide into the objects which are peculiar to a special sense and those which without being the special objects of any one sense, are perceived by all the senses."

Let us endeavour to reconstruct the procedure of the *lectio*. The lectures averaged about three each day, two in the morning and one in the afternoon. The lecture periods varied greatly and might be anything from one to three hours according to the subject-matter. The lecture room consisted of a wooden building with an earthen floor. As classes frequently started at 5 a.m. or 6 a.m. light was needed in winter and this was supplied by candles. The students sat cross-legged on the floor which was strewn with straw to overcome the damp and the cold. The master was seated in a hard wooden chair with a rough lectern before him. Sometimes a bachelor occupied a chair at his side. After a short prayer, the master began by reading from his manuscript the portion of the text selected for study. The students did their best to write down the words of the text in abbreviated Latin. Often the master would speak too rapidly for the students to get down the text. The authorities discouraged students from taking down *verbatim* the master's lecture. The statutes of Paris attempted to regulate the exact speed at which the master should speak. He was not to speak too slowly, drawlingly (*tractim*) but rapidly (*raptim*) as though nobody was taking notes. The students had their own way of dealing with this problem. A master who was inaudible or gabbled his lecture had to endure groans, and cat calls, and even showers of stones.

After the reading of the text, the master gave a sketch of the topics covered by the author. The above example shows how carefully an experienced master would proceed in his analysis of the subject-matter. He would then deal in detail with each topic set out in his preliminary analysis. Space will not permit a sample of a complete lecture to be reproduced but the following translation of the first paragraph of St Thomas' lecture on the above text will be sufficient to show the method.

"In this chapter, Aristotle expounds his theory about each kind of sense object which he has named in the text. He starts by describing what is meant by the proper objects of a sense. This is defined as follows: the sense object proper to a sense is one which is perceived by that sense only and not by any other sense. Sense is not subject to error when it is concerned with its proper object. For example, the proper object of the sense of sight is colour. In a similar way, sound is the proper object of hearing and the sense of taste perceives a flavour which is in a liquid. But the sense of touch has a number of special objects. It perceives the hot and the moist, the cold and the dry, the heavy and the light, and many other tactile qualities of a similar nature. The point to notice is that each one of these senses judges its proper sense object and in doing so is not subject to error. For instance, the sense of sight is not deceived when it perceives a colour nor is the auditory sense deceived about sound. The sense objects perceived *per accidens* or which are common to more than one sense are able to deceive the senses. Thus the eye may be mistaken when it judges that this coloured object before me is a man or is in a particular place. In a similar fashion, a person may be mistaken when he hears a sound and concludes from this the nature of the object which has produced the sound. We see, therefore, that the characteristic of the objects proper to each sense is that they do not give rise to error." The reader should notice how St Thomas as a skilled lecturer leaves no doubt in the mind of his hearer which is the vital point in the text, namely, that when a sense organ is dealing with the proper object of that particular sense, there is no possibility of error. He enlarges upon the account given by Aristotle by means of additional illustrations and then uses repetition to clinch the main idea of the passage.

There was a definite connection between the *lectio* and the *disputatio*. The link was provided by the *quaestio*. When the master had read and explained his text, certain difficulties might arise. The information given in the text might not be complete; the expression of the writer might lead to misunderstandings, or problems might occur to the students which had not been dealt with either by the text or in the lecture. In cases like these, the student would naturally ask questions. He was always free to ask questions and if he did not, the master would frequently put questions to him. The student might not be satisfied with the answer given by the master and might press him for a fuller explanation. He might, on occasions, as Abelard often did with his masters, completely disagree with the solution given in class. Here, then, was the genesis of the discussion or *disputatio*.

In the mediaeval universities a definite discussion technique developed. Just as nowadays there are certain definite rules which govern the procedure, so in mediaeval times the discussion had its common form which differed considerably from the modern technique. In the first place, the discussion was carried on in Latin. It was not the Latin used by Cicero and other writers of the golden age in Roman literature. It was the colloquial Latin of the Middle Ages which could hardly have been understood by the Roman of classical times. Often it was ungrammatical and its vocabulary included many words which had been coined for the occasion. Nevertheless, the language used was adequate for the purpose, and when the *disputatio* was reported and written out in a literary form, the result was a Latin which was both vigorous and sufficiently flexible to convey the meaning intended. Secondly, one must recollect the tremendous influence exercised by the Aristotelian logic. Just as at the present time all remarks have to be made to or through the chairman, so in the mediaeval *disputatio*, the thesis had to be set out in strict logical form, generally as a syllogism and all objections to it were required to be cast into the same form. Hence, St Thomas defined the *disputatio* as a syllogistic activity carried on between one person and another in respect to some proposition which has been enunciated. It is important, therefore, to realise that the *disputatio* at its best was a natural psychological development. In the hands of incompetent masters and certainly in the later part of the Middle Ages it became a formal activity but the same may be said of the lecture, the lesson, or any other type of teaching method.

In its fully developed form, the ordinary *disputatio* began with a *quaestio* or problem proposed by the master. Often it was a problem which arose from his lecture course. The *quaestio* was circulated in writing some days before the actual discussion took place in order to give students an opportunity to ponder over it. The disputation itself occupied at least two days. On the first day ˙he master was in the chair but the bulk of the work fell upon the ɔachelor. This was part of his apprenticeship for the work of a master. Questions were put and difficulties (*objectiones*) with regard to the thesis were formulated by the masters and students present at the *disputatio*. The bachelor grouped the objections in as logical a sequence as possible. Then assisted by the master, he furnished arguments for the support of the thesis. The second day was taken up by the determination of the master. He began by giving a reasoned exposition of his point of view and concluded by resolving each objection in order.

The statutes of the University of Paris required every master to hold disputations during the session. During the first three years of his professorship, St Thomas presided at disputations on two mornings each week and even when in later years he was busy writing his treatises, he found time to hold a disputation once a fortnight. The type of disputation described above was the ordinary disputation which formed a regular part of the university course. Frequently the disputations conducted by a particular master would be organised into a sequence and closely related to the lecture course which he delivered. In some cases they extended over a complete session or more rarely over several sessions. Thus St Thomas held 253 disputations on problems connected with the topic of Truth (*De Veritate*). His usual practice was to arrange for his disputations to be reported and for the written account to be submitted to him for correction and revision before publication. In their literary form they were termed *Quaestiones disputatae*.

The *Disputationes quodlibetales* were extraordinary discussions which took place about twice a year, during Advent and Lent, and were so named because members of the audience could propose for discussion any topic that they wished. There was no necessary connection between the questions submitted, although in the published form, *Quaestiones quodlibetales*, the master grouped them in the best sequence possible.

The following example from the *Summa Theologica* has been selected to show the procedure of the disputation reduced to a literary form. The reader will be able to trace the resemblance of its structure to the *Sic et Non* of Abelard and the *Sentences* of Peter the Lombard. The example chosen is the first Article of Question XCI in the first Division of the second part of the *Summa Theologica*. Each question represents a topic, in this case, it is the different kinds of law. Every question is divided into a number of Articles which are the particular problems to be discussed. This Article raises the problem whether there is an eternal law.

We proceed thus to the First Article : —

Objection 1. It seems (*videtur*—the formula used by St Thomas to state the initial argument against the thesis) that there is no eternal law. Every law is imposed on someone, but there was not someone existing from eternity on whom a law could be imposed; for God alone existed from eternity. Therefore, no law is eternal.

Objection 2. Moreover (*praeterea*—the formula which introduces additional arguments against the thesis) promulgation is necessary to law. But promulgation could not be from eternity. Therefore, etc.

Objection 3. Moreover, a law implies an ordering to an end. But nothing which is ordered to an end is eternal, for it is only the ultimate end which is eternal. Therefore, etc.

On the contrary (*Sed contra*—the formula stating the thesis which is to be maintained. It generally consists of a quotation from some authority which may be Holy Scripture; an extract from a Church Father or theologian; the decree of a Council of the Church; a quotation from Aristotle, Avicenna, or some other philosopher) Augustine says (*De Lib. Arb.*, Book I, chapter 6, a little beyond the middle) the Law which is called the Supreme Reason cannot be understood otherwise than unchangeable and eternal.

I answer that [*Respondeo dicendum quod*—This introduces the main body (*corpus*) of the Article in which the reasons for accepting the thesis are set forth. It corresponds to the master's determination in the actual disputation] as stated above (*Quaest*. XC, articles 1 and 4—a reference to the previous Question) a law is none other than a dictate of practical reason which proceeds from a ruler who governs a perfect community. It is clear that if one grants that the world is ruled by Divine Providence, as was said in the 1st Part of this work (*Quaest*. XXII, articles 2 and 4), then the whole community of the universe is governed by the Divine Reason. Therefore, the very idea of the government of things in God the Ruler of the existing universe, has the nature of a law. Because the Divine Reason cannot conceive anything in time but in eternity, as is said in *Proverbs*, viii, 23, a law of this kind must be termed eternal.

Reply, Objection 1. (*Ad primum ergo dicendum*—this indicates the beginning of the reply to the first argument which was not approved.) Those things which are not in themselves, exist with God, in so far as they are foreknown and pre-ordained by Him, as is said in *Rom*., iv, 17: "Who calls those things which are not, as those that are. Therefore, the eternal concept of the Divine Law has the nature of an eternal law, inasmuch as it is ordained by God to the government of things which are foreknown to Him".

Then follow the replies to the second and third objections.

The disputation was also used as an examination test. As a regular university exercise and as an examination test, the disputation survived the Renaissance, and Reformation, and at Oxford in the eighteenth century its forms still continued when they had outlived their usefulness and lost their original meaning.[1]

SUGGESTIONS FOR FURTHER READING

The standard work on the universities during the mediaeval period is Hastings Rashdall's *The Universities of Europe in the Middle Ages*. This work was first published in 1895. A new edition was prepared in 1936 and edited by Sir F. M. Powicke and A. B. Emden (O.U.P., reprint, 1942). Rashdall's theory of the foundation of the University of Oxford was severely criticised, especially by

---

[1] For an account of Oxford examinations in the eighteenth century, see, Vicesimus Knox, *Essays, Moral and Literary*, Essay No. 77, *On some parts of the Discipline in our English Universities*, 8th edition, London, 1786.

A. F. Leach. The notes and corrections in the new edition are extremely valuable. Rashdall was rather addicted to sweeping generalisations and since the original edition there has been a considerable advance in our knowledge of the mediaeval universities. These points have been kept in mind by the editors of the 1936 edition.

N. Schachner, *The Medieval Universities* (George Allen and Unwin, 1938) is a more popular account of the development of the universities of mediaeval Europe. It is largely based upon Rashdall and repeats many of his more sweeping generalisations. It is a very readable book but in certain details it is inaccurate. A concise account of the historical development of the universities is given in S. J. Curtis, *History of Education in Great Britain*, chapter 2 (University Tutorial Press). This work is a companion to the present one and provides the factual and historical background which has not been repeated in this chapter. S. J. Curtis, *A Short History of Western Philosophy in the Middle Ages* (Macdonald, 1950), contains a chapter on Mediaeval Universities and Schools. An account of the thought of St Thomas Aquinas, including his contribution to psychology, is given in chapters 9 to 11. The life and work of St Thomas Aquinas has been described in the novel by Louis de Wohl, *The Quiet Light* (Victor Gollancz, 1950).

CHAPTER VI

THE HUMANISTS OF THE RENAISSANCE

During the Middle Ages intellectual education was in the hands of the Church, and the scholastic method prevailed throughout Europe. It is true that by the end of this phase the need for learning had expanded, and that the method itself had become as sterile as Abelard had feared it would, but these are no grounds for assuming that education was poor in quality or that it was restricted to the few. Some authorities consider that elementary education was much more thorough and widespread in pre-Renaissance times than it was for many years after the Reformation. It is certainly true that in England the rise of universities belongs to this middle period when the Renaissance was only beginning; it is equally true that in the same period Roger Bacon went a step beyond the schoolmen in pointing the way to the inductive method of discovery. It appears, also, that in England the path to higher education was by no means closed to the "masses", for it is said that Grosseteste, Bishop of Lincoln, and distinguished scholar, was probably the son of a serf, and that Breakspear, later Pope Adrian IV, was the son of a menial.

It is worthy of note that intellectual training was only one of the kinds of vocational education available. The apprenticeship system ensured the utilitarian education of craftsmen and tradesmen, while for the young page and squire there was education in chivalry which equipped them with the accomplishments needed in their station in life: skill in physical pursuits such as archery, riding and hawking, and familiarity with social graces such as verse making and chess playing. Thus when England had its foretaste in the fourteenth century of both Renaissance and Reformation, it is very probable that education was fairly widespread and of a very fair standard. The century which produced Chaucer as a writer, Humphrey of Gloucester as a patron of learning, and Wyclif as a pricker of England's conscience, was, in fact, the period which saw the first signs of revolt against scholasticism and Church control, not, however, because all that existed was bad, but because the time was ripe for progress and change.

Thus, by the dawn of the sixteenth century, which saw the expression of this change in the work of a group of educators, the impulses generated a century earlier had gained power and momentum throughout Europe. The example set by the fourteenth-century literary giants stimulated interest in modern languages, an interest fostered by the urge to travel in search of culture and knowledge. The increasing appreciation of Greek writing did much to engender a new humanistic philosophy in students. Moreover, it served to elevate to respectability the study of the physical, factual world which had become a topic of particular interest during this period of trade and discovery. Above all, perhaps, the candle lit by Wyclif and Huss was now burning brightly in spite of the frequent application of snuffers, and revision of political ideology was in process. All these factors are of significance in estimating and evaluating the contribution to educational ideas made by Tudor thinkers, but it would be interesting to know how far the latter were influenced by two factors of more direct educational import. Firstly, how much did John Colet and Erasmus know of the theory and practice of Vittorino da Feltre, and secondly, how far were their innovations in teaching method due to the vastly improved supply of copies of books, made possible by the recent invention of printing?

Vittorino da Feltre (1378-1446)

Vittorino lived before this invention, but he is not undeserving of the title of first Christian Humanist in education. He belongs to that Little Renaissance when Duke Humphrey was encouraging the interchange of brilliant students between Italy and England. In the first part of the fifteenth century he conducted in Mantua a court school attended by the children of the ruler and other selected pupils, and he worked out a system of teaching far ahead of his time, both in philosophy and method. His country had already broken with the mediaeval Christian ideal and the zest with which the new modes and morals had been adopted was already degenerating into exaggeration and over-indulgence. Vittorino, however, upheld the Christian life, although he went to the ancients for his educational methods. Thus he aimed at harmony of mind and body and he gave much time to physical pursuits in his curriculum. He went beyond the later, narrow Humanists in accepting science, music, and mathematics, as desirable subjects, although he gave that emphasis to language teaching which is characteristic of humanism. Some authorities consider that Vittorino followed Quintilian very closely and it is, perhaps, unfortunate that the former left no writings to prove or disprove this assumption.[1] If the Tudor thinkers knew of Vittorino's work, it must have been through hearsay or from his pupils' writings, but it cannot be entirely accidental that they echo so frequently so many of his views on teaching. He abhorred the idea of corporal punishment; he laid great stress on strict moral training; he emphasised the good influence of the teacher, and the importance of personal relationships between teacher and pupil and, moreover, he believed in discovering the interests and aptitudes of pupils in order that attractive and agreeable ways of teaching and learning might be devised. He is an outstanding example of the fine scholar and brilliant teacher who achieves, in his own methods, success which cannot be gained by imitators. Teachers throughout Europe tried to emulate his use of Ciceronian style in Latin teaching and so, a half-century later, earned the derision of Erasmus.

High tribute must be paid to Vittorino as a contributor to the development of education, not only for his integrity and his sound standards but also for the part he played in the training of so many young people who were destined to spread the revived Greek learning and the new Humanist outlook. Not only was he responsible for the education of future Italian rulers, clergy, professors, and state officials but perhaps even more important, he was the Latin teacher of many Greek scholars who came from the East, and who did so much to give to Western Europe, not only a wealth of Greek manuscript, but also the knowledge by which it could be understood. Until this time there were few teachers of Greek, and thus hardly any Greek grammars, so that development was slow at first.[2] It is interesting to find that Humphrey of Gloucester, England's greatest bibliophile of the early fifteenth century owned only one book in Greek—a dictionary.

In passing, recognition should also be given to other Italian teachers of the period, particularly Vergerius and Guarino, teachers of Vittorino. The former was a professor at Padua when Vittorino

---

[1] Contemporary writers report that Vittorino frequently discussed Quintilian's *Institutio*. Platina says of him, *Quintilianum ut optimum vitae atque eruditionis auctorem miris laudibus extollebat.*

[2] Greek had never been completely lost. Scotus Erigena was a competent Greek scholar in the ninth century. Robert Grosseteste and Roger Bacon were largely responsible for the revival of Greek in England in the thirteenth century.

was a young student at the university, and during those years of the turn of the century the older man was taking up with enthusiasm the study of Greek. It is said that he sat with the boy students under Chrysoloras, the Greek, in order to learn the elements of the language. It is significant that while Vittorino was a student, Vergerius was preparing a treatise *On Character and Liberal Studies* (1404), and it is no coincidence that he expressed in words so much that Vittorino later expressed in practice. He wrote: "We call those studies liberal which are worthy of a free man; those studies by which we attain and practise virtue and wisdom; that education which calls forth, trains, and develops, those highest gifts of body and mind which ennoble man and which are rightly judged to rank next in dignity to virtue only". Thus he turns to the Greek pattern of "liberal" education by selecting subjects allied to the Quadrivium —literature, history, philosophy, rhetoric, poetry, music, logic, and mathematics. He recommends a somewhat Spartan physical training, although admitting that the child's capacities must be considered, and that due attention must be paid to recreative and social games, and to the development of good habits and gracious, pleasant manners.

Guarino was the Italian son-in-law of the same Greek Chrysoloras who taught Vergerius, and he had spent several years in Constantinople before he met Vittorino, who was his pupil in Venice. Later he conducted the court school in Ferrara, along lines which later, were further developed by Vittorino. Guarino's son, Battista, who became his colleague in teaching, described his father's method of teaching Greek—which the latter attributed to Chrysoloras—in a tract *Upon the Method of Teaching and of Reading the Classical Authors* (1459). This work is the first to emphasise the importance of Greek studies, and perhaps, the first to indicate clear-cut teaching method—the reading aloud, the grammatical analysis, the study of meaning, the careful summarising, the eventual memorising of lovely passages, and discussion of interesting points. It is perhaps not to be wondered at that the later Humanists were preoccupied with language teaching.

Largely as a result of Duke Humphrey's patronage of Oxford scholars, young English students soon came to consider their education incomplete without a period of study in Italy. In mid-century an Oxonian named William Tilley studied in Padua and Bologna, and returned to England to spread the new learning as Prior of

Christ Church, Canterbury, and Master of the school. Among his pupils was Thomas Linacre, who in turn studied at Oxford, and in Italy, where he qualified in medicine. Scholars from most countries of Northern and Western Europe were making similar pilgrimages— men such as Reuchlin and Agricola, who were later to contribute much of the Humanist movement. Linacre returned to England to practise as a physician while, at the same time, teaching Greek at Oxford. In this latter work one of his colleagues was William Grocyn, also an old Oxonian with Italian interests. To these great teachers came young John Colet who was later to join them as a colleague. By this time Caxton's printing press was producing books which were to enable Colet to pursue the teaching methods in which he believed.

John Colet (1467-1515)

Although much has been written about Colet as Dean of St Paul's and founder of the great school, his influence as an educational thinker is rarely given adequate consideration. The absence of any treatise by him on the subject may be the main reason for this neglect. A brief examination of his place in the early Tudor scene, therefore, may serve to emphasise his great contribution to the European reservoir of educational ideas.

He was the son of a prosperous merchant who had held office as Lord Mayor of London, and it is very probable that he attended one of the city schools, for he condemned these establishments later in no uncertain terms: "Though there ought to have been the greatest care in appointing the masters, those given the post are generally a shabby, broken-down set of men, sometimes hardly in their senses. So mean the place, so miserable the pittance, you could say that pigs were being reared there, and not that respectable people's children were being taught". He proceeded to Oxford, where he made strides in mathematics—"there was no part in which he was not seen above his years"—and also studied widely the ancient philosophers as far as they could be read in Latin. By good fortune, Linacre and Grocyn started the first public teaching of Greek in England during Colet's days as a student, and he was inspired to follow their example in seeking the new learning by making a pilgrimage to Italy. He not only pursued the study of Greek—in which he never became fully proficient—he also seized every opportunity to study men, modes, and morals, through France and Italy. Whether or not he visited Savonarola, as is reported, there is no doubt that he agreed most emphatically with the great monk's opinion of the decadence of the clergy, and the evils of life in pleasure-loving, prosperous Italy.

These experiences deepened his desire to find a true philosophy of life and on his return to England he took orders and returned to Oxford as a lecturer in divinity. His first course of public lectures was on the Epistle to the Romans, which he described as "The earnest words of a living man addressed to living men, and suited to their actual needs". Such a concept and such a treatment of the Bible, was quite new to his hearers, who, like their predecessors in the Middle Ages, had heard and discussed only short extracts and single texts instead of the whole vivid human narrative which alone could convey to the individual the true spirit and significance of the Holy Word.

Colet's fame soon spread, and students went to Oxford to sit under him, for he took his place beside Grocyn and Linacre as a scholar of international repute. Erasmus, who came to Oxford to learn Greek, found himself learning much more than Greek from Colet, to whom he wrote: "Such is your learning that even without the recommendation of your high character you would be of necessity admired by all. Such is the holiness of your life that, even if you had no learning to recommend you, you could not fail to be held in love and respect and reverence by everyone. Why should I now mention how much I have been struck and delighted by your quiet, composed, simple style welling forth like a clear fountain from a richly stored mind? You say what you mean, and you mean what you say". Colet replied with an offer to engage in disputation with Erasmus, and the latter, who had delighted in this practice since his schooldays, received yet another stimulus to his developing concepts of new ideals in education, for Colet then made it clear that he deemed valueless the schoolmen's manner of disputation which aimed merely to display skill in argument. He pointed out to Erasmus: "We seek not for victory in argument but for truth". This passionate desire for truth has earned him recognition as a herald of the Reformation, but it should also win for him a place among great educators who, in times of uncertain values, have stood firm for the highest ideals of the human race, and, moreover, who have dedicated themselves to the handing on of those ideals, both to fellow-men and to posterity.

Perhaps it will be doubted that Colet's ideas and influence signified any step forward in the evolution of educational ideas. It may be said that he contributed nothing new. Are such arguments answered, then, by saying that he stopped the rot? By proving himself a fine practical teacher of scholars, of ordinary parishioners, and of small boys, he gained the confidence of his disciples and pupils, imbuing them with his own fine spirit of service, truth-seeking and simplicity in everyday life. His success in inspiring men to study the Bible was not achieved by mass-lecturing alone. He did not begrudge the time given to quiet tutorials or discussions with any who sought his help. Thus it is told that in these early days many a scholar came privately after hearing the lectures to ask for guidance in studying St Paul's Epistles. One priest had copied out all the Epistles for himself—thus showing how scarce even Bibles were in those days—and Colet went through the first part of the little book with him, not merely as an instructor, but as a fellow-seeker of the wisdom contained in it. Colet said of St Paul: "He appears to be in his single person a boundless sea of wisdom and piety". It cannot be doubted that this gentle tuition, and this genuine enthusiasm for his "teaching matter" was equally a characteristic of his later dealing with younger pupils.

In 1505 he became Dean of St Paul's in London, where he continued his success as a preacher and teacher, and where his audience of laymen and ordinary citizens was much larger. He was firm in his dealings with the lazy, luxury-loving clerics of the Cathedral and set them an example in his own frugal, austere life and impeccable conduct, thus convincing all of the sincerity of his hope that his reforms would lead men back to the simplicity and integrity of the early Christians. He wore a plain black gown instead of the rich vestments of his office, and his hospitality, although wide and generous, was of the plainest except for the rich intellectual sustenance provided by brilliant and distinguished guests. The writings of the times, particularly those of his friend, Sir Thomas More, indicate that Colet earned the complete confidence of his congregation and subordinates as well as their obedience and love. He enjoyed the goodwill of the King and the respect of the Church, and although he did not hesitate to subject both to severe verbal trouncing on occasion, his integrity was such that his own position remained unassailable.

Thus, when asked to preach at a meeting of convocation summoned to discuss measures for the suppression of the Lollard heretics, he denounced, not the latter, but the assembled clergy themselves, whose ambition, self-seeking, and ignorance offended his principles. He denounced, too, the King's warmongering, but Henry VIII responded by seeking discussion with him; and although not deterred from his French expedition, the King confirmed his high opinion of the Dean by saying: "Let every man have his own doctor, and let every man favour his own, this man is the doctor for me". Needless to say, his uncompromising disapproval of corruption, injustice, and superstition earned him enemies, and many hoped that his apparent leanings towards heretical opinion would prove his downfall. It is true that he read all heretical books and, according to Erasmus, he would not have found Luther's doctrines unacceptable. He was profoundly irritated by many Catholic practices and customs, particularly the collection of relics of saints and the undue reverence paid to them. In fact, he was a true leader of the English Reformation, and it may be that his denunciations were more heeded by the King than has been recognised in the past, for Henry's activities in matters religious are usually attributed to political motives. Colet's influence on educated opinion may well have produced a generation of Englishmen of whom some moved far towards Protestantism without actually severing the link with the Roman Church, while others, though proclaiming themselves Protestant, still felt the ties of tradition and old customs. If this be so, it goes far towards explaining the apparent inconsistency of many Tudor worthies, including benefactors of education such as Sir Andrew Judd who, although Protestant, won high office under Mary and Phillip.

The story of St Paul's School is told elsewhere, but it is perhaps fitting to conclude this brief estimate of Colet's influence by relating how he used the fortune inherited from his father to found a school in St Paul's Churchyard, a school which derived its name, not from the Cathedral, but from St Paul himself to whom it was dedicated as a sign of Colet's admiration for the apostle. It was a "grammar school", that is a school for boys, 153 in number, who could already read and write, and who had shown aptitude for study. Although the first school, opened in 1510, consisted of only a large room divided into two by a curtain, it afforded good conditions according to the standards of the day. Both Erasmus and Colet felt strongly on the subject of school buildings, and indeed, the former, who was horrified at the dirt and squalor he found even in English upper circles, must have encouraged Colet in no uncertain degree to provide the best possible hygienic conditions.

The task of compiling a special Latin grammar for the school was undertaken by Colet himself because the book Linacre produced at his request, seemed to be too difficult for young boys. Into Colet's preface can be read much of his teaching philosophy: "Albeit many have written and have made certain introductions into Latin speech . . . in such plenty that it should seem to suffice, yet nevertheless, for the love and zeal that I have to the new school of St Paul's and to the children of the same, I have also . . . of the eight parts of grammar made this little book . . . in which, if any new things be of me, it is only that I have put these 'parts' in a more clear order, and I have made them a little more easy to young wits than, methinketh, they were before: judging that nothing may be too soft nor too familiar for little children, especially learning a tongue unto them all strange. In which book I have left many things out of purpose, considering the tenderness and small capacity of little minds. . .". Colet and Erasmus were mainly responsible for this book, but a contribution was made by Lily, St Paul's first master, himself an Oxford scholar and close friend of Colet. The book was used in schools for many years under the name of *Lily's Latin Grammar*.

Before he died of a disease caused by the filth of sixteenth-century London, Colet was able to direct the running of his school for eight years. He drew up wise statutes for its management and entrusted its government to the Mercers' Company. Although it was to be a secular school with a married man as headmaster, it was to cherish Christian ideals. Erasmus, one of the first visitors, suggested that a schoolroom picture of Christ teaching should bear the inscription: "Audite Eum". It is probable that Colet, after several severe illnesses, retired for the last few days of his life to a little cell he had built near a monastery, thus maintaining, as his friend Erasmus did, his loyalty to his Church. His friends, particularly Erasmus, and More, mourned him deeply, and wrote with feeling on the great loss sustained by England. "For centuries," said More, "we have not had among us any man more learned or more holy". He might have added, "—or more clear-sighted as an educator", for even Erasmus spoke on education only what he had gained from Colet: that its aims are true scholarship and spiritual values, and that its means are those suited to the individual's interests and capacity.

Thus it may be claimed that John Colet's contribution to educational thought was not insignificant. He was a pioneer teacher of the new interpretation of Scripture, helping students to break away from the traditional mediaeval practice of seeking mystical and allegorical meanings. Although he believed in the mental discipline of Greek and Latin studies, Colet held as important above all else, the seeking of rules of life in the Scripture. He says: "In the choice and well-stored table of Holy Scripture all things are contained that belong to the truth". To reach this goal he taught students to throw away ready-made ideas which it had become customary to read into the text and to interpret the words and ideas simply and naturally. To Colet the New Testament was the only true guide for living, and he expressed this frankly in a commentary on one of the Epistles. "If we seek to feed on the wisdom of the heathen which is devilish, not Christian, we lose the principles of our Lord ... those books in which Christ is not found are but a table of devils. Do not become readers of philosopher companions of devils." He despised many classical writers whose works revealed "all barbary, all corruption . . . which ignorant blynde folis brought into this worlde", and he forbade the use of such works in school, even as he forbade the teaching of the dog-Latin of the schoolmen. "I say that fylthynesse and all such abusyon which the later blynde worlde brought in, which more rathyr may be callid blotterature thenne litterature I utterly abbanysh and exclude oute of this scole." He also banished extra holidays—there were already 153 holy days when work was suspended—and he forbade cock-fighting and similar unseemly behaviour which was fashionable in those days. He was indeed, the apostle of simplicity and high endeavour in study, and of gentleness and austerity in living.

Desiderius Erasmus (1466-1536)

The name of Erasmus deserves a high place on the roll of those scholars who, by keeping England in touch with trends of European thought during the revival of learning, ensured that the Tudor period was to see a remarkable flowering of education in both practice and theory. His contribution to the cause of the Protestant Reformation often overshadows his influence on pedagogy. for he probably achieved more than any other individual in breaking down long-established prejudices, and thus in opening men's minds to the new doctrines. The wider aspects of his influence and the factors contributing to his success are of acknowledged importance, so that it only remains to examine his activities and ideas in relation to the main thesis of this work.

He was the illegitimate son of a prosperous Dutchman, and he was educated at Dutch schools of which he retained memories and impressions not entirely pleasant. The grammar school must have been a good establishment of its kind for several school-fellows of Erasmus were to achieve fame and power. One was a future Pope. It would seem that lively, original, and sensitive boys were likely to be fish out of water in typical fifteenth-century schools where learning was, supposedly, inculcated by harsh discipline. Erasmus relates that the headmaster whipped the boys because, in his opinion, flogging was good for them whether they deserved it or not. Nothing, however, could quench the ardour of the boy for learning, and he not only read voraciously, but also tried his skill in disputation with his colleagues, challenging them to argument as students did at universities.

At a crucial stage of his education his parents died leaving enough money to start their two sons on careers, but the banker and schoolmaster, who were appointed guardians, neglected their duty. They thought to rid themselves of responsibility by sending their wards to an establishment which prepared boys for monastic life. In his writings Erasmus suggests that he submitted to pressure because he was finally persuaded that as an Augustinian novice he could be free to devote himself to study. Thus in youth and early manhood he found himself in the grip of a strong, relentless system which, within a few years, made him a priest in spite of himself. In the year of America's discovery he was ordained, but it was clear to his colleagues, and his superiors, that he was not reconciled to the simplicity and limitations of a monk's life. He was not satisfied with a few books in a cell for he had a passionate desire to seek knowledge widely. Perhaps of equal significance was his dislike of the food eaten by the monks, especially the large quantities of fish. He said later that his heart was Catholic but his stomach Lutheran. It is possible that his reactions to the severity of monastic life were comparable to his reactions to school discipline but, fortunately for posterity, his Prior was more understanding than his masters. However, he was determined to escape, but before he could bring his courage to the point of revolt, the Prior introduced him to the Bishop of Cambrai, who took him as a secretary. After two years, the Bishop, recognising the young man's ability and keenness, gave him enough money to go to Paris and study Greek.

As most poor scholars of the time, he augmented his allowance by tutorial work, and it was a young pupil, Lord Mountjoy's son, who first persuaded him to visit England at the turn of the century. As he was still pursuing Greek it was almost inevitable that he should visit Oxford, where Grocyn and Linacre had set up one of the few schools of Greek outside Italy. Here he not only fell in love with England, but also made a great friend, John Colet, who was then lecturing in Oxford. Erasmus writes: "The air of England is soft and delicious. The men are sensible and intelligent. Many of them are even learned, and not superficially either. They know their classics, and so accurately, that I have lost little in not going to Italy. When Colet speaks I might be listening to Plato. Linacre is as deep and acute a thinker as I have ever met with. Grocyn is a mine of knowledge, and Nature never formed a sweeter and happier disposition than that of Thomas More". Although Erasmus did not stay in England, he left a number of firm friends behind, particularly Colet, Mountjoy, and More. They had introduced him to influential people, among whom it is not unfitting to number a small boy, Prince Henry, who did not forget the great scholar.

In 1500, Erasmus published in Paris, his first book, the *Adagia*. It was a heterogeneous collection of shrewd and witty jottings, notable mainly for the inclusion of penetrating critical comments on Catholic clergy, and it achieved success because general opinion was in agreement. It paid, however, no better than the scholarly books of to-day so that Erasmus lived in poverty while struggling to perfect his Greek and to complete a Greek New Testament.

After five years he came to England again—and again met Prince Henry—but he could not rest until he had been to Italy, and he seized the opportunity engineered for him to chaperone the sons of the King's physician, and later to tutor the son of James IV of Scotland on a visit to Italy. In Rome he was welcomed as a celebrated scholar, and he had the opportunity to gain a comfortable place at the corrupt court of the Pope, but his independent spirit triumphed over poverty and a weak stomach. His decision to keep his freedom of thought and movement ensured that his attack on the old ways of education would be written, for Mountjoy and More persuaded him to return to England on the accession of young Henry to the throne, and while staying with More, he wrote *Praise of Folly*, containing a significant contribution to ideas on educational practice. It does not deal exclusively with education, for it is aimed at all the foibles and weaknesses of mankind—superstition, false religious duties, extortion, ambition, aggression—and he spared neither Prince nor Pope nor Everyman. That the book ran into seven editions suggests that the awakening conscience of Europe was provoked by his home truths.

His attack on the prevalent system of school teaching embraced buildings, methods, and masters—"A race of men the most miserable, who grow old in penury and filth in their schools—*schools* did I say? Prisons, dungeons I should have said—among their boys, deafened with the din, poisoned by the foetid atmosphere, but, thanks to their folly, perfectly self-satisfied so long as they can bawl and shout to their terrified pupils, and box and beat and flog them, and so indulge in all kinds of ways their cruel dispositions".

It was exactly at this time—1509-10—that Colet, now Dean of St Paul's, was laying the plans of his new school, plans not merely for buildings, but also for methods and textbooks. It is not too much to assume that the discussions between the two friends were responsible for much of the material of *Praise of Folly*, and for many of the rules of St Paul's School. It is certain that Colet valued highly all suggestions of Erasmus, and that Erasmus and Colet wrote more of *Lily's Grammar* than Lily himself.

It is extremely likely that had Henry VIII not been too busy with his war with France to remember his resolution to patronise Erasmus, England might have enjoyed the latter's inspiration in matters educational for many years. As it was, although he was appointed to teach Greek at Cambridge, and given the income from a living by Archbishop Warham, Erasmus could not make ends meet and, moreover, he begrudged the time spent in teaching, time which he would have preferred to give to his great work, the translation of the Bible from Greek into Latin. In 1514 he left England, for loss of students upon an outbreak of plague swayed him to accept a generous offer by the prince who afterwards became the Emperor Charles V.

Although he enjoyed this patronage for the rest of his life, it was not to be a life of quiet study and undisturbed peace. His version of the Bible, with its explanatory comments, its paraphrases, and its inflammatory preface, set Europe ablaze, for it not only underlined the opinions of all thinking people on the decadence of the clergy, but it also set the whole of the Bible before those people who hitherto had been permitted to hear only certain carefully selected portions. The rest of the story does not belong to a study of education except in so far as the tremendous clamour for reform stimulated the desire and demand for education. Erasmus was perhaps the most loved and hated man in Europe. He received pensions, presents, and furiously hostile abuse. Pope Leo X, a man of liberal ideas, saw the sincerity of the great scholar's belief in the Catholic Church, but the revolt of Luther precipitated a bitter struggle which ended the hope that the internal reform of the Church might be achieved peaceably. In the heat of partisanship, many could not understand why Erasmus stood aloof, unable to approve Luther's methods, unable to condone the faults of the clergy, but above all, unable to stop the headlong rush of Europe into violence. Until his death in 1536 he was revered by many as the greatest scholar of his day, and he wielded tremendous influence not only through the products of his own unflagging pen, but also as editor for a great European publishing firm. The worth of his character, the quality of his scholarship, and the sincerity of his motives, have been topics of controversy throughout the centuries.

During the last twenty years of his life his great literary output included works on education, and his frequent journeys included visits to England. The friendship of Erasmus and Colet was undoubtedly inspiring to both men—Colet in his school, which Erasmus visited, and the latter in his books, which reveal the influence of Colet. Erasmus did not fail to admit his indebtedness to the friend who first drew him away from scholasticism.

This monk, who was released by the Pope from his monastic vows, expressed fully in his educational ideas the new spirit called humanism, which emphasised that life in this world was worth living. Of education he says: "The first and principal function is that the tender spirit may drink in the seeds of piety, the next that he may love and learn thoroughly the liberal studies, the third is that he may be informed concerning the duties of life, the fourth is that from the earliest childhood he may be habituated in courteous manners".[1] Thus we see how the concept of Plato's liberal education was grafted on to a stem of Christian ideals. But even as Erasmus lashed his Catholic colleagues while himself remaining Catholic, so he criticised his fellow-Humanists, who, lacking the understanding and breadth of vision of the greater thinker, poured forth wordy, shallow literature aping the classical authors, particularly Cicero.

The philosophy of education expressed by Erasmus, accepted the Aristotelian evaluation of reason as the guiding force in human nature. The function of education was to enable human beings to enjoy life to the full, but as both nature and capacity varied from person to person, education could not expect to achieve success by employing mass methods—particularly those methods which implied the antithesis of enjoyment for the pupil.

However, even as in wider issues he took a stand for improvement and progress rather than change and revolution, so in educational practice, he accepted the ancient methods of teaching the humanities on the assumption that the art of good teaching was the gaining of skill in applying such methods correctly and efficiently. In *The Order of Study* (*De Ratione Studii*, 1516) published six years after the opening of St Paul's School, Erasmus puts forward those points on classics teaching which he must have discussed with Colet during the compilation of the accidence to *Lily's Grammar*, and during their deliberations on the needs and capacities of small boys. The manner of studying classical authors was to be the same as the great classical teachers had ordained, but Erasmus added that human interest and value should be given to the study by a consideration of the life and era of each author, his personal attributes, and the characteristics of his style. In addition, no opportunity was to be missed to examine the worth of the writings in terms of Christian values.

In his later educational work, *The Liberal Education of Children* (*De pueris statim ac liberaliter instituendis*, 1529) Erasmus gives some simple rules for teaching which might well be found in a modern treatise: "First, do not hurry, for learning comes easily when the proper stage is reached. Second, avoid a difficulty which can be safely ignored, or at least postponed. Third, when the difficulty *must* be handled, make the boys' approach to it as gradual and as

[1] W. H. Woodward, *Erasmus concerning Education*, p. 73, C.U.P. 1904.

interesting as you can".[1] His whole approach to teaching is that of the psychologist who would arrange material in stages of difficulty and who would ensure that revision and repetition be achieved by each pupil in a meaningful manner, that is to say, in the pupil's own way rather than in a slavish reproduction of the original. At a time when the practice of rote learning was no less prevalent than it was in the era of cheap education for the masses, Erasmus pointed the way to true study and learning by insisting that the gaining of knowledge could be achieved only by intelligent purposeful thinking on the part of each individual. His maxim: "Understand, arrange, repeat", although intended to apply, primarily to the intellectual activity of learning languages, might well serve for the learning of many things at most stages, and it is certainly not inconsistent with Professor Whitehead's concept of learning processes.

Although it would thus appear that Erasmus was ahead of his time in recommending so much of what appears modern in methodology, it is interesting to remember that he set out, not to devise new methods, but to emphasise the significance of the best methods of the great teachers. Infusing these methods with the philosophy of humanism, he arrived at a consideration of the needs and characteristics of the individual pupil, and hence he could not accept as either humane or fruitful the cruelty of the lifeless academic system he had endured as a boy, and which he saw prevailing in sixteenth-century schools.

In rejecting the rote learning of grammatical rules he was emphasising, as did the Greeks, the need for language to convey ideas, to discuss matters of interest—though it be merely the humble interests of very small boys—and he was utilising, as did the Romans, the human situation of the moment to stimulate individuals to effort and achievement. While it is clear that the introduction of the rod would serve only to prevent the flowering of that essential natural interest, it is hardly just to attribute the gentleness of Erasmus to mere tricks of teaching method. Although his pioneering appears to have achieved little in the general educational practice of Europe, his plea for an end to prevalent cruel practices was perhaps his greatest contribution to the cause of education.

Harsh treatment of children appears to have been accepted as essential in upper-class families, perhaps one of the less fortunate outcomes of the acceptance of the Christian doctrine of original

[1] W. H. Woodward, *op. cit.*, p. 217.

sin. For their education, boys, and sometimes girls, were sent either to schools or into noblemen's houses, or taught at home by tutors, and it was rarely a happy period for the children, although many parents were at heart as kind and loving as those parents of whom Plato complained that they spoilt their young by inconsistency and over-indulgence. Erasmus wrote in a letter: "I do the more lament that soch wittes commonlie be either kepte from learning by fond fathers, or bet (beat) from learning by lewde scholemasters".

In his *Liberal Education* he says: "Let us see to it that the rod we use is the word of guidance or of rebuke, such as a free man may obey, that our discipline be of kindness and not of vindictiveness". He would have the rod used only as an extreme resort, after the utmost patient efforts on the part of the teacher, and if it appeared that the pupil had neither aptitude nor desire for learning, he should not be kept at it. The prevailing "payment by results" system made it hard for tutors and schoolmasters to accept such a ruling, and this, no doubt, explains why Erasmus and his successors pleaded in vain for the freedom of the child. He himself realised that unskilled, inadequately prepared teachers were not only incapable of putting his methods into practice, but were also too poor to risk losing pupils voluntarily.

No doubt it was such obstacles to progress which contributed greatly to the conviction of Erasmus that education should be a public concern. Again, this was no new idea, but it was new and shocking to his age. He believed education to be no less important a national essential than military defence—a contention still not fully accepted in this country. Yet, as in teaching and in the Church, he wanted no sudden change. He hoped that State, Church, and individual enterprise would, by parallel efforts, succeed in fulfilling the need, and he pointed out that for the sake of the nation the intellectual resources of the humbler classes of the community should be tapped. Such developments came considerably more slowly and less efficiently than he would have wished.

He believed formal education could start even earlier than at the age of seven, so that his arguments apply not only to what is now called "secondary" education, but also to the "primary" years, and it is here that the gulf between sixteenth-century and twentieth-century concepts appears at its widest.

Thus in *De pueris* Erasmus emphasises that teaching should begin at a tender age, preferably before seven, not only in order to inculcate the maximum amount of knowledge during childhood, but also to train children in good habits of study—in fact, to leave them no leisure or opportunity to imitate bad examples. He goes so far as to say that he would rather risk the child's health than his education, and he speaks more than once of the danger of a late start. Nevertheless, pressure in the shape of harsh discipline is highly undesirable. Such methods he believes are the antithesis of "liberal education", and there must always be full consideration of the pupil's abilities and interests. The skill of the teacher lies in guiding the individual pupil by reason, training him along desirable lines, and giving him practice in acquiring knowledge and experience. Erasmus admits that teachers of such skill are rare beings, and it is here he mentions the responsibility of the state for seeking out suitable men and ensuring an adequate supply of good teachers. One of his remarks to teachers was heeded by only a few during the next four hundred years: "Wholly wrong are those masters who expect their little pupils to act as though they were tiny adults".

His ideas on teaching methods are somewhat confused although they embody the essence of modern "play-way" activities. Thus he writes: "In England I heard of a father who taught his boy to aim with a bow and arrow at Greek or Roman letters painted on a target; a hit meant a cherry for the archer". In the early stages, he would use, as Quintilian, cut-out alphabets in bone or even in edible biscuits, and later he would use pictures to stimulate discussions in Latin.

He would have no rote learning, but at the same time he would abolish from the schoolroom games such as chess—which waste time to no purpose—nonsense such as riddles, and all songs and stories in any way related to the vernacular and particularly to folk lore. Thus it is clear he had many "blind spots", for closer investigation shows that he would include some methods and material more fantastic and less profitable. His selection, it is clear, is based on his preoccupation with antiquity, the study of which was to lead to social reform. He was keenly eager to see Latin such a living useful language that it would become unnecessary to use the vernacular, and it was to this end that all connections with the pupils' native tongue—folk lore and traditions—were to be avoided.

Erasmus had a fine faith that a universal language would bring men together, and he set out to foster education for world

citizenship which he believed could be achieved by classical literature as the instrument and with the knowledge of Christ as the aim.

Juan Luis Vives (1492-1540)

It is relevant to consider briefly the life and works of Vives
because it is worthy of note that in giving his philosophy and his
principles of educational method to Western Europe, he was, in fact,
interpreting to the continent those ideas and ideals which appear to
have been accepted by the friends and disciples of John Colet. If
any generalisations are possible about the contributions of individual
men to the progress of educational thought, perhaps it may be said
that Colet had the power to inspire, Erasmus to propagate, and
Vives to intellectualise the spirit and method inherent in the teaching
philosophy of the Christian Humanists. There seems little doubt
that Vives was the most brilliant scholar of them all, but, partly
owing to the power of the system of patronage for both good and ill,
Vives achieved neither the prosperity nor the fame of Erasmus.

Vives was a Spaniard, but little is known of his youth, except
that he left Spain somewhat hurriedly at about seventeen because
the Inquisition was too active for his liking. He studied in the
University of Paris, but, disliking both the hurly-burly of the city
and the sardonic temper of its inhabitants, he made his home in
Bruges to which town he always returned after his many journeys,
visits, and "residential posts". One of his early appointments was
as tutor to an extraordinary young man who was a Cardinal and
Archbishop at the age of nineteen. This took him to Louvain,
where in 1519 he was appointed professor at the university. He
was attached to the college of the castle and he became acquainted
with Erasmus, then a senior member of the university. There is
no doubt that the latter had a great influence upon the young man,
for Vives in many ways reflects strongly the attitudes and modes of
thought of Erasmus. When Vives lost his protector in 1521, Erasmus seems to have given little practical help but it cannot be ignored
that Erasmus himself was largely dependent on patronage, and that
there were many poor scholars needing assistance at that time.
Vives made many journeys, seeking in vain the patronage of rich
nobles—the equivalent, one supposes, of the present application for
scholastic positions—and finally came to England probably to take
up an appointment at Corpus Christi—one of the new Oxford
colleges. The part Erasmus played in obtaining this work for Vives

can only be guessed, but it is certain that he encouraged, advised, and helped in the publication of a commentary on St Augustine's *City of God* in 1522.

It was in the following year that Vives took up the post in Oxford and also dedicated to Catherine of Aragon his new work, *De institutione feminae Christianae*, which advocated education for the inferior sex. Whether it was the idea of instruction or that of inferiority which sold this book through forty editions is a debatable point. He was, it must be admitted, somewhat ahead of his time in suggesting that education should fit a woman for marriage as a partner in the "ownership of the whole of life". That he was no misogynist is shown by his stubborn partisanship of Catherine, who had treated him with great benevolence, and also by his marriage on one of his several visits to Bruges from England. It is said that he was, during that time, tutor to Princess Mary, for whom he wrote, within his first year, two letters, *De ratione studii puerilis*. Having been made a Doctor of Laws, his work was to lecture in philosophy at Oxford, and no doubt his contact with adolescent students helped to clarify his ideas on education.

Vives had the courage of his convictions, and accordingly paid the penalty of his loyalty to Catherine during the episode of the divorce. He wrote in the Queen's defence, and so lost the King's favour and, moreover, his comfortable position. After being confined to his house for several weeks he was banished, and returned to Flanders where he received appeals from Catherine for his further intervention. Whether it was discretion or loss of interest which caused him to turn his back on the whole matter it is hard to judge, but is is not likely that it was lack of courage. Although he had not the power and influence of Erasmus, he adopted very much the Dutchman's attitude during the wars of religion, and thus brought upon himself suspicion and distrust which affected his career far more than it had harmed Erasmus. He tried to take up work again at Louvain, but it must be assumed he was not very successful for he spent most of the rest of his life in retirement in Bruges.

He made an adequate living from his writing, his books on devotion being particularly successful although he also wrote on political economy, philosophy, and education. His first work, the commentary, *De Civitate Dei*, had shown his quality as a critical thinker, and had antagonised conventional theologians by pouring scorn on ancient commentators—incidentally it had also displeased Erasmus by its prolixity. Now he directed his scathing criticisms against the scholastics and their absorption with the authority of Aristotle, thus taking his place with the best of the Humanists, and at the same time pointing the way to the concepts which crystallised a half-century later in the ideas of Francis Bacon.

However, Vives's immediate task on his return to Flanders was to outline a scheme for the relief of poverty by the exclusion of beggars and poor strangers from the community, and the introduction of public apprenticeship systems, lunatic asylums, and foundling schools. His scheme also envisaged the compulsion of members of the community to work, and the collection of heavy taxes from churches and monasteries. Ypres and several other cities put similar schemes into practice despite much opposition, and thus the responsibility of Vives for the project did not serve to endear him to his own Catholic brethren, particularly the Franciscans, whose lifework was dependent on the existence of the poor. An interesting work of a decade later, *De communione rerum,* is, to some extent, a continuation of Vives's theorising on community problems, and he shows some uncertainty as to the desirability of private ownership of property.

In 1531, a considerable work in twenty books, *De tradendis disciplinis,* was published, and among the welter of ideas on many subjects contained therein, it is possible to find the essence of Vives's philosophy—not fully developed and defined, it is true, but nevertheless indicating the main sources of his inspiration. In brief, he accepted much from the past, particularly from Aristotle, including a theory of knowledge which was almost identical with the latter's sensism. It is clear that his theories of the world and matter are based on a concept of evolution. His treatise, *De anima et vita,* published in 1538, gives his philosophy from another angle and has often been called one of the earliest books on psychology. He discusses the inductive method of discovery in philosophy, and this long before Bacon argued that only empirical scientific methods were of value. He stresses that man should not be concerned with the nature of the soul, but with its manifestation, and that he should not seek to study the essence of mind, but rather the actions of men. His main theme is that knowledge is of value only when it is put to use. Thus it is not surprising that students of Vives's philosophy would rank him with Bacon as a pioneer of realism.

De disciplinis deserves recognition as an outstanding treatise on education of the Renaissance period. It sets out to formulate rules of style in rhetoric and literature, but, even as it includes much discussion of philosophy—a philosophy which bears directly on educational theory—so it also embodies principles for both curriculum and method in education. Thus, for instance, the aim and scope of history is discussed in some detail, the relevance of all human activity being emphasised. It can only be as suspected that Vives found the history teacher of his day to be as obsessed with battles as some teachers have been within living memory.

Perhaps the most notable innovation in educational thought is found in the discussion of science in education. Vives advocates nature study for a boy, because to understand what he sees does not call upon knowledge and experience which he lacks. The study will exercise his imagination and judgment so long as it is first hand experience and not merely the reading of other men's findings. The principle is, of course, entirely acceptable to-day, but although Vives doubtlessly saw the relationship between interest and activity, his main concern was to find some harmony between his religion and the scientific bent of his own mind. He points out that the study must not be expected to reveal absolute reasons for everything in Nature. Men's limited intelligence on the one hand, and the teachings of religion on the other, are bounds beyond which the student should not attempt to wander. Thus he should not meet the ideas of "hard and difficult" men like Pliny and Aristotle, ideas which always demand explanation, nor should he be confused by inconsistent opinions or biased arguments such as are found in classical writings. "In all the philosophy of natural history," he says, "the boy is to learn such knowledge as far as he can test it by his own judgement, experience, and diligence."

Following this description of the basic method of study are suggestions which also express another great principle of modern education: "At first should be shown that which is more easily perceivable by the senses, for the senses are the sources of all cognition". The boy should study what he can see and feel, the sky, the weather, fire, air, water, and earth, with perhaps the help of one of the more harmless little geography books of Aristotle or one of his disciples. He should on no account be required or permitted to engage in the old practice of disputation on nature topics: "There is no need of disputations, only the silent contemplation of Nature.

The scholars should rather ask and seek what is true than wrangle and discuss".

In this way Vives interpreted in other spheres of learning the great newly-revived concept of study by personal investigation and experience which Colet and Erasmus had advocated for the study of Scripture and languages. His campaign against the practice of dialectics proceeded in other works such as *In pseudo dialecticos*, where he sums up his attitude thus: "Does an artist spend all his life preparing his brushes and colours?" He speaks even more strongly of "this cursed babel which has corrupted every branch of knowledge". The treatise, *De causis corruptarum artium*, was similarly concerned with the evils of traditional habits of study, but by this time many of the bad habits had arisen from the cult of humanism itself—the unintelligent acceptance of classical authority and the aping of classical writers in style and ideas.

The list of reading books given in *De disciplinis* to accompany the study of nature, is so full of classical names that Vives might well be considered somewhat inconsistent. It needs to be borne in mind that books for individual reading were now playing a full part in education and, moreover, that the main purpose of reading, as generally accepted, was to obtain mastery of a classical language, usually Latin. Thus Vives, being aware of the relatively narrow choice open to the teacher or tutor, discussed books at some length, not in contradiction of his former precepts, but in order to give such words of warning and advice as "The pupil must not learn things which ought to be avoided". Moreover, he should study not only certain classical works, but also "pore over maps" and study the recent Spanish voyages and discoveries. The most advanced study must revert again to personal observation and investigation, by travel and by seeking information from "gardeners, husbandmen, shepherds, and hunters, for any man cannot possibly make all observation without help". It is clear that Vives would have given to nature study a higher place in education than it achieved for many years. "It is at once school and schoolmaster," he says, "for it presents something a man can look at with admiration and at the same time his culture is advanced by it."

There is much more which is worthy of study in *De disciplinis*, but it must suffice to add that he subscribed to Erasmus's opinion that the best of established teaching methods should be studied and adapted. He advocated the study of teaching method by observation of many different teachers with the aim of evolving rules of teaching as a result of such investigation. He made a practical contribution to language teaching by producing *Exercitatio Linguae Latinae* (1538) which apparently became popular, for it passed through ninety-nine editions. It has already been indicated that he contributed also to psychological theory, and indeed, much that is modern can be found in *De anima.* He discusses the association of ideas, the nature of memory, the principle of mnemonics, the function of "simple apprehension" and the nature of the emotions, a list of topics not usually associated with sixteenth-century educational theory. Thus even a general survey of such brevity may serve to show that Vives was a thinker of rare depth, of considerable breadth of vision, and of undoubted understanding of educational problems. It is possible that hitherto the extent of his influence may have been under emphasised.

Vives synthesised the best of the ancient teachers with the best of contemporary thought and, moreover, he added so much from his own genius that he might well be set apart as belonging to no group and to no age. From Quintilian he accepted a great deal that is acceptable to-day about children—the significance of play, the importance of the senses, and the existence of differences of many kinds between one individual and another. From the Greeks he took his theory of the association of ideas which he put forward to show that pupils need to be taught connections between ideas: thus the teacher should use "play-way" methods. From Erasmus he "caught" his great interest in international understanding, but added as his own contribution, an insistence upon the inclusion of modern languages, history, and geography in the curriculum. With Luther he demanded the preservation of the vernacular and the establishment of state education for both boys and girls. If only he had become a schoolmaster the fate of many a small European might have been vastly different.

John Sturm (1507-1589)

There is hardly a country in Europe which did not produce a reformer, a schoolmaster, or an interested nobleman, intent upon the improvement of education in the sphere best known to himself. Not all were completely humanistic in outlook. Rabelais, although usually grouped with the Humanists, shows many characteristics of the later Realists, while the views of Melancthon and Luther were not unconnected with their religious convictions.

No consideration of sixteenth-century educational ideas would be complete and balanced without a brief note on the work of John Sturm, the Strasbourg schoolmaster, who, imbued with enthusiasm for the new learning and Humanist philosophy, put into practice a system which spread to the limits of the civilised world. It is one of the sad lessons of history that it was a system which could have served only a limited purpose, but which in being applied to general education offered wide scope for misuse and abuse. Thus the least important, least universal, and least permanent principles of humanism made a crushing impact on educational practice and so stimulated the growth of protest culminating in the teaching of Comenius.

Sturm passed through a school of the Brethren of the Common Life, as did Erasmus, and through the University of Louvain as did Vives. He lectured in Paris with such success that Strasbourg invited him to take up a Latin school post. He soon became a headmaster and held the post from 1538 to 1581, being dismissed in his old age because his religious views differed from those of the governing party. In forty-three years, however, he created the fashion for an intense concentration on Latin teaching at all stages of education, even the primary stage. His own aim was to prepare the children of citizens and nobles for professional careers in which fluency, grace, and style in Latin speech would be a primary requisite. Firstly, it was a vocational skill, and secondly, it was a cultural attainment essential to the progress of civilisation.

Thus in order to achieve proficiency, children must start to learn Latin even as early as five years, and to achieve style they must read and emulate the classical stylists, particularly Cicero. It will be remembered that Erasmus had uttered fierce warnings against this method which led to slavish imitation. Sturm no doubt avoided many of the faults of which his disciples and successors were guilty, for he was an outstanding example of a successful schoolmaster who could teach well by his own method. Moreover, he was a competent organiser so that his school ran efficiently, and put on a good show for visitors who came to get ideas for running similar establishments elsewhere. He was also more enlightened than at first appears, for it is said he introduced some mathematics and science, and also lively classroom methods unusual in those days. His book, *De litterarum ludis*, gained wide popularity.

Sturm's imitators were rarely of similar calibre, and there followed, throughout Europe, the lifeless language teaching, the learning by rote, the neglect of physical education, and the ignoring of the mother tongue which characterised the grammar school purporting to prepare boys for the higher education most of them would never receive.

French Renaissance Writers—Francois Rabelais (1495?-1553), Michel de Montaigne (1533-1592)

The Renaissance movement, late in reaching France, was not firmly established until the Reformation in Germany had begun. The University of Paris was one of the main causes of the delay because of its support of the Scholastics and its resistance to the influx of Protestant opinions from Germany. Even the encouragement of Francis I was not sufficient to silence the opposition and the result was that each side clung tenaciously to its own beliefs. Two of the outstanding supporters of the Renaissance spirit in education were Rabelais and Montaigne.

The former is said to have been the son of a lawyer who sent him at the age of nine to a Franciscan convent. Some years later, Rabelais entered a Benedictine monastery where he was granted greater freedom for his studies and for visiting French universities. Eventually he left the monastery to become a secular priest and also qualified as a physician. Rabelais had little experience of teaching, but through the influence of Erasmus and Sturm, he became interested in education and expressed his views about contemporary practice in his satire, the *Life of the Great Gargantua*. The title was derived from popular romances dealing with the adventures of the giants, Gargantua and Pantagruel. The writings of Rabelais are associated in popular thought with the qualities of buffoonery, coarseness, and indecency, but beneath this is a vein of earnestness coupled with learning and a shrewd wit. His works are frankly a caricature intended to draw attention to current abuses and seek to drive home his criticisms, which are constructive as well as destructive.

The ideas of Rabelais represent the revolt against the decadence of the Scholastics of his age. In keeping with his more liberal outlook, Rabelais protested against the "grammar grind", and characterised the education of Gargantua as making him into "a fool, a sot, a dolt, and a blockhead". Gargantua's father is repre-sented as growing dissatisfied with the kind of training which developed only the memory and determined to place his son in the charge of a tutor who possessed the new spirit in learning. Under the direction of his tutor, Gargantua entered upon a strenuous course of study, and beneath the burlesque it is clear that Rabelais envisaged a scheme of training which aimed at the education of the whole man. The course of study pursued by Gargantua is obviously an impossible one, but as Dr Boyd points out, "The element of bur-lesque is obvious in this outline of Gargantua's education: it is a gigantic task for a gigantic nature, not a course for ordinary men. But with the burlesque there are some serious ideas".[1]

These serious ideas are more clearly expressed in the letter which Gargantua sent to his son, Pantagruel. Gargantua advised him to learn Greek, Latin, Hebrew for the sake of the Scriptures, and then Chaldee and Arabic. Classical literature, music, athletics, the works of nature, art, manual work, and the study of the Bible find a place in this curriculum which aimed at training the pupil to think for himself. The encyclopaedic nature of the course has obvious affinities with the schemes later proposed by Milton and Locke. This is not surprising because, although Rabelais seems to have exercised little influence upon the schools of the period, his works were known to Montaigne, Milton, Locke, and Rousseau. S. S. Laurie summed up the aim of Rabelais as "the expansion and enrichment of the human mind as opposed to the overloading of it with subtleties and superfluous details of a formal grammar, and a still more formal scholasticism".[2]

In some ways Montaigne is a contrast to Rabelais. He agreed with Rabelais in his condemnation of the medieval outlook, but he was no scientist, and was equally critical of the old and the new in education. He realised that the danger of the new learning was its tendency to turn the individual into a pedant, and in his *Essay on Pedantry* he wrote: "We are for ever asking, 'Does he know Greek or Latin? Can he write verse or prose?' But the important point is if he has grown better and wiser; and that point lags behind".[3]

[1] *The History of Western Education*, p. 219, sixth edition, A. & C. Black, 1952.
[2] *Studies in the History of Educational Opinion from the Renaissance*, p. 47, C.U.P., 1903.
[3] G. E. Hodgson, *The Teacher's Montaigne*, p. 85, Blackie, 1915.

Montaigne's birthplace was in the neighbourhood of Bordeaux, and he came from a well-to-do family. He described his own education as follows: "My late father made all the inquiries a man could, among people of intelligence and understanding, to find an excellent method of education, because he was aware of the blemishes in the ordinary method. He was told that the length of time we spend in learning languages imperfectly is the one and only cause why we never attain to that greatness of soul, and to that knowledge which distinguished the Greeks and Romans. I do not think myself that it is the sole cause. But anyhow, this is the plan which my father discovered: before I had learned to speak, while I was still at nurse, he gave me to a German—who was quite ignorant of our tongue, but very well versed in Latin. This man, whom he had brought expressly, and whom he paid very highly, carried me about constantly. There were two others, less learned, who were about me, in order to relieve him: all of these only spoke to me in the Latin language. As for the rest of the household, it was an inviolable rule that neither my father, my mother, nor man nor maid servant ever spoke in my presence any words save those Latin ones which they learned in order to chatter to me. It is marvellous what progress they all made: my father and mother learned sufficient Latin to understand and even to speak it if they wished, and also did those servants who were specially attached to me. In fact, we were all 'latinised', so that the villages round about us began to abound with it; and still there are many Latin names of workmen and tools which by long habit have taken root".[1]

After this experiment in the direct method of learning Latin, Montaigne was sent at the age of six to the College of Guienne. He left at the age of thirteen, by which time his Latin had deteriorated through lack of use. He developed a taste for reading from perusing the stories of Ovid's *Metamorphoses* at the age of seven or eight, and this led him to read Virgil, Terence, Plautus, and the Italian comedies, "lured ever onwards by the attractiveness of the contents". At a time when most boys left the college with a loathing for books, the young Montaigne became an assiduous reader.

At his father's death, Montaigne became the owner of the château of Montaigne, and although occupied in public service, he had sufficient leisure to write the first two volumes of the *Essays*

[1] G. E. Hodgson, *op. cit.*, pp. 142-3.

which were published in 1580. He produced the third book of the *Essays* in 1588.

The key note to Montaigne's views is his conviction that education should be concerned with the whole man. "It is not a mind, it is not a body we are educating, it is a man; we must not cut him in half; and, as Plato says, we must not cultivate one without the other, we must develop them equally, like a pair of horses harnessed to the same pole." [1]

He would like to see teachers "really educate our understandings". As an omnivorous reader, he valued books, but he placed great reliance upon foreign travel and intercourse with other folk,— "in order that we may learn about the manners and customs of other peoples, and that we may rub our wits and our shoulders against other men's. I would have a child travel from his infancy; and first of all—so as to kill two birds with one stone—among those nations whose speech is most unlike our own, to which, unless you begin early, you will never mould his tongue". [2]

The young person should be accompanied by a tutor, who should be a man "whose head is well furnished rather than stuffed full: and, though one desires both, yet that he should possess character and understanding rather than knowledge: and, lastly, that he should train his pupil on a novel plan". [3] "The tutor, according to the capacity of the pupil should develop him, make him approach things, choose, discriminate amongst them for himself: sometimes showing him the way, sometimes leaving him to find it. I would not let the tutor be the only person to speculate and talk : I would have him listen to his pupil, turn and turn about". [4] Montaigne believed that the pupil should be trained to think for himself and not accept an opinion on trust or because of authority. This principle, he thought, was especially applicable to the study of history, which is not merely the memorising of events and dates. The boy should be trained to judge rather than learn history. Above all, the individual should be taught "to know himself and to know how to die well and live well".

Montaigne severely criticised the harsh life and methods of the schools of his period. "Instead of inviting children to learning, we really accustom them to horror and cruelty. Let me have no

---

[1] G. E. Hodgson, *The Teacher's Montaigne*, p. 130, Blackie, 1915.
[2] *ibid.*, p. 110.   [3] *ibid.*. p. 105.   [4] *ibid.*, pp. 195-6.

more violence and driving: in my opinion there is nothing else which so brutalises and dulls a high-mettled nature.—How far more seemly that their classroom should be decently strewn with flowers and leaves than with blood-stained birchen rods".[1]

On the other hand, Montaigne would not pamper the pupil but would inure him to hardships and deprive him of all luxury in clothes, bed, food, and drink, so as to avoid his becoming soft. He had no use for formal studies such as grammar or logic which are concerned with words rather than things. He did not despise book learning, but believed the acquisition of wisdom rather than learning should be the aim of education. The pupil's book is the world. Montaigne's *Essays* were widely read, both in his own country and in England, and many of his ideas were developed by Locke and Rousseau.

The English Scene

John Colet was a boy of ten when Caxton set up his printing press so that by the time he founded his school the new books had become a major factor in a rapidly changing world. Books became more and more accessible at a reasonable price; and the population was consequently becoming more literate and a demand was grow-ing for a popular press. Spelling was being standardised and reference books were being compiled and thus the nature of teaching and learning was very seriously affected. Pupils now had paper for written exercises and it became possible for "reading and writ-ing" to take the place of "speaking and doing"—a change by no means entirely for the better.

Within twenty years of Colet's death England was cut off from the Roman Church, and although this stimulated the development of the vernacular as a scholarly and official language, there were adverse results such as the disappearance of schools with the closing of the monasteries and chantries. Colet's old friend, More, pictures in *Utopia* some of the other ills brought about, not only by the dissolution of the monasteries, but also by the Enclosure Acts, and the decline of the guilds. Poverty increased, the sources of charity dried up, and the educational system suffered a setback which was perpetuated for many years. Such factors may have played a predominant part in hindering the spread and development of ideas and practices favoured by Colet and his disciples. Of the strength of their interest in education there is no doubt. Sir Thomas More

[1] G. E. Hodgson, *op. cit.*, pp. 130-1.

experimented with his "school" of young people, and wrote in terms which reveal his agreement with Colet and Erasmus. His wide circle of friends and acquaintances included two young men, Sir Thomas Elyot and Juan Luis Vives, who continued in their writings the interpretation of much-discussed principles. Cardinal Wolsey, who helped Vives and Elyot in their early careers, was no mean patron of education, being responsible for the founding of a college, and the authorship of a treatise of education. Thus the ferment was there, but in England the times were unfortunate, for Henry VIII's quarrel with the Pope, and the troubles it brought in its train, distracted from matters educational all these brilliant men. More lost his head, Wolsey met his downfall, Vives was banished, and Elyot suffered a permanent setback in his career through his friendship with More.

Thus the propagating of the new ideas and ideals was left to continental scholars and it can only be conjectured what eminence England might have gained had the King permitted the continuance of the happy intellectual circle of Colet and More. The latter did much to spread understanding of Colet's attitude and teachings, and moreover he adopted Colet's custom of keeping open house for interesting people, and developed his method of training a few boys in the household. The story of More's "school" for boys and girls may be read elsewhere, for here it must suffice to suggest the probable extent of the influence of the two friends. Even were their spirit not glowing in the writings of Vives, his adoption of their ideas would be obvious from the fact that like Colet, he reproached the King for warmongering, and that, like More, he wrote upon the makings of an ideal community.

Sir Thomas Elyot (*c.* **1490-1546**), who was neither priest nor professor, wrote about education, admitting his indebtedness to Erasmus and More. He married Margaret Barrow, a student of More's "school" so that it is not unlikely that a member of the inferior sex helped to shape his ideas on education. His main book, *The Gouvernour* (1534), although said to be based on two Italian works, Pontano's *De Principe* and Patrizzi's *De Regno*, contains much that is neither in these nor in another contemporary Italian work with which it is often compared—*The Courtier*, of Castiglione.

That all these works are concerned with the upbringing of young nobles and princes does not indicate their contents to be entirely irrelevant to education in a wider context. Their topic is a reflection of the significant historical fact that by this time the upper classes were no longer holding learning in such high esteem as a half-century earlier. Scholarship was now considered necessary only for the clergy and certain officials. Thus these several works on education were designed to persuade men with power and money that it was a duty to ensure a sound and thorough Christian education for future rulers. It is not surprising to find in Elyot's work the essential characteristics of humanism. He accepts the Platonic idea of an all-round "liberal" education, with its insistence on the protection of the young pupil from undesirable influences, and its emphasis on the danger of excess in emotional experience and in physical and manual pursuits. He accepts much from Quintilian and Plutarch, but at the same time, he holds to the Humanist view of the importance of teaching classical languages from the earliest years. Unfortunately, in England as in Europe, the wider ideals of humanism were never applied in general to the teaching of children. The true concept of "liberal" education was thrust aside, and the language "grammar grind" became a bad habit which served only a temporary vocational purpose.

Elyot, in choosing to outline the education of a well-born child, appears to be making not a class distinction but a plea for the best conditions obtainable. He believes with the classical writers and the Humanists that childhood should be a period of training in "sweet manners and virtuous customs", but he would have children "sweetly allured" into learning, for he deplores—while accepting —the necessity for children to start learning at an early age. They should be taught Latin "in most gentle manner", and should hear only "pure and elegant" language whether it be Latin or English. Play-ways and conversation methods should be used in the early years, but at seven a sterner régime should prevail, for boys should be "taken from the company of women" and given into the charge of an "ancient and worshipful man"—preferably a learned one.

Elyot advocates the pursuit of music, drawing, and various manual crafts, according to the interests and aptitudes of pupils, purely as recreative activities, although such skills, once acquired, prove useful in later life. He envisages that little boys will learn Latin, Greek, and French, quite easily so long as they are not tired by tedious study of grammar. The Humanist practice of studying not only the style but also the subject matter of classical writings, is to be followed. Elyot is particularly partial to the poets although oratory and rhetoric are to be studied intensively from the age of fourteen. Cosmography figures in Elyot's curriculum as in Vives's, but its function is only to enlighten the study of classical history which is a subject of great moral value "whereby our wits may be amended and our personages be more apt to serve our public weal".

From seventeen onwards the boy is to study philosophy, and this period until he comes of age should not be spent in premature vocational training. Wrestling, running, swimming, hunting, riding, hawking, archery, and other physical activities should be carefully organised to strengthen the youth and develop his skill and courage. An inferior tutor cannot organise adequately such experiences for the pupil, nor can he generate in the young man a spirit of admiration and emulation. Thus Elyot stresses constantly that the prevailing niggardliness and negligence on the part of noble parents is to be deprecated because it has caused the decay and decline of the teaching profession. "Lord God," he says, "how many good and clean wits of children be nowadays perished by ignorant schoolmasters!"

The significance of Elyot's educational writing is twofold. Firstly, it epitomises the best of Humanist thought, embodying as it does, not only most of the principles of Colet and Erasmus, but also the spirit and substance of Vittorino's humanism, derived by Elyot from his Italian studies. Secondly, he was the first English writer on education of the modern period and so was responsible for handing on much of the best of humanism to English teachers, and at the same time, for setting the example, unusual in a Humanist, of writing in his own native language. It cannot be doubted that young Ascham, who took his degree at Cambridge in the year of publication of *The Gouvernour*, must have been well acquainted with Elyot's ideas, although in his own writings, his frequent references to his friend, Sturm, might give the impression that he followed continental rather than English trends of thought.

Roger Ascham (1515-1568) became a teacher of Greek in his own university and gained recognition as a scholar and writer who was not too proud nor too faint-hearted to use his own language as a vehicle for his learned ideas. His first book was in praise of archery as a noble pastime, and as he himself was passionately fond of music, it is not surprising to find that he did not omit a consideration of the Greek gymnastic from his educational theory. In that book,

Toxophilus, he says: "The best wits to learning must needs have much recreation, and ceasing from their books, or else they mar themselves", and complains of the decline of singing in the country.

These two small examples alone suggest that, in spite of his visit to Sturm's gymnasium, he remained at heart a disciple of the English school, which, as exemplified by Elyot, had blended the best of humanism with the best of the old training of chivalry. His close association with young members of the English nobility may have strengthened his opinion in this respect. He taught penmanship to Edward VI, he was tutor to Princess Elizabeth, and he knew many other young people including the ill-fated Lady Jane Grey, who provided him with one of his strongest arguments against the harsh treatment accorded to children, not only by teachers, but also by parents. His book, *The Scholemaster*, was the result of a discussion with Sir Richard Sackville on the severity of school punishments, and on the practice of sending boys abroad to be educated. It was written during the last few years of his life, and was published by his widow in 1570, two years after his death. Throughout the book Ascham frequently reverts to his main plea: "Gentleness in teaching" and "gentleness allures to learning".

The Scholemaster in its title, reveals its main difference from *The Gouvernour*. Ascham, although himself a tutor of individual children, wrote about school education. In the first part, *The bringing up of Youth*, he asks: "What shall we say when now in our days, the schoolmaster is used both for Praeceptor in learning and Paedagogus in manners?" He regrets that no longer can each boy have a "grave governour" to control his learning, his behaviour, and his movements, but he feels it all the more necessary for a schoolmaster to make the school "a sanctuary against fear", and to breed up in children both love of learning and "good order of living". To remedy the decline of learning he would have beating abolished except for moral offences, but he would have adolescents more strictly disciplined in behaviour and morals, and would not allow youngsters to wander without tutors on the continent, indulging in dissipation, and earning a bad name for the Englishman.

The second part of *The Scholemaster* concentrates more specifically on language teaching, but even in this *Ready Way to the Latin Tongue*, the same two dominating principles, gentleness and control, are stressed many times. Languages are the basis of his education, as might be expected, but he would not hasten so quickly as some Humanist teachers to the stage of composition, for he feared the development of bad habits. It is evident that he is striving, like his predecessors, for good style. The vernacular is to be used for two-way translations, which process he stresses as preferable to the prevailing single translation. But his writings made very little impression upon the English grammar school of his day. Other celebrated educators, however, including Buchanan and Mulcaster, pay tribute in their own work to Ascham's influence.

Richard Mulcaster (1530-1611) was an Eton boy who, after spending several years at both English universities, achieved a reputation for his skill in Greek and Hebrew. In 1561 he became Master of Merchant Taylors' School where he remained for twenty-five years. He then spent twelve years at St Paul's School, so that he was undoubtedly the first English writer on modern education whose ideas evolved through over thirty years of schoolmastering. He taught many famous men in their boyhood, and there exists much interesting evidence as to his quality and personality. Thomas Fuller reports : "In a morning he would exactly and plainly construe and parse the lessons to his scholars; which done, he slept his hour (custom made him critical to proportion it) in his desk in the school, and woe betide the scholar that slept the while! Awaking, he heard them accurately, and Atropos himself might be persuaded to pity as soon he to pardon when he found just fault". His curriculum included not only Latin, Greek, and Hebrew, but also mime and drama—records show that his boys performed plays at Court.

Although Mulcaster's educational writings are a practical teacher's interpretation of humanism they also indicate in no uncertain way the movement of thought towards a new philosophy.[1] Thus while he is not the first to advocate the use of the vernacular in school, he is the first to emphasise its importance as a national asset and to claim that "Whatsoever shall become of the English State, the English tongue cannot prove fairer than it is at this day". He would include English in the curriculum, and have it studied before Latin, which, therefore, should be started at a much later age than suggested by all Humanist teachers. Again, he agrees with Elyot and Ascham about physical training, but he would extend physical activities to girls and also to the teachers. He would follow Elyot in teaching both music and drawing, but he does not agree with Ascham that the study of mathematics has little value.

[1] 1581 *Positions Wherein Three Primitive Circumstances be examined which are necessie for the Training up of Children either for Skill in their booke or health in their bodie;* 1601 *The Elementarie which entreateth Cheeflie of the right writing of our English tung.*

Mulcaster agrees with Vives that the pupils should not be pushed too hard or too quickly, and he believes, with Erasmus and Elyot, that the status of the schoolmaster should be raised; but he goes further in suggesting that the most skilled and highly paid teachers should teach the lower classes which should be smaller than those at the top of the school. He agrees with Vives that girls should be educated, but he would even admit them to higher education. For other principles he appears to have moved outside the limits of the Humanist code as generally interpreted—he restates Luther's ideal of education for all and, moreover, equal opportunity for all. Above all, his reaching out beyond the conventional ideals of his time is shown by his demand for training colleges. When he asks, "Is the framing of young minds and the training of their bodies so mean a point of cunning?" he probably saw more clearly the implications of such a concept than did Comenius a generation later.

SUGGESTIONS FOR FURTHER READING

Most of the general histories of educational thought contain useful references to the long and full period covered by this chapter. The few books listed hereunder will serve to supplement the chapter, and to give it reality through the actual words of great thinkers.

W. H. Woodward, *Vittorino da Feltre and Other Humanist Educators*, C.U.P., 1912.

F. V. N. Painter, *Luther on Education*, Lutheran Publication Society, Philadelphia, 1889.

W. H. Woodward, *Desiderius Erasmus concerning the Aim and Method of Education*, C.U.P., 1904.

K. L. Born (Editor), *The Education of a Christian Prince by Erasmus*, Columbia University Press, 1936.

F. Watson, *Vives on Education*, C.U.P., 1913.

Sir T. More, *Utopia*, Arber English Reprints, 1869.

Sir T. Elyot, *The Boke named the Gouvernour*, Ed. H. H. S. Croft, London, 1883.

R. Ascham, *The Scholemaster*, Arber English Reprints, 1895.

R. Mulcaster, *Positions*, Ed. R. H. Quick, 1888.

Mulcaster's Elementarie, Ed. E. T. Campagnac, O.U.P., 1920.

G. E. Hodgson, *The Teacher's Montaigne*, Blackie, 1915.

CHAPTER VII

JESUIT EDUCATION—THE LITTLE SCHOOLS OF PORT-ROYAL—LA SALLE

The topic of Jesuit education is an unusually difficult one because the violent antagonisms which have been engendered by religious and political controversy have tended to obscure the educational principles which governed the work of the Jesuit schools and colleges. It should not be forgotten that some of the severest critics of the Jesuit system of education have been found amongst Roman Catholics, and that many Protestant writers have been loud in their praise of the work accomplished by the Jesuits.[1]

Although the bitter controversies of past ages have almost died out the same cannot be said about old habits of thought. Even now, the phrase Jesuit education produces in the minds of some people the picture of unscrupulous agents whose adherence to the doctrine that the end justifies the means led the Jesuit to adopt any method that gave him an ascendancy over the minds of the young. The average English dictionary bears witness to the truth of this statement. Thus, Chambers' Dictionary, after defining a Jesuit as a member of the Society of Jesus, gives as the popular meaning of the word, "a crafty or insidious person, an intriguer, a prevaricator". The writers of this work are not concerned with the religious and political disputes which gave rise to the emotional tinge attached to the name Jesuit. Their object is to attempt to give an impartial and purely objective account of Jesuit education. Any criticism or approval of the aims and methods of the Jesuits will be based on educational grounds alone.

The formation of the Society of Jesus by St Ignatius Loyola in 1534 (the infant society received Papal recognition in 1540) is so well known that there is no necessity to enter into detail about the conversion of its founder, which occurred after a severe wound received on the ramparts of Pampeluna. The important fact which had so great an influence upon the organisation of the Society of

---

[1] Francis Bacon's judgment in Book I of the *Advancement of Learning* is well known. "Of the Jesuit Colleges, although in regard of their superstition I may say, '*Quo meliores eo deteriores*', yet in regard of this and some other points of learning and moral matters, I may say, as Agesilaus said to this enemy Pharnabaces, '*Talis cum sis, utinam noster esses*'."

Jesus is that Loyola began his career as a soldier. After his conversion, he visited the Holy Land, inspired by missionary zeal to bring the Mohammedans into the Christian fold. When he discovered that this project could not be realised, he returned to Spain to enter upon a course of study which led him from the grammar school at Barcelona to the University of Paris. Loyola was deeply affected by the evidences of decline in the University of Paris which from the position of the greatest centre of learning in Europe, had been reduced to a condition of enfeeblement and chaos by the policy of the French kings. One idea, however, developed in his mind. He had dedicated himself as a soldier of Christ, and he was persuaded that if he wished to carry out his object successfully, he must take advantage of everything that higher education could offer. Whilst at Paris, he gathered about him a small group of six young men (amongst whom was St Francis Xavier, the future Apostle of the Far East) who shared his outlook and ideals. It was this small company of earnest Christians which formed the beginnings of the Society of Jesus, and it was their selfless devotion and zeal which made possible its astonishingly rapid growth.

Three important features of the Society call for attention. In the first place, its aim was not, as has often been stated, that of combating Protestantism. When the idea of the Society first occurred to Loyola, he knew nothing at all about Luther and German Protestantism. His aim was *Omnia ad maiorem Dei gloriam*— All for the greater glory of God—and when he offered the services of the Society to the Pope, his chief concern was that of reforming the morals of the people and amending the ignorance of the clergy in countries that still remained loyal to the ancient Church. Later, the Society became a leading factor in the movement generally known as the Counter-Reformation, but this was rather the result of circumstances than the pursuit of a prearranged plan.

The Society was organised on a military basis. Another name for it was the "Regiment of Jesus". Its chief officer was the General of the Order and to him all members gave that implicit obedience which an officer naturally expects from his subordinates. Loyola's training as a soldier had much to do with the success of his venture. A good soldier has to make up his mind about his objective and the means he is going to adopt to achieve it. For a military commander who lacks a clear idea of what he should do, and who changes his tactics from moment to moment, the campaign is already lost before it has begun. The soldiers' point of view has both strength and weakness. If the military point of view involves a clear insight into the nature of the objective and the steps necessary for its attainment, this very fact may restrict its range and tend towards autocracy. Fortunately, Loyola and his immediate successors were preserved from this danger. They were imbued with the love of learning, and overwhelming zeal for service to the Church and a human sympathy and understanding which enabled them to know exactly how to encourage the minds of their subordinates and to employ their special interests and abilities in the most effective way.

Perhaps the most important thing as regards our purpose was that the Society of Jesus put education in the forefront of its activities. "St Ignatius was the first to assume the education of youth as a special part of the work of a religious order, as a special ministry, a special means of obtaining the ends of his society."[1] This does not mean that education was an unimportant part of the activity of previous orders of regular clergy. During the mediaeval period, both Franciscans and Dominicans, particularly the latter, had been greatly concerned with higher education in the universities. The schools of the Brethren of the Common Life were famous during the closing years of the Middle Ages, and that of Deventer was responsible for the education of three outstanding thinkers, the philosopher, Cardinal Nicholas of Cusa, the devout St Thomas à Kempis, and the great Renaissance scholar, Erasmus. The Jesuits, however, recognised that the education of the young was one of its more important objectives and was to be carried out by "teaching catechism to children and the ignorant; lecturing on philosophy and theology in the universities; by instructing youth in grammar schools and colleges".

The growth of the Society of Jesus was most remarkable. Even before the death of its founder, Jesuit colleges had been established in many Italian towns, in Spain, Portugal, Austria, and France. By 1610 there were over 300 schools and colleges taught by the Jesuits, some of which were in the New World. This expansion was partly due to the sanctity and wholeheartedness of purpose which distinguished the lives of St Ignatius and his successors, partly to the efficient instruction given in the Jesuit institutions, and partly to the outstanding ability and scholarship of so many members of the order.

[1] R. Schwickerath, S.J., *Jesuit Education*, p. 87, B. Herder, 1903.

The most important contribution made to education by the Jesuits was in the realm of organisation and method rather than in that of educational theory. As regards organisation, the order was divided into provinces, and each province comprised all the schools and colleges in a certain country or district. A Provincial was appointed by the General of the Order to take charge of the province. He was responsible to the General who had a small council of five assistants. The constitutions of the Order could only be changed by the General Congregation, which was composed of the General, the Assistants, the Provincials, and two deputies elected from each province. This body may also be regarded as limiting the power of the General, and so preventing the growth of an autocracy. The government of a Jesuit college was in the hands of a Rector, who was assisted by a Prefect of Studies, in charge of everything connected with the instruction, and a Prefect of Discipline, responsible for the maintenance of good order and discipline. So effective was this organisation that in its essentials it remains unchanged at the present day. The constitutions of the Society were drawn up by Loyola in 1541, and only the fourth part deals specially with education, and then on general rather than detailed principles.

When Loyola died in 1556, his constitutions were carefully examined, and were accepted without any alteration. He had, however, suggested that the details of the educational organisation should be discussed and events soon showed the wisdom of this. The growth of Jesuit colleges and schools demonstrated the necessity for some degree of uniformity in administration and teaching method. At first, these institutions adopted the methods in use in the countries in which they were situated, though they introduced modifications which appeared desirable. Some tentative schemes were prepared but when a request for more detailed guidance came from the teachers and heads of colleges in the provinces, it was felt that a general scheme should be issued. These requests were sent to Aquaviva, who was General of the Society from 1581 to 1615. The result was the issue of the *Ratio atque Institutio Studiorum Societatis Jesu.*

This document received its final form after fifteen years careful study and deliberation. Probably no educational scheme has ever been drawn up with such meticulous care. A start was made in 1584 when Aquaviva summoned six prominent Jesuits to Rome and charged them with the task of preparing a report on existing organisations and methods based on a careful study of writers and systems of education in different parts of Europe. The report was completed after nearly a year's concentrated work. It was then despatched to the provinces, and at least five men of learning in each province were ordered to examine it and make comments on it. The suggestions emanating from the provinces were examined at Rome and a revised scheme was prepared. Once again this was sent to the provinces to be tried out in practice. Further modifications were suggested, and after another period of careful deliberation, the *Ratio Studiorum* was issued in 1599.

The term *ratio* as used by mediaeval writers had such varying meanings that it is often difficult to find an exact English translation for it. In this particular case it denotes methods of teaching rather than theoretical principles. The latter had been discussed in the earlier reports but the *Ratio* of 1599 was essentially a set of rules for the organisation and teaching of the Jesuit colleges.[1] As Rusk remarks: "So comprehensive, systematic, and exhaustive are the regulations that the modern reader is inclined to forget that the *Ratio Studiorum* is one of the first attempts on record at educational organisation, management, and method, at a time when it was unusual even to grade pupils in classes; and one is tempted to compare it, not always to the disadvantage of the *Ratio*, with the regulations of a modern school system which have only after some generations been evolved and perfected".[2] All Jesuit colleges and schools were governed by the *Ratio Studiorum* of 1599, until 1832.

One criticism that has been levelled at Jesuit education is that it was solely concerned with secondary and higher education and neglected elementary. This is only partially true. The Jesuits maintained elementary schools, not only in the mission field, but in certain European countries. It is true, however, that the Jesuits decided to specialise in the teaching of older pupils, and they were probably wise in adopting this policy. A serious entry into elementary education would have needed a much greater man-power than the Society had at its disposal, and in view of the learning and qualifications of its members, it seemed that they could be more effectively used in the higher branches of study.

---

[1] A summary of the rules for the government of colleges and regulations for the work of the different professors is given by Schwickerath, *op. cit.*, pp. 114-15.
[2] R. R. Rusk, *The Doctrines of the Great Educators*, p. 74, Macmillan, reprinted 1945.

It has been said that in the Jesuit system, both the teachers and the pupils were excessively supervised. No doubt any educational system can suffer from too rigid and elaborate an organisation, and too much supervision. Both Quick and Kinloch suggest that the amount of supervision was akin to spying, and had for its aim, the attempt to "gain complete control over a human being, so that he becomes a mere instrument in the hands of his superior".[1] An over-zealous Rector or Prefect of Studies may have been tempted to fall into this error, but one should bear in mind that a similar criticism has at times been made concerning our modern English school system. Teachers in our national schools are required to follow a definite syllabus, to enter the work they have done in a record book, and they receive periodic visitations from the head of the school and from local inspectors and H.M.I.'s, who look at every aspect of the school life and recommend methods which they consider will produce an improvement in the work of a particular class or in the school as a whole.

This criticism raises also the whole question as to how far the teacher should make use of his personality in the training of his pupils. He cannot help doing so unconsciously, but it has been debated whether he is justified in deliberately influencing his pupils through the exercise of his personality. Arnold of Rugby, Thring, and Sanderson, certainly did this, and they, and especially Arnold, have been criticised for it. Many modern writers believe that the teacher should be more in the background and unobtrusively stimulate the pupils to develop their own individual characters and personalities. Even now, opinions are divided on this matter, and there are some who maintain that the teacher should come boldly out into the open and exercise a vigorous leadership.

A further criticism is that the *Ratio Studiorum* deprived the individual teacher of his freedom and initiative because no deviations from the rules were permitted. Such a statement needs

---

[1] See R. H. Quick, *Essays on Educational Reformers*, p. 38, new edition, Longmans, Green, 1902. The quotation is from T. F. Kinloch, *Pioneers of Religious Education*, p. 41, O.U.P., 1939. Kinloch asserts, p. 37, that Loyola derived much of his system from Sturm and Vives. There is no evidence to show that this was so. The similarities between these different systems of education may be explained in another way. Sturm had studied in the school of the Brethren of the Common Life at Liège and Vives, whom Loyola met at Bruges, had spent many years in the Netherlands. It is probable that all three drew ideas from a common source, the schools of the Brethren, and the University of Paris.

qualification. New methods and studies were not entirely prohibited. When the Society was first recognised the nature of the
instruction to be given in the colleges was qualified by the phrase
"as shall seem expedient to them, according to the circumstances
of persons, places, and times". There is no doubt that Aquaviva
was not prepared to countenance a rash adoption of novelties.
Hence the *Ratio*, while not prohibiting deviations, adopted a cautious attitude. "As according to the difference of country, time, and
persons, there may be a variety in the order of studies, in the hours
assigned to them, in repetitions, disputations and other school
exercises . . . if [the Provincial] should think anything more conducive to the greater advancement of learning in his province, he
shall inform the General in order that, after all, special regulations
be made for all the particular needs; these regulations should, however, agree as closely as possible with our general plan of studies."

One may think that this policy was ultra-conservative, but on
the other hand the history of education in England during the last
fifty years may seem to show that modern teachers have erred in
an opposite direction. Anyone who has had a long experience in
educational practice will know how the fads and fancies which are
fashionable at the moment tend to dominate certain schools. He
will have seen, occupying in turn, the educational stage, such fads
as observation, physical training, graded series of occupations (now
revived under the name of activity methods), expression work, and
training for citizenship (now taking the form of emphasis on social
studies). It is not that these studies or methods are in themselves
undesirable. All of them are worthy of consideration by the
educator. The error is that the enthusiastic advocates of these particular ideas put a partial truth in place of the whole and so distort
the educational pattern; they tend to see their own particular fancy
as the end of the educational process rather than a means to the
end.

In a religious order one would expect religious education to be
placed foremost. This was so with the Jesuits. Space forbids an
account of the religious education and also of the university education given by them.[1] For the modern educator, the chief interest

---

[1] The reader who is interested in the religious education given in Jesuit
colleges is referred to the account of Kinloch, *op. cit.*, pp. 39-47. One statement
on p. 40 calls for comment. "Teachers were told to busy themselves each
night in examining the conscience of individual pupils." This would seem quite
an impossible task as the statistics show that most colleges contained upwards

will probably be found in the curriculum and methods of what is equivalent to the secondary school of to-day (*studia inferiora*). Instruction was free, but in schools where boarders were accepted, fees were charged for their keep, except in cases of hardship. The "lower studies" were organised as follows: Three grammar courses each lasting a year and named Lower, Middle, and Upper Grammar, respectively, a course in the Humanities, and a course in Rhetoric, which lasted two years. The instruction has been criticised as being predominantly classical. This was so for the Jesuits excelled in classical studies, but the same criticism applied to the grammar schools of Elizabethan England. Actually the studies of the Jesuit colleges were more liberal than those of corresponding schools. Thus, history was taught in all five classes and in the two upper classes it included ecclesiastical and modern history. Geography was also studied, not only of the district in which the college was situated, but the pupils were kept informed about recent discoveries, and the work of the Order in the mission field. In the course in philosophy which followed that in "lower studies", mathematics was taught to quite an advanced level and, in addition, as much of the physical sciences as was known at the time. All these subjects, however, were subordinate to those in the classical languages. The Jesuits published numerous textbooks dealing with school studies.[1]

There were certain features which were characteristic of the Jesuits. They aimed at thoroughness in learning. This was secured both by the care taken in preparing the teacher for his work and by the methods actually employed in the classroom. The full course for a Jesuit teacher lasted for seventeen years. At each stage, he was required to be able to teach one stage beyond that in which he was actually engaged. Thus he was only permitted to teach philosophy when he had completed his studies in theology. Skill in teaching was considered to be of equal importance as scholarship.

of a thousand pupils. Moreover, most of the pupils were day boys. Boarders on a large scale were not encouraged until the nineteenth century. Kinloch seems to have drawn the wrong conclusion. Teachers were instructed to be always available so that boys could approach them for elucidation of their particular moral or religious problems. Naturally the Jesuits encouraged boys to frequent confession, but the pupil's confessor was not necessarily, and in general was not, one of his masters.

[1] The writer has in his possession a textbook of geography (1646) and one of mathematics (1675). Like all school books of that period, they are written in Latin. The latter book demonstrates the method of multiplication which was introduced into England by Dr Robert Recorde who was physician to Queen Mary. For an account of the method, see S. J. Curtis, *History of Education in Great Britain*, chapter 3.

When a new professor was required, the person selected went to an experienced teacher for one hour each day for instruction in the art of teaching. In the early days of his work, he received frequent visits from the Rector, and once a fortnight the Prefect of Studies came into his class to listen to a lesson.

The *Ratio Studiorum* gave detailed guidance to the teacher on the subject of lecturing so that students could take notes; the order in which classical authors should be read, and how the text should be explained; how the discussion at the close of a lesson should be conducted, and the methods to be used in the periodic revision. Fr Jouvancy published the *Ratio Discendi et Docendi* in 1703, which may be regarded as an official amplification of the *Ratio Studiorum*.[1]

The form of instruction recommended for the classical and literary course was the *Praelectio*. It was really a combination of the lecture and the explanation, and as its name implies, served as an introduction to the lecture method in the courses of higher studies. Unless it was too long, the professor began by reading to the class a passage from an author. He then outlined the argument, and when necessary, connected the content with the preceding lesson. Each sentence was then examined in turn, and any difficulties of grammar or subject matter elucidated. In translations into the mother-tongue, it was recommended that the Latin word order should be retained and then the rough version polished up till it became a model for imitation. Finally, the teacher should give any notes he considered necessary, and spend the last part of the period in a revision of the whole lesson. The teacher was instructed to make a frequent examination of pupils' note-books to ensure orderly notes and neat writing.

The *Ratio* emphasised the necessity for constant repetition, especially with the younger pupils. The Jesuits believed in laying a firm foundation during the early stages of learning. As a rule, every lesson began with a revision of the preceding, and ended with a repetition of the ground covered. One day a week was given up entirely to revision, and during the second six months of each year, the whole of the work of the first half was gone over a second time. One may wonder if the constant repetition "staled" the work, and tended to stifle interest. Much would depend upon the personality

---

[1] T. Hughes, S.J., describes the directions given to young teachers by Jouvancy in *Loyola and the Educational System of the Jesuits*, pp. 163-6 (Great Educator Series), W. Heinemann, 1892.

and skill of the teacher, but we shall see that he used certain incentives to avoid this danger. It is instructive to compare the thoroughness of Jesuit instruction with its lack in some of the basic studies in certain modern schools, if one may believe what some critics have to say about them.

Considerable importance was attached to regular examinations and tests. At the end of each year, every class was given a formal examination, oral and written. In order that pupils should not be unduly frightened at the prospect of examination, they received instruction on the method of answering questions. Perhaps the best known incentive to study was the Jesuits' use of competition or emulation. It might be between individuals or groups. Each pupil was allotted a rival or *aemulus*. When a question was addressed to a pupil, his rival was on the alert for mistakes or inadequacies, and ready to rush in with the correct answer. Sometimes the class was divided into two camps or armies such as Romans and Carthaginians. Each had its captain who kept a record of the successes scored by his side. One should compare this with the form teams which are now characteristic of many English schools, and contrast it with the attitude of Rousseau, who firmly refused to make any use of emulation. Other incentives were used, such as the award of titles, badges, and prizes.

Another device which was recognised as being of a superior type was the Academy. This was a voluntary association of students who met regularly under the master to read translations, discuss topics in literature or philosophy, or even deliver lecturettes. One may compare the Academies with the various societies found in most English secondary schools. It was thought to be a signal honour to be elected a member, and the work of the Academy provided practice for the disputations which were a feature of the higher courses.

Discipline in Jesuit colleges was not unduly severe. They presented a contrast in this respect in the public and grammar schools of England in the sixteenth and seventeenth centuries in which flogging was the universal punishment for offences. The Jesuits did not hesitate to administer corporal punishment when it was necessary, but the *Ratio Studiorum* warned the teacher not to be too zealous in finding occasions for punishing pupils. The teacher was forbidden to strike a boy, and all corporal punishment was inflicted by the Prefect of Discipline, who was not a member of the Order.

If this did not produce the desired reformation, the offender was expelled from the school. The *Ratio* impressed upon all teachers that their duty was to win the affection of their pupils.

Jesuit education did not escape the deterioration which spread to most schools and universities during the eighteenth century, although even in this period their institutions compared favourably with others. The same dull grind at the classical languages was to be found in them, and like the other schools they were growing out of touch with the needs of the time. In France, especially, some members of the Society took to meddling with politics which involved it in a fierce struggle with the Bourbon monarchs. They were also bitterly and sometimes unjustly attacked by Pascal in his *Provincial Letters*. The reports of La Chalotais on the *Constitution of the Jesuits* eventually brought about the expulsion of the Order from France in 1764. Their enemies were bitter and persistent, and brought their influence to bear upon the Pope, who suppressed the Society in 1773.

The points at issue were mainly political and do not concern us in this work. The Jesuit colleges were revived in 1814, and one of the first tasks of the refounded Society was to revise the *Ratio*, and bring it into line with modern needs. The revised *Ratio* was issued in 1832. Some very significant changes were made. It should be realised that the revised *Ratio* did not establish a new system of education. The fundamental principles of Jesuit education remained unchanged, but they were adapted to modern needs, and incorporated developments which were occurring in institutions outside the Order. Thus, the classical core of the curriculum was retained, but increasing emphasis was to be placed upon the teaching of the mother-tongue. The claims of science were recognised, and more time was to be devoted to the study of history, geography, and mathematics, and in the higher studies. Aristotle lost the dominance which through his philosophy he had previously enjoyed. In fact, the changes made in 1832 were similar to those recommended by the Public Schools Commission in England some thirty years later. These changes were only a beginning. Later in the century, more attention was given to the study of modern foreign languages, and the teaching of mathematics and science had made great strides at a time when these same subjects were struggling to obtain a place in the curriculum of the English grammar schools.

The suppression of the Society had resulted in the loss of endowments, buildings, and libraries. It could no longer provide free instruction, and in the re-established colleges, boarders were more numerous. The Society received yet another setback later in the century when its activities were suppressed or curtailed in certain European countries: Italy in 1860, Germany in 1873, and France in 1901. This loss was more than compensated by the development of its educational work in Great Britain, the Dominions and Empire, the United States, and South America.

In England, Jesuit colleges have accommodated themselves to the general educational system. Their pupils are prepared for the same examinations as those from the independent public schools and the grammar schools within the national system, and with the exception of the emphasis placed upon religious education, the curriculum of the Jesuit colleges is in line with that of other institutions. The spirit of the *Ratio* is still alive and vigorous as evidenced by the emphasis upon well-trained teachers, thoroughness in learning, and the friendly relations which exist between teachers and taught.

The remaining section of this chapter is concerned with certain developments in France during the seventeenth century, and chronologically belongs to a later stage in this book, but because the ideas which inspired these movements originated from the Church it is convenient to deal with them at this point. In France, during the seventeenth century, a distinct interest in secondary education manifested itself. It was largely the outcome of the activities of the Teaching Congregations or Societies connected with the French Church. The Jesuits formed the largest of the teaching communities, but they were international rather than definitely French. Two congregations arose which owed a great deal to the new view of life and education associated with the philosophical outlook of Descartes (1596-1650). The first was founded by Pierre de Bérulle (1575-1629). It was known as the Oratory of France, and was originally instituted in 1611 with the aim of reforming the life and learning of the French clergy. The idea was derived from the Italian Oratory founded at Rome by St Philip Neri (1515-1595), and it was intended as a free society of priests devoted to the training and education of those who wished to be ordained, and also for men who were already in orders. De Bérulle thought of his society as a national institution working under the supervision of a superior-general at Paris. Special importance was attached to the power of prayer (*oratio*) and this accounted for the name adopted—*Oratorium Jesu Christi Domini nostri.*

The Oratorians grew rapidly and spread beyond France to Belgium, Spain, and even Rome.[1] The Oratorians differed from the Jesuits in another way. They were an organisation of secular priests. As the work of the congregation developed, its educational activities were no longer confined to aspirants to the priesthood. The Oratorians acceded to the request that they should open schools for young men of noble birth. Many of the Fathers were men of great culture and liberal views and who expressed admiration for the philosophy of Descartes. Professor H. C. Barnard gives a list of thirty-six Oratorian colleges in France, with the dates of their foundation and a map to show their distribution.[2] When the Jesuits were expelled from France, seven of their colleges were handed over to the Oratorians.

These colleges present an interesting example of the development of municipal activity in the cause of education which may be compared with the growth of the Burgh schools in Scotland. In many cases the stimulus came from the civic authorities who invited the Oratorians to found a college, and promised to contribute to its upkeep from the municipal funds. In some towns, a similar arrangement was made with the Jesuits. As the municipality made a grant to the college, it insisted upon inspection, and a certain measure of control. As was pointed out in Chapter III, municipal control of schools during the later Roman Empire was fairly common, and the above example from seventeenth-century France shows that the idea of local interest and control in education was by no means an innovation of the closing years of the last century. In some Oratorian schools instruction was given gratis, but boarders were charged for their maintenance. The consequence of local influence was that the schools did not conform to a single type, but each reflected local conditions. At the same time, all the schools accepted the general principles set out in the *Ratio Studiorum* of the

---

[1] The Oratorian Fathers were noted for their special interest in Church music. Palestrina was a disciple of St Philip Neri and had composed Masses for the Congregation at Rome. Some have derived the word "oratorio" from this fact.

[2] *The French Tradition in Education*, Appendix H, C.U.P., 1922.

Oratory which was published in two parts, in 1634 and 1645, respectively.

Although the instruction was based upon the study of Latin, the Oratorians approached Latin through the medium of the vernacular. The fact that Descartes wrote his *Discours* in French was one of the reasons which accounts for this departure from accepted practice. In addition, pupils before the age of twelve received instruction in the mother-tongue. The Latin teaching emphasised the reading, and explanation of authors more than the learning of grammar and the writing of Latin prose and verse. Greek, although taught, was not invested with equal importance. In a few schools a certain amount of Hebrew was taught. Perhaps the greatest innovation of the Oratorians was the importance attached to the study of history. Boys began with the study of Biblical and Church history; they then learnt Roman and Greek history, and in the upper classes they were given a three years' course of French history. Pupils kept history note-books, some of which are still extant,[1] and the writing of notes and exercises was regarded as a valuable training in the use of the mother-tongue. Geography was also taught, and in one school each classroom possessed a good supply of maps which were hung on the walls of the room. In many schools, the study of mathematics was given an honoured place. One textbook, written by Bernard Lamy, the most distinguished of the Oratorian teachers, has an ultra modern outlook. It dealt with mathematics as a whole, and did not divide the study into separate branches such as arithmetic, algebra, geometry, and trigonometry.

During the eighteenth century, the Oratorian schools were affected by the universal apathy and decay. The preference for the philosophy of Descartes and Malebranche (the latter became a member of the Oratory in 1660), and a leaning towards the theological views of Jansenism provoked the hostility of the Jesuits. Moreover, the Oratorians lost favour with Louis XV. The Oratorians, however, were always open to new ideas and they at first welcomed the French Revolution, and were exempted when the religious Orders were suppressed. This respite was only temporary, and in 1792 the Congregation was suppressed. Professor Barnard speaks very highly of the work of the Oratory. He writes: "In point of numbers and influence the Oratory is, of course, eclipsed by the Society of Jesus; but as regards the character of the education given

---

[1] H. C. Barnard, *op. cit.*, pp. 164-5.

by the two institutions the Oratory easily wins the suffrages of the modern critic. The emphasis which its members laid on the teaching of history, mathematics, and science, their spirit of free enquiry, their freedom from political aims, the mildness and sanity of their discipline—all these characteristics give the Oratorians a claim to be considered the most 'modern' of French educators of their time".[1]

Although the work of the "Little Schools of Port-Royal" was short lived, its influence was perhaps more pervasive than that of the Oratory. The Abbey of Port-Royal was founded in 1204, about eighteen miles south-west of Paris. The original aim of the foundation placed under the supervision of the Cistercians, was the education of girls, but this seems to have been ignored by the later Middle Ages and Renaissance. Reform began with the appointment in 1602 of Jacqueline-Marie Arnauld as abbess at the age of eleven. Her conversion occurred some years later, and her efforts at reform were supported by Cardinal Richelieu, but the unhealthy situation of the Abbey, on the site of a stagnant pond, necessitated its removal to Paris in 1626. The brother of the abbess made the acquaintance of Jean Du Vergier De Hauranne (1581-1643), better known as the Abbot of Saint Cyran. In 1635 he became spiritual director at Port-Royal. Saint Cyran had studied at Louvain where he met Jansen, afterwards Bishop of Ypres. Both men were studying the works of St Augustine, and became interested in his views about original sin. They concentrated upon Augustine's controversy with the Pelagians in which he had emphasised the doctrines of Grace and Predestination in a rigorous way that later appealed to Calvin at Geneva. Such theological points may seem irrelevant in a work on the theory of education, but they not only provide a clue to the attitude of the Port-Royalists, but they explain the reason for the determined opposition of the Jesuits to the Little Schools.

The Jansenists taught that the Fall had resulted in a permanent estrangement between man and God, and that by his own efforts, man is unable to raise himself. So far they were following the accepted view. Man is therefore dependent for his salvation upon the operation of Divine Grace, but at this point the doctrine of Predestination enters. God does not confer His Grace freely upon mankind, but only to those whom He wills shall be saved. God chooses the elect, and when an individual is converted, the change

[1] *op. cit.,* p. 181.

in his state is entirely due to Divine Grace. The Jesuits denied this conclusion, and asserted that God gives sufficient Grace to all mankind. Whether an individual ultimately reaches a state of salvation depends upon whether by the exercise of his free-will he chooses to avail himself of the Grace so freely offered. They taught that Christ did not suffer for a limited number of the elect, but for the whole human race, and that the individual's acceptance of Grace made it efficacious for his salvation.[1]

The gentlemen of Port-Royal were faithful to their belief in Predestination, and this fact explains their particular view about the function of education. They agreed that original sin is washed away by the Sacrament of Baptism, but afterwards, every precaution must be taken to preserve the soul from the assaults of the devil after baptismal innocency has been secured. They thought that education was the most effective means to this end; its function was preventative, and it could only be effective if the child was under the constant supervision of the educator. The latter needed special Grace for his work so that in the end the result depended upon the arbitrary will of God. From the modern point of view this is a most repellent doctrine, but it should not blind us to the undoubted merits of Port-Royal education.

Saint Cyran gathered round him a small but devoted circle of outstanding men, amongst whom were at least two members of the Arnauld family, and this small group gave themselves freely to a life of meditation, study, and work. Saint Cyran had always been noted for his ardent love of children, and he may be regarded as the founder of the Little Schools. They commenced with a handful of boys in 1637, but early in the following year they were transferred to Paris. The movement suffered a severe blow when Saint Cyran was arrested and imprisoned for his Jansenist views. The little community was forced to leave Paris and take up its quarters outside the city at Port-Royal des Champs. Saint Cyran, from his prison cell, continued to direct its educational work, and his influence persuaded Dr Arnauld to join the movement and accept ordination. Dr Arnauld's pamphlet on *Frequent Communion* raised

---

[1] A similar controversy divided the Church of England. Article XVII whilst upholding the ideas of Predestination and Election emphasised God's purpose as predestination to eternal life. Andrews, Laud, and their supporters, adopted the view of the Dutch divine, Arminius, which was in all essentials similar to the teaching of the Jesuits. This school of thought gained the ascendancy and may be regarded as representing the position of the Church of England.

a storm of controversy. The Jesuits attacked it on the ground that it favoured non-communicating attendance at Mass. Saint Cyran died in 1643 when the schools were in their infancy, but his ideas were the inspiration which guided the work of his followers.

As has been said, the Little Schools of Port-Royal had a very short life. They were not fully organised until 1646; they had to encounter the fierce opposition of the Jesuits because of their views about Predestination, and they were finally dispersed by Louis XVI in 1661. Yet in this short period they were able to introduce ideas which have been an abiding force in French education. Saint Cyran would have agreed with Locke in his condemnation of the large classes in the public schools. True to his theological beliefs, he considered that five or six boys constituted the maximum that a master could supervise, since he would have to keep them under constant surveillance day and night, lest the devil possessed himself of their souls. This limited the number of boys who could be educated in the schools. It has been estimated that at no time were there more than fifty pupils in the schools. Their importance should not be reckoned in terms of numbers, but rather by the influence of certain eminent teachers who set forth their educational principles in writing, and so perpetuated them long after the closure of the schools.

The name Little Schools (*petites écoles*) has nothing to do with the number of pupils who were being educated. It originated in the Middle Ages. A distinction was made between the "great" or Latin schools in which boys only were taught, and the "little" or French schools which were attended by boys and girls. The former corresponded to secondary, the latter to primary schools. At a later period the term *écoles petites* was used to mark the distinction between the primary schools and the colleges of the University of Paris. The schools of Port-Royal, although in fact secondary schools, used the title *petites écoles* to emphasise that they did not compete with the University of Paris nor with the secondary schools of the Jesuits. In this way they hoped to avoid opposition from the two most influential organisations which supplied secondary education.

The death of Saint Cyran was in some ways a severe blow, but it had the effect of delivering the schools from the harsh and narrow theology which affected their educational outlook. They were continued by a band of younger men, which included Claude Lancelot, an exceedingly able teacher who was responsible for the publication of a number of "Methods" for learning Latin, Greek, Italian, and Spanish; Pierre Coustel, whose *Rules for the Education of Children* provides the main information about the theory and practice of the Port-Royalists; and Pierre Nicole, who collaborated with Dr Arnauld in writing the *Logic of Port-Royal*. The *Treatise on the Education of a Prince* was also produced by Nicole. Pascal and his sister, Jacqueline, joined the community at a later date. If Arnauld's treatise on Frequent Communion irritated the Jesuits, Pascal's biting sarcasm in his *Provincial Letters* damaged to such an extent the reputation of the Society in France that they determined to bring about the downfall of Port-Royal. The writings of the Port-Royalists were read outside France. They were certainly known to Locke, and there is reason to believe that his views on learning by heart were influenced by Nicole. Rousseau read the *Logic*, but though he may have been indebted to these thinkers for certain details there is no evidence that they influenced the main doctrines of the *Emile*.

The Port-Royalists, although they did not pay as much attention to the teaching of mathematics, science, and history, as the Oratorians included these studies in the curriculum of the Little Schools. Their main contributions to educational theory and practice consisted in their ideas about the study of languages and their insistence that the teacher should base his work on an intimate knowledge of the child's nature. In England, Germany, and France, during the seventeenth century, not only was the instruction given in the schools and universities confined to the classics, but the Latin tongue was the medium in all learning and even in casual conversation. Thus the Jesuits insisted that both within and without the classroom, everything should be in Latin. English schoolmasters such as Lily, Mulcaster, and Brinsley, followed the same rule. Sturm, in the Gymnasium at Strasbourg, was solely concerned with the speaking and writing of Latin, and paid no attention to the mother-tongue.

The Oratorians and Comenius, it is true, approached the study of Latin through the vernacular, but they based their schemes of secondary education upon the learning of the classical languages. The gentlemen of Port-Royal regarded the study and use of the mother-tongue as essential. No doubt they were influenced by Comenius and the Oratorians, but they went a step further than these when they proclaimed that the vernacular was worth studying for its own sake. Like the Oratorians, they were impressed by the philosophy of Descartes, and the fact that he wrote some of his most important works in French was not lost upon them. Both Lancelot and Nicole were familiar with the *Janua Linguarum* of Comenius but they thought it unsuitable as a school textbook. They believed that the aim of learning a second language was to read the authors as soon as possible and that the long vocabularies of Comenius were almost as useless for this purpose as the rules in the ordinary Latin grammars.

The Port-Royalists emphasised the importance of acquiring a good French style. Thus they encouraged the reading of good French authors, and considered that it was more important for a pupil to be able to translate a passage from a Latin writer into good French than to turn French sentences into Latin or Greek. Professor Barnard quotes the following from Coustel's *Rules*: "It is not enough to read carefully good authors, to make judicious extracts from them, and if desired, to learn their most beautiful passages by heart, if, with all that, one does not thereby fit oneself for making use of them, when opportunity offers, by means of translation; this, indeed, it is which makes passages in Latin and Greek books, which are beautiful and striking, appear as such in our own language also. It may be said that this is the sum total of the advantages to be derived from study, for of a thousand people who leave college, not four will find it necessary to speak or write Latin. But everyone should be able to make himself understood in French; and he, who in good society is unable to do this, is put to shame. Children must therefore be especially practised in the art of translation, because the concentration needed for weighing all the phrases, and discovering the meaning of a Latin author, exercises both their intellect and their judgment at the same time, and makes them appreciate the beauty of the French as much as that of the Latin".[1]

At the same time, this group of teachers believed that all sound instruction must be based on a thorough knowledge of the child's nature, and that the teacher's art should include devices for removing difficulties from the path of the learner. Professor Barnard speaks as follows about their work in this connection: "Coustel lays down as a first principle of successful teaching that the master

[1] *The Little Schools of Port-Royal*, p. 122, C.U.P., 1913.

should study the individual psychology of his pupils and adapt his teaching methods accordingly; . . . It is unquestionable that they should not all be treated in the same manner. If a physician cannot prescribe remedies suitable for the healing of the body, without knowing its various temperaments, and if a farmer ought not to set about sowing a field without knowing the quality of its soil, then beyond doubt a schoolmaster should also know the different kinds of intellect which he has to educate. Coustel goes on to enumerate the various types of child mind and the manner in which each should be treated, quite in the style of an up-to-date American educational psychologist".[1]

The endeavour to avoid needless difficulties in the studies of children led the teachers of Port-Royal to stress the use of play methods in the education of young pupils, and the value of concrete illustrations and pictures. Special attention was paid to the teaching of reading and writing. A phonetic method of teaching reading was used and this invention was attributed to Pascal. One last point is worthy of note. Although Quick is not strictly accurate when he says that the gentlemen of Port-Royal banished every form of rivalry,[2] it is true that they were well aware of the dangers which may follow unrestricted emulation. Quick was dependent for his information on Pascal, who, although a member of the community, was not fully aware of the details of the classroom procedure in the schools. The Port-Royalists, whilst not indeed forbidding the use of emulation, preferred to encourage the pupil to surpass his own achievements of the past. Rousseau had read the *Pensées* of Pascal, and it was probably this which led him to declare that he would make no use of rivalry in the education of children. We know from records of pupils that a modified form of emulation was permitted in the schools, but it was not carried to anything like the degree practised by the Jesuits.

The latter part of the seventeenth century witnessed in France a development in the field of elementary education which bears some likeness to the Charity School movement in England. This was associated with the efforts of the Brethren of the Christian Schools, a religious community of teaching Brothers who at the present day form the largest religious teaching order in the world. This development sprang from the work of Jean Baptiste de La Salle (1651-1719). A member of a noble family, he was appointed when quite young

[1] *op. cit.*, pp. 90-1.   [2] *Educational Reformers*, p. 181.

to a canonry at Rheims. He was a wealthy man but when on the threshold of middle-age, he abandoned all the comforts he had previously enjoyed and devoted the remainder of his life to the work of educating poor children. He started as adviser to a group of young laymen who were organising charity schools for boys, but eventually he united them in the religious community known as the Institute of the Brothers of the Christian Schools, 1684. The Brethren depended upon charity for their support, and pledged themselves to refuse any kind of remuneration for their teaching. Each member took the vow of obedience for one year only, and could renew it annually. In order to concentrate attention upon elementary instruction, the Brethren were forbidden to teach Latin, though at a later period this prohibition was removed. The organisation was at first confined to the diocese of Rheims, but after 1688 it spread to Paris where it became associated with the famous church of St Sulpice. In modern times, the Brethren are to be found in all parts of the world, and are especially strong in the United States. The details of the educational work of La Salle may be read elsewhere.[1] There are, however, certain features of his work which are of special interest for the student of the history of educational ideas. La Salle was essentially an organiser and administrator rather than a theorist. His most important publication was the *Conduct of the Schools*, a work which may be compared with the *Ratio Studiorum* of the Jesuits. It was mainly concerned with the conduct and administration of the schools and the methods of instruction to be employed.

La Salle's contributions, therefore, were in the realm of practice rather than theory. He has been credited with the invention of the method of simultaneous instruction of class teaching. This is not strictly true, for the method had been recommended by Comenius in the *Great Didactic*, and we know that certain English schoolmasters of Elizabethan and Stuart times used similar methods. It was, however, the earliest example of class teaching methods employed on a large scale, for they were common to all the schools of the Institute.

La Salle attached great importance to the employment of trained teachers, and he was responsible for opening one of the earliest seminaries or training colleges in France. He may have been influenced by the example of the seminary founded in the diocese of

[1] W. J. Battersby, *De La Salle, A Pioneer of Modern Education,* 1949.

Lyons some years earlier. Another innovation was the establishment in the parish of St Sulpice of a school which Adamson suggests resembled in its aims and methods the modern Continuation School.[1] The curé had been much troubled by the drinking and gambling of many young men in his parish. He consulted La Salle about this matter, and on his advice, a Sunday School was opened, and young men below the age of twenty were admitted up to a maximum of two hundred. The younger pupils were given instruction in reading, writing, spelling, and arithmetic; the older ones were taught drawing and geometry. Religious instruction was naturally an important feature of the school. This institution differed from the Sunday schools of Robert Raikes in the following century because it aimed at giving these young people an education which should be a continuation of their previous course in the primary school and which would be of value to them in their work.

La Salle was a pioneer in another field altogether. The President of the Parliament of Normandy asked him to take under his wing a number of young offenders who had broken the law for the first time. This resulted in the establishment of what would now be called a reformatory school. A special boarding establishment was opened at St Yon for these young delinquents, and they were given a course of instruction which included the practical arts of the carpenter, the wood carver, and the locksmith. Another boarding school in the same town may be regarded as a forerunner of the secondary modern school. Each form had its own writing and arithmetic master, and other teachers gave instruction in modern languages, drawing, music, and bookkeeping. Classical studies were rigidly excluded. La Salle's attitude towards the study of Latin was similar to that of the schools of Port-Royal. He believed that pupils ought to have a thorough grounding in the mother-tongue before they proceeded to learn another language.

Adamson sums up the achievements of La Salle as follows: "While it is not possible to place the founder of the Institute amongst the highest class of original thinkers on education, he has an indisputable claim to stand with those whose actual concrete services to educational administration have been very considerable indeed. Original he may not be, yet his mind was of no common order, as is proved when one considers the readiness with which he accepted reforms, and the effectiveness with which he put them into

[1] J. W. Adamson, *Pioneers of Modern Education*, p. 222, C.U.P., reprint, 1921.

practice. It is a debatable point whether such minds (practical in the best sense, because they are accessible to ideas) do not confer greater benefits upon humanity than do the thinkers of a loftier type".[1]

SUGGESTIONS FOR FURTHER READING

A good deal has been written about the educational work of the Society of Jesus, but it is difficult to find an account which is free from partisan feeling. Thus Quick's account in his *Essays on Educational Reformers*, new edition (Longmans, Green, 1902), and Kinloch's description of the religious education of the Jesuits in *Pioneers of Religious Education* (O.U.P., 1939), although in the main reliable, have a definite bias. The chapter on Jesuit Education in R. R. Rusk, *The Doctrines of the Great Educators* (Macmillan, reprinted 1948), is recommended. It gives a purely objective assessment and pays considerable attention to the Constitution of the Society of Jesus. T. Hughes, S.J., *Loyola and the Educational System of the Jesuits* (Great Educator Series, W. Heinemann, 1892), and R. Schwickerath, S.J., *Jesuit Education* (B. Herder, 1903), are partisan, but nevertheless valuable. The latter gives a good account of modern Jesuit education, especially in the United States.

For the Oratorians, the chapter in H. C. Barnard, *The French Tradition in Education* (C.U.P., 1922), is recommended. Quick has a section dealing with the Port-Royalists, but some of his references to particular writers are inaccurate. The best study of Port-Royal is H. C. Barnard, *The Little Schools of Port-Royal* (C.U.P., 1913).

Adamson has a good chapter on La Salle in *Pioneers of Modern Education* (C.U.P., reprinted 1921). W. J. Battersby has recently published two studies of La Salle; *De La Salle, A Pioneer of Modern Education* (Longmans, 1949), and *De La Salle, Saint and Spiritual Writer* (Longmans, 1950). The former deals with the educational work of La Salle and describes his association with Adrian Nyel, Barré, and Madame Maillefer, and the latter with his spiritual influence. La Salle's *Conduct of the Schools* has been translated by F. de la Fontainerie, and is published by McGraw Hill, New York, 1935.

[1] *op. cit.*, p. 236.

CHAPTER VIII

COMENIUS

On the continent, during the early years of the seventeenth century, problems of education were engaging the attention of both scholars and rulers. **Wolfgang Ratke (1571-1635),** a Holsteiner, achieved some celebrity as an innovator, by presenting to the Imperial Diet in 1612 a *Memorial* which pronounced his ability to introduce a quicker and more efficient method of language teaching than any then in use. In addition he described a scheme for a school where all subjects would be taught in High German, as well as in other languages—an obvious revolt against the domination of Latin. Moreover, he suggested that the Diet might care to consider how there might be "conveniently introduced and peacefully established throughout the whole Empire a uniform speech, a uniform government, and a uniform religion". Later he submitted an *Elucidation* of his scheme, emphasising the principles that education should be based on the vernacular, and that the Bible should be the first and main textbook in language teaching.

Germany was ready to listen to Ratke, for his contemporaries recognised the need for a revision of prevailing methods. His scheme was much discussed and generally appreciated, and it must have been about this time that it became known to the young Comenius, who embodied in his own pedagogy several of Ratke's basic maxims. In 1614 Ratke was invited to reform the educational system of the city of Augsburg, but it appears he was less successful as an organiser than as a theorist. His reputation was still such, however, that the Princes of Onhalt and Weimar offered him protection, and he settled in Köthen, where he was provided with a school of boys and girls. He received visiting teachers and trained them in his methods at the school. These methods show how the same scientific spirit was moving in Germany as in England, but they also reveal that the teaching of Vives had not been in vain. Ratke's main principle was that there should be no rote learning of words without knowledge of the things represented by words. Learning should follow "the order and course of nature", and should be pursued all the time by personal investigation, experiment, and analysis. The process of learning was to Ratke a process of pursuing one thing at a time and becoming familiar with that one thing by re-examination and repetition, before proceeding to the next.

Another educator who influenced profoundly the young Comenius was **Johann Heinrich Alsted (1588-1638)**, who became a teacher at the high school of his native town of Herborn, in Nassau. His own education, although on traditional lines, had included some arithmetic, music, and German, a factor which may well have played a part in the evolution of his ideas on education. He had made the traditional pilgrimage of the scholar from university to university in Northern Europe, and he now displayed such brilliance in his philosophical and theological writings that his reputation was quickly established, so that by the time Comenius came to Herborn he had achieved the rank of professor of philosophy, and later, in 1619, that of professor of theology.

His most famous work, the *Universal Encyclopaedia*, published in 1630, is a great treatise which reveals his genuine interest and skill in the actual practice of teaching, as well as his sound scholarship and progressive theoretical concepts. He pleads for a recognition of the importance of vernacular schools which should exist everywhere for both boys and girls. "The teacher must be clad with patience like a corselet, and with humility and wisdom,"[1] and his aim should be to inculcate piety and good habits of behaviour, as well as to teach reading and writing. Children should enter the vernacular school at five, but boys and girls should not sit together in mixed classes. They should all have copies of the same textbook which the teacher should divide into fixed lessons. The method advocated—reading by the teacher and repetition by the pupils—is traditional enough, but Alsted suggests that the teacher should encourage effort by offering small rewards, and he should make learning easier by giving memory exercises in rhyme—even on religious topics. Although only four hours' schooling a day is adequate, the work which is done in that period should be thorough, particular attention being paid to grammar because it is the basis of all language learning.

Latin schools are, in general, for "boys whose parents are in such a station that they may hope for a more fruitful intellectual

[1] P. R. Cole. *A History of Educational Thought*, p. 209, O.U.P., 1931.

culture",[1] and if they find learning difficult, the teacher should devise play-ways and should teach through the vernacular. The curriculum should include Latin, Greek, music, arithmetic, and logic, and each day's work should contain "exercises of piety, composition, and relaxation of the mind". In a six-year course, the first three years should concentrate on the acquisition of skill in language construction, and the second three years—the "humanities" period —should introduce the pupils to rhetoric, poetry, oratory, and a wide range of classical literature. Arithmetic and music should be started in the middle school, and continued in the upper school, while in the top form the elements of logic should be studied. Alsted has no great opinion of the capacities of girls, but he allows that some "noble" women could well take up study as a hobby.

Alsted was, above all, a leader of the Protestant campaign for education as an ennobling factor in human experience. He accepted the classical concept of the child as a "tabula rasa", and he pleads, "O ye schools, inscribe the characters of piety and humanity!"

Comenius

Long before the period usually associated with the Reformation, several religious groups in central Europe claiming to owe their origin to the Greek and Oriental churches, incurred the displeasure of the Papacy by aspiring to a measure of freedom and independence that appeared to border on heresy. John Huss and Jerome of Prague, in the fifteenth century, followed Milicius, another Bohemian preacher of the fourteenth century, in leading the opposition to Rome which culminated in the deplorable "inhumanity of man to man" during the centuries which followed.

One sect calling itself "The Unity of the Bohemian Brethren" survived in remnants in the sixteenth century, mainly in the wild mountain country of Moravia. The members were not Protestant in the Lutheran sense, for they preserved an ecclesiastical system somewhat similar to the English. In a Moravian village, probably Nivnitz or Komna, a son, John Amos, was born to the Potter[2] family in the year 1592, and the boy was brought up for twelve years in the security of a small trademan's family amidst a deeply

---

[1] P. R. Cole's translation.

[2] According to Benham, the German family name, Töpfer, had to be concealed as a security measure when the persecution began, but there are other versions of the origin of the great educator's name.

religious community. His entrance to Latin school was delayed by the death of his parents and, according to his own report, the neglect of his guardians, but when he started his classical education at sixteen, he found study very much to his taste, and he learnt rapidly and with enthusiasm. He asserts that even at this tender age he was seized with the desire to find "some means whereby more might be inflamed with the love of learning, and whereby learning itself might be made more compendious". It is not unlikely that in spite of his own aptitude for learning, he was irked by the pressure of the grammar-grind common to European Latin schools following the leadership of John Sturm. Thus the above remarks, which appear in the preface to the *Prodromus*, are followed by an expression of hope that "the youth might be brought by a more easy method, unto some notable proficiency in learning".

The young man proceeded[1] in 1612 to Herborn High School, in Germany, where his determination to become a teacher was reinforced. It is likely that he found his study at Herborn particularly fruitful, for there the great Professor Alsted had developed a "department of education" where intending schoolmasters could study their craft. He went on to Heidelburg, and later on a tour of the Netherlands, continuing his study of Latin, Greek, philosophy, and theology. It is said he finally walked home to Prague after an illness which had used up his funds.

Thus in the early years of his life circumstances had combined to generate in this boy of keen intellect and gentle character an unshakable faith in Moravian survival both as a religious group and as a nation. His interest in the vernacular, for which he was to become celebrated, had its origin in an early desire to write books in the Bohemian language for the benefit of his countrymen. He started to compose a lexicon while he was at Herborn. Another important event of his Herborn period was the publication of a description of a new plan for teaching devised by Ratke, the German scholar, who, in his various experiments, showed no great aptitude for putting into practice excellent principles partly inspired by the "new philosophy" of Bacon.

At twenty-two John Amos was too young to enter the Church, but he was given charge of one of the Brethren's schools which

---

[1] Benham suggests he was probably sent by a group of the Brethren because the local schools were poor owing to "the persecuting spirit of the times". Keatinge suggests that the University of Prague was controlled by the Utraquists who submitted to the Roman Church.

immediately provided him with the opportunity to experiment along the lines of Ratke's suggestions. Apparently he sent some enquiries to the great man himself, but received no reply. It is interesting that his early attempts to improve education were similar to those of many predecessors—the writing of "simple grammatical rules". In two years he became pastor of the town of Fulneck in the Carpathians, one of the oldest centres of the Brethren. He became superintendent of the local school in 1618, and again embarked, with enthusiasm and considerable success, on the teaching of the classics, following his own precept, "children acquire a knowledge of words by objects . . . while learning words they should also be taught things". At the same time he wrote much in his native language on topics of nation-wide urgency, such as liberty of conscience, and there is no doubt that such writings served to fan the flame of revolt against the Holy Roman Empire.

Hostilities broke out in 1618, and became acute during the next few years. John Amos Komensky (of Komna) was driven from his church in 1621, and suffered the loss of his library and manuscripts at the hands of Spanish troops. Soon the Brethren ordered him to go into hiding because of the danger of personal persecution, but he remained near his home and his congregation, although he suffered severe privations and also the loss of his wife and son. During this period his main writing was *The Labyrinth of the World and the Paradise of the Heart*, of which *Pilgrim's Progress* is somewhat reminiscent. In 1624 an imperial mandate banished the evangelical clergy so that Komensky had to take refuge with a sympathetic nobleman in a mountain retreat. The Brethren soon decided that the younger ministers should travel to sympathetic countries to solicit help. Komensky went to Poland and Berlin on this mission and then returned to his retreat where he studied classical poetry, and also, at the request of a colleague who was teaching the sons of their protector, wrote *Some canons of a better method*. The main stimulus to further thought on teaching was, however, the reading of Bodin's *Didactica*, newly received from Germany. An edict forbidding the protection of Brethren and ordering religious conformation, brought an end to this period, for the whole fraternity had to flee into Poland. Komensky was not destined to return to his native country. He was to gain international repute as a scholar and educator under the Latinised name of Comenius.

The destination of the Brethren was the Polish town of Lissa or Lezna, not far from the Silesian border. Largely through the support of the ruling Lescynski family, it had become a place of refuge for Protestants of all kinds—and a large and prosperous centre. A congregation of Brethren already existed, and its school offered opportunities for the genius of Comenius. It is probable that he was in complete charge of the community's education and perhaps developed an elementary as well as a secondary school. He read widely, particularly on methods of language teaching, and he corresponded with such specialists as would reply to his letters. Bishop Andreae of his own church was pleased to find a successor who shared his interests. Comenius was encouraged to proceed with his plan to write a general methodology extending over all subjects and all stages of teaching. He confessed himself to be but "a man of moderate ability, and of almost no learning" with heart so simple that "it matters not to me whether I teach or be taught", and there is no doubt that he wrote his *Didactica Magna* in a humble spirit, using his native language in the hope that it would be useful to teachers in his own country when the freedom of Moravia and Bohemia should be achieved.

At the same time Comenius pursued the task of finding a quick way of teaching Latin, so that school children might have time to learn other useful things. Bathe's *Janua Linguarum*—originally in Latin-Spanish—had by this time been published in eight languages, and the scheme of the book appealed to Comenius in spite of its inclusion of unnecessarily difficult words and its failure to give alternative meanings, faults which he set out to remedy. The various *Nomenclators* gave him the idea of a selected vocabulary arranged in sentences and classified under headings "in a manner suited to the capacity of boys", and with a "short, compendious, simple and easy grammar". The little book aimed to teach *words* through *things* and things through words in a simple graded order, and although the author hoped it would prove useful, he did not consider it perfect. Probably nobody was more surprised than he when it achieved immediate success on its publication in 1631. It was translated into all European languages and into several Asiatic tongues. Comenius followed it up with *Vestibulum*, which was intended as an elementary textbook for use before the *Janua*.

In 1632 Comenius was elected Bishop of the Moravians, and thus gained great influence over Brethren scattered throughout

Europe. Among the most remarkable achievements of a long life was his unfailing attention to his episcopal duties and his prolific writings on theological topics. It is clear that he must have continued his teaching work and that he gained wide recognition as a successful educator, for in 1638 the Swedish authorities invited him to reorganise their schools. Although he felt unable to undertake the task personally he offered to give advice and suggestions. It is probable that as a result of this he was impelled to reconsider his manuscript of the *Didactica*, and finally to make a Latin version for publication.[1]

At the same time this extraordinary man was scribbling his private notes on his growing philosophical concept of education as a mighty instrument for universal brotherhood and Godliness. This great idea which he called, in its early stages, *Pansophia*, was the subject of correspondence between Comenius and his friends, one of whom, Samuel Hartlib of London, waxed so enthusiastic as to publish without the writer's consent a long letter in which Comenius outlined his pansophic project.[2] This pamphlet, published at Oxford in 1637, aroused wide interest and some criticism, so that Comenius felt it necessary to write a more adequate summary of his ideas. Tassius of Hamburg, in a letter to Hartlib said: "A philosophic ardour flames in every corner of Europe, and with it zeal for a better Didactic. If Comenius had done nothing more than scatter such fruitful seeds in the minds of all, he would have done enough". In England the seeds were so fruitful that Hartlib succeeded in winning considerable support for his idea of inviting Comenius to England to supervise the foundation of a pansophic college. Unfortunately, although the Long Parliament had given general approval to the college project, it failed to issue any official invitation to Comenius, so that when he arrived in 1641, he found himself dependent on the patronage of sympathetic Englishmen while parliament was prorogued, and later while it was preoccupied with troubles in Ireland and incipient rebellion at home.

Although Comenius returned to the Continent after less than a year's sojourn in England, his visit was not entirely fruitless. He gave much to English education through his conversations and

---

[1] The usual date given for its first publication is 1657 but the *School of Infancy* was published in 1633 at Lissa, in German.
[2] *Conatuum Comenianorum Praeludia*, Oxford, 1637.

discussions with many English teachers, writers, and patrons of education. The long list of names of men interested in the suggested reforms of the trio, Comenius, Hartlib, and Dury, indicates that concern for the country's education was not confined to any religious sect, political party, or class of society. Due tribute must be paid to the Puritan contribution to educational progress, but in these matters, thinking Englishmen of all parties and professions felt the need to make personal contribution. Hartlib had the gift of moderation in religion and politics, and was able to hold the friendship of those with more extreme opinions. Dury was essentially a propagandist for the resolution of religious differences, while Comenius was not only in himself the advocate of moderation and brotherliness, but was also a member of a church more acceptable to the orthodox Englishman than any other in Protestant Europe.

Comenius lived in England on a fund made up of small subscriptions from merchants, nobles, schoolmasters, clerics, and university lecturers.[1] Among these supporters were members of the scientific discussion group which later developed into the Royal Society. Plans for a new college[2] were discussed, and Comenius was so pleased by such evidence of the headway gained by his pansophic ideas that in *Via Lucis*, written during this period, he suggested England as the ideal region for the first pansophic experiment.

The next six years of the life of Comenius exemplify not only the international character of scholarship at that time, but also the power of patronage in the collection of knowledge and the extension of learning. The visit of Comenius to Sweden in 1642, to gain the approval of a new patron, was very similar to a modern scholar's journey to be interviewed for an appointment. He found he had to decide whether or not to undertake a definite assignment which would prevent him from pursuing his pansophic work, for as the Swedish chancellor, Oxenstiern, disapproved of pansophism, the main task was to be the production of books on teaching, textbooks,

[1] Some details of these subscriptions may be found in *Hartlib, Dury, and Comenius* by G. H. Turnbull, Liverpool, 1947.

[2] R. F. Young, *Comenius in England* (1932), gives a statement by Comenius indicating that Parliament discussed this matter in 1641: "They communicated their plans for assigning to us some college with its revenues, whereby a certain number of learned and hard-working men, called from all nations, might be honourably maintained either for a term of years or permanently. There was even named for this purpose the Savoy, Winchester College, and Chelsea College".

and lexicons. His English friends were shocked by his decision to accept the work,[1] and Comenius was by no means happy in his tedious labours, especially as they occupied six years of his time, instead of the two he had planned.

These years were spent in Elbing, in Prussia, a Hanse port with a cosmopolitan population which included a Moravian congregation. Nevertheless, Comenius had little time for his friends or his countrymen, for it needed all the efforts of the leader and four or five assistants to get through the work. Comenius was often short of funds, for although his patron, de Geer, appears to have been most generous, it was expensive to keep assistants, and while Comenius was loath to ask for more money in the early days, de Geer failed later to realise that his allowance was inadequate for the rapid production of books. It appears that Comenius accepted a few engagements to tutor rich men's sons, and also attended big religious conferences in fulfilment of his ecclesiastical duties. De Geer grew restive at repeated delays, but he was, at heart, convinced of his protégé's integrity in spite of his annoyance at the latter's reluctant journey to the Thorn Conference on the proposed unification of the Catholic and Protestant Churches.[2] Indeed, de Geer expressed his penitence for unfair reproaches by sending a generous allowance, and a further donation for Moravian exiles.

In spite of great privation, and several changes of personnel owing to unpleasantness and inefficiency, the little team of scholars finished the assignment in 1646, but the Swedish committee which approved it, required a revision in preparation for publication, a task which appears to have weighed heavily on Comenius for various reasons.[3] He wrote to Hartlib: "My thoughts were arranged and expressed in preface full fourteen years ago . . . but since we began to come before the public, to expect help from man, and to attempt a display . . . the vigour of our mind appeared to be shaken and moved from its centre, to waver and be unsteady, whilst we were confused with the multitude of different counsels, and hence

---

[1] It may be that one factor in his decision was the financial straits of Hartlib and the poverty of Moravian exiles in Poland. His new patron, de Geer, agreed to send some money. It is probable that a representative from Richelieu also approached Comenius with an offer of employment.

[2] Comenius was not against this proposal but he realised that more extreme sects would bring the scheme to failure. He himself believed, "Christians, provided they would truly and seriously *be* Christians, can easily live in concord".

[3] The main treatise of the Elbing period is *Methodus Linguarum Novissima* containing important sections on the theory of language and on teaching method.

our progress was evidently retarded . . . The primary ideas still prevail, and we proceed rather slower with assistants than without them . . . I am thoroughly ashamed at having to write such begging letters . . . So also I feel shame at being compelled to remind my patron, who has promised to help me this year, that I am in want".

In 1648, Comenius returned to Lissa, and from there conducted an unsuccessful campaign on behalf of his sect, whose plight had been ignored by the signatories of the Treaty of Westphalia. Sweden proved a broken reed, and the Brethren saw religious toleration granted in Germany but not in Bohemia. Comenius, now Senior of the Brethren in Lissa, was fully occupied by his activities on behalf of the new floods of exiles and refugees. His wide reputa- tion served him well in his search for posts for Moravian scholars, teachers, and artists. Through his unofficial employment bureau the Brethren were spread over Protestant Europe, but he made little progress with his educational writings.

In 1650, however, he received an invitation from a Transylvanian princess to undertake the organisation of a school system in her realm. At the age of fifty-eight, with an excellent reputation and relative security achieved but with heavy responsibilities on his shoulders, he deliberated whether to engage again in direct educational work. He was still under de Geer's patronage, and his church duties were onerous, but he decided to accept the proposal of the princess, who had afforded protection to many Moravian exiles. He stayed with his family in Saros-Patak for four years, during which he enjoyed the freedom to develop schools according to his own ideas, and to write with the concentration and single-mindedness of his youth. In spite of some frustration and disappointment, this was a most fruitful period, and he produced some valuable contributions to his *Didactica*[1] in addition to the famous and successful school book, *Orbis Pictus*. This was a veritable realisation of his didactic principles, ensuring, by a careful arrangement of pictures and des- criptive text in two languages arranged in parallel columns, that the meaning of words would be learnt through the sense of sight. More- over, each "thing" was numbered in both picture and text to ensure complete accuracy of comprehension. Although illustrated text- books had been produced previously by Eilhard Lubinus and prob- ably by others, *Orbis Pictus* surpassed them in clarity and usefulness. Like the *Janua* it was put into many languages, the best known

[1] *Scholae Pansophicae Delineatio.*

English version being by Charles Hoole, a schoolmaster, who "Englished" it in more ways than one.[1]

After the return of Comenius to Lissa in 1654, further misfortune came within two years, for in the course of a struggle between Sweden and Poland, Lissa was sacked and burnt, and Comenius lost everything, including the modest savings he had put by for his children during his recent period of relative prosperity. He himself asserted that he lost manuscripts representing forty years' work as well as his whole library.[2] He spent the rest of his life in Amsterdam, organising relief for his people,[3] giving private tuition to the sons of rich merchants, and writing at leisure and in relative comfort under the kindly patronage of de Geer's son. In 1657, his *Opera Omnia Didactica* was published in fine folio, probably a small edition. The size and expense of this work were such that only a few rich, interested men would be likely to buy it. Had there been a cheap abridged edition, teachers in England and on the continent might have given a fair trial to the methods it suggested. It included by no means all the didactic writings of Comenius, some of which remained in manuscript and were lost for two and a half centuries after his death, until discovered in 1935 by Professor Czysczewskij. They include the *Pampaedia*, which purports to be "the art of teaching everybody to learn everything, and to put it to its correct use, according to its purpose".[4]

Comenius also lived to see the publication, in 1668, of his *Via Lucis*, written twenty-six years earlier. In the dedication he pays tribute to "the splendid establishment of the Royal Society", and urges the continuance of group effort for human betterment. Unfortunately, the tendency to extreme idealism which produced that somewhat mystical essay, drew him in his old age to a belief in prophecy and revelation. After his death, his later religious tracts were used by his opponents to destroy his reputation, and until the middle of the last century he was regarded as a charlatan by educated men who had not troubled to read his books.

---

[1] He included, for instance, pictures and text on games played by English schoolboys.

[2] His main losses were *Sylva Pansophiae* containing "The definition of all things", and his dictionary of the Bohemian language.

[3] In 1665 the Earl of Pembroke sent £50 for the personal use of Comenius and £100 for Moravian relief.

[4] *Schools in the Pampaedia of J. A. Comenius* by A. Turek, Research Review of the University of Durham Institute of Education, September 1951.

The Philosophy of Comenius

By the seventeenth century, philosophers had become concerned with the problem of gaining ascertainable knowledge rather than hearsay and opinion. New discoveries, both geographic and scientific, accelerated the movement away from the mediaeval tradition. Much of the accumulated knowledge of the past had been proved false, and it had become vitally necessary to devise a method of discovering truth. Bacon and Descartes led the way, and although Comenius rarely refers to their philosophic ideas, it may be assumed he was acquainted with those ideas. He was a great admirer of Bacon, and it is probable that he met Descartes,[1] so that even had the new philosophy not been a subject of discussion among European scholars, it might be expected that Comenius would have given some thought to the ideas of the two men.

Comenius enjoyed Bacon's *Instauratio Magna* because it was in accordance with his own convictions that nature was a great laboratory, and that the ancients could no longer provide answers to all the queries and problems set by the new mighty and complex world. "Do not we ourselves dwell in the garden of nature as well as the ancients?" he asks, "Why should we need other teachers than these our own senses. Why should not we instead of these dead books lay open the living book of nature?" It is probable that he did not fully understand Bacon, for the latter had no confidence in human senses, nor in the power of the mind unless disciplined to accurate observation and to methods of rational procedure.

Comenius had absorbed too much of the mediaeval spirit to throw it off completely and lightly. His adherence to the concept of universality was but a re-interpretation of the old doctrine that man was the centre of the universe. The confidence that the whole realm of Nature was for the use and benefit of man persisted at least until the nineteenth century when it was somewhat of an obstacle to the acceptance of the idea of evolution. Comenius was a mediaevalist in this respect.

He assumes that the nature or essence of a thing is its end or purpose rather than its actuality at any given moment, so that any adequate interpretation of his ideas must indicate the specific use of the term "nature". He offers a definition himself: "By the word

---

[1] Comenius did not consciously accept any of Descartes' ideas, for he wrote several refutations of the Cartesians. Apparently most of these documents were burnt at Lissa.

nature we mean not the corruption which has laid hold of all men since the Fall . . . but our first and original condition to which, as to a starting point we must be recalled".[1] Thus he reconciles his belief in innate goodness and his acceptance of the doctrine of original sin. "The seeds of knowledge of virtue and of piety," he writes, "are naturally implanted in us, but the actual knowledge, virtue, and piety are not so given. These must be acquired by prayer, by education, and by action."

In his wider concepts—his idea of the whole system of nature— he reveals the influence not only of his religious convictions but also of mediaeval philosophy. To Comenius all Nature has a purpose, being not merely man's instrument but rather the whole of which man is a part. Knowledge to him is not an abstraction from reality as it is to Plato; it is rather the revelation of reality and of God, and therefore he feels that the understanding of Nature brings the understanding of God. He is thus at one with the philosophers who see in reasoning and the power of thought only a means for discovering the essence of Nature which is by implication, perfect in itself. Comenius probably derived as much from the mediaeval thinkers as from Bacon, in shaping his methodology in which so large a role is given to Nature.

Again, it may have been from his predecessors as well as from his personal history that he developed his consciousness of a need for communal effort and experience. The Humanists had broken down belief in the function of monastic withdrawal from the world, and the search for knowledge and understanding of the self had now widened to include the whole of man and the whole of Nature. Campanella, himself a monk, had concluded that a man cannot observe his own self in isolation; he needs to study its activities and its changes which occur only through contact with other people, and with new experiences. And only by studying all men and all environment, and relating their reactions and characteristics to personal experience, can the self be truly found. Such conclusions inspired the conception of an ideal community, *The City of the Sun*, the precursor of More's *Utopia* and Bacon's *Atlantis*, as well as of the many less skilful imitations of the seventeenth century. It is hardly likely that Comenius had read none of these works;[2] he

---

[1] Quotations in this section are from Keatinge's translation of the *Didactic*.
[2] In his *Physics*, Comenius refers to Bacon and Campanella as "The two Hercules who have vanquished the monster Aristotle".

admits to extending Bacon's broad concept of universality but he also pays frequent tribute to Vives who was infected with the Colet-More spirit and attitude.   Thus it is not surprising that in his pedagogy Comenius reflects many of More's Utopian requirements, such as, teaching in the vernacular, teaching by concrete examples, and teaching through the senses.

Although Bacon's influence on Comenius is seen mainly in the latter's aims and curricula, there was also some percolation, in methodology, of the principle of practical experiment.   In teaching method itself, however, Comenius was not an experimentalist in the sense that Pestalozzi was, in a later age.   His function was that of a reformer who provided ready-made methods which could be applied by any other teacher, and which would unfailingly bring better results than the old.   He felt it essential to justify these methods, not merely by providing evidence as to their results, but by giving "demonstrative proof that it is possible to imbue all the young with knowledge, virtue, and piety".   In view of the particular function of Comenius as an educator it is difficult to discover or estimate how far he himself appreciated, or even understood, inductive empirical method.   On the other hand, he shared Bacon's distrust of the ability of the human intellect to attain knowledge unaided, and he went much further than Bacon in considering the details of various ways of collecting and disseminating knowledge, even at the lowest stages and with the humblest pupils.   There is no doubt that the principles of his teaching method are based on Bacon's generalisations—for instance, Bacon says in *Instauratio Magna*, "Upon the whole, men do not hitherto appear to be happily inclined and fitted for the sciences, either by their own industry, or the authority of authors . . . The only clue and method is to begin all anew and direct our steps in a certain order from the very first perception of the senses", and it is very clear that Comenius truly endeavoured to ensure a beginning anew and a progress in a given order.

In his search for a method which would lead men to truth, it is unlikely that Comenius depended entirely upon earlier generations of thinkers.   Bacon had inspired him during his professional apprenticeship in early manhood, but by the middle of the century other philosophers had expounded ideas which, even when unprinted, usually spread through Western Europe by that extraordinary grapevine of seventeenth-century intellectualism.   Comenius asserted:

"We must take strong and vigorous measures that no man in his journey through life may encounter anything unknown to him that he cannot pass sound judgment upon it and turn it to its proper use without serious error", while Descartes was formulating his views that "the end of study should be to direct the mind towards the enunciation of sound and correct judgments on all matters that come before it".[1] The concept of the interconnection and interdependence of all things which contributed to the evolution of Comenius's encyclopaedism, was also a fundamental of the philosophy of Descartes, who says: "Since the sciences taken all together are identical with human wisdom which always remains one and the same . . . there is no need for minds to be confined at all within limits; for neither does the knowing of one truth have an effect like that of the acquisition of one art and prevent us from finding out another, it rather aids us to do so . . . Hence we must believe that all the sciences are so interconnected, that it is much easier to study them all together than to isolate one from all the others".[2] That Comenius believed with Descartes not in mere accumulation of knowledge, but in its use for the development of reason, understanding, and judgment, is often forgotten or ignored by those who consider the Moravian's pansophism to be mere sentimental idealism.

Comenius was, in fact, moving in his scientific study of education along the same lines as Descartes was moving in the study of philosophy. One of the latter's *Rules for the Direction of the Understanding* was, "There is need for a method for finding out the truth . . . certain simple rules such that if a man observe them accurately he shall never assume what is false as true . . . but will arrive at a true understanding of all that does not surpass his powers". Comenius maintained equally firmly that it would be possible to find one right and efficacious method in education. Descartes's definition of method as "the order and disposition of objects towards which our mental vision must be directed", and the breaking down of difficult ideas into simple and progressive steps, is extraordinarily reminiscent of the *Didactica*, while the philosopher's later rule that imagination, the senses, and memory, need to be brought to the aid of the understanding, is reflected in the

---

[1] Haldane and Ross, *Philosophical Works of Descartes*, p. 1, C.U.P., 1911-12.
[2] *ibid.*, p. 2.

Orbis Pictus and in a dozen points of teaching method given by Comenius.

It is unlikely that there was any close contact between these two thinkers, but it is very probable that both were interpreting the social needs of their age. The rapid growth of all branches of knowledge, and the lack of specialised techniques for dealing with it, turned the attention of thinking men to the problem of enabling mankind to derive some immediate benefit from these new developments.[1] Comenius and Descartes were but two of those who arrived at encyclopaedism as a solution, although neither would have admitted that his schemes were based on this utilitarian consideration. Comenius advocated the search for knowledge to ameliorate the physical condition of man, but to him its spiritual value was in the progress of the individual towards God.

It is the strong and distinctive religious motive in the whole life and works of Comenius that must now be considered as an all-powerful factor in the evolution of his teaching philosophy. Believing as a good Protestant that each man is made in the image of God and is responsible directly to his God, he had no doubts as to the essential educational requirements of the ideal commonwealth, and he had no hesitation in advocating as a practical possibility, reforms which must have appeared fantastic in the extreme to contemporary Europe and, no doubt, somewhat ridiculous to those worthy professors who rescued his writings from oblivion in the nineteenth century. To-day the idea of universal education is accepted, and we are engaged in a life and death struggle to bring into being a world organisation based on ideals of brotherhood and the capacity of all men for nobility and virtue.

The preoccupation of Comenius with religion, and with the task of elevating mankind nearer to God's perfection, blinded him to the value of certain aspects of education deemed significant to-day. True, he appreciated that education is concerned with the whole man and not only with his intellect, but in emphasising that the school's function is to inculcate morality, and that the university should give vocational training for public service, he ignored individual need for creative activities and aesthetic experiences. In addition—in the

---

[1] There is some evidence that the secret society of Rosicrucians also did much to spread the idea of encyclopaedism, and even pansophism. Comenius's friend and teacher, Andreae, was a member, and so were many English reformers. Although Comenius attacked the Rosicrucians in *The Labyrinth of the World* it appears he later adopted some of their pansophic ideas.

absence of a science of psychology—he "organised" human development somewhat arbitrarily to accord with his general scheme. He would have four equal periods of education from birth to the twenty-fourth year. In the first period, the senses were to be trained; in the second, the imagination and memory fostered; in the third, the intelligence developed; and in the fourth, the will was to be disciplined. In spite of its artificiality, it is clear that such a plan was devised with some definite consideration of the relation between age and ability. Although in the light of present knowledge much of Comenius's psychology is crude and faulty—and often less sound than that of Vives a century earlier—it was, at least, a reasonable attempt to translate into practical form the generally accepted philosophical theories on the direction of the understanding. At the same time it was an attempt to introduce a humane system of child education at a time when harshness and arid instruction still prevailed in most schools.

In the pursuance of his ideals, Comenius, with much of the fervour of the modern "planner", allowed little true freedom to the individual. Perhaps unconsciously, he held fast to many of the tenets of Plato and Aristotle, and sought to inculcate in all children the habits of thought, behaviour, and activity which would later ensure the fulfilment of the duties and responsibilities of citizenship and of Christianity. On the other hand Comenius was entirely free from class or racial prejudices, and he even accepted and advocated the extension of education to girls. But the age of equality and fraternity had not yet arrived. His essay, *Via Lucis*, written in middle life, affords an adequate, though incomplete, summary of his hopes for mankind.

Via Lucis

The way of light of Comenius was a middle way, not a safe way, nor a well-trodden way, but a knife edge. Even as throughout his own life he steered resolutely between the Roman and Lutheran churches, and maintained the right of small nations to freedom from tyranny while urging the principle of world-citizenship, so his scheme for the betterment of all men rested on the concept of world peace without indifference, world order without stagnation, and world-wide search for knowledge, experience, and truth, without rejection of the lessons of the past. Comenius had such faith in the existence of eternal truths and permanent values that he had no fear that new experiments, theories, and discoveries would have power to destroy them, and so he advocated the seeking of new knowledge even though it might lead to re-interpretation of the highest laws and values of tradition.

This wide search for new knowledge should not be limited to the material. The physical world is important, but human societies and their problems even more so. Above all, the realm of the soul of man demands the seeking of truth. Man—that is to say, each and every man—needs to study all these aspects of life, so that, achieving the degree of understanding his capacities allow, he may gain harmony within himself yet not cease his striving. Comenius, aiming at finding short cuts to this harmony in order to save men from the uncertainty of their own ignorance, sought for guiding principles for the work of improving all human affairs. He states his basic assumptions clearly in his dedicatory preface to the *Way of Light*: "All men alike have innate principles of three kinds, matching the necessities of all kinds of action, knowing, willing, and achieving. In every man there are innate the common notions and the stimuli of desire, which we name common instincts; and the organs for doing everything, which it may be permissible to call common faculties . . . Hitherto philosophers have spoken only of common notions; not any one of them has ever brought these into order . . . We have thought that these first streams of wisdom should be traced to their proper sources, and directed according to their kinds. We have tried, therefore, to set forth not only notions, but also instincts and faculties by an entirely new method in fables or pictures; the study of which must make it evident that all men are necessarily united in these roots of human general intelligence".[1]

Pansophia was therefore "a comprehensive scheme of human omni-science—of all the things under heaven which it is granted to us to know, to say, to do", and it was designed to allocate all human experiences of life to these three categories "in an order inviolable", so that man's path of duty and happiness should become clear to him and yet leave him free to explore the unknown. The task of Comenius was "to enquire into the ways and means by which that universal wisdom may be procured for every human being born, so that there may be no minds left uncultivated or allowed to be out of line with the general harmony, all alike tinged

[1] All quotations from *Via Luris* are from Professor Campagnac's translation, Liverpool, 1938.

with pansophic light". Believing that the truth of things is within us and that religious faith is dynamic and creative, Comenius assumed that man's growing understanding of a seemingly chaotic universe would bring increased individual wisdom and social harmony, so that religious and political strife would no longer trouble the world. It is not too much to say he was at one with Socrates in believing that if men know "the good" they will inevitably pursue it, and he deems it his mission to reveal to all men both "the good" and "the way", and to persuade them "to covet and pursue happiness". In *Via Lucis* he asks his disciples to ensure that in the continuance of the pansophic scheme, nothing but ascertained and tested truths be considered worthy of inclusion in the store of knowledge, so that high and reliable standards will be set and men will "learn to dread mistakes and errors".

In this great school of the world, "made up of an order of teachers, learners, and disciplines", every person has an innate desire to learn, to discover, then to pass on his knowledge to others by persuasion or even by compulsion. Each can achieve wisdom by following after the truth of things and contemplating their inner reasons and principles, and each has a will of his own by which he can, if he chooses, seek only the good. In his search he will encounter many things "remote from the intellect, and will need to have them brought near and examined at close quarters", or else he must "take the telescope of panharmony" by the help of which a thing which cannot by itself and directly become an object of knowledge is nevertheless made known, as far as possible, by things which are similar and parallel to it. The wonderful invention of printing has accelerated this process, bringing to men the wisdom of the past so that they are stimulated "to cultivate their own minds . . . in the search for fresh discoveries". In addition, living men have been brought more closely together by exploration and by improvements in navigation, and thus a major task will be to ensure that methods of mental communication, speech, and books, are both accurate and trustworthy.

Still more urgent is the need to make available true knowledge of God. "They are grievously at fault," says Comenius, "who, as Augustine tells us in the *De Origine Animae*, declare that it makes no difference to the truth of faith what opinion any man entertains about created things, so long as the right opinion is entertained concerning God." The new attitude should accept that "the more clearly and fully Nature is revealed the more clearly and fully will the majesty of the Creator of Nature shine forth". Nevertheless, the revelation of Nature and therefore of God may be hindered if the "inferior, insufficient, confused, ill-ordered, noisy, impetuous" philosophy of the Greeks is not replaced by a new philosophy. It is necessary that people should learn both good and evil, for a knowledge of evil enables it to be hated and avoided—"Ignorance is in itself an evil because it is darkness; but knowledge, even of evil, is good because it is light".

It is important that people should learn not merely for the sake of learning, but for the sake of knowing well enough to gain guidance in the active search for truth. In general, the more a man learns "the richer harvest he reaps"—but only if the knowledge is truly his own and not merely accepted from another man without the exercise of his own reasoning powers. To forward the extension of knowledge to all men it is hoped that there may be established "universal books, universal schools, a universal college, and a universal language". All these ideas need much planning and preparation in order that they shall be as near perfection as possible, and without vulgar ostentation. The first universal book will be *Pansophia*, setting forth in strict order and agreed arrangement "all things that are necessary for man for this life and the future life to know, to believe, and to hope". The second, *Panhistoria*, will gather together the history of Nature and show the continual struggle in nature and in human affairs, but the wickedness of past generations must be buried in the darkness of oblivion. The third book, *Pandogmatica*, should contain, as an orderly record, the "quintessence of authors" from age to age, from land to land. The opinions should be written truly, "without any colour", so that the original sense is not obscured.

Universal schools should enable each individual to rise out of the darkness of ignorance and barbarism, and should give an introduction to the elements of the universal books. It should be possible to achieve this with the "delighted acquiescence" of the pupils. Parents need guidance in early methods of instruction and discipline, teachers need to learn the art of teaching, and rich men need to realise their debt to the state and the community by educating poor children with their own.

The task of the universal college and its professors will be to act as architects and builders in the furtherance of the universal scheme.

Many able men will be needed and each nation should appoint at least one honorary professor to serve under a head who shall reside in the most accessible spot to be found. Drake's voyages have shown the possibility of the inter-communication of nations, and Bacon's writings have shown the desirability of co-operation for universal reform of the sciences. Thus England has ample claim to be the most suitable location for the college—which needs large financial resources to pursue its work of producing books, and ensuring that schools be set up in every town and village. The professors should "make it their business to ensure the proper management of the schools, and prevent abuses from creeping in, and keep them from going to sleep".

The creation of a universal language presents problems. Although Vives, having similar ideas, advocated the use of Latin, it would be better to find a simpler, more regular and richer language. It might be necessary to invent a rational, analogical, and harmonious language, but this should not be attempted until Pansophia is established. It is urgently necessary that the support of churches and states and rich men be given to the establishment of the scheme. Funds are needed for the production of books, and for their testing in schools to discover "whether or not by them knowledge is really instilled more easily than it was in the past". After these preliminary experiments the whole scheme should rapidly come to fruition throughout the Christian world, and the problem could then be faced of "giving to the barbarians a taste of the harmonious and universal wisdom".

The Pedagogy of Comenius

Space will permit but a brief account of the ideas on education expressed in the prolific writings of Comenius. For deeper study, Keatinge's version of *The Great Didactic* is an invaluable classic but it does not cover the whole field of his works, and even at the time of writing it is probable that there is still more to be gained from manuscripts as yet not translated into English. It is reasonable to suppose, however, that further discoveries will but serve to confirm our impression that the writer was steadfast in his adherence to principles worked out in the schools of Lissa, and checked over in the schools of Saros-Patak. While it would be interesting to know whether a Latin version of his early *Didactica* had reached

England ahead of him,[1] it probably matters little one way or another, for, unfortunately, his "publicity value" lay in his pan-sophic concepts which were grand and exciting to Englishmen, particularly to that group of scientists who were to found the Royal Society. Nevertheless, many who shared his interest in schools and young people, no doubt learnt much from discussion with him during his stay in England. Some even wrote pamphlets and treatises embodying ideas borrowed from Comenius.

While many regretted his acceptance of the Swedish assignment to produce a series of didactic works, his own regret was not that the work was to be didactic, but that according to the terms of the agreement he could not develop his pansophia at the same time. Later, as an elderly scholar in Amsterdam he still wrote about teaching as well as about his grandly simple philosophy. The first "omnibus edition" of his main educational works was published at Amsterdam in 1657. Its four sections correspond to the four main writing periods of the author. Thus the first book includes his early *Didactica,* the *School of Infancy,* the *Vernacular School,* the *Janua,* and the *Vestibulum,* as well as the *Prodromus Pansophiae* (his summary of pansophia), and other early works. The second section covers the Elbing period, and is somewhat thin, being mainly an extension of language method. The manuscripts lost at the burn-ing of Lissa probably belonged to this period. The third section covers the Transylvanian period, and includes a full and clear-cut account of how to organise, conduct, and teach "pansophic" schools, together with three particularly interesting additions to language textbooks—the *Atrium,* the *Orbis Pictus,* and the *Schola Ludus.* The fourth section covers the three years in Amsterdam which preceded publication of the *Didactica,* a period during which he wrote at length, saying little new but putting forth commentaries on matters religious, educational, and pansophic. One delightful title is typical of the writer's modesty and sincerity: "*The art of wisely withdrawing one's own assertions*".

Throughout his long career Comenius did not waver in his belief that a "didactic art" was essential for the preparation of the indi-vidual and all mankind for the best in this life and the next. "It is our duty," he says, "to study how young people may be stirred to

[1] The chapter headings, at least, were known in England after the visit, for in 1642 Hartlib included them in his *Reforme of Schooles.*

vigour of mind and to love heavenly things." His pansophic philosophy required that education should help man to learn all things, and to achieve power over these things and discipline of himself. The analogy of education and husbandry was not originated by Rousseau, for Comenius likens man to a rich soil in which the seeds of knowledge, morality, and religion are planted by Nature. Good tillage will bring the seeds to fruition, but neglect will result in a crop of weeds.

Comenius is confident that this "cultivating" could and should be given to all children "save those whom God has denied intelligence", and moreover, that it can be done, within the space of a normal childhood and adolescence, "without blows, severity, or compulsion, but most lightly, gently, and spontaneously". It can be done only if the "natural order" for education is discovered and applied in schools. Admitting that in his time, life was too short for the learning of all things, and that, as yet, specialists had not reduced knowledge into easily comprehensible forms, he yet had faith that a right order of learning could be found, that a right presentation of material would "unlock the mind", and that a right way of teaching would "sharpen the understanding", so enabling learning to proceed "surely, easily, solidly".

In elaborating these general principles, Comenius reveals considerable psychological insight so that a true interpretation of his precepts would not be inconsistent with modern theories of method. It may seem obvious, for instance, to say that nothing should be taught "except when it can be comprehended", but a great deal of modern research aims to discover what is suitable for children to learn at different ages. Similarly the problem of avoiding teaching words before things is a vital concern of experiments in activity methods, environmental studies and similar attempts to ensure the use of the senses in learning about real things. It would be agreed to-day that the "sure" way to learning is by regular attendance, by enjoying school, by meeting no insuperable obstacles, by learning one thing at a time, and by proceeding in steps to tasks of greater difficulty. It would be more difficult to ensure, in a modern community, that scholars should have no access to irrelevant literature or that they should be kept out of bad company.

Easy learning, says Comenius, can be induced by stirring up in children the desire to learn: "Let the method of teaching lessen the labour of learning so that nothing be a stumbling block to the pupil.

and deter from perseverance in study". Children are willing to learn if they see the immediate use or purpose, and if they are taught things they can understand in an interesting way. Their tasks should be graded in difficulty, and should involve learning through the senses in the first place. Lessons should be few, and should be adjusted to the capacities of the pupils, who should not be required to memorise more than a few very important things. Punishment for bad work should be avoided, for it is the teacher's fault if a child does not learn. Children learn through all the senses, not through the ears alone, so that the teacher must use drawings, pictures, wall writing, and other aids, and also encourage pupils to write down their own records. The schoolroom should be light, clean, and pleasant, and the teachers kind and encouraging. Given really good teachers, it is preferable that pupils should not experience too many changes of teacher. Similarly, in order to foster a sense of security and ensure smooth progress, methods should be consistent throughout the school, and confusing changes of textbook should be avoided.

Solid learning depends partly on factors already mentioned as, for instance, the pupil's enjoyment of the work, and his appreciation of its utility and purpose. In addition, it is necessary to avoid including useless study: new studies should grow out of the old, and be relevant to them. This thoroughness of all learning should be ensured by coherent arrangement of material, and by continual repetition and exercises. Moreover, true learning of true things cannot be achieved by the acceptance of other people's written or spoken ideas or descriptions. It is necessary for each student to arrive at truth for himself, either through his senses or by reasoning.

These general principles are, on the whole, acceptable to present-day moderate opinion, but other points might be subjects of contention. The suggestion that procedure should be from the general to the special—the outline of the subject should be given before going on to the particular—might be interpreted as the converse of those present-day theories which require that generalisation grow slowly from the study of detail. On the other hand, Comenius may have meant by "general" only that pupils should be shown rapidly the shape and purpose of the study before proceeding to the investigation of interesting details. His requirement that there should be a standard method of instruction for all scientific subjects and, similarly, a method for arts and a method for languages, might be challenged by subject specialists, and by experimenters in "activity methods". It is reasonable to suppose, however, that Comenius wished to see sciences taught by the observation of data, and languages to be taught through the vernacular and by using suitable authors and examples before grammars and rules. His adherence to the principle of deduction in scientific studies shows that he read Bacon critically. Perhaps he saw the flaws in Bacon's arguments about inductive methods. His main object in his didactic writings was not to suggest methods of scientific research, but to indicate how existent scientific knowledge could be absorbed quickly and with true understanding.

In order that the greatest possible benefit should be derived from the school course, Comenius wished to see much attention paid to curricula and the arrangement of syllabuses. He was, it is true, too preoccupied with the need of pupils to imbibe a great deal of information, but this does not invalidate his argument that it is desirable to have a detailed plan for the school course. This is but a normal part of school management to-day, as are the large classes and the planned use of textbooks, material, and apparatus. Opponents of class teaching would wish, perhaps, that seventeenth-century teachers had not advocated the class system which eventually replaced the prevalent tuition of small groups. While he considered that a teacher could teach a very large class successfully, Comenius realised the problems involved, and would have grouping in tens, each group under the supervision of a bright boy capable of checking exercises. Moreover, class lessons were to be held for only half the day, the remainder being occupied by private study in school.

The practical suggestions of Comenius for class teaching are, again, not obsolete as long as teachers teach large classes at desks in sparsely equipped classrooms. The teacher should command attention, question skilfully, arouse the competitive spirit, and give an opportunity for pupils to ask questions, but far more significant than these points, are the suggestions that pupils should be enabled to learn through the senses, and should always be pleasantly stimulated to interest in a profitable topic at the beginning of each lesson. Comenius would have placed little reliance on the ingenuity and originality of the teacher, but some educational systems to-day embody his ideas on the need for carefully constructed standard textbooks and strictly regulated syllabuses and time tables so that "the same thing is done by all at the same time".

The anxiety of Comenius to ensure that as much as possible should be learnt and well learnt, caused him to consider closely the function of many kinds of school activities, and he perceived that in many cases they could fulfil dual purposes under skilful direction. Thus the learning of language, whether foreign or the vernacular, would also serve for the learning of general facts about the world and its inhabitants. By combining "words and things" the old, arid, fruitless grammar-grind would be avoided, and pupils would not only learn two things at once, but would learn more quickly because they would be more interested. Even exercises in literary style should embody some useful matter deliberately selected, and exercises in reading and writing should always go hand in hand. All learning should be made sure by frequent repetition, but it is interesting to observe that most instances of repetition involve, on the pupil's part, activities of a different kind. Pupils might teach others what they have learnt, and they might have competitions between themselves. Moreover, the play-element is emphasised by the indication that such activities might be of a practical nature, such as plant collecting. Similarly, rewards for success might be the awarding of titles used in the outside world—perhaps the dawn of the concept of the school as a microcosm of society; or perhaps an imitation of Jesuit methods? The awarding of titles—kings, councillors, doctors, and others—was reflected a century later in the play-methods of David Manson. While such methods of stimulating interest were considered essential by Comenius, he would have the teacher constantly on guard against the introduction of irrelevant, superfluous material and activities which might retard progress.

In examining the precepts of Comenius, it is necessary to bear in mind that he aimed at the improvement of current practice, so that many suggestions, which now fail to convince, were based originally on very real needs. The fruitless, meaningless language teaching of the day needed changing; teachers' deep ignorance of science needed remedying by the collection of a definite and true body of knowledge; and the teaching profession needed reformation not by the addition of more mediocre teachers, but by the devising of methods by which good teachers could teach more pupils. It is equally necessary to avoid being misled by the partiality of Comenius for seeking analogies with Nature. It was an affectation of his times as well as a result of his philosophy, and although the analogies now appear artificial and often ridiculous, the resultant points on teaching are usually worth noting.

Above all, it is necessary to avoid accepting a first reading of a generalised account of his teaching principles, as a true and adequate interpretation of his real meanings. If an examination in greater detail finds his repetitiveness tiresome, further study will find that same repetitiveness illuminating. It may be discovered, for instance, that the teacher must know the needs and capacities of each member of his large class, because he needs to judge what is irrelevant and superfluous for each. This interpretation immediately widens the whole concept of education, for it appears that, after all, each pupil is not expected to learn "all things", but he is to be allowed to pursue subjects for which he has an aptitude. He is not to waste time on subjects for which he has neither liking nor aptitude. Similarly, it is not proposed to teach everything within the scope of each subject. Too much detail is irrelevant and superfluous, and only confuses pupils, and for this reason textbooks should contain only as much as is necessary for sound learning and understanding.

Briefly, Comenius advocates methods which foster learning by experience, whether it be experience of observing, touching, and smelling in science lessons, writing, reading, making things in arts' subjects, or speaking about interesting things in language lessons. The acquirement of knowledge is essentially based on activity followed by reasoning; the acquirement of morality and piety is based on habituation, imitation, and the avoidance of evil.

In his search for the right order of teaching, Comenius gave much attention to the school system and to syllabuses. Throughout his career he advocated a division of education into four stages, suggesting that the careful training of infants within the family circle should be followed, not by an introduction to Latin, but by a six years' course in a primary school—a course which should aim to develop a full and accurate use of the native language. Writing— usually neglected in elementary schools of the time—should be taught as well as reading, and even in the first year pupils should pass from slates to washable horn tablets, and finally to ink and paper.[1] Pupils should be taught to make simple measurements and calculations, and to work at simple crafts according to their aptitude.

[1] One of the recovered manuscripts is on the teaching of reading and writing.

They should be taught geography and history, and above all, morality, and all this with the help of books with attractive titles, and by the expenditure of only four hours a day on lessons—two hours in the morning for the exercise of the understanding and the memory, and two in the afternoon for activities using hands and voice. Singing should be taught, but whether as an art or as a pious accomplishment is open to question.

From twelve to eighteen the Latin school should provide an encyclopaedic course—the vernacular, Latin, Greek, Hebrew, physics, mathematics, ethics, dialectics, geometry, music, astronomy, and theology, related and unified, it appears, by the permeation of history through the whole curriculum. Although class lessons are still to occupy only four hours a day the pupils are to race through the *Vestibulum* and the *Janua* at a spanking pace, learning the vernacular, Latin, science, and general knowledge all at the same time, and pausing at the end of each term to give forth their knowledge in dramatised form.[1] In addition to sound and rapid learning, there should be acquired in this school both self-discipline and good social manners. At Patak, Comenius wrote *On Manners* and *Laws of a well-ordered school* which not only indicate that he had in mind a boarding school, but also emphasise his demand for civilised behaviour, adequate classroom accommodation, co-operative parents, and a headmaster who attends to his proper duties. Boys should not put elbows on the table at meals, take food out of their mouths, or pick their teeth with their nails or forks; nor should they play dice, eat between meals, nor, strangely enough, go swimming or lie on their backs in bed.[2]

The academia or university should, in the opinion of Comenius, admit only brilliant students and retain only those who are industrious as well as able. Furthermore, he believes, with Bacon that although the university should offer opportunities to study any subject, an important function of its academic staff should be to produce books. The highest standards should be maintained in all activities—disputations, tutorials, and public examinations—and positions of honour should be given only to those who have completed their university course with success.

Provision should be made for specialisation in one subject by

---

[1] *Schola Ludus* is Comenius's dramatisation of the *Janua* made in Saros Patak.
[2] In one of Charles Hoole's little books of Latin-English sentences for children, there is a section on manners which includes many of the same points.

those who give an adequately good performance in an examination
to be taken at the end of the Latin school course. A few students
of exceptional talent should be encouraged to pursue all the
branches of study, "that there may always be some men whose
knowledge is encyclopaedic". Plenty of books of university
standard should be made available, especially "epitomes". Even
as maps "present to the eye huge tracts of sea and land on a small
scale so that they can be taken in at a glance", so epitomes of
authors would enable the student to discover quickly the field of
study which held particular interest for him.

If university education is treated somewhat briefly, the function
of travel is summarised in a few words. "We are at one with
Plato, who forbade the young to travel until the hot-headedness of
youth had passed away, and they were sufficiently versed in the
ways of the world to do so with advantage." This adds the final
flourish to Comenius's appeal that rate of maturation be taken into
account in planning education. His "stages" appear commonplace to-day, but in his own times, he was proposing to change the
whole nature of existing systems in suggesting that there should be
a "common core" of primary education, that no child should learn
a foreign language before twelve unless particularly interested and
able, and that boys should not be thrown into the hurly-burly of
university life and foreign travel until after eighteen. This insistence
on proceeding slowly and surely in the main stages of education
as well as in the detailed processes of learning, is a major contribution to educational progress; for this reason alone it is worth
examining in greater detail his careful tracing of child development
through one of his major phases of education.

The School of Infancy[1]

This delightful little work is addressed to "pious Christian
parents, tutors, guardians, and all upon whom the charge of children
is incumbent", and it purports to suggest to them their duties, based
on three main principles: that children are precious gifts, that their
education should be designed with Christian purpose, and that they
need good education so greatly that "failing it, they must, of
necessity, be lost". In amplifying these principles Comenius reveals something of his philosophy. Thus, for instance, he describes

[1] Quotations from translation of D. Benham, *Comenius's School of Infancy*,
London, 1858.

children as "being innocent, with the sole exception of original sin; they are not yet the defaced image of God", and he quotes Jonah in asserting that they are "unable to discern between good and evil, between the right hand and the left". He also says: "He who takes little children in his arms may be assured that he takes angels", and he concludes by quoting Matthew: "Unless ye become as little children . . .", in support of his contention that in children we may see "modesty, courteousness, benignity, harmony, and other Christian virtues", and thus that we owe them "the most diligent attention".

In elaborating his principle of the parents' responsibility for ensuring the right kind of education, Comenius quotes Plutarch as saying: "Those persons valued the shoe more than the foot", of parents who give their children false values and inadequate spiritual sustenance. He summarises the purposes for which children should be educated as faith and piety above all, then moral uprightness, and lastly—in importance as well as in order—knowledge of languages and the arts. He is briefer and more incisive in his treatment of the principle of the child's essential need of a "right" education, but one passage in particular is worthy of quotation in full. After describing how, through the incompetence, preoccupation, or indifference of parents, children since remote times, have been given into the charge of Paedagogues, "leaders not drivers of children", who gathered pupils into schools—"retreats of *ease* and places of literary *amusements*"—Comenius delivers his broadside attack on the prevailing system: "It being designed by this name to indicate that the action of teaching and learning is of itself, and in its own nature, pleasing and agreeable; a mere amusement and mental delight. This gladsomeness was, however, altogether departed from in subsequent times, so that schools were not as their name previously indicated, places of amusement and delights; but grinding houses and places of torture for youth among certain peoples, especially when youth were instructed by incompetent men, altogether uninstructed in piety and the wisdom of God; such who had become imbecile through indolence, despicably vile, and affording the very worst example, through calling themselves masters and preceptors; for these did not imbue the youth with faith, piety, and sound morals, but with superstitions, impiety, and baneful morals, being ignorant of the genuine method, and thinking to inculcate everything by force, they wretchedly tortured the youth; of which we are reminded by the singular though trite dialogues: 'He appears to have got a very rich vintage of blows upon his shoulder blades', and 'He was repeatedly brought to the lash'. For other mode of instruction than with severity of rods and atrocity of blows, was unknown".

In the short, succinct dissertation which follows this indictment Comenius explains why and how, in his opinion, parents should supervise closely the upbringing and education of their children, especially during the first six years of life, which are of utmost importance. Although he confuses heredity and early nurture, and uses some ridiculous examples from pseudo-history to prove his contentions, his basic arguments are indubitably sound and reasonable, and when examined in detail, might be mistaken for a rough draft of part of Locke's *Thoughts Concerning Education*. He intends to convey that, although some human characteristics are innate and unchangeable—"for who can amend that which was born lame ?"—there is a need for careful and constant attention in the early years to ensure that each little person is given the opportunity to develop as fully and finely as possible, "since it is impossible to make the tree straight that has grown crooked".

He contends that education begins at birth. Indeed, he goes further, and touches on many truths now taken for granted by modern doctors and psychologists, in his discussion of the need of pre-natal care by the mother's attention to her own emotions, diet, and exercise. In the intervening centuries it has not always been held that a pregnant woman should "perform with all agility her usual employment". His plea for natural feeding of babies by mothers is not only a protest against the practices of the day, it is also a premonition of the modern discovery of the close psychological bond between mother and nursed baby. Moreover, although he puts piety at the head of his list of virtues to be inculcated by good parents, he does not treat it first except to imply that the baby should be surrounded by love, and respond with love and obedience, not only towards his parents, but towards the benign power called God. His main concern is for the physical welfare of the little being. He uses the old tag about a sound mind in a sound body as intelligently as Locke, whose ideas on child training are usually assumed to be revolutionary in his age. Such a gift, Comenius asserts, must be won by effort, and when the parents have taken every precaution against rich, highly seasoned foods, external injuries, and chills, and lack of adequate exercise and play, the child himself must be helped to learn how to eat sensibly to keep himself clean, and "to acquire an aversion to indolence".

His plea for regularity of habits in eating, sleeping, "daily exercise and excitements"; his demand for safe places where children may run about; and his suggestion of the need for "guardians of health, nurses, and baby carriers", have found their answer in the modern nursery and nursery school. His argument that parents should be vitally concerned with all aspects of the child's development is still valid. Perhaps his most pleasing injunction to parents is that they "ought to be especially careful never to allow their children to be without delights". While urging Platonic moderation in all things he suggests that the baby should be cuddled and kissed, the small child played with, and pleased by music and pictures, and, indeed, given "some little occupation . . . for its eyes, ears, and other senses". Nothing pleasing should be denied to the child unless it is "adverse to piety and upright morals". It is very probable, in spite of this last proviso, that he would have allowed children pleasures and freedom unthinkable to Puritans and Pietists.

In discussing the nature of instruction during infancy, Comenius lays down a principle which has hardly yet been accepted in this country—that it can be achieved informally during the first six years, so that there must be no formal teaching, regimentation or apportioning of "instruction precisely to certain years", because it is essential to allow for differing rates of development from child to child. His suggestions on "how children are to be exercised in the knowledge of things" have sometimes been accounted ridiculous because he speaks of the learning of "optics", "astronomy", "geography", and even "history". A reading of the text would have revealed to critics that Comenius suggests only those observational activities which are now recognised as the essential foundation for later fruitful learning. He differentiates between "natural knowledge" such as eating, drinking, sleeping, digesting, and growing which "affect not their intellect", and knowledge gained with the help of the intellect, such as ability to differentiate between people, between foods, between animals, and between other parts of the environment perceivable through the senses. From very early days the duty of parents and nurses is to help the children to gain and consolidate this knowledge, and to learn the names and uses of "things". The study of "optics" implies merely looking at interesting things, so that the adult should "show them the beauty of the heavens, of trees, of flowers, of running water . . . bind corals to their hands and neck", should take them to see orchards, fields, rivers, and windmills, and should give them picture books, adorn the walls with pictures and, indeed, allow children every opportunity to see things which are "pleasing to them".

Astronomical studies are those observations of the sun, its rising and setting, the moon and its quarters, the variations in length of days and such elements known to modern five-year-olds. Geography comes naturally to children right from birth, "when they begin to distinguish their cradles and their maternal bosom". Comenius, not Pestalozzi, was the true pioneer in geography teaching. The learning of position and routes in the known environment, the understanding, through personal experience, what is meant by a village, a field, a forest, a river—these elementary exercises are now deemed by geographers to be essential for the acquisition of standards of measurement. Similarly, the primary requirement of history learning is the comprehension of time, and this is developed by reflection upon known and experienced periods of time, such as is stimulated by simple questions: "What did you do yesterday?" Nor is it unreasonable to consider important the learning of economics, "the due performance of household duties". Small children can understand something of the function of different members of the family, and the need for care of clothes, and respect of furniture, especially if they have toys which help them to play at "houses" and "mothers and fathers" for, says Comenius, "this way is to teach the youth according to their own way, and by presenting these little things before their eyes, they will not be ignorant of the greater things which they represent".

A warning is given which teachers to-day might apply to all primary education. Little of politics is needed by children "for although they hear the names of sovereigns, governors, judges, yet inasmuch as they do not visit the places where these functions are performed, they cannot comprehend them, and could not if they did; inasmuch as they exceed their capacity". It is amusing to find that the development of a sense of humour and shrewdness in assessing whether or not others are joking, are deemed useful elements in the learning of "politics".

Lest conscientious parents should imagine that all this knowledge can be acquired only by their own direct teaching, Comenius adds advice which is, in fact, implied in most of his other suggestions which rest on the assumption that learning takes place in a social context. He indicates that children learn better in groups which are more or less homogeneous because "they sharpen each other more effectually since the one does not surpass the other in depth of invention, there is among them neither assumption of superiority of the one over the other, or force, or dread, or fear, but love, candour, free questioning, and answers about anything".

Many other child activities may be turned to educational purpose. "Boys ever delight in being occupied with something," says Comenius, "let them be like ants, continually occupied in doing something, carrying, drawing, constructing, and transposing". They need toys, constructional material, space to "run and jump, to kindle and extinguish, pour out water, carry things", to build, draw with chalk, and even to write and to count. Suggestions for learning arithmetic and geometry are surely the precursors of much nursery school apparatus. For instance, the principles of geometry are being learnt when the differences are discovered between large and small, short and long, wide and narrow. Similarly, weights and measures should be learnt by practical methods. Making music "is especially natural to us" and children should be encouraged to sing—if only to expand their chests—and to play toy musical instruments if they wish. The soothing effects of music are mentioned but no real consideration is given to the creative function of music.

Of major significance, however, is the correct development of speech and language. Training should start from the first meaningful utterances of "Mama" and "Papa" by encouraging clear and correct articulation, and rectifying, by play methods, any tendency to lisping. Later, conversation about their observations and activities, together with playful practice of tongue-twisters, should ensure clear speech, while stories and poems recited to children with appropriate facial expression and gestures, will awake in them a love of melody and rhythm. "The roots of all sciences and arts arise as early as in this tender age," says Comenius, "and on these foundations it is neither difficult nor impossible for the whole superstructure to be laid".

The small section of the treatise dealing with training in morals and virtue is full of restrained, reasonable contentions, largely based on Platonic principles. Thus, the whole household should present to the child good examples of temperance, neatness, cleanliness, courtesy, and honesty, because all children are imitative. At the same time their attention needs to be drawn to good examples, and they should be reprimanded by words for bad behaviour. Mild corporal punishment should be used if reprimand fails to produce improvement, but whenever willingness to improve is shown, praise should be given. Comenius has no use for the over-indulgent parent, and he regards with disapproval slack discipline, greediness, and disrespect on the part of their children. Obedience to parents, truthfulness, and respect of property are essentials for later virtue, and great care should be taken to avoid small deceits and to expect humble confession of faults. Unselfish giving should be encouraged by appreciation of small generous gestures. The virtues of industry, polite silence, patience, quick, cheerful co-operation in little duties and services, courtesy and good manners—all these are mentioned as desirable, and it is implied that even small children under six should be trained in such niceties of civilised behaviour by example, by precept, and if necessary, by the rod.

The inculcation of piety is similarly a matter of habituation in childhood. Children should be told simply about God as a loving father, and should be taught to pray, but in the Moravian doctrine, as in many others, there is over-much emphasis on punishment and the fear of God. However, apart from some insistence on the rote learning of prayers and commandments, not unknown to-day, training in piety was to be largely a matter of guarding against evil, for "first impressions adhere most firmly to our minds", and "the brain can by no means be forced to lose what it has once received".

Finally, Comenius warns against the curtailment of this period of nursery education. He admits that some children may be ready to proceed to school before six, and that others may need to spend a further year or more at home, but it is best to take expert advice and steer a middle course, lest "the parent who would have a Doctor before the time will scarcely have a Bachelor, and occasionally may have a Fool". When parents decide the time is ripe, children should be prepared for the new venture, not by warnings of severity to come, but by encouragement to look forward to a pleasant experience. "Whatever can be devised to excite in them a love of school ought not to be omitted. Similarly the child should be made to feel that the new teacher is a friend of the parents, and therefore of the child, for when to children the school becomes an amusement, they will make proficiency with delight."

SUGGESTIONS FOR FURTHER READING

The classic study of Comenius is M. W. Keatinge's *The Great Didactic of Comenius* (2 vols., Black, 1896), which contains not only the gist of that work, but also a well-written biography and valuable critical essays. S. S. Laurie's earlier study, *John Amos Comenius* (C.U.P., 1881), gives a useful summary of the *Didactic* and discusses the influence of Bacon and Ratke on Comenius. M. Pattison's lecture, *Comenius* (Blackie, 1892), was prepared before Laurie's book. It is stimulating, and it contains useful pointers on the language textbooks of Comenius and his predecessors. R. H. Quick's *Essays on Educational Reformers* (Longmans, Green, 3rd edition, 1904) include a biography and appreciation of Comenius and also a summary of Ratke's ideas.

Two books showing the historical setting of the work of Comenius are W. S. Monroe's *Comenius and the Beginnings of Educational Reform* (Heinemann, 1900) and R. F. Young's *Comenius in England* (O.U.P., 1932). A commemorative booklet of essays by leading educators and scientists was published three hundred years after the Moravian's visit to England—*The Teacher of Nations*, edited by J. Needham (C.U.P., 1942). Another more recent study is *John Amos Comenius*, by M. Spinka (Chicago, 1943).

CHAPTER IX

THE COMENIAN AGE IN ENGLAND

It now becomes increasingly difficult to select from the many writers on education those who must not be omitted from a book which can be little more than a review of the progress of ideas. Few would deny that Comenius is the outstanding advocate of the "new" attitude to learning and teaching which developed in the seventeenth century, although the essential germ may be found in Vives and his contemporaries. Opinions will vary, however, as to the amount of originality and real understanding contained in the writings of Comenius, even as they will differ as to the extent of the influence of other thinkers, particularly Bacon and Ratke, on the evolution of the ideas of Comenius. While recognising that many other names would be included in a more detailed consideration of seventeenth-century educational thought, it is not intended to attempt more than a brief survey of trends of ideas in England.

The main impetus to the movement away from decadent humanism and lingering scholasticism was given by Sir Francis Bacon, thirty years the senior of Comenius, and the source of inspiration of several continental educators whose influence on the ideas of Comenius is evident. **Francis Bacon (1561-1626)** was a statesman by profession, not a patron of education in the same sense as was his father,[1] nor an educator with practical knowledge and understanding of teaching problems. Professor Laurie at the turn of the present century said Bacon was "the man of genius who gathered up those hints, anticipations and aspirations which constitute a 'tendency' and gave them shape".[2] Professor Fowler wrote in the late nineteenth century: "The more special object of Bacon's method was to overcome the subtlety of nature, and extort from it some account of its secrets".[3] These two quotations summarise the main contribution of Bacon to education, for both *The Advancement of Learning* (1605) and *Novum Organon* (1620), in

---

[1] Sir Nicholas Bacon, a patron of St Alban's School.
[2] S. S. Laurie, *Educational Opinion from the Renaissance*, C.U.P., 1888.
[3] T. Fowler, Introduction to *Locke's Conduct of the Understanding*, Clarendon Press, 5th edition, 1901.

surveying the whole sphere of human knowledge, emphasised that education itself was one of those sciences which needed study so that "the rightness of the way" might be discovered.

Although his inductive method of scientific study has hardly stood the test of time, its expression represents a stride forward in human progress, for Bacon was using it as a weapon to confound "two sorts of rovers, the one with frivolous disputation, confutations, and verbosities, the other with blind experiments and auricular traditions and impostures".[1] It is to be remembered that he lived at a time when abuse and decadence prevailed in the universities, and when many people of all classes still believed in magic and witchcraft. Bacon was seeking support in high political circles for concepts such as teacher-training, reform of method and curriculum, the progress of studies and the value of present realities, but his ideas were destined to gain little ground in England, although lip service was paid to his intellectual leadership. In the schools a few teachers, such as Brinsley of Ashby-de-la-Zouch, were finding their own way, through experience, to similar conclusions without the help of philosophical abstractions.

John Brinsley (1585-1665) wrote several school books which achieved success, mainly translations of Cicero, Vergil, and Cato, and a Latin grammar called *Posing of the Parts*. His chief work was *Ludus Literarius*, written after many years of schoolmastering, and published in 1612. It purports to show "how to proceede from the first entrance into learning to the highest perfection required in the Grammar Schooles", but its value to-day is as a record of a licensed grammar schoolmaster's methods of teaching and class management in the early seventeenth century. Arranged in the form of a dialogue between two schoolmasters, the matter is essentially concerned with practicalities, with a description of methods that "work" under conditions generally prevailing at the time.

Brinsley accepted as desirable large classes and an early introduction to study; he had no complaint against the classical curriculum, for much of the dialogue is taken up with the teaching of *Lily's Latin Grammar*. On the other hand, he avoided many of the problems of large classes by encouraging both co-operation and competition within the classroom; he specified that when children start school at five they should not have general lessons, but only play activities; in his curriculum he gave Greek, Hebrew, and

---

[1] Francis Bacon, from a letter to Lord Burleigh.

religion, almost equal place with Latin; and he emphasised the importance of English and arithmetic. He made a plea for the development of true understanding instead of mere rote learning, and at the same time he advocated that teachers should carefully select for their pupils' study only such topics and books as "whereof they may have the best use, and that perpetually in their learnings, or in their own life".

Ten years later he published another work—*A Consolation for our Grammar Schooles : or a faithfull and most comfortable incouragement for laying of a sure foundation of all good learning in our schooles and for prosperous building thereon*, wherein he speaks of his long experience of "the manifold evils which grow from the ignorance of a right order of teaching". He feels he has gained "some gracious taste of the sweetness that is to be found in the better courses truly known and practised", and he suggests that the instruction of schoolmasters in "good methods" and "the right order" is essential so that they will not suffer "endless vexation" while inflicting on their pupils "extreme labour and terror . . . with enduring far overmuch and long severity". Thus Brinsley reached the same conclusion as Mulcaster, another practising teacher of long experience, so that it is unnecessary to claim for Comenius any originality in advocating training colleges. Comenius was, similarly, a practising schoolmaster for long periods of his life, and it is hardly to be wondered at if he, too, felt that young teachers could be helped to find better ways of teaching.

Towards the end of the second decade of the century Brinsley was suspended from teaching because his religious and political opinions had a pronounced Puritan tang. He may be considered one of the advance-guard of the great Puritan campaign on behalf of the education of ordinary people. Leadership towards reform was not, however, entirely in non-conformist hands, for there are many schoolmasters whose names are worthy of mention, although two examples must suffice. **Thomas Farnaby (1575-1647)** was a famous and highly successful master of private schools during this period. Starting as a poor Jesuit-trained "abecedarian", or elementary teacher, he rose to be master of a flourishing London grammar school which included many future celebrities among its three hundred pupils. Farnaby had sailed with Drake, so it is hardly likely that his popularity as a teacher was entirely based on the fashionable grammar grindstone, or that, having seen so much of the world and its living geography, he would be satisfied to confine his pupils' studies to ancient geography. Unfortunately his written works—mainly grammars and versions of the classics—give little indication of his teaching methods.

On the other hand, the writings of a distinguished member of the diplomatic service indicate clearly that educators in England were feeling their way towards a revision of the curriculum, and improvement in method even before the ideas of Comenius became known in England. **Sir Henry Wotton (1565-1639),** after a year of successful service abroad, found himself, through the efforts of enemies, out of the King's favour and in financial straits, but he eventually gained security, albeit seclusion, as Provost of Eton, which office he filled ably and cheerfully. He was intelligent and well-read, but he was no hermit scholar, for he enjoyed entertaining and was a particularly enthusiastic fisherman. Through his former contacts with upper class families, he drew many noble youths to Eton, including the Boyle brothers, one of whom was to become the celebrated scientist. Although he accepted the prevailing bias of the school, and although his own interests appear to have been artistic and literary—he was an admirer of Milton's poetry— he was well aware of the new realist attitude to science. Bacon had sent him three copies of the *Novum Organon* in 1620, and he dabbled in scientific experiments himself, so that it is not surprising to find his arguments on education based on scientific realities rather than classical maxims. He was an observer of children, taking the trouble to become acquainted with the pupils by bringing them to his table and into his house. He listened and watched, and so came to his conclusions as to the character and temperament of each individual.

He followed Bacon's lead in rejecting the dictatorship of the classical writers whom he does not hesitate to criticise. It cannot be doubted that his idea of a balanced curriculum would have included modern languages, modern geography and history, and arts and handicrafts, but unfortunately, his writings[1] are incomplete, and we have only the brief *Survey of Education* and *Aphorisms of Education* by which to judge the quality and nature of his educational concepts. As far as is known, he put down his ideas on paper during the third decade of the century, before Hartlib published the summary of Comenius's *Great Didactic* in 1642, so that it is

[1] Isaac Walton, *Reliquiae Wottonianae*, 1672.

unlikely he had heard or read anything of the Moravian's pedagogy. Milton, on the other hand, although Wotton's contemporary, did not produce his *Tractate* until 1644, and therefore must inevitably have heard a great deal about Comenius, although he refers with scorn to "Modern *Januas* and *Didactics*".

Another development in English education before the visit of Comenius in 1640, must be mentioned—the beginning of experiments in language teaching, or perhaps it would be more accurate to say the appearance of signs of revolt against the tyranny of *Lily's Grammar*. In 1588 John Higgins had published an English version of the *Nomenclator* of Hadrian Junius, one of several attempts to collect from Greek and Latin authors the names of material things. Higgins's *Remembrancer*, covering "the names of things" from over three hundred authors, was the forerunner of the first textbook of Comenius. Another forerunner was the *Janua Linguarum* of William Bathe, a Jesuit priest, born in Ireland, and educated in Spain. The first edition was in 1611; another English version was produced by William Wilde in 1615, and another by John Harmar, Head of St Alban's School, in 1626. Bathe's *Janua* included all common Latin root words, formulated into over a thousand short maxims such as, "Repentance is the companion of a wrong judgment". Each word was used only once, and the original arrangement was in two columns, Latin and the vernacular side by side. The first English publication of Comenius's *Janua* (1631), under the name of "John Anchoran", had three columns, Latin, English, and French. Thomas Horne, later Master of Tonbridge School, published another version in 1633, perhaps at the instigation of Hartlib, a disciple of Comenius. Thus it is probable that many English schoolmasters had become well acquainted with the Comenian elements of language teaching before the visit of Comenius, and certainly long before the publication of the *Didactica*. Apart from this, methods and curricula were very much as in the preceding century. The few elementary schools taught only a smattering of the three R's, unless they had a "vocational bias" such as kersey knitting and spinning. The grammar schools were still preoccupied with ancient languages. The main sign of "progress" was the inclusion of Greek and Hebrew.

The third decade of the seventeenth century saw the strengthening of demands for the reform and extension of education.

The Puritan influence played its part in this movement, but although many leaders were either Puritan or inclined to Puritanism, the issues were never primarily religious, although the story of the vicissitudes of schools and schoolmasters during the next fifty years might point that way. The patrons, teachers, and writers of the period are far too numerous to mention here, but a brief consideration of outstanding figures may serve to set the English stage.

Samuel Hartlib (1600-1662 c.), the son of a Polish merchant of Elbing, came to England when he was about twenty-eight, and earned for himself within a few years a considerable reputation as a propagandist in several matters of public welfare, but particularly in education. His means of subsistence are uncertain—he probably relied entirely on casual employment, occasional patronage, and official promises—but there is no doubt that he gave of his best to the cause of educational reform, and may be acknowledged a benefactor of English education if only in that he gave nearly forty years of unstinted effort without any real hope of pecuniary recognition. It is almost certain that he died in poverty, never having received the pension granted to him by the state in 1646. Yet he was not an austere, puritanical man. He and his family lived in luxury, and entertained lavishly in times of affluence, and adapted themselves philosophically at other times to more straitened circumstances.

It is very probable that either he or his relatives in Elbing were acquainted with Comenius and his work, for Hartlib's main educational task in the third decade of the century was the interpretation of many of the Moravian's ideas to Englishmen interested in education.[1] From 1633 he was a friend and supporter of the Scots reformer, John Dury, sharing his views on both the need for the union of all Protestant churches and the need for school reform and teacher training. These opinions were very closely allied to those of Comenius, and in 1637 and 1639, Hartlib presented accounts of the ideas of Comenius. Indeed, it was probably his publication without the writer's permission, of a résumé of the *Pansophiae* that led to the visit of Comenius to England. Although this visit produced no immediate tangible result, Hartlib published in 1642 a treatise, *A Reformation of Schools*, an interpretation of the *Didactica*,

---

[1] Comenius knew something of Hartlib's early activities in England, for in the original *Didactic* he refers to an experiment in education in an English castle—one of Hartlib's short-lived ventures.

and a few years later wrote an account of Cyprian Kinner's experiments along Comenian lines. During this period, he also persuaded Milton to write his *Tractate of Education,* a pamphlet which shows at least that there was a ferment in the minds of thinking men interested in education.

Hartlib set out to make himself "acquainted with the literary, scientific, theological, and political information of the day", and hoped that in showing the value of organised enquiry and collection of information, he would win official recognition, and perhaps gain appointment as head of a national bureau of education. In 1647, he presented to Parliament *Considerations tending to the happy accomplishment of England's Reformation in Church and State,* in which he proposed the establishment of a labour exchange, and also a kind of international bureau for religious and educational matters. Furthermore, he suggested a Patent Office to disseminate knowledge of new inventions for the good of mankind.

This great bureau or "Office of Address" was to be centred in one of the Oxford Colleges, but even the *Further Discovery of the Office of Public Address,* in 1649, failed to generate any real enthusiasm at Oxford, probably because the plan was too sweeping in requiring the appropriation of college revenues for the work of a "universal college", as Comenius would have called it. Hartlib's complete acceptance of the ideas of Comenius expressed in *The Way of Light* is shown by his obstinate and persistent advocacy of those projects which had fallen through during the visit of Comenius to England. The main functions of the "Office of Address" were to be the putting into practice of Bacon's suggestions, and the development of the schemes of Comenius for better teaching and for universal schools. In 1652, Hartlib, realising that Oxford would not experiment for him, revived the idea of a universal college in the existent buildings of Chelsea College. He now described the project as "a public centre of good intelligence and correspondence with foreign Protestant Churches in the cause of religion and learning", and he reshaped, but nevertheless, repeated, his pleas for the inclusion of Fellows from all Protestant nations—men whose duty should be to disseminate the newly-collected knowledge and ideas to their own peoples, in their own languages, through their own churches.

His loyalty to the ideals of Bacon and Comenius emerges yet again in his own philosophical effort, *Macaria,* published in 1646.

In his imaginary kingdom he painted a picture of human happiness based on a social interpretation of the educational pansophia of Comenius. He realised, however, that the "reformation of the whole world" must be attempted from many angles, and he encouraged the propagation of many ideas, simple and complicated, concrete and abstract, humble and scholarly, on a number of aspects of "universal education". His own contributions were varied; thus, he wrote in 1651 an *Essay for Advancement of Husbandry Learning; or propositions for the erecting of a College of Husbandry,* and in 1654 he produced *A True and Readie Way to Learn the Latin Tongue,* which included extracts from Lubinus, Richard Carew, and Montaigne.

Most of the writers on education of the day either wrote at Hartlib's suggestion or published with Hartlib's support. The long list includes clergy, such as Bishop John Hall, and the divine, Hezekiah Woodward; schoolmasters such as George Snell and John Webster; and state officials such as Sir William Petty. Diarist John Evelyn was also associated with him, as was Abraham Cowley, and many other celebrated men, but he was also a patron, in a modest way, of talented unknowns such as Plattes, a writer on agriculture and chemistry, Pell, a mathematician, and Adam Speed, a writer on education and husbandry, and cousin to Thomas Horne, head of Tonbridge and later of Eton. Indeed, as Milton's biographer has truly said: "Everybody knew Hartlib . . . He is interesting both for what he did himself and also on account of the number and intimacy of his contacts with other interesting people".[1] Many other names could be added, but two alone, Boyle and Locke, will serve to indicate the significance of Hartlib's great work of collecting and interpreting a wealth of educational ideas for the use of his contemporaries and his successors.

John Milton (1608-1674) was a Londoner, who, as a boy attended St Paul's School. Before and during his schooldays his father, a scrivener by profession, and a musician by inclination, kept him under the tutelage of one Thomas Young, who held Presbyterian views. Milton proceeded to Christ's College, Cambridge, and after some delay through being "sent down" for an offence, he graduated, but instead of turning to religion as he had intended, he joined his father who had retired to Buckinghamshire. Here he spent five years enjoying, as he said, "a complete holiday

[1] D. Masson, *Life of Milton,* London, 1895, vol. 3.

in turning over Latin and Greek authors", but at the same time writing some of his best known works. He then went on the scholars' traditional pilgrimage to the Continent, and on his return lived in London for three or four years before he "commenced schoolmaster" to the sons of some of his friends. He was then already thirty-five.

It is doubtful whether his "school" ever grew larger than a dozen pupils.[1] The children were expected to study, before the age of fifteen, a wide range of difficult subjects—Latin, Greek, Hebrew, Chaldean, Syrian, Italian, French, arts, sciences, and "practical" subjects such as military science, architecture, and agriculture. Most of the textbooks used were in Greek and Latin. It is not surprising to find that his main writings on education show that he had no real appreciation of the qualities and capabilities of ordinary children. It would seem he attempted to fuse Humanist aims with Puritan principles; there are few signs of the true realist attitude although it has been claimed that Milton reconciled realism and classicism.

The famous *Tractate of Education*, was published at the instigation of Hartlib in 1644. It aimed to stimulate Puritan youth to great effort during the Civil War, and its spirit of high endeavour and noble ideals is certainly its most valuable characteristic, especially when it is in conjunction with an emphasis on the responsibility of the individual before God. It ought, perhaps, to be studied side by side with a much later work which reveals that during the succeeding years Milton smoothed away many of the flaws, such as certain undemocratic views, which mar his earlier scheme. This work was *A Ready and Easy Way to Establish a Free Commonwealth*, published in 1660.

Milton pays scant attention to the education of girls, and none at all to the education of young children. He concentrates on the boy between twelve and twenty-one. Before sixteen, Latin grammar —with careful attention to pronunciation—should predominate in the curriculum, and Milton would aim "to lead pupils . . . draw them into willing obedience, inflamed with the study of learning, and the admiration of virtue; stirred up with the high hopes of living to be brave men and worthy patriots, dear to God, and famous in all ages". All other studies—arithmetic, geometry, agriculture, geography, astronomy, and natural philosophy—are to be subsidiary

[1] Masson, in his *Life of Milton*, suggests eight to twelve pupils.

and contributary to the main study of languages, and these subjects are thus to be studied through the ancient writers and not, apparently, through the new scientific writings.

Between sixteen and eighteen, the boy, having achieved some skill in languages, should now concentrate on the classical poets who deal with practical subjects, and should dig deeper into scientific and technical studies—trigonometry, fortification, architecture, engineering, navigation, natural science, anatomy, and medicine—and here Milton follows Vives in advocating practical investigation of the environment and experiment in workshops. The third stage, between eighteen and twenty-one, continues similar activities to advanced levels.

To balance these excessive but unoriginal suggestions, Milton makes a commendable plea for the full and accurate use of the vernacular as the basis of education. He says: "Though a linguist should pride himself to learn all the tongues that Babel cleft the world into, yet, if he has not studied the solid things in them as well as the words and lexicons, he were nothing so much to be esteemed a learned man as any yeoman or tradesman competently wise in his mother dialect only". In discussing the making of a free commonwealth, he advocates schools "wherein children may be bred up to all learning and noble education, not in grammar only, but in all liberal arts and sciences. This would soon spread much more knowledge and civility—yea religion—through all parts of the land".

It is not unlikely that Milton's ungracious attitude towards Comenius may have been occasioned by some slight envy combined with umbrage. Comenius was famous by this time, and thus a target for criticism. He was no stylist, and probably not a scholar of Milton's calibre, yet he had won a world-wide reputation while Milton had not exactly swept England with his *Tractate*. Indeed, Cheyney Culpeper, a gentleman interested and active in educational reform, wrote to Hartlib in 1645: "There are some good sprinklings in his letter of education, but there is not descending enough into particulars but rather a general notion of what experience only can perfect".

John Dury (1596-1680), friend and colleague of Hartlib and Comenius, was linked to them not only by zeal for the reformation of church and school, but also by the possession of mutual acquaintances, especially in the Prussian port of Elbing where Hartlib's family lived, where there was a large group of Moravian brethren, and where Dury lived for a few years as minister of a reformed church of the English colony. Dury was born of a Scots family, who went to Europe in his infancy to escape religious difficulties in Scotland. The boy was educated at Sedan and Leyden, and after entering the ministry spent a great deal of time and effort trying to effect a reconciliation between the Reformed and Calvinistic churches. He had at heart throughout his life this question of the unification of the Protestant churches, although on his return to England in 1632 he entered the Church of England under the patronage of Archbishops Ussher and Laud, and played a part, as a member of the Assembly of Divines, in the drawing up of the Westminster Confession and Catechism in 1643.

He was very closely associated with Hartlib and Comenius during the latter's visit to England, and there can be no doubt that all three men found the association fruitful and stimulating in the extreme. Thus, while Dury would have been an outstanding personality and thinker of integrity under other circumstances, his debt to Comenius becomes obvious on examination of the content of Dury's educational writings between 1645 and 1654, during which period he remained in England. Hartlib wrote a preface to his main treatise on education, *The Reformed School*. His firm religious convictions form the basis of his educational ideas, for he advocates the formation of communities specially designed to ensure the Reformed School. The communities were to be Christian groups making strict rules of living and developing co-operative effort for the realisation of essential projects, including education. The new schools should train pupils to be "good Commonwealth's men" with experience and some skill in vocational activities, for the societies would need farmers, sailors, tradesmen, and administrators.

Dury's ideal is a small boarding school for boys, well staffed—four teachers to fifty boys—and having the aim to bring up Godly, healthy, well-mannered young people. Although the form of the school resembles Milton's ideal rather than that of Comenius, the latter's aims were identical with those of Dury, and both men added the acquisition of knowledge only as the "last and least part of true education". Dury discusses education at some length, expressing views in close agreement with those of his friend. Thus he speaks of making learning enjoyable so that nothing should be "tedious and grievous to the children". He discusses the need to learn "things and words" together, and urges, in particular, the study of science.   Moreover, the natural capacities of children should be studied in order that teaching could be adjusted to their needs.   A further indication of Dury's discipleship of Comenius is another work, *The Reformed Librarie Keeper*, which, no doubt, stimulated the development of many school libraries.

Comenian Ideas in England

When he was an old man of nearly seventy, Comenius still had the power to stir men to enthusiasm for teaching by demonstrating his methods.   Doubtless he would have inspired many English schoolmasters had time permitted, but in a few months he could do little to help teachers to grasp his principles.   Moreover, the most valuable writings on teaching method were never generally available, and the brief summaries published by Hartlib were inadequate. None of his disciples and imitators displayed genuine understanding of his fundamental concepts, but it is possible that a few intelligent teachers who met him were able to improve considerably their own teaching methods.

His main contributions to English education were in the encouragement of school foundations, the improvement of Latin teaching, and the recommendation of libraries for schools.   The list of school foundations—by patrons, by parishioners, and by the state—in the troubled years which followed, suggests a marked increase in elementary and grammar school education.   The success of *Orbis Pictus*, even if it did not necessarily bring in its train the improvement of teaching, showed that schoolmasters were giving thought to the matter.   The records of many school library foundations pay tribute to the inspiration of Dury and Comenius.

Charles Hoole,[1] who made the most popular version of the *Orbis Pictus*, held traditional ideas on curriculum, but his discussion of "The Petty School" in his work, *A New Discovery of the Old Art of Teaching School*, suggests that he was not unfamiliar with the ideas of Comenius on primary education.   Moreover, he recognised the value of practical observation and scientific study, for during his later teaching days in London he conducted his pupils on expeditions to Tradescant's museum of antiquities and curiosities. Thomas Horne, Master of Tonbridge Grammar School from 1640 to 1649, established a library at the school, thus following up the

[1] For some years Master of Rotherham Grammar School.

ideas acquired from his friend Hartlib, who, during his earlier days, had helped to "settle his spirit on . . . schooling".[1] The library still exists, and catalogues dated 1640 and 1680 recently came to light.[2] The first is a very short list of books, the second is long.

John Pell, the mathematician, and one of the most faithful correspondents of Comenius, had a sister, Mrs Bathsua Makin, who became a pioneer in the reform of girls' education. Her *Essay to Revive the Antient Education of Gentlewomen*[3] is largely a justification of her contention that girls can learn foreign languages as intelligently as boys, but she pays glowing tribute to "Mr Comenius", and indicates in various references, that she is familiar with his ideas. She was a tutor to royalty, a recognised teacher of gentlewomen, and thus, presumably, a member of the established Church. At the same time Adam Martindale, a Presbyterian preacher and teacher, forbidden by law after 1662 to keep a parish school, was demonstrating practical work in mathematics by taking the boys of Warrington Grammar School into the fields to practise surveying. Martindale also enjoyed reading the books of "Mr Comenius".[4]

Moreover, the knowledge of, and interest in, the ideas of Comenius on teaching, remained alive in England in the eighteenth century. Lest this should be doubted, in view of the considerable body of opinion to the contrary, the following extract is quoted from the preface to the eleventh edition (1727) of Hoole's translation of the *Orbis Pictus*, now in the writer's possession: ". . . Yet it were heartily to be wish'd, some Persons of Judgment and Interest, whose Example might have an influence upon others, and bring them into Reputation again, would revive the *Comenian Method* which is no other than to make our Scholars learn with Delight and cheerfulness, and to convey a solid and useful Knowledge of Things, with that of Languages in an easy, natural, and familiar way. His Didactic Works (as they are now collected into one volume) for a speedy attaining the Knowledge of Things and Words . . . for forming the Mind, and settling good Habits, may doubtless be look'd upon to contain the most reasonable, orderly, and complete System of the Art of Education, that can be met with".

[1] G. H. Turnbull, *Hartlib, Dury, and Comenius*, Liverpool, 1947.
[2] They were found in an old book by the writer during her visit to the Skinners' Library.
[3] Published in 1673.
[4] *Life of Adam Martindale*. Chetham Society, 1845.

Pietist Schools in Germany

No doubt there were similar cries in the European wilderness, but true Comenian thought was lost to Continental education because it was opposed by religious sects and frustrated by the inflexibility of State educational systems. Later, the Enlightenment grew bright enough to attract many wavering pedagogic moths, but before this happened, the turn of the century was not without its educational experiments and innovations. One of these is considered by some historians to have inspired the leaders of the English Charity School Movement, and as the Movement was undoubtedly an indirect outcome of the Comenian ferment, the new German scheme demands comparison with its predecessor.

During the last decade of the seventeenth century a sect of Lutheran Germans known as the Pietists became known, not only for their somewhat extreme religious views, but also for their considerable educational activities. To them, religion was very much a personal and individual concern and therefore they devoted much time to individual prayer, pious exercises, and the study of the Bible. Their austerity was extreme, for all worldly pleasures were abhorrent to them, and even in dealing with children they appear to have lacked the gentleness and broadmindedness of a Colet. Of their leaders, Jacob Spener and **August Herman Francke (1663-1727),** the latter was mainly responsible for the establishment and successful development of the schools of Halle which made his name as an educator. He was professor of Oriental Languages at Halle, and also pastor of a nearby village, but between 1694 and 1714 he poured forth his Pietist energy in a practical way, by founding and endowing several schools, an orphanage, and a training college for teachers. The schools catered for a wide age-range and for all classes, not together, it is true, for the school for poor children appears to have been separate from the school for townsmen's children. There was also the traditional Latin school for boys, but moreover, there was a secondary school for girls. It is said that there were over two thousand children in the institutions under his management at the time of his death.

As Francke's main aim was the provision of a good religious education for poor children, it is not surprising to find that his orphanage and elementary schools were very large, nor that his curriculum gave more than half the time to religion. School hours were seven to eleven and two to five in summer, and two hours less in winter, so that there were still several hours a day left for the learning of other subjects, especially as there were no intervals, no half-days, and no holidays. Writing and reading—mainly Luther's catechism and the New Testament—necessarily occupied much time, but arithmetic was introduced when pupils could read, and there was also some instruction in natural science and German literature and language. There was also some vocational training in manual activities.

In 1702 Francke published *Short and Simple Instruction: How Children are to be guided in True Piety and Christian Wisdom*, which emphasises the function of education as a means of conquering the wickedness of human nature. The Pietist attitude led to the application of a measure of strictness and severity in training that would never have won the approval of Comenius. Although some manuscripts of Comenius may have found their way to Halle, there is no real evidence that the Pietists used either his methods or curricula. Their main achievement was in showing that efficient education for all was a practical possibility.

Zinzendorf, the German noble who was later to lead the Moravian revival, was sent to Francke with a parental report that he was quick and intelligent, but that it would be necessary to keep a sharp rein on him "lest he should become too proud and presume too much upon his talents". Zinzendorf himself, wrote later that he had been punished severely for minor offences at school and had been made ridiculous in the eyes of his fellows. Nevertheless, the strong religious bias of the life at Halle fostered his natural inclination to study the religious basis of life, although in his later leadership of the Herrenhut community he found the gentler Comenian philosophy more satisfying than Pietism.

Moravian Schools in England

During the eighteenth century, Moravian missions organised by Zinzendorf's community, brought to England not only the Comenian spirit of brotherhood but also the Pietist practice of austerity. The schools, which were established in these new religious communities, appear to have been rather more comprehensive in curriculum and progressive in methods than the average eighteenth-century school. Some boys were prepared for trades, others grounded in the Classics; each boy's welfare was discussed at Staff meetings, and his moral, physical, and intellectual progress fostered with persistence and no little affection. There are reports of trips to Kirkstall Abbey; there is the chequered history of the building of an adjoining girls' school. There is much in these records which appears Comenian, but much also which reflects the bleak austerity of institutional life and the sentimental instability of the "enthusiast" temperament.

SUGGESTIONS FOR FURTHER READING

Several reprints of original texts are available and will repay further investigation. Bacon's *Advancement of Learning* has been reprinted by C.U.P., O.U.P., Dent, and Macmillan, and Milton's *Tractate of Education* by C.U.P. and Macmillan during the present century. Brinsley's *Grammar Schools* and Hoole's *New Discovery of the Old Art of Teaching School* have been edited by E. T. Campagnac (Liverpool, 1917 and 1913).

Of educational reformers in England, surprisingly little has been written. There are two studies of Hartlib, both somewhat scarce: *A Biographical Memoir of Samuel Hartlib*, by H. Dircks (Smith, 1865), and *Samuel Hartlib, a Sketch of his Life*, by G. H. Turnbull (Milford, 1920). Professor Turnbull has written more recently *Hartlib, Dury, and Comenius* (Liverpool, 1947), which presents recently rediscovered letters in a manner which gives the reader a personal acquaintance with the great men. R. F. Young's *Comenius in England* (O.U.P., 1932) throws light on the English educational situation.

Two books which emphasise vividly and vigorously the intense and widespread concern with education in the seventeenth century are Foster Watson's *Beginnings of the Teaching of Modern Subjects in England* (Pitman, 1909), and W. A. C. Vincent's *The State and School Education, 1640-1660* (S.P.C.K., 1950).

CHAPTER X

JOHN LOCKE, 1632-1704

John Locke was but a child when Comenius came to England. He was born into the professional classes, his father being a lawyer who joined the Parliamentary army. Little is known of his early upbringing, but his whole life appears to have been singularly free from feminine influence although he earned the respect and friendship of cultured women such as Lady Masham.[1] It is doubtful whether he shone in social life but he conformed to the conventions of behaviour and social intercourse of his day, winning approval as a guest and respect as an acquaintance, particularly in scientific circles. He was never robust, and as a weakly boy he hated Westminster School and its rough-and-tumble. In his *Thoughts* on education he writes: "What qualities are ordinarily to be got from such a troop of play-fellows as usually assemble together from parents of all kinds that a father should so much covet, is hard to divine. I am sure he who is able to be at the charge of a tutor at home may there give his son a more genteel carriage, more manly thoughts, and a sense of what is worthy and becoming, with a greater proficiency in learning into the bargain, and ripen him up sooner into a man, than any school can do".

Later, as a reserved young student at Oxford, he criticised the university practice of disputation, partly because of its artificiality and falsity, and partly, no doubt, because he did not enjoy such enforced self-display. His intellectual qualities, however, brought him success, and it is ironically significant that after taking his Master's degree he became a tutor at Christ Church, Oxford—and even reader in Greek and rhetoric. He was drawn towards philosophical studies and found Cartesian ideas particularly acceptable, but, having been left adequately provided for by his father, he was able to take his time in deciding on a career. He considered holy orders, medicine, and public affairs, in turn, and, having tried the last for which he was ill-fitted in health and temperament, studied medicine. Although he lacked paper qualifications owing to a

[1] Daughter of Cudworth, Cambridge Neo-Platonist, friend of Worthington, Master of Jesus, who handled Hartlib's papers after the latter's death. The papers included letters of Comenius.

disagreement with University authorities, his skill as a doctor in accomplishing a delicate operation, won him the friendship of a patient—Lord Ashley. It was this nobleman—later the first Lord Shaftesbury—who, not only gave Locke his first teaching post, but also, through his own political schemes and adventures, caused the near-persecution and exile of Locke, who seems to have dabbled in politics with no clear convictions or enthusiastic effort.

Locke was tutor to Ashley's son during a somewhat short period of his adolescence, and this poor specimen, who at the age of seventeen was pushed into marriage by his tutor, no doubt started Locke thinking about the problems of education. It seems probable that his own boyhood experiences, together with his difficulties in training this weakly boy, were fundamental causes of the "revolutionary" ideas on child education which later earned such wide recognition on the Continent and led directly to the even more unconventional theories of Rousseau. There were, however, other factors, by no means unimportant, which contributed to the development of Locke's ideas on education, and among these factors should be included his appreciation as a medical man of the physical needs of the individual child. Quite apart from the problem of the weakling in school, English schools were particularly bad for all boys at that time—as indicated by the "Children's Petition" presented to Parliament in 1669, "a modest remonstrance of that intolerable grievance our youth lie under in the accustomed severities of the school discipline of this nation". So ineffective was this petition that in 1698 a second appeal sought an Act "to remedy the foul abuse of children at schools, especially in the great schools of this nation".

Locke, however, had neither inclination nor opportunity to investigate existing conditions as a schoolmaster, for his connection with the Ashley family threw him into public life in spite of increasing ill-health.[1] Eventually, in 1675, he sought a milder climate and spent a few years in France during which he tutored a merchant's son for a time, and also made many contacts with scientists and doctors. When he obeyed Shaftesbury's summons to return to England, it was with reluctance and regret. His forebodings were fulfilled when, probably in all innocence, he was involved in his patron's political intrigues. He decided, being a

[1] His patron, while Lord Chancellor, appointed him Secretary of Presentations and Secretary to the Council for Trade and Foreign Plantations.

cautious man, to flee to Holland where he stayed for six years,[1] although the climate was too severe for him. He suffered attacks from England from time to time—for instance, his name was included in the list of "traitors and plotters" against the life of James II which was sent to the Dutch Government. Nevertheless it was in Holland that he first started to publish his philosophical and educational ideas. In addition to writing for a magazine, he almost completed a work of several years—*Essay Concerning the Human Understanding*. It was, however, his correspondence with a friend in England on the subject of the upbringing of the latter's son, which eventually gave to the world Locke's educational ideas. A few years after his return to England he was persuaded to publish these letters, together with some additional essays, as *Some Thoughts Concerning Education* and to this work he constantly made additions for the rest of his life.

William and Mary thought highly of Locke, whom they brought back to England, and he might have gained the highest diplomatic appointments had he not now been firm in his determination to avoid public life. In 1690 he published *Essay Concerning the Human Understanding*. He lived with the Masham family in Essex where he had opportunity to tutor Frank Masham from his fourth year and thus was enabled to test his theories more thoroughly than hitherto.

Although there appears to be no direct evidence that Locke owed any of his ideas to Comenius, it is difficult to believe that he had neither read the *Great Didactic* nor discussed education with men who had known the Moravian. It is certain that Locke was well known in scientific circles as a knowledgeable critic of conventional thought and practice in science and medicine. He was acquainted with scientists such as Goddard[2] and Boyle[3] who had shown interest in education from the time of the visit of Comenius to England. Both were members of the Committee for the Advancement of Learning set up in 1653. It is probable that the Royal Society itself was a direct result of discussions and correspondence of scientists with Comenius, for in the 'forties and 'fifties

---

[1] 1683-1689.

[2] Gresham Professor of Physic. His special interest in optical glasses may have inspired Locke's suggestion that glass-polishing would be a gentlemanly hobby.

[3] The Hon. Robert Boyle was a great friend of Hartlib and Dury. He was guardian of the latter's grandchildren for a time.

informal meetings in London and Oxford drew the giants of the scientific world and thus eventually emerged the Society which obtained its Charter in 1662. News of this success pleased Comenius greatly, for it was a partial realisation of his own great project—a Pansophic institution.

Apart from this possible link with Comenius through science, Locke must have learnt much of him from Hartlib with whom he was well acquainted. Nor is it unreasonable to suppose that he may have read Milton's views on education, and that he may even have read Charles Hoole's partial interpretation of the methods of Comenius. It certainly seems most unlikely that he would not have read the English summaries of Comenius's ideas, several of which were published during the years when Locke was developing his own educational ideas. In addition, during his six years in Holland in the 'eighties, he met many scholars, some of whom must have known Comenius who had died among them a decade earlier. This is not to suggest that Locke drew his inspiration from Comenius. Even those who had the closest contact with the latter seemed unable to comprehend the full significance of his educational theory, and in some ways, Locke's philosophy and methods are completely opposed to those of Comenius. It is possible, however, to see in the ideas of both men the trend of the thought-streams of their age.

The Philosophy of Locke

It is not possible to estimate adequately Locke's educational philosophy by an examination of the collection of rules and hints contained in his *Thoughts on Education.* His greater work which, as already indicated, was completed only after many years' labour, was not in any strict sense an educational treatise, nor were his educational views the logical outcome of the philosophical thought it contains. Yet Locke's philosophy, as expressed in the *Essay* coloured his ideas about education, and must be taken into account when analysing the *Thoughts.* His account of the origin of the great treatise is instructive in that it distinctly expresses its aim—an aim which has since frequently been misunderstood. In the Epistle to the Reader, he explains: "Were it fit to trouble thee with the history of this Essay, I should tell thee, that five or six friends meeting at my chamber, and discoursing on a subject very remote from this, found themselves quickly at a stand, by the difficulties that rose on every side. After we had awhile puzzled ourselves, without coming any nearer a resolution of these doubts which perplexed us, it came into my thoughts that we took a wrong course; and that before we set ourselves upon inquiries of that nature, it was necessary to examine our own abilities, and see what objects our understanding were, or were not, fitted to deal with. This I proposed to the company, who all readily assented; and thereupon it was agreed that this should be our first enquiry".[1]

His aim, therefore, was to examine and determine the nature and possible extent of human knowledge: his empiricism and theory of ideas are important subsidiaries to his main purpose. Obviously the conclusions at which he arrived were found to be significant for his views on the subject of education. The first book of the *Essay* is a polemic directed against the theory of innate ideas as taught by Descartes, Malebranche, and certain English thinkers of his age. Having given his reasons for rejecting this view, Locke proceeds in the second book to elaborate his own opinions. "Let us then suppose the mind to be, as we say, white paper, void of all characters, without any ideas:—How comes it to be furnished? Whence comes it by that vast store which the busy and boundless fancy of man has painted on it with an almost endless variety? Whence has it all the materials of reason and knowledge? To this I answer, in one word, from EXPERIENCE."[2]

Mental activities are primarily concerned with either the objects of the external world or with the operations of the mind. A knowledge of the external world is arrived at through the activities of the sense organs. The mind also perceives its own operations such as perception, thinking, doubting, believing, reasoning, knowing, and willing. The source of the former contents of the mind, Locke terms sensation; of the latter, reflection. The contents of the mind are indiscriminately termed ideas. He appeals to the reader's own experience to support his view. He says, "He that attentively considers the state of a child, at his first coming into the world, will have little reason to think him stored with plenty of ideas, that are to be the matter of his future knowledge. It is *by degrees* he comes to be furnished with them . . . But all that are

[1] *An Essay Concerning Human Understanding*, edited by H. C. Fraser, vol. 1, p. 9, Clarendon Press, 1894.
[2] *ibid.*, pp. 121-2.

born into the world, being surrounded with bodies that perpetually and diversely affect them, variety of ideas, whether care be taken of it or not, are imprinted on the minds of children. Light and colours are busy at hand everywhere, when the eye is but open; sounds and some tangible qualities fail not to solicit their proper senses, and force an entrance to the mind; but yet, I think, it will be granted easily, that if a child were kept in a place where he never saw any other but black and white till he were a man, he would have no more ideas of scarlet or green than he that from his childhood never tasted an oyster, or a pineapple, has of those particular relishes".[1]

Ideas derived from sensation are first in the child's experience. Then when he grows older he begins to contemplate the operations of his own mind. The ideas which enter consciousness from these two sources are termed simple ideas. Locke analyses them into ideas that come from one sense only; those which are the result of the stimulation of more than one sense; those which originate in reflection alone; and those which are produced by a combination of all the ways of sensation and reflection. It is from the last that we obtain our notions of pleasure and pain, power, existence, unity, and succession.

This account does not exhaust the catalogue of the mind's contents. The mind is passive in the reception of simple ideas but once it has received them, it is able to act upon them in various ways, either by combining them into a compound idea, or by setting them side by side and so perceiving the relation between them, or by separating them from all accompanying ideas, that is, by "abstraction". It is in this way that complex ideas are formed. Ideas of beauty, of substance, and of relations are complex ideas but they have all grown out of the simple ideas which sprang from experience.

It is irrelevant to follow Locke into the distinction he draws between primary qualities such as solidity, extension, figure, motion, and number, which are inseparable from a body, and the secondary qualities such as colours, sounds, and tastes which are not in the objects themselves but which are produced in man by the primary qualities of objects. There are, however, certain features of Locke's account which call for comment. In the first place, it should be

---

[1] *An Essay Concerning Human Understanding*, edited by H. C. Fraser, vol. 1, pp. 125-6, Clarendon Press, 1894

noted that the passivity and receptivity of the mind is emphasised by this theory. Objects of the external world affect the sense organs and the mind passively receives the reports made by them. It is true that the mind is active in combining simple into complex ideas, though it is difficult to conceive how a mind which is a *tabula rasa* can be active at all. To *be*, the mind must *do* something. Locke has dismissed innate ideas but it might be urged that he has not disposed of the view that the mind is furnished with certain innate capacities which need experience before they can become explicit. As Kant was to show in the following century, the idea that every effect has a cause cannot be derived from experience but depends upon the nature of the mind itself. Locke's view of experience as a passive process was responsible for the traditional title of the "Five Gateways of Knowledge" as applied to the senses—a view which was both soundly and humorously criticised by Adams in his *Herbartian Psychology*. In truth, Locke had not adequately analysed what he meant by the term "experience" and it was the merit of Dewey's philosophy that it stressed the dual nature of experience as possessing both an active and a passive aspect.

Locke was perhaps unfortunate in using the term "idea" to cover the whole of mental content. Plato had restricted the term to those universal notions which he ascribed to an extra-mental existence. By the seventeenth century it had undergone a considerable development and was being applied in diverse ways; some limited and restricted, others very wide in their extent. Thus some thinkers limited "idea" to the realm of sense perception and imagination. Even in this case, ambiguity existed. Did the term apply to the process of cognition, or to the mental content, or to both ? The Cambridge Platonists had reverted to the older meaning of the term as found in the Platonic Dialogues.

Locke adopted the terminology of Descartes who employed the word "idea" to cover all mental content. As he said in his letter to Stillingfleet, it represented "whatever is meant by phantasm, notion, species, or whatever it is which the mind can be employed about in thinking". Descartes's own usage was derived from Aquinas and the schoolmen.

Aquinas in his theory of knowledge had distinguished between two modes of being which an object can possess by the use of the terms *esse naturale* and *esse intentionale*, that is, being as an object of nature and being as an object of thought. Thus, a tree has a primary existence as an object of the external world but it also exists as an object of thought in the minds of those who perceive it. Descartes was following a similar line of thought when he used the term *esse objectivum* to denote the existence of anything as an object of thought. The *esse objectivum* or objective reality of my idea of an oak consists of the qualities which are attributed to the oak when I think of it. The term "objective" as used by Descartes should not be interpreted as indicating that the idea asserts anything corresponding to it in *rerum natura*. The qualities I attribute to a fabulous animal such as the unicorn constitute the objective reality of my idea of unicorn. It is true that Locke did not employ the terminology of Descartes when speaking of ideas, though he must have been acquainted with it, but he followed the French philosopher in making the term "idea" apply to any mental content.

When he deals with the ideas which are derived from sensation, Locke teaches a doctrine of representative perception. This is the view that the idea signifies or represents the object perceived. The scholastic view was that in both perceptual and conceptual thinking, the individual attains to a knowledge of the essence of objects. Locke rejects this and asserts that ideas are signs or representations of a world of things external to the mind. A. N. Whitehead criticises this theory in a well-known passage. "Thus the bodies are perceived as with qualities which in reality do not belong to them, qualities which in fact are purely the offspring of the mind. Thus nature gets the credit which should in truth be reserved for ourselves; the rose for its scent; the nightingale for his song; and the sun for his radiance. The poets are entirely mistaken. They should address their lyrics to themselves, and should turn them into odes of self-congratulation on the excellency of the human mind. Nature is a dull affair, soundless, scentless, colourless; merely the hurrying of material, endlessly, meaninglessly."[1]

Locke defined knowledge as consisting in the perception of the agreement or disagreement between our ideas. He gave so wide an extension to the meaning of the term "idea" that he failed to distinguish between the idea as a notion and the mental image. He wrote, "Does it not require some pains and skill to form the general idea of a triangle (which is yet none of the most abstract,

[1] *Science and the Modern World*, pp. 68-9, C.U.P., 1927.

comprehensive, and difficult) for it must be neither oblique nor rectangle, neither equilateral, equicrural, nor scalenon; but all and none of these at one ".[1] In other words, the general idea is a kind of composite image compounded from all the varieties of triangle. Berkeley, who like Locke confused abstract and general ideas with sensuous images, had no difficulty in starting from the same premises and confuting Locke's assertion. "If any man has the faculty of framing in his mind such an idea of a triangle as is here described, it is vain to pretend to dispute him out of it. All I desire is that the reader would fully and certainly inform himself whether he has such an idea or not—and try whether he has, or can attain to have the general idea of a triangle which is neither— etc."[2] It was not until Aveling's investigation which was described in his *Consciousness of the Universal*[3] that the image was clearly distinguished from the universal idea and the function of imagery in conceptual thinking fully explained.

Of the Conduct of the Understanding

Locke was not entirely satisfied with his *An Essay Concerning Human Understanding* in spite of the years of labour spent on it. Seven years after its publication he turned over in his mind possible additions to the *Essay* and decided on a chapter to be called "Of the Conduct of the Understanding" which, he reported to his friend Molyneux, might turn out to be the largest chapter of the *Essay*. As he wrote, however, it grew into a short treatise which is, in many ways, complementary to the *Thoughts Concerning Education*, for while the latter considers the upbringing and training of young gentlemen by tutors and parents, the *Conduct* presents to those same young gentlemen principles and methods for their further self-development at the university stage. Professor J. W. Adamson ranks the *Conduct* with the great "courtesy" books of the sixteenth and seventeenth century. The treatise appears to be incomplete, and it was not published during Locke's lifetime.

Locke's main contention is that man's understanding determines so completely his attitude and his achievements that it must be carefully trained in order that it may guide him truly. It is even more important than the will, for it must come into play before

[1] *An Essay Concerning Human Understanding*, Book IV, c. 7, para. 9.
[2] *Introduction to the Principles of Human Knowledge*, Berkeley's Complete Works, vol. 1, p. 246, Clarendon Press, 1901.
[3] Aveling, *Consciousness of the Universal*, Macmillan, 1912.

any voluntary action in order to provide a reason for that action. The understanding has the task of passing judgment on the ideas and images in the mind, thus each man ought to train his own understanding and not depend on "rules that have served the learned world these two or three thousand years". Locke points out that Bacon had urged the search for truth through the better use of the individual mind, and he joins with his predecessor in advocating the study of the differences between men, and the factors operating in the processes of understanding. This appears to be a plea for the organisation of that body of knowledge now called psychology.

Locke contradicts one of his former contentions in asserting that men are born with different capacities and aptitudes. In the *Thoughts* he puts forward the *tabula rasa* concept of many of his predecessors, but now he admits, "Amongst men of equal education there is great inequality of parts", and on the other hand, "the woods of America, as well as the schools of Athens, produce men of several abilities in the same kind". Nevertheless very few men, even those most gifted by nature, reach the full and accurate use of their powers, because most people depend on a few misapplied rules of logic for the conduct of their understanding. Faults in this faculty of the mind may "keep them in ignorance and error all their lives".

One of the main faults is the misuse of reasoning power. Some people merely accept as valid what others think, some use not reason to decide their actions and beliefs, but their own inclinations and self interest. Still other people do their best to reason soundly, but because they lack "large sound, roundabout sense", they do not know enough to give balanced judgment and so often see only one side of a matter. Even the most able people are liable to this failing, the remedy for which is contact with other minds by discussion. Those able men who yet make little advance in their search for truth, usually talk to men of their own kind, and read "but one sort of books", and so are set in their one-sided notions. To reach truth it is essential to hear and examine all points of view, for "to prejudice other men's notions before we have looked into them is not to show their darkness, but to put out our own eyes". The reason of man enables him to sift the gold from the dross but this faculty is "spoiled and lost by assuming prejudices" when it is not fully exercised. Locke attributes the lack of sympathy between classes and between professions to man's habit of becoming "muffled up in the infallibility of his own sect". Particularly in philosophy and religion it is essential to explore widely. "I do not say to be a good geographer", says he, "that a man should visit every mountain, river, promontory, and creek upon the face of the earth, view the buildings and survey the land everywhere as if he were going to make a purchase; but yet every one must allow that he shall know a country better that often makes sallies into it and traverses up and down, than he that like a mill horse goes still round in the same track".

In addition to this width of experience, man needs exercise in the correct use of his mental faculties, for although "we are born with faculties and powers capable of almost anything", only practice and the acquisition of good habits will bring those gifts to fruition, whether the result is a physical skill, artistic achievement, or mental agility. Thus although there may be innate differences from man to man, in the capacity to understand, the differences which are actually observable are the result of habits over a considerable period, for "nobody is made anything by hearing of rules or laying them up in his memory". The stupidity of most men in discussions on religion is but one instance of lack of practice, for they are usually "dexterous and sharp enough in making a bargain". Moreover, it is essential to ensure that whether in contemplation or discussion, the true relationship between ideas and the words which represent them, is realised—a matter discussed at greater length in the *Essay*. Principles likewise must be examined, for it is not enough to hold an opinion without a sound reason for holding it. Hasty, unconsidered generalisations, as, "This is a new idea, therefore it must be false" are dangerous, being based on "wrong measures". Men who adhere earnestly to false principles are at least preferable to those who are always wavering and uncertain. Neither have had exercise in the particular kind of reasoning involved, and, indeed, most men so lack this skill that they do not realise their inability. Even in business matters men are prone to blame others for failure rather than themselves. How much greater is their failure and ignorance of failure, in other matters. Indeed, "You may as well set a countryman, who scarce knows the figures and never casts up a sum of three particulars, to state a merchant's long account, and find the true balance of it".

At this point Locke introduces his main remedy for this lack of training in reasoning—the study of mathematics. There is a strong hint of the idea of transfer of training here, but although the aim is to exercise the mind "in observing the connection of ideas and following them in train", it is also to show the student that he cannot expect to reason well in all things without practice. Practice in reasoning in one sphere is no guarantee of ability to reason soundly in another, although that ability may be achieved by practice. Thus it is desirable for young men to have as much practice as possible in a variety of fields, for it is not so easy to find time for such practice later on. "The lucky chance of education" offers a man opportunities to develop his understanding.

The main advantage to be gained from the study of mathematics is not so much advanced skill in the subject, as the experience of searching for truth, for "where a truth is made out by one demonstration, there needs no further inquiry, but in probabilities where there wants demonstration to establish the truth beyond doubt, there it is not enough to trace one argument to its source, and observe its strength and weakness, but all the arguments after having been so examined on both sides, must be laid in balance one against another, and upon the whole of the understanding determine its assent". The practice of disputation in universities accustoms students to decide truth or falsehood on a basis of one argument, and it would be a great advance if the habit of taking into account many views instead of one, could replace the existent danger of "error by presumption, laziness, or precipitancy".

In addition, the study of mathematics will make a man aware of the limitations of his powers of reasoning, for he will not always be successful, and he will not be so apt to think "that there could be nothing added to the acuteness and penetration" of his understanding.

While admitting "nobody is under an obligation to know everything", Locke deplores the general English attitude to religion. He deems the French peasants to be much more knowledgeable and understanding in such matters than English gentlemen, whose ideas are usually limited to those gained through the senses. They should take care to furnish their minds with moral and more abstract ideas, and, moreover, to exercise their reasoning on these matters. Their own views should be examined before those of other people are criticised, for few are free from "the prejudices imbibed from education, party, reverence, fashion, and interest". Locke points out that no one who has reasoned within himself to reach his own opinions need fear putting them forward for examination and criticism by others. In testing the ground on which his arguments stand he will discover whether he has reached the truth or whether his opinions are based on mere custom or prejudice.

Locke believes it is possible to test and re-test reasoning processes to ensure that skill in conducting the understanding has been achieved. It is essential to find true principles, for "to be indifferent whether we embrace falsehood or truth is the great road to error". In education, particular care should be taken that students are made aware of the characteristics and consequences of faulty understanding. Reading, which plays a great part in education, has a dangerous tendency not only to inculcate the faulty, biased, unsound opinion of the writers, but also to encourage the formulation of conclusions too hastily on too little evidence, and often with too little effort. While distrusting the result of encyclopaedic learning, he admits that a man of affairs, with the best intentions, has little time to do more than study "the business of his particular calling in the commonwealth and of religion which is his calling as he is a man in the world". At the same time he regrets that more people cannot have enough leisure to examine many branches of knowledge and to experience the various ways of enquiry and reasoning necessary in wide studies. This would remedy the common failing of the specialists—the application of the standards, techniques, and modes of thought of the one thing to all other things. The mind needs "a fair and equal view of the whole intellectual world", and such can be given as part of education, the function of which is not to make boys perfect in any one subject but "to open and dispose their minds as may best make them capable of any when they shall apply themselves to it".

It is not enough, however, merely to read widely, accepting the opinions of writers and learning facts by rote. It is the teacher's task to show pupils how to exercise judgment in reading, for few young people have the ability to weigh up written arguments without help. Thinking about what is read should become a habit through exercise and it will not long be "a clog and rub" to the reader, for he will soon find his reading much more enjoyable.

Much of the rest of the treatise continues this discussion of profitable reading. Many pitfalls for the shallow reader are indicated —faulty arguments and opinions, misleading words, wrong association of ideas, and also readers' faults such as the wandering of attention which, says Locke, afflicts the most earnest of us. Books, he asserts, are often a hindrance to learning, yet some men "scarcely allow themselves time to eat or sleep, but read and read and read on, yet make no great advances in their intellectual faculties". Always he reverts to his contention that we cannot profit from other men's opinions "till we ourselves see it with our own eyes, and perceive it by our own understandings". We must persevere in our efforts to perfect our own reasoning faculties and not be led astray by emotional weaknesses, among which he numbers despondency, lack of perseverance, over-anticipation, indecision, and what is called to-day, wishful thinking. We must search constantly for fundamental verities, for "truth . . . is the measure of knowledge and the business of the understanding".

Some Thoughts Concerning Education

Because our faculties and abilities can develop in any direction, says Locke, it is important to ensure the exercise only of those powers which give us skill in the "right" direction. These powers are of the body as well as of the mind, and thus both body and mind must have practice in activities which develop desirable qualities. Although natural endowments and tendencies may contribute in a small degree to the make-up of the adult person, environmental factors play by far the greatest part, whether for good or ill. This basic assumption explains why Locke sets the acquisition of good physical habits side by side with the development of mental capacities in his scheme of education. His preliminary preoccupation with the child's habituation to austere conditions may also be due partly to his medical interests, and partly to his knowledge of Greek ideas on education. It is certainly related to the struggle of the "new" scientists to dissuade the layman from old practices based on ignorance and superstition. Medical science was still sadly inadequate according to modern ideas, while standards of hygiene in both home and street were still crude and primitive. Waves of plague swept over the country from time to time; water was scarce and usually polluted; clothing was hand-made and voluminous, therefore valuable, and it could not be sent to the cleaners. There appears to have been a high incidence of child mortality, for in the correspondence and literature of the times there are frequent references to sickly, ailing children.

John Locke, therefore, set out to encourage the protection of children from the factors of the environment harmful to their physical welfare. Because the strictures on this matter are given first in *Some Thoughts*, it is customary to conclude that he ranks vigour of body as a main aim of education together with his other main aims—morality and knowledge. Lest too much emphasis be laid on this arrangement as a possible innovation resulting from his own medical knowledge, a weakly childhood and criticism of current convention, the reader may do well to glance again at the summary of the *School of Infancy* of Comenius. It will then be clear that although Locke mentions in none of his works the name of Comenius, nor acknowledges his debt to any other educational thinker, he had, in fact, adopted wholesale not only the opinions of the seventeenth-century reformers, but also the essential principles of Comenian child welfare and education.

Perhaps Locke's main original contribution to education—as distinct from philosophy—is his principle of "hardening" both the body and the mind. Thus where Comenius would have great care taken of the small child lest it should be hurt or feel too keenly the elements, Locke would accustom the child to discomfort, to simple, light clothes in winter, and even to leaky shoes. Comenius, of course, had in mind the children of poor, frugal, exiled brethren, while Locke knew only those small rich folk weighed down with heavy replicas of their parents' garments. In other matters of health, however, Locke reproduces most of the Moravian's rules— constant dosing with medicine to be avoided, plenty of sleep and exercise to be ensured, food to be simple, and drink not to include wine, but to consist mainly of light ale.[1] While Comenius indicates mildly but frequently that education should train children in self-restraint and discipline in these matters, Locke voices his prohibitions in strong terms. Both, however, believe, as Locke expresses it, "The great thing to be minded about Education is what Habits you settle".

Moreover, Locke does not intend the hardening process to be dangerous to children. He wishes to free them from "clothes that pinch", and from food which spoils the teeth, but he also wishes

[1] Comenius suggested milk.

to deter them from foolish actions such as lying on the cold ground when hot after exercise, and eating too much fruit. His whole object is to ensure restraint, moderation, and regularity in physical habits for he attributes to over-indulgence the delicacy and weakness of constitution so often found in gentlemen's children. The child should eat and drink just enough, should sleep long enough but not too long in a hard bed, should take care "to go constantly to the Necessary House" so that purging, weakening physic will not be needed. Rousseau over half a century later accepted Locke's "hardening" principle, commenting that Nature does not coddle.

Locke would have an exactly similar treatment in the inculcation of good manners and virtuous habits of mind, for a further great aim of education is to produce well-bred young people, wise in conduct, and honest, courteous, and sincere in attitude. "To deny himself his own desires" is the quality of a virtuous man, and the only way to educate children to such virtue is to refrain from condoning slack behaviour even in the very young. If children learn that crying gains "Grapes or Sugar Plumbs", that aggressive actions go unchecked, that parents are vain, untruthful, and intemperate, it can hardly be expected they will be self-disciplined; but on the other hand, undue severity, even in a righteous parent, will achieve no greater success, for they will be "wicked in private".

"If, therefore," asserts Locke, "a strict Hand be kept over Children *from the Beginning*, they will in that Age be tractable, and quietly submit to it, as never having known any other". It is important that they should hold parents in awe and respect from the earliest years, for "it will cost Pains and Blows to recover it, the more the longer it is deferred". In keeping children in "fear and awe" parents ensure opportunities for the development of self-control, for "every man must some time or other be trusted to himself and his own conduct". Education—and Locke means, in this instance, habit training—should put into a child "what is to sway and influence his life", so that his attitude and behaviour will be honest and dependable. Firmness in this habit-training, however, does not entail harsh punishment, which does more harm than good. The function of education is to help the child to learn how to use his reason more and more in the making of decisions, thus it is useless to keep the child too submissive and too sheltered, for enterprise and courage are qualities to be encouraged. Too many prohibitions, and too frequent application of the rod not only indicate laziness on the part of the teacher, but also train the child to behave well *with the wrong motives*.

Locke believes that unhappy experiences cause children to dislike those parts of learning with which the experience is associated. If beaten or scolded, the child may submit to the teacher's will either temporarily, until the latter is not present, or permanently as a spiritless nonentity. Yet, firmly but kindly instructed, he might have found the desirable course of action much to his own taste, or he might have reasoned that it would be a wise course for him to take. Rewards are as dangerous as punishments, for again it means that there is a wrong motive behind the child's obedience, and, moreover, the granting of rewards tempts the parent into over-indulgence. The only way to ensure the right kind of effort on the part of the child, in any aspect of learning, moral or otherwise, is to establish authority firmly and quickly—by the rod if necessary—and then to depend upon the results of esteem and disgrace to regulate the child's behaviour, for he is extremely sensitive to the attitude of elders he loves and respects. Praise and commendation of a child may well be most effective in the presence of other children, but his faults are best reviewed in private for he then knows he still has the good opinion of others and will do his best to keep it.

"Playing, and childish actions are to be left perfectly free and unrestrained," says Locke, for such activities are necessary, and restraint will come naturally in time; though children should have enough sense and courtesy to stop a noisy game at a look from a parent. That is to say, the authority of the parent should be absolute but nevertheless easy, friendly, and indeed, hardly noticeable. To be burdened by rules is an unhappy state for children, for they cannot be expected to remember words and ideas which they often do not understand. Right ways of behaviour are ensured by experience itself under parent's or tutor's guidance. Adults should beware of making rules which it is beyond the capacities of children to keep. If there must be rules, let them be "rather fewer than seem absolutely necessary". The guidance already mentioned should be by kind words and "gentle admonitions", and also by training in one habit at a time by repeated practice. Most important of all, the guidance should be based on a study of "natures and aptitudes", for the aim is not to turn all children out to the same pattern, but "to make the best of what Nature has given".

On the other hand, parents owe it to their children to see they are well versed in accomplishments and manners of conventional society, but this can be done mainly by setting them good examples to imitate so that they will take pleasure and pride in "making a leg", dressing neatly, and speaking politely. They will grow into such behaviour naturally and gracefully, and will not appear affected as they might if good manners were only assumed on special occasions. More important than polite accomplishments are those qualities of character expressed in "respect and good will to all people"— qualities which cannot be developed by "occasional lectures", but which emerge through "reiterated actions fashioned beforehand into the practice of what is fit and becoming".

Perhaps the essence of Locke's theory lies in the words he uses in discussing this topic. "We are all a sort of chameleon that still take a tincture from things near us; nor is it to be wondered at in children, who better understand what they see than what they hear." One is reminded of Aristotle's warnings about the dangers of leaving children in charge of servants, for Locke frequently refers not only to the likelihood of spoiling and inconsistency—the undermining of parental authority—but also to the "ill examples" met with among "the meaner servants", especially in habits and language. He finds the same dangers in schools, and asserts that parents risk their sons' "innocence and virtue for a little Greek and Latin". He puts forward an interesting argument that since girls show no backwardness or lack of assurance by being educated at home, why should it be considered essential for boys to have the wider experience of school ? "Virtue is harder to be got than a knowledge of the world," says Locke, "and if lost in a young man is seldom recovered".

Schools, he believes, cannot give adequate personal supervision to each boy, so that the other aspects of education apart from book-learning, are neglected. The boys do not learn much of one another. Although he advocates no reform of schools, his arguments for the necessity of moral education might have been written yesterday, especially those dealing with the decay in religion and morals of the times, and the "acquired improvements" of society. He pleads that the foundations of the great virtues must be "laid in the education and principling of the youth". Only the tutor, a man of integrity as well as learning, can take the place of the parent in laying those foundations through his close personal relations with an individual pupil whose book-learning, social experience, and moral training can be carefully organised and guided.

Moreover, the tutor, unlike the schoolmaster, can find ways of giving his pupil "a liking and inclination to what he proposes to be learnt". He can observe his interests, and moods, and take opportunities not open to the schoolmaster, for the pupil will "learn three times as much when he is in tune . . . Children might be permitted to weary themselves with play and yet have time enough to learn what is suited to the capacity of each age". Such is his faith in the power of a good tutor that he asserts, "a child may be brought to desire to be taught any thing you have a mind he should learn", and because children love to be busy there is hardly any limit to what can be achieved by skill and gentleness. There should be no need for coercion except in cases of obstinate and continued disobedience.

This leads to a consideration of the opportunities offered, in dealing with small misdemeanours, for simple exercises in the use of the reason. By explaining to him "in very few and plain words", the tutor not only pleases the child by this man-to-man treatment, but also ensures that he obtains practice in reasoning within the limits of his immature capacities. This contention that children should be treated as rational creatures is one of Locke's great contributions to educational thought. He states clearly that he does not suggest they can reason from remote principles, but they ought to have experience in simple reasoning from the earliest possible age. This does not mean that the way of teaching by suggestion and example shall be abandoned when discussion is embarked upon, for good examples are of utmost importance at all stages of education—an additional reason for the selection of a tutor of very high moral calibre and knowledge of the world. Locke's ideal tutor would be, indeed, a paragon versed in "an art not to be learnt nor taught by books".

Locke's principles of education have a distinct Aristotelian flavour, especially in the general and persistent requirement that the immature human being shall not be sheltered from the physical, mental, and spiritual dangers of environment and society, but should be so carefully introduced to them, and so skilfully induced to reason about them, that he achieves balance and self-control in all aspects of behaviour and thought. His guides—tutor and father—

should set an example of upright living in a real but faulty world, and the tutor, in particular, should not only be a man of high intellectual and moral quality, and accurately developed reasoning power, but should also be a man who has lived in society and has gained its accomplishments while resisting its temptations. "The only fence against the world," asserts Locke, "is a thorough knowledge of it, into which a young gentleman should be entered by degrees, as he can bear it; and the earlier the better, so he be in safe and skilful hands to guide him". These skilful hands should "fashion the carriage and form the mind" so that the boy acquires not only good habits, but also the capacity to recognise virtue and wisdom, and a willingness to emulate only the best that he sees in the "little view of mankind" shown him by his tutor. Yet from time to time Locke emphasises that the pupil will learn little of value as a mere onlooker. He must experience the kind of discomfort, problems, and evils to be encountered in the adult world, but he must meet them under such conditions, that to withstand, to solve, to conquer, is within his capacity if he makes the effort necessary in all learning and developing.

This general argument is the basis of all Locke's more detailed considerations. Even as Plato criticised the inconsistency and foolishness of Athenian parents, so Locke deplored the two extremes he observed in the society of his own day—harshness to children in the inculcation of knowledge, and excessive indulgence in matters of food, dress, and behaviour within the family circles. Both educators, however, were concerned only with upper class children and parents, though this main principle might well be worthy of wider application, if only because it involves essentially the treatment of the pupil as an individual. For instance, Locke suggests observation of the child at play in order to discover "predominate passions and prevailing inclinations", for the make-up of each child is different, and the adult attitude and methods of training must be adjusted accordingly. The reason he gives for an early study of the child's nature is interesting and significant, for it is sometimes forgotten that his acceptance of the *tabula rasa* concept has certain reservations. He admits, like most modern psychologists and educators, that Nature contributes a persistent though perhaps not a controlling factor to the sum total of the characteristics of the human adult. Thus education should always work with Nature, fostering good qualities and modifying weaknesses, for "after all is done, the byass will always hang on that side that Nature first plac'd it".

A further implication of Locke's general principle is that true education is the gaining of self-control by the individual. Unlike the Herbartian teacher, the tutor does not so much mould the pupil as induce and encourage him to mould himself. Locke's tutor would provide "learning situations" just as carefully as would the tutor of "Émile". The main differences are that Locke's pupil would face more discomforts and dangers at an earlier age than Rousseau's pupil, and the former would be expected to rationalise from his sense experience and from human situations much sooner than the latter. The former would learn to control his impulse to play with fire by mild personal injury, and similarly he would control his irrational fear of the strange and the ugly by being brought again and again into contact with things to which he shows aversion: if he runs away from a frog he must be made to look at it again and finally to handle it. Intellectual self-control should be fostered by giving experience and practice. The tutor should answer his questions truthfully whenever the thirst for knowledge appear genuine, and should reason with him calmly and kindly about his own small faults and failings. Physically, morally, and mentally the pupil needs to face up to minor difficulties, so developing himself for the facing of greater problems as he grows older.

Locke's insistence on the self-development of the pupil impinges on yet another principle accepted in modern education, for it follows that self-development results from constant activity of one kind and another. "Children generally hate to be idle," says Locke, thus the tutor's task is to tempt or trick them into worth-while pursuits but the suggestions as to how this may be accomplished are not always convincing. Some modern parents would agree that to set a child to one kind of play activity for long periods every day is the surest way of tiring him of it, but fewer would believe either that the modern child would submit to such "business required of him" or that he would inevitably turn to his books or other educational pursuits. One point, however, might well be heeded to-day —the suggestion that skill, ingenuity, and enterprise should be developed by the making of most of their toys by children themselves.

Having dealt—at some length and with frequent repetition—with methods of ensuring that the young human being obtains practice in self-control, Locke considers the content of education. It is hoped to develop in the pupil virtue, wisdom, breeding, and learning, in that order: —

Virtue: —   "There ought very early to be imprinted on his mind a true notion of God . . . from whom we receive all our good, who loves us and gives us all things."

"Having laid the foundation of virtue . . . as far as this age is capable, by accustoming him to pray to Him, the next thing is to keep him exactly to speaking of truth and inclining him to be good natured."

Wisdom: —"This is the product of a good temper, application of mind and experience together and so above the reach of children. To accustom a child to have true notions of things and not to be satisfied till he has them, raise his mind to great and worthy thoughts and to keep him at a distance from falsehood and cunning, is the fittest preparation of a child for wisdom."

Breeding: —"Two things are requisite: First a disposition of the mind not to offend others: and secondly, the most acceptable and agreeable way of expressing that disposition. From the one men are called civil; from the other well-fashion'd . . . The other part, which lies deeper than the outside is that general good-will and regard for all people which makes any one have a care not to show in his carriage any contempt, disrespect or neglect of them."

Learning: —"I think it is the least part . . . When I consider what ado is made about a little Latin and Greek, how many years are spent on it, and what a noise and business it makes to no purpose, I can hardly forbear thinking that the parents of children still live in fear of the schoolmaster's rod which they look on as the only instrument of education. How else is it possible that a child should be chain'd to the oar seven, eight, or ten of the best years of his life to get a language or two, which, I think might be had at a great deal cheaper rate of pains and time, and be learn'd almost in playing."

It is clear to Locke that the first three parts of education are best acquired from example rather than from precept, and that the protection of the pupil from bad company and undesirable example should be the prime task of tutor and parent. Children must not be infected with fear of the unknown, especially of the spirit world; they should not be driven to lying through fear; they should not be praised for showy expositions of superficial wisdom, and they should not be perplexed by the manners of the fashionable world which often shows polite conventions such as "putting off hats" and "making legs" in association with ugly behaviour such as ridicule, contradiction, and affectation.

The business of acquiring knowledge is more straightforward but equally open to error and abuse. Early learning can be made pleasant for children and they will even "seek it as another sort of play" if lessons and books are not forced upon them, and if the attitude of the parents suggests that learning is a privilege and a pleasure. The kind of toys Locke describes as suitable for teaching children to read and count, are not unlike the toys suggested by Comenius and earlier writers. Children may be cheated into learning but not hastened against their own inclination. Any small restrictions and corrections should be in cases of untruthfulness or other ill-behaviour, and not for unwillingness to learn. When a child is ready to read, however, he should be given only books suited to his capacity and at the same time excellent in style and moral content. "If his Aesop has Pictures in it," says Locke, "it will entertain him much the better, and encourage him to read when it carries the Increase of Knowledge with it: for such visible Objects children hear talked of in vain and without any Satisfaction whilst they have no Ideas of them; those ideas being not to be had from Sounds, but from the Things themselves or their Pictures". This again, reflects the main didactic principles of Comenius. Similarly Locke's insistence on the careful teaching of writing resembles Comenius's emphasis on the right way of holding a pen and making strokes.[1] Locke's main original contribution is a suggestion that a boy showing interest and manual dexterity may be allowed to go on to drawing.

As soon as a boy can speak English he should start learning French because it is a living language and "people are accustomed

---

[1] Brinsley had paid much attention to the teaching of writing at the beginning of the century (*Ludus Literarius or the Grammar School*).

to the right way of teaching that Language, which is by talking it into Children in constant Conversation and not by grammatical rules". He should proceed to Latin in a year or two, preferably by the same method, but care must be taken to keep up his English reading. "Latin I look upon as the absolute necessary to a Gentleman," says Locke, thus summarising the attitude of his times which had seen the production of many new editions of *Lily's Grammar*, and many *Januas*, as well as the unique *Orbis Pictus*. As he admits, custom had made Latin "so much a part of Education" that the schools continued to impose it upon boys who would never need it or relish it in after life. The schools, he points out, were full of boys intended for trade, commerce, and farming, who would be better equipped were they able to write a good hand and cast accounts. Yet their fathers expected their boys to be taught Latin "as if their children had scarce an orthodox education unless they learned Lilly's Grammar".

Apart from this, however, the grammar school method of teaching is at fault says Locke. A skilled teacher could make the learning of Latin as pleasant and easy as the learning of English, and moreover, he could ensure that the pupil "might have his mind and manners formed, and he be instructed to boot in several sciences such as are a good part of geography, astronomy, chronology, anatomy, besides some parts of history, and all other parts of knowledge of things that fall under the senses". It is difficult to believe that such a suggestion comes not from Locke's contact with Comenian educators, but solely from his rational philosophy. The direct or conversational method advocated by Locke enables the tutor to take into account the varied and transient interests of children and so win their attention and co-operation without exercising "such an austerity (as) may make their government easy to themselves, but of very little use to their pupils". Locke holds the teaching of grammar to be fruitless; he points out that Englishmen who have never studied English grammar are able to use their own language efficiently in ordinary human intercourse. The study of grammar is for the mature student. Some written exercises, such as translating from Latin to English, are useful if pupils gain scientific knowledge in the process, "beginning still with that which lies most obvious to the senses". The themes, declamations, and verses which it is customary to demand of pupils in schools, are harmful in the extreme. To set pupils a theme is

"to bid them make bricks who have not yet any of the materials",
and moreover, that artificial, set style of speech was no longer
fashionable in English so why require such compositions in Latin ?
" 'Tis thoughts they search and sweat for, and not language," says
Locke, in urging that if it is desired to exercise and stimulate the
pupils' imagination and flow of ideas, it is better to set an English
composition.

Latin verse-making is even less desirable, for " 'tis the most unreasonable thing in the world to torment a child and waste his time
about that which can never succeed . . . the reading of the excellent
Greek and Roman poets is of more use than making bad verses
of his own in a language that is not his own". The practice of
learning by rote is equally fruitless if it is pursued without discrimination so that the pupil's head is stuffed with "the furniture
of a pedant", but the learning of short, carefully selected passages
may serve to "exercise the memories of schoolboys". Their
learning will be more thorough and meaningful if they are interested
in the passages and see the relevance of their labours to their
general education.

Although Latin is of importance, its acquisition should no
longer be regarded as a long and difficult task for the pupil, whose
mother "may teach it him herself if she will but spend two or three
hours a day with him". There should be ample time for the learning of arithmetic, geography, chronology, history, and geometry.
The geography Locke suggests is the old "Cape and Bay" topography, but the constant use of the globe is a practice which might
be imitated more widely to-day. His story of the small boy who
could find the longitude and latitude of any place before he was six,
suggests that a modern child of nine or ten ought to be at least as
familiar with the globe. Arithmetic—counting and elementary
number work—should be started soon after geography, so that
within a short time the two subjects may go hand in hand in the
further study of the globe—even as far as advanced exercises on
the solar system. Locke's admonition, again repeated, to "begin
with that which is plain and simple" and "give them first one
simple idea" is an amusing indication of his inability to envisage
what is truly "simple" to the mind of a child.

A little geometry—a mere six books of Euclid—comes next,
again in association with globe study, a reasonable suggestion
except that Locke assumes that the normal child will find these

studies easy. His limitations are revealed again in his proposals for chronology and history, which subjects are to be learnt from books in Latin, as indeed are "the knowledge of virtue" (ethics) and civil law. He is doubtful of the value of the traditional rhetoric and logic, for he feels that good speech and eloquence depend on much wider study and experience, and that reasoning is developed only by careful and graded practice in thinking about problems which interest and concern the pupil. Disputation is an artificial way of arguing and leads not so much to the discovery of truth as to "a captious and fallacious use of doubtful words". Good style and true sentiment are best acquired through the native tongue.

As to science in education, Locke, himself a scientist by inclination, could not see ahead to the time when "natural philosophy" would give birth to many daughter sciences capable of being "methodised into a system". "The works of Nature," he says, "are contrived by a Wisdom and operated by Ways too far surpassing our faculties to discover or capacities to conceive, for us ever to be able to reduce them to a science". Thus the "knowledge of the principles, properties, and operations of things as they are in themselves" should be made available to pupils to enlarge their minds "towards a truer and fuller comprehension of the intellectual world to which we are led both by reason and revelation". A history of the Bible especially written for young children might be the best kind of textbook in such studies, for there are so many natural phenomena that can only be explained by the "Will of a superior Being" so ordering it.

Locke, understanding little of normal child nature, is vague in the extreme about the arrangement of subjects and subject-matter according to the age of the pupil. Presumably at the "secondary stage" a young gentleman may be allowed to read controversial views on the systematising of natural philosophy. A sounder suggestion is that "rational experiments and observations", should be studied—writings such as Boyle's and Newton's, and other contemporary books on "husbandry, planting, and gardening". A brief comment on the method of studying this body of knowledge reminds us again of his association with Comenian thought:—"The order of Nature, . . . in all progression is to go from the place one is, then into that which joins and lies next to it; and so it is in the mind, from the knowledge it stands possessed of already, to

that which lies next and is coherent to it, and so on to what it
aims at, by the simplest and most uncompounded parts it can divide
the matter into." Thus he appears to accept that the part is always
simpler to understand than the whole.

Several other accomplishments are necessary for young gentlemen, asserts Locke. Greek, the foundation of our learning can be
left to the inclination of the mature young man, but dancing is
essential from the earliest days to give manly grace, confidence, and
naturalness in the performance of conventional gestures, such as
"making a leg". Music cannot claim similar priority, for few
boys are gifted, and performance on an instrument is not a major
social skill; its value is purely as recreation and relaxation. Fencing
and riding on the other hand, are not only useful as physical
exercises, they are also essential social accomplishments. Care
should be taken not to "make a business" of these pursuits, for
they can be distracting and even dangerous. The young man could
employ part of his leisure more profitably in acquiring the practical
knowledge and manual skill involved in the learning of a craft such
as gardening, iron work, or carpentry, according to the interest
and aptitude of the pupil. Such activities provide both exercise and
recreation, and may serve to keep the boy from cards, dice, and
other idle, useless pastimes. While not wishing to deny a youth
the innocent diversions suited to his age, Locke feels he should be
encouraged to follow a hobby based on one of the many manual
arts, for even if the more strenuous occupations have no appeal for
him he may like to try his skill as a lapidary, an engraver, or a
polisher of optical glasses. "A young man will seldom desire to
sit perfectly still and idle, therefore parents should not deny him
these opportunities on the grounds that such work is only for the
lower orders. Parents are reminded that they would readily agree
to the learning of accounting by their sons, for although "merchants'
accompts" belong to the "disgraceful name . . . of trade", a knowledge of their working is valuable to a young gentleman not only
in helping him to manage efficiently his estate in later life, but also
in giving him training in "rational thought" both in the laying
out of his pocket money and in the regulation of his pleasures and
entertainments.

Finally, Locke considers the question of foreign travel, which
was still in his day deemed an essential part of a gentleman's education. While admitting its general value, he criticised the custom of

sending boys abroad between seventeen and twenty-one because their foreign accent has become too fixed, and because it is the period of wilfulness and insubordination. The best ages for travel would be either between seven and sixteen under a tutor, or after twenty-one without a tutor. He repeats the criticism of prevailing fashion, previously uttered by Ascham and Bacon, when he asserts, "So many young gentlemen come back so little improved by it". He considers that they remember best the "worst and vainest practices" they have seen, and appear to have gained nothing in knowledge, virtue, or breeding.

Locke's importance as an educator is, perhaps, above all, in his insistence on the study of the individual pupil and the adjustment of method to suit him. "There are a thousand other things that may need consideration," he admits, "especially if one should take in the various tempers, different inclinations, and particular defaults that are found in children, and prescribe proper remedies . . . there are possibly scarcely two children who can be conducted by exactly the same method". Apart from this important factor of personality, children are "as white paper or wax to be moulded and fashioned as one pleases"—thus he emphasises the great responsibility of the teacher. His second outstanding contribution to educational thought is his theory of the development of reasoning which, although not entirely acceptable to the modern psychologist, has significance and validity in modern education.

Locke's Other Educational Writings

Locke wrote other brief essays on educational topics, but all except one follow the familiar lines of argument. *Instructions for the conduct of a young Gentleman*, concerns training in virtue and good manners, while *Thoughts concerning Reading and Study for a Gentleman* continue his thesis on reasoning, its training and function. The essay, *Of Study*, written in his journal during his stay in France, is a plea for balance and common sense in the pursuit of knowledge: men should find study a delightful recreation if they select subjects which accord with their interests and suit their natural abilities. The search for truth is all-important, so that, again, sound reasoning and judgment are skills to be cultivated assiduously, but not at the expense of bodily health and temper.

Vastly different in topic and content is his description of his scheme of *Working Schools*.[1] This curious little essay—a forecast of Mrs Trimmer's School of Industry—shocks the modern reader into a realisation of the immense gulf between the classes in Locke's day. He proposes that working schools should be established by law. The children of all working people seeking parish relief should be required to attend, and thus relieve their parents of the necessity of providing for them. All children over three years old were to attend the schools where they would be fed on bread, augmented in cold weather by a little warm water-gruel. He argues that as they rarely eat anything but bread and water at home, it would be unnecessary to vary this diet, for its greater regularity would ensure healthy development. A saving of parish money would be effected in that whereas "relief" was handed out with no return, the amount expended on food and teaching in school would be covered by the profits on the cloth, knitted garments, or other goods made by the children in school. Apart from the teaching of a particular industrial skill or craft, the teacher's task would be to train children in religion and morality, and ensure their attendance at church on Sundays.

The master-craftsmen and farmers of the locality should be required to accept without premium some of the boys as apprentices. The boys should be taken at an age decided by the master, and they should be bound until the age of twenty-three, so that in their maturity, their work would "make amends for the usual sums" paid for apprenticeship. The boys still remaining in school at fourteen should be accepted as apprentices by gentlemen, yeoman, or farmers of the district, but not more than two at a time to each master. There should be facilities for parents to learn crafts at the school, material being provided from the poor rate.

Locke's writings won for him wide European recognition throughout the eighteenth century, and it is probable that his reputation as an educator was somewhat unduly enhanced by the weight of his *Essay*. He was a philosopher with a point of view, and because the great minds of Europe respected him to the point of reverence, his unorganised, repetitive *Thoughts* were accepted, even by Rousseau, as new and original. The ideas contained in his collection of letters and in his suggestions for working schools

---

[1] Hartlib, Rawlin, and Petty had advocated such a scheme, but in a more philanthropic spirit.

were, in fact, by no means of his own inception. His contribution to education was in the application of his shrewd realist philosophy to the opinions on child training which had been formed by English intelligentsia who welded together Puritan-Comenian ideas and emigré-aristocratic standards. Had Sir William Petty published his later educational ideas[1] they would certainly have been similar to those of Locke, and it must be suspected that Locke gained much from men like Petty and Boyle.

Nevertheless, he gives in the *Thoughts* a very fair picture of the new concept of "gentleman", a self-disciplined person, speaking with lucid simplicity—as the scientific "Vertuosi"[2] had ordained—and not disdaining those manual skills associated with scientific activities. His picture of "education for poverty", however realistic it may be, is disappointing in view of the grandly democratic tone of his *Treatise on Civil Government*, in which he developed a theory of constitutional government based on the freedom and equality of all men. His suggestion that only personal labour can give men the right to private property—as far as there is enough left for others—would lead one to expect him to show recognition of the right of all men to equal educational opportunity. Like too many men of affairs he gives no indication that education is a matter worth considering in planning the welfare of a nation.

Trends in Education at the end of the Seventeenth Century

John Locke's writings reflect the growing tendency of the English upper classes to give their children a wider education than that offered by the grammar school. After the Restoration it was feared that the latter fostered sedition, and although Christopher Wase emphasised, in his *Considerations concerning Free Schools as settled in England*,[3] that it was a short-sighted policy to neglect the schools, the practice of employing tutors flourished even after the Revolution of 1688. Perhaps it was this withdrawal of a considerable section of the child population from the common schools which led to their decay in the next century. Perhaps it also led to the more favourable attitude on the part of the ruling classes to the extension of elementary education by means of school foundations. Group philanthropy, as expressed in such organisations as

---

[1] They existed as mere jottings in manuscript among his papers.
[2] Or "Ingeniosi" as Wren designated the members of the Royal Society.
[3] Published in 1678.

the Society for the Propagation of Christian Knowledge (founded in 1698), was to begin a new era of elementary education. The increase in provision for girls' education in this movement may be very largely due to the development of gentlewomen's education as indicated by the writings of Bathsua Makin and Mary Astell— the latter publishing her startling demand for higher education for women a few months after Locke's *Thoughts* appeared in print.

In France, a similar plea had already been made. François de Salignac de la Mothe **Fénelon** (1651-1715), born of a noble provincial family, found himself as a young priest entrusted with the spiritual care of women converts and repentent sinners. It would be interesting to know how far ten years of such work provided him with the ideas expressed later in his *Traité de l'Éducation des Filles* (1687), which he wrote in his middle thirties while he was head tutor to the King's three grandsons. Possessed of many of the better qualities of the courtier, combined with no little integrity, Fénelon was an excellent tutor, both in his personal relations with these difficult boys and in his working out of a scheme of education—notably his code of graduated moral lessons. The same independence of thought which, soon after he became Archbishop of Cambrai, earned the displeasure of Rome, produced in his educational theory a liberal, pacific, almost democratic naturalism that was even more unorthodox in his day than his religious opinions. Compared with the suggestions of Locke, his general ideas on education are conservative, but there are so many points of agreement that it seems likely the two writers—setting down their ideas on child training about the same time—were drawing upon an established body of continental opinion. Where Fénelon moved ahead of Locke was in opening the campaign for girls' education. Their contributions to education were comparable in that while neither was original or even new, both were forceful and impressive enough to make an immediate impact on general thought and practice. While Locke is quoted in almost every eighteenth-century treatise on education, Fénelon is the inspiration of the many works on girls' education of that period.

Fénelon advocates the education of girls not as "femmes savantes", but as future teachers of small children. This is perhaps the firmest principle in an inconsistent, often contradictory, preamble and it is reinforced by the lengthy consideration given in the treatise to the upbringing of youngsters, irrespective of sex. The task of the mother or governess has much in common with that of Locke's tutor—to be kindly, even tempered, consistent, just, virtuous, and knowledgeable, to organise enjoyable learning, to study individual needs of children, to train them in good physical habits and supervise their social experiences.

Emphasising that much teaching is achieved by example, Fénelon clearly hopes to see a generation of young gentlewomen modest in dress, restrained in speech and emotional display, skilled but not ostentatious in polite conversation and social arts, unaffected, prudent, devout, and highly skilled in household management and education. In fact, the young woman needs to know domestic economy even as Locke's young man needs to learn estate management. The curriculum designed to equip the girl with such skills and knowledge includes the grammar of the mother tongue, arithmetic, the principal rules of justice, history, needlework, painting, a little music, and, perhaps, some Latin. Really well-to-do girls should be taught their duties to their dependents, how to avoid abuses, how to set up schools, charitable organisations, and local industries, and how to foster the extension of useful knowledge and Christian conduct.

British Educational Thought in the Eighteenth Century

The high repute of Locke as a philosopher served to gain for his *Thoughts* a wider public than any educational writings had won since the Restoration. Fénelon's ideas were brought to England by returning émigrés. Early in the eighteenth century, eminent scholars, such as Jonathan Swift and Isaac Watts, wrote in much the same vein about the education of both boys and girls. Watts emphasised particularly the need for training the understanding, writing, "Take every occasion to guard them against prejudices and passing a judgment on men and things on insufficient grounds".[1] Perhaps more immediately important than such treatises in stimulating controversy on the new ideas and introducing them to a wide public was the invention of the periodical journal, an instrument which introduced personalities to the general public much as radio has done in this century. The editors of *The Spectator* were profoundly interested in education, and the early numbers contain many such comments as, "I am confident that no boy who will not be allured to letters without blows will ever be brought

---

[1] Watts, *On the Education of Children and Youth*, 1710, Chapter III.

to anything with them".[1] The *Tatler* incited discussion by such statements as "A private educator promises in the first place virtue and good breeding, a public schoolboy manly assurance and an early knowledge into the ways of the world".[2] In the years which followed, both journals printed articles and letters on controversial educational topics—the uselessness of the classical curriculum, the need for examinations to ascertain ability and aptitude, the question of corporal punishment, the needs of the "blockhead", vocational training, the reform of school education, the importance of English language, and the danger of slang. That education had become a "popular" subject by mid-century is indicated by its infiltration into the world of the novel. Thus, Richardson's *Pamela* joins the tutor-or-school controversy, pointing out, "It is hardly possible for anyone with talents inferior to those of Mr Locke himself, to come up to the rules he has laid down upon this subject".[3] Fielding makes his *Joseph Andrews* say, "Public schools are the nurseries of all vice and immorality".[4] Goldsmith not only expressed his views from time to time in his better-known writings, but also wrote a shrewd little essay on education.

Of the main educational treatises of mid-century those of two Scottish school masters are worthy of mention. James Barclay, of Dalkeith,[5] recommends the use of Fénelon's moral stories, and expresses appreciation of Locke's point about school education. Being a grammar school master he feels that the evils of school life may be avoided by adequate supervision. He urges the reform of classics teaching and the basing of education upon a firm training in the English language. He approves the widening of the curriculum to include arithmetic, history, and geography, taught in the vernacular, and he demands that teachers should be adequately qualified in such speech, scholarship, and worldly experience before being allowed to teach. He lays stress on the stimulations of the pupils' natural curiosity by encouraging discussion, and he suggests that the task of the educator is not to work "against nature", but to "prescribe the proper means for accomplishing her intention".[6] One of Barclay's assistants, George Chapman, paraphrased these views in his own treatise thirty years later, when he was Master of Dumfries Grammar School.

[1] Richard Steele, *The Spectator*, Vol. I, August 30th, 1711.
[2] *Tatler*, Vol. IV, No. 13, February 28th, 1712.
[3] Samuel Richardson, *Pamela*, Vol. II, Chap. XCII, 1740.
[4] Henry Fielding, *Joseph Andrews*, 1742.
[5] *A Treatise on Education*, Cochran and Co., Edinburgh, 1743.
[6] Barclay, *A Treatise on Education*, p. 40.

David Fordyce, also a Scottish schoolmaster, challenges some of Locke's tenets in his *Dialogues Concerning Education* (1745-1748), especially the *tabula rasa* concept. He prefers to compare the mind to "a seed which contains all the Stamina of the future Plant and all these Principles of Perfection to which it aspires in its Aftergrowth". Thus he sees education's function as to improve Nature, "to give Form and Proportion and Comeliness to those unwrought Materials".[1] Much of the rest is a restatement of Locke—the training of the understanding, preparation for living in the world, the wider curriculum, the pleasant methods of teaching. "Instruction", he writes, "must have a smiling appearance".[2]

The middle of the eighteenth century is also notable for the number of writings on education by people whose connection with that profession were somewhat remote. Thus, in 1753, James Nelson, Apothecary of Red Lion Square, London, laid down in his *Essay upon the Government of Children* that parents of all ranks have a joint responsibility for the training of their children in healthy habits, in good manners, and in the acquisition of skills and knowledge necessary to their station and future employment. It is thoroughly in the vein of Locke, even to the conclusion that there should be "something of Sparta" in education. The following year the Honourable Juliana Susannah Seymour made known her view *On the Management and Education of Children* in the fashionable style of "Letters written to a Niece". She recommends attention to physical habits and diet; she doubts the value of the learned languages, especially as many writings are "infamous and dangerous"; she stresses the need for character training, preferring that youngsters should be "a little less finished in the Heads",[3] than contaminated by undesirable influences. She points out that children frequently perform dull, repetitive actions in their play, and that it is the task of the tutor to capture this "Industry and Emulation" by removing the feeling of compulsion and making the work pleasurable. Mrs Seymour's remarks on the education of girls are less noteworthy than those of her better-known contemporary, Hester Chapone, who was widely quoted by the next generation of educational writers.

A colourful figure of the same period is Thomas Sheridan, actor father of the playwright. Educated at Westminster and Trinity

---

[1] Fordyce, *Dialogues Concerning Education*, pp. 116-17.
[2] *ibid*, p. 204.
[3] *Essay Upon the Government of Children*, p. 195.

College, Dublin, he was accepted by fashionable, intellectual, and social circles. Moreover, he was awarded honorary masterships by Oxford and Cambridge. Yet he achieved little more than a mediocre career as a teacher of elocution although, once embarked on this pursuit, he developed theories about education in general, inspired perhaps by the spirit of his school master father, but more likely by his actor's instinct to put on a good show to draw in the patrons. There is no doubt that his two books were written in the hope that public money would be forthcoming to set him up in a school. He proclaimed the decadence of contemporary society and the need for a "right" system of education aiming at the reform of manners and morals. It is not surprising that in his scheme oratory looms largely in the curriculum. Only through good oratory by priests, statesmen, and scholars could the principles of religion be spread among an illiterate populace. In *British Education* he discusses Locke's system as "only an attempt to mend and patch our present system".[1] In his *Plan* he asserts that Locke's methods would be likely to produce good men but not good citizens.[2] Education should be based on English and, therefore, the language should be refined, ascertained, and fixed. After a basic course in the lower school—a wide curriculum and the fostering of "Memory, Fancy and Judgment"—boys should proceed to an upper course which would include vocational training. He envisaged a multilateral academy preparing boys to enter the Legislature, Law, the Church, the Army, Trade or Estate Management. Apart from the emphasis on oratory, perhaps the most interesting suggestions are that teaching groups should not be larger than ten, that the rod should not be used, and that motivating forces should be "Honour, Shame, and Delight". He is one of the few writers of his day to challenge the traditional system strongly enough to imply that education should be in keeping with the constitution of the State and should change with it.

A notable contribution was made to educational thought in the 1760's by no less a person than Adam Smith, the great economist. Cherishing a great respect for the teaching of the Greeks, he was not concerned with belittling what remained of their influence, nor was he preoccupied with the practical details of child education. He had no quarrel with Locke's pedagogy, nor with the new

[1] *British Education*, 1756, p. 12.
[2] *Plan of Education*, 1769.

utilitarian spirit in education. He had met Rousseau but was not greatly influenced by his educational ideas, except in that the concept of liberty happened to agree with his own theory that greater liberty in human life generally would lead not to chaos but to the emergence of a natural order. This main theory caused him to regard contemporary education with little favour—the enforced study, the harsh discipline, the inefficient teachers. But for his theory he might have clamoured for State education for all. As it was, he advocated education for all, but not free education. Parents who could afford to pay school fees should pay teachers according to their success in teaching. For poorer children the State should provide school buildings and should pay part of teachers' salaries. Again, the rest of the payment should be by results, so that teachers would always be on their mettle. School fees would be "so moderate that even a common labourer may afford it". Smith's reason for favouring universal education was that an informed proletariat would bring security to Government because people would no longer be influenced by "delusions of enthusiasm and superstition".

Another spate of treatises on education came in the last quarter of the century, by which time Rousseau's writings had become known and new concepts of liberty and responsibility were being considered with reference to various aspects of human life. Yet, until the Edgeworths and their circle tried out parts of the Rousseau plan, educational writings and practice remained obstinately conservative—mainly the kindly Utilitarianism of decadent versions of Locke, but occasionally sterner pleas for the revival and purification of the old classical tradition, now deemed "liberal" because it was not vocational or useful. The anonymous *Proposals for the Amendment of School Instruction* (1772) is a deliberate attempt to apply Locke's strictures to School education, but it also pleads for universal education so that even poor children may learn according to ability. David Williams's *Treatise on Education* (1774) is also largely a restatement of the *Thoughts*, expressing disapproval of school education although he himself was a Chelsea school master. He founded a "Society for Promoting Reasonable and Humane Improvement in the Discipline and Instruction of Youth". In 1777, John Ash, a Baptist minister, published a collection of *Sentiments of Education*, giving much space to Locke's ideas on the wider curriculum, play-way methods, and language technique. To make his book thoroughly up to date he points out that trade and commerce and agriculture are no longer to be despised as callings and, therefore, as subjects for study. He quotes Fénelon, Watts, and Mrs Chapone on the education of girls, and adds that they should study botany and zoology.

Dr Joseph Priestley was another contributor to the fund of educational literature.[1] As a scientist and a non-conformist there could be no doubt as to his views on the wider curriculum, as a minister he could not minimise religious education in his scheme, yet as a one-time school master he would not deny the value of Latin and Greek, recommending Latin as a basic subject. He considered history another essential subject and would not neglect science, French, and geography. He favours universal education, pointing out that a liberal education through these "new" studies would lead to a higher form of patriotism in both leaders and people.

Of the traditionalists, the outstanding protagonist is Vicesimus Knox, Master of Tonbridge School. His *Liberal Education* of 1795 is a lengthy but skilful plea for the reform of Latin teaching and the restoration of Greek. His "reform", however, envisaged a return to Lily's Latin Grammar, an early beginning of study, insistence on application, regular Latin verse-making, and the learning of English grammar *after* Latin. Discipline was to be firm but not harsh. Masters were to be skilled and kindly and pupils were to enjoy work and play. Play-acting should be excluded from their activities and parents should be asked to be consistent and firm during vacations.

Published later, but compiled several years before the publication of Knox's work, William Barrow's *Essay on Education*[2] makes practically all the same points, refuting many of Rousseau's contentions although calling him to support his claim that the young child has no powers of judgment. He goes part of the way with Locke in his views on infant training and elementary schooling, accepting as valuable some additions such as arithmetic and geography, but his system is essentially in the old tradition, the classics providing, to his mind, all the incentives to application, to developing the memory, the imagination, and good taste. Moreover, they serve as a foundation for the study of other languages and improve the study of the sciences. Above all, they benefit the

[1] *Miscellaneous Observations Relating to Education,* 1780.
[2] *An Essay on Education,* 1802.

morals of the pupils so long as the teacher points out the occasional ethical lapses.   Barrow suggests the official licensing of teachers and the improvement of their prestige and financial condition.

In surveying educational writings of the eighteenth century, the conclusion cannot be avoided that among the forests of verbiage there are but a few saplings of new wisdom.   Yet the enthusiasm of the writers is surely an indication that education was no more static than were social, economic, or political conditions.   It is true that many schools were at their worst during the century, either through abuse and neglect or through their own bondage to the past.   It is true that most would-be reformers are tiresomely repetitive throughout the century, and appear dominated by Locke —even when they venture to contradict him—without having a true understanding of his basic principles.   Nevertheless, there came about changes in attitudes and practice which, although sometimes for the worse, opened up the way to future progress.   Except in the Latin-yoked schools, the wider curriculum was a *fait accompli* by the end of the century.   Hundreds of private schools, efficient and otherwise, were advertising their modern methods of making middle-class children into gentlemanly but calculating business men.   To satisfy fashionable requirements many schools employed visiting teachers of dancing and French, and occasionally engaged a peripatetic scientist for a lecture-demonstration.

There were also many private schools which claimed to train middle-class girls in the manners and accomplishments of the fashionable world as well as in the domestic skills necessary for running ordinary households.   The writers on female education express no great enthusiasm for prevailing practice, but their suggestions are concerned with the refinement of that practice rather than with any fundamental reform or change.   Almost a century elapsed between Mary Astell's outcry in the wilderness and Mary Wollstonecraft's defiant demand for woman's equality with man.

This latter contribution belongs to the end of the century and deserves mention for its courage and scholarship as well as for its note of prophecy.   Miss Wollstonecraft was not a mere theorist or agitator.   As a young woman she kept school with her sister in a London suburb and later, during a period as governess to a nobleman's children, she wrote *Thoughts on the Education of Daughters*.[1]

[1] 1787.

Then she broke away from the conventions still limiting the experiences of impecunious but genteel young women. She worked for a publishing firm, and in 1792 produced her *Vindication of the Rights of Women*, a plea for the recognition of women's intellectual powers, and for the provision of adequate educational opportunities. In 1797, she married William Godwin, the philosopher and novelist, only to die after childbirth the same year. By her untimely death at thirty-eight, the cause of women's education lost a provocative and stimulating pioneer thinker.

More immediately successful were those writers who helped to bring about a change in the attitude towards the elementary education of the poor. Charity schools, although still playing their part in the provision of instruction in reading and religion, could not solve the problem of the growing masses of child factory workers in the industrial areas. During the last two decades of the century the Sunday School Movement was firmly established by the work of such enthusiasts as Robert Raikes, Hannah More, and Sarah Trimmer, who, in their writings, aimed only to justify their own belief in education as a force for social regeneration. The more abstract consideration of the value and function of universal education was the prerogative of the economists and philosophers. The temper of the age is indicated by such men as Paine[1] and Malthus,[2] who pointed out that an ignorant populace was a danger to the State.

SUGGESTIONS FOR FURTHER READING

Most of the *Thoughts* and *Conduct of the Understanding* are included in *The Educational Workings of John Locke*, by J. W. Adamson (Longmans, Green and Co., 1912). Adamson's commentary and criticism are stimulating and enlightening. In R. H. Quick's edition of *Some Thoughts on Education* (C.U.P., 1895), the essay *Of Study* is included and the working schools' project outlined. T. Fowler's introduction to *The Conduct of the Understanding* (Oxford, 1880) is worthy of study, while S. S. Laurie in his *History of Educational Opinion from the Renaissance* gives more attention to Locke—"The English rationalist"—than to any other thinker. The first two chapters, though somewhat brief, of W. Boyd's *From Locke to Montessori* (Harrap, 1917) show the relationship to Locke's ideas of Condillac's writings of the eighteenth century.

[1] *The Rights of Man*, 1792.   [2] *Essay on Population*, 1798.

CHAPTER XI

ROUSSEAU

An out-and-out charlatan, an individual swayed by successive waves of emotion, stable in one thing only, his own self-love, a writer whose thought teemed with inconsistencies and contradictions, and who relied upon paradox to hold his readers, a thinker who when not giving expression to his feeling of the moment, utilised other men's ideas, a man who can be held responsible for most of the wrong turnings taken by education in the last hundred years. On the other hand, a highly original thinker who burst the bonds of convention, who in his political philosophy may be termed the father of modern democracy, and whose views on education were so revolutionary that they have influenced theory and practice ever since. Which of these two verdicts passed on Rousseau is the correct one ? Obviously they are extreme points of view and probably the truth, as is often the case, lies somewhere between the two. Rousseau's character and personality were so complex that they affect different people in different ways, and even the same person may feel inclined to change the emphasis of his judgment according to his mood at the moment.

After reading that frank and illuminating document, the *Confessions*, one is tempted to describe him as one of the most despicable characters who has ever lived. No doubt such a judgment is very near the truth, although even in the *Confessions* there are passages which suggest that Rousseau's moral character was not altogether selfish and depraved, and that he possessed certain generous, and perhaps noble traits, which tend to make the reader revise his first impression. In judging Rousseau's achievements, however, one should in justice put on one side the effect his moral character produces. It must be acknowledged that Rousseau had read fairly widely even if his reading was often superficial and undisciplined, and that he had the ability to say the right thing in the right way and at the right time. As a consequence his influence upon the course of education has been more profound than that of any other eighteenth-century writer, perhaps even more than that of any other single thinker.

Rousseau's ideas about education are bound up with the general attitude which colours his political philosophy, and cannot properly be understood without reference to the former. Three main influences combined to shape his outlook. In his earlier years at least, he was a true child of that movement which is often termed the "Enlightenment"; the extremely varied experience of his life strengthened ideas he had already formed, and his impulsive and emotional nature did the rest.

Although it may be convenient to speak of the Enlightenment as a movement, its essence consisted in a change of spirit, and the adoption of another attitude towards life. In this aspect it presents a parallel to the Renaissance. Even as the outward signs and effects of the latter took the form of an enthusiastic and overwhelming love of classical literature and thought, especially that which emanated from ancient Greece, so the Enlightenment was characterised by the appeal to reason; in fact this period in the history of thought is sometimes styled the Age of Reason. The cause of this change of attitude is not difficult to discover. Like all great visions which have inspired the human race, the Renaissance started forth accompanied by a tremendous wave of enthusiasm, and as with all other great inspirations, the original impetus gradually grew more feeble with the progress of time, until it flickered out in a spirit of disillusionment. The dreams of the scholars of the fifteenth and sixteenth centuries seemed as far away as ever from being fulfilled. The Renaissance had held out the promise of attaining the perfection of knowledge. In many respects, the Dr Faustus of Marlowe's tragedy pictured the hopes and beliefs of the Renaissance scholar. In moments of sober reflection it became apparent that these rosy expectations had not met with success. When thinkers in ancient Greece became convinced of the sterility of earlier philosophical speculations, the Sophists arose and turned men's minds to the contemplation of human nature and its problems. A parallel feeling developed in the latter years of the seventeenth century and is perhaps most perfectly expressed in Pope's dictum that the proper study of mankind is man.

The appeal to reason was especially strong in the eighteenth century. "The most obvious features of the Enlightenment are its practical and unimaginative character, its hatred of vague enthusiasm, and misty ideals and ideas, its determination to apply the test of a severely accurate reason to everything, and reject out-right whatever will not stand the test, and the constant reference in all this, as the court of final appeal, to the one undoubted fact—the individual himself, with his rights, and his rational powers of understanding."[1] The Enlightenment focused attention upon the individual and this interest became the dominant factor in philosophical and educational thought, an influence which persisted throughout the nineteenth century, and which has met with serious challenge only since the period of the two World Wars.

The change of attitude first began in England. This may seem curious because English thought in the past has often lagged behind that of the continent, but the explanation lies in the greater stability of life and institutions which was enjoyed after the Restoration. Hobbes and Locke may be regarded as pioneers of the new move-ment which became so popular in France in the eighteenth century. The centralised autocracy of Louis XIV, the corruption which in-fected both the Church and the nobility, the utter degradation of the lower classes, and the checks imposed on the liberty of the middle classes, all contributed to a spirit of opposition which eventually found its outlet in the French Revolution.

The thinkers of the Enlightenment in France were not all of the same stamp. Two broad divisions may be discerned in their ranks. One wing was represented by Condillac, Helvetius, Voltaire, and the encyclopaedists; the other by Rousseau. Dr Boyd points out that it was the philosophical publications of the former group of thinkers which influenced Rousseau. They did not develop their educational theories until after the publication of the *Emile*.

Condillac, who adopted the sensationalism of Locke, developed a psychology based on the senses, which in some ways was a fore-runner of the modern behaviourist point of view. He illustrated his theory by supposing a statue which developed the sense of smell, and from this one faculty acquired all the other senses. His next step was to argue that our conceptual activity developed from a combination of the sense powers. Hence he stressed the importance of training in observation and reasoning. The common eighteenth-century view that the child is an adult in miniature was accepted by Condillac. He believed that the child could study the same subjects as the adult except that the material should be simplified

[1] A. K. Rogers, *A Student's History of Philosophy*, pp. 387-8, revised edition, Macmillan, 1920.

to bring it within the grasp of his feebler powers of understanding, and presented in smaller doses. Rousseau was to administer a rude shock to this belief, but in spite of its absurdity, it lingered in England through the greater part of the Victorian era.

Helvetius, starting from the same premises as Condillac, drew a quite different conclusion. Since all the faculties of the mind have developed from the senses, each person's endowment at birth is exactly the same. The reason why individuals as they mature become different is because their environment has been different. Choose any two individuals and bring them up in the same environment, subject to the same educational influences, and they will hardly be distinguishable as regards their characteristics. This view entirely ignored the effect of heredity, and Helvetius attributed the depravity and the degradation of a great part of mankind to a faulty education. In his opinion, *L'Education peut tout*.

It is interesting to note that in the early nineteenth century, Robert Owen shared the same belief in the power of environment to fashion the individual's character and personality. It is a view similar to this which G. B. Shaw held up to ridicule in *Pygmalion*. Voltaire (1694-1778) was perhaps the most influential figure of this group. His views had been shaped by the new scientific ideas of Newton and the Royal Society, and the writings of Locke, with which he became acquainted during his exile in England. Voltaire's caustic wit was used as a weapon of attack on the manifest abuses of Church and State. The French monarchs, in their desire to maintain the reputation enjoyed by France as the centre of culture, tolerated criticism so long as it was general in character. If any literary man overstepped the bounds and became too particular in his remarks, there were ways and means of dealing with him.

The encyclopaedists consisted of a group of brilliant French writers, including Diderot, D'Alembert, and Grimm, who were engaged in the production of a great encyclopaedia which would contain the sum of all human knowledge at that time. In their articles, they seized every opportunity of criticising the conventions of the artificial society in which they lived, in terms which would not bring upon them persecution from Church or State. Rousseau at first threw in his lot with Voltaire and the encyclopaedists. His own opinions had been strongly influenced by his reading of Hobbes and Locke, and he felt that his attitude coincided with that of the encyclopaedists. Later he broke with them. A man of his emotional and passionate tendencies had little in common with those who based their faith upon cold and dispassionate reason. He also felt that the criticisms passed by this school were negative and destructive, and offered in return very little by way of constructive ideas. Some of those who most freely accepted the sensationalist teaching of Locke were moving towards the idea of State control of education. Rousseau has often been cited as an example of a fervent individualist who was opposed in principle to any system of public education. This statement is true within limits. He was convinced that social institutions in the huge and unwieldy nation-states of the eighteenth century were artificial and corrupt, and that under these conditions, the only true form of education was that which the boy received in isolation from social influences.

This was the view which he stressed in the *Emile*. There was, however, another side to Rousseau's thought. What he opposed in the case of the existing social system he was ready to approve in the ideal state. He was not so blind to facts as to fail to see that the individual must be a member of some kind of society, and enter into social relations with his fellows. Everything depended upon the type of society. What was both possible and desirable in the city-states of Greece and in his own small republic of Geneva could not be realised in the nation-states of his own day. Thus in the *Emile*, he declared: "The public institute does not and cannot exist, for there is neither country nor patriot". In his *Letter to Dr Tronchin*, written in November, 1758, when he was entering upon the composition of the *Emile*, Rousseau expressed his view that the home and public education of Geneva produced not only the efficient workman, but the good man and the good citizen. He said: "You make a very wise distinction between the Greek republics and our own in regard to public education; but this does not prevent such education having its place in our city, and having it from the mere force of our conditions, whether we wish it or no . . . I received this public education, not indeed in the shape of formal instruction, but of traditions and maxims, which, handed on from generation to generation, gave to my early boyhood the knowledge which it required and the feeling which it needed".[1]

That Rousseau was not opposed to the idea of public education is attested by the two following extracts from works, one of which

[1] From Professor Archer's translation in *Rousseau on Education*, p. 69, Edward Arnold, 2nd impression, 1928.

was produced at the beginning, and the other towards the close of his literary career. "Public education, according to regulations prescribed by government, and under magistrates appointed by the supreme authority, is therefore one of the fundamental requirements of popular government."[1] The second extract is taken from his tractate *Considerations on the Government of Poland* which was written in 1772 in response to the request of a Polish nobleman for advice about the reform of the Polish government. "It is education which must shape their minds in the national mould, and which must direct their tastes and their opinions, till they are patriotic by inclination—by instinct—by necessity . . . Whatever system of state education is adopted . . . it is desirable to establish a committee of officials of the highest rank who shall have the supreme control and shall appoint, dismiss, and change at will all principals and heads of colleges . . . as well as all physical instructors, who should be encouraged to a careful and zealous performance of their duties by the hope of promotion to higher posts, which will or will not be allotted to them according to the manner in which they have carried out their existing duties. As it is on these institutions that the hope of the state, the reputation, and destiny of the nation depends, I attach to them, I admit, an importance which I am very surprised to find is not accorded to them in any other quarter."[2]

Although Rousseau was not opposed to a state system of education in principle and was aware of the social implications of education, it must be admitted that his intense solicitude for the rights and well-being of the individual overshadowed the former and constituted one of the least satisfactory features of his theory. These two points of view were never fully reconciled in Rousseau's thought, and to a certain extent they were reinforced by his own life experience. The details of his life are fully described in his *Confessions*. All that is possible here is to draw attention to certain events in his life which have a direct bearing upon his educational ideas. He was born in 1712 in the small city-state of Geneva. His mother died at his birth, and he was brought up and received his early education at the hands of his father. The latter seems to have been a most unwise parent. Rousseau's sensitive and emotional nature seems to have been derived from the father, and his lack

---

[1] W. Boyd, *The Minor Educational Writings of Jean Jacques Rousseau*, p. 45, Blackie, 1911.
[2] R. L. Archer, *op. cit.*, pp. 64, 68.

of the sense of responsibility was largely the result of his upbringing. He never had the experience of being a pupil in a class, and his next stage in education was under the care of a tutor. His early life was most unsettled. He tried all manner of occupations and failed in each of them. As an adolescent, he was apprenticed to an engraver, but he was so unhappy that he ran away from his master. Among the occupations he tried was that of tutor. He was not successful, but the experience awoke in him a lasting interest in the problems of education.

It was during the course of a journey to Lyons that an incident occurred, which, according to Rousseau, made a profound impression upon him. Feeling extremely hungry, he knocked at the door of a peasant's cottage and asked for a meal, offering to pay for it. He received some skimmed milk and coarse barley bread. The peasant excused his lack of hospitality by asserting that it was all he had. When he saw that the young man was genuinely hungry, he relented and disappearing through a trap-door, he emerged later from his private store with a white loaf and a bottle of wine. The peasant refused to take the money offered to him, and explained with considerable emotion that he had to make a pretence of abject poverty in order to escape the rapacious demands of the tax gatherer. Rousseau afterwards recorded: "What he said to me on this subject (of which I had not the smallest idea) made an impression on my mind that can never be effaced, sowing seeds of that inextinguishable hatred that has since grown up in my heart against the vexations these unhappy people suffer, and against their oppressors. This man, though in easy circumstances, dared not eat the bread gained by the sweat of his brow, and could only escape destruction by exhibiting an outward appearance of misery".[1]

At the age of about twenty-five, Rousseau had a serious illness and either just before or during his breakdown, he commenced a course of reading which was influential in forming his ideas. It was at this time that he studied Hobbes and Locke, and although they affected his attitude, they were not the only influences which helped to form his views. He also read a number of distinguished French authors, such as Montaigne, Pascal, Fenelon, and Voltaire, and studied the philosophers, Malebranche, Leibnitz, and Descartes. These tempered the influence which the English writers exercised

---

[1] *The Confessions of Jean Jacques Rousseau*, vol. 1, p. 169, translation published by J. B. Lippincott Co., 1891.

upon him. Rousseau hoped for a literary career, and after unsuccessful attempts his opportunity arrived. One day, during the summer of 1749, he chanced to see an announcement in the *Mercure de France* to the effect that the Academy of Dijon offered a prize for the best essay on the topic: "Has the progress of sciences and arts contributed to corrupt or purify morals?" Rousseau resolved to compete, and the following year he was awarded the prize for the *Discourse on the Arts and Sciences.* His own estimate of the work was a just one. "As soon as the discourse was finished, I showed it to Diderot. He was satisfied with the production, and suggested some corrections. However, this work, though full of force and fire, absolutely wants logic and order. Of all I ever wrote, it is the weakest in reasoning, and the most devoid of number and harmony."[1]

In 1753, the Academy of Dijon offered another prize for a discourse on the subject: "What is the origin of inequality among men, and is it authorised by natural law?" This time Rousseau was not successful, but he published the work in 1755 under the title of a *Discourse on the Origin and Foundation of Inequality among Men,* and dedicated the book to the Republic of Geneva. He sent a presentation copy to Voltaire, who replied: "I have received your second book against the human race for which I thank you. Never was such ability used in the endeavour to make us all stupid. On reading your book, one longs to walk on all fours". In spite of adverse criticism, Rousseau was becoming acknowledged as a man whose views mattered. About the same time he wrote the article on "Political Economy", which was printed in the encyclopaedia in 1755. The next five years saw the composition of Rousseau's major works, *The New Héloïse,* published in 1761, *The Social Contract,* in 1762, and the *Emile,* a few weeks later. The latter work is that which consolidated Rousseau's reputation as an educational theorist, but it should be realised that his minor treatises form a most valuable introduction to the teaching of the *Emile.* The publication of the *Emile* produced a universal outburst of indignation. The book was condemned, and ordered to be publicly burnt. At the same time an order for the arrest of its author was issued. The *Emile* mortally offended two influential groups, Voltaire and

[1] *The Confessions of Jean Jacques Rousseau,* vol. 2, p. 5, translation published by J. B. Lippincott Co., 1891.

the encyclopaedists, and the Church, which was indignant at the theology expressed in the Savoyard clergyman's confession of faith.

Rousseau was warned by his friend, the Duchess of Luxembourg, that the authorities intended his arrest. He resolved to seek refuge in Switzerland, but as Geneva would not receive him, he decided to live in the canton of Neuchâtel, which was part of the territories of Frederick the Great. He was kindly welcomed by the governor, Marshall Keith, an exiled Scottish Jacobite. Here he remained for over three years. He seems to have set the people of the district against him, with the result that he found it wise to go elsewhere. After a stay of six weeks in Berne, he was ordered to leave as quickly as possible. He then made up his mind to seek refuge in England with David Hume, and settled at Wooton in Derbyshire. During his stay in England he began the writing of his *Confessions*. By this time, Rousseau, through brooding over his misfortunes, developed a persecution complex, and was persuaded that even his best friends were plotting to betray him. In this mood he accused Hume of treachery. Needless to say, nothing was further from Hume's mind, but Rousseau's suspicious and querulous attitude produced a violent quarrel. After three years wandering from place to place, he returned to Paris in 1770. The warrant for his arrest was still in force, but it was intimated that it would not be executed. It was during these last years of his life that he wrote the second part of the *Confessions*, the *Dialogues* and *Rêveries* and certain minor works. He died suddenly in 1778.

The *Discourse on the Arts and Sciences* was not in itself an important work. Its value to the modern reader is that in it Rousseau's ideas on political philosophy were first expressed in a somewhat crude form, and then elaborated in later treatises. In this essay Rousseau contended that all the ills and miseries of civilisation should be attributed to a departure from a state of Nature. Rousseau's philosophy is usually designated by the term Naturalism. To a considerable degree this name is justified provided that one also bears in mind that he was indebted to more than one school of philosophy when he was formulating his ideas. Hence Rusk has reason for placing Rousseau amongst the idealists. He says: "When we trace the sources of Rousseau's anti-social bias, and of his return to Nature as the cure for all the world's troubles, which are merely the obverse and converse sides of the same principle, we are confirmed in our view that Rousseau's standpoint is idealistic".[1]

The anti-social attitude to which Rusk refers, appears in the *Discourse on the Arts and Sciences*, and there is no reason to believe that Rousseau was insincere when he wrote it. His own explanation was that he took the advice of Diderot, and boldly expressed opinions that in his time were decidedly unconventional. He argued that the development of the arts and sciences was largely responsible for the departure from the state of Nature. Thus he wrote: "Where there is no effect, it is idle to look for a cause: but here the effect is certain and the depravity actual; our minds have been corrupted in proportion as the arts and sciences have improved. Will it be said that this is a misfortune peculiar to the present age ? No, gentlemen, the evils resulting from our vain curiosity are as old as the world. The daily ebb and flow of the tides are not more regularly influenced by the moon, than the morals of a people by the progress of the arts and sciences. As their light has risen above our horizon, virtue has taken flight, and the same phenomenon has been constantly observed in all times and places".[2]

Rousseau then appealed to the testimony of history in support of his theory and in characteristic fashion, distorted the facts of history to lend force to the argument. There is no doubt, however, that his own unfortunate experiences, and his strongly emotional nature decided the line he adopted, whatever he attributed to the advice of Diderot, and that he used the appeal to history as a means of rationalising his conclusions. Professor Adams and Dr Boyd both emphasise this.[3]

[1] *The Philosophical Bases of Education*, p. 148, University of London Press, 1928.

[2] J. J. Rousseau, *The Discourse on the Arts and Sciences* in *The Social Contract and Discourses*, pp. 133-4, Everyman edition, J. M. Dent.

[3] "Without doubt Naturalism in education came to its zenith in the reaction associated with the name of Jean Jacques Rousseau. How far he was sincere in his preference for the natural man is very difficult to determine. His whole theory of education, however valuable it may be in itself and however much truth it may include, was in all probability in its origin nothing more than the reaction of his temperament on his surroundings. That temperament belongs to the class psychologists call contrary. His was one of those natures that have a constitutional bias towards contradiction, and particularly towards a vigorous opposition to the existing order of things. The chance of a prize competition directed him to the consideration of the relation between the development of society and the result in moral progress. His temperament drove him to accept the less obvious of the two possible alternative positions. This inevitably led to the views adopted in the *Emile*." J. Adams, *The Evolution of Educational Theory*, pp. 252-3, Macmillan, 1912.

"Consider the terrible destitution of Rousseau in all the vital human relations. Whether as child or man, he had never known what real home life meant.

Rousseau included education among the influences which corrupt mankind. He wrote: "If the cultivation of the sciences is prejudicial to military qualities, it is still more so to moral qualities. Even from our infancy an absurd system of education serves to adorn our wit and corrupt our judgment. We see, on every side, huge institutions, where our youth are educated at great expense, and instructed in everything but their duty. Your children will be ignorant of their own language, when they can talk others which are not spoken anywhere. They will be able to compose verses which they can hardly understand; and without being capable of distinguishing truth from error, they will possess the art of making them unrecognisable by specious arguments. But magnanimity, equity, temperance, humanity, and courage will be words of which they know not the meaning. The dear name of country will never strike on their ears and if they ever hear speak of God, it will be less to fear than to be frightened of Him. I would as soon, said a wise man, that my pupil had spent his time in the tennis court as in this manner; for there his body at least would have got exercise.

"I well know that children ought to be kept employed . . . But what should they be taught? This is undoubtedly an important question. Let them be taught what they are to practise when they come to be men; not what they ought to forget".[1]

At the back of Rousseau's mind when he wrote the essay was the antithesis of Nature and society, but although he made occasional references to Nature, it is obvious that at this stage of his thought the precise meaning of the term was not clear to him. It was a useful word to mark the opposition between the highly artificial life of society, and the simple existence led by primitive man. In the next essay, the *Discourse on the Origin and Foundations of Inequality among Men*, the idea of "Nature" was developed from a mere negation to one that contained a positive content. If we are to understand the origin of the inequalities of man as they are

Again and again, he had sought congenial employment, and had always failed to establish himself as a worker. He was proud to call himself a citizen of Geneva, yet was condemned by circumstances to live in permanent exile from it. And even the kindly relations of neighbourliness, which sometimes go a long way to make good other social deficiencies, were denied him by his own unhappy nature. Surely no one was ever more a solitary in the midst of society than he— who could more effectively lead the attack against social life than one who owed so little to the great social institutions of family, profession, and state that mean so much for more ordinary men?" W. Boyd, *The Educational Theory of Jean Jacques Rousseau*, pp. 59-60, Longmans, Green, 1911.
[1] *Discourse on the Arts and Sciences*, pp. 147-8.

manifest in society, it is imperative to know man as constituted by nature in distinction from the artificial modifications produced in him by society. The essay, therefore, introduces a consideration of man in the state of Nature. Rousseau is at pains to show that the state of Nature is a hypothesis, and not a fact of history. "The investigations we may enter into, in treating this subject, must not be considered as historical truths, but only as mere conditional and hypothetical reasonings, rather calculated to explain the nature of things, than to ascertain their actual origin; just like the hypothesis which our physicists daily form respecting the formation of the world."[1]

At this stage in the development of his thought, natural man meant the primitive savage whom Rousseau, in contradiction to fact, spoke of as a noble and magnificent creature, free to develop his own nature without any interference. His downfall started when the ownership of property arose. "The first man, who, having enclosed a piece of ground, bethought himself of saying, this is mine, and found people simple enough to believe him, was the real founder of civil society."[2] From this point man began to sink further and further into the state of slavery. The remedy is a return to Nature.

In idealising natural man, Rousseau was obviously opposed to Hobbes's conception of man's life in the state of Nature as "solitary, poor, nasty, brutish, and short". On the other hand in his more sober moments, Rousseau realised the impossibility of annihilating society, and suggested that a reconciliation between natural and civilised man could be reached if society could be completely re-fashioned. Thus, in the appendix to the *Discourse*, he states that the corruptions of society have gone too far to make feasible a return to Nature. Some form of society is inevitable, and the problem is to discover a state of society in which man's natural freedom will as far as possible be restored. Even at this time, we find him asserting that society is based on "a real contract between the people and the chiefs chosen by them; a contract by which both parties bind themselves to observe the laws therein expressed, which form the ties of their union".[3]

In *The Social Contract*, the idea of the state of Nature is allowed to fall into the background, while that of the origin of society

---

[1] *Discourse on the Origin of Inequality*, pp. 175-6.
[2] *ibid.*, p. 207.
[3] *ibid.*, p. 228.

becomes predominant. The treatise opens with the well-known words, "Man is born free; and everywhere he is in chains. One thinks himself the master of others, and still remains a greater slave than they. How did this change come about ? I do not know. What can make it legitimate ? That question I think I can answer". The theory of *The Social Contract* was the answer Rousseau gave.

It is not relevant to our purpose to enter into the details of Rousseau's social philosophy or the complications involved in his doctrine of the general will, but it is important to notice a change in his attitude towards society which affected the educational views expressed in the *Emile*. He has now abandoned his belief that the life of the savage is the ideal, and seeks a moral and political equality for man which can only come to fruition in society. The following passage illustrates the change in his thought. "The passage from the state of Nature to the civil state produces a very remarkable change in man, by substituting justice for instinct in his conduct, and giving his actions the morality they had formerly lacked . . . Although, in this state, he deprives himself of some advantages which he got from Nature, he gains in return others so great, his faculties are so stimulated and developed, his ideas so extended, his feelings so ennobled, and his whole soul so uplifted, that, did not the abuses of this new condition often degrade him below that which he had left, he would be bound to bless continually the happy moment which took him from it for ever, and, instead of a stupid and unimaginative animal, made him an intelligent being and a man . . . What man loses by the social contract is his natural liberty, and an unlimited right to everything he tries to get and succeeds in getting; what he gains is civil liberty and the proprietorship of all he possesses."[1]

One should read the opening sentence of the *Emile* in the light of this development in Rousseau's thought: "God makes all things good; man meddles with them and they become evil". It is also necessary to avoid accepting Rousseau's statement too literally. The *Emile* is a treatise on education cast into the form of a romance in which there are at first two characters: Emile, who may be regarded as Rousseau when a boy, and his tutor, who is obviously Jean Jacques as a man. Later a third character appears, that of Sophie, who is destined to be the mate of Emile. This combination of romance and treatise was not a new experience for Rousseau.

[1] *The Social Contract*, pp. 18-19.

He had already tried it out in *The New Héloïse*, which was published in the previous year, 1761. The method possessed certain advantages. The author was able to create his own background, and so develop his characters in what we should now term a "planned environment". By arranging his background, Rousseau was able to express more clearly his ideals of education. Two unfortunate consequences followed his choice of method. A treatise disguised as a romance tends to fall short of perfection in both aspects. It has been truly said: "It is enough of a story to spoil it as a treatise, and so far more than enough of a treatise to spoil it as a story".[1] The second disadvantage turned out to be more serious. Many critics of Rousseau, because they failed to recognise the dual form of the *Emile*, have made the mistake of confusing the building with its scaffolding. Thus, both Rousseau's contemporaries and some of his modern critics have taken the provision of a tutor who devotes his whole activities to the education of one boy as an essential part of the theory of education expressed in the *Emile*. Hence, some have dismissed Rousseau's ideas as absurd and impracticable. It should, however, be admitted that some passages in the *Emile* afford a certain amount of justification for this misconception.

Although, as we have already seen, Rousseau was not opposed in principle to a national system of education, he was convinced that the nations of his day were totally unfit to supervise or control the education of their future citizens. Not only were the states of Europe far too large, but the kind of society which they fostered was unnatural and needed a complete transformation. An ideal education can only be conducted in an ideal environment, and as Rousseau was unable to find in the real world the type of society which he desired, he used the artifice of the romance to show what the process of education could be if it was carried out in a suitable environment. He attached a high value to the educational influence of a good family, and in the *Emile* he indicated his belief which he expressed later in a letter to Prince Louis Eugene of Wirtemberg that "it is only a father who can give a father's care, and only a mother who can give a mother's care".

It is not intended, even if it were desirable, to give a running commentary on the *Emile*. The reader is advised to study it for himself and to read in conjunction the account of the education of

[1] H. Graham, *Rousseau* (Foreign Classics for English Readers), Edinburgh, 1882.

Julie's children described in Part V of *The New Héloïse*. All that space permits is a summary of some of the more important ideas that Rousseau contributed to educational theory. Speaking of the *Emile*, Lord Morley described it as "one of the seminal books in the history of literature, and of such books the worth resides less in the parts than in the whole. It touched the deeper things of character. It filled parents with a sense of the dignity and moment of their task. It cleared away the accumulation of clogging prejudices and obscure inveterate usage, which made education one of the dark formalistic arts. It admitted floods of light and air into the tightly closed nurseries and schoolrooms. It effected the substitution of growth for mechanism . . . It was the charter of youthful deliverance".[1]

It is the last sentence of this passage which expresses the most important influence that Rousseau exercised upon education. One may justly hail him as the discoverer of the child. This is not to forget that educational thinkers of the ancient world, the mediaeval period, and the Renaissance, had many kindly, sympathetic, and helpful ideas about the training of children. In their view the child did not come first. They fixed their eyes upon what he was to be in the future and the curriculum they approved and the methods they recommended were coloured by this attitude. Rousseau, on the other hand, emphasised that the prime factor to be considered in education is the child and his present nature as a child. He wrote: "Nature wants children to be children before they are men. If we deliberately pervert this order, we shall get premature fruits which are neither ripe nor well flavoured, and which soon decay . . . Childhood has ways of seeing, thinking, and feeling, peculiar to itself, nothing can be more foolish than to substitute our ways for them".

So important did this principle seem to him that he repeated it in the *Emile*.[2] In the Preface to the *Emile*, he wrote: "We know nothing of childhood; and with our mistaken notions, the further we advance, the further we go astray. The wisest writers devote themselves to what a man ought to know, without asking what a child is capable of learning. They are always looking for the man in the child without considering what he is before he becomes a

---

[1] Lord Morley, *Rousseau*, pp. 391-2, Chapman and Hall, 1883.
[2] W. Boyd, *The Minor Educational Writings of Jean Jacques Rousseau*, p. 57, Blackie, 1911. The passage is repeated in *Emile*, Book II, p. 54 (Everyman translation).

man . . . Begin thus by making a more careful study of your scholars, for it is clear that you know nothing about them". He carried out this advice in the *Emile* by expressing the view that education is a continuous process which begins at birth and which can be divided into four consecutive stages. Thus, Book I deals with the infant; Book II with childhood; Book III with the pre-adolescent between the ages of twelve and fifteen; and Book IV with adolescence.

These stages of development correspond to the progress made in the history of the human race. To all intents and purposes, the infant is living at the animal level. The child can be compared with primitive man. Boyhood is a period of self-sufficiency whilst at adolescence, the sex impulses ripen, social behaviour becomes possible, and the young person is able to conduct his life according to moral principles.

It is an easy matter to criticise Rousseau's account of the child's development from the standpoint of present-day child study, but it is essential to bear in mind that in the eighteenth century he was a pioneer in this field. His exposition was rendered less effective by his adherence to a faculty psychology, but in his defence, one could urge that this was the dominant view of his time. The continuity of the child's development may seem to be broken by the emphasis placed upon the emergence of new faculties, for example, at adolescence, the pupil appears to make a complete break with his former life. One may dispute Rousseau's statement that the most dangerous period of human life lies between birth and the age of twelve, but when these partial criticisms have been made, the fact remains that he concentrated attention upon the child and his nature rather than upon the subject and the pupil's future occupation. This was one of the most revolutionary steps that educational theory had so far taken.

Most previous thinkers had explicitly or implicitly subscribed to the doctrine of original sin. Rousseau took an entirely opposite point of view. "Let us lay it down as an incontrovertible rule," he wrote, "that the first impulses of nature are always right; there is no original sin in the human heart, the how and why of the entrance of every vice can be traced".[1] No argument was produced in support of this statement, but it is obvious that Rousseau contradicted all thinkers of the type of St Augustine to whom the presence

[1] *Emile*, p. 56 (Everyman translation).

of the taint of original sin was a solemn and awful thought. Rousseau's suggestion was that all deviations from virtue can be traced to the influence of the child's environment and in particular to ill-advised direction by the parent or teacher.

Many previous writers on education had firmly held to the doctrine of original sin which they interpreted so narrowly as to regard the natural impulses of children as contaminated at their source. The logical outcome was the belief that the main objects of moral education were the suppression of the pupils' natural impulses and the substitution of good habits in their place. Abelard, indeed, had shown that the popular view of original sin was open to grave objections when it asserted that human nature was so depraved as to render it impossible for an individual to act rightly without the assistance of Divine grace. He regarded original sin as an explanation of the weakness of human nature which renders the individual susceptible to evil influences which he can conquer by exercising his will in accordance with the light of conscience. Abelard, however, was suspect as a theologian and the harsher view prevailed. The most obvious way of suppressing the inborn tendency to sin seemed to be the use of corporal punishment. Hence portraits of mediaeval and Elizabethan schoolmasters usually depict them with the birch, and even a kindly man like Brinsley, described the rod as "God's instrument to cure the evils of their condition".

Rousseau's denial of original sin and his statement that all is good as it comes from nature, led him to adopt an equally extreme position, namely, the doctrine of discipline through natural consequences. If Emile broke his bedroom window, he would have to sleep in a draughty room and the cold which followed would warn him of the folly of giving way to passion. Rousseau ignored the fact that the cold might develop into pneumonia so that the consequences would be out of all proportion to the offence. Rousseau's overemphasis, however, had the effect of bringing about a more kindly and sympathetic way of dealing with children's misdemeanours. As Dr Boyd says, "Under the shelter of the theological exaggeration of human depravity, there had grown up, and become firmly established, a harsh repressive system of education which ignored childhood and did violence to all that was best in human nature; and there was no possibility of any better education until the fundamental conceptions of the method had been challenged and made suspect . . . Even though men were not prepared to follow Rousseau in the new way he had indicated for them, it was impossible for them henceforth to go back wholeheartedly to the old".[1]

Rousseau contended that the education of the child ought to accord with nature. It should be noticed that this term had undergone another transformation in meaning. He believed that the education of the child should be based upon his nature, *i.e.* his needs as a child, his powers and abilities, interests and outlook as a child. Most modern educators would agree with this view though they might question whether Rousseau's idea of the nature of the child was the correct one. His views about the early education of the child represented quite a new departure. They could be summed up in the two words "freedom" and "activity".

Although Rousseau had handed over the care of his own children to a foundling hospital, he made in the *Emile* one of the most passionate appeals to parents to convince them of their own obligations towards their children. Perhaps nowhere is there a greater divergence between Rousseau's own practice and the precepts he recommended. His criticisms of the denial of freedom were sound, and he realised that swaddling clothes and all the restrictions that went with them ought to be discarded. Infancy is the age when the child develops through free activity and the employment of his senses. Hence all premature attempts at a formal education should be discouraged. "Exercise his body, his limbs, his senses, his strength, but keep his mind idle as long as you can."[2]

Rousseau was well aware of the defects of eighteenth-century schooling. If in England, the prevailing tone of the schools had reached its lowest level, the same was to a large extent true of France.[3] Rousseau thoroughly agreed with Locke about the narrow and barren nature of the usual school curriculum. Like Locke he vehemently denounced the all-pervading tendency to verbalism. "What do they teach?" he cries, "Words, words, words . . . To conceal their deficiencies teachers choose the dead languages, in which we have no longer any judges whose authority is beyond dispute . . . If the master's Greek and Latin is such poor stuff, what about the children? They have scarcely learnt their primer by heart,

[1] *The Educational Theory of Jean Jacques Rousseau*, p. 316, Longmans, Green, 1911.
[2] *Emile*, p. 58.
[3] For conditions in English public and grammar schools, see S. J. Curtis, *History of Education in Great Britain*, chapter 4.

without understanding a word of it, when they are set to translate a French speech into Latin words; then when they are more advanced they piece together a few phrases of Cicero for prose or a few lines of Vergil for verse".[1] Rousseau's disgust with the traditional methods of education led him to assert: "Reverse the usual practice and you will almost always be right".

From the age of two to twelve, the child may be considered as akin to the primitive savage. Indeed, if he has been born amongst savages or peasants, there is no need for him during the first twelve years of his life to have any other education than that provided by his life experience. Such a course is impracticable with Emile, who is a member of a civilised community. It will be necessary to protect him against those evil influences which proceed from a decadent society. Hence the education of the earliest years will be mainly negative. "It consists, not in teaching virtue or truth, but in preserving the heart from vice and from the spirit of error."[2] This does not mean that the educator has nothing positive to teach in this period. He will not, however, give his pupils formal lessons. There is no need for the tutor to worry because his pupil can neither read nor write. "Do not save time, but lose it," wrote Rousseau. These are the years during which the child will naturally learn through play and through the exercise of his senses. Rousseau's long discussion of sense training in the *Emile* (pp. 97-127) shows the importance he attached to this aspect of education and it contains many maxims which were novel at his time but are now commonplaces. "Measure, count, weigh, compare." Children will always do anything that keeps them moving freely. Emile is to learn to draw "not so much for arts' sake, as to give him exactness of eye and flexibility of hand". The influence of Locke is apparent in much of this section of the *Emile.* "It is the time to learn to perceive the physical relations between ourselves and things. Since everything that comes into the human mind enters through the gates of sense, man's first reason is a reason of sense-experience."[3]

Rousseau is very sceptical about direct moral teaching at this age. He would exclude the fable as a vehicle of instruction since the pupil will, in most cases, draw the wrong lesson from it. His principles lead him to favour the environment as the most effective teacher of morals. Hence the importance he attaches to planning the pupil's environment so that he will derive the right moral lessons

[1] *Emile*, pp. 72-3.   [2] *ibid.*, p. 57.   [3] *ibid.*, p. 90.

from the situation which has been so carefully prepared for him. The examples of the gardener and the beans (pp. 62-3) and the value of controlling one's temper (pp. 60-1) are good illustrations of Rousseau's method. It never occurred to him that children are extremely acute in sensing a situation that has been carefully staged for their benefit.

From twelve to fifteen is the period of boyhood or pre-adolescence. Rousseau realised that this is the practical stage of the child's development when he estimates the value of everything in terms of its use to himself. The boy's curiosity is strongly developed and he is anxious to find out the How and Why of the things he experiences. We can, therefore, begin to teach him science, not indeed to make a scientist of him but "to give him a taste for the sciences and methods of learning them when this taste is more mature".[1] Rousseau advocates what was later known as the Heuristic method: "Put the problems before him and let him solve them himself. Let him know nothing because you have told him, but because he has learnt it for himself. Let him not be taught science, let him discover it".[2] He should make the apparatus he needs and verbal explanations and books should only be used as a last resort. "Teach by doing whenever you can, and only fall back upon words when doing is out of the question."[3] With these principles in mind, Rousseau shows how he will stimulate Emile to learn geography and astronomy, and at a later stage, physics.

Emile should also learn a practical craft. Rousseau chose the art of the carpenter: "It is clean and useful, it may be carried on at home; it gives enough exercise; it calls for skill and industry, and while fashioning articles for everyday use, there is scope for elegance and taste".[4]

Until this stage of his development, Emile has not been encouraged to read books. "I hate books," cried Rousseau, "they only teach us to talk about things we know nothing about". As Emile can now read, his tutor has to face the problem of the kind of book which is suitable. Rousseau would limit him, for the time being, to one book, *Robinson Crusoe*. This is a valuable account of the life and activities of a person, who, because he has been shipwrecked upon a desert island, is obliged to be self-dependent. "Robinson Crusoe on his island, deprived of the help of his fellow-men, without the means of carrying on the various arts, yet finding

[1] *Emile*, p. 135.   [2] *ibid.*, p. 131.   [3] *ibid.*, p. 144.   [4] *ibid.*, p. 163.

food, preserving his life, and procuring a certain amount of comfort;
this is the thing to interest people of all ages, and it can be made
attractive to children in all sorts of ways." [1] During this stage of
self-sufficiency, Emile's knowledge will be restricted to Nature and
objects. His grasp of social relations will not go beyond the
economic aspects of society. He will be given no lessons in history,
and the explanations of the moral relations between men will be
postponed until adolescence.

Up to this point, Emile's education has been a preparation for
the real education which begins in adolescence. The negative
rather than the positive aspect of education had been emphasised,
but now the latter comes into its own. Rousseau was fully aware
that adolescence is a critical period for many young people. His
description of the characteristics of the adolescent is probably the best
which appeared before the rise of a more scientific method of child
study. He pointed out that the first tasks for Emile will be to learn
how to control the new passions which are surging within him. Now
is the time to stimulate the social sentiments. His previous training
had "made him a worker and a thinker: we have now to make him
loving and tender-hearted, to perfect reason through feeling". It
would seem that the study of history affords the best means of
obtaining a knowledge of the ways of men, for it enables the adolescent to view human activities from the standpoint of a spectator.
Unfortunately, the accounts presented by the historians are consciously or unconsciously biased. Also the more scientific our
conception of history, the more it tends to be concerned with the
study of great movements rather than the activities of great men.
Rousseau's intense individualism peeps out when he recommends
the study of biography in preference to reading national history.

Emile is now ready to receive religious instruction. Rousseau's
ideas on the content of this teaching and the method to be employed
are illustrated in the creed of the Savoyard priest. The views
expressed in this long section of the *Emile* (pp. 228-78) were largely
responsible for the condemnation of the book by the authorities.
Space does not permit an examination of these doctrines. Rousseau
summed up his purpose by reminding the reader that he has "tran-
scribed the document not as a rule for the sentiments we should
adopt in matters of religion, but as an example of the way in which
we may reason with our pupil . . . so long as we yield nothing to

[1] *Emile*, p. 147.

human authority, nor to the prejudices of our native land, the light of reason alone, in a state of nature, can lead us no further than to natural religion; and this is as far as I should go with Emile. If he must have any other religion, I have no right to be his guide; he must choose for himself".[1]

Rousseau clearly recognised the importance of sex instruction during adolescence, and although his attitude was that of a healthy realism in contrast with the hypocrisy of the Victorian age, his teaching is by no means satisfactory. This is chiefly apparent in Book V which deals with the education of Sophie, Emile's future mate. Rousseau's personal dealings with women had been unfortunate and marred his exposition from the very start. Book V represents a complete anti-climax. In spite of the amorous adventures described in the *Confessions*, Rousseau really knew very little about women. Lord Morley summed up this last book of the *Emile* in the following words: "We are confronted with the oriental conception of women. Every principle which has been followed in the education of Emilius, is reversed in the education of women . . . The whole education of women ought to be related to men: to please them, to be useful to them, to make themselves loved and honoured by them, to console them, to render their lives agreeable and sweet to them,—these are the duties which ought to be taught to women from their childhood . . . Woman is created to give way to man, and to suffer injustice. Her empire is an empire of gentleness, mildness and complaisance. Her orders are caresses, and her threats are tears ".[2] Hence it is not surprising to find that whilst the education of Emile followed a line which at least was original, that of Sophie was distinctly conventional, and the views which Rousseau expressed on the subject of women and their education aroused feelings of indignation and contempt in most English women of the time who read his account.

Rousseau's influence upon later thinkers was perhaps more far reaching than that of any other writer on education. Even those who disagreed with some of his principal doctrines, borrowed much from him. The immediate influence of the *Emile* was greatest in Germany and Switzerland. Basedow, Salzmann, and Campe, put into practice many of the ideas of Rousseau. Pestalozzi and Froebel, whose importance as educational reformers merit separate treatment, took many of their main ideas from the *Emile*. In fact,

[1] *Emile*, p. 278.   [2] *Rousseau*, pp. 387-8.

there were but few educational thinkers of the nineteenth century who were not influenced in one way or another by Rousseau.

The influence of Rousseau in Germany is particularly interesting because through the work of the Philanthropinum the State system of education in Prussia arose at a time when in this country Bell and Lancaster were struggling to provide national education by means of voluntary effort. Earlier in the eighteenth century, Prussia had made certain experiments in regard to compulsory elementary education. In 1717, Frederick William I enacted that in country districts wherever schools were available, children should attend regularly during the winter months and as often as possible in the summer at times when they could be spared from their agricultural work. The King actively supported the building of new schools in rural districts. This policy was continued by Frederick the Great who issued the *General Code of Regulations for Rural Schools* in 1763, a document which may be regarded as marking the birth of the Prussian elementary school system. Athough Frederick had in view the establishment of a national system of education, he was content to leave the schools under the direction of the Church. The development of State control received a great impetus from the work of Johann Bernhard Basedow (1723-90) and his followers who were warmly supported by Baron von Zedlitz, the minister of Frederick.

Basedow was the son of a Hamburg wig maker. His father was severe and brutal and the treatment the young boy received may provide some explanation of his erratic behaviour in later life. His interest in education was aroused when he became tutor to a young boy in Holstein. Through the influence of the father of his pupil, Basedow received the appointment of Professor of Philosophy in a Danish academy, but his somewhat unorthodox views in theology brought about his dismissal. The next few years were taken up with writing an incredible number of phamplets on religious topics, but at length, when he grew tired of religious controversy, he found a new interest through the introduction of Rousseau's works into Germany. In 1768 he published *An Address to Philanthropists and Men of Property on Schools and Studies and their influence upon the Public Welfare*. In this publication he appealed for subscriptions to enable him to produce a textbook and to organise a school which should be conducted on reformed lines

The appeal met with a remarkable response which bore witness to the universal dissatisfaction with the schools and their traditional methods. The fund quickly amounted to 15,000 thalers. The *Address* also outlined Basedow's proposals for reform in education. He asked for the appointment of a National Council of Education to control not only the schools but every kind of educational agency including books and the theatre. His plea for State control of education reflected the opinions of La Chalotais who in his *Essay on National Education* had claimed that education was a matter for the State and not for the religious bodies. Basedow's theological views had brought him into conflict with the leaders of institutional religion in Denmark and Germany. This accounts for his declaration that the schools ought to be strictly non-sectarian and for the support his plan received from all sections of the community.

Basedow's proposals for the reform of the curriculum formed a mixed bag the contents of which were drawn from the works of Comenius, Locke, and Rousseau. They were fully described in his *Book of Method for Fathers and Mothers of Families and of Nations* (1770) the publication of which was made possible by the large subscriptions he had received. The same year saw the publication of the first version of another work which was revised in 1774 under the title of *The Elementary Work* (*Elementarwerk*). The attention given in the book to pictorial illustration is evidence of the influence of Comenius. In spite of this extraordinary jumble of material the book had a wide sale and found its way into all regions of Germany.

Basedow's next venture was the establishment on 1774 of his model school, the Philanthropinum at Dessau. The ideas of the reformed school method attracted a number of able teachers, but unfortunately they found themselves unable to work with a man of such capricious and unstable temperament as Basedow. The school was never a large one and through Basedow's mismanagement and general incompetency it rapidly declined in numbers. In 1784 the school was reorganised and continued to exist under new management until it finally disappeared in 1793. Nevertheless, the importance of the Philanthropinum is not to be reckoned in terms of the length of time it endured, but rather by the fair promises of educational reform it seemed to offer. The ideas for which it stood caught on and a wave of enthusiasm which may be likened to that which accompanied the inception of the Charity School movement in England spread throughout Germany and even to France and Switzerland.

Philanthropinums sprang up everywhere. They varied greatly in value. Some were obvious frauds, but others, conducted by teachers who had been connected with the original Philanthropinum, were strikingly successful. Basedow's failure may be attributed entirely to his unsuitable character. He has been described as a man who was "vulgar, immoral, intemperate, given to the vices of the peasantry from which he sprang without possessing their fundamental virtues; above all it cannot be doubted that he was in some respects an imposter and a mountebank".[1] Like Rousseau, however, his personal character had little effect on the movement he started, and his experiment attracted the attention of Kant and Goethe. Some writers have regarded the teaching of Pestalozzi as an extension of the movement initiated by Basedow.

The most successful of Basedow's followers was Joachim Heinrich Campe (1746-1818). He founded a Philanthropinum at Hamburg and later became a Councillor of Education in Brunswick. One of Campe's most noteworthy achievements was his German translation of the educational works of Locke and Rousseau. He was a most prolific writer, and in addition to producing books for the use of teachers, he commenced a series intended for children which has been termed the "Campe Children's Library". One of the best known was a revision of *Robinson Crusoe* which served as a model for the more famous *Swiss Family Robinson* of Wyss.

Perhaps a more practical exponent of Basedow's ideas was Christian Salzmann (1744-1811) who opened a school in 1784 in a farming district of Saxe-Gotha. The school was limited to sixty pupils in order to maintain the family atmosphere, and its earliest scholar was Carl Ritter who has been claimed as the father of modern geography. Salzmann made a serious attempt to put into practice the principles of Locke and Rousseau. The "hardening" process recommended by these writers was exemplified by the amount of time devoted to physical pursuits which included swimming and skating. Nature study, school gardening, and excursions for the study of geography and local history were prominent features of the school. Salzmann also wrote a large number of books dealing with education. Like Campe, he combined the

[1] P. Monroe, *Textbook in the History of Education*, p. 580, Macmillan, 1907.

principles he inherited from Rousseau with a moralising and religious tendency which exhibited eighteenth-century Lutheranism at its worst. Those who read *Swiss Family Robinson* in their childhood will realise how the sickly sentimental religious strain detracts from what might have been an ideal book for pre-adolescent boys.

Another experiment in a very different direction was attempted by Baron von Rochow (1734-1805) in Prussia. He was deeply touched by the miserable conditions under which so many of the peasants lived and which seemed to him to be the result of ignorance and improvidence. He believed that the remedy was to be found in the extension of elementary education. With this aim in view he opened a model farm school on his estate. The experiment was so successful that it attracted the attention of the Prussian authorities and similar schools were established in other parts of the country.

Rochow used ideas which came to him through the writings of Basedow and he himself was responsible for a number of books designed both for teachers and children. His experiments were warmly supported by Zedlitz who had already shown his appreciation of the movement initiated by Basedow. Shortly after the death of Frederick the Great, Zedlitz was appointed president of the central administrative board set up in 1787. This council, known as the *Oberschulcollegium*, represented an important stage in the transition from Church to State control of education.

The reactionary movement which set in soon after Frederick's death, drove Zedlitz from power, but the realisation of a national system of education only received a temporary setback. In 1794 the revised Prussian legal code was issued and all schools and colleges were declared to be State institutions subject to examination and inspection by State officials. The final step was taken in 1803 when the code came into operation. Whilst religious instruction was retained, the schools were opened to all children irrespective of the religious communities to which they belonged. This laid the foundation of the important developments in Prussian education which occurred in the period following the defeat of Jena in 1806.

One of Rousseau's followers in Geneva was Mdme Necker de Saussure (1765-1841), a pioneer of systematic child study. She kept a diary of the progress and development of her own children and later published her ideas about education in a work entitled *Progressive Education* (1836-8). This treatise is interesting because

Rosmini drew largely upon it for the composition of his *Ruling Principle of Method*. Maria Edgeworth also met and exchanged views with Mdme Necker de Saussure. In her book, Mdme Necker de Saussure showed that she did not altogether see eye to eye with Rousseau. She rejected his thesis that the child is born essentially good and as a corollary emphasised that it is demoralising to allow him to do exactly what he likes. He needs training and careful supervision. Whilst she recognised the importance of basing all education on the child's nature, she did not accept the sharp distinction which Rousseau had drawn between the stages of the child's development. Above all, she refused to subscribe to Rousseau's views about the education of girls. They appeared to her one-sided and narrow, and she supplemented them by insisting that the girl's education should be liberal in character so as to afford her an opportunity of developing her own personality and fitting her to discharge intelligently her duties as a member of society.

SUGGESTIONS FOR FURTHER READING

Those who wish to make a further study of Rousseau are strongly recommended to read him at first-hand. English translations of his principal works are readily accessible in the Everyman Series, published by J. M. Dent: *The Social Contract and Discourses,* and *Emile.* His minor educational writings can be studied in W. Boyd, *The Minor Educational Writings of Jean Jacques Rousseau,* Blackie, 1911, and R. L. Archer, *Rousseau on Education,* Edward Arnold, 2nd impression, 1928. A good translation of *The Confessions of Jean Jacques Rousseau* was published by the J. B. Lippincott Co. in 1891.

Much has been written about Rousseau's contributions to education. Lord Morley's *Rousseau,* Chapman and Hall, 1883, should be read by all who wish to gain a general impression of his life and philosophy. The most complete study of Rousseau as an educational thinker is that of Dr W. Boyd, *The Educational Theory of Jean Jacques Rousseau,* Longmans, Green, 1911. T. Davidson, *Rousseau and Education according to Nature,* stresses the impulsive side of Rousseau. It was published in the Great Educator Series, W. Heinemann, 1898. Davidson is extremely biased and holds the view that Rousseau's theories are essentially immoral and are responsible for all the errors in educational practice after his time. Shorter accounts of Rousseau's doctrines will be found in Helen Wodehouse, *A Survey of the History of Education*, chapter 10, Edward Arnold, 1929; R. R. Rusk, *The Doctrines of the Great Educators*, chapter 8, Macmillan, reprinted 1948; and R. H. Quick, *Educational Reformers*, chapter 14, Longmans, Green, new edition, 1902. The last book contains a chapter on Basedow and the Philanthropinum, and includes an account of the visit of Goethe to Basedow and a description of the direct method of teaching Latin in the Philanthropinum.

CHAPTER XII

IMMANUEL KANT AND WILLIAM WORDSWORTH

The two thinkers discussed in this chapter are writers who in the strict sense were not professional educators but who were affected by the ideas of Rousseau. Kant's work on education, *über Pädagogik*, was a small treatise which he did not publish himself. Its origin was as follows: When Kant was Professor of Logic and Metaphysics in the University of Königsberg, the terms of his appointment stipulated that he should lecture on certain subsidiary subjects of which paedagogics was one. Following tradition, he chose as his text a book by Professor Bock, but his actual lectures were quite independent of his text. When his health began to fail, Kant handed the manuscript of his lectures to his friend, Theodor Rink and they were not published until 1803, the year before Kant's death. Kant never considered himself well qualified for lecturing on education. Earlier in his career he had acted as a private tutor for nine years during which period he was reported to have said that he never applied the maxims he taught later in his public lectures. The publication of the *Emile* made a great impression upon him. Kant had the reputation of being the most punctual of men and it is said that only on one occasion he lapsed from his habit, that being the day that the *Emile* came into his hands. Kant differed in almost every respect from Rousseau as regards character, temperament, and habits, but in the *Pädagogik*, he not only refers to Rousseau, but adopts many of his ideas. Thus he employs the term "education according to nature", but he has in mind the rational nature of man and he emphasises that in bringing up a child it is essential to treat him as a child and not as an adult in miniature.[1]

Man, according to Kant, is the only creature who needs education. The animals are provided with instincts and therefore do not need any formal process of education though he acknowledges that young birds learn their characteristic songs from their mothers. Education includes nurture, discipline, moral training with a view to the formation of character, and instruction. It should start in infancy because the young child is unable to make plans for himself

---

[1] R. R. Rusk goes so far as to say that "for Educational purposes it is also better to approach the writings of Kant from the standpoint of Rousseau than from that of Hume or Leibniz, as is customary in Philosophy". *The Philosophical Bases of Education*, p. 164, University of London Press, 1928.

and consequently others have to do this for him. It ceases when the individual is old enough to have children of his own though Culture (*Bildung*) may still continue. Education is either physical or practical, *i.e.* moral. For the former, nature should be the chief directing influence. Discipline is extremely important in the education of young children. Their animal impulses without the restraining influence of discipline would lead them to rush wildly and rashly into danger. Man is naturally unruly and when young he has to be brought to obey the laws of mankind. The young child is but little above the animal stage of development and it is education that will develop his humanity. Hence young children are sent to school to learn to do what they are told rather than to be instructed. Discipline is therefore the negative aspect of education and will take predominance, when the child is young, over instruction, the positive part. It should be noticed that although Kant uses concepts he gained from reading Rousseau, his interpretation is quite different. Thus it is true that the young child is in the animal stage of his development but Kant does not share Rousseau's enthusiasm for the "noble savage". The aim of education is to develop in each individual a true human nature.

Kant was optimistic as regards the future of education. "It is delightful to realise that through education human nature will be continually improved, and brought to such a condition as is worthy of the nature of man. This opens out to us the prospect of a happier human race in the future."[1] His remark that a theory of education, although it had not so far been worked out, is a glorious ideal and quite practicable, makes one wonder whether Kant, if he had become interested in education at an earlier stage in his career, might have produced a critique of educational theory worthy to take its place amongst his major philosophical works. His subsequent remarks seem to support this supposition. He wrote, "Hence the greatest and most difficult problem to which man can devote himself is the problem of education. For insight depends upon education, and education in its turn depends on insight. It follows, therefore, that education can only advance by slow degrees, and a true conception of the method of education can only arise when one generation transmits to the next its stores of experience and knowledge, each generation adding something of its own before

[1] *Kant on Education, a translation of the Pädagogic*, by Annette Churton, p. 8, Kegan Paul, Trench, Trubner, 1899.

transmitting them to the following".[1] As Kant in his old age was not prepared to make systematic study of educational theory, he was content to throw out certain ideas which he considered might be of value to other thinkers.

Amongst these was the importance he attached to experiment in educational method. He wrote: "Experimental schools must first be established before we can establish normal schools. Education and instruction must not be merely mechanical; they must be founded upon fixed principles . . . People imagine, indeed, that experiments in education are unnecessary, and that we can judge from our reason whether anything is good or not. This is a great mistake, and experience teaches us that the results of an experiment are often entirely different from what we expected".[2]

Kant was well acquainted with the experimental system of education carried out in the Philanthropinum at Dessau by J. H. Basedow in 1774. When he gave his first course of lectures in education, Kant had used Basedow's *Methodenbuch*, and in 1777 had written an appreciation of the work carried out at Dessau. Apart from this influence of Basedow, that of Rousseau was the most significant. Kant shared with the latter the belief in the degeneracy of eighteenth-century society. He bitterly complained that parents whose eyes were fixed upon the worldly success of their children ignored one of the most important principles of education, namely that children ought to be educated, not for the present, but for a possibly improved condition of man in the future. He agreed with Rousseau that children are born with a definite inclination towards goodness. "Evil is only the result of nature not being brought under control. In man there are only germs of good."[3] Kant was not an advocate of state control. He believed

---

[1] *Kant on Education, a translation of the Pädagogic*, by Annette Churton, pp. 11-12, Kegan Paul, Trench, Trubner, 1899.

[2] *ibid.*, pp. 21-2.

[3] *ibid.*, p. 15. Compare with the following passage from T. K. Abbott, *Kant's Theory of Ethics*, p. 326, Longmans, Green, 1909. "Later, but much less general, is the . . . opinion, which has perhaps obtained currency only amongst philosophers, and in our times chiefly amongst instructors of youth: that the world is constantly advancing . . . from worse to better (though almost insensibly); at least, that the capacity for such advance exists in human nature. This opinion, however, is certainly not founded on experience, if what is meant is *moral* good or evil (not civilization), for the history of all times speaks too powerfully against it, but it is probably a good-natured hypothesis of moralists from Seneca to Rousseau, so as to urge man to the unwearied cultivation of the germ of good that perhaps lies in us, if one can reckon on such a natural foundation in man." Kant's belief was that man has the capacity for the exercise of freewill and moral goodness and badness only exist in reference to his free actions.

that education could best be improved through the effort of private individuals who were themselves experienced educationists. "The management of schools ought, then, to depend entirely upon the judgment of the most enlightened experts."[1] Evidently the English system as it has existed since 1902 would not have found favour in his eyes and he had not considered that sometimes the so-called expert views matters from the narrowest possible angle and his opinions often express the fashionable craze of the moment.

As the child grows older, the positive side of education becomes more important. Kant decided in favour of school education rather than training under a private tutor. When a tutor is employed there often arises a conflict between the authority of the parent and the tutor. Although the early training of the child should aim at inculcating habits of mechanical obedience, there should be a gradual progress towards freedom and the child should be encouraged to think for himself. "One of the greatest problems of education is how to unite submission to the necessary restraint with the child's capability of exercising his freewill."[2] Kant's solution of the problem is that the pupil should be accustomed to a certain amount of restraint but at the same time he should be trained to use his freedom in the right way.

Kant followed Rousseau in regard to the nature of physical education. He emphasised the mother's duty of suckling her own babes and deprecated the use of swaddling clothes as not only useless but as being definitely harmful because they restricted free movement. Early education is mainly negative because we do not add to the provision of nature but merely see that such provision is carried out. Like Locke and Rousseau, he believed in hardening the child. Rocking is bad for him, and leading strings and go-carts are superfluous. If the child is allowed to crawl when he shows a desire to do so, he will gradually learn to walk himself. Our rule should be to use as few aids as possible in teaching the child, and encourage him to learn things by himself. Learning to write is an illustration of this principle. At some point in the early history of the race some person discovered writing for himself. The child should be encouraged to do the same.

[1] *Kant on Education, a translation of the Pädagogic,* by Annette Churton, p. 17, Kegan Paul, Trench, Trubner, 1899.
[2] *ibid.,* p. 27.

The positive side of physical education consists mainly in the exercise of the mental faculties. "What has to be done is to see that natural ability is cultivated. Sometimes instruction is necessary; sometimes the child's mind is inventive enough, or he invents tools for himself."[1] We should choose such physical exercises as will develop strength, ability, quickness, and self-confidence as is the practice in the school at Dessau. Every encouragement should be given to children to climb, run, jump, lift, and carry weights, throw at a mark, wrestle, and dance, though simple rather than elaborate dances should be chosen. Games which involve the activity of throwing are excellent in developing the sense of sight. Kant mentions a number of games which he approves—blindman's buff, spinning tops, cutting a reed to make a musical instrument, swinging, and flying a kite. Through playing games the child learns endurance, but there is also a social value in play. The child learns to co-operate with others and to tolerate other people's opinions. In this connection, Kant quotes from Sterne. "Toby in *Tristram Shandy* says to a fly which has been annoying him for some time, and which he at last puts out of the window, 'Go away, tiresome creature: the world is large enough for us both'."[2]

Kant's exposition is sometimes marred by his adherence to a faculty psychology but his analysis of play and work activities points the way to the views of later thinkers on this subject. He did not agree that everything should be made easy for the child. Thus he wrote: "Various plans of education have been drawn up by different people, in order to discover the best methods—a most praiseworthy undertaking. One among others suggests that children should be allowed to learn everything as it were in play. (He probably had Basedow in mind.) A child must play, must have his hours of recreation; but he must also learn to work".[3] The difference between play and work may be summed up by saying that play is pleasant in itself and is undertaken without regard to an end, but work is not always pleasant in itself and is directed to an end. Man needs both kinds of activity.

The child should be taught early to differentiate between right and wrong actions. His sense of morality has not yet developed,

---

[1] *Kant on Education, a translation of the Pädagogic*, by Annette Churton, p. 59, Kegan Paul, Trench, Trubner, 1899.
[2] *ibid.*, p. 65.
[3] *ibid.*, pp. 67-8.

but he should be trained to obey and to conform to rules. When he is older he will perform right actions not merely because of habit but through an understanding of the moral principles involved. In his early years, however, it is essential that he should be trained to adhere strictly to rules of conduct even when he is unable to understand why he should do so. Kant did not entirely support Rousseau's view of punishment through natural consequences. Sometimes, he agreed, the natural consequences of an action may be a sufficient deterrent but he realised that the aftermath might be delayed so long that the child forgot the sequence. When a child becomes ill through over-eating the connection between the events is clear enough. In other cases disobedience ought to be followed by an artificial punishment. This should never be inflicted with signs of anger. Punishment should never be vindictive, but its aim should be the improvement of the child.

Physical education is followed by practical education. The latter consists of three parts: the ordinary curriculum of the school which develops the child's ability and fits him for success in the vocations of life; discretion by which is meant training in the social arts and citizenship; and character training. At all stages the educator must remember that he is dealing with an immature person and he should obey the maxim: "Let a child be clever after the manner of children; let him be shrewd and good-natured in a childish way but not cunning (*listig*) like a man. The latter is as unsuitable for a child as a childish mind is for a grown-up person".[1] Unfortunately Kant does not deal with the ordinary school curriculum. He gives some general principles such as: skill must be thorough and not superficial and that it is better to know a few things thoroughly than many superficially, but his chief interest, as one would expect from the author of the *Metaphysic of Morals* and the *Critique of Practical Reason* lies in the training of character.

One cannot say that the principles Kant prescribes for the moral training of the young flow directly from his system of moral philosophy, but there are certain allusions to his ethical teaching. He naturally insists that the child's duties should be shown him through rules and examples of conduct. He should be taught that his duty to himself is to maintain the dignity of mankind in his own person. If he grasps this principle he will realise that

[1] *Kant on Education, a translation of the Pädagogic*, by Annette Churton, p. 32, Kegan Paul, Trench, Trubner, 1899.

intemperance, uncleanliness, and lying contravene this end. One of the child's chief duties towards his fellows is to reverence and respect their rights. Kant thought that the schools should teach a kind of catechism of right conduct explaining how the principles of morality apply to the situations of daily life. His belief that moral actions are confined to those where duty is the motive appears in his statements that children should be trained to help others from a sense of duty, and that benevolence is not an absolute obligation. Actions performed from the motive of love and benevolence, although very desirable, were not moral actions in the eyes of Kant. They are done as duty directs, but not because duty directs.

Like Rousseau, he could find no place for competition and rivalry. Children should be warned not to compare themselves with others but only with an ideal standard of right and wrong. One quotation is reminiscent of his moral philosophy. "But is man by nature morally good or bad ? He is neither, for he is not by nature a moral being. He only becomes a moral being when his reason has developed ideas of duty and law. One may say, however, that he has a natural inclination to every vice, for he has inclinations and instincts which would urge him one way, while his reason would drive him in another."[1]

Is it practicable to give children religious ideas early in life? Kant's reply is characteristic of his philosophical position. Religious ideas depend upon a theology, and young people cannot be taught theology until they come to know themselves and have experience of the world. How can a boy who knows nothing about duty understand his duty to God ? It is necessary to distinguish between theory and practice. Theoretically the best course would be to teach children about ends and aims concerned with mankind and give them instruction about the order and beauty to be found in nature. This would lead to the idea of a Supreme Being, the Author and Lawgiver of nature. In practice this would not work out because children in their everyday life pick up certain ideas about religion. They are just as liable to get hold of false ideas as true ones. To counteract this it is necessary to present religious ideas quite early in the child's life. Kant did not believe in the teaching of religious formularies or catechisms which appeal to memory and imitation. Our method must be in accordance with

[1] *Kant on Education, a translation of the Pädagogic*, by Annette Churton, p. 109, Kegan Paul, Trench, Trubner, 1899.

nature. "Children will understand—without abstract ideas of duty, of obligation, of good and bad conduct—that there is a law of duty which is not the same as ease, utility, or other considerations of the kind, but something universal, which is not governed by the caprice of man. The teacher himself, however, must form this idea."[1]

The next step is to bring the child to an understanding of the nature of God. This can be done by analogy, for children will grasp the Fatherhood of God by comparison with their experience of their own fathers. The teacher can then point out that all mankind forms a unity under God the Father. Kant is very insistent upon one thing. Religion is really morality applied to the knowledge of God. Therefore, the correct method is to begin with morality which will lead to religion. We must begin with the moral law within the child, *i.e.* his conscience which is the representative of God. By uniting the ideas of duty and God, the child will learn, for example, to be kind to animals and that he should always try to discover good in evil.

In the case of Kant, the influence of Rousseau is fairly clear, but when one comes to consider Wordsworth's ideas about education, the relation between them and the doctrines of Rousseau is more of a general than of a specific character. It would be a grave error to look upon Wordsworth as being merely a disciple of Rousseau. He had certainly read the *Emile* and during a very impressionable period of his life he was in contact with a number of people who were fervent admirers of Rousseau. If his standpoint presents some similarities to the doctrines of the *Emile*, it is still true to say that most of his vital ideas were products of his own temperament and experience. In some instances, he differed considerably from Rousseau and was also severely critical of those, who in this country, attempted to put into practice the theories of the *Emile*. Professor Helen Wodehouse summed up the relations between the ideas of the two men when she wrote: "Wordsworth's childhood had much in it which conformed, not with Rousseau's extravagancies or pedantries, but with his best mind".[2]

---

[1] *Kant on Education, a translation of the Pädagogic,* by Annette Churton, pp. 110-11, Kegan Paul, Trench, Trubner, 1899. Kant explained elsewhere the method he would adopt in presenting the conception of duty to young people. See *Kant's Theory of Ethics* translated by T. K. Abbott, pp. 253-5, 6th edition, Longmans, Green, 1909.

[2] *A Survey of the History of Education,* p. 114, Edward Arnold, 1929. In § 6 of her chapter on Rousseau, Professor Wodehouse gives a number of

Although Wordsworth's views about education are not by any means confined to *The Prelude*, this work may be regarded as the chief source for the study of them. It was composed between 1799 and 1805, revised in 1832, but was not published until 1850, a short time after the poet's death. *The Prelude* was dedicated to Coleridge. Its sub-title is *The Growth of a Poet's Mind*, and Wordsworth himself described it as an autobiographical poem. In keeping with this aim, he deliberately selected for inclusion those events which contributed most to the shaping of his life and character. Apart from its interest to the student of English poetry, its significance for the theory of education lies in the fact that it presents the growth and development of Wordsworth's mind from childhood to maturity. Many of the ideas expressed were not grasped by educationists of the nineteenth century, but through the modern emphasis on the social implications of education, they have acquired a fuller meaning for present-day readers.

Wordsworth spent his schooldays at Hawkshead Grammar School where he learnt Latin and mathematics. He then entered St John's College, Cambridge, where he completed his undergraduate studies if not with distinction, yet satisfactorily. He wrote: "Of my earliest days at school I have little to say, but that they were very happy ones, chiefly because I was left at liberty then, and in the vacations, to read whatever books I liked. For example, I read all Fielding's works, *Don Quixote, Gil Blas*, and any part of Swift that I liked—*Gulliver's Travels* and the *Tale of the Tub* being both much to my taste". Thus the experience of his childhood were far different from those of Rousseau. His own torment and agony of mind and spirit were to come later.

School and university, however, were not the chief formative influences in Wordsworth's development. It was the natural beauty

interesting parallels between the thought of Rousseau and that of Wordsworth. The following quotations support the view adopted by Professor Wodehouse:

"Much has been written on the influence of Rousseau on Wordsworth's theories of education, but though he had certainly read *Emile*, and as a young man was surrounded by warm advocates of Rousseau, he based his views solely on his own experience, and only seems to refer to Rousseau when he differs from him." *The Prelude*, edited by Ernest de Selincourt, p. 528, O.U.P., 1926.

"There is little evidence that Wordsworth had studied the theories of Rousseau seriously; but the ideas and spirit of Rousseau were, 'in the air', and to get clearly the significance of some parts of *The Prelude*, it is useful, it is even necessary, to compare the two writers." James Fotheringham, *Wordsworth's "Prelude" as a Study in Education*, p. 53, Horace Marshall, 1899.

amidst which he spent his boyhood and the simple character of the people living in the neighbourhood which had the greatest effect upon him. Everyone who has dipped into Wordsworth's lyrics recognises that he is the poet of nature *par excellence*, but a deeper study of his works is necessary before one can realise that his claim to this title does not merely rest upon the descriptions he gave of the scenery in his beloved Lake District.

In his undergraduate days, Wordsworth paid several visits to France, then passing through the early stages of revolution. The imaginative and idealistic strain in the young man's nature brought him into wholehearted sympathy with the aims of the Girondists, but then came in swift succession the execution of the King and Queen, the Reign of Terror, in which the supporters of the Gironde were led to the guillotine where Wordsworth might have followed if his tutor had not commanded his return, and the war with England. Wordsworth's mind was filled with agonising doubts. Was not his own country fighting to suppress the pioneers of freedom ? His whole being was wracked by the torments of a mental conflict, but helped by his friends, he found peace for his troubled spirit by the return to the scenes of his childhood. It was not the mere change of scene and occupation which brought tranquillity. It went far deeper than that. The dark night of doubt and uncertainty melted away before the advent of his vision. His vision was his inspiration for some years and was responsible for his finest poetry. As he grew older, the brightness of the vision dulled and only occasionally did his work reflect the freshness of his former efforts. It is not Wordsworth the poet, however, with whom we are primarily concerned, but Wordsworth's theory of education.

It is easy to say that Wordsworth's vision consisted in his discovery of nature, but it is more difficult to determine the exact significance of this discovery and the meaning it had for him. One can dismiss immediately the idea that nature meant for Wordsworth nothing more than the hills and crags, the trees and gushing mountain streams, and the quiet lakes. These were but symbols of a presence which was for him both intensely real and spiritual.

> "And I have felt
> A presence that disturbs me with the joy
> Of elevated thoughts; a sense sublime
> Of something far more deeply interfused,
> Whose dwelling is the light of setting suns,
> And the round ocean and the living air,
> And the blue sky, and in the mind of man :

A motion and a spirit, that impels
All thinking things, all objects of all thought,
And rolls through all things . . ."[1]

There is no doubt that when he wished, Wordsworth could be a most accurate observer of nature as the poem, the *Green Linnet* shows.

R. D. Havens writes: "He was not a sentimentalist but a hard-headed, keen-eyed, matter-of-fact man, impatient of inaccuracy in observation or expression".[2]

There are really two schools of thought about Wordsworth's philosophy of life. The first would include him in that group of writers on philosophy and education whose teaching is usually described as Naturalism. According to this point of view, Wordsworth would be a materialist. Thus A. Beatty, who is the leading exponent of this school of thought,[3] believes that Wordsworth's philosophy was based on Locke and David Hartley. The latter in his *Observations on Man*, 1749, developed certain doctrines which had already been taught by Locke. Hartley's importance in the history of English thought lies in the influence he exercised upon the psychology of James Mill. According to the *Autobiography* of J. S. Mill, his father was indebted to Hartley for the theory of the association of ideas which was a cornerstone of the Utilitarian school of philosophy. Like Locke, Hartley taught that all our ideas are developed from sensation. Our senses receive impressions from external objects. Some of these persist as simple ideas of sensation. From these by a process of compounding arise all our other ideas. Thus complex ideas are formed through association of simple ideas. Man, however, is not a mere machine. The activity of the human mind through the operation of pleasure and pain gives a personal value to our experiences.

As an illustration of Wordsworth's reliance upon Hartley for his psychology, Beatty cites the theory of the three ages of man: childhood, the period of sense impression; youth, the age of feeling; and maturity, which is characterised by the development of thought. Whatever we may think of Beatty's view, he does at least recognise that Wordsworth's philosophy is important for the evaluation of his work, and in doing so, runs counter to the interpretation of

[1] *Lines composed above Tintern Abbey*, 93-102.
[2] *The Mind of a Poet*, John Hopkins Press, 1941.
[3] *William Wordsworth, His Doctrine and Art in their Historical Relations*, University of Wisconsin Press, 1927.

Matthew Arnold. The latter wrote: "The Wordsworthians are apt to praise him for the wrong things, and to lay too much stress upon what they call his philosophy. His poetry is the reality, his philosophy, . . . is the illusion . . . In Wordsworth's case, at any rate, we cannot do him justice until we dismiss his formal philosophy ".[1]

The interpretation given by Beatty has been rejected by the alternative school of thought. Thus A. N. Whitehead regards Wordsworth as a typical representative of the reaction against the prevailing attitude of the eighteenth century. He writes: "Wordsworth in his whole being expresses a conscious reaction against the mentality of the eighteenth century. This mentality meant nothing else than the acceptance of the scientific ideas at their full-face value. Wordsworth was not bothered by any intellectual antagonism. What moved him was a moral repulsion. He felt that something had been left out, and that what had been left out comprised everything that was most important".[2]

Many commentators who adopt this point of view emphasise that the contributions made to Wordsworth's thought by Plato, Spinoza, and Kant, have been entirely ignored. To what extent had Wordsworth studied Plato? Lack of evidence prevents a decisive answer from being given. There is good reason to believe that Wordsworth had read Thomas Taylor's translation of Plato which appeared in 1804. Without doubt, Wordsworth would have been familiar with the teaching of Plato and the Neo-Platonists through his long discussions with Coleridge. The *Intimations of Immortality* is distinctly Neo-Platonic in its thought and quite foreign to the philosophical outlook of Hartley. Some thinkers of this school also draw attention to the influence of German mysticism which they believe affected Wordsworth's thought in two stages: in the *Prelude* and the poems written before 1805, the influence of Spinoza may be traced, but in the *Ode to Duty* and the *Excursion*, Kantian thought becomes more prominent.

Two points emerge from the above discussion. In the first place, both schools of thought are agreed that Wordsworth developed a definite philosophy of life and this is important because it was bound to affect his theories about education. Secondly, the

---

[1] *Preface to Poems of Wordsworth*, p. xix, Golden Treasury Series, Macmillan, 1893.
[2] *Science and the Modern World*, p. 96, C.U.P., 1927.

two schools of thought are not necessarily antagonistic. Each one emphasises a definite aspect of Wordsworth's philosophy. In his earlier period he was a supporter of the philosophy propounded by Locke and Hartley and in this respect may be termed an adherent of Naturalism. As a result of his mental and emotional conflict, he experienced what one can only describe as a mystic or spiritual vision, and his task became one of combining this with his naturalistic outlook, a process which was assisted by ideas he received from Neo-Platonism and German mysticism. H. W. Garrod seems to point to this solution when he writes: "Wordsworth's poetry is essentially mystical. But whereas the mysticism of other men consists commonly in their efforts to escape from the senses, the mysticism of Wordsworth is grounded and rooted, actually in the senses".[1]

The two factors, therefore, which constitute the philosophy of Wordsworth and which govern his views about education would seem to be the sensationist and associationist teaching of Hartley and his mystical interpretation of nature which was mainly a consequence of his own experience and type of mind reinforced by ideas supplied by the Neo-Platonists, Spinoza, Kant, and the German transcendentalists. He seems to suggest this himself. The passage from *Tintern Abbey* quoted earlier to illustrate his spiritual interpretation of nature is immediately followed by the lines below which indicate the naturalistic point of view.

> "Therefore am I still
> A lover of the meadows and the woods,
> And mountains; and of all that we behold
> From this green earth; of all the mighty world
> Of eye, and ear,—both what they half create,
> And what perceive; well pleased to recognise
> In nature and the language of the sense
> The anchor of my purest thoughts, the nurse,
> The guide, the guardian of my heart, and soul
> Of all my moral being." (102-111)

If the reconciliation suggested between the opposing schools of thought be accepted, it would seem convenient to deal with Wordsworth's ideas about education as they spring from his emphasis upon the activities of sense and of feeling, and then to consider the mystical element in his philosophy and its influence upon his

[1] *Wordsworth*, p. 105, Clarendon Press, 1927.

theories.   Wordsworth would most certainly have agreed with the
Kantian view that conception without perception is empty.
Thought cannot work in a vacuum.   The content of thought is as
important as its form and if the thinking of the mature individual
is to be fully effective, it must be based on a rich variety of content
developed from a full range of sensory experiences and their accompanying feelings.

The stage of early childhood is characterised by the intense
activity of the senses and by vivid imagery.   The small child is a
newcomer in a strange and wonderful world.   His power of sensing
is his means of finding his way about this world and getting to
know it.   From all quarters, impressions pour into his mind by
way of his different sense organs.   He also takes great delight in
the exercise of his senses and the interplay of sense activity and
feeling assist him in building up experiences.   The process of turning events into experiences is not merely passive.   Receptivity and
creativeness go hand in hand.   Experiences result, either consciously
or unconsciously, in a modification of his mind and in this way,
the sense impressions and his reaction to them form what he will
afterwards become.

Wordsworth is emphatic that the adult who has become
estranged from the life of vivid sensory experience and fundamental
feeling that fashioned his childhood and youth, has lost the essential
source of inspiration that invests life with its meaning and sense
of worthwhileness. This is the message of the ode, *Intimations of
Immortality*.   Professor W. R. Niblett puts this idea very plainly.
"The *Immortality* ode is engaged in establishing, not the doctrine
of pre-existence, but the vividness and visionary quality of the
experience and memory of the child.   If the mind of the child is to
retain sensitiveness, coherence, and consistency in the values it
sets upon experiences it must not be forced and regimented by
town life, or schools organised to push it, to make it scientifically
analytical, to put it into friendless competition with other minds.
The child cannot make adaptations with the speed of a machine,
for he is a creature essentially of the soil; and if he is forced to
do so, he will grow up superficial, unimaginative, insensitive of
heart."[1]

[1] *Wordsworth and the Child*, in Education Papers, p. 61, No. 3, vol. 5, King's
College Education Society, Newcastle-upon-Tyne.

In the *Immortality* ode, it is the disillusioned adult who opens by complaining:

"There was a time when meadow, grove, and stream,
    The earth, and every common sight,
            To me did seem
        Apparelled in celestial light,
    The glory and the freshness of a dream.
    It is not now as it hath been of yore;—
        Turn wheresoe'er I may,
            By night or day,
    The things which I have seen I now can see no more".

The *Excursion* takes up the same theme. If the adult has missed the true line of his development, how is it possible for him to regain it ? The answer given is that it is only possible if we have the power to go back to the days of childhood and the vital experiences we then enjoyed. This idea is constantly with Wordsworth.

"Our childhood sits,
Our simple childhood sits upon a throne.
That hath more power than all the elements."
                        (*Prelude*, v, 506-8.)

Even more significant is the poem:

"My heart leaps up when I behold
    A rainbow in the sky:
So was it when my life began;
So is it now I am a man;
So be it when I shall grow old,
        Or let me die!
The Child is father of the Man;
And I could wish my days to be
Bound each to each by natural piety".

The last three lines have often been criticised and some have seen in them little more than a poetic licence which borders on the ridiculous. How can the child be father of the man ? Wordsworth had completely broken with the eighteenth-century view that the child was the adult in miniature. Like Rousseau, he believed that the child thinks as a child, feels as a child, and that the childish outlook on life is quite different from that of the adult. And yet the adult was once a child. Now he is a grown man, but unless he can be true to the fundamental principles of his childhood, his mature life will lose its inspiration, and it will follow the wrong path which can never lead to the acquisition of true wisdom. The phrase "natural piety" emphasises the truth that in his development the individual must adhere to the right order of life. As James Fotheringham wrote: "We must value the great simple things of life and nature, the primitive and general principles and powers of mind and heart".[1]

In the *Prelude*, Wordsworth states his conviction that a purely intellectual education is not only ineffective but is also deadening because it ignores what he terms the "vital feelings of delight". Knowledge is not a mere acquisition or possession, a number of facts stored up in the memory. If knowledge is to be a real power in life it must be a living organic growth which has been absorbed completely by the individual. "I believe," writes Professor Niblett, "that the most important kind of knowledge of all—perhaps the only kind that matters ultimately—is not intellectual in its nature. It is something quite different from information, let alone knowledge acquired for examination purposes. Just as it is possible to make a ball roll by applying a hand to it, so it is possible to make a child's mind revolve and work by artificially exercising it. But the sort of knowledge which matters is not to be gained in this way.

"The truest sort of knowledge is absorbed almost organically. It becomes a living part of the mind which takes it in, growing and developing within and gradually changing and creating the person of whom it has become a part. Wordsworth often shows his knowledge of this truth in his poems about childhood incidents".[2]

If Wordsworth represented a reaction against the outlook of the science of his day, he was just as much opposed to the educational practice of the early nineteenth century. The grammar schools, bound by the literal interpretation of their founders' intentions, had failed to move with the times. The unhappy pupils were condemned to what Professor Huxley termed "gerund grinding". Rousseau had raised his voice against the artificiality which had emeshed the curriculum and teaching of the schools. Wordsworth was at one with his protest. Many schoolmasters thought that the more difficult the subject, the more distasteful it was to the pupil, the greater the benefit he derived from studying it. Wordsworth was wholeheartedly opposed to this creed. He wrote:

> "And—now convinced at heart
> How little those formalities, to which
> With overweening trust alone we give
> The name of Education, have to do
> With real feeling and just sense". (*Prelude*, xiii, 168-172.)

[1] *Wordsworth's "Prelude" as a Study of Education*, p. 21, Horace Marshall, 1899.

[2] "Essential Education" in *Educational Issues of Today*, p. 22, University of London Press, 1947.

Wordsworth was convinced that the acquisition of mere knowledge can never be the end of education. Its end is life itself. True knowledge is developed and grown by the individual himself. It is creative, not acquisitive.

> "In Nature's presence stood, as now I stand,
> A sensitive being, a creative soul." (*Prelude*, xii, 206-7.)

Education, he believed, was justified in so far as it increased the individual's capacity for living.

He was contemptuous of what passed for education in the elementary schools but he was not opposed in principle to the idea of national education. Indeed, he wrote in the *Excursion*:

> "O for the coming of that glorious time
> When, prizing knowledge as her noblest wealth
> And best protection, this imperial Realm,
> While she exacts allegiance, shall admit
> An obligation on her part to *teach*
> Them who are born to serve her and obey;
> Binding herself by statute to secure
> For all the children whom her soil maintains
> The rudiments of letters, and inform
> The mind with moral and religious truth,
> Both understood and practised,—so that none,
> However destitute, be left to droop
> By timely culture unsustained; or run
> Into a wild disorder; or be forced
> To drudge through a weary life without the help
> Of intellectual implements and tools;
> A savage horde among the civilised,
> A servile band among the lordly free". (ix, 293-310.)[1]

Wordsworth recognised the necessity for school attendance. He was also well aware of the place book-learning should occupy in education. Unlike Rousseau, he did not despise the pupil's study of books provided that they were used in the right way. He knew full well the joy and pleasure that he had experienced from his own reading in the days of his youth, and in the *Prelude* he tells us:

[1] Matthew Arnold, contending that it was Wordsworth's poetry which mattered and not his philosophy, wrote: "One can hear them being quoted at a Social Science Congress; one can call up the whole scene. A great room in one of our dismal provincial towns; dusty air and jaded afternoon daylight; benches full of men with bald heads and women in spectacles; an orator lifting up his face from a manuscript written within and without to declaim these lines of Wordsworth; and in the soul of any poor child of nature who may have wandered in thither, an unutterable sense of lamentation, and mourning, and woe!" (Preface to Poems of Wordsworth, p. xxi, Golden Treasury Series, Macmillan, 1893.)

> "And when thereafter to my father's house
> The holidays returned me, there to find
> That golden store of books which I had left,
> What joy was mine! How often in the course
> Of those glad respites, though a soft west wind
> Ruffled the waters to the angler's wish,
> For a whole day together, have I lain
> Down by thy side, O Derwent! murmuring stream,
> On the hot stones, and in the glaring sun,
> And there have read, devouring as I read,
> Defrauding the day's glory, desperate!" (v, 477-487.)

He also retained pleasant memories of the classics of his childhood days for he tells us:

> "Oh! give us once again the wishing-cap
> Of Fortunatus, and the invisible coat
> Of Jack the Giant-killer, Robin Hood,
> And Sabra in the forest with St George!
> The child, whose love is here, at least, doth reap
> One precious gain, that he forgets himself".
>
> (*Prelude*, v, 341-6.)

On the other hand, Wordsworth had little use for the planned environment which so captivated Rousseau's mind. He asks:

> "But who shall parcel out
> His intellect by geometric rules,
> Split like a province into round and square?"
>
> (*Prelude*, ii, 203-5.)

He disliked intensely the earnest disciples of Rousseau whom he describes as:

> "These mighty workmen of our later age,
> Who, with a broad highway, have over-bridged
> The froward chaos of futurity,
> Tamed to their bidding; they who have the skill
> To manage books and things, and make them act
> On infant minds as surely as the sun
> Deals with a flower; the keepers of our time,
> The guides and wardens of our faculties,
> Sages who in their prescience would control
> All accidents, and to the very road
> Which they have fashioned would confine us down,
> Like engines; when will their presumtion learn,
> That in the unreasoning progress of the world
> A wiser spirit is at work for us,
> A better eye than theirs, most prodigal
> Of blessings, and most studious of our good,
> Even in what seem our most unfruitful hours?"
>
> (*Prelude*, v, 347-363.)

This explains his criticisms of the infant schools of the early nineteenth century. In spite of their obvious defects, Wordsworth preferred the much despised dame schools. He wrote: "I will back Shenstone's Schoolmistress by her winter fire and in her summer garden seat against all Dr Bell's sour-looking teachers in petticoats that I have ever seen".[1] If the children who attended the dame school acquired little in the way of accomplishments, they at least had the benefit of personal contacts. This also reveals why Wordsworth had no love for the solitary Emile and his tutor. He was firmly convinced of the value of the social life such as his own schooldays had provided. The boys at Hawkshead were typically English in their behaviour and outlook.

> "We were a noisy crew; the sun in heaven
> Beheld not vales more beautiful than ours;
> Nor saw a band in happiness and joy
> Richer, or worthier of the ground they trod."
>
> *(Prelude, i, 479-82.)*

Wordsworth's ideal was:

> "A race of real children; not too wise,
> Too learned, or too good; but wanton, fresh,
> And bandied up and down by love and hate;
> Not unresentful where self-justified;
> Fierce, moody, patient, venturous, modest, shy;
> Mad at their sports like withered leaves in winds;
> Though doing wrong and suffering, and full oft
> Bending beneath our life's mysterious weight
> Of pain, and doubt, and fear, yet yielding not
> In happiness to the happiest upon earth.
> Simplicity in habit, truth in speech,
> Be these the daily strengtheners of their minds;
> May books and Nature be their early joy!
> And knowledge, rightly honoured with that name—
> Knowledge not purchased with the loss of power!"
>
> *(Prelude, v, 411-25.)*

In the elementary schools of the nineteenth century, knowledge was too often purchased by the loss of power. Teachers were obsessed by the idea of imparting information and filling children's minds with "minute, remote, or trifling facts in geography, topography, chronology, etc., or acquisitions in art or accomplishments which the child makes by rote and which are quite beyond its age, things of no value in themselves, but as they show cleverness".[2]

Pestalozzi deplored the emphasis the schools placed upon words to the neglect of things. Wordsworth puts his complaint in

---

[1] *Memoirs of William Wordsworth*, by the Rev. G. C. Wordsworth (Canon), vol. 2, p. 182, Edward Moxon, 1857.
[2] *ibid.*, p. 169.

another way. The methods in vogue robbed the child of opportunities for experiencing and feeling. When he could have gone direct to the objects of nature, he was put off with counterfeits. "The diet these schools offer is not the natural diet for infant and juvenile minds—Natural History is taught in infant schools by pictures stuck up against walls and such mummery. A moment's notice of a redbreast pecking by a winter's hearth is worth it all."[1]

Wordsworth has been charged with inconsistency in his views on education. We have seen that he looked forward with approval to a state system of education, and in a note he wrote on the passage from the *Excursion*, already quoted, he said, "The discovery of Dr Bell affords marvellous facilities for carrying this into effect; and it is impossible to overrate the benefit which might accrue to humanity from the universal application of this simple engine under an enlightened and conscientious government".

When, however, he had gained some experience of the work of the Monitorial schools, he modified his opinions. He believed that the education of the feelings is as important, if not more so, than the education of the intellect. At the present day, intelligence is at a premium, possibly because it seems to be more easily measured than the emotions. Modern writers have sensed this defect in English education as clearly as Wordsworth. They have called attention to the gap which seems to exist between thought and emotion. Thus, Victor Murray writes, "Progress in education inevitably widens the gulf between thought and emotion and puts asunder that which God has joined together. We progress on the intellectual plane while standing still or even receding on the emotional. So much is this the case that everything becomes, so to speak, intellectualised and intellectual values predominate. For a feeling we substitute the idea of a feeling or even the name of a feeling, beauty becomes something not so much to be respected and enjoyed as to be analysed . . . There are even eminent scholars and well-known divines, and thousands of hard-headed business men who are emotionally as immature as children".[2]

Professor W. R. Niblett writes in the same strain. "Wordsworth was declaring more than a century ago that if schools came to look upon themselves as institutions, as factories for making human beings a certain mental shape, then humanity was doomed. For they would be using up the capital of the human spirit in order

[1] *Memoirs of William Wordsworth*, p. 186.
[2] A. Victor Murray, *The School and the Church*, pp. 86-7, S.C.M. Press, 1944.

to pay out dividends of memorised skill and information. For Wordsworth the chief problem was that of the growth and preservation of an inward life. The end of education is not learning but an intensified power to live."[1]

The other aspect of Wordsworth's thought, namely, his mysticism, remains for consideration. R. D. Havens speaking of Wordsworth's "trance-like states of consciousness", says: "Anyone who is familiar with the literature of mysticism will recognise them as examples of the brief periods of ecstasy, insight, and oblivion to be met within all races and all periods of history which are known as mystic experiences".[2] His view is that Wordsworth himself did not recognise his experiences as belonging to this class but confused them with the imagination. "He did not see that in his greatest moments, when the light of sense went out, imagination had no part."[3]

Wordsworth has been described as a Christian pantheist, an ill-chosen term which perhaps was intended to mark the distinction between the tendencies of his vision and his approval of institutional religion which became more evident when his vision began to fade. He was throughout life a loyal member of the Church of England, and it perhaps furnishes the reason why in his later years he altered the text of certain passages in the *Prelude* so as to give them a more definite theistic emphasis. He was both poet and mystic. The purist may object to the classification of Wordsworth as a mystic. It has, however, the support of one of the most prominent

---

[1] *Wordsworth and the Child in Education Papers*, vol. 5, p. 63, No. 3, King's College Education Society, Newcastle-upon-Tyne. In a letter to Mr Tremenheere, one of the inspectors appointed by the Committee of Council on Education, Wordsworth comments on the Minutes of the Committee in the following terms: "Let me ask you, dear Sir, whether throughout the Minutes too little value is not set upon the occupations of Children out of doors, under the direction, or by permission, of their Parents, comparatively with what they do or acquire in school? Is not the knowledge inculcated by the Teacher, or derived under his management, from books, too exclusively dwelt upon, so as almost to put out of sight that which comes, without being sought for, from intercourse with nature and from experience in the actual employments and duties which a child's situation in the Country, however unfavourable, will lead him to or impose upon him? . . .

"It struck me also that, from the same cause, too little attention is paid to books of imagination which are eminently useful in calling forth intellectual power. We must not only have knowledge but the means of wielding it, and that is done infinitely more thro' the imaginative faculty assisting both in the collection and application of facts than is generally believed". (*The Letters of William and Dorothy Wordsworth*, edited Ernest de Selincourt, vol. 3, No. 1590, Clarendon Press, 1939.)

[2] *The Mind of a Poet*, p. 159-60, John Hopkins Press, 1941.

[3] *ibid.*, p. 169.

modern authorities on mysticism, Dr D. R. Inge, who writes, "The greatest prophet of this branch of contemplative mysticism (Dean Inge is speaking of Nature-mysticism) is unquestionably the poet Wordsworth. It was the object of his life to be a religious teacher, and I think there is no incongruity in placing him at the end of the roll of mystical divines who have been dealt with in these lectures".[1]

Even Miss Evelyn Underhill, who is usually most meticulous about those whom she would assign to the ranks of the mystics, speaks of Wordsworth as a mystical poet and quotes the final stanza of the "Daffodils" as an example of the imaginary vision of the mystic which differs in degree but not in kind from Suso's vision of the dancing angels.[2]

The temptation comes to ask what Wordsworth's mysticism has to do with his views about education. The answer is that unless one has some understanding of and sympathy with mysticism, much of what he has written will appear as sheer nonsense. Some critics have not hesitated to affirm this. Thus Dr Hayward describes as "nonsensical and pernicious" the lines:

> "One impulse from a vernal wood
> May teach you more of man,
> Of moral evil and of good
> Than all the sages can". (*The Tables Turned*, 21-4.)

The view expressed in this stanza is not peculiar to Wordsworth. As long ago as the twelfth century, St Bernard, who is acknowledged as one of the greatest of the mediaeval mystics, wrote to Henry Murdach, later third Abbot of Fountains and Archbishop of York, as follows: "*Experto crede*, you shall find a fuller satisfaction in the words than in books. Trees and rocks shall teach you that which you cannot hear from masters".[3]

Dr Hayward's objection sprang from the fact that he surveyed nature with the eyes of a scientist and had no patience with the mystic, whether he be a religious, a philosopher or a poet. In one of his books he wrote a chapter entitled *Nature Light and Nature Moonshine*, in which he made a slashing attack upon Wordsworth and upon certain similar views of Froebel. He blamed Rousseau

---

[1] *Christian Mysticism*, p. 305, Methuen, 1899.
[2] *Mysticism*, p. 342, 11th edition, Methuen, 1926. The vision of the dancing angels is described in *The Life of Blessed Henry Suso by himself*, translated by T. F. Knox, c. 7, Methuen, 1913.
[3] Quoted by K. E. Kirk, *The Vision of God*, p. 311, 2nd edition, Longmans, Green, 1932.

for Wordsworth's attitude and rejoiced that he was afforded the opportunity "of protesting against the pernicious and extraordinary influence of this thief, parasite, rogue, and voluptuary of Geneva".[1] In saying this he showed how little he knew about the origin of Wordsworth's ideas.

Because some writers have taken Wordsworth's references to nature in a purely literal sense, they have stigmatised them as completely untrue to scientific fact, and have quoted with obvious relish the lines of Tennyson, "Tho' Nature red in tooth and claw".[2] Let us hear what Wordsworth himself had to say about the realistic attitude of the scientists of his day: "If the time should ever come when what is now called science, thus familiarised to men, shall be ready to put on, as it were, a form of flesh and blood, the Poet will lend his divine spirit to aid the transfiguration, and will welcome the Being thus produced, as a dear and genuine inmate of the household of man".[3]

Space will not permit a lengthy discussion about the meaning of mysticism and the nature of the mystic's quest. The reader who is interested in this subject is recommended to study the works of Miss Evelyn Underhill. It is sufficient to say that the mystic believes from personal experience that he can attain to a more intimate knowledge of and communion with ultimate Reality than is possible through the senses and the intellect. The latter are quite adequate to carry out the purpose for which they were designed, the exploration of the physical world. Man, however, possesses a higher power, which if used aright, will lead him more surely to his goal. To put the mystic's quest in other words, we may say that he is convinced that he can attain union with God by way of the heart rather than the head, through love and not through reason. The passage from the ordinary experience of life to the ecstatic union of the lover with the beloved is marked by stages. As regards mental and spiritual activity, the mystic passes from the intellectual consideration of Reality by means of meditation and then forsakes this for the higher activity of contemplation. In terms of experience, the mystic passes through the stages of purification and illumination until he reaches the consummation in the unitive life. Dean Inge by reference to the *Prelude* suggests

---

[1] See F. H. Hayward, *The Educational Ideas of Pestalozzi and Froebel*, c. 111, Ralph Holland, 1905.
[2] *In Memoriam*, lv.
[3] *Prefaces. Poems of William Wordsworth*, O.U.P., 1916.

that Wordsworth had experienced all these stages and that he warned the beginner against the danger of prematurely passing from a lower to a higher stage.[1]

The modern nature mystic of which Wordsworth is an example, differs considerably from the older mystics of the Church. The majority of the latter believed it necessary to withdraw from the sense world before starting on the mystic pilgrimage. The unknown writer of the *Theologia Germanica* in a beautiful passage, reminds us that man has been created with two eyes. One has the power of looking into eternity, the other of perceiving time and creatures. Both eyes cannot function at the same time. "If the soul shall see with the right eye into eternity, then the left eye must close itself and refrain from working, and be as though it were dead. For if the left eye be fulfilling its office toward outward things; that is, holding converse with time and creatures; then must the right eye be hindered in its working; that is in its contemplation."[2] The mediaeval mystic found ultimate Reality by looking within himself. The modern nature mystic looks with both eyes and sees God in all things and all things in God. He tends to stress the immanence rather than the transcendence of God and this, if pushed to extremes, always carries with it the tendency to express his thought in terms which savour of pantheism.

The central point of Wordworth's teaching is that he stresses the essential bond between man and nature rather than the antithesis of the two. In this respect he differs entirely from Rousseau although at times both men seem to speak the same language. Human nature is a part of nature and this is the reason why the human mind and external nature are synchronised. We are not strangers in the world. The same eternal spirit who created the beauties of nature has also created the human soul. Hence man can go to nature as his teacher. As Campagnac wrote: "And just as in himself, Wordsworth was simple, orderly, disciplined, so he came to see in the simplicity, the order, the discipline of Nature, in the wide sense which he would have given to the word, not merely the Unity of Law and Principle, but another Personality, answering to his own, a Mighty Being, awake, breathing, listening, speaking to him—a personality not less real than that of human friends, vast, and yet not vague".[3]

[1] *Christian Mysticism*, pp. 307-9, Methuen, 1899.
[2] pp. 22-3, Macmillan, 1901.
[3] E. T. Campagnac, *Poetry and Teaching*, pp. 34-5, Constable, 1910.

Wordsworth's use of the symbolism of nature was no mere echo of Rousseau's education according to nature. He was expressing in poetic form St Paul's doctrine that "the invisible things of God from the creation of the world are clearly seen, being understood by the things that are made". (Rom. i, 20.) The visible objects of nature lead the mind which contemplates them to love and understanding of the God of nature. God works in and through natural phenomena and in the human heart.

> "A gracious spirit o'er this earth presides,
> And o'er the heart of man; invisibly
> It comes, to works of unreproved delight,
> And tendency benign, directing those
> Who care not, know not, think not what they do."
>
> (*Prelude*, v, 491-5.)

Wordsworth's mystical vision of nature, then, provides an additional reason why he regarded education as something much more than the imparting of information, and why he felt he had little in common with the Monitorial schools of Dr Bell. He was convinced that true education should bring to the individual moral and spiritual insight. He feared that the elementary schools of his day might produce characters like Peter Bell within whose breast "these silent raptures found no place".

> "He roved among the vales and streams,
> In the green wood and hollow dell;
> They were his dwellings night and day,—
> But Nature ne'er could find the way
> Into the heart of Peter Bell.
>
> In vain, through every changeful year,
> Did Nature lead him as before;
> A primrose by a river's brim
> A yellow primrose was to him,
> And it was nothing more."

SUGGESTIONS FOR FURTHER READING

Kant's *Pädagogik* is available in English—*Kant on Education*, translated by Annette Churton, Kegan Paul, Trench, Trubner, 1899. The most easily accessible translation of Kant's works on moral philosophy is Kant's *Theory of Ethics*, translated by T. K. Abbott, Longmans, Green, 1909. Kant is not easy reading for the beginner and the student who is not already acquainted with the Kantian philosophy is advised to read the *Metaphysic of Morals* rather than the more difficult *Critique of Practical Reason*.

There is no easily accessible work on Wordsworth's theory of education. For preliminary reading the student is recommended, H. Wodehouse, *A Survey of the History of Education*, § 6 of the chapter on Rousseau, Edward Arnold, 1929. E. T. Campagnac's *Poetry and Teaching,* Constable, 1910, is a most stimulating little book for the young teacher.

In *The Use of Imagination, Educational Thought and the Literary Mind*, Chatto and Windus, 1959, Professor W. Walsh deals with Wordsworth, Coleridge, and Keats, and also discusses the contributions of E. M. Hopkins, Mark Twain, Henry James, D. H. Lawrence, Walter de la Mare, W. B. Yeats, and T. S. Eliot.

CHAPTER XIII

PESTALOZZI

Pestalozzi was an original thinker and experimenter owing little to the inspiration of his predecessors in pedagogy, but it would be wrong to suppose that the whole of the eighteenth century was barren of experimental educational practice until the great man's ventures at Neuhof and Stanz. Some of his predecessors have been considered in the preceding chapter, many others must be left to the further researches of the reader, but two little known educators are truly deserving of recognition as Pestalozzi's precursors, the one in experiments in method and the other in the sociological significance of his work and his pioneering in infant education.

The earlier experimenter was **David Manson (1726-1792)** who, from about 1750 onwards, kept a private school in Belfast for many years, probably spending on the school the bulk of his modest income—derived from a small brewery run as a sideline. By his efforts to make childhood happier and poverty less dire, he won the affection of the town, expressed at his funeral towards the end of the century by a torchlight procession. Unfortunately we know little of Manson's educational theories and principles except by report and assumption, but from his brief writings it is clear that he had read Locke intelligently and critically, and it seems very likely, in view of his intense interest in child education and the special characteristics of his method, that he had read widely. Certain characteristics of his play methods are identical with those of Comenius—as, for instance, the awarding of places and offices according to success in repeating lessons. The boys and girls repeating the longest morning lessons became kings and queens and received two tickets each. The hierarchy continued downwards to the humblest effort of the "undertenant". The lazy who achieved nothing were designated "sluggards". A somewhat complicated system of prestige-earning by both performance and behaviour was worked out; the tickets (marked F.R.S.—Fellow of the Royal Society) could be lost for noisiness or poor spelling, but they were well worth collecting because ten gained a half-guinea medal. Moreover a boy or girl keeping the position of king or queen for a week, earned a guinea medal. Such generosity when fees were but a few shillings a term may well account for the decline in Manson's fortune which is to be suspected from the scattered evidence.

Interesting though these details may be, there is no real evidence that this experiment to generate interest in dull or rote learning, to build up self-regard, and to give experience in living in a civilised community, was ever extended to a wider curriculum than "English grammar, reading, and spelling" which were the subjects offered in Manson's advertisements in the local newspaper. His own little books, *A New Pocket Dictionary*, a *Spelling Book*, and a *Pronouncing Dictionary* indicate what he considered the most important matter of learning, although he himself had taught mathematics to adults; moreover he established liaison with specialist teachers living nearby, or willing to visit his school, so that parents could have their children taught other subjects.

Manson's contribution was not limited to the play-way teaching of reading and spelling; there are three other aspects of his work equally significant. Firstly he is a true pioneer in the campaign for the abolition of corporal punishment, although some might consider his unorthodox methods of dealing with naughtiness equally undesirable! He argues that Locke erred in assuming that positive commands might be given to pupils. If they are given a choice their decision does not weaken the teacher's authority. If they make the wrong choice the teacher's task is to show how desirable the other course would have been, so that the pupils seek to be allowed to take it. Moreover, crying should be treated by ridicule, and aggression by planned retaliation of a similar kind, so that when the pupil objects he can be "reasoned with" and shown the nature of his own offence. Freedom of choice ranked high in Manson's priority list of child needs, but we are not told how he persuaded offenders to choose freely a boxing bout with a large wooden figure—the "natural consequence" of the most serious offences.

The second great principle of Manson was the importance of physical exercise of a recreative nature. His aim was to teach children "without the discipline of the rod, and by intermixing pleasurable and healthful exercise with their instruction". For this he provided a special playground and various pieces of apparatus, including a velocipede. His third principle was the improvement of the condition of the poor by vocational education. His main concern was for the poverty-stricken hand-loom weavers of the town, who he hoped would augment their subsistence in small-scale farming by the latest methods. He wrote a book to help them, but as few could read, it probably achieved little. This versatile man also invented an improved spinning wheel to help the spinners push up their output, and for many years his original model was preserved in the town.

A few years after the publication of Rousseau's *Emile* another neglected educator started his work in a quiet Alsatian valley. **Jean Frédéric Oberlin (1740-1826),** son of a Strasbourg professor, had been educated for the army but had preferred the Church. From the age of twenty-seven to the end of his long life he held the position of pastor of the Ban-de-la-Roche where he developed a remarkable educational system initiated with the same motive which fired Pestalozzi—the improvement of the condition of a poor and ignorant populace. His success was not achieved easily or quickly, for so great was the opposition and suspicion he encountered, that his life was threatened more than once. By great effort and perseverance he erected five schools in the parish, which was a large, sparsely-populated area, and he instructed and trained suitable people as teachers for these schools, where reading, writing, arithmetic, and singing were taught to all pupils. In the upper classes many other subjects were taught including drawing, history, geography, physics, geometry, astronomy, the duties of citizens and public officers, and the elements of business methods.

Oberlin was not content to leave infant education in the hands of mothers—perhaps because it was easier to make schools for the children than to educate the parents. Thus he is recognised as a pioneer in infant school education but he was just as truly a pioneer in further education, for his instruction of his parishioners in improved methods of agriculture and land reclamation earned him the gold medal of the Royal Agricultural Society of Paris.

Jean Heinrich Pestalozzi (1746-1827), was born into a world of increasing economic prosperity and intensifying social disunity and inequality. His native town of Zurich flourished like the other main Swiss towns, and its government was apparently liberal and enlightened. The sick were tended, the poor afforded aid and shelter, orphans were given institutional care, and minor miscreants were sent to "houses of correction"; there were fine libraries, museums, and high schools. Yet in spite of an appearance of benevolence in government, and freedom from persecution and strife, the Swiss States were controlled by autocracies based either on hereditary rights—the succession of son to father in a certain office —or on the restriction of official appointments to freemen of a city.

In the sixteenth century it had been customary to consult the largest class of the population—the peasants—on major state issues, and now these poor members of the community were serfs to all intents and purposes although from the legal viewpoint more were freemen than bondmen.

There was, it is true, a system of popular schools but they appear to have been counterparts of the English "dame" schools, though often in even less skilled hands so that the education of all the poorer people was limited to that which could be given by uneducated teachers—nothing but the inculcation of passages from the Bible. The revolt had to come from those who had not been denied the opportunity to think and learn, and by the middle of the eighteenth century, the need for reform was being realised by some members of the many cultural, artistic, and scientific societies which existed in all the towns. Switzerland was a meeting place for the progressive intellectuals of the day—men of all nations, including Gibbon, Voltaire, and Goethe, spent much time in that country, thus affording to intelligent middle-class Swiss the opportunity to keep well abreast of European thought and to arrive at a realisation of their country's needs. Through newspapers and pamphlets there was an increasing interchange in Western Europe of ideas concerning the liberty of man, ideas expressed in their most impressive form in Rousseau's *Social Contract* published in 1762.

Pestalozzi was born into a Protestant family of Italian origin— a middle-class family enjoying the modest comfort of a professional man's home. His father, a surgeon and oculist, died early in his son's childhood, leaving his wife and family by no means well provided for, so that Pestalozzi's early recollections were of the constant struggle to keep up appearances made by his mother and a devoted woman servant. In spite of tragedy and the ensuing straitened circumstances, the boy had a happy childhood, and there is little doubt that his mother was immortalised in his writings as the wise Gertrude who taught her children through play and through family activities—a loving teacher who trained childish fingers and eyes, and taught by example and precept both virtue and good manners.

This early upbringing failed only in so far as it lacked a father's influence. Pestalozzi confessed that it kept him rather too soft, too sheltered, so that his early schooldays were not entirely successful. He appears to have had no aptitude for spelling and arithmetic, and no doubt his genteel breeding had not prepared him for lively boyish games. His Latin school experience was happier, for now appeared that capacity for bubbling enthusiasm which was in the future to carry him through so many nerve-racking experiments, and to sustain him through periods of great disappointment and poverty. Later he was inclined to blame his schooling for failing to exact the thoroughness and practice requisite to all sound learning: "The *wish* to be acquainted with some branches of knowledge that took hold of my heart and my imagination even though I neglected the means of acquiring them, was, nevertheless, enthusiastically alive within me; and, unfortunately, the tone of public instruction in my native town at this period was in a high degree calculated to foster this visionary fancy of taking an active interest in, and believing oneself capable of the practice of things in which one had by no means had sufficient exercise".

At about fifteen the boy entered a college which prepared boys for the professions, and here he encountered some excellent and inspiring teachers capable of handing on something of their own love of Greek, of history, of politics. Yet again, Pestalozzi saw this training in retrospect as elevating and inspiring, but ineffective because it omitted the "solid and sufficient training of the practical ability" which was essential equipment in any struggle for independence and freedom. The students were imbued with ideals of beneficence, self-sacrifice, and patriotism which were impractical and unrealistic, so that it is hardly to be wondered at if the youths joined the newly formed Helvetic Society in which Catholics and Protestants worked together for the improvement of education, and for the reform of government. Needless to say, Rousseau's political ideas were discussed at meetings so that the young Pestalozzi's mind was ready for the impact of *Emile* when he encountered that work, and according to his own report, the idea of finding a right way of teaching as a "universal remedy" for the ills of society, grew steadily within him from that time.

The oligarchs of Geneva did not like either the Helvetic Society or Rousseau's writings. The journal issued by the Society was eventually suppressed and Pestalozzi, after a brief imprisonment, found his health failing because he not only gave too much of his zeal and energy to his idealistic activities, but he also tried to prepare himself for future struggles by a too severely Spartan régime—including vegetarianism and sleeping on the floor. He had already given up the idea of entering the ministry, for which he had been intended—probably because he showed no great aptitude for that profession after his interests became centred elsewhere. He turned to law, but although some essays he wrote at the time testify as to his high intellectual capacity and unremitting thoroughness in investigating topics related to the principles of good government and similar abstractions, there is no evidence that he would have ever become a good practical lawyer. The new concepts of freedom obsessed him and his studies were focused on the enlightenment of those problems nearest to his heart. The function of education gained in importance and definiteness with every new essay he wrote. Already his main concept of education as fitting the individual for his place in society, had evolved from his observation of the inefficiencies of public officials and the lack of technical skill of the labouring classes.

Medical opinion, combined with the influence of Rousseau's naturalism, caused the young man to give up his studies and engage in farming, first as an apprentice and then as a small farmer experimenting with new agricultural methods on some waste land near Zurich. In 1769, before the result of the venture became clear, he married a very fine young woman, built a house—"Neuhof"—and started a family. Although his lack of practical ability and the unsuitability of the land made financial failure inevitable, the ensuing period was fruitful in more important aspects of life, for Pestalozzi began to develop his fundamental educational concepts through his own experience in observing and training his small son. When the child was only three, the father wrote in his diary: "I drew his attention to some water which ran swiftly down a slope . . . I walked a little lower down and he followed me, saying to the water: 'Wait a minute, I will come back soon'. Shortly afterwards I took him to the bank of the same stream again; and he exclaimed, 'Look, the water comes down too; it runs from there and goes down and down'. As we followed the course of the stream I repeated several times to him, 'Water flows from the top of the hill to the bottom'".

Pestalozzi discovered for himself the principles of experimental method in teaching science—snow was brought into the house to observe the change into water, plants were collected in a garden— in fact, the essentials of Comenian method appear to have been followed, although, there is no clear evidence that Pestalozzi had read much on education except *Emile* and Plato. He learnt how to study an individual child, how to weigh up whether or not he was deliberately answering wrongly "for fun" or to show independence of will. He learnt that words must be taught through things, otherwise words are learnt merely by rote and are entirely meaningless and uninteresting to the child. "Why have I been so foolish," he asks, "as to allow him to pronounce these important words without taking care to connect them at the same time with a clear idea of their meaning?" He learnt that the voice and attitude of the teacher affect the response of the pupils, and that a child learns by activity, by imitating, by drawing, by collecting, and above all, by observing nature: "When he hears a bird sing or an insect hum on a leaf, then you should stop talking".

It was not long before he became critical of Rousseau's theoretical methods. He felt that the achievement of self-control entailed the application to tasks and the suppression of natural desires from the earliest years. "Liberty is a good thing," says Pestalozzi, "and obedience is equally so. We should re-unite what Rousseau has separated. Impressed by the evils of an unwise constraint that only tends to degrade humanity, he has not remembered the limits of liberty". Nevertheless, life for the young child should be happy and free, and education in self-control should be gradual and careful. Punishment and restraint should rarely be necessary, pressure to learn beyond the child's natural pace is harmful, and the denying of opportunities to learn by trial and error retards the development of character as well as of learning. Thus Pestalozzi had already arrived at a belief in teaching words through things, in following and observing nature, and in learning through activity. He had realised that concentration, effort, and perseverance are needed in thorough learning and that these and other qualities need to be developed in character training. He was beginning to evolve ideas on language and number teaching and was giving thought to the needs and order of child development.

Although his financial position was little improved by the help given from time to time by friends and relatives, Pestalozzi and his wife conceived the idea of devoting their efforts to "the simplification of the instruction and the domestic education of the people" by taking in some waifs and strays and giving them education, training in a vocational skill and, above all, the advantages of family life in a good home. It was a practice of the times for such children to be put in the charge of farmers who usually used them as slave labour, but Pestalozzi aimed to use their labour not for profit but only as much as was necessary to make the venture self-supporting. They were to work in the fields in summer and to spin cotton in winter and in bad weather, but part of each day was to be given over to education, first, by the stimulation of speech, and then by the teaching of reading, writing, and arithmetic.

The group was twenty strong, and many more children would have come had there been room. In all ways but financially the experiment was at first successful. The children, enjoying the same care in every way as the founder's son, were happy, skilful, and well-behaved, and it was so obviously a genuine piece of social reform that Pestalozzi's *Appeal to the friends and benefactors of humanity*, published in a journal in 1776, won a satisfactory response so that with the help of bodies such as the Bern Council of Commerce and the Bern Agricultural Society it became possible to accept more children and to continue the work until 1780. Pestalozzi succeeded in no small degree in his aim to teach not only reading, writing, arithmetic, and religion, but also new farming methods to the boys and useful household skills to the girls. It may have been this very success which laid the foundation of eventual failure, for during the last two years of the experiment the parents of many of the potential wage-earners proved a great hindrance and menace. Not only did they persuade the children to run away before the end of the agreed period—five or six years—but they also spread untrue reports and encouraged the children to persist in their old bad habits. Pestalozzi's lack of practical efficiency in business matters, together with a drop in subscriptions, brought the venture to an end at the cost of the health of both organisers and the loss of every penny they had. Only the generosity of friends saved the house for them and they lived in extreme poverty and debt, without income from the farm because the land had to be let to pay creditors.

Then followed another extraordinary phase of Pestalozzi's long life. Harassed by creditors, treated with contempt by those who formerly praised his efforts, tortured by the thought that he had lost all his wife's money as well as his own, he was no longer able to serve society in an active capacity, yet the eighteen years he spent, almost as a hermit, thinking and writing, seem to have provided opportunity for the slow, full cross-fertilisation of the ideas gained as a student and as a young father. Through the good offices of a college friend, his first small writings appeared in 1780 in a journal edited by this friend. He was reshaping and restating his basic principles, as, for instance, "The intellectual powers of children must not be urged on to remote distances before they have acquired strength by exercise in things near them"; and "The circle of knowledge starts close round a man and stretches out concentrically". The following year, with the encouragement of another friend, he tried his hand at story writing although he confessed later that he could "scarcely write a line without committing grammatical errors". His book *Leonard and Gertrude* achieved such a success that his old supporters came to appreciate his qualities again. The Agricultural Society of Bern gave him a gold medal which he sold almost immediately.

The success of the book depended on factors which were much less evident in later works of the same kind—the interest and humanity of the story, the drama, the humour, and the character drawing. The moralising and the propaganda on behalf of education were but incidental and subsidiary, though nevertheless extremely impressive and significant because the presentation was so skilful. Gertrude's efforts on behalf of her weak-willed husband, her influence in village life, her careful training of her children—all these threads of the story contributed towards the educative element in an entertaining novel. In addition, however, they offered to the discerning reader a complete picture of the writer's concept of the true function of education. The author was saying, in effect, that ordinary life can be used to educate—that a school should provide the same companionship and duties as a good working-class home. He was emphasising that the development of the individual and that of the group are bound up together—that the individual can grow in mind and spirit only within a social setting, that a child needs help and guidance in obtaining the fullest intellectual and spiritual benefits from experience.

He depicted Gertrude as the perfect working-class housewife, fulfilling her natural function as the first teacher of her children, training them through their senses, guiding their observations of nature and drawing them into work-activities contributing to the family's welfare. Through her example, the leader of the village came to realise that the proper education of the child was the only way of bringing about reform and improvement, and a village school was set up on lines in harmony with home education. Pestalozzi aimed to show how education should be an integral part of community life, and also how both Church and government should co-operate in the forwarding of this major social service.

Feeling that the general public had missed his major point that progress and reform depended on education, Pestalozzi published in

1782 *Christopher and Elizabeth,* which aimed, through discussion in dialogue form, to bring home to readers the main points in the first book. This was too didactic to have any wide appeal so he continued the adventures of Leonard and Gertrude in three more volumes in 1783, 1785, and 1787, never fully recapturing the narrative style of his earlier work.

Another result of his first literary success was a newspaper venture, which, although it lasted only a year, gave further proof of the strength and independence of his opinions. In rewriting his ideas in the form of allegories and fables he continued to develop his philosophy and to expand his concept of the ennobling force of education in human society.

After a few years, although never really prosperous, Pestalozzi was able to take up farming again. Meanwhile, evidence of a growing reputation came in the form of correspondence with influential people in all parts of Europe who wrote for advice and opinions on educational and social matters. It is said that he influenced the course of educational development in Denmark and Austria as well as in his own country, and he was certainly invited to France, Austria, Italy, and Germany. He visited the last country in 1792, meeting many celebrated Germans, including Goethe and Fichte. In the same year he was declared a "Citizen of the French Republic", a fact which reminds us that by this time much of Europe had accepted the political theories he had supported in his youth, while in his own country the reform party had prevailed, and was not unmindful of the services he had rendered through his pen.

His last effort to express his philosophy in print before engaging in active experiment was published in 1797. Written at the instigation of Fichte, the German philosopher, it was entitled *Investigations into the Course of Nature in the Development of the Human Race,* a clumsy title which, perhaps partially accounts for its small sales. He attempted to set out the basic principles of human life as he saw them in the light of his own experience and his own life. To him it was a work of major importance but he admitted: "This book is to me only another proof of my lack of ability; it is simply a diversion of my imaginative faculty, a work relatively weak—no-one understands me'. Although somewhat obscure and fanciful it is notable as one of the first sociological evaluations of education. He argues that the progress of civilisation towards human betterment depends on man's effort to raise himself to "the moral state", motivated by benevolence and love. It must be truly individual effort, for "Morality is quite an individual matter—no man can feel for me that I am moral . . . A man must possess himself before he can really possess anything else".

When the new Swiss Government[1] came into power, Pestalozzi had the opportunity to edit a newspaper designed to enlighten the people and make known the new principles and policy, but he preferred to offer his services as a teacher to help in the "improvement of the education and schools of the people". His request for "three or four months' experience" found an immediate answer, although not in the way anticipated by either Pestalozzi or the Swiss leaders. The French army, in passing through Switzerland to attack Austria, destroyed the town of Stanz, and Pestalozzi was given the task of setting up and conducting a home for the destitute and homeless children of the town, most of whom had passed several weeks in dire need and misery before the arrival of Pestalozzi. The decree of December 1798 confirming the establishment of the "poor-house" directed that all children should be over five and should work in the fields and house, but Pestalozzi was allowed complete freedom to plan the time-table—lessons from six to eight in the morning, and from four to eight in the afternoon and evening. There was no building in the place fit for habitation but the outbuildings of a convent were to be repaired to accommodate eighty children. The whole of the winter, however, was spent in one room, with only one woman to help with domestic arrangements. He related afterwards: "For the first few weeks I was shut up in a very small room. The weather was bad and the alterations which made a great dust and filled the corridors with rubbish, rendered the air very unhealthy. The want of beds compelled me at first to send some of the poor children home at night, and they came back next day covered with vermin". The children included not only those brought up in poverty but also those who had known good homes, not only those of low intelligence but also those of considerable ability. In spite of filth, vermin, and sickness the spring saw the development of the children into happy, co-operative, disciplined pupils, and in the achievement of this success Pestalozzi had gained the experience which confirmed most of his theories. He wrote: "My children soon became more open, more contented, and more susceptible to every good and noble influence than anyone could possibly have foreseen . . . I had incomparably less trouble to develop those

---

[1] Le Grand, one of the new Swiss Directors had been associated with Oberlin and was eager to make use of Pestalozzi's services in similar work.

children whose minds were still blank than those who had already acquired inaccurate ideas . . . The children soon felt that there existed in them forces which they did not know . . . they acquired a general sentiment of order and beauty . . . the impression of weariness which habitually reigns in schools vanished like a shadow from my classroom. They willed, they had power, they persevered, they succeeded, and they were happy".

The inhabitants of the locality were not favourably disposed towards the new venture, partly because Pestalozzi was a supporter of a government unpopular in the region and, moreover, he was a Protestant in a predominantly Catholic area. He wrote to a friend that the friars and nuns gave more help and sympathy than any others except perhaps the sub-prefect, who made urgent appeals to headquarters for the granting of a larger staff and better facilities. Of Pestalozzi he reported: "This excellent man has both firmness and gentleness, but unfortunately he often uses them at the wrong time". It is difficult to estimate whether the establishment could ever have been organised on a permanent basis. In June the experiment was brought to an end by the retreat of the French troops and the taking over of the convent for a military hospital. Although after the evacuation some weeks later twenty-two children returned, Pestalozzi, whose old tubercular trouble had recurred under severe privation and exposure to disease, was in no condition to take up the work again. He spent some time in the mountains until his lung healed before taking up his first real teaching appointment at Burgdorf. Looking back, he said: "I felt that my experiment proved the possibility of founding popular instruction on psychological grounds; of laying true knowledge gained by sense-impression at the foundation of instruction". He was convinced more firmly than ever of the child's power to learn through the known and the seen, for he had discovered how empty and useless their earlier learning—"one-sided letter-knowledge"—was to his pupils.

It is difficult to understand why those leaders who recognised the value of Pestalozzi's work then gave him only an assistantship in a school conducted by a shoemaker, or why they permitted him to be relegated from there to an infant school for children between four and eight. His own explanation was that rumours were spread that he could not write, work accounts, or read, but as his reputation as a writer cannot have been unknown to everybody in Burgdorf, perhaps this may be regarded as another instance of his own habit of underestimating himself. He writes: "Popular reports are not entirely destitute of truth . . . For thirty years I had read no book . . . I had no language left for abstract notions . . . in my mind there was nothing but living truths brought to my conscious-ness in an intuitive manner in the course of my experience".

Whatever the cause of his transfer to the infant school he found there the opportunity he needed. The old schoolmistress gave him a free hand, and after eight months so remarkable was the change in the school that the Burgdorf School Commission sent him a public letter of commendation. "The surprising progress of your little scholars of various capacities shows plainly that every one is good for something if the teacher knows how to get at his abilities and develop them according to the laws of psychology. By your method of teaching you have proved how to lay the groundwork of instruc-tion in such a way that it may afterwards support what is built on it . . . Between the ages of five and eight, a period in which accord-ing to the system of torture enforced hitherto, children have learnt to know their letters, to spell and read, your scholars have not only accomplished all this with a success as yet unknown, but the best of them have already distinguished themselves by their good writing, drawing, and calculating. In them all you have been able so to arouse and excite a liking for history, natural-history, mensuration, geography, etc., that thus future teachers must find their task a far easier one if they only know how to make good use of the preparatory stage the children have gone through with you."

As a result of this success Pestalozzi gained the mastership of the second boys' school of the town, but his old complaint over-took him and caused his resignation. When he recovered his health he found that friends had been active in forming a "Society of the Friends of Education" which provided funds to equip as a school the castle of Burgdorf, loaned by the Government. Towards 1799 Pestalozzi opened school with the help of a young village school-master named Krüsi. The latter had been teaching a group of orphan war-victims in the castle, and he was to continue this work while Pestalozzi built up a boarding school for more fortunate children. The castle had already been allocated for use as a train-ing college and only lack of funds had delayed its development, so Pestalozzi seized the opportunity to start the work of building up an educational institution which should be a centre for research, teacher-training, and school-book preparation. Krüsi's school—a day school—was to be enlarged and developed, a boarding school for children of prosperous families, was to exist alongside, a "normal school" or teachers' training college was to be set up, and an orphan asylum was to be established in the castle. The orphanage was to be financed by private subscription and by profits from the boarding school and the sale of books.

In 1801 Pestalozzi wrote and published *How Gertrude Teaches her Children, an Attempt to give Directions to Mothers how to Instruct their own Children.* This is not another story of Gertrude, but an account of his experiments and an exposition of his theories. In the same year he issued from the institution at Burgdorf *Help for Teaching, Spelling, and Reading,* and during the next two years the whole staff—the two principals, an assistant writing master, and an assistant drawing master—wrote a set of textbooks issued in 1803 as "Pestalozzi's Elementary Books". These were six little books, three on *Intuitive-instruction in the Relations of Number,* two on *Intuitive-instruction in the Relations of Dimensions,* and one called *The Mother's Manual or Guide to Mothers in Teaching their Children how to Observe and Think.*

While not a little diffident about his own skills and capacities, Pestalozzi had not the slightest doubts as to the efficacy of the methods he was evolving, and with the single-mindedness of the pioneer he never hesitated to advertise those methods or to admit visitors to see them in operation. There is ample independent testimony of his success. Those who entered the schools in a sceptical frame of mind emerged fully convinced. He would not allow them to go away thinking that the quality of the education provided was in any way due to his own personal capacities—it was, he asserted, due to the use of a method which could be used by all teachers. The Society of the Friends of Education reported: "Pestalozzi's pupils learn to spell, read, write, and calculate quickly and well, achieving in six months results which an ordinary village schoolmaster's pupils would hardly attain in three years . . . It appears to us that this extraordinary progress depends less upon the teacher than the method of teaching". An independent visitor wrote: "In six to ten months the children have learnt writing, reading, drawing, and a little geography and French, and have also made astonishing progress in arithmetic. They do everything cheerfully and their health seems perfect . . . The success the method has already obtained should suffice to convince any impartial thinker of its excellence". A Nuremberg merchant confessed himself

amazed when he saw the children "treating the most complex calculations of fractions as the simplest matter in the world. Problems
which I myself could not solve without careful work on paper they
did easily in their heads . . . They seemed quite unconscious of
having done anything extraordinary". A public commission
reported after its inspection that Pestalozzi had discovered the real
and universal laws of all elementary teaching, and it was also noted
that the moral and religious life was praiseworthy and that the discipline was based on affection. A Berlin visitor of 1802 reported
that there were at that time ten masters and several foreigners studying the method. He was particularly struck by the insistence on the
greatest possible liberty for the children, who were to be checked
only when they took advantage of that liberty. The experimenting
with different methods, material and appliances, was also an outstanding feature of the institute.

At the time of greatest promise, the political tide turned and
almost swept away the new educational edifice. Through his work
at Burgdorf, Pestalozzi had won fame abroad and popularity and
respect in his own country so that when a crisis arose through the
French announcement that a new constitution was to be framed for
Switzerland, he was sent to Paris as one of the deputies charged with
the task of putting forward Swiss views. Napoleon would not see
him and in the changes which followed, he lost his castle and his
main support, for the former was requisitioned for the canton
government offices, and the latter, which had been the central
national authority—the "Executive Directory"—was abolished.
This was in 1804, and for the rest of that year the school was
divided, the lower school being sent to an old monastery at München
Buchsee and the upper school to Yverdun castle. The former came
under the control of Fellenberg, another well-known teacher, and
a report of this experience by a pupil-teacher, serves to emphasise
the difference between Pestalozzi's happy muddling and the cold
efficiency of the typical "good school" of the time. The young man
wrote, "We missed more than anything else the love and warmth
which vivified everything at Burgdorf and made everybody so
happy. With Pestalozzi himself it was the heart which dominated
everything; with Fellenberg the mind . . . nevertheless, there was
more order there and we learned more than at Burgdorf".

In 1805 the whole institute was reunited at Yverdun, the scene
of Pestalozzi's unremitting efforts for twenty years. The original
scheme for the institute was dropped, and the teaching of children

—and research on method—engaged the whole attention of the staff. Pupils as well as visitors came from most European countries. The visitors included deputations commissioned to report on the work, teachers with their students—Froebel, Dr Mayo, von Raumer—and individuals of distinction—Herbart, Ritter, Maria Edgeworth, Brougham, Robert Owen, Andrew Bell, and many others. Seventeen students were sent from Prussia for a three-year course of training as teachers. In 1814 the Czar of Russia sent a decoration in recognition of Pestalozzi's services to education. Thus Yverdun came to be regarded by the whole of Europe as the educational Mecca of the day—and this in spite of the cumulative problems and difficulties arising during the first ten years at the castle. In 1809 at the request of Pestalozzi and his staff, the Swiss Diet agreed to arrange an examination comparable to the full inspection of an English school by Her Majesty's inspectors. Three commissioners spent five days at the school, after which they gave a mildly favourable report on the standards attained but made no comment on the value of the aims and principles which influenced the methods.

It may have been partly the effect of this report which led to a greater concentration on the striving for results than had been characteristic of the earlier work. This "restless pushing and driving", described by a teacher who had been a pupil under the old system, was no doubt due to the ambition of individual members of staff, even as many of the other disagreements appear to have been due to the impatience of colleagues who may have been more efficient than Pestalozzi but who nevertheless lacked his true understanding of the essential needs of childhood. The place had grown too big for Pestalozzi. As the benevolent head of a family he could keep his finger on its pulse and could smooth out minor difficulties before they had the opportunity to become major ones. But now the family atmosphere was lost; the leader could no longer have the same personal contact with each individual, while his deputies, although submitting to his system of communal living—which would be considered extreme even to-day—were not resigned to the selfless, unrewarded service which Pestalozzi himself was prepared to give. It would serve no useful purpose, however, to describe at length the tribulations which finally led to the closing of Yverdun in 1825, when Pestalozzi was eighty years old. That the school existed for so long and earned such fame is an amazing enough record—a tribute not only to the great leader who found his vocation only in his old age, but also to the men who worked with him.

It is true that Krüsi, his loyal admirer, and Niederer, his most skilled disciple, left the school in 1816 and 1817 respectively, and it is also true that the personal differences between members of staff gained undesirable publicity in Switzerland, but this did not prevent the fulfilment of the school's major task of fostering the extension and improvement of education. Not only did teachers prepare manuals on arithmetic, geometry, drawing, and singing, but even the students turned their hand to this work—thus Henning, one of the young Prussian students, wrote a manual of elementary geography. Joseph Schmid, mathematician and business manager, revised and improved the *Elementary Books* of the Burgdorf Institute. Schmid was a product of Pestalozzi's own training which was, perhaps by its very freedom and informality, the cause of some of the clashes of temperament which disturbed Yverdun. Although Pestalozzi, maintaining his friendliness towards all his old colleagues, later paid tribute to Schmid's invaluable work as business manager, the latter appears to have been tactless in his dealings with colleagues and visitors—for instance, the withdrawal of twenty-four French student teachers by their master after only a year was said to have been due to Schmid's attitude.

The training of students and the receiving of visitors were even more important than the preparation of textbooks in the spreading of educational ideas in Europe. Yet it was the development of this work which brought about the partial failure of the true Pestalozzian teaching schemes. At Burgdorf the happy family atmosphere and the pleasant methods which gave adequate results, drew students willing to study how to achieve similar success. It would, no doubt, have taken the most inspired and competent staff several years to have developed a reasonable teacher-training course based on the practising school. Neither competent staff nor period of years was given to Pestalozzi and Krüsi for this work. First, more teachers for the school itself had to be trained, but there were no skilled trainers of teachers to train them; moreover there were few good teachers in the whole of Europe from whom teaching standards might be sought. The students were likely to be either bewildered by lack of pedagogical teaching, or too confident in the supreme merit of their own ideas. In decent privacy and segregation from the world, even these faults might have been remedied by staff conferences and by the permeation of the fundamental humility and geniality of the Pestalozzian research attitude, but too early exposure to an adulatory world ruined any remaining hope that stability, unity, and genuine pedagogical thoroughness would be achieved.

The tendency to aim at results has already been mentioned. This was partly due to the scholarly instinct which often finds it difficult to be satisfied with "the child's natural rate of progress" but a further cause was undoubtedly the understandable desire to "put on a good face" before visitors. Rarely a day passed without the arrival of visitors expecting to see the school at work, and moreover, displaying such interest in the methods used, that the children's lesson times were very frequently wasted while the teachers explained and answered the strangers' questions. Dr Mayo during his stay at Yverdun with several pupils in 1819 reported that many English people came, including Lord and Lady Elgin and family, and Lady Ellenborough and friends. It almost seems that a trip to Yverdun was not to be missed by the best people holidaying in Switzerland.

Pestalozzi realised all to well the difficulties and dangers of the period, but carried on by his own enthusiasms, he had no power—perhaps no will—to counteract them at the time. He later referred to "the great delusion . . . that all those things in regard to which we had strong intentions and some clear ideas, were really as they ought to have been and as we should have liked to make them . . . We announced publicly things which we had neither the strength nor the means to accomplish". Of the disunity brought about by the interaction of these and other factors he speaks with even deeper regret: "Led aside by worldly temptations and apparent good fortune from the purity, simplicity and innocence of our first endeavours, divided among ourselves in our inmost feelings, and from the first made incapable, by the heterogeneous nature of our peculiarities, of ever becoming of one mind and one heart in spirit and in truth for the attainment of our objects, we stood there outwardly united, even deceiving ourselves with respect to the real truth of our inclination to this union. And unfortunately, we advanced, each one in his own manner with firm, and at one time with rapid steps along a path which, without our being really conscious of it, separated us every day further from the possibility of our ever being united". His humility in including himself as an offender is typical of his generous attitude.

At the age of seventy-two this remarkable man set up a Poor School at Clindy, a neighbouring hamlet. Here twelve necessitous boys enjoyed the same experience as the poor children at Neuhof, but within a few months the success of the old man's work brought the frustration of its true purpose, for his colleagues at Yverdun prevailed in bringing about the conformation of the school to the Yverdun curriculum, the introduction of other teachers and of fee-payers, and finally the transfer of the school to Yverdun. Yet in spite of his submission, Pestalozzi still dreamed of a poor school, now at Neuhof, where he began. He worked to transfer the Clindy poor boys to Neuhof but his colleagues had done their work all too well, and not one boy remained in the school. Nevertheless, at the closure of Yverdun through debt and internal dissension, he returned to Neuhof where he spent the last two years of his life. He wrote *Swan's Song* and *My Fortunes as Superintendent of my Educational Establishments at Burgdorf and Yverdun*, two important works; but he was not content with writing—he taught in a village school, ordered the building of a Poor School, negotiated for the publication of his works in English and French in order to get funds for the school, attended conferences and visited schools and orphanages. Moreover, he was elected President of the Helvetic Society for which he wrote an address *On Fatherland and Education*. Less than three months before his death he presented a paper, *An Attempt at a Sketch on the Essence of the Idea of Elementary Education*, to an educational society, and was working at a fifth volume of *Leonard and Gertrude*, a supplement to his *Book for Mothers*, and an elementary Latin book. Unfortunately the last— and unfinished—writings of his life were refutations of attacks made on him in newspaper revivals of the Schmid-Niederer controversy— revivals occasioned by the publication of Pestalozzi's own story of Yverdun. While it must be regretted that his last days were shadowed and made unhappy by useless recriminations, his passionate zeal can only be admired and wondered at.

Pestalozzi's Educational Practice

The simple broad aims of Pestalozzi have been indicated sufficiently in the foregoing brief account of his life and work, and it only remains to attempt some evaluation of those methods and teaching principles which he himself regarded as the most important results of his various experiments and observations. His opinion on such matters is worthy of respect, lacking as they do the pardonable egoism of most innovators. His humility would not permit him to say, "I am a good exponent of my methods. If you consider my teaching successful, copy me". He confesses that it was only in his own imagination that he saw the ideal school community and the perfect teaching method. He would have agreed with his old pupil, Ramsauer, that his classroom method often left much to be desired, especially when he became so carried away that his spate of words poured over his uncomprehending pupils. He did not present a "good example" to his pupils in appearance, for he dressed with great negligence and untidiness; nor did he present to them a picture of the well-behaved, completely-controlled adult, for he was disposed to "temper-tantrums" in front of classes of pupils when he discovered teachers not working satisfactorily, or when they incurred his displeasure for any reason.

He would have admitted freely all these failings but it is doubtful whether he would have presumed to offset them by a statement of his own achievement in gaining a spiritual ascendancy over pupils, staff, and students. For this achievement he merits recognition as a great educator, yet he himself did not wish to admit that good teaching might be bound up with such qualities of greatness, for he hoped above all that he was helping to show the world its need for many trained teachers, rather than just a few "born" teachers.

That there was much truth in his contention that good teachers could be "made" was proven by the extraordinary fruitfulness of his ideas in both the old and new worlds. It was shown at Yverdun itself, although it might be argued that there the methods were hardly given a fair trial and that it was the spirit of the leader which gave that centre its unique quality. It was certainly something more than a mere inculcation of methodology which ensured the acceptance of communal living conditions by the staff. Each teacher lived with his own group of pupils—slept and ate with them, supervised their duties, personal hygiene and books, and spent his free time with them whenever they showed a desire for his company.

The first lesson of the day was at six o'clock in the morning and the last finished at eight in the evening. Apart from a few brief breaks between lessons, the times for recreation and exercise were about an hour or an hour and a half at mid-day, and a similar period from four-thirty. Wednesday and Sunday afternoons were given over to conducted excursions. In bad weather recreation and excursion time was spent in a gymnasium. This carefully regulated life and simple food ensured the good health of the pupils, but it also prohibited any extensive freedom for the staff. It is true that few of the younger teachers appear to have sought time to read and study, perhaps because Pestalozzi so often stressed that good teaching could not be learnt from books, only from practice. On the other hand they were encouraged and expected to attend their colleague's lessons as a means of remedying any deficiency of knowledge. Froebel is reported to have sat in class with the boys, learning along with them.

A description of Yverdun by a former pupil, Roger de Guimps, is worthy of quotation because it indicates its remarkable similarity to the modern conception of a "progressive" school. After describing how, in spite of the spread-over of lessons, there was ample time for playing, bathing, and tending the little garden plot given to each pupil, he relates that there was complete liberty of egress and ingress, a privilege not abused by the children. "Not one lesson was longer than an hour," he continues, "and they were all followed by a short interval during which the classes usually changed rooms. Some of the lessons consisted of gymnastic exercises or some sort of manual work or gardening. The last hour of the day was a free hour, given up to what the pupils called their own work. They could do anything they wished—draw, read geography, write letters, or arrange their note-books . . . The end of the year was devoted to making New Year albums to send to parents, containing drawings, maps, mathematical problems, fragments of history, descriptions of natural objects and literary compositions. On New Year's Day the pupils of each class decorated their room, transforming it into a woodland scene, with cottage, chapel, ruins, and sometimes a fountain, which was so arranged as to play when Pestalozzi came in. Fir-branches, ivy and moss were fetched in large quantities from the neighbouring forests, and transparencies with emblems and inscriptions were secretly prepared; for the decoration of each room was to be a surprise, not only to Pestalozzi, but to the pupils of the other classes . . . The principal idea in most of the inscriptions was: 'In summer you take us to see nature; to-day we try to bring nature to see you'. Frequently on this day the pupils performed a dramatic piece, the subject generally being one of the great episodes from Swiss history of mediaeval times. For these plays the actors made their own costumes and weapons from coloured paper and cardboard".

The curriculum included religion, history, classical and modern languages, physical science, natural history, mathematics, geography, spelling, perspective drawing, and singing, and although only the last five subjects were taught according to Pestalozzi's method, the width of the range of subjects is sufficiently remarkable to merit the term "reformed curriculum". It would seem that Locke's plan for the individual little gentleman was now being applied with a considerable measure of success to the group education which he deplored. An outstanding but inevitable problem arising from this was one which still exists—the problem of teaching each pupil so that every step fits his developmental needs. True, at Yverdun the situation was even more complicated by the fact that between them the pupils had half a dozen native languages— German, French (prayers were read in both), English (and American), Spanish, Italian, and Russian. Perhaps even more serious, however, was another problem shared by most schools to-day—that the preceding training and education of the pupils varied so greatly.

Pestalozzi's Educational Theory

Pestalozzi saw education as a means of social reform but not solely as an ameliorating influence. His plea was, in truth, an appeal for equality of opportunity—it was a duty of society to develop each man's abilities to the full; this could only be accomplished by providing good schools, high moral standards, and sound teaching methods. Moreover, the education itself should be such as would prepare the individual for his future place in life, not in the sense of class distinction but in the sense that he should be able to find satisfaction in his occupation and in his domestic life. Pestalozzi does not envisage early education as vocational, however, but he would have the school reflect the best of the family atmosphere typical of the social grade to which its pupils belong. Presumably if the child gains a good general education closely related in pleasures, duties, responsibilities, and activities to a good home training—and based on association with the social environment, not on segregation from it—then he will become a fully developed, balanced, disciplined adult who will easily move out from his native society should his skills and abilities make it possible.

In *On Infants' Education* Pestalozzi describes the end of education as "not a perfection in the accomplishments of the school, but fitness for life; not the acquirement of habits of blind obedience and of prescribed diligence, but a preparation for independent action", and, moreover, he emphasises in the same work: "We have no right to shut out the child from the development of those faculties also, which we may not for the present conceive to be very essential for his future calling or station in life". His own repeated efforts to draw to him under the same four walls children of all classes, indicate that his various statements on this topic were not mere rhetoric. He truly believed that the rich child missed much of the best of family education by being excused family chores and responsibilities, and also by being so often put in the charge of unimaginative nurses and tutors instead of receiving the best kind of maternal training. In his school-family he aimed to reproduce those conditions of precept and practice, example and experience, which he considered to be the most likely to fulfil the right of all people to "a general diffusion of useful knowledge, a careful development of the intellect, and judicious attention to all the faculties of man, physical, intellectual and moral".[1]

This emphasis on physical education is reminiscent of Locke and perhaps came to Pestalozzi through Rousseau, but it cannot be doubted that his own health problem and his experience with the orphans of Neuhof and Stanz taught him far more than any writings. He was not content to let Nature educate at her own speed in any sphere of development, so that although he accepted Rousseau's standards of simplicity in dress and living conditions, he included in his scheme a very considerable element of physical exercises allied to modern gymnastics, and in addition allowed much time for free out-of-door activities. Specialists accept his ideas as penetrating deeply into the nature of physical education. He aimed to develop strength and control of the limbs through exercises and, in addition, grace through rhythmic movement. "Exercises may be devised for every age and for every degree of bodily strength, however reduced,"[2] he wrote, and although this viewpoint has not always been fashionable, it is not disdained to-day by the boxer, the ballet dancer, the typist, and many other specialists in arts and occupations demanding some physical dexterity.

Not the least among his educational aims in physical training, in addition to the remedial and preventive aspects, is its contribution to moral education—comparable to that he attributes to music, indicating, perhaps, that he was not entirely forgetful of his early reading of Plato.[3] He writes of gymnastics as promoting cheerfulness, comradely spirit, frankness, courage, and perseverance, and

[1] On Infants' Education.
[2] ibid.
[3] He refers to Greek education in several works, aims, and principles in On the Idea of Elementary Education, and the Socratic method—its unsuitability for children—in How Gertrude Teaches her Children.

he describes music as striking at the root of "every bad or narrow feeling, of every ungenerous or mean propensity, of every emotion unworthy of humanity".[1]

The foundations of moral education, however, are formed by the mother and she awakens in her child feelings of love, confidence, gratitude, and obedience. By her constant loving care, her firmness, her consistency, and her simple teaching about God, the child gains feelings of security and confidence combined with habits of obedience both to her and to the father. The great task of the educator is to preserve these virtuous feelings and habits: "Here you must not trust nature; you must do all in your power to supply the place of her guidance by the wisdom of experience".[2] Thus life itself forms the beginning of moral education, and its continuation, through the development of the will to goodness, should also be based on real experience and not on mere homilies and sermons, for "words alone cannot give a real knowledge of things . . . will cannot be aroused by mere words". Children need to have noble sentiments "engrafted on their hearts", by example and by experience. This is clearly an adaptation of Plato's method of habituation to goodness, but there is a greater emphasis on the need to *give* love and kindness to children, to make unceasing efforts to broaden their sympathies, and to develop their good judgment and tactfulness. Pestalozzi emphasises the threefold nature of moral education—the arousing of noble feelings, the exercise of self-control, and the formation of personal standards.

The basic elements of intellectual education are comparable to those of physical and moral education although Pestalozzi suggests that the natural laws for the development of human powers are not the same for the heart, the mind, and the body.[3] In fact, the different needs of each side of man's nature account for the basic principle of Pestalozzi's method, best indicated by an extract from an address he gave on his seventy-second birthday: "Each of our moral, mental, and bodily powers must have its development based upon its own nature and not based upon artificial and outside influences. Faith must be developed by exercises in believing and cannot be developed from the knowledge and understanding only of what is to be believed; thought must grow from thinking, for it cannot come simply from the knowledge and understanding of what

[1] *On Infants' Education.*
[2] *How Gertrude Teaches her Children.*
[3] *Swan's Song.*

is to be thought or the laws of thought; love must be developed by loving, for it does not arise merely from a knowledge and understanding of what love is, and of what ought to be loved; art also, can only be cultivated through doing artistic work and acquiring skill, for unending discussion of art and skill will not develop them. Such a return to the true method of Nature in the method of the development of our powers necessitates the subordination of education to the knowledge of the various laws which govern those powers".[1]

Pestalozzi emphasises that the three aspects of education need to go hand in hand for the harmonious development of the individual, but it is in his ideas on the training of the intellect that are most clearly defined his principles for "improving the tendencies and powers of humanity according to the course of Nature".[2] The mother and the teacher can do no more than "assist the child's nature in the effort which it makes for its own development".[3] Therefore the first task of educational research should be the discovery by observation of the child's unfolding powers and changing needs, and the arrangement of the whole range of human knowledge in an order adapted to those powers and needs. Pestalozzi would deem forced precocity as undesirable as backwardness, for he believes child development should proceed like that of plants— according to the "norm" for each stage. This attitude accounts for his indifference to the actual attainments of his pupils in the traditionally "important" subjects. He was more concerned with discovering "the unbroken chain of measures originating in . . . a knowledge of the constant laws of our nature".[4]

Pestalozzi's concept of intellectual education is related to Locke's principle for the conduct of the understanding—a development of reasoning by the practice of reasoning. The mind receives impressions from the outside world and it analyses, compares, and combines those impressions. Education must foster this process by following the course of nature—for the first mental impression is received immediately after birth, so that much has been stored up by the time formal education begins. To the fundamental processes of the mind of Pestalozzi gave the name *Anschauung*, a term which does not bear translation by one equivalent, since it embraces all and any of the various stages of the evolution of ideas. Sometimes

---

[1] Quoted in H. Holman, *Pestalozzi*, pp. 170-1, Longmans, Green, 1908.
[2] *Swan's Song.*
[3] *How Gertrude Teaches her Children.*
[4] *On Infants' Education.*

it is the process of reception by the mind of a sense-impression and the resultant production of an idea—an idea of softness, of prickliness, of warmth, of dullness—independent of a knowledge of the appropriate word used to describe it. Sometimes it is the process of idea-formation through a combination of sense-impression and observation—the latter term implying intellectual awareness or attention. Sometimes it is the immediate mental realisation of an idea without the intervention of external things. These three versions of *Anschauung* explain its translation as "sense-impression" or "observation" or "intuition". Pestalozzi intended it to have a very wide meaning: "Anschauung is the immediate and direct impression produced by the world on our inner and outer senses—the impressions of the moral world on our moral sense and of the physical universe on our bodily senses".

From Pestalozzi's definition of education as the art of assisting natural development, it is clear that he assumes the existence of inborn tendencies to form ideas through *Anschauung*. The simple ideas gained from early experience build themselves up into complex powers of reasoning and abstract thought, so that the educator's task is not to put knowledge or reasoning power into the pupil, but to provide the best conditions for his full development—to tend him as a gardener tends a plant, removing noxious weeds from his vicinity, and supplying healthy, fertile soil and the right degrees of sun, water, and shelter. In fact, the pupil develops himself through self-activity—he develops speech through speaking and thought through thinking. The highest and best form of any human skill, accomplishment, or virtue is achieved through performance and practice in the right conditions, from the elementary beginnings initiated by natural human impulses.

The justification for education is, therefore, that even as a plant's growth may be uncertain or retarded in neglected soil, so man, without education, is prevented from achieving full mental and moral stature. The accidental, ill-arranged experiences of life permit but limited development, so that both parents and teachers need to order and plan the environmental experiences of the young—here we see a measure of agreement with Rousseau. Later, as the young person takes his place in the world, the state, or society itself, should take the place of parents and teachers in ensuring that he is not denied the opportunity of suitable work and conditions of life, for on these depends his continued development in the perception of moral values, the realisation of duty, and the appreciation of goodness and justice.

Pestalozzi does not suggest that complete development can be achieved without conscious effort on the part of the learner. He needs to study—to direct his own search for knowledge—and he needs to seek constant exercise of his powers of reasoning and judgment. Nevertheless, such activity starts from much experience in weighing up and estimating simple impressions gained from things. Practice and maturity bring increased capacity to proceed from the known to the unknown. The use of this mental capacity to weigh up impressions, to compare and contrast them, to put them into categories, is the activity which results in the formation of ideas, whether simple or complex. The baby in the hot bath-water gains an "idea" of heat without knowing the word and without consciously relating it to other ideas. The nurse testing the bath-water with her elbow could, if necessary, describe her experience, but, more important, she can gain very quickly an idea of exact temperature because, through the practice of comparing and judging past experiences of a similar kind, she has gained an insight into the real nature of hot water—she has a distinct and accurate idea of it. The probationer, through lack of practice in identifying the particular grades and categories of water-testing experiences, may have only a vague, confused idea, or even a completely wrong idea, of the correct temperature for baby's bath. The tutor does not insist that each attempt at testing be analysed into its elements and the temperature deduced accurately. It will be enough to give the probationer guidance and to provide adequate opportunities for the involuntary development of skill in differentiating between temperatures.

As it is through the formation of ideas through *Anschauung* that the highest intellectual processes can be attained, it is important that the teacher should guide and foster the production of clear, accurate ideas at each stage. To ensure this accuracy, two factors are essential—perfection and completeness of the original sense-impression (or intuition, or observation) and the achievement, through practice, of facility in reasoning and judging at that level before proceeding to the next stage which involves more difficult and more complex ideas. This repetition and practice at each stage needs to be based upon a series of the most representative experiences in that particular category. The implications of this theory

in class teaching are simple but nevertheless of fundamental significance. Assuming that Pestalozzi's requirement—educational research—has been fulfilled, the teacher should be able to plan a
syllabus graded according to difficulty. Each study should begin
with observation of the object or the external physical manifestation
of the topic—which should be a normal, representative specimen,
or series of specimens. If it is unavoidable, the real specimens may
be replaced by pictures—*but never merely by words.* The teacher
helps the pupils to name the object, to investigate and name its
parts and properties, and, after due consideration of this description,
to formulate a definition representing their distinct idea of the
object. The teacher's function is to train pupils in habits of accurate
observation, not in the memorising of words. However true the
teacher may know those words to be, they have no reality or truth
for the pupil unless based on his own perceptions. The inspiration
of Herbart's theory of apperception probably lies in Pestalozzi's
belief that the association of like ideas—gained from like objects—
serve to weaken the non-conforming ideas gained from unrepre-
sentative objects in a category. Therefore it is important that plenty
of worthy, noble, and correct ideas are formed for they will surely
oust the unworthy, ignoble, and incorrect.

The teacher encourages the pupil in the development of language, observation, and mental skills which proceed from the "three
elementary powers"[1] of making sounds, forming images, and
imagining concepts, powers on which Pestalozzi based his whole
educational practice. In aiming to make education "a steady,
unbroken development of these fundamental powers", and to ensure
certain progress "from obscure to definite sense-impressions, from
definite sense-impressions to clear images, and from clear images to
distinct ideas", he seeks to base all teaching on sound, form, and
number. He postulates that the natural tendency of the mind, when
presented with a confused mass of objects, is to sort them out into
separate objects and to group them in categories—that is, to number
them; the mind also notices the shape of the objects and seeks to
apply to them some name already in the mind through previous
experience. The properties of number, form, and name are common
to all things, and all other properties which are not thus shared are
nevertheless related to those three elements. He contends, "whatever ideas we may have to acquire in the course of our life, they

---

[1] *How Gertrude Teaches her Children.*

are all introduced through the medium of one of these three departments".[1]

From such a conviction grew his methods in elementary education. All activities were planned to enable correct ideas of number, form, and language to be developed from good and full perception. Reading, writing, and arithmetic were not the bases of instruction but merely subsidiary activities: "It is well done to make a child read and write, and learn and repeat—but it is still better to make a child think".[2] That is, these elementary skills are useful only in so far as they can be employed in the pursuit of further knowledge. Moreover, the activities through which they are acquired are far more important than the skills themselves, and so in place of the old "words and things" learning, Pestalozzi substituted the approach to the three R's through the object lesson.

Some of the best teachers of English of the present day have reverted to the Pestalozzian principle that talking is more important than reading. Until children have learnt to feel and think, and until they have acquired some knowledge of the world around them, there is no purpose in learning to read. From the first they have the capacity to feel intuitively the meaning of sound. They need guidance in expanding this capacity of intuitive understanding, guidance also in the conscious acquisition of a vocabulary, and, not least, guidance in the ability to describe things accurately in speech. The natural place for this early guidance is in the home, and later in the school. The study of grammar should come only after a long, thorough, carefully graduated course in language-using. A very large area of advanced thought is dependent on a wide knowledge of language for its clear and meaningful functioning, even as another large area of thought is dependent on mathematical symbols. Hence, language teaching should consist of giving exercise in "describing accurately" at the appropriate child level. In the early stages, the sense-impressions made by objects or pictures will give rise to discussion and simple definitions of properties and characteristics, and pupils will easily recall their findings about objects with similar properties.

Constant exercise in describing what he sees, feels, and hears, and what he has seen, has felt, and has heard, will give a child increasing command over language both in vocabulary and construction. Pestalozzi accepted as a fundamental that a whole sentence is simpler than its component parts, yet when he planned the

[1] *On Infants' Education.*   [2] *ibid.*

teaching of spelling and reading he started from syllables—he assumed that the "natural" process was the formation of single sounds into words, and words into speech. His system had the great advantage over the later elementary routine, that much directed and guided talking preceded any learning of spelling and reading. Had he been content to regard his artificial syllable-learning as mere exercise for the articulating organs, it might have been suspected that he had studied the evolution of infant speech, its combination of consonants and syllables, as shown in our own day by Dr M. M. Lewis.[1] While deeming the alphabet but "dead signs", he yet found it desirable to learn letters separately, and he devised play-way methods and apparatus for this purpose.

The teaching of "form" was an interesting attempt to combine measuring, drawing, and writing on the assumption that the "natural order" involved these activities in this order. Practice in measuring and drawing gives clearer, more accurate ideas of shapes of objects, but the pupil should not be employed in making copies of copies. He should measure and draw real things. For some time Pestalozzi and his colleagues experimented with a scheme for teaching "the simple elements of the laws of form", supposedly essential before drawing could be undertaken. This curious "alphabet" of geometrical forms repeated the same mistake as the division of words into syllables but its defects were more obvious and the inventors eventually modified it. A knowledge of, and practice with, the fundamental lines, angles, and curves, were supposed to facilitate the learning of writing and to prevent the development of bad habits. Again, in addition to arranging the letters in order of difficulty (of lines, angles, etc.), Pestalozzi devised ways of helping the pupils and of making the work more interesting. Exercise books could be cut into strips so that the work to be copied could be placed immediately above the line to be written; the work could be checked by the pupils themselves by placing over their work transparent horn sheets bearing perfect strokes and letters. Writing is much more than a mechanical exercise, however. Penmanship is a skill which enables speech to be written down, thoughts to be expanded and clarified, and imagination to be exercised.

In number teaching Pestalozzi set out to find ways of helping children really to understand number, and not merely to develop speed and accuracy in the mechanical working of examples. He wanted children to discover for themselves the elementary

[1] M. M. Lewis, *Infant Speech*, Kegan Paul, Trench, Trubner, 2nd edition, 1951.

mathematical rules through activities based—like all other learning activities—in the first place on sense-impressions. "Any number, whatever be its name," wrote Pestalozzi, "is nothing but an abbreviation of the elementary process of counting", and so the counting of real objects, the grouping, the adding, the subtracting were the essential basic activities of early number work, in order that the primitive constitution of numbers should be deeply impressed upon the mind without being complicated and confused by written symbols. Pupils would gain "an intuitive knowledge" of the real properties and proportions of numbers—a useful illustration of the Pestalozzian meaning of the term "intuition"—a knowing in the mind independent of sense-impression or reasoning. Pestalozzi's description of his method: "I make him go over the same numbers again . . . with beans, pebbles, or any other objects which are at hand", reminds us that nursery and infant schools to-day use a great deal of number apparatus in a similar way. True, much of it aims to enable the child to gain experience in counting, grouping, adding, and subtracting without the teacher's guidance, but the principle—the use of units, at first solid and later as marks on paper —is exactly the same.

To facilitate progress to division, multiplication, and the understanding of fractions, Pestalozzi devised his Table of Units in which the unit adopted was the square, a figure which lends itself to simple visual subdivision and partition. Through activities with these divisible squares, pupils gain an "intuitive knowledge" of the proportions of the different fractions and so can proceed later to their symbolic representation with clear ideas of their true significance. Although the details of the scheme were too full and elaborate to suit the modern fashion for "freedom", the operation of the scheme produced results which evoked more wonder and admiration from visitors to Yverdun than any other aspect of the school's work, perhaps because arithmetical skill was a newer and more impressive accomplishment than fluent, vigorous speech. The pupils were not only quick but remarkably accurate in the working of practical arithmetic.

This then, was Pestalozzi's basic curriculum, but as we have seen, his scheme also opened up wide fields of knowledge and experience. Not only did he provide an education which even according to modern standards was "general"—and this at a time when child education was still closely hedged in by tradition—but he also made praiseworthy attempts to apply his *Anschauung* principle to the teaching of all other subjects. Even where he failed, or where the method became cluttered up by over-elaboration, his insistence on individual experience as the basis of all learning might well be imitated by many more educators of children. Perhaps the most striking example of an excellent lead, ignored by many generations of teachers, was his work in geography teaching. From his experience with his own son—illustrated by his story of the river— he developed a method which the best teachers are struggling to put into practice to-day—the guided observation of the local area and the introduction to maps, not through maps made by strangers, but through the activities of making large-scale models and maps of the locality. An old pupil described this work: "We were taken to a narrow valley, not far from Yverdun . . . After taking a general view, we were made to examine the details until we had obtained an exact and complete idea of it. We were then told to take some clay which lay in beds on one side of the valley . . . and on our return we took our places at the long table and reproduced in relief the valley we had just studied . . . In the course of the next few days more walks and more explorations each day on higher ground and each time with a further extension of our work. Only when our relief was finished were we shown the map, which by this means we did not see till we were in a condition to understand it". The basic idea is as valid to-day as a century and a half ago. Equally worth while is Pestalozzi's view that geography should be closely co-ordinated with related subjects. Karl Ritter, one of the most appreciative of Pestalozzi's pupil-teachers was the great German pioneer in geography teaching, who had a wide and lasting influence on German elementary education in his day. Germany had in the nineteenth century by far the best geography teaching in the world. Many of its best characteristics—including *heimat kunde*—persisted into the twentieth century.

Of other subjects there is space to say little except that subjects based on *Anschauung*, such as science, were approved by Pestalozzi, and those which were not so easily related to experience—such as history—were less favoured. Languages, including Latin, should be learnt on the same principles as the vernacular—by talking and not by grammar—but language work should be as carefully planned as other studies because, in Pestalozzi's view, it should be the link between sense perception and the true faculty of thought. Handicrafts and other manual activities[1] were accorded equal status with

---

[1] Gardening, bookbinding, model-making, shooting, etc.

other ways of learning. Indeed, Pestalozzi suggested that an "alphabet of practical abilities" should be sought so that manual work and physical exercises could be analysed into elements, and teaching schemes devised to develop skill in elementary movement in graded order. This suggestion was taken up by Pestalozzi's disciples, and, as in some other subjects, the process was often carried to the point of absurdity.[1]

In view of the absence of a science of psychology in his day, and in view of the humility and frankness of his reports and suggestions, it would be mere carping to attempt to summarise the weaknesses of Pestalozzi's educational theory. Indeed, those failings which have been subjected to critical comment by other writers may be put forward alternatively as points of strength, if only in that their courageous deviation from the traditional and conventional permitted experiment which might not otherwise have taken place for another century. The same points are among those which have preserved and enhanced his reputation and have given his contribution a permanent significance. For instance, it cannot be established that he and his staff would have taught better or found "short cuts" had they read other men's opinions on education. As it was, they were thrown into true research method. Again, while it may not be entirely true that "anyone can teach", the adoption of the idea of training teachers has, in fact, resulted in the handing on of methods evolved through research, to thousands of teachers coming from the walks of life on which Pestalozzi wished to draw. Again the criticism—contemporary, it is true—that his pupils were "too little under restraint", has been confounded by the modern attitude to school discipline. His experiments in methods of self-government have been followed and developed, and now, after a phase of somewhat extreme freedom at some stages of education, general opinion tends to agree with him that firmness and consistency on the part of the teacher are desirable, although his first duty is still "to be interested and interesting".[2]

Many critics have torn to shreds the language-form-number theory, but even if based on faulty psychology and hazy philosophy,

---

[1] The writer's colleague in this work has in his possession an English publication of 1865, *Calisthenics or the Elements of Bodily Culture on Pestalozzian Principles*, which attempts to reduce bodily movements to their elements and succeeds only in setting out large numbers of purposeless exercises.

[2] H. Holman, *Pestalozzi*. p. 294, Longmans, Green, 1908.

surely it deserves recognition as the first attempt to develop knowledge and goodness systematically out of child experience? Pestalozzi himself said: "I am but the initiator—and depend upon others
to carry out my views". That his followers had not the vision to
expand and improve his concepts was the real cause of the tedious
oral repetition and the stereotyped object lesson which were the
characteristics of the narrowed application of Pestalozzian methods.
How far they created the essential "family atmosphere", how far
they aimed to foster goodness rather than merely to repress evil,
how far they graduated their exercises according to child-under-
standing, are questions not easily answered. It is extremely
doubtful, however, whether any but the few pioneers and contemporary disciples had any true insight into Pestalozzi's heart.
English teachers had the opportunity to learn, for Dr Biber's book
was published in English in 1831.[1] It was a fair book although its
author had been a bitter critic of Pestalozzi.

Of all the English people who visited Pestalozzi at Yverdun
none did more to interpret directly and fully Pestalozzi's ideals and
principles in England than the **Rev. Charles Mayo (1792-1846),** who
spent nearly three years from 1819 as English chaplain at the school.
He had deliberately sought leave of his college—he was a Fellow
of St John's, Oxford—in order to make this visit, so that it is clear
he had a genuine interest in education even before he became a
whole-hearted disciple of the Swiss educator. On his return, fired
with the desire to introduce to England the methods and principles
he had learned, he set up a private school at Epsom and later moved
it to Cheam, where he stayed for the rest of his life. Not only did
he put into practice the new methods, he also took every opportunity
to spread information about them and understanding of them—as,
for instance, by his lecture in 1826 on the life of Pestalozzi given at
the Royal Institution. He emphasised that the essence of the
method was that all subjects and studies should arise from the
experience of the pupil, and that the teacher's function was to guide
the child through educative experiences from the less advanced
intellectual stage to the more advanced. Reiner, a pupil of Pestalozzi, joined the staff of the school to teach mathematics and science,
and Mayo's sister Elizabeth also taught in the school for several
years. Dr Mayo himself wrote several school textbooks for use
in his school, Reiner wrote *Lessons on Number* and *Lessons on
Form*, and Miss Mayo collected together her own lessons and

[1] E. Biber, *Henry Pestalozzi and his Plan for Education*, London, 1831.

published them in two books, one on objects and one on shells, both of which ran into many editions. Miss Mayo left the school in 1834 to introduce Pestalozzian ideas into the training college and schools of the Home and Colonial Society,[1] an institution in which her brother was extremely interested. Both Mayos contributed to the society's publications. Miss Mayo appears to have had considerable scope to criticise and direct the method and content of the courses taken by the student teachers and the lessons given by them. She gave "demonstration lessons" and she was thus probably the first woman tutor in the practice of education in the history of English teacher-training.[2]

In America, Pestalozzian schools were set up even earlier than in England. Joseph Neef, who had been on the staff at Yverdun, opened a school at Philadelphia, and later taught in Indiana. Although several other private schools claimed to use the new methods there was no general extension of them until the second half of the century when the "Oswego Movement" brought popularity to the English version of Pestalozzianism. The enterprising superintendent of the Oswego schools set up a training class for teachers and appointed staff from England, first a Miss Jones and then Herman Krüsi, both from the Home and Colonial Institute. Krüsi stayed at Oswego twenty-five years, during which time he saw his students become trainers of teachers and spread the methods widely throughout America.

In both England and America the interpretation of Pestalozzi's ideas was much too limited to give a true Pestalozzian education, and it was inevitable that the formalism and artificiality of the "object lesson" and the objective language method, should come under fire as soon as the younger educational thinkers formulated their principles. Spencer criticised the English version, and Horace Mann, the American educator, compared the American mechanical interpretation of Pestalozzianism extremely unfavourably with the truer version practised in Prussia.

SUGGESTIONS FOR FURTHER READING

Dr Biber's book is difficult to obtain but R. de Guimps' *Pestalozzi*, translated by J. Russell (Swan Sonnenschein, 1890, 2nd edition), is usually available in libraries and is rich in detail. R. H.

[1] Krüsi's son taught at this institution for five years before going to America.
[2] See Canon Mayo's *Genealogical Account of the Mayo and Elton Families*, 2nd edition, 1908.

Quick's *Educational Reformers* (Longmans, Green, new impression, 1904) contains a very readable account of Pestalozzi's life and work, while H. Holman's *Pestalozzi, his Life and Work* (Longmans, Green and Co., 1908) is arranged in an interesting manner and includes evidence from many sources. John Russell's *Pestalozzi* (reprint, Allen and Unwin, 1926) was written in 1888 by a Victorian schoolmaster as an appreciation and a vindication rather than a critical assessment. H. Barnard's *Pestalozzi and His Educational System* (Bardeen, Syracuse, U.S.A.) contains useful information on Pestalozzian movements both in Europe and America. *Pestalozzi's Educational Writings* (J. A. Green and E. A. Collie, Arnold, 1912) gives extracts from books, pamphlets, and letters. *Leonard and Gertrude* (translated by E. Canning, Heath and Co., 1901) and *How Gertrude Teaches her Children* (translated by Holland and F. C. Turner, Swan Sonnenschein, 1894) are fairly easily available.

CHAPTER XIV

HERBART, FROEBEL, AND ROSMINI

Although it may prove difficult to evaluate adequately in one chapter the ideas and efforts of the two greatest German educators of the early nineteenth century, it is impossible to omit a brief consideration of some other great leaders of thought during an era of intellectual ferment. The outstanding philosophers of the Revolutionary period had no little influence on the educational theories of both Herbart and Froebel, who, in spite of apparent wide divergence of opinion on many points, have so much in common that their debt to contemporary thinkers must be recognised—quite apart from the debt owed by both to Pestalozzi.

Neither could escape the impact of the ideas of **J. G. Fichte** who dominated German philosophy during at least three decades of political and social upheaval and change. Having received a theological training at Jena and Leipzig, he became a tutor and served in private families for several years. His appointment to a post in Switzerland in 1788 was a turning point in his life, for in the next few years he not only read *Emile* and took up the study of Kant's philosophy, but also visited Pestalozzi. It is hardly surprising that in consequence, the later development and expansion of his own philosophy was bound up with the evolution of strong convictions as to the nature and function of education. Between the years 1794, when he was appointed to the chair at Jena, and his death in 1814, his influence as a professor of philosophy was very great.

He made a special study of the writings of Pestalozzi whom he had encouraged in his literary activities. The last four years of his life were spent as professor of philosophy at the new University of Berlin, a position gained after the publication of his highly successful *Addresses to the German People*. His educational ideas were expressed a few years earlier in *Aphorisms on Education*. Fichte was not uncritical of Pestalozzi's ideas, but he appreciated the greatness of the spirit behind them and he accepted several major concepts—in particular, the function of education as a social regenerative force, the idea of the school community, and the importance of the teacher in the wider community. He saw teachers as men fitted to direct workers into jobs suited to their ability and class, and he saw them as advisers of individuals and groups on ethical and moral problems. It is clear that Herbart accepted much of his doctrine on the teacher's responsibility and on the need for moral education, although the younger man rejected his idealism and suggested, moreover, that the *Addresses* contained "a mass of educational nonsense".

Fichte's view—sometimes self-contradicted—that society is corrupt, while man is innately good, reflects his study of Rousseau, while his rejection of family education suggests a study of Plato. Perhaps from the same source is his insistence that a man's education should render him incapable of leaving undone what he knows to be good. His educational theory[1] was undoubtedly moulded to integrate with his political philosophy, itself influenced profoundly by the political upheavals and uncertainties of a period when Germany was groping towards nationalism. A series of wars and invasions had emphasised the need for a strong Germany, and the stern inflexibility of Fichte's idealism fitted the mood of the times. He postulated that the State should set up an ideal and strive to realise it, that citizens must work with their might towards the same goal— the strengthening of Germany and the extension and expansion of the benefits of German culture and way of life. In spite of his attempt to define the working of free will in individual citizens it is clear that he wished to see the production of a German citizen-type, with sentiments moulded to pattern by education and conforming to a State system which demanded unquestioning effort and administered stern punishment. The seeds of Nazism appear to exist in Fichte's philosophy, but his contribution towards the raising of the status of education was by no means insignificant.

Wilhelm Hegel, born in 1770, and educated for the Church, became a teacher not through interest but in order to break away from his appointed path and gain time for the study of philosophy. This largely explains why, although he had much more experience as a tutor and teacher than Herbart, he had no consuming interest in pedagogy as such, but there are other reasons for the contrast between the two men. Professor Mackenzie writes: "Hegel . . . approached the subject more from the metaphysical and sociological sides . . . the first points upon which he wished to be clear were the

[1] See G. H. Turnbull, *The Educational Theory of J. G. Fichte: a critical account together with translations*, Liverpool U.P. and Hodder & Stoughton, 1926.

more general ones of the relation of education to the process of the world's evolution—to the State, to the family".[1]

At thirty, Hegel was freed from the necessity of teaching for a living by a small legacy, and he lost no time in joining his friend and fellow-philosopher, Schelling, at Jena. They worked together for a few years but Hegel soon evolved his distinctive philosophy, a blend of Christian spiritualism and Greek realism which diverged sharply from the mysticism of his friend. In 1807 he published *Phaenomenology of the Spirit* which not only expresses his new philosophy but also indicates his educational theory. The latter, being based on abstruse metaphysics, had little immediate impact on education but it may have helped to win its author the directorship of the High School at Nuremberg in 1808. In 1816 he became professor of philosophy at Heidelberg and two years later won the coveted chair at Berlin where he remained as a leader of German philosophical thought for thirteen years.

Less concerned than Fichte with questions of politics and the nationalistic needs of Germany, he made a lasting contribution to educational thought by considering education as the science of the ideal development of the spirit. His absolute idealism is an unfailing guide to Hegelian educators in the interpretation of education as a science. He was the first philosopher to express the concept of external reality as thought itself rather than as the antecedent of thought. In following up the Greek effort to reconcile mind and matter he took a great step towards the clear definition of the unity of thought and of being. The path now lay ahead for other thinkers, who have continued further along it during the past century.

While educators had been feeling towards the concept of the self-regeneration of the spirit, philosophical guidance had failed to support this line of thought because education was assumed to be but the fortuitous *furnishing* of many little finite personalities. Hegel's view of reality as a process of *becoming*, and his concept of human personalities as the true realities of an absolute and infinite personality, revolutionised the philosophic attitude towards education. From this time it was to receive its due recognition as a generative process and as a positive factor in universal spiritual progress. Pestalozzi had anticipated Hegel with his theory of intuition, and Froebel interpreted Hegel in his theory of action.

[1] M. Mackenzie. *Hegel's Educational Theory and Practice.* pp. 16-17, Swan Sonnenschein, 1909.

Herbart, as will be seen, aimed to set up a rival school of philosophy but he could not escape, nor ignore entirely, the great flow of Hegelian thought.

Johann Friedrich Herbart (1776-1834)

Professor Adams wrote of Herbart, "He has no history. Philosophers seldom have. It is a compensation".[1] Yet it would be doing Herbart less than justice to omit the story of his career and work.

He was the son of an Oldenburg lawyer and his cultured, talented wife, a couple who were later divorced. A delicate boy, he was educated by a tutor under his mother's supervision, and through this careful guidance he made extraordinary progress, especially in mathematics, physics, and music. It is said that he began logic at eleven and metaphysics at twelve. He then proceeded to the gymnasium at Oldenburg and later to the University of Jena. Here he neglected his main studies in law in order to read philosophy under Fichte—then among the most influential scholars in Europe—but he soon outgrew the latter's idealism and began to develop an independent system of philosophy. At twenty-one he left the University without completing his course, and he undertook the private tuition of three boys in the house of a Swiss nobleman. One condition of his appointment was that he should write a full report of the progress of these boys every two months, a requirement which no doubt served to direct his keenly critical mind towards the consideration of educational principles. A few of the letters which still exist contain many of his chief educational ideas to which he held throughout his career.

During the two years of this tutorship he visited Pestalozzi's school, thus gaining experience which not only confirmed his growing interest in education but also inspired him with a lasting desire to make a major contribution to a new science. After resigning his post he spent two years studying philosophy with special reference to education. His writings of this period—mainly educational—include some appreciations of Pestalozzi's works. In 1802 he took his doctor's degree at Göttingen and accepted a lectureship in philosophy and pedagogics. During the four years which followed he not only wrote on logic and metaphysics but also

[1] J. Adams, *The Herbartian Psychology Applied to Education*, p. 45, Heath, London, 1907.

produced several educational works, including *The Aesthetic Revelation of the World* and *The Science of Education and General Pedagogy deduced from the Purpose of Education.* In 1809 he succeeded Kant as professor of philosophy at Königsberg. During his twenty years in this University he lectured in philosophy and pedagogics. It has sometimes been assumed that his greater enterprise and success in the latter subject was due to his greater interest in it, but it cannot be overlooked that he wrote several philosophical works which aimed to establish him as leader of a school of thought of similar pre-eminence to Kant and Hegel. The latter was now the accepted leader of the day, however, and Herbart was frustrated in his ambitions. In pedagogy he achieved much, even though it did not bring him the wide recognition he might have gained as a philosopher. The Ministry of Education supported his proposal for the foundation of a training college and his work in teacher-training drew many students to Königsberg. He not only lectured on education, he also made it a principle to teach in the practising school himself for an hour every day. In spite of his success in this work, he failed in his application for Hegel's chair at Berlin, and in 1833 he returned to Göttingen as professor, continuing here until his death in 1841. In 1835 he published his *Outline of Pedagogical Lectures.*

Herbart's Philosophy and Psychology

As a philosopher Herbart was overshadowed by the giants of the age in spite of his shrewdness and originality. Thus his philosophy is of significance mainly in relation to his educational ideas rather than in more general application, although he is regarded by many as the equal of Kant and Hume in his capacity for deep and accurate thought. His contribution to criticism is undoubted.

His early rejection of Fichte's idea that the self creates its own world strengthened into a realist approach to metaphysics, in strong contrast with the fashionable idealistic attitude. His ethics are not opposed to Kant's, but instead of the latter's Categorical Imperative he holds to five practical or moral ideas—the Ideas of Inner Freedom, Perfection, Benevolence, Right, and Equity. His psychology postulates not the soul endowed with native faculties as envisaged by his predecessors, but a simple soul or mind subject to presentations and impressions. Philosophy he assumes to be the refining and elaborating of empirical conceptions by reflection, and he argues that as some conceptions become more distinct, it becomes more difficult to reconcile their constituent parts without the intervention of metaphysics, for which he evolved a method of relations comparable to Hegel's dialectic.

Herbart's theories on the nature of mental life are of particular significance, not for their validity or success, but because they indicated the way for further thought and experiment by later investigators. The soul as a simple unity about which nothing is known, except that it is the area of operation of "presentations", was a concept which gave scope for the first attempts to measure mental states. According to Herbart the primary presentations of the soul are simple; ideas are born through the effort involved in the process of suppression and reconciliation necessary to unite these presentations; the mind is thus constantly seeking equilibrium and the conscious part of the mind is concerned with those presentations which never acquire equilibrium. Once the conflict is resolved they sink into the subconscious. Thus, emotions and volitions are states resulting from the interaction of presentations in the conscious mind. Desires are presentations striving to reach consciousness; when they succeed they become volitions. The self is a mass of presentations; self-consciousness is the result of interaction among these presentations; their permutations, interactions, and combinations make up the whole range of mental activity and life. Herbart failed in his attempt to apply quantitative laws to the working of presentations, but his association of mathematics with the study of mental life no doubt stimulated the experiments of Fechner and others.

The Herbartian "soul" is real, unchangeable, independent, and without faculties; the contact of this soul with the reality of the body brings about the thought and motivation of the live man. The consciousness becomes filled with ideas which, according to certain mechanised laws, either blend or displace one another. Thus tensions exist in the mind, and man is made aware of them as sensations. The will, for instance—or rather an expression of the will—is an idea which has been subjected to tension and which, although inhibited, has remained alive and active. The concept of discipline illustrates the function of such ideas: "We ought to arouse many desires, but in no wise permit any of them to rush unrestrained on its object. It ought to seem as if an immeasurable store of will-power lay locked in a mental reservoir which can be opened by reason only, when, where, and how it wills".[1]

Education is both the beginning and the end of Herbart's philosophy. He claims the end of education to be ethical—the formation of moral character which requires the will to goodness. This ideal character is best achieved by the balanced, harmonious development of the individual through "many-sided interests". The process of education should thus be concerned with the exercise of all the capacities and capabilities of pupils by methods which accord with the fundamental Herbartian doctrine of "apperception" and "interest". Apperception is the assimilation and identification of a new idea by the mass of ideas already in the mind—the term "idea" being used widely to include sense-impressions as well as intellectual and emotional impressions. Progress in knowledge is a process of apperception, the nature of new perceptions being determined by those which have gone before. No knowledge results from the first sensation experienced by a human being, and its "presentation" to the mind or soul merely sinks below the surface of consciousness until it is roused and recalled into the conscious mind by the next sensation presented. The first presentation then modifies the reception of the latter and blends with it. The compound presentation sinks below the threshold of consciouness awaiting the arrival of the next presentation, upon which another rise above the threshold and another assimilation occurs. As the collection of ideas in the mind becomes larger and more complex, the ease and degree of assimilation vary considerably. Thus Herbartians feel it essential, in education, to direct the process of apperception by the careful selection and arrangement of sensations and impressions to be experienced by pupils. Their minds consist of nothing but the ideas received, and therefore those ideas must be those considered desirable in the building up of character and knowledge. Undesirable presentations must be excluded from the pupils' experience, so that later there will be no ideas in the mind friendly to other harmful ideas. Ideas, sensations, and impressions may be apperceived or assimilated when partially familiar—they "fit in" to the relevant mass; a foreign idea finds the mind but a glass wall on which it can gain no foothold.

[1] J. F. Herbart, *Aesthetic Revelation of the World*, trans. by Felkin, together with *Science of Education*, Swan Sonnenschein, 1892.

The main factor in human behaviour concerned in the process of apperception is interest, which depends on the existent content of the mind in any given situation. There is a reaction between knowledge and interest; the latter not only ensures voluntary attention, it also renders more acute involuntary attention. It thus guides human observation and even human will, and is, in consequence, a major aim of Herbart's pedagogy, not merely a subsidiary factor. He envisages that "many-sided interest" has complete power to counteract evil and prejudice, and thus is to be sought as the highest quality of the ideal moral character. Wickedness and evil spring from ignorance and therefore education should give the individual pupil that wide, integrated knowledge and experience which ensures that the "circle of thought" will lead to wise and virtuous activity.

Thus Herbart, no less than Plato, held that the purpose of education was "virtue". He believed the means of education should be government, discipline, and instruction. The first of these would ensure the necessary order and the aversion of evil, the second would lead the pupils towards virtue by building up the will and forming good habits, and the third would cultivate systematically those ideas which would ensure individual morality. Methods of instruction based on Herbartian psychology proceed by first isolating an individual concept to ensure "clearness", then connecting it with related concepts to bring about "association", then arranging these concepts in a "system" of relationships, and finally perfecting the relationships by the "method" of self-activity or practice. The balancing of varied interests is needed to ensure harmony in development: "Those only wield the full power of education who know how to cultivate in the youthful soul a large circle of thought closely connected in all its parts, possessing the power of overcoming what is unfavourable in the environment and of dissolving and absorbing into itself all that is favourable".[1]

Herbart's ideal man would be one who had achieved the highest moral character through a many-sided interest. This concept alone indicates that Herbartian doctrine is by no means antagonistic to idealist modes of thought. He believes, with Kant, that man cannot know the world as it really is, but that although human understanding cannot get to the real nature of experience which lies behind appearances, the experience itself involves much more

[1] *The Science of Education*, p. 92, trans. Felkin, Swan Sonnenschein, 1892.

than is apparent. To Herbart it involves a plurality of "reals" of which the soul is only one. In their relations with each other all reals strive to maintain their original nature and to resist being changed by the impact of other reals. This impact and the resultant interactions give rise to what is known as experience, and the effects of these interactions stay with man as ideas which keep him in contact with reals he absorbs in the future; thus all his new learning is in terms of the old, through the process of apperception.

Herbart's Pedagogy

In the practical organisation and methodology of school education, the predominating principle controlling the experiments of Herbart and his disciples is that of correlation, with which are associated the formal steps of instruction. The curriculum should permit the correlation of the various courses of study; the content of the courses should be so arranged that the topics to be treated in the different lessons given on one day, or in one week, should be related to one another. In addition, subsidiary topics should be arranged in concentric circles round a main subject. The reason for such arrangement lies in Herbartian psychology which postulates that similar ideas blend and reinforce one another, while dissimilar ideas repel each other so that some may fall over the "threshold of consciousness" if there is no "apperceptive mass" in the mind to absorb and reinforce the new ideas. A child will not be likely to give much attention to the factors in his environment which convey only ideas not "apperceived"—that is, about which he has no previous knowledge which helps him to absorb those ideas. Therefore the most complete and speedy learning is to be ensured by arranging the new teaching with relation to the existing background in the pupil's mind. The presentation of new experience will be followed by speedy association if related to the main "apperception masses" already developed by the pupil. The stronger and wider these masses, the more sure and speedy the learning will be, because conflicts between dissimilar reals will be avoided. Thus the absorption of ideas and facts will be facilitated if there is a common thread to all the material and topics presented to pupils in the various lessons which make up the time-table.

A strange, unrelated idea—using the word in its widest context —introduced to the pupil's mind, will not be able to maintain itself for long above the threshold of consciousness; that is, the pupil will not be interested in it. A new idea related to an existent apperception mass, causes that mass and the idea to exert their drawing-power; that is, the pupil will show interest. The factor of interest is therefore not incidental or superficial in learning, but fundamental and integral. Herbart gave a twofold interpretation to the word. It was the force which facilitated the apperception of new presentations, and it was the feeling of pleasure arising from the completion of a successful association of old and new ideas. John Dewey later asserted that interest could not fulfil these two functions in a Herbartian scheme, which, he believed, could not employ it as a motivating force.

The task of the Herbartian teacher, then, was to discover how to progress from one concept to another and how to ensure the assimilation of new ideas to old. Herbart himself proposed that teaching method should proceed in four steps, but these were elaborated by later Herbartians into five: The first step, "Preparation", ensures a revision—a bringing back to consciousness—of old knowledge with which the new is to be related. "Presentation", the second step, seems to indicate that the teacher will now tell the new facts, illustrate the new procedure, or demonstrate the new experiment. The third—"Association"—in a class lesson, corresponds to the stage when the teacher helps the class to analyse the new knowledge or experience and to compare and contrast it with the old. The teacher's task is to ensure that psychological apperception is securely achieved—good teaching depends on efficiency at this stage. The fourth stage of the Herbartians is "Systematisation" which, for the modern teacher, is mainly a matter of recapitulating or reviewing what has been learnt, and coming to some conclusion about it with reference to its wider significance. The consideration of further subsidiary evidence may be involved, particularly in science and the humanities. The final stage, "Application", is clearly the practising of the new skill, the use of the new knowledge in other contexts, the use of the discovered rule to solve other problems.

Owing, perhaps, to the efforts of later disciples, Herbart's "steps" are usually discussed in relation to the formal classroom lesson, which, although still predominant in our schools, is frowned upon by many who regard it as an anachronism kept alive only by the shortage of schools and teachers. Be that as it may, there still remains in Herbart's doctrine, some wider stimulus for the discerning teacher. Herbart was a reader of Rousseau and a disciple of Pestalozzi. He rejected the former's naturalism, protesting that it was a "mere folly to leave man to nature",[1] and he went beyond and away from Pestalozzi in his psychological concepts, but he had, nevertheless, their belief in the importance of self-activity and in the function of the teacher as a guide of that activity. They differed mainly in their opinion as to the extent and nature of the teacher's direction of the pupil's self-activity; they were agreed that the teacher must speed up learning. Herbart's way was not the antithesis of modern "activity methods". His particular and individual contribution to thought on this problem was his conviction that interest—which involves self-activity—is the outcome of apperception and that, therefore, the best teacher is one who calls forth that self-activity, not one who merely gives instruction in useful knowledge while receiving from the pupils a passive attention which is not true interest.

Herbart accepted, with reservations, Rousseau's criticism of contemporary society and he believed that well-educated individuals would make a good society. He demanded, however, that society itself should make possible the self-determination of each member by providing a clear-cut system of civil administration. Thus his school society would be based on firm but enlightened government and its aim would be to mould its members in the shape approved as virtuous by the larger society. "A healthy mind in a healthy body" was a prerequisite to the complex, more advanced education of the citizen. This latter was to be achieved by a careful training of the sentiments and the development of "right" attitudes—willingness to co-operate, a sense of justice, control of aggressive tendencies, good-will towards others, and obedience to law and authority.

In the early stages of education, external control must be at its strongest because the pupil has not yet built up the knowledge of responsibilities and values necessary to lead him to control himself. Early education should make children aware that life exacts penalties for non-conformity with law, so that although learning through apperception and interest cannot be started too early, it needs to be accompanied by training in good behaviour. Herbart points out,

[1] J. F. Herbart, *Science of Education*, pp. 135-6, D. C. Heath and Co., Boston, 1892.

however, that it is useless to restrain undesirable activity unless some new activity is supplied to take the place of the one inhibited. He thus stresses the need for activity though its purpose may sometimes be only to keep order. The young child should have much freedom to choose what he wishes to do, but once a task or occupation is started, he should learn that he is expected to finish it.

Such a framework of government and discipline suggests that Herbart was making provision for the maturation factor in individuals, and probably in society itself. A pupil acquires higher qualities, such as moral insights, gradually and at a mature stage— so perhaps, does society. His good society would not be composed of obedient nonentities all cut to the same pattern, but of individuals with character and initiative. Moreover, an important part of the educational process itself is brought about by experience in groups —particularly homogeneous groups. In *The Science of Education* Herbart writes: "Those who grow up merely passive as obedient children, have no character when they are released from supervision", and he indicates the educative discipline of the group thus: "When human beings, big or little, rub against each other, the relationships with which those moral perceptions are connected, develop abundantly and spontaneously . . . Never disturb what exists among children without good reason".

The question of curriculum was discussed by Herbart only in principle. Only a wide and balanced curriculum could give the full scope for the many-sided development he desired, for the limiting of fields of study would cut out some aspects of human experience. Although one subject might arouse several kinds of interest, it would almost certainly arouse more of one kind of interest than another. Some subjects arouse simple wonder, some stimulate the search for reasons and causes, some have aesthetic appeal, some help the mind to consider human relationships, some give experience in group activities, and some foster interest in religion. All these ways of learning are of importance and value, and should be experienced by the pupil through variety of method within the subject as well as through variety in the curriculum and school activities. This wide curriculum must be co-ordinated, in order that apperception masses may be built up and the circle of thought be constantly enlarged and "connected in all its parts".

In *Aphorismen zur Pädagogik* Herbart writes: "There is a length and breadth of instruction formed respectively by those subjects which must be learned together and those which must follow each other. The breadth of instruction must be greater than the length, which is prolonged through several years. But there are only two main threads which can and ought to be spun out in both directions —knowledge of nature and knowledge of humanity; languages are but the instruments". There is no uncertainty about this dethronement of grammar learning. If any one study was to be elevated in its place it was to be history—not the history of facts and dates but the history of human adventure and endeavour. Not that the classics were to be neglected, but they were to be learnt only by pupils with special aptitude. In importance Greek and Latin rank somewhat lower than religion, science, mathematics, geography, and the mother-tongue, although classical literature might well be used to good effect in the training of the sentiments. The language itself might possibly be acquired incidentally, as it were, to the study of literature. Herbart relates that as a young tutor he achieved this by introducing his pupils to the *Odyssey*—they learned Greek easily although they disliked Latin intensely.

Herbart had no illusions that success in education could be achieved by following rules on curricula, syllabuses, and methods. The personal factor could not be eliminated. "Even the best method," he wrote, "cannot secure an adequate degree of apperceiving attention from every pupil; recourse must accordingly be had to voluntary attention, that is, to the pupil's resolution".[1] But that resolution should not be called into play unnecessarily by dull, uninteresting teaching. "Tediousness is the greatest sin of instruction," he asserts, "It is the privilege of instruction to fly over steppes and morasses; if it cannot always wander in pleasant valleys, it can at least exercise in mountain climbing and reward with broad fields of view".

The Herbartian Teacher

Herbart's theory of learning implies that the pupil has no innate tendencies and abilities to be guided and fostered by the teacher. The latter's task is first to decide, by reference to ethical principles, what must be taught and learned in order to produce the "moral man". Then he must consult the findings of psychology to learn how best to manipulate these essential ideas to set the mental processes working with the greatest speed and efficacy. He is to be a

[1] A. F. Lange and C. De Garmo *Herbart's Outlines of Educational Doctrine*. p. 71, Macmillan, 1904.

true "organiser of learning", for without his skill in selecting ideas and weaving them into the texture of the mind, the pupil will not achieve that "many-sided" balance and understanding which gives him inner freedom—that is, release from conflict between what he thinks he should do and what he actually does. Herbart's "psychology of habit"[1] demands that the teacher should organise learning so that desirable ideas become fixed in their associations, preserving the "circle of knowledge"—the interconnection of all knowledge in the mind. Yet at the same time the teacher needs to be constantly alert to find paths from what is known to what is not yet known, so that the new knowledge is drawn within the circle, and may be used as a means of finding more paths to more new knowledge, for "the circle of thought contains the store of that by which gradual interest will lead to desire, and desire to volition and action".

If it is borne in mind that Herbart deems attention and interest to be practically synonymous it is clear that the Herbartian teacher needs to ensure that each individual pupil is brought into contact with material, whether physical or mental, which he can recognise as related to that previously absorbed. Herbart's view that interest follows learning may perhaps be better interpreted by reference to attention. He does not assume that a "presentation" connected with previous learning will always arouse in the pupil spontaneous attention, but he does believe that the teacher can more easily induce willing voluntary attention by showing the relationship of the new topic to knowledge already mastered. Although not specifically discussed by Herbart, the question of the relationship between success in learning and interest in further learning, is one which occurs to the modern student of psychology. Whitehead's indication of the need of the individual to achieve success in each "cycle of learning" supports a Herbartian definition of interest which has often been rejected by later thinkers. Again, Dewey's definitions of spontaneous attention and reflective attention accord with Herbart's belief that attention to new studies may be generated either by presenting associations so that attention is involuntary, or by winning the co-operation of pupils willing to apply themselves deliberately to study. Both thinkers would agree that artificial stimuli of interest and attention—rewards and competition—should play no part in education, for the main need is that the mind of the

[1] P. R. Cole, *Herbart and Froebel*, p. 69, Columbia, N.Y., 1907.

pupil shall take active hold of the new idea. The will to learn—to acquire understanding and belief in knowledge, in modes of behaviour, in ethical concepts—evolves only through the activity, the ferment, in the mind.

In the process of instruction and training, the educator needs not only to select what ought to be learnt—in all aspects of learning—but also to evolve methods of generating the necessary mental processes. Thus presentations must be as vivid and stimulating as possible. They may be made through pictures or stories, or through direct observation or experiment—at this stage the teacher is an organiser of pupil-experience, a stage manager. Secondly, he is to lead the pupils through the analysis and the reconstruction in wider relationships—a process which his followers formalised into steps, but which Herbart did not intend as a "lesson scheme" limiting the initiative and personality of the teacher. Thirdly, the teacher's task is to foster many-sidedness of interest by organising "the conveyance of difference within the framework of repetition", in which terms Whitehead describes the educational process. Fourthly, the educators must arrange for the widening of the web of thought by the correlating of the curriculum, a task calling for endless effort, ingenuity, and the observation of individual pupils, in order to ensure unbroken, steady, upward progress, with no marking time and the minimum waste of energy on haphazard, unguided activity.

When Herbart writes: "Let us look on the Odyssey as the point of touch in a fellowship between pupil and teacher", he reminds us that the cold jargon of educational and psychological theory can be—and must be—interpreted in terms of real human relationships. Those who consider Herbart over-emphasises intellectual education, forget that his concept of "mind" and "ideas" involves more of man than his intellect. Sentiments and attitudes are not always based on intellectual understanding in the narrow sense, and Herbart believes that the "ideas"—or perhaps "feelings"—of pupils are shaped by the subtle, silent presentations of the teacher who has succeeded in establishing a "good pupil-teacher relationship". Again, although Herbart's theory appears to postulate that personalities can be manufactured to type by the teacher, he indicates frequently his acceptance of individual differentiation and his consciousness of variation and change in individual needs and capacities from childhood to maturity.

Some time after the death of Herbart, his educational ideas achieved great popularity especially in Germany, largely owing to the efforts of his disciples Ziller and Stoy who demonstrated the practical value of Herbartian methods in schools. Dr Stoy, working in Jena, the nursery of so many great German intellects, embarked upon the application of Herbart's principles in elementary schools and eventually he was joined by Frick who, after experience as director of the orphan school at Halle, now undertook to develop Herbartian methods in secondary schools. Ziller set up a training college and practising school at Leipzig where he won fame, not free from criticism, for interpreting Herbart's ideas somewhat freely. He expounded the doctrine of "culture stages", similar to the theory that the stages in the development of the embryo and the young of a species recapitulate the history of animal evolution. He also put forward the idea of interest as a "protection against the passions". Dr Rein, who succeeded Stoy at Jena followed Ziller rather than his predecessor. The extension of Herbart's principles aroused much controversy, but it also drew interested students to Jena, particularly from America. The cult of Herbartianism flourished in the United States for many years, in spite of the onslaughts of critics who originated the term "soft pedagogy" to describe the flabbiness they claimed to be inherent in the doctrine of interest.

In the late nineteenth and early twentieth centuries much was written of a controversial nature on the question of the validity of Herbart's concepts. To-day these controversies have less significance, especially in view of the growth of interest in the accumulation of psychological data, but his theory still provides food for thought for teachers who seek to reach a decision on the extent of their powers and responsibilities. Many would disagree with the mechanical view of the mind implicit in Herbartian theory, for they would consider it too determinist, having no place for individual responsibility and free will. Yet Herbart was not so mechanistic as the English Associationists and he was somewhat contradictory in emphasising the need to develop the individuality of the pupil—an individuality which, according to his theory has no real existence. Some thinkers feel that the ethical aim of self-culture is false, and moreover, that Herbart lays a mistaken stress on knowledge and culture as "virtue". Again it might be debated whether "many-sided interest" is an infallible indication of moral fibre.

On the other hand few would deny the soundness of Herbart's wish to establish psychological laws, and his search for rational rather than empirical principles. The value of interest is taken for granted to-day, while the ethical function of education and the need for a wide culture are matters discussed in most modern writings on educational ideas. Not the least contribution of Herbartianism to the modern world is its assumption that education is a potent force in society and that the teacher's vocation ranks high.

Friedrich Froebel (1782-1852)

Of Froebel it was written towards the end of the last century "All the best tendencies of modern thought on education . . . culminate in what was said and done by Friedrich Froebel".[1] This high esteem amounting to reverence, which was characteristic of educational opinion half a century ago, goes some way towards explaining the tendency to over-estimate his undoubtedly splendid contribution to educational progress. That he is linked in this chapter with Herbart as a fellow-disciple of Pestalozzi, and that in consequence he is accorded briefer treatment than the great Swiss teacher, is not to be interpreted as a protest against such over-estimation; it is rather an attempt to put into perspective the work of two great educators who, by their own admission, owe so much to Pestalozzi. In view of the existence of some differences of opinion on the value and quality of the latter's contribution to educational ideas, it may be well for the student to bear in mind that the writer regards Pestalozzi as the greatest figure of a great trio, whose ideas when considered deeply and in detail are strikingly in accord, although much has been written defining their differences.

Froebel's early life was a not unimportant factor in the evolution of his ideas. His mother died when he was a baby and he spent a rather lonely childhood, browsing in the countryside of his south German mountain home. His brother was given a good education by his pastor father, but Friedrich had to attend the village girls' school until, at ten, he was sent to his mother's brother. During his few years at the village school near his new home he gained little except some small skill in arithmetic. He was still a lonely boy, fond of nature but not very good at games with his fellows.

---

[1] R. H. Quick, *Essays on Educational Reformers*, p. 384, Longmans, Green, 1904, 3rd edition.

At fifteen he was apprenticed to a forester—a poor equivalent to his brother's university education. He was supposed to receive instruction in mathematics and in the assessment and valuing of land and timber, as well as the craft itself, but the boy learnt little in two years except what he gained from geometry books. He gave much time to the observation and study of plants and insects—experience significant in his later philosophy with its tendency to pantheism. At seventeen he had the opportunity to go to Jena to see his brother who was studying at the University, and so imbued with interest in biology and mathematics had Friedrich now become, that he found ways of staying there for some time, taking university courses until he ran into debt so seriously that he was clapped into the University prison for nine weeks. At that time Goethe, Schiller, and Fichte were lecturing at Jena, but the young man was attracted by Schelling, whose philosophy appealed to him, and by Batsch, the zoologist, one of the pioneers in ideas of evolution. As he was ill-prepared for university work, Froebel did not get very far in his studies but the experience was enough to show him the main trends of his interests and capacities. Nevertheless, he did not find his true vocation for some time and it was not until the master of a normal school in Frankfurt invited him to teach drawing —he had taken up the study of architecture—that he gained the experience which he found truly satisfying. Later, from 1807 to 1810, he tutored three boys, spending most of the period at Yverdun with his pupils. In his autobiography he summarised the results of that experience—a great inspiration to go on experimenting and perfecting a "method"—"The powerful, indefinable, stirring, and uplifting effect produced by Pestalozzi set one's soul on fire for a higher, nobler life, although he had not made clear or sure the exact way towards it nor indicated the means whereby to attain it."[1]

Froebel continued his self-education at Yverdun, sitting in class with the boys. At the same time, his flexible and critical mind absorbed the ideas of Pestalozzi and noted the details of Yverdun practice—absorbed and noted in order to refine, perfect, and correct by his own thought and experiment. First, however, he set out to ensure that his mind was equipped to undertake such a task, and, being a scientist by natural inclination, he embarked on the study of sciences which had recently made rapid strides. Not only

---

[1] F. Froebel, *Autobiography*, p. 79. trans. E. Michaelis and H. K. Moore, Syracuse, N.Y., 1889.

physics, chemistry, and geology, but also philology engaged his attention[1] as well as his early study, mathematics. The trends of scientific progress were all towards a world unity holding a great appeal for Froebel and shaping his philosophy, which thus emerged from his study of the empirical sciences rather than from speculation. This phase of activity led him into an intensive specialisation in mineralogy, which won him an assistant curatorship under a famous research professor at the Berlin Museum. He was even offered a professorship in mineralogy, but on the reopening of war with France, Froebel joined the army until the end of the war, and then returned to Berlin.

In 1816 he opened his first school[2] which was moved in the following year to Keilhau, the Thuringian village generally associated with his name. Here during the next nine years, Froebel, in partnership with two friends, worked out the principles of his educational theory and practice. The school was not particularly successful financially and Froebel proved little more efficient than Pestalozzi, but when in 1826 *The Education of Man* (*Menschenerziehung*) was published, another milestone of educational progress had been passed. Having evolved his law of human growth and education—"the reconciliation of contrasts"—he set out to provide his pupils with activities designed to train them in accordance with the laws of human development. He argued that man is an active organism, needing to engage in contrasting or opposing activities which it is the task of education to reconcile. On the one hand are individual interests and resultant activities, and on the other hand are activities with others, undertaken as part of group efforts for group purposes. The educated personality has achieved harmony in these opposing activities.

In view of such a theory, it is not surprising to find that Froebel's pupils were to learn through co-operative work and play, by living together and by engaging in group and individual activities largely based on contact with nature and the environment. The school was another Yverdun—more Pestalozzian than Yverdun ever succeeded in becoming, and it differed only in emphasis. Outdoor work, for instance, was more important in practice as well as in theory. The boys spent much time gardening. The form of government was

---

[1] At the Universities of Göttingen and Berlin.
[2] The first pupils were the three orphaned sons of his favourite brother, two nephews and the son of one of his partners.

patriarchal and benevolent, as at Yverdun, but there was a somewhat greater measure of self-government. The curriculum was wide and flexible, and interesting methods were developed, including the use of Herbartian ideas in classics teaching.

Like Pestalozzi, Froebel dearly wished to take poor children into his school, a desire which he pursued even though internal dissension and external famine, at one stage, brought the school near bankruptcy—only averted by the financial help of a young teacher. Froebel also had a dream of an all-purpose institution—a whole range of schools including a technical college, a school for mothers, and a nursery school for orphans—but the prospective patron withdrew. In 1831 Froebel left Keilhau to his partner and accepted an appointment in Switzerland as a trainer of teachers. In 1835 he had the opportunity to build up a training establishment and a demonstration school at Burgdorf, Pestalozzi's old centre, and it was in the course of this work that he grew more and more aware of the importance of the early stages of education.

Convinced that only by the right education of young children would be achieved his aim of a commonwealth of good, co-operative people, he set his heart on studying and developing infant teaching. The illness of his wife strengthened his decision to break away from his work and in 1836 one of his partners took his place at Burgdorf. He spent some months visiting German infant schools founded by disciples of Oberlin, but he found them to be little more than day-nurseries for children of working mothers. From that time onwards Froebel bent all his efforts to the task of working out methods of teaching young children. The mountain village of Blankenburg in his native Thuringia was the scene of his new venture—"a school for psychological education"—which, within a few years, he was inspired to call by the name which has survived—"the Kinder-Garten". Here he experimented in the organisation of materials and activities through which children might express their natural capacities while cultivating their powers of observation and understanding. For more than a decade he was able to develop his methods and extend his ideas, so that by 1850 many kindergartens were founded, many infant teachers trained, and much apparatus created for use in the new schools.

It was not in Germany that the widest acceptance of Froebel's ideas became evident, for only a few Germans could understand and accept his essentially democratic views. In 1851 the Minister of Education on behalf of the Prussian Government proscribed the kindergarten and, despite the efforts of several influential well-wishers, the ban was still imposed when Froebel died the following year. Although according to report, the action arose from official dislike of the socialistic views of his nephew, and perhaps even from a confusion of identity, the mistake, if such it was, prevented the development of kindergartens in Prussia for another decade, but after the withdrawal of the prohibition in 1861 they soon became established. Elsewhere Froebelian methods had been taken up with enthusiasm largely owing to the propaganding zeal of Froebel, his colleagues, and their students. Thus, for instance, in Saxony a "Women's Kindergarten Union" had been formed in 1840 in the enthusiasm aroused by demonstrations given by some tutors and pupil-teachers from Keilhau. One tutor, Frankenberg, settled down in Dresden to conduct a highly successful "play school".

Froebel himself not only issued a small weekly journal and gave demonstrations in several large towns, he also received many students and visitors at Blankenburg. Here, for perhaps the first time in the history of educational experiment, are found women playing a major part in the propagation of ideas and in the pioneer work of founding schools. In London, Bertha Rongé set up a kindergarten which she opened to visitors during the educational exhibition organised by the Society of Arts in 1854. Kindergartens were opened in Manchester by Adèle von Portugall and Eleanore Heerwart, the latter being a founder of the International Kindergarten Union. The Baroness von Marenholtz Bülow did excellent work as a propagandist in Germany, England, France, Italy, and the Netherlands; Henriette Breyman worked mainly in Switzerland. Many more young women took part in this great campaign, a considerable number having been trained by Froebel himself, particularly from 1845 after the publication of *Mutter-und-Kose-Lieder* which it had taken several years to complete. It is noteworthy that the first edition of this work was called *A Family Book for Developing the Self-Activity of Children*, a title which gives the clue to Froebel's view of education.

The later growth of the Froebelian movement in England was largely due to the work of Madame Michaelis who came to England in 1874 after much experience of kindergarten teaching in Switzerland and Italy. Within a year she had founded the Froebel Society. Her teaching work in England was preceded by a period of lecturing to the School Board teachers in Croydon. Then she set up the Croydon Kindergarten and Preparatory School, which she conducted for sixteen years, until she opened a training college for kindergarten teachers at Notting Hill. In America a Froebelian school was opened as early as 1838 by Caroline Frankenberg, a student of Froebel's, but she returned to Germany after only a year and it was not until Henry Barnard published in 1856 a description of the kindergarten at the 1854 exhibition in London that the movement made any progress. In the decade which followed the need for kindergarten teachers made itself felt and several Continental teachers set up training schools in America. Their successful work, combined with the efforts of enthusiasts like Pauline Agassiz Shaw and Susan E. Blow, won wide recognition of the value of kindergartens—many of which were set up by public authorities before the end of the century. Experimenters such as Felix Adler and Emily Huntington achieved some success during the same period in adopting kindergarten methods to the teaching of older children. John Dewey adopted Froebelian principles in the conduct of his University Elementary School and he pays direct tribute to Froebel in his *Elementary School Record* published in 1900.

Froebel's Philosophy

Froebel lived at a time when Germany was leading the world in philosophical thought. He was both student and scientist by nature, so that his own educational theory was developed from a combination of observational method—learned from Pestalozzi—and study of the ideas of other educators and philosophers. It has already been suggested that Froebel leaned towards pantheism, but such a statement needs to be qualified, for his philosophy has a deeply religious foundation, maintaining, as it does, that all material things are expressions of God's creative will. His constant aim to realise his concept of all-sided unity drove him to seek an understanding of the laws underlying human experience and knowledge. Such a driving force in a man of undoubted intellectual calibre enabled him to pursue scientific research not only in the older, more orthodox sciences, but also in the science of language, and, above all, in the science of the human mind. As a research worker Froebel heeded factors deliberately ignored by Pestalozzi, factors which often help the researcher to find short cuts—the results of previous research and the opinions of specialists. That Froebel studied research and opinions on science as well as education explains to a considerable degree the trend of his philosophical conclusions. The growing interest in, and knowledge of, evolution in nature, undoubtedly helped him to shape his educational theories as well as to evolve a philosophy which was strongly individual and not merely one adopted piecemeal from his great contemporaries.

At the same time, this commendable capacity to keep abreast of contemporary thought, and this somewhat remarkable ability to synthesise new science and philosophy for himself, led to "advanced" thinking, which, by reason of Froebel's historic setting could not be "advanced" enough to satisfy those who were destined to evaluate and criticise his ideas. After his time the nature of scientific thought and investigation changed rapidly, so that critics of the later nineteenth century were often puzzled by the curious aura of pseudo-mysticism lent to his writings by the fascinating but immature scientific concepts which he accepted. So long as the state of science in the early nineteenth century is borne in mind, it is not difficult to appreciate Froebel's philosophy and to understand how he interpreted it in educational theory and practice.

The main factor of his philosophy—a factor hardly even implied by any previous educator—was the view that life is an evolutionary process. Like Pestalozzi he assumed that the improvement and elevation of group and individual go hand in hand, and that the opportunity is offered to man to reach higher and higher stages of goodness and perfection through a never-ending evolutionary process which had already brought him so far from the rest of the animal world. Education, in its widest sense, was the active, fermenting element in this process, an element which man, at his present evolutionary level, now had the power and understanding to manipulate for his own welfare—that is, for the acceleration of the rate of development of the human race. The old definitions of education were thus as obsolete as the old methods. No longer was it enough to aim primarily at the inculcation of habits, knowledge, and values esteemed by past generations, although such might be gained incidentally in the main process. No longer was it enough to offer the pupil opportunities to develop only a certain narrow range of skills, and to seek in him the signs of conventionally desirable capacities. Again, the development of skills and special abilities might be an integral part of the educational process, but none of these traditional activities should obscure the main aim or confuse the methods designed to achieve it. The new aim must be to produce a new "harmonious personality" with a capacity for spontaneity, a person of fully developed individual abilities and rich, well-adjusted social relationships. Education should make a world of people looking not to the past but to the future, aware of their responsibilities and privileges, and contributing to the betterment of mankind.

Froebel's God is an active source of continual creation in both nature and mind. This self-active, creative spirit, emerging as physical force and mental activity in the two realms of human experience, was, for the great educator, a completely satisfying concept, because it enabled him to reconcile the body-mind, physical-spiritual dualism, and also to fit in to the existent pattern the many new manifestations of newness and change which were becoming known *and which had yet to become known,* whether in the realm of the new sciences of the physical world, or in the sphere of study of the human mind.

This was truly an answer to the old metaphysical viewpoints which allowed for change only within limits. The famous—and often misunderstood—"doctrine of unity" rests on this concept although its explanation is usually, and quite reasonably, based on the scientists' version of the functioning of an organic "whole". Froebel's major "organic whole" is the universe with God as the unifying factor, but it is composed of myriads of small "wholes" or unities, complete and independent in themselves but nevertheless as much functioning parts of the larger whole as are the smallest cells of a large body. Whether in the largest whole or the smallest, there must be balance, proportion, and function maintained by the control of a unifying power; so, in brief, the unity called man needs to maintain balance, proportion, and efficiency of function in order to contribute his utmost to the great organic process of development.

Educators before him—Pestalozzi, Rousseau, and even Comenius —had likened education to the cultivation of plants, but none had interpreted this argument in such clearly defined biological terms. Froebel conceives of God as the original organism creating an entire, changing universe, in which men and all else contained in it, are thus part of God himself. Once this is comprehended, the rest of the biological analogy is straightforward. The perfect development

of any whole is dependent on the full, balanced, relevant functioning of each small, essential portion. Each person, as a small,
essential portion, contributes to God's purpose in so far as he performs his part as a smoothly functioning, balanced unity. The
performance of his part involves not only contributing to the
efficiency and integrity of his social group, but also mobilising
his own powers into an integrated whole. The greater the strength
and variety of these mobilised powers and the more complete the
harmony of their operation, the fuller the contribution of the
individual to the upward evolution of humanity. No longer is it
enough for the human body-mind to be merely a vehicle for the
conveyance of past ideas, values, and traditions into the future.
The basic elements must be conveyed—as they are worth con-
veying—much in the same degree as physical characteristics of the
human race are transmitted. But the past cannot determine the
future, it can only influence the trend of human development.
Here, indeed, is the germ of Whitehead's later theory which
attributes a major part in the learning process to "the conveyance
of difference within a framework of repetition".

Such a concept clearly rejects the division into educational
compartments of the several sides of man's make-up. Froebel
holds firmly to the idea that functional unity involves the exercise
of physical and mental activities *together*; therefore education,
aiming to achieve harmony, yet freedom, in the realisation of human
potentialities, is only to be achieved, in his opinion, through *productive* activity which calls into play both physical and mental
capacities and aptitudes. The emphasis on productivity carries the
organic analogy a stage further—the natural functioning of an
individual or a group is purposeful and productive (that is, leading
to change), so that training designed merely to exercise a set of
muscles or a type of reasoning, or a certain sense, is not only out
of date but may well be harmful, because the attempt to develop
separate faculties conflicts with the idea of unity and harmony
within the organism. If this idea of unity is borne in mind, it is
not difficult to work out Froebel's basic assumption that the education of the hand or brain can only be full and significant when
related to the education of the whole body and spirit, and that the
true education of the individual is only possible when its relationship
to the education of all society is realised. Each small unity in the
universe has a distinctive function and purpose. It maintains its

unity only as it is related to other similar unities and to the larger unity which contains them all. That larger unity may be but part of a still larger unity. Any unity which suffers severance from its large unity loses its function and disintegrates. Such is Froebel's explanation of individual integration and the social cohesion of human groups.

No less significant in Froebel's educational theory is his idea of development—of unfolding, of evolution—according to a universal law or creative force. Again accepting the biological principle, Froebel saw each unity—whether animal, vegetable, or mineral, whether physical or mental—as having a "drive" to develop along those lines fitted to its characteristics. The fundamental force was the same throughout the universe, the lines of development were the same throughout each category, but the possibilities for change through evolution were unknown and unending. The natural development of the tree is to flower and fruit, but the natural law by no means prohibits the evolution of modified types of flower and fruit. The geomorphological history of a river may show its developmental relationship to other rivers, but it may yet evolve new and unique characteristics. Human fingers grow and acquire skill at a certain general rate, but there are individual differences in manual dexterity, and, moreover, there is the possibility of discovering completely new activities for the fingers. The reasoning power of modern man has developed from a simple power of primitive man and an elementary power of animals; it can go still further forward. The political sense of human groups is developing from the simpler concepts of chieftainship and feudalism and the more complex but by no means perfected concepts of democracy. All aspects of human life, moral and ethical as well as physical, are subject to the same law of development; all aspects of man's environment are similarly kept to a process of orderly evolution by the same force. Moreover, according to the same doctrine, the highest and most complex product of the evolutionary process is man, who now has achieved understanding of his own potentialities and limitations and who therefore must devote his superior powers to the deliberate, rational, and scientific fostering of the process itself.

Froebel's Pedagogy

That Froebel saw the problems of education against a sociological background is frequently revealed in his writings. In a letter of 1834, he wrote: "No community can progress in its development while the individual who is a member of it, remains behind; the individual, who is a member of the whole body, cannot progress in his development while the community remains behind". He saw the school and kindergarten as socially significant institutions, fostering the emergence of individuality through the experience of group relationships and activities. He believed as fervently as Pestalozzi in the importance of family education and in the need for a firm link between home and school. With Comenius he believed that parents should be trained in the home education of their children, and at one period he envisaged the foundation of a school for mothers.

While not approving of the vocational and utilitarian education favoured by some thinkers—including Pestalozzi—he saw the school as a nursery of future citizens—not the fervent patriots of Fichte's ideal, but group-members prepared to put their special abilities to the best service of the community.

Froebel's central idea for all stages of child education is expressed in the term *Darstellung*, a wide concept of expression and expressive activities, hardly realised in its entirety by the "expression work" of the modern primary school. Perhaps the nearest translation is "creative self-expression", for it is the process whereby is satisfied the innate urge of the organism to push out to greater life, and to make its adjustments and contributions to the greater unity of which it is a part. The impulses welling up in the pupil need to be "lived out" through activities which offer best opportunity for this development and adjustment. Children may express ideas, feelings, and purpose in activities which at the same time give them knowledge and experience—constructing, play-acting, writing, painting, calculating, story-telling, and a hundred other pursuits, some individual and some needing co-operation in groups. Froebel had no use for the formal sense-training of Pestalozzi and earlier educators, for he saw that sense perception would develop through *Darstellung* which is purposive and progressive. Methods and materials devised by the teacher are therefore not to be imposed on the pupil but are rather to be available for his use, under guidance.

For this purpose, Froebel's "gifts" were devised for use in the first period of education. These were solid shapes, the basic forms being the sphere, the cube, and the cylinder, augmented for constructional activities by triangles, squares, rings, and sticks. He selected these shapes because in his view they represented typical forms in nature and art, and thus together signified the unity of nature and art created by the greatest Unity. Were it not that he emphasises with some vehemence this mystical concept, it might be legitimate to ignore the symbolism of the gifts and to assume that the habit of observation acquired at Yverdun had taught him that children need plenty of constructional material. But he calls his wooden blocks "symbols which unlock his (the child's) soul for the thought or spirit which is innate in everything that has come out of God's creative mind", and he claims he can make perceptible to children "absolute existence" through his "system of games and occupations".[1] The latter included, at the earlier stages, besides play with the gifts, dancing, singing, number games, drawing, and games involving speech. For older children the scheme offers such activities as gardening, building boats and other useful objects, exploring, and reading, the need for both individual and group experience being kept in view. At this stage the acquisition and care of personal possessions is to be encouraged because the child is now eager to collect. Similarly, more group activities are to be provided at this period when the gang spirit is strong. In adolescence, the tendencies fostered by these earlier activities should gradually modify into the normal attitudes of active and enterprising young adulthood.

Stated thus baldly, it might appear that the school has the task of producing educated youngsters through a time-table of unlimited free play. Nothing was further from Froebel's thoughts, yet it is here that his ideas have sometimes been misinterpreted. It is true that Froebel is the great exponent of the fundamental use of play in education, but he envisaged activities both guided and progressive. By stressing the purposive element in activity he made possible the identification of play and work as one. The teacher's task is to organise and guide the free and continuous development of the pupil through play—a gradual development of self-activity, never forced. He is to encourage the awakening senses, to help the pupil to find words to express his ideas and mental images, and to ensure the retention of such knowledge by play-way methods. Froebel saw in

[1] Quoted in S. E. Blow's *Educational Issues in the Kindergarten*, pp. 52-3, Appleton, 1908.

the imitative games of children innate human virtue stretching out towards the instinctively desired goal of social order and good. He had faith that the play experiences of children would enable them to achieve confidence and balance in an orderly world, a process which he called "rounded life harmony" (*allseitige Lebenseinigung*).

Although they held strongly contrasted philosophical views, Herbart and Froebel made contributions to educational thought which are not altogether incompatible. Both believed that education should fit the individual for full life within the group, and although Herbart's emphasis was on intellectual exercise and Froebel's on practical activity, they both aimed to open up to the pupils the whole wide range of human knowledge and experience. Both stress the "relatedness" of knowledge, Herbart's method of correlation in teaching being by the co-ordination of equally balanced topics, and Froebel's method rather the concentric arrangement of learning round one main topic. Herbart's "formal steps" may be considered not as lesson divisions but as a psychological approach to the pupil, while Froebel, in seeking to bring out the impulses of each pupil, was no less a psychologist. Both aimed to develop character and would avoid vocational education except in its widest sense.

Both thinkers have often been misunderstood and misinterpreted and their ideas subjected to scathing criticism. For this the "movements" themselves were responsible, for they were widespread and so all teachers could not have complete understanding, vision, and competence. However, as they started a ferment of ideas and spate of experiment, the unimaginative Herbartians and rigid Froebelians did no disservice to education. Perhaps "unimaginative" is hardly the word to use for one specimen Herbartian syllabus quoted by Charles De Garmo[1] the American Herbartian. It was devised by Professor F. McMurry, a trainer of teachers, not, presumably, with his tongue in his cheek. The Fifth Grade, studying John Smith in history, Chesapeake Bay in geography, and in science the tobacco plant and the oyster, is to pursue the following edifying investigation in arithmetic: "Quantity of tobacco chewed by one person per year, in a lifetime; quantity smoked; its value. Weight of ashes of cigar compared with weight of cigar; one is what per cent. of the other, etc.". Froebelians were no less prone to exaggerate the outward forms of their

---

[1] C. De Garmo, *Herbart and the Herbartians*, Heinemann, 1899.

doctrine. Professor Adamson refers to their "almost superstitious or pedantic use of one definite set of apparatus". In losing sight of the principle behind the "occupations" they failed to bring about development.[1] Most modern teachers would believe with Herbart that life and experience teach, and with Froebel that development comes from within. Both ideas—many-sided learning and self-activity—are Pestalozzi's.

Italian Educators of the Early Nineteenth Century

Although Herbart and Froebel were the giants of the period, educators in other countries were thinking and experimenting in ways which were often similar to those of the Germans. The work of the Italians, Aporti and Rosmini, illustrates this point. **Ferrante Aporti (1791-1858)** developed his educational ideas when, as a young man, he found himself engaged in two strongly contrasted types of educational work. He was not only Professor of Church History at the Seminary of Cremona, but also at the same time, superintendent of the town's schools, and it was through this latter work that his concern for the welfare of the poor was generated, and his belief in the need for infant schools developed. In 1827 he opened the first infant school, an example which was quickly followed by other Italian towns. Aporti spent much time visiting and guiding these schools, and in 1833 he published *Il manuale per le scuole infantili*, followed in 1837 by *Sillabario per l'infanzia*. He raised primary education to the dignity of a university study by giving courses on teaching methods at the University of Turin, and in his old age he became Rector of that university and a senator of his country.

Antonio Rosmini-Serbati (1797-1855), a native of the Tyrol, became a philosopher and theorist rather than an administrator or a teacher. He studied theology at Padua and after inheriting considerable property from his father, he was ordained priest in 1820. He had set himself two aims in life and the next six years he spent

---

[1] The English Herbartian, F. H. Hayward, wrote *Pestalozzi and Froebel* (Holland, 1904) in which he quoted an American satire:—

> They taught him how to hemstitch, and they taught him how to sing,
> And how make a basket out of variegated string.
> And how to fold a paper so he wouldn't hurt his thumb;
> They taught a lot to Bertie—but he couldn't do a sum.
> They taught him how to mould the head of Hercules in clay,
> And how to tell the difference 'twixt the blue bird and the jay,
> And how to sketch a horsie in a little picture frame,
> But, strangely, they forgot to teach him how to spell his name.

in concentrated study in his native town in order to prepare himself for his life's work. His objects were to construct a coherent system of philosophy which would constitute a basis for the study of revealed religion and to found an institution for the training of priests and teachers. At that time, the Italian Tyrol was under Austrian rule and Rosmini, as a patriotic Italian, was in sympathy with the liberation movement. Thus he incurred the hostility of the Austrian government and of the Jesuits who thought that his teaching savoured of heresy. After several years of wandering, he finally left Austrian territory and took up residence at Stresa. An old friend of his became Pope under the title of Gregory XVI and officially recognised the new Order, the Institute of the Brothers of Charity. Rosmini was caught up in the political ferment which followed the year of revolution, 1848, and found it advisable to seek refuge in Naples. It was during this period of his life that he was offered the post of Minister of Public Instruction in the Liberal government which had been forced on the Pope. He declined the offer but a few years later the Jesuits accused him of heresy. His writings were examined by the Congregation of the Index and in 1854, the year before his death, he had the satisfaction of knowing that they were completely cleared of the charge.

The activities of the Rosminian Order were confined to Italy and England. In 1835 Rosmini sent an envoy to Prior Park to found an English Province of the Order. This resulted in the opening of a mission at Loughborough in 1841, and the foundation of Ratcliffe College at Syston, near Leicester, two years later. The college was opened in 1846. Missions were also started at Newport, 1847, Rugby, 1850, and Cardiff, 1854. The novitiate at Rugby was moved to Wadhurst, near Bexhill-on-Sea. A preparatory school for Ratcliffe was built at Grace Dieu, near Coalville, Leicestershire. The Rosminians also established a reformatory school at Market Weighton in the East Riding of Yorkshire which was handed over later to the Brothers of the Christian Schools and eventually became a Home Office approved school.

Although in his philosophical works, Rosmini made many references to education, his most important contributions are contained in his *Ruling Principle of Method in Education*. The work was commenced in 1839 and is a fragment of a much larger book which was designed to deal with the education of the human being from birth to old age. The latter was never completed. We only possess Books I and II (less the last two chapters) and some notes which indicate the lines on which the rest of the work would have followed.

The part which was completed deals with education in what we now call the nursery, infant, and junior school stages but sufficient was written to show quite clearly the nature of Rosmini's educational ideas. The book was written with a practical purpose in view. In 1839, Anna Maria Bolorgaro handed to the Institute of Charity the charge of an elementary school which her grandfather had established at Stresa. Rosmini's intention was to write a treatise for the guidance of elementary school teachers but later reflection suggested the idea of a work which would exhibit the theory of education as an integral part of his philosophical system. The latter was in the main that body of doctrine which had been inherited from St Thomas Aquinas and other scholastic thinkers of that period. It is important to realise that Rosmini was not only familiar with scholastic philosophy, but was also acquainted with the works of Descartes, Spinoza, Leibnitz, Kant, and Hegel; the English school represented by Locke and Berkeley and the Scottish philosophers, in particular, Hume, Reid, and Stewart.

Rosmini regarded educational method as a branch of logic. Truth is the supreme object of the human mind and it is in relation to truth that it exercises its noblest functions. One of these is concerned with the communication of truth to others and it is this aspect which is the main object of education. Rosmini regretted that in his day (early nineteenth century), education suffered from a lack of an agreed method or rather from having no method at all. As regards countries like Prussia where the State controlled education, he reminds us, "Though education under the control of the state is carried on with greater regularity, on the other the schools placed under these uniform and unchangeable rules are almost always the last to admit improvements, and either oppose any attempt to introduce them, by excluding the experiments which might lead to them, or, if any foreign discovery be adopted, its external form only is taken, while the kernel and inner spirit of it is left aside".[1]

Rosmini's first objective is to discover the ruling principle of educational method. His conclusion is one that seems very familiar to those who have studied Sanderson and Dewey and have read the Hadow Reports, but one has to remember that it was given when

[1] *The Ruling Principle of Method in Education*, translated by Mrs William Grey, p. 6, D. C. Heath, 1889.

scientific child-study had scarcely begun. Education must be determined by the child, his nature and outlook which are continually changing as he grows from babyhood to manhood. His principle put in a concrete form may be described as follows. If one studies the development of the child, he will notice that although the growth from birth to maturity is continuous, yet it is possible to discover a number of fairly well marked periods in it. They are differentiated not by age but by certain psychological factors which are characteristic of each stage. Moreover, the duration of any one stage varies with different individuals—some develop more quickly than others. Hence our problem is not to fit the child to a preconceived curriculum but to base the latter upon the changing psychological make-up of the child.

It is essential to discover the law which governs the development of the human mind. Rosmini's method is to start with any one thought, reduce it to its elements, and trace the thoughts which have preceded and those which must follow it. He analyses an example of thinking to demonstrate the principle involved. Suppose I see a certain variety of yellow rose. Before I can recognise it as a flowering plant, I must know the distinction between a flowering and other plants. When I say that it belongs to the family *Rosaceae*, I must know the difference between this family and other flowering plants. If I add that it is a China rose, then I must be aware of the distinction between this and other members of the *Rosaceae* family and, finally, if I call it an Adelaide of Como, I must understand how it differs from other China roses.

How is this to be taught to a child? Should one start with the individual and progress to larger and larger classes, *i.e.* use an inductive and synthetic method, or ought one to begin with the most general and work towards the particular, *i.e.* adopting a deductive and analytic method? The first will concentrate the child's attention upon the differences; the other upon the resemblances. Rosmini is quite sure of the answer. The second procedure agrees with the way in which the child actually learns. He begins with the idea of a plant and analyses his experience into its components. The child notices resemblances first and gradually comes to a knowledge of the distinctions between things, breaking up the genus into progressively smaller classes until he arrives at knowledge of the individual. "The mind first conceives the general and then the particular —first the thought blocked out, as it were in the rough, then in definite outline, then finished and perfected; first the necessity for a division, then the form to be given to it."[1]

This is the natural order in which objects present themselves to the mind and, by a study of the child, it is possible to discover a definite sequence in his thoughts or cognitions. Rosmini claims that in using this method the educator is following nature. He criticises the methods of teaching prevalent in the schools because they create a needless confusion in the child's mind. In what way ought this procedure to be employed? Rosmini answers that there is a definite order in the child's cognitions. "Present to the mind of the child, first, the objects which belong to the first order of cognitions; then those which belong to the second order; then those which belong to the third, and so on successively, taking care never to lead the child to a cognition of the second order without having ascertained that his mind has grasped those of the first order relative to it, and the same with regard to cognitions of the third, fourth, and other higher orders."[2]

It may be as well to pause at this point in order to compare Rosmini's doctrine with that of other educators. He had not only read Rousseau, but occasionally quotes from him. He was well acquainted with the work of Mdme Necker de Saussure and with the writings of the Edgeworths. *The Ruling Principle of Method*, however, was contradictory to the teaching of Pestalozzi and that

---

[1] *The Ruling Principle of Method*, p. 32.
[2] *ibid.*, p. 40.

Rosmini's scheme may be tabulated as follows:

PERIOD	CHARACTERISTICS
1. Birth to 6 or 7 weeks.	A period of passive sensation and purely instinctive activity—ends with the first smile of the baby which indicates that he has noticed something.
2. Babyhood—up to two years.	First order of cognitions—the simple perception of objects as existing.
3. Early infancy.	Second order of cognitions—early stages of speech—perception of the sensible qualities of things—ends at three years or later.
4. Middle infancy.	Third order of cognitions—power of attributing qualities to objects perceived.
5. Later infancy.	Fourth order of cognitions—appearance of judgments of appreciation—these involve comparison of two or more objects with a preference given to one of them. Beginnings of the moral sense (Conscience).
6. Early childhood.	Fifth order of cognitions—conception of the ego and self-identity.
7. Later childhood.	Development of reason—knowledge of moral obligation—lasts to end of thirteenth year.
8. Adolescence.	Fourteen to twenty-one.
9. Maturity.	

of Froebel in his earlier days. They sought to break down the sub-ject-matter of instruction into its simplest elements and begin by teaching these. Rosmini thought that the child starts with the wholes of experience and learns by analysing them. This is in agree-ment with the conclusions of modern child study. It is now generally acknowledged that in the pre-school child, the three main kinds of learning, namely, the acquisition of bodily skill, the growth of knowledge, and the development of social behaviour go on side by side. The infant approaches his world as an unanalysed whole, and by exploring it in all directions begins to acquire knowledge of it in greater and greater detail. The parent and the teacher can help the child by guiding this process of exploration.

It is significant that no order of cognition is mentioned in con-nection with the first period. The reason is that the newly-born baby is only aware of, to use William James's description, a big, blooming, buzzing confusion. He lives on the level of sensation and instinct. His sensations come from two sources; the impressions produced by external objects such as the touch of his mother and the glare of the sun, and from his own body which contributes both pleasurable and painful feelings. His sensations set up in him blind unreasoning wants. Thus a pain in his stomach produces a blind want for food. Instinct provides a means of satisfying his want. All that the baby experiences is a feeling of restlessness and irrita-tion. Then comes a stage when these wants are supplemented by the dawning of intelligence. Following Mdme Necker de Saussure, Rosmini considers that this happens when the baby smiles for the first time which indicates the recognition of a something and usually occurs at the age of six or seven weeks.

From what does the first order of cognitions take its rise? This question can only be answered by reference to Rosmini's philosophy. It is impossible, even if desirable, in the space available, to examine his philosophy in detail. One can only present a summary of some of his main ideas which bear upon his educational theory. His views are developed in the three volumes of the *New Essay on the Origin of Ideas.*[1] This treatise was intended as a reply to Locke's *Essay Concerning Human Understanding.* During the eighteenth century the teaching of Locke and Condillac had become popular in Italy. Rosmini naturally begins his work with a consideration of the problem of knowledge. He opens his discussion by adopting the rule: "To explain the facts of the human mind, we must not

---

[1] English translation published by Kegan Paul, Trench, 1883.

assume less than is necessary for that explanation . . . but we must not assume more than is necessary". He thinks that philosophers may be divided into those who assume too little and those who assume too much. In the former category are Locke, Condillac, Reid, and Stewart. The second group includes Plato and Aristotle, the Arabian thinkers, Leibnitz, Kant, and Hegel. Aquinas is accorded a preferential treatment and Rosmini tends to think of St Thomas as feeling his way towards the position adopted in the *New Essay*.

Rosmini considers that among modern thinkers Kant arrived nearest to the truth, but his assumption that all human knowledge has its origin in sense experience led him to a faulty statement about the theory of knowledge. Kant perceived the distinction between sense perception and conceptual thinking and was also correct in concluding that the raw material supplied by sense activity needs elaboration before it can become knowledge. His error was to assume too much and formulate the doctrine of the forms of the outer and inner sense, *i.e.* space and time, and the categories of the understanding, *e.g.* cause and effect. All this scaffolding, Rosmini believes to be unnecessary. Rosmini also desires to avoid Locke's confusion between perceptual and conceptual thinking, which was a consequence of using the one term, idea, to describe all the contents of the mind. Thus, in the *New Essay*, he is at pains to distinguish between sensation and sense perception. The former is a modification produced in a sentient subject either through the action of an external object or through the internal occurrences of mind and body, and is essentially passive. In sense perception, the subject refers to its appropriate cause and this necessitates the activity of mind. Hence, like Dewey, Rosmini believed that sense experience has a passive and an active aspect.

During the first few days of his life, the baby receives a multitude of sensations of which only a few are singled out for notice because they are accompanied by a feeling of want. The latter sets going the instinctive nature of the baby and leads to definite kinds of activity such as crying, grasping, and sucking. Another way of stating this is to say that the mind attends to certain sensations. Two more principles are necessary to account for the origin of ideas. The first is the fundamental feeling by which Rosmini means the general diffused feeling of our own bodies which constitutes us sentient beings. Without it we could not notice the modifications of feeling which are sensations. The second principle is the intuition of being. This is innate and takes the place of the Kantian categories which are really deductions from it. As Rosmini says: "The first and most imperfect affirmation inwardly pronounced by the child is that which, if formulated by us in words as yet unknown to him, would be expressed thus: I feel, I have the sense of, an entity".[1]

Stated in its simplest form, Rosmini's doctrine is that the mind must think under the form of being. Our ideas are really judgments in which we affirm that so and so is so and so. Every judgment possesses a subject and a predicate and unless I possessed the first and most general predicate, namely, that something is and which is of the very constitution of the mind, I could not advance to particular judgments by which I assert that a certain object exists. I cannot think any object without thinking of it as being. This is an intuition because it is an idea which is not derived from experience but is grounded in the structure of the mind itself, or as Rosmini puts it: "It is the formal element in our knowledge and the source of all *a priori* cognitions".[2] The material element, the content of our ideas, is furnished by sense experience. Hence in the first period of life the child is only potentially capable of knowledge and the first order of cognitions, the simple recognition of objects as existing, represents the first stage in knowledge and is coincident with the second period of the child's life. The act of attention actualises this potentiality and Rosmini writes: "The object of instruction is to bring the young to know, and it may therefore be called the art of properly directing the attention of the youthful mind".[3]

Space will only permit a few references to Rosmini's theory of education. In the earliest years the teacher should concentrate on the training of the senses and then the development of spoken language. He says: "The child should be provided in abundance with objects to look at, touch, examine, and experiment upon, . . . in a word, to perceive, and perceive ever more and more accurately. The objects chosen should be those which most attract his attention, which will also be those which satisfy his wants, his desires, and give him pleasures: for it is only by these that his attention is

---

[1] *The Ruling Principle of Method*, p. 46.
[2] Rosmini wrongly considered that his doctrine was in agreement with St Thomas Aquinas. The latter refused the suggestion that the idea of being is innate and believed that it sprang from the first contact of the mind with reality.
[3] *The Ruling Principle of Method*, p. 45.

aroused". They must be presented in a proper sequence. "The seven colours of the rays of light, one after the other; also white and black; . . . Let him hear, in the same way, the seven primary notes, first in succession, then by degrees in their harmonic intervals and chords; then give him regular solids to play with, to the proportions of which, in form and measurement, his eye and hand may become accustomed, at the same time that they impress themselves on his imagination. Later on, but not till much later, the child may be familiarised with more colours, more sounds, more forms harmoniously combined, but always by degrees, and never passing on to a new play till he shows weariness of the old".[1] The resemblance of this scheme to the Froebelian Gifts and Occupations will at once be noticed.

Rosmini is at one with Pestalozzi and Froebel in the importance he attaches to play as an educative influence and the emphasis he places upon the child's delight in listening to, and later in reading stories. The stimulus to the imaginative play of childhood includes not only the vividness of his imagination but also his pleasure in free activity and his delight in his own creations. Rosmini was a pioneer in perceiving that imaginative play is nature's way of teaching the child about "human nature and its modes of action".

SUGGESTIONS FOR FURTHER READING

Although not essential to a study of Herbart and Froebel the two small books on the educational ideas of Fichte and Hegel mentioned in the text are well worth reading. Of the many works of Herbart, Sir J. Adams's *The Herbartian Psychology Applied to Education* (Heath, 1907) should not be missed, and De Garmo's *Herbart and the Herbartians* (Heinemann, 1899) gives biography, summary of ideas, and a sketch of the Herbartian movement up to his own day. Herbart's *Science of Education* was translated by the Felkins about the same time (Swan Sonnenschein, 1895) and at the turn of the century A. F. Lange translated, and C. De Garmo annotated, *Outlines of Educational Doctrine* (Macmillan, 1901). F. H. Hayward wrote in 1903 a lively account of the development of Herbartianism, including critical reviews of many contemporary books on education: *The Critics of Herbartianism* (Swan Sonnenschein, 1903).

[1] *The Ruling Principle of Method*, p. 82.

A brief biography of Froebel as well as the main parts of *Die Menschenerziehung* are given in W. H. Herford's *Student's Froebel*, 2 vols. (Isbister, 1893), while some useful extracts from other writings appear in *Froebel's Chief Writings on Education* (Longmans, Green, 1912) by S. S. Fletcher and J. Welton. Quick includes Froebel in his *Education Reformers* (Longmans, Green, 1904, 3rd edition) but gives no space to Herbart. Susan Blow's *Educational Issues in the Kindergarten* (Appleton, 1908) gives the American Froebelian viewpoint at the height of the movement. F. L. Hayward's *Pestalozzi and Froebel* (Holland, 1905) makes a critical but fair examination of Froebel's theory and includes an interesting appendix relating the "pantheism" of Froebel to that of Wordsworth. In 1880, Emily Shirreff wrote a small book of considerable historic interest in the development of women's education: *The Kinder-garten, Principles of Froebel's System and their bearing on the Education of Women, also Remarks on the Higher Education of Women* (Sonnenschein and Allen). The National Froebel Foundation has recently published *Friedrich Froebel and English Education*, edited by E. Lawrence.

Although somewhat difficult for students with no background knowledge of philosophy, P. E. Cole's *Herbart and Froebel, an Attempt at Synthesis* (Columbia, N.Y., 1907) is stimulating.

CHAPTER XV

ENGLISH EDUCATIONAL WRITERS OF THE NINETEENTH CENTURY

(1) THE EDGEWORTHS, BENTHAM, THE MILLS, AND SPENCER

One of the prominent characteristics of English thought from the seventeenth century until quite recent times has been a preference for the practical outlook which has sometimes been accompanied by suspicion and distrust of theory, unless the latter could be shown to be directed towards some useful end. This tendency is not only discernable in writers on the subject of education but also in those concerned with philosophy, theology, and politics. With few exceptions, English philosophy has exhibited a strong common sense and practical bias until English thinkers became influenced by the philosophical systems of Kant and Hegel. Thus philosophers of the eighteenth and nineteenth centuries were specially interested in psychology, morals, and logic. Hobbes, Locke, Hartley, and the Utilitarians, were typical of the practical outlook of English thought and Berkeley's interest in metaphysics was really no exception, for one of his chief aims was to show that the existence of a Divine Mind was the guarantee of the being of the objects of the sense world. This attitude presents not only a contrast to Continental thought but also to Scottish philosophers of the same period, Hume, Stewart, and Sir William Hamilton. The same characteristic appears in English writers on religion and political theory and is perhaps not unconnected with the national genius for devising compromise solutions.

Until the closing years of the nineteenth century, English educational thought was more concerned with practical problems of the curriculum, teaching method, and school organisation, and whether schools should be maintained by voluntary effort or by the State, than with educational theory and philosophy. It is significant that when English educators visited Pestalozzi at Yverdun, the external aspects of his work impressed them more strongly than his principles. The same applied to Froebel. The kindergarten was introduced into this country only in 1851, the year before Froebel's death and it was not until the close of the century that his ideas were fully grasped by English infant teachers. No doubt the lack of adequate translations of Froebel's works was a contributary cause of the tardy acceptance of his theories.

The group of educational writers to be considered in these two chapters—the Edgeworths, Bentham, the Mills, Herbert Spencer, T. H. Huxley, John Ruskin, and Matthew Arnold—are practical educators rather than educational philosophers and the theories they present are strictly subordinate to practical considerations. It is, therefore, not surprising to find that the work in which the Edgeworths set out their views about education was called *Practical Education* and that the later book by R. L. Edgeworth was entitled *Professional Education.*

The Edgeworths were a remarkable family who exercised considerable influence upon the educational thought of the early nineteenth century. Their books have been forgotten and it is a sad commentary on English educational thought to find that many of the methods which at the present day are styled "modern" or "progressive" were advocated in *Practical Education* which was published as long ago as 1798.

The head of the family, R. L. Edgeworth (1744-1817), was born at Bath and later settled in Ireland at Edgeworthstown, Co. Longford. He was married four times and raised a family of eighteen, excluding several children who died in infancy. His first wife was Anna Elers. The marriage can scarcely be called a success. Edgeworth was a very able, well-educated man who was also something of an inventive genius. It is said that Anna could hardly write her own name. Two of the children of this marriage, Richard and Maria, were noteworthy for quite different reasons. The first-born was Richard and his story is one of failure. At this time, Edgeworth had been reading Rousseau and he was so captivated by the doctrines of the *Emile* that he resolved to bring up his child on the pattern set forth by Rousseau. Edgeworth's enthusiasm for Rousseau was fully shared by his friend, Thomas Day, the author of *Sandford and Merton,* who attempted to model his adopted children on the ideas of the *Emile* with as little success as Edgeworth. When Edgeworth's experiment failed, he was stimulated to adopt the method of recording observations on the development of his other children with the hope that he might discover something better.

Richard turned out to be a self-willed, independent child, quite undisciplined and resenting any form of control. His father described him as having "all the virtues of a child bred in the hut of a savage and all the knowledge of things which could be acquired by a boy bred in civilized society". In Richard's case, however, the damage was already beyond repair and the strict discipline of the school to which he was sent failed to undo the effects of his early training. Edgeworth must have breathed a sigh of relief when his son declared his intention of going to sea. It seems that when Richard was eight, his father thought it would be fitting to display to Rousseau a child brought up on his own principles. On the occasion of a visit to Paris, he introduced his son to Rousseau. "Here was a boy educated upon his own system—not very far removed from the self-expressionism of our own day—and it would surely interest him to observe its results. Not that it was a system Rousseau applied to his own children since he invariably relegated them to a Foundling Institution, but Edgeworth may have been unaware of this when he presented his son to the Master. But the boy was found wanting. When going for a walk with Rousseau he would exclaim: 'That is an English horse ! or, that is an English carriage !' Rousseau deplored this display of national feeling and party prejudice in one so young."[1]

Edgeworth's second wife, Honora Sneyd, was a very remarkable woman. She looked upon education as an experimental science and kept a diary in which she recorded regular observations on the progress of her children. After her death, Edgeworth continued the diary and many of her observations were used in the compilation of *Practical Education*, and also in the *Parent's Assistant*, a series of stories written by Maria in 1796. Honora Sneyd died in 1780 and Edgeworth married her sister Elizabeth. One of the children of the second marriage, Lovell Edgeworth, was responsible for the chapter on chemistry in *Practical Education*. Elizabeth died in 1797 and Edgeworth's final matrimonial adventure was his marriage to Francess Anne Beaufort who survived him and died in 1865, sixteen years after the decease of his daughter, Maria (1767-1849).

Practical Education was the joint work of Edgeworth and his daughter Maria. The title was deliberately adopted as a challenge to the educational practice of the schools. The influence of Rousseau is still apparent in it but it is considerably modified by

[1] Isabel C. Clarke, *Maria Edgeworth*, p. 21, Hutchinson, 1949.

ideas taken from Locke, the American writer Benjamin Thompson, and Joseph Priestley. Edgeworth's decision to write on educational subjects was confirmed by the advice of another member of the circle, Dr Erasmus Darwin. The latter had corresponded with Rousseau and had published in 1797, *A Plan for the conduct of Female Education*, a work which showed a modern outlook on the physical education of girls in the emphasis it placed on the value of fresh air, exercise, and suitable dress.

Practical Education was a serious attempt to put the psychology and practice of education on a scientific basis. Maria was enthusiastic about her father's ideas and recorded: "I claim for my father the merit of having been the first to recommend, both by example and precept, what Bacon would call the experimental method in education". The aim of the work was sufficiently stated in the opening paragraphs of the Preface. "We have chosen the title of *Practical Education*, to point out that we rely entirely upon practice and experience. To make any progress in the art of education, it must be patiently reduced to an experimental science; we are fully sensible of the extent and difficulty of this undertaking, and we have not the arrogance to imagine that we have made any considerable progress in a work, which the labour of many generations may, perhaps, be insufficient to complete; but we lay before the public the result of our experiments, and in many instances the experiments themselves."

The first chapter on "Toys" was based on suggestions made by Dr Beddoes who married Edgeworth's daughter, Anna.[1] It begins with a condemnation of the very elaborate toys which neither appeal to the senses, the imagination, nor to the initiative and inventive powers of children. Hence such toys are either neglected or broken up because the child has a natural desire to see how they are made. Edgeworth obviously understood children for his conclusion is: "A boy who has the use of his limbs, and whose mind is untainted with prejudice, would in all probability prefer a substantial cart, in which he could carry weeds, earth, and stones, up and down hill to the finest frail coach and six that ever came out of a toyshop".[2]

---

[1] Beddoes was an able man who in a great many ways was extremely unconventional. Thus he insisted upon taking cows into the bedrooms of patients suffering from lung complaints under the belief that their breath was beneficial to the sufferers.

[2] *Practical Education*, p. 2, London, 1798.

After his criticism of fashionable toys, Edgeworth makes some constructive suggestions. The playthings which are most suitable for infants are those which can be grasped without danger and which cannot easily be swallowed. Ivory or wooden sticks, pieces of wood cut into different sizes and shapes, steel buttons tied together are likely to attract the baby and stimulate him in the exercise of his senses. The older child needs toys which will draw out his activity. "A nursery or a room in which young children are to live, should never have any furniture in it which they can spoil; as few things as possible should be left within their reach which they are not to touch, and at the same time they should be provided with the means of amusing themselves, not with painted or gilt toys, but with pieces of wood of various shapes and sizes, which they may build up and pull down, and put in a variety of different forms and positions: balls, pulleys, wheels, strings, and strong little carts, proportioned to their age, and to the things which they want to carry in them, should be their playthings."[1]

The period of childhood is one in which the boy or girl is intensely interested in doing and making things. Hence Edgeworth recommends such occupations as drawing, cutting out shapes, modelling in clay or wax, basket-making, weaving and play with tops, kites, and balls, which present a challenge to the child's dexterity. Ownership of a garden, a set of carpenter's tools, miniature models of contrivances, chemistry and cookery sets, conjuring outfits, blowing bubbles with soap suds, are all things which at one time or another will afford the child endless and profitable amusement.

From play, Edgeworth proceeds to consider tasks. He strikes a very modern note in criticising the desire of parents to teach reading and writing to their children as early as possible. One of the common results of introducing children to reading prematurely is the establishment of a habit of dislike towards books. It has already been said that Edgeworth was an inventive genius. If he had received an adequate technical training, he would probably have contributed in a major fashion to the scientific and mechanical progress of his age. As it was, he invented a sailing carriage, a velocipede, the forerunner of the modern bicycle, a telegraph, and self-winding clocks. His enthusiasm for invention is displayed in numerous places in *Practical Education*. He clearly grasped the

[1] *Practical Education*, p. 11, London, 1798.

defects of the alphabetic method of teaching reading and spelling and invented a phonetic alphabet as a means of teaching children the sounds of the letters. At the same time, he emphasised the importance of visual work in learning to spell and also the value of constant exercise in reading and writing. He thought that the danger to be avoided was that of over-burdening the memory and he therefore recommended the learning of not more than five or six new words each day.

The break away from the views of Rousseau is very apparent when he attacks the view that children should be left entirely at liberty and that they will learn everything better than one can teach them. He remarks: "It has been the fashion of late to attempt teaching everything to children in play, and ingenious people have contrived to insinuate much useful knowledge without betraying the design to instruct; but this system cannot be pursued beyond certain bounds without many inconveniences".[1] He added: "The truth is, that useful knowledge cannot be obtained without labour, that attention long continued is laborious, but without this labour nothing excellent can be accomplished". Hence he makes the significant distinction between teaching children in play and making learning a task.

Like many reformers of this period, Edgeworth was opposed to the practice of learning words without understanding the things and the ideas which they represent. "Words without correspondent ideas are worse than useless, they are counterfeit coin, which imposes upon the ignorant and unwary; but words, which really represent ideas, are not only of current use, but of sterling value; they not only show our present store, but they increase our wealth by keeping it in continual circulation; both the principal and the interest increase together."[2] Space prevents reference to the many practical and common-sense views about learning which are expressed in *Practical Education*. Edgeworth believed that learning should never be forced but the pace should be adjusted to the age and ability of the pupil. He stressed the value of the conversational mode of teaching and the necessity of restricting the amount which the child should learn by rote. The multiplication tables were an exception because unless they were perfectly memorised little progress in the art of arithmetic could be made.

[1] *Practical Education*, p. 53.
[2] *ibid.*, p. 64.

The Edgeworths were very concerned with training the minds of children to habits of alert attention and they realised that this was not possible unless the teacher provided the pupils with adequate motives to attend. The inventive ability of Edgeworth can clearly be seen in the chapters on arithmetic, geometry, and mechanics. Emphasis was placed on demonstration, experiment, and accurate observation and detailed instructions were given for the making of the apparatus needed for the experimental study of the principles of the lever, the wheel and axle, the pulley, the inclined plane, and the screw. The chapter on chemistry, written by his son Lovell, was certainly an innovation in 1798. There is little doubt that the work of Dr Priestley was an important influence in this respect.

Practical Education was largely based upon the psychology of Locke whose influence is clear in the authors' adoption of the criterion of utility in estimating the value of particular studies. The chapter on geography and chronology again illustrates Edgeworth's inventive ability. He preferred to use the globe in place of ordinary maps and the following passage is typical of his outlook. "Might not a cheap, portable, and convenient globe be made of oiled silk, to be inflated by a common pair of bellows ? . . . It might be hung by a line from its north pole, to a hook screwed into the horizontal architrave of a door or window; and another string from its south pole might be fastened at a proper angle to the floor, to give the requisite elevation to the axis of the globe. An idea of the different projections of the sphere may be easily acquired from this globe in its flaccid state, and any part of it might be consulted as a map if it were laid upon a convex board of a convenient size. Impressions from the plates which are used for common globes, might be taken to try this idea without any great trouble or expense; but we wish to employ a much larger scale, and to have them five or six feet diameter. The inside of a globe of this sort might be easily illuminated, and this would add much to the novelty and beauty of its appearance."[1]

Practical Education was widely read and although Adamson is correct in stating that it is impossible to single out any one institution which was directly influenced by the Edgeworths, many educated people were affected by their ideas and the ingenuity of such devices as that described above appealed to practical minded

[1] *Practical Education*, p. 421.

teachers. "In Edinburgh," writes Isabel Clarke, "they made the acquaintance of a Doctor Birkbeck who was about to give a lecture to children having taken the idea from *Practical Education*. At his house they were shown several curious machines but the thing that interested them most was a large globe of silk lighted by a lamp inside which when swelled out in a darkened room displayed a map of the world—a suggestion he had adopted from the same source".[1]

The Edgeworths agreed with Locke that the cultivation of good habits and the production of character were prime aims of education and in her children's stories, Maria Edgeworth was always most careful to point the moral. Father and daughter alike were convinced that utility and improvement were the principles which ought to govern the curriculum and the methods of teaching. They seemed to have kept religious education so much in the background that the *Quarterly Review* drew attention to the fact. There were other defects in their curriculum. Edgeworth was unduly optimistic and believed that a child of ordinary intelligence should have no difficulty in learning reading, writing, and spelling. This opinion led him to underestimate the importance of memorising in education. Even more serious was his disparagement of the imagination. In his anxiety to "improve", he ignored the development of the aesthetic responses through the study of music, art, and poetry. Father and daughter combined in expressing their contempt of the fairy stories and nursery classics which had nourished the imagination of generations of children. Maria recalls that her father's antagonism was always aroused at the mention of Puss-in-Boots or Jack and the Beanstalk.

Considering the period in which they lived, the Edgeworths held very liberal views about the education of girls and had many caustic comments to make on the "accomplishments" which it was thought young ladies should possess. Although they set great store on the advantages of a good home education, they recognised the benefits to be gained from public education and they advised parents "to send their children to large public schools, to Rugby, Eton, or Westminster; not to any small school: much less to one in their own neighbourhood".[2] This passage is important historically because it heralds the restricted application of the term

[1] *Maria Edgeworth*, p. 75.
[2] *Practical Education*, p. 502.

"public" to certain of the institutions which had hitherto been known as "the great schools".

One should not pass on from this brief sketch of *Practical Education* without quoting the Edgeworths' views about the essentials of a good teacher. "Before any person is properly qualified *to teach*, he must have the power of recollecting exactly how *he learned*: he must go back step by step to the point at which he began, and he must be able to conduct his pupil through the same path without impatience or precipitation. He must not only have acquired a knowledge of the process by which his own ideas and habits were formed, but he must have extensive experience of the varieties of the human mind. He must not suppose, that the operations of intellect are carried on precisely in the same manner in all minds; he must not imagine, that there is but one method of teaching, which will suit all persons alike. The analogies which strike his own mind, the arrangement of ideas, which to him appears the most perspicuous, to his pupil may appear remote and confused. He must not attribute this to his pupil's inattention, stupidity, or obstinacy; but he must attribute it to the true causes; the different associations of ideas in different minds, the different habits of thinking, which arise from their various tempers and previous education. He must be acquainted with the habits of all tempers: the slow, the quick, the inventive, the investigating; and he must adapt his instructions accordingly. There is something more requisite: a master must not only know what he professes to teach of his own peculiar art or science, but he ought to know all its bearings and dependencies."[1] This would serve as an excellent introduction to a talk delivered to young students of the present day who are about to embark on their first period of practical teaching in school.

Essays on Professional Education (published 1809) was the work of Richard Lovell Edgeworth alone. Its object was a consideration of the kind of education suitable for the country gentleman, the professional man who seeks a career in the Church, the Services or the law, the statesman, and the prince. This work is a later member of a family of treatises produced by Castiglione, Elyot, Milton, and Locke which deal with what W. H. Woodward terms "the doctrine of courtesy". By this time Edgeworth's views had developed and the breach between his teaching and that of the

---

[1] *Practical Education*, pp. 542-3.

Emile had become more apparent. He strongly expresses his opinion that "children should not be thus suffered to run wild like colts for a certain time, and then be taken and broken in by the most harsh, violent, and unskilful methods. Parents should with real kindness and affectionate foresight, begin as early as possible to prepare their children for school education".[1]

From the historical point of view, *Professional Education* is noteworthy for furnishing the *Edinburgh Review* with the opportunity of attacking the classical curriculum of the ancient universities.[2] It was this criticism which provoked the spirited reply of Copleston in 1810.[3]

Another member of the Edgeworth circle was Mrs Barbauld (1743-1825), a writer of poems and children's books. Her stories for young children were long used as elementary reading books. She taught in her own private school and included in her curriculum geography which was quite neglected in the majority of schools. Maria Edgeworth is now chiefly known as a novelist whose tales of Irish life established her literary reputation.

The next group of educational writers to be considered are better known because of the particular school of philosophy they represented, namely, Utilitarianism. The members of this school who contributed to educational ideas were Jeremy Bentham (1748-1832), James Mill (1773-1836), and John Stuart Mill (1806-1873). Bentham was the founder of the school. He was one of those infant prodigies who seem to have been common in the eighteenth and early nineteenth centuries. Before he was four, it is

---

[1] *Professional Education*, pp. 38-9.

[2] Edgeworth wrote the following paragraph:—"The principal defect in the present system of our great schools, is that they devote too large a portion of time to Latin and Greek. It is true, that the attainment of classical literature is highly desirable; but it should not, or rather need not, be the exclusive object of boys during eight or nine years". (*Professional Education*, p. 47.) This produced the following comment from the *Edinburgh Review*:—"That vast advantages, then, may be derived from classical learning, there can be no doubt. The advantages which are derived from classical learning by the English manner of teaching, involve another and a very different question; and we will venture to say, that there never was a more complete instance in any country of such extravagant and overacted attachment to any branch of knowledge, as that which obtains in this country with regard to classical knowledge. A young Englishman goes to school at six or seven years old; and he remains in a course of education till twenty-three or twenty-four years of age. In all that time, his sole and exclusive occupation is learning Latin and Greek . . . If you have neglected to put other things in him, they will never get in afterwards;—if you have fed him only with words, he will remain a narrow and limited being to the end of his existence". (Vol. 15, 1809-10, p. 456.)

[3] For the details of the controversy, see: S. J. Curtis, *History of Education in Great Britain*, chapter 12.

recorded that he ordered the footman to bring him a folio *Rapin* because he wanted to read history. At the age of four he was learning Latin grammar, and in his later childhood he became a voracious reader. In 1755 he was sent to Westminster where his industry was the means of saving him from the birch. He entered Queen's College, Oxford, at twelve, graduated at fifteen, and received his M.A. at eighteen.

The Bentham family had made up their minds that the young Jeremy should be a lawyer but he entertained other ideas about his future. Later, he became a member of a club which R. L. Edgeworth supported. As a result of his legal studies he became convinced that both the law and the government were hopelessly corrupt and needed a drastic overhaul. Although he conceived that he had a mission to reform them, in his earlier years he was at heart an aristocrat in his views and had little time to spare for democratic ideals, until, as Halévy has shown, circumstances and the influence of James Mill led him into the radical camp.[1] This explains why the Radicals looked upon him with considerable suspicion. From law he turned to the study of philosophy and started by reading Locke and Helvetius. He then passed to Hume. This reading strengthened his determination to be a reformer and the ideas he derived from his studies led to the formation of what is generally known as the principle of Utility.

This doctrine was concisely stated in the opening paragraph of the *Introduction to the Principles of Morals and Legislation*, 1789. "Nature has placed mankind under the governance of two sovereign masters, *pain* and *pleasure*. It is for them alone to point out what we ought to do, as well as to determine what we shall do. On the one hand, the standard of right and wrong, on the other the chain of causes and effects, are fastened to their throne. They govern us in all we do, in all we say, in all we think; every effort we can make to throw off our subjection will serve but to demonstrate and confirm it. In words a man may pretend to abjure their empire : but in reality he will remain subject to it all the while. The *principle of utility* recognises this subjection, and assumes it for the foundation of that system, the object of which is to rear the fabric of felicity by the hands of reason and law. Systems which attempt to question it, deal with sounds instead of sense, in caprice

---

[1] Elie Halévy, *The Growth of Philosophic Radicalism* (Trans. by Lady Morris) Part II, Chapter III, 1, reprint of 1952, Faber & Faber.

instead of reason, in darkness instead of light." This doctrine is generally known as Psychological Hedonism. Bentham believed that man is so constituted that all his actions are determined by the desire to seek pleasure and avoid pain. By pleasure he understood pleasant feeling. The word "ought" did not appear in the scheme at all. There was no point in postulating that the individual ought to seek his greatest pleasure when in point of fact he could not help doing so.

The consequence of this view was that Bentham regarded morality as an exact science. The determination of an individual action is entirely governed by the amount of pleasure or pain which he thinks will follow it. Bentham thought that the amount of pleasure and pain could be exactly measured and that a calculus of pleasure-pain could be fashioned. Differences in the quality of pleasures did not count. All that mattered was quantity. "Push-pin is as good as poetry". The quality of the pleasure was not to be taken into consideration. The legislator could employ the principle of utility by visiting certain types of behaviour with sanctions. To put the matter crudely, if you want to reform a burglar you must impress upon him that his crime will inevitably be discovered and that the punishment which will follow will be more painful than the pleasure he obtained from his burglary.

Bentham was greatly interested in the reform of the Poor Law and he urged that education should be provided for the poorer classes which should include moral and intellectual training and the teaching of a trade. He became interested in prison reform and advocated the establishment of a model prison which he named the Panopticon. "This idea was invented and first applied in Russia by his brother Samuel, whom Bentham visited at Crichof in 1786. It was the idea of the Panopticon, a prison in which the inspector has *the faculty of seeing at a glance everything that is going on;* a circular prison where one inspector, or at most a very small number of inspectors, is in a position to supervise all the cells which are arranged concentrically round a central pavilion : a system of blinds makes invisible the inspector who sees everything . . . He recommended that the principles should be extended to factories, mad-houses, hospitals, and even to schools, for the supervision of children during class hours and hours of recreation". Dr N. Hans writes : —"It is interesting to note that Russian prisons during the Tsarist period, and the Russian concentration camps during the Soviet régime, were built and organised according to the Panopticon model. Bentham even advocated placing a swivel gun in the central circle on an elevation to control the whole prison in case of revolt. The machine-gun in a central tower controlling the concentration camp is only a modern adaptation of the same idea. His Chrestomathic School in a Panopticon building was the educational equivalent of his prison".[1]

The term Chrestomathia means useful learning, and Bentham's *Chrestomathia* was a collection of papers (published 1815-17) in which he stated his views on the organisation of the school, the curriculum, and the general aims and principles of education. He suggested a building on the Panopticon model, but the organisation of the school was based on the monitorial system of Bell and Lancaster. The Headmaster took the place of the prison governor. Pupils would not be assigned to a particular class or form. Each pupil would be a member of different classes according to the degree of attainment he had made in the different studies. This classification was actually adopted in the early days of University College School, London.

The Chrestomathic Day School was intended for the "middling and higher ranks of life", *i.e.* it was a secondary school. The curriculum was based on the principle of utility, and Bentham's ideas about it were nearly as encyclopaedic as those of Milton and the Dissenting Academies. After some difficulties about a site, that of Queen's Square Place was finally approved. Fortunately for English education, the project never matured. William Allen persuaded Bentham to invest money in Owen's establishment at New Lanark. Leslie Stephen suggests that Bentham took pleasure "in Owen's benevolent schemes for infant education, and made money by his investment, for once combining business with philanthropy successfully. Probably he regarded New Lanark as a kind of Panopticon. Owen had not as yet become a prophet of Socialism".[2]

James Mill (1773-1836) was Bentham's lieutenant. His father was a village cobbler in Forfarshire, and he was destined by his parents for the ministry. With the assistance of Sir John Stuart, Mill was able to obtain an education superior to his status in life, and he entered the University of Edinburgh in 1790 where he

[1] *Pioneers of English Education*, edited by A. V. Judges, p. 90, Faber and Faber, 1952.
[2] *The English Utilitarians*, Vol. 1, p. 211, Duckworth, 1912.

studied Greek, theology, and philosophy. He seems to have gained some experience as a tutor in several wealthy Scottish families, but his career as a minister was not a success. After a brief journalistic experience, he met Bentham in 1808. The friendship which sprang up between the two men ripened and Bentham desired to have his new disciple living near him. "With his 'need of someone to admire', which made him the ideal disciple for Bentham, a dreaded master, with his genius for logical deduction and exposition, which gives a kind of originality to his works even when they are expressing someone else's ideas, Mill rendered to Bentham as much service as Bentham rendered Mill. Bentham gave Mill a doctrine, and Mill gave Bentham a school." [1]

Mill found that the support of a family, which eventually included nine children, was a strain on his resources, but by the exercise of rigid economy, he managed to keep out of debt. He had started the *History of British India* in 1806, and at the outset he judged that its composition would take about three years, but as at the same time he undertook the education of his own children, this period actually became protracted to nearly three times the original estimate. There is no doubt that the friendship with Bentham was of financial assistance to Mill. He accepted the offer of a house belonging to Bentham, for which he paid a reduced rent. Bentham also entertained the Mills for half of each year at his country houses at Barrow Green and, later, at Ford Abbey, Chard.

Mill became Bentham's devoted follower in spite of the fact that his stern and rigid outlook on life was a marked contrast to the spirit of instability which was at the root of Bentham's conduct. During the later years of Bentham's life, Mill threw himself heart and soul into the Utilitarian movement. His earlier beliefs suffered a profound change and he became an agnostic. He was not only friendly with William Allen, the Quaker, one of the early supporters of Owen at New Lanark, and Francis Place, the Radical tailor and prominent worker in the Chartist cause, but also made the acquaintance of Wilberforce and Zachary Macaulay.

Allen persuaded Mill to take an interest in the work of Joseph Lancaster, and when the Royal Lancasterian Institution was founded in 1809, Allen was one of the trustees and Mill was a member of the financial committee. At this time a bitter controversy

---

[1] E. Halévy, *op. cit.,*p. 251.

was in progress between Joseph Lancaster and Andrew Bell which was heightened by the support which was given to Bell by Mrs Trimmer. The latter was a devoted adherent of the Established Church and was suspicious of Lancaster because he was a Quaker and favoured undenominational religious teaching in the schools. Bell was warmly supported by the Tories. Mill, as a Radical, naturally rallied to Lancaster. He was associated with Place in the organisation of a West London Lancasterian Association which adopted the motto, *Schools for All*. Mill published a pamphlet in 1812 in support of this principle: *Schools for All and not Schools for Churchmen only*. Apart from furnishing useful statistics for the Report of Brougham's Royal Commission, according to Leslie Stephen, the Association became a failure. "As the committee, according to Place, included four infidels, three Unitarians, six Methodists, two Baptists, two Roman Catholics, and several members of the Established Church, it was hardly a happy family. To add to the confusion, Sir Francis Burdett, who had contributed a thousand pounds, had taken it into his head that Place was a Government spy. The Association, as is hardly surprising, ceased to exist in 1816, after keeping up a school of less than three hundred children, and ended in hopeless failure." [1] After this, Mill gave all his support to Bentham and the proposed Chrestomathic school.

All this time he had devoted every moment he could spare to the completion of the *History of British India*, which eventually appeared in 1817. The *History* was as dull and dry as Mill himself, but it was a solid achievement and immediately received recognition as the standard work on this subject. Mill had never visited India but he reasoned that this was really an advantage because it ensured that his account was wholly impartial. Nevertheless, his reputation was so enhanced that he was given a post in the India Office, and by successive promotions he reached in 1836 the rank of Examiner, which carried with it a salary of £2,000 a year.

Although they described themselves as Radicals the Utilitarians were not truly democratic in their outlook and both Bentham and James Mill found themselves in opposition to the reformer Cobbett and the socialistic views of Owen. If they were to achieve any

[1] *The English Utilitarians*, Vol. II, James Mill, p. 21, Duckworth, 1900.

measure of success it would be necessary for them to state their opinions clearly and convincingly. Mill undertook this task by contributing between 1816 and 1823 a series of articles to the *Encyclopaedia Britannica.*

It was at this time that Mill became interested in the scheme to create a University of London which had been advocated by the poet, Thomas Campbell, in 1824. He associated himself with Brougham, Zachary Macaulay, Joseph Hume, and Dr Birkbeck, the leading members of the "education mad party". He was also elected a member of the Committee of the Society for the Diffusion of Useful Knowledge, 1827, which published many works of educational interest. One might think of the Society's work as similar to that of the Extra-Mural Department of a modern university.[1]

Mill's chief contribution to the development of educational ideas lies in his psychology which was developed in the *Analysis of the Phenomena of the Human Mind,* 1829, and in his article on "Education" which appeared in the fifth edition of the *Encyclopaedia Britannica.* The latter was reprinted by Roebuck in 1836 at the price of fourpence a copy as propaganda in his campaign for popular education.

Bentham had contributed to moral philosophy the principle of Utility. In the *Analysis of the Human Mind,* Mill developed the fundamental conception of Utilitarian psychology, the theory of the Association of Ideas. The "mental chemistry" implicit in this theory not only dominated Mill's exposition but proved to be a baneful influence which affected the development of English psychology throughout the greater part of the nineteenth century. The principle of utility combined with the doctrine of the association of ideas held in thrall the psychological views of the next three or four generations and the work of James and MacDougall may be regarded as a reaction to the prevailing belief. Mill's psychology was largely adopted by Alexander Bain (1818-1903) who for many years was examiner in Mental and Moral Science at the University of London, and thus ensured the predominance of the associationist point of view. The result was that psychology tended to concentrate on the intellectual processes at the expense of the emotional; it viewed the experience of the child in the light of the adult.

[1] The account of the foundation of University and King's Colleges and the University of London is given in S. J. Curtis, *History of Education in Great Britain,* chapter 12.

Mill declared that his intention was to make the workings of the human mind "as plain as the road from Charing Cross to St Paul's", and however laudable such a motive might be it was attended by considerable danger. If one attempts to simplify that which by its very nature defies simplification, the result is bound to contain a considerable amount of error. There is no doubt about the origin of Mill's doctrines. He had carefully studied both Locke and Helvetius but it was Hartley who was responsible for the doctrine of association. The theory had a certain validity provided always that it was not overworked, and Mill's mistake was to lay more on its shoulders than it could sustain. In fact, the doctrine of association served Mill in a way somewhat similar to the "conditioned reflex" utilised by J. B. Watson and the Behaviourists. If we grant that the association of ideas is the fundamental principle of mental activity, by obeying this law, it would seem possible to control the whole development of the individual from the cradle to the grave.

The two principles of utility and of the association of ideas colour Mill's article on education. He states that the aim of education is that of rendering the individual happy both to himself and to others. He endeavours to base the practice of education upon psychology. In this attempt, however, he was a pioneer in the scientific treatment of education. We shall see that some of the principles suggested in the article were not carried out in the education of his son. For example, although he stressed the value of physical education, the young John Stuart was never given opportunities for playing with other children and his recreation consisted chiefly in the daily walk in company with his father.

Mill's conception of an educational science was not new. Basedow had used experiment in the Philanthropinum at Dessau and Kant had been firmly convinced of the necessity of establishing experimental schools. The Edgeworths had also emphasised that education should be an experimental science. Mill's ideas, however, represented a very important advance on those previous thinkers. The latter had been concerned with discovering and formulating a scientific educational method. They did not question the aims of education as generally understood. Thus the Edgeworths had assumed that everybody would agree that the aim of education is the acquirement of useful knowldege and the training and disciplining of the mental faculties to render the pupil capable of assimilating further doses of useful knowledge. It is to Mill's credit that he saw the importance of coming to a conclusion about the aims of education and this attitude was developed by J. S. Mill who clearly stated that psychology should be concerned only with the means and that by itself it is unable to give guidance about the ultimate purposes of education. He believed that the latter fell within the province of philosophy, in particular, moral philosophy and the social and political sciences.

Although Mill believed that the aim of education is to secure the happiness of each individual who is being educated and then the happiness of his fellows, he acknowledged that the nature of happiness was still a matter of controversy amongst philosophers. Nevertheless, he was confident that it is possible to ascertain "the means which are at the disposal of man for endowing the human mind with the qualities on which the generation of happiness depends".[1] The qualities he selected as being conducive to happiness were drawn from the cardinal virtues of Greek philosophy: intelligence (knowledge and sagacity), temperance (command of the natural appetites and desires), justice and generosity (summed up in the eighteenth-century term benevolence). One may ask if the nature of happiness had not been determined, how it could be possible to decide upon the qualities which would produce it?

Mill related these desirable qualities to the agencies which are responsible for education and adopted a threefold classification— the family, the school, and "the mode in which the mind of the individual is acted upon by the nature of the political institutions under which he lives".[2] These agencies are concerned with what he terms domestic, technical or scholastic, and social, education, respectively.

One of the main criticisms of Mill's article is that he expressed a purely academic and bookish point of view. Education, he thought, is concerned with the mind and therefore physical education is important in so far as the body exercises a beneficial or harmful influence upon the intelligence. Although he stressed the importance of good health, adequate nourishment, and freedom from excessive manual exertion (he was thinking of the workers in the early days

[1] F. A. Cavenagh, *James and John Stuart Mill on Education*, p. 25, C.U.P., 1931.
[2] *ibid.*, p. 4.

of the Industrial Revolution), he did not conceive of these as goods in themselves but only in relation to intelligence. Adamson has, therefore, considerable justification for his remark that Mill "places the body outside the province of education".[1] In particular, Mill never appreciated the function of play in the development of the child. The article on "Education" was a purely theoretical one. Mill started with a number of psychological and educational principles and deduced from them what education should be and do, but he showed no first-hand knowledge of what was actually taking place in the schools. His views provide an example of what occurs when a complete divorce is brought about between theory and practice.

One aspect of Mill's thought does, however, anticipate modern tendencies, namely, his acknowledgment of the relation between society and education. He was also opposed to the idea that knowledge has a value in and for itself. He wrote: "The highest measure of knowledge is therefore required. But mere knowledge is not enough: a mere magazine of remembered facts is a useless treasure. Amid the vast variety of known things, there is needed a power of choosing, a power of discerning which of them are conducive, which not, to the ends we have in view".[2]

Mill's faith in the power of education to reform society led him to identify himself with the work of Brougham both in regard to the formation of the University of London and to the diffusion of useful knowledge amongst the masses. If he had lived a generation or two later, he would no doubt have been a zealous supporter of the University Extension movement.

John Stuart Mill (1806-1873) was trained to take the place of his father and Bentham as the leader of the Utilitarian party. With this end in view, his father undertook the education of his son. J. S. Mill described in detail his early education in his *Autobiography*, chapter 1. This account is well worth reading for it shows quite clearly one way in which a child should not be trained. Although he had a great respect for his father one can see that Mill, when looking back on his early years, was not altogether in agreement with his father's methods. The elder Mill taught his son when he was busy writing the *History of India* and in bringing up a large

---

[1] *English Education*, 1789-1902, p. 107, C.U.P., 1930.
[2] F. A. Cavenagh, *op. cit.*, p. 21.

family. J. S. Mill records: "During the whole period, a considerable part of almost every day was employed in the instruction of his children in the case of one of whom, myself, he exerted an amount of labour, care, and perseverance rarely, if ever, employed for a similar purpose, in endeavouring to give, according to his own conception, the highest order of intellectual education".[1]

The last phrase indicates the major fault of James Mill. The education he gave his son was purely intellectual. J. S. Mill thought that his first lessons in Greek began about the age of three. When he was eight, he began to learn Latin but by this time he had already read a considerable number of Greek authors including the whole of Herodotus and Xenophon and six dialogues of Plato. Mill commented on his course of instruction as follows: "But my father in all his teaching, demanded of me not only the utmost that I could do, but much that I could by no possibility have done".[2] He realised later the main deficiency of this training and tells us that his father accomplished his end by keeping him away from the companionship of other boys. "The deficiencies in my education were principally in the things which boys learn from being turned out to shift for themselves, and from being brought together in large numbers . . . I grew up healthy and hardy, though not muscular but I could do no feats of skill or physical strength, and knew none of the ordinary bodily exercises. It was not that play, or time for it, was refused me. Though no holidays were allowed, lest the habit of work should be broken, and a taste for idleness acquired, I had ample leisure in every day to amuse myself; but as I had no boy companions, and the animal need of physical activity was satisfied by walking, my amusements, which were mostly solitary, were, in general, of a quiet, if not a bookish turn, and gave little stimulus to any other kind even of mental activity than that which was already called forth by my studies: I consequently remained long, and in a lesser degree have always remained, inexpert in anything requiring manual dexterity; my mind, as well as my hands, did its work very lamely when it was applied, or ought to have been applied, to the practical details which, as they are the chief interest in life to the majority of men, are also the things in which whatever mental capacity they have chiefly shows itself."[3]

[1] J. S. Mill, *Autobiography*, p. 3, Longmans, Green.
[2] *ibid*., pp. 3-4.   [3] *ibid*., pp. 20-1.

The result of this training was that by the age of fourteen, the young Mill had covered more than a complete university course in the classics, in philosophy, and in mathematics. Small wonder, then, that shortly before he came of age, Mill passed through a severe mental crisis which endured for a considerable time. Two important events contributed to the restoration of mental peace. The first was his introduction to the poetry of Wordsworth. He wrote: "What made Wordsworth's poems a medicine for my state of mind, was that they expressed, not mere outward beauty, but states of feeling, and of thought coloured by feeling, under the excitement of beauty. They seemed to be the very culture of the feelings, which I was in quest of. In them I seemed to draw from a source of inward joy, of sympathetic and imaginative pleasure, which could be shared in by all human beings; which had no connection with struggle or imperfection, but would be made richer by every improvement in the physical or social condition of mankind. From them I seemed to learn what would be the perennial source of happiness, when all the greater evils of life shall have been removed".[1]

The other turning point of his life was his meeting with Mrs Taylor, the lady who later became his wife. She possessed all those qualities of imagination, sympathy, and human understanding, which had been stunted in himself by his early education. The result of these influences was that although Mill became the recognised leader of the Utilitarian philosophy (he attached this title to the school himself), his personality, far richer than that of his father or Bentham, led him towards views which were inconsistent with strict Benthamism. Torn between loyalty to the system in which he had been reared and the promptings of his own liberal and generous nature, he read into Benthamism an extension of meaning which it was unable to carry and this caused the many inconsistencies in his teaching. He was a great man but not great enough to discard entirely the Utilitarian policy and start afresh.

Thus, although he was a staunch defender of the Utilitarian theory of morals, he introduced into his exposition certain qualifications which were at variance with the views he was supporting. A. D. Lindsay comments as follows: ". . . we find him in all his books enunciating with firmness the Utilitarian principle, then compelled by his fairness and openness of mind to admit exceptions and

---

[1] J. S. Mill, *Autobiography*, p. 85.

insert qualifications which the older Utilitarianism, complete but narrow, had never recognised. The resultant picture is much fairer to the facts, but presents much less of a consistent doctrine, and the critical reader is always wondering why, if Mill admits this or that, he persists in maintaining general principles with which the facts admitted are clearly inconsistent".[1]

Considerations of space will permit of but one example of what Lindsay had in mind. In *Utilitarianism* (p. 6) Mill describes his principle as follows: "The creed which accepts as the foundation of morals, Utility, or the Greatest Happiness Principle, holds that actions are right in proportion as they tend to promote happiness, wrong as they tend to produce the reverse of happiness. By happiness is intended pleasure, and the absence of pain; by unhappiness, pain, and the privation of pleasure". So far, this is perfectly orthodox Benthamism. Mill, however, proceeds: "It is quite compatible with the principle of utility to recognise the fact, that some *kinds* of pleasure are more desirable and more valuable than others. It would be absurd that while estimating all other things, quality is to be considered as well as quantity, the estimation of pleasures should be supposed to depend on quantity alone.

"If I am asked, what I mean by difference of quality in pleasures, or what makes one pleasure more valuable than another, merely as a pleasure, except its being greater in amount, there is but one possible answer. Of two pleasures, if there be one to which all who have experience of both give a decided preference, irrespective of any feeling of moral obligation to prefer it, that is the more desirable pleasure. If one of the two is, by those who are competently acquainted with both, placed so far above the other that they prefer it, even though knowing it to be attended with a greater amount of discontent, and would not resign it for any amount of the other pleasure which their nature is capable of, we are justified in ascribing to the preferred enjoyment a superiority in quality, so far outweighing quantity, as to render it, in comparison, of small account."

One might ask how this statement is to be reconciled with Bentham's hedonistic calculus. If some pleasures are preferable to others because they are of a higher type, the criterion is no longer pleasure pure and simple, but some other quality which

---

[1] In his Introduction to *Utilitarianism, Liberty and Representative Government*, p. viii, Everyman edition, J. M. Dent.

makes them more desirable. Commenting on Mill's admission, Hastings Rashdall writes: "All this tends to show how completely the admission of qualitative differences in pleasure abandons the Hedonist point of view. As a popular mode of expression, the doctrine that pleasures differ in kind is a true and useful formula; but it should be recognised that this is not Hedonism. For it means precisely this—that we ascribe value or worth to states of consciousness for other reasons than their pleasantness, although a certain amount of pleasantness might be a characteristic of all states of consciousness which are capable of being desired".[1]

Mill, though he would never have admitted the fact, had really departed from Psychological Hedonism and had gone a considerable way towards the doctrine of Ethical or Rational Hedonism. Hence, Rashdall asserts that Sidgwick, who held the latter view, starts from where Mill left off.

Once he admitted the ideas of obligation, of differences in the quality as well as the quantity of pleasures, and claimed Conscience as the ultimate moral sanction, he had dealt a death blow to the system which his father and Bentham had raised with so much care. The tension is not so apparent in his views on education, but there are several divergencies from his father's position. His views are expressed in the *Essay on Liberty* (1859) and his *Inaugural Address as Rector of St Andrew's University* delivered in 1867. Mill, in common with the other members of the Utilitarian school, was an individualist and regarded with apprehension the increasing concern of the State with the life of the individual. Hence he did not believe that the State should take responsibility for the education of the people. He wrote: "That the whole or any large part of the education of the people should be in State hands, I go as far as any one in deprecating. All that has been said of the importance of individuality of character, and diversity in opinions and modes of conduct, involves, as of the same unspeakable importance, diversity of education. A general State education is a mere contrivance for moulding people to be exactly like one another: ... An education established and controlled by the State should only exist, if it exist at all, as one among many competing experiments, carried on for the purpose of example and stimulus, to keep the others up to a certain standard of excellence".[2]

[1] *The Theory of Good and Evil*, p. 26, Clarendon Press, 1907.
[2] Essay "On Liberty" in *Utilitarianism, Liberty and Representative Government*, p. 161, Everyman edition, J. M. Dent.

Mill, however, was not prepared to exclude the State entirely from the field of education. He granted to it the function of requiring and compelling the education, up to a certain standard, of each of its citizens. The obligation to educate his children should be the parent's and the State should only intervene when the parent neglected his duty. "Were the duty of enforcing universal education once admitted there would be an end to the difficulties about what the State should teach, and how it should teach, which now convert the subject into a mere battlefield for sects and parties, causing the time and labour which should have been spent in educating to be wasted in quarrelling about education. If the government would make up its mind to require for every child a good education, it might save itself the trouble of providing one. It might leave to parents to obtain the education where and how they pleased, and content itself with helping to pay the school fees of the poorer classes of children, and defraying the entire school expense of those who have no one else to pay for them." [1]

Mill's *Rectorial Address to the students of St Andrew's* is one of a group of essays dealing with the meaning of a liberal education which appeared during the nineteenth century. Sir Walter Moberly regards them as representing the Christian-Hellenic traditions which governed the outlook of the universities during the first seventy years of the nineteenth century.[2] Whewell's essay *On the Principles of English University Education*, 1837, was a forerunner but the most widely read of these treatises is J. H. Newman's *Idea of a University*, 1852.

Mill was elected Rector of St Andrew's in 1865. His permission had not been sought and he actually asked to withdraw, but eventually he was persuaded to accept the office and postpone his inaugural address until 1867.[3] The address was memorable for its length alone. It lasted for three hours. The writer once knew an elderly lady who was a friend of J. S. Mill and who described the

---

[1] Essay "On Liberty" in *Utilitarianism, Liberty and Representative Government*, p. 161, Everyman edition, J. M. Dent.

[2] The *Crisis in the University*, pp. 30-1, S.C.M. Press, 1949. Whewell's essay is discussed in S. J. Curtis, *History of Education in Great Britain*, chapter 12.

[3] The office of Rector of St Andrew's is a survival of the medieval custom by which the Rector represented the doctors, masters, and scholars of the university, and was elected by the *Comitia* or general congregation of the university. The congregation voted by nations, Lothian, Britannia, Albany, and Angus. In the sixteenth century the place of Britannia was taken by Fife. By the nineteenth century the Rectorship had become a titular office and the delivery of one or more addresses was the main duty of its holder.

somewhat damping effect that Mill's austere and ascetic, one might almost say, forbidding appearance, and his thin reedy voice had upon his audience. Mill, himself, had not passed through a university course and therefore he regarded a university as primarily an institution for the dissemination of knowledge rather than a society possessing a strong intellectual and social life. Although in certain parts of the address, Mill departed from orthodox Benthamism, it is true to say that the marks left by his early education are plainly discernable.

Mill commenced by distinguishing two aspects of education. In its widest meaning, "whatever helps to make the individual what he is, or hinders him from being what he is not—is part of his education".[1] In the narrower sense, education consists in the "culture which each generation purposely gives to those who are its successors, in order to qualify them for at least keeping up, and if possible for raising the level of improvement which has been attained". Mill thought that the work of a university was mainly concerned with the latter aspect. He emphasised that a university was not an institution for providing technical and professional training. That should be obtained at schools of medicine, law, engineering, and the industrial arts. The real function of a university was to give its students a general or liberal education. "Men are men before they are lawyers, or physicians, or merchants, or manufacturers; and if you make them capable and sensible men, they will make themselves capable and sensible lawyers and physicians. What professional men should carry away with them from an university, is not professional knowledge, but that which should direct the use of their professional knowledge, and bring the light of general culture to illuminate the technicalities of a special pursuit." [2]

The ideal position, he believed, would be that in which the school took the responsibility for providing the elements of knowledge whilst the university busied itself with inculcating the philosophy of knowledge. Unfortunately, in Scotland, the schools have not carried out their functions and it therefore falls to the universities to concern themselves with the teaching of the subjects which the schools have neglected. England, he asserts, is in a far worse condition than Scotland. "Youths come to the Scottish Universities ignorant, and

[1] *J. S. Mill's Inaugural Address at St Andrew's* in F. A. Cavenagh, *James and John Stuart Mill on Education*, p. 133, C.U.P., 1931.
[2] *ibid.* p. 137.

are taught. The majority of those who come to the English Universities come still more ignorant, and ignorant they go away." [1]

Mill then passes to the controversial topic whether education should be scientific or literary. His answer to the problem is quite decided. "This question, whether we should be taught the classics or the sciences, seems to me, I confess, very like a dispute whether painters should cultivate drawing or colouring, or, to use a more homely illustration, whether a tailor should make coats or trousers. I can only reply by the question, why not both? Can anything deserve the name of a good education which does not include literature and science too?" [2] Mill deprecates the efforts of those educational reformers (he has Herbert Spencer in mind), who would abandon the study of the classics and put science in their place. His own classical training was still influential in directing his thoughts and explains the reason for his vigorous defence of a classical foundation.

Mill was quite aware of the dangers which attend excessive specialisation. He shows that this had been caused by the rapid growth of knowledge in recent years so that one who endeavours to know any one subject with minute accuracy "must confine himself to a smaller and smaller portion of the whole extent". Such a state, he believes, is worse than simple ignorance. Mill was living at a time when the public examination system was only in its infancy. His comments on the present day situation in the upper forms of the grammar schools and in the universities would probably have been forceful. His own solution is that the individual should combine a detailed and accurate knowledge of one subject with a general knowledge of many things and he is at pains to avoid a confusion between general knowledge and superficiality.

Space will not admit of a detailed account of Mill's views about a suitable curriculum for the university. He does, however, express opinions which would have been completely condemned by his father and Bentham, namely, the value of aesthetic training carried out through the medium of poetry and the fine arts. He asks : "Who does not feel a better man after a course of Dante, or of Wordsworth, or, I will add, of Lucretius or the *Georgics*, or after brooding over Gray's *Elegy*, or Shelley's *Hymn to Intellectual Beauty*?" [3] The passage which follows is a complete refutation to

---

[1] *J. S. Mill's Inaugural Address at St Andrew's* in F. A. Cavenagh, *James and John Stuart Mill on Education*, p. 137, C.U.P., 1931.
   [2] *ibid.*, p. 138.   [3] *ibid.*, p. 193.

those, who like Herbert Spencer, would relegate the fine arts to a position of minor importance. Mill's discussion of the university curriculum is coloured by his belief in the doctrine of "formal training" which leads him to stress the disciplinary values of subjects and to describe them as "sharpeners of the intellectual faculties".

Herbert Spencer (1820-1903) is an example of a thinker who was so much overestimated by the later nineteenth century that the tendency of the present day is to write off the contributions he made to philosophy and education. He, himself, was partly to blame for this neglect. Spencer in his early years had a brief experience of teaching but on finding that he was not particularly successful, he followed for ten years the profession of railway engineer. As this did not afford him permanent satisfaction, he turned his abilities in the direction of a literary career and accepted the post of sub-editor of the *Economist*. He held this appointment until 1853 when he resolved to devote himself to independent literary work.

No one will dispute that Spencer possessed talents of a high order and he might have secured a more permanent appreciation from succeeding generations but for certain weaknesses. He was a natural rebel, independent, self-confident, and vigorously assertive. In later years he admitted his failures. Like R. L. Edgeworth, he had a capacity for invention which ranged from ideas about aerial locomotion to a new fork for toasting bacon.

His intellectual independence, which Dewey termed "his singular immunity from all intellectual contagion", led Spencer to ignore the views of other thinkers except in so far as it happened they coincided with his. He was not ignorant of this tendency and in his *Autobiography*, published the year after his death, he records that he could never settle down to study Plato. "Time after time I have attempted to read, now this dialogue and now that, and have put it down in a state of impatience with the indefiniteness of the thinking and the mistaking of words for things: . . . When I again took up the dialogues, I contemplated them as works of art, and put them aside in greater exasperation than before." [1]

Locke and Kant were treated in a similar manner. How far this intellectual isolation was complete is difficult to determine. Adamson states in regard to his essays on education that "they completed a chain which had united French and English theorisers during three centuries. Montaigne's essays had informed and

---

[1] *Autobiography*, vol. 2, p. 442, Williams and Norgate, 1904.

inspired Locke's convictions respecting the upbringing of youth; the Englishman in turn built a foundation upon which Rousseau constructed this conception of educational method and Spencer gave *Emile* an English nineteenth-century setting".[1] It is probable that Spencer had never read Rousseau but he had studied Pestalozzi some of whose theories he developed in his characteristic one-sided way, and he certainly owed much to August Comte.

Spencer is almost unique in the history of English philosophy because of his attempt to construct a complete system of speculative thought in which everything would fall into place under the governance of the principle of evolution. As early as 1860 he published the *Programme of a System of Synthetic Philosophy* and devoted the rest of his life to working it out in detail. Although he was hampered by constant ill-health, he resolutely adhered to his plan and before his death he had written works on biology, psychology, sociology, and ethics. It is a sad commentary on such single-minded industry and perseverance that present-day second-hand booksellers have in stock numerous copies of his various *Principles* which they would be glad to sell if they could only find customers who were willing to buy them. No doubt Spencer's early training as an engineer was a potent factor in developing his ability for classification. As W. R. Sorley wrote: "He built a system as he might have built a bridge. It was a problem of strains and the adaptation of material".[2]

Spencer also possessed a fully developed critical faculty which led him to pick holes in other people's work without appreciating their constructive contributions and he was loth to acknowledge that other writers had influenced him in the views he finally adopted. He was upright and conscientious in all that he did or taught and was completely fearless when stating his own belief. His relations with his fellows were marked by a domineering spirit for he was intolerant of their defects. He was not interested in persons; ideas alone appealed to him. His views on art and literature revealed a lack of sympathy and understanding. Moreover, he claimed not only to be able to perceive all the problems but to know all the answers. Rarely in the history of human thought has such a high degree of intellectual power been exercised to so little lasting purpose.

Spencer's chief contribution in the realm of educational ideas consists of four magazine articles written between 1854 and 1859.

[1] *English Education* (1789-1902), p. 296, C.U.P., 1930.
[2] *A History of English Philosophy*, p. 270, C.U.P., 1920.

They were collected and published in book form in 1861 under the title of *Education, Intellectual, Moral and Physical*. The popular edition (republished by Williams and Norgate, 1911) contains as a foreword, a quotation from Leslie Stephen. "Balston, our tutor (Eton, 1842-5) was a good scholar after the fashion of the day and famous for Latin verse; but he was essentially a commonplace don. 'Stephen major,' he once said to my brother, 'if you do not take more pains, how can you ever expect to write good longs and shorts? If you do not write good longs and shorts, how can you ever be a man of taste? If you are not a man of taste, how can you ever hope to be of use in the world?'" The quotation provides the key to the position adopted by Spencer in his first chapter which is called, "What knowledge is most worth?"

One is tempted to ask immediately, "Of most worth to whom, the individual or society?" There is no doubt about the meaning Spencer attached to that question. He was even a more convinced individualist than the Utilitarians and was always suspicious of State interference with the life of the individual. The chapter begins with a frontal attack on classical studies which he relegates to the class of ornaments and decorations because in his eyes they have no direct use in the lives of the majority of people. When one considers the lamentable state into which the teaching of the classics in our grammar schools had fallen and which a few years later was revealed to the public in the reports of the Clarendon and Taunton Commissions, one can quite understand Spencer's attitude.

The discussion of the defects of a classical education leads Spencer to formulate his well-known definition of education as a preparation for complete living. Taken by itself, such a definition is too general and vague to be of much value to those who are actually engaged in the work of teaching. Spencer, however, does attempt to clarify it by his analysis of the activities of life into those which directly and those which indirectly minister to self-preservation; those which have for end the rearing and discipline of off-spring; those involved in maintaining the right kind of social and political relations and those which fill up the leisure part of life.

Spencer asserts that the scientific studies, especially those concerned with self-preservation and the maintenance of good health, are of most importance and should therefore come first in the curriculum. Literary studies are placed at the bottom of the scale as leisure time pursuits. In adopting this order of values, Spencer makes the unproved assumption, so common in the works of eighteenth- and early nineteenth-century thinkers, that the self and the social interests are to a great extent antagonistic. It is in this chapter that an oft-quoted fallacy occurs: "When a mother is mourning over a first-born that has sunk under the sequelae of scarlet-fever—when perhaps a candid medical man has confirmed her suspicion that her child would have recovered had not its system been enfeebled by over-study—when she is prostrate under the pangs of combined grief and remorse; it is but small consolation that she can read Dante in the original".[1]

History comes in for very drastic criticism. The only history with which Spencer was acquainted was that which dealt with kings and queens, court intrigues, and plots. Hence one would support his verdict that this kind of history is useless for school pupils. It throws no light upon the development of society and institutions, nor is it of use to the individual in helping him to form thoughtful opinions about current political events and situations. Spencer would suggest as a substitution what he terms descriptive sociology. Since his time the value of social and industrial history has been recognised and it is to be found in the history syllabus of most modern schools. The treatment of the "leisure time activities" reflects Spencer's own psychological make up. One would agree that science and mathematics enter into poetry, fine art, and music, but it is easy to exaggerate, as Spencer certainly does, and regard them as essentials and not accessories. Like J. S. Mill, Spencer was a believer in the disciplinary value of subjects but in this respect he would give the primacy to the sciences rather than the languages and arts.

The second essay on "Intellectual Education" attacks learning by rote, the misuse of object lessons, and the substitution of words for things. Spencer says much that had been said both before and after his time. He acknowledges his debt to Pestalozzi but at the same time he is rightly critical of the application of Pestalozzi's methods in English education. Spencer introduces his well-known maxims of method. These are formulated as follows: (1) Proceed from the

---

[1] This fallacy was termed by Aristotle *ignoratio elenchi* which consists in ignoring the original question and substituting another in its place and then proceeding to answer it. The most common form which is exemplified by Spencer's argument is the appeal to prejudice and passion, the *argumentum ad populum*. In law suits it is often used by an examining counsel to discredit the evidence of a witness but fortunately most judges are sufficiently astute to draw to it the attention of the jury.

simple to the complex; (2) from the indefinite to the definite; (3) from the concrete to the abstract; (4) that the education of the child should accord "both in mode and arrangement with the education of mankind, considered historically", (Racial Recapitulation); (5) proceed from the empirical to the rational; and, finally, (6) in education, encouragement should be given to the process of self-development.

At first sight these principles appear to represent a notable advance in ideas about method but on closer examination, one realises that they are as often false and misleading as sound and helpful. They represent the standpoint of the subject of instruction rather than that of the age, abilities, needs, and outlook of the child at different stages of his development. They are mainly based upon logic and not upon the psychology of the child. One exception seems to be the theory of Racial Recapitulation which does claim to be based upon the mental development of the child. Modern thought, however, has only accorded a limited approval to this theory. It is only fair to Spencer to state that he regarded it as a broad generalisation and he should not be held responsible for the applications of the theory by a later generation of educators.

The chief criticism of Spencer's maxims is that they are too general and vague to be of much use to the teacher who if he follows them as guides may in his application be as often wrong as right. For example, the maxim *proceed from the simple to the complex* may be entirely misleading unless the terms simple and complex are understood to be relative to the age and mental development of the child. A young child may be confronted with a situation which appears to him to be simple because he accepts it as a whole and therefore does not realise its complexity. If the teacher applies the maxim literally it might lead him to the mistaken notion of analysing the subject-matter for the child and then teaching the elements which then have to be combined into more complex wholes, *e.g.* the alphabetical method of teaching reading or an introduction to geometry which begins with definitions, axioms, and postulates.

The fallacy which affects the whole outlook of Spencer is that he assumes that the possession of knowledge necessarily confers power. He tends to ignore the fact that the ability to use knowledge and to develop a right judgment is far more important than the mere accumulation of information. The latter may not be necessary if the individual has access to a book of reference or is able to consult an expert. A. N. Whitehead's criticism of inert ideas would be pertinent in this connection. When Spencer attempts to assess the value of the subjects of the curriculum he takes the adult point of view and does not realise that a study which may be very valuable in later life can be quite useless to the child who has not reached the stage of development which will enable him to comprehend it.

Spencer was right in pressing the claims of science at a time when scientific studies found no place in the majority of schools in spite of the advances made in the various branches of science and their important applications to industry. He weakened his arguments by his exaggerations and by his failure to recognise that much of the scientific teaching he advocates is suitable only for older pupils or for the specialist. Nevertheless, some useful suggestions are to be found in the first two chapters. Thus there is the emphasis on the "heuristic" method, already in germ in the *Emile*. "Children should be led to make their own investigations, and to draw their own inferences. They should be told as little as possible, and induced to discover as much as possible." [1] Again, his views on the right use of the object lesson as a means of exercising the senses, the methods to be employed in teaching drawing, and the first steps in acquiring geometrical knowledge show that Spencer had ideas which were in advance of current practice.

The essay on "Moral Education" definitely stamps Spencer's educational philosophy as the type usually known as Naturalism. He starts by the adoption of the Utilitarian view that "conduct whose total results, immediate and remote, are beneficial, is good conduct; while conduct whose total results, immediate and remote, are injurious, is bad conduct. The ultimate standards by which all men judge of behaviour, are the resulting happiness or misery". [2] It would follow from this that all conduct which brings pain as a consequence is bad. Pain is nature's way of teaching the individual to avoid certain kinds of conduct. One should note the confusion in Spencer's thought between the natural and the moral order.

In respect to moral training, Spencer adopted the discipline of natural consequence as his guiding principle. Although he had not studied Rousseau there is a remarkable resemblance between Spencer's doctrine and that of the *Emile*. Spencer writes: "Nature illustrates to us in the simplest way, the true theory and practice

[1] H. Spencer, *Education, Intellectual, Moral and Physical*, p. 93 (popular edition), Williams and Norgate, 1911. [2] *ibid.*, p. 137.

of moral discipline".[1] He then proceeds to make certain claims for his views of punishment. The natural consequences uniformly follow the action; they are proportionate to it, and the individual cannot escape from the results of his wrong doing. Unlike artificial, natural punishment does not endanger resentment nor create a feeling of injustice in the child's mind. He comes to regard it as the working out of the law of cause and effect.

Spencer's next step is to illustrate how the discipline of natural consequences can be applied. The child who refuses to put away his toys at the end of his play will find that his mother refuses to let him have them when he wants, on a future occasion, to play with them. The little girl who is never ready to accompany other children for a walk will be left behind. The boy who carelessly loses or breaks his penknife has to suffer being without one. Spencer would recommend following this rule in regard to more serious offences. He declares that the principle of justice demands that "a wrong act shall be undone by a right one; and in the case of theft this implies either the restoration of the thing stolen, or, if it is consumed, the giving of an equivalent: which, in the case of a child, may be effected out of his pocket-money".[2] Spencer does not realise that there is no meaning to the phrase "principle of justice" unless the relation of the individual to the community is considered. If this is done, one would be forced to acknowledge a second principle, equally, if not more valid, than the discipline of natural consequences.

Strictly speaking, one could say that the examples supplied by Spencer do not illustrate his principle but represent a manipulation by the parent to give the punishment the appearance of being the natural consequence of wrong doing. Even Spencer had to confess that the principle has its limitations. He writes: "During infancy a considerable amount of absolutism is necessary. A three-year old urchin playing with an open razor, cannot be allowed to learn by this discipline of consequence; for the consequences may be too serious".[3]

Spencer's doctrine is open to criticism on other grounds. As a convinced individualist, he failed to see that in many cases the essence of punishment lies in the social disapproval of the action. The doctrine is thoroughly individualistic: it is negative and prohibitive, deterrent rather than educative. T. H. Huxley was far

[1] H. Spencer, *Education, Intellectual, Moral and Physical*, p. 136 (popular edition), Williams and Norgate, 1911.   [2] *ibid.*, p. 160.   [3] *ibid.*, pp. 169-70.

wiser when he wrote: "Like all compulsory legislation, that of Nature is harsh and wasteful in its operation. Ignorance is visited as sharply as wilful disobedience—incapacity meets with the same punishment as crime. Nature's discipline is not even a word and a blow, and the blow first; but the blow without the word. It is left to you to find out why your ears are boxed".[1] Not only are the consequences often out of all proportion to the offence but as Kant showed: "Punishment, then, is a physical evil, which, though it be not connected with moral evil as a *natural* consequence, ought to be connected with it as a consequence by the principles of a moral legislation".[2]

Spencer's last essay, "Physical Education", is the most valuable in the book. It was written at a time when little attention was given to such matters as food, clothing, play, and sleep. He criticises severely the absurd restrictions placed upon growing girls in the "Establishments for Young Ladies". His remarks had a considerable influence upon the succeeding generation. In particular, his ideas coupled with the teaching of J. S. Mill and John Ruskin, were responsible for the attention given by Almond at Loretto to the provision of fresh air, good food, sensible clothing, and physical exercise.

SUGGESTIONS FOR FURTHER READING

The works of the Edgeworths, *Practical Education and Professional Education*, are not easy to obtain. Isabel C. Clarke, *Maria Edgeworth*, Hutchinson, 1949, is a fascinating account. The standard works on the Utilitarian school are Leslie Stephen, *The English Utilitarians*, Duckworth, 1900 (reissued 1912), and Elie Halévy, *The Growth of Philosophic Radicalism* (translated by Lady Morris, 1928, reprinted with corrections, 1952), Faber and Faber. F. A. Cavenagh in *James and John Stuart Mill on Education*, Landmarks in the History of Education series, C.U.P., 1931, gives the text of James Mill's article on *Education*, the *Rectorial Address of John Stuart Mill*, and extracts from the latter's *Autobiography*. The essays on *Utilitarianism* and *Liberty* can be obtained in the Everyman series, J. M. Dent.

There are numerous editions of Herbert Spencer's *Education*.

---

[1] *Collected Essays*, vol. 3, p. 85, Macmillan, 1905.
[2] *Kant's Theory of Ethics*, Abott's translation, 6th edition, p. 127, Longmans, Green, 1909.

CHAPTER XVI

ENGLISH EDUCATIONAL WRITERS OF THE NINETEENTH CENTURY

(2) J. H. NEWMAN, JOHN RUSKIN, T. H. HUXLEY, MATTHEW ARNOLD

English educational ideas during the two or three decades after the middle of the nineteenth century were focused upon the problems of the curriculum in the public schools, the endowed grammar schools, and the universities. During the preceding half-century, Britain had passed through changes in the social, political, and industrial spheres which were so far-reaching as almost to merit the title of a revolution, but the schools and the universities had done little to keep in step with the new developments. The Reform Act of 1832 had resulted in the transference of political power to the middle classes, and it was not to be long before the skilled artisans and finally the labouring classes were to be admitted to participation in the government of the country. Scientific discovery and invention had progressed at an astonishing rate and the new scientific ideas were being applied in industry. The *laissez-faire* attitude of the earlier years of the century was being subject to criticism from many quarters and, although a good deal of suspicion of State intervention in the life of the people remained, it was becoming obvious that the absolute independence of the individual could not continue in the form in which it had been exercised at the beginning of the century.

It is true that certain eminent headmasters, such as Butler at Shrewsbury, and Arnold at Rugby, had through their personal examples infused a measure of life into the time-honoured curriculum of the public schools, and that at the universities, reforms were making headway, albeit, very slowly. In most of the endowed grammar schools, the position had, if anything, grown worse since the beginning of the century. One has only to read the account given by Carlisle in the *Endowed Grammar Schools of England and Wales*, 1818, and compare it with the findings of the Taunton Commissioners in 1868 to realise, that little, if any, progress had taken place. Indeed it was the widespread dissatisfaction with the school curriculum which was one of the factors which called into being the Clarendon and Taunton Commissions.

Thus it is not surprising that writers of the period under consideration show much concern about the curriculum and, whether they are discussing secondary or university education or education in general, they are keenly interested in the factors which should constitute a liberal education. In line with the Clarendon and Taunton Commissioners, they draw attention to the restricted nature of the curriculum and the inferior position occupied by the study of the natural sciences, modern languages, history, and geography. The reader will have noticed J. S. Mill's treatment of the question whether higher education should be literary or scientific, and Herbert Spencer's vehement advocacy of the claims of science.

The group of writers now to be considered represent different standpoints but they are all concerned with clarifying the meaning of the term "liberal education".

It is important to realise that the idea of a liberal education had become modified since the days of Plato and Aristotle, and of the teaching of the Seven Liberal Arts which western Europe had inherited from the Greeks. In the mediaeval grammar school a liberal education consisted of the subjects of the Trivium with an emphasis upon the study of Latin grammar. Renaissance educators had expanded this restricted curriculum by their insistence upon the study of the classical writers and the importance they attached to the development of style in the writing of prose and verse. Grammar became the means for the study of classical literature and was no longer an end in itself. The growing use of the vernacular in the affairs of daily life had weakened the utility motive for the study of Latin. Most grammar schools of the eighteenth century paid lip service to this idea but in practice only a minority of pupils in the larger schools achieved such mastery of the classical languages which enabled them to read and appreciate Latin and Greek literature. In most schools the teaching of Latin consisted in a dull and uninspiring grind at grammar so that at length the pupils could with difficulty construe one or more prescribed authors. In the smaller schools, Greek had practically disappeared, and many country grammar schools were in reality nothing more than rather inefficient elementary establishments.

As the utility value of Latin declined, the schools and universities and society in general attached a so-called cultural value to a classical education. The ability to include in any public speech a few quotations from classical authors was considered to be one of the marks of the gentleman who had received a good education and who was a man of taste. Thus at the end of the eighteenth century, it was generally understood that a liberal education and an education based on the classics were synonymous terms.

In spite of the general sterility of the education given in the schools it must not be assumed that there were no signs of progress during the first half of the nineteenth century. In fact a revival was developing within the realm of classical studies themselves. The new intellectual outlook is usually known as Classical Humanism. Amongst schoolmasters, Thomas Arnold reflected the new spirit. Whilst maintaining the old ideal of classical scholarship, he believed that a study of the classics undertaken in the right way would materially assist the pupil in his understanding of the problems of modern life. He therefore sought to utilise the classics as means of teaching history, literature, philosophy, ethics, and politics. In their respective spheres, Cardinal Newman and Mark Pattison represented the classical humanist position in the universities.

The progress of the movement in England was influenced by the revival of Greek studies in Germany which had taken place after the middle of the eighteenth century. On the Continent it had gathered strength from the work of Wilhelm von Humboldt (1767-1835) who was put in charge of the Prussian Bureau of Education in 1808. At this time the urgent problem which confronted the Prussian government was that of creating a new national movement which should banish the dejection and disillusionment caused by the defeat of Jena. Humboldt was convinced that the study of the civilisations of Rome and Greece, particularly the latter, could furnish the inspiration that was needed. If pupils of the gymnasium could recapture the spirit and ideals of the ancient world and harness them to modern needs, a great force for the regeneration of the Prussian people would be created. Hence his synthesis took the line that a liberal education was a general education based on the study of classical culture but which at the same time should not exclude modern subjects. Although Humboldt's term of office expired in 1810 and his system was modified by the reactionary officials who succeeded him, it is true to say that when Matthew Arnold visited the schools in 1866, they still bore the imprint of Humboldt's ideas. Humboldt's achievements were important for this country because they strongly influenced the views of the Clarendon and Taunton Commissioners and helped to form the ideas about the nature of a liberal culture which were expressed by Matthew Arnold.

Two other important points should be grasped before considering the views of particular writers. In the first place, it is possible to distinguish at least four schools of thought, if one may employ the phrase, amongst educationists of the mid-Victorian era.

(1) The enlightened defenders of a liberal education based upon the classics. Thomas and Matthew Arnold, Mark Pattison, Cardinal Newman, and the group of writers who contributed to *Essays on a Liberal Education*, edited by Dean Farrar, 1867, are representative of this school.

(2) An extreme right wing typified by Dr G. Moberly, Headmaster of Winchester, who wholeheartedly supported the traditional teaching of the classics.

(3) The supporters of the claims of science. These may be divided into writers like Spencer, who would relegate classical studies to the background, and those like T. H. Huxley and J. S. Mill who believed that a balanced curriculum should contain both literary and scientific studies.

(4) The majority of grammar school teachers, who had not seriously thought about the issue and who through ignorance or complacency were prepared to continue with the restricted curriculum and the unsatisfactory methods of teaching which had been employed for several centuries. Unfortunately this group formed the majority of secondary school teachers and it was to be many years before they were completely eliminated.

The second point is that during the clash of ideas the conception of a liberal education became greatly modified. From a general education with a classical core it became a general education resting upon a harmonised, well-balanced curriculum in which both arts and sciences had their place and in which the antithesis of culture and utility tended to break down. The final stage was reached when it was suggested that English studies might replace classical as the core of the curriculum.

As regards university education the most important contribution of this period is Newman's *Idea of a University*, a series of lectures originally delivered in 1852. When the Oxford Movement in the Anglican Church started in 1833 as a result of John Keble's sermon on "National Apostasy", Newman soon became its acknowledged leader. The persecution directed against the movement, intensified after the publication of Newman's *Tract 90*, caused a number of the Tractarians to secede to the Church of Rome   In 1843 Newman resigned his living of St Mary's and was formally received into the Roman Church in 1845. When the Irish hierarchy decided in 1852 to establish a Catholic University of Ireland in Dublin, Newman gave the series of lectures which embody his ideas about the function of a university. R. L. Archer describes the series as "a masterly harmonisation of Catholicism and contemporary Oxonianism, and it remains the outstanding and classic exposition of the latter".[1]

Newman was appointed Rector of the new institution. The Catholic University was not a success, partly because it was a private venture without State support, and partly because Newman himself was not endowed with the qualities which produce the able administrator. In order to understand the position adopted by Newman in his course of lectures it is necessary to review in outline events in Ireland before 1850 when the scheme for a Catholic University was first discussed. In the early part of the century, religious controversy between Protestants and Catholics was even more bitter than the feud between Anglicans and Nonconformists in England. The Established Church had always been a minority body even in Northern Ireland where a large number of Protestants preferred the Presbyterian form of church organisation. During the eighteenth century the penal laws against Roman Catholics were in full force. Catholics were forbidden to teach a school, or even take a post as a private tutor, under pain of transportation, and if the individual returned after his period of exile, he was liable to be tried for high treason. The penal Acts were repealed in 1782 but the Government refused to recognise Catholic education and continued to vote money to support schools connected with the Established Church.

As in England, a number of schools had been opened by voluntary societies, *e.g.* The Incorporated Society for Promoting English Protestant Schools in Ireland, 1733, the Association of Discountenancing Vice, 1800. Irish education had been discussed by several Royal Commissions and Parliamentary committees. The most noteworthy of these was the Commission of 1806 which included R. L. Edgeworth as a member. This Commission was in favour of a "mixed" education system under which Catholics and Protestants would be educated together without any interference with their respective religious beliefs. The experiment was tried by the Society

[1] *Secondary Education in the Nineteenth Century*, p. 39, C.U.P., 1932.

for Promoting the Education of the Poor, 1811 (Kildare Place Society). The scheme adopted was similar to that of the Lancastrian system in England. The schools of the Society received a Government grant after 1814, but they received no support from the Catholic clergy. University education was provided by Trinity College, Dublin (founded by Elizabeth I in 1592), but this institution was connected with the Established Church.

In 1832 the Government adopted a scheme of national elementary education and made a grant of £30,000 to enable the Lord-Lieutenant of Ireland to assist the education of the people. A board of national education was set up in Dublin on which Catholics and Protestants were represented. The policy adopted was similar to that recommended by Edgeworth; the provision of literary and moral education in common with separate religious instruction for the different denominations. The Presbyterians welcomed the scheme but it was coldly received by both the Catholics and the majority of the clergy of the Established Church. One contemporary summed up the scheme in the following words: "While the whole system is crumbling to dust under their feet, while the Church is prostrate, property of all kind threatened, and robbery, murder, starvation, and agitation rioting over the land, these wise legislators are debating whether the brats at school shall read the whole Bible or only parts of it".

Further provision of higher education was made by the foundation of the Queen's Colleges at Belfast, Cork, and Galway between 1845 and 1849. They were incorporated as the Queen's University in 1850. They hoped to solve the religious difficulty by providing purely secular instruction. Very few Catholics entered these institutions. In addition, a college had been established at Maynooth in 1795 for the training of Catholic clergy. It received grants from public funds. In 1845 Sir Robert Peel presented a Bill designed to increase the grant paid to Maynooth to £30,000. This roused intense opposition and in the parliamentary debates which followed, the violent language used by the Protestant party has seldom been exceeded. The Maynooth Bill was one of the causes of the downfall of Peel's administration. Mr Gladstone immediately resigned because he deemed that support of the Bill was incompatible with the opinions he had expressed in his essay on the relations between Church and State. It was in these circumstances that the Irish Catholic hierarchy decided to found a Catholic University which would be quite independent of the Government.

The Government held the view that a "mixed" education was possible through the operation of a conscience clause. It was thought that religious instruction could be given apart from the other subjects of the curriculum because the influence of religion upon secular studies was negligible. Newman strongly disagreed with this view. Believing that all knowledge is one, he was concerned to show that the study of theology cannot logically be omitted from the university curriculum. He started his argument as follows: "A university, I should lay down, by its very name professes to teach universal knowledge: theology is surely a branch of knowledge: how then is it possible to profess all branches of knowledge, and yet to exclude not the meanest, nor the narrowest of the number?"[1] One may object to both premisses of this argument. The reader will have noticed the mistake in the derivation of the word "university". There are also many who would not be prepared to grant that theology is a branch of knowledge and they are not necessarily atheists nor agnostics. Thus St Peter Damian in the eleventh century believed that theology is a matter of revelation and, therefore, not knowledge in the accepted sense.

Newman sums up his position by stating: "I lay it down that all knowledge forms one whole, because its subject-matter is one; for the universe in its length and breadth is so intimately knit together, that we cannot separate off portion from portion, and operation from operation, except by a mental abstraction; ... sciences are the results of that mental abstraction—being the logical record of this or that aspect of the whole subject-matter of knowledge. As they all belong to one and the same circle of objects, they are one and all connected together; as they are but aspects of things, they are severally incomplete in their relation to the things themselves, though complete in their own idea and for their own respective purposes; on both accounts they at once need and subserve each other".[2]

In his fourth lecture, Newman turns to his idea of the meaning of liberal knowledge, and hence a liberal education and considers the function of a university. He believed that a university is essentially an institution concerned with the diffusion and extension rather than with the advancement of knowledge. Research should

---

[1] *On the Scope and Nature of University Education*, p. 11, Everyman edition, J. M. Dent.
[2] *ibid.*, p. 42.

be carried on in special institutions which are not universities. Speaking of the university as a place of education, he says: "An assemblage of learned men, zealous for their own sciences, and rivals of each other, are brought by familiar intercourse and for the sake of intellectual peace, to adjust together the claims and relations of their respective subjects of investigation. They learn to respect, to consult, to aid each other. Thus is created a pure and clear atmosphere of thought, which the student also breathes, though in his own case he can only pursue a few sciences out of the multitude. He profits by an intellectual tradition, which is independent of particular teachers, which guides him in his choice of subjects, and duly interprets for him those which he choses. He apprehends the great outlines of knowledge, the principles on which it rests, the scale of its parts, its lights and its shades, its great points and its little, as he otherwise cannot apprehend them. Hence it is that his education is called 'Liberal'. A habit of mind is formed which lasts through life, of which the attributes are, freedom, equitableness, calmness, moderation, and wisdom; or what in a former discourse I have ventured to call a philosophical habit".[1]

Liberal knowledge with which the university is concerned is an end in itself. This distinguishes it from useful knowledge which is pursued for some ulterior end. Newman quotes from the *Rhetoric* of Aristotle to illustrate the distinction. "Of possessions, those rather are useful, which bear fruit; those liberal, which tend to enjoyment. By fruitful, I mean, which yield revenue; by enjoyable, where nothing accrues of consequence beyond the use." Hence liberal knowledge "stands on its own pretensions, which is independent of sequel, expects no complement, refuses to be *informed* (as it is called) by any end, or absorbed into any art, in order duly to present itself to our contemplation".[2]

Newman's conception of knowledge is quite different from the view held by Edgeworth and Brougham and the members of the Society for the Diffusion of Useful Knowledge. He opposes the idea that knowledge consists in an accumulation of facts, mere information which can be culled from books. It is an illumination, a habit, a personal possession, and an inward endowment. Corresponding to the distinction between useful and liberal knowledge we

[1] *On the Scope and Nature of University Education*, pp. 92-3, Everyman edition, J. M. Dent.
[2] *ibid.*, p. 99.

can differentiate between instruction and education. A person is said to be instructed in a trade or a manual exercise. A university is concerned with education, which "implies an action upon our mental nature, and the formation of a character; it is something individual and permanent, and is commonly spoken of in connection with religion and virtue. When, then, we speak of the communication of knowledge as being education, we thereby really imply that that knowledge is a state or condition of mind; and since cultivation of mind is surely worth seeking for its own sake, we are thus brought once more to the conclusion which the word 'Liberal' and the word 'Philosophy' have already suggested, that there is a knowledge, which is desirable though nothing come of it, as being of itself a treasure, and a sufficient remuneration of years of labour".[1]

The modern schoolmaster will find that Newman's words are worthy of his close attention. In these days when there is an increasing demand for vocational training and technical instruction, it is easy to confuse the acquisition of information and technical skill with education in its truest sense. An individual may have learnt a great deal about steam, gas, electricity, radio-activity, and their applications; his mind may constitute a veritable storehouse of facts, mathematical, historical, geographical, and scientific, and yet he may be essentially uneducated. The real test lies in the effect his learning has had upon his mind, his character, and his outlook on life.

Newman had no quarrel with useful education as such. He recognised that it is both valuable, and necessary, and if he were living now he would probably be one of the first to point out that such a training has within itself the possibilities of a culture as important as that which is usually associated with literary pursuits. He made his position quite clear when he wrote: "There are men who embrace in their minds a vast multitude of ideas, but with little sensibility about their real relations towards each other. These may be antiquarians, annalists, naturalists; they may be learned in the law; they may be versed in statistics; they are most useful in their own place; I should shrink from speaking disrespectfully of them; still, there is nothing in such attainments to guarantee the absence of narrowness of mind. If they are nothing more than well-read men, or men of information, they have not what specially

[1] *On the Scope and Nature of University Education*, p. 105, Everyman edition J. M. Dent.

deserves the name of culture of mind, or fulfils the type of Liberal Education".[1]

Liberal knowledge, Newman insists, does not aim at making men better. Its purpose is neither religion nor morality, and "Liberal Education viewed in itself, is simply the cultivation of the intellect as such, and its object is nothing more or less than intellectual excellence".[2] Liberal education seeks to produce a healthy state of mind. This is a good in itself in the same way that a healthy body is a good. What, then, are the characteristics of this healthy mental condition ?

Newman tells us that it "consists, not merely in the passive reception into the mind of a number of ideas hitherto unknown to it, but in the mind's energetic and simultaneous action upon and towards and among those new ideas, which are rushing in upon it. It is the action of a formative power, reducing to order and meaning the matter of our acquirements; it is a making the objects of our knowledge subjectively our own, or, to use a familiar word, it is a digestion of what we receive, into the substance of our previous states of thought; . . . We feel our minds to be growing and expanding *then*, when we not only learn, but refer what we learn to what we know already. It is not a mere addition to our knowledge which is the illumination; but the locomotion, the movement onwards, of that mental centre, to which both what we know and what we are learning, the accumulating mass of our requirements, gravitates . . . It possesses the knowledge, not only of things but also of their mutual and true relations; knowledge, not merely considered as acquirement, but as a philosophy".[3]

He knew full well that such a view would not meet with popular approval in mid-Victorian days when the demand was growing for instruction in those subjects which were of use. The industrial progress, the mechanical inventions, the development of new forms of transport, and the material prosperity enjoyed by the wealthier members of the community constituted in Newman's eyes a very real danger. It is true that these tendencies were only in their infancy; much more was to come, but Newman was sufficient of a prophet to realise that the liberal, classical humanism of the older universities was threatened by the desire for vocational and professional instruction. This explains why he was at such pains to

[1] *On the Scope and Nature of University Education*, p. 127, Everyman edition, J. M. Dent.
[2] *ibid.*, p. 113.   [3] *ibid.*, pp. 126-7.

labour the distinction between a useful and a liberal education, and why he did not then realise that what he called a useful education if given in the right way could also produce in the recipient the "enlargement of mind" to which he attached such importance.

When he delivered his addresses he had in mind the record of the University of London which in those days was mainly an examining body.   Hence the famous passage: "If I had to choose between a so-called university which dispensed with residence and tutorial superintendence, and gave its degrees to any person who passed an examination in a wide range of subjects, and a university which had no professors or examinations at all, but merely brought a number of young men together for three or four years, and then sent them away as the University of Oxford is said to have done some sixty years since, if I were asked which of these two methods was the better discipline of the intellect—mind, I do not say which is *morally* the better, for it is plain that compulsory study must be a good and idleness an intolerable mischief—but if I must determine which of the two courses was the more successful in training, moulding, enlarging the mind, which sent out men the more fitted for their secular duties, which produced better public men, men of the world, men whose names would descend to posterity, I have no hesitation in giving the preference to that university which did nothing, over that which exacted of its members an acquaintance with every science under the sun".[1]

He then gives the reason for his decision.   "When a multitude of young persons, keen, open-hearted, sympathetic, and observant, as young persons are, come together and freely mix with each other, they are sure to learn one from another, even if there be no one to teach them; the conversation of all is a series of lectures to each, and they gain for themselves new ideas and views, fresh matter of thought, and distinct principles for judging and acting, day by day."[2]   These two extracts show that Newman really understood the essentials for a healthy university course and subsequent events have endorsed his view.   All our modern provincial universities and university colleges have been busy in extending their halls of residence, and in bringing into operation some form of a tutorial group system as a supplement or even a substitute for lecture courses.

[1] *On the Scope and Nature of University Education*, pp. 137-8, Everyman edition, J. M. Dent.
[2] *ibid.*, pp. 138-9.

In the last two discourses, Newman returns to the subject of the relation of liberal knowledge to religion and the duties of the Church towards liberal knowledge. In his view, the Church supplies the unifying principle. Newman expresses his admiration of the thirteenth century when the Church exercised the steadying influence he advocates, and by bringing Aristotle into line with Catholic truth made possible the great synthesis of faith and reason accomplished by St Thomas Aquinas. He ventures upon the prophecy that the time will come when once again a similar reconciliation will be needed and can be made in a university in which the study of theology is recognised and which has the support of the Church. Newman delivered his lectures in 1852. Darwin's *Origin of Species* was published in 1859.

Newman's lectures represent the greatest defence of a liberal education as understood and practised at Oxford in the nineteenth century. Within a few years of their delivery there appeared on the scene another thinker who in many ways held opposing views, but who may be regarded as a prophet inasmuch as he pleaded for many developments in education, the majority of which have been realised in the present century. He was John Ruskin (1819-1900), whose name is not immediately associated with education but rather with a philosophy of art, the defence of the paintings of Turner, and a pleasing, semi-poetical style in English prose. In reality, education was always very close to Ruskin's heart. He had a considerable experience in both teaching and examining. When in 1858, Oxford instituted the Middle-Class Examinations, later known as the Oxford Local Examinations, Ruskin was appointed examiner in drawing. He held decided views about the place of art in general education and, in *The Stones of Venice*, he urged the inclusion of art as a subject for undergraduates. Ruskin was not only well known as a critic and teacher of art but he was intimately associated with the movement for adult education which resulted in the establishment of the Working Men's Colleges. When F. D. Maurice became Principal of the London Working Men's College, Ruskin offered to teach drawing. He joined with Maurice in his advocacy for secondary and higher education for girls and women, and his influence was one of the factors which induced Felix Slade to endow chairs of fine art at Oxford, Cambridge, and London. For several years, Ruskin held the appointment of Professor of Fine Art.

He was a voluminous writer but he did not produce a single work entirely devoted to the discussion of education. At the same time nearly all his books and pamphlets contain references to education and certain of them deal with the subject at some length. Thus the student who wishes to assess Ruskin's influence on education will find it necessary to read all his books, pamphlets, and letters. His main teaching is contained in the four books: *Unto This Last* (1862), *Sesame and Lilies* (1864), *Time and Tide* (1867), and *The Crown of Wild Olive* (1866-9).

Like Wordsworth, Ruskin was a severe critic of the educational ideas and practices common in his time. He accused the majority of people as valuing education merely as a means of improving the position of the individual. This was connected with the idea of competition to which Ruskin was opposed. He was never tired of preaching the virtues of co-operation. Hence he complained that there was no real desire for education for its own sake. He wrote: "The cry for it among the lower orders is because they think that, when once they have got it, they must become upper orders. There is a strange notion in the mob's mind now-a-days ... that *everybody* can be uppermost; or at least, that a state of general scramble in which everybody in his turn should come to the top, is a proper Utopian constitution; and that, once give every lad a good education, and he cannot but come to ride in his carriage ... And very sternly I say to you ... and say from sure knowledge—that a man had better not know how to read and write, than receive education on such terms".[1]

Besides criticism, however, Ruskin had a number of constructive ideas to offer. In the preface to *Unto This Last*, he outlined the principles which ought to govern the new social order of which he dreamed. "First—that there should be training schools for youth established, at Government cost, and under Government discipline, over the whole country; that every child, born in the country should, at the parents' wish, be permitted (and, in certain cases, be under penalty required) to pass through them; and that, in these schools, the child should (with other minor pieces of knowledge hereafter to be considered) imperatively be taught, with the best skill of teaching that the country could produce, the following three things: —

(*a*) The laws of health, and the exercises enjoined by them;

(*b*) Habits of gentleness and justice; and

(*c*) The calling by which he is to live."[2]

[1]*Time and Tide.* Letter XVI.   [2] *Unto This Last.* Preface. pp. xvi, xvii.

Ruskin's emphasis on the laws of health and physical exercise reinforced the similar plea which a few years earlier had been made by Herbert Spencer. He gave moral training a very high priority and was not afraid to recommend vocational training. All through his life he was an opponent of every kind of commercialism and dependence upon machine-made products. In the *Crown of Wild Olive*, he eloquently urged the revival of hand industries and the recovery of the true spirit of craftsmanship which he believed was associated with them. His message to the members of the R.A. Institution at Woolwich was: "Educate or govern, they are one and the same word. Education does not mean teaching people to know what they do not know. It means teaching them to behave as they do not behave. And the true 'compulsory education' which the people now ask of you is not catechism but drill. It is not teaching the youth of England the shapes of letters and the tricks of numbers; and then leaving them to turn their arithmetic to roguery and their literature to lust. It is, on the contrary, training them into the perfect exercise and kingly continence of their bodies and souls. It is a painful, continual, and difficult work; to be done by kindness, by watching, by warning, by precept, and by praise—but above all— by example.

"Compulsory! Yes, by all means! 'Go ye out into the high-ways and hedges, and *compel* them to come in.' Compulsory! Yes, and gratis also. *Dei Gratia*, they must be taught, as, *Dei Gratia*, you are set to teach them. I hear strange talk continually, 'how difficult it is to make people pay for being educated!' Why, I should think so! You do not expect *them* to pay you for your teaching, except by becoming good children. Why should you expect a peasant to pay for his, except by becoming a good man?"[1]

He was no believer in a uniform system of education. Schools should fall into three general classes. "Your schools will require to be divided into three groups; one for children who will probably have to live in cities, one for those who will live in the country, and one for those who will live at sea; the schools for these last, of course, being always placed on the coast. And for children whose life is to be in cities, the subjects of study should be, as far as their disposition will allow of it, mathematics and the arts; for children who are to live in the country, natural history of birds, insects, and plants, together with agriculture taught practically; and for children

[1] *Crown of Wild Olive*, pp. 185-6.

who are to be seamen, physical geography, astronomy, and the natural history of sea fish and sea birds."[1]

Ruskin had his own contribution to make to the controversy about the nature of the curriculum. He was not prepared to accept the classical curriculum as the ideal. He wanted every pupil to become familiar with the greatest literary works of the world and to have experience of the finest music and art. He also believed in introducing the pupil to the wonders of nature and of physical science. In fact, one could almost call him the founder of modern nature study. He wished that all schools could have the right kind of environment. Instead of the dingy buildings in the slums of the great cities and the pseudo-Gothic or Tudor schoolhouses of the country, he would like to see the schools "in fresh country, and amidst fresh air, and have great extents of land attached to them in permanent estate. Riding, running, all the honest, personal exercises of offence and defence, and music, should be the primal heads of this bodily education".[2]

He also had strong convictions regarding the place of literature in the curriculum. His ideas about the right use of books are to be found in *Sesame* and the importance he attached to accuracy in the use of words is illustrated by his famous exposition of how to study an extract from Milton's *Lycidas*. The second part, *Lilies*, contains a criticism of the shallow and restricted ideas about the education of girls in the mid-nineteenth century. Like Spencer, Ruskin believed: "The first of our duties to her—no thoughtful persons now doubt this—is to secure for her such physical training and exercise as may confirm her health, and perfect her beauty". Girls, he insists, must be made happy if they are to be lovely, and he quotes with approval Wordsworth's phrase "vital feeling of delight". He scorned the select establishments for training young ladies. Their education should be as important as that of their brothers. "Let a girl's education be as serious as a boy's. You bring up your girls as if they were meant for sideboard ornaments and then complain of their frivolity. Give them the same advantages that you give their brothers—appeal to the same grand instincts of virtue in them; teach *them* also that courage and truth are the pillars of their being: do you think that they would not answer that appeal, brave and true as they are even now, when you know that there is hardly a girls' school in this Christian kingdom

---

[1] *Time and Tide*, Letter XVI.   [2] *ibid.*, Letter XVI.

where the children's courage or sincerity would be thought of half so much importance as their way of coming in at a door."

No doubt many hard-headed business men in the days when the Revised Code was being administered with maximum severity, dismissed Ruskin as a dreamer, perhaps a prophet. And a prophet he was. If he had lived to the present, he would have rejoiced to see most of his dreams coming true, and his prophecies being fulfilled. The great advances made in school building in recent years, the provision of playgrounds and playing fields, the attention given to art, handicrafts, and nature study, the importance attached to medical inspection and treatment, and physical pursuits—all these represent ideals which Ruskin had in mind and his only complaint would be that far too many schools of the type with which he was familiar are still allowed to exist.

While the Taunton Commission was investigating the state of affairs in the endowed grammar schools, there appeared in 1867 a collection of *Essays on a Liberal Education* which was edited by the Rev. F. W. Farrar, at that time teaching at Harrow, and later to become Dean of Canterbury. This publication not only supported the reforms suggested by the Taunton Commissioners as regards the curriculum, but in its constructive recommendations went a stage further. The eminence of the contributors to this volume procured for them a respectful hearing. The modern reader should keep in mind when assessing their views that they accepted the prevailing faculty psychology with its corrolaries of mental discipline and the transfer of training. Perhaps the most closely reasoned essay was written by H. Sidgwick who was a Cambridge professor and a philosopher of some reputation. One of the stock arguments advanced by the defenders of a purely classical education was that it was indispensable to the better understanding of English. Sidgwick made a devastating reply to this argument. He wrote: "An artificial education is one which, in order that a man may ultimately know one thing, teaches him another, which gives the rudiments of some learning or accomplishment, that the man in the maturity of his culture will be content to forget".[1] In addition to classical studies, Sidgwick recommended: "I think, that a course of instruction in our own language and literature and a course of instruction in natural science, ought to form recognised and substantive parts of our school system. I do not venture to estimate the

[1] *Essays on a Liberal Education*, edited by F. W. Farrar, p. 87, Macmillan, 1867.

amount of time that ought to be apportioned to these subjects, but I think that they ought to be taught to all, and taught with as much serious effort as anything else. I think also that . . . more stress ought to be laid on the study of French".[1]

Professor J. Seeley, the author of *Ecce Homo* and *The Expansion of England*, supported the views of Sidgwick, but perhaps the most significant contributions were those of E. E. Bowen, master at Harrow, who was responsible for the creation of a "modern" side and who is widely known as the author of the Harrow school song, *Forty Years On*, and J. M. Wilson, then science master at Rugby and afterwards Headmaster of Clifton College.

Bowen attacked the grammatical approach to the classics. He drew an imaginary picture of the consequences that would follow if a professor of chemistry followed the traditional procedure. "Proceeding upon the classical principles, he will first commit the whole of his knowledge to a volume, which he will draw up in a dry and technical style, and if possible, in a dead language. Of this he will ask his class to learn a certain portion every day, and to believe the time may come when they may want it. He will perform a few experiments, every detail of which he will refer to their position in the book. He will urge as carefully as he can that the phosphorus takes fire, not because chemical force is set at liberty, but because the book says it shall. He will introduce into his book-lessons the rarest metals and the most elaborate combinations, not because the pupils will commonly use them in the laboratory, but because his system is not complete without them. And when he finds that his disciples hate their work, and, in practice, hardly know an acid from a base, he will believe that the fault lies not in his mode of teaching, but in the unfortunate incompleteness of his book."[2] In conclusion, Bowen stated: "Now it is certain that a large proportion of boys dislike the work they have to do. Some like it; some are indifferent; a great many simply hate it. We maintain that an educator of boys has no business to be satisfied as long as this is the case".[2]

Wilson stood for a point of view which even at the present time all schools have not adopted. He believed that as a school study, physics was preferable to chemistry. He put himself in the place of the pupil. Chemistry could easily become a "cram" subject.

[1] *Essays on a Liberal Education*, edited by F. W. Farrar, p. 187-8, Macmillan, 1867.
[2] *ibid.*, p. 200.

From his textbook the pupil could memorise the properties of the common elements and compounds, the action of certain acids and alkalis, and give satisfactory answers to the questions set in the London Matriculation Examination, without ever having performed by himself even the simplest chemical experiment. This was no overstatement, for the Bryce Commissioners found that at Knaresborough Grammar School, quite satisfactory passes had been obtained by pupils who had never handled a test tube.

Wilson believed quite rightly that the value in learning science consists not so much in the acquisition of scientific facts as in the insight into scientific method that the pupil receives and that for this purpose, physics and biology were more effective than much of the chemistry taught in nineteenth-century schools. From the standpoint of a practising schoolmaster, Wilson criticised the policy of the majority of headmasters. They divided their schools into classical and modern sides and placed all the dull pupils in the latter. Because a great many of these pupils failed to pass in the public examinations they drew the conclusion that science was an inferior kind of mental discipline. On the constructive side, Wilson recommended that the head of a school who wished to introduce science into his curriculum should make a start with the middle forms. Each year he should extend the teaching into the next lower class until he reached a point where effective teaching could no longer be given. From this zero point he could work upwards to the higher forms in which pupils were ready to specialise.

J. W. Hales, Fellow of Christ's College, Cambridge, was in general agreement with the other writers. He stated: "What I should wish to propose is, that the linguistic studies of all our schools should begin with English, should then proceed with the dead languages in the case of boys who are likely to have leisure to study them to any profit, and in other cases should proceed with English and living languages".[1]

The general view of the contributors represented a revolt against the idea that the classics must necessarily constitute the core of the curriculum. They were feeling their way towards the position which regarded English studies as replacing the classics. Also, each one agreed that a systematic teaching of sciences and modern languages was desirable. It never occurred to them whether a core to the curriculum is essential or whether there is any other way of relating subjects.

[1] *Essays on a Liberal Education*, edited by F. W Farrar, p. 301, Macmillan, 1867.

Another voice was soon added to the discussion, that of Robert Lowe. His name has become so associated with the Revised Code of 1862 that his views about the curriculum of the secondary school have received scant attention. Lowe, himself, was no mean classical scholar but he was in total disagreement with the way in which these studies were conducted in the schools. He was convinced that the narrow linguistic tradition with which he was familiar required considerable modification. Although his actions with regard to elementary education have been almost universally condemned, it is difficult to see what other course was open to him at that precise period. We are not, however, concerned with his administration but rather with his ideas. He had a deep dislike of superficiality and believed that the education provided for the poorer classes of the community ought to differ materially from that which the upper and middle classes received. His views on middle-class education were expressed in the pamphlet *Primary and Classical Education.*

This pamphlet was the published account of an address delivered to the Philosophical Institution of Edinburgh in 1867. At that time the prevailing view was that elementary education was a charity which the more well-to-do sections of the community provided for the poorer people who did not possess the means to pay for the schooling of their children. In addition, the political situation of the time must be taken into account. The Reform Act of 1867 had extended the franchise to a large section of artisans, the "leap into the dark" as Disraeli termed it. Lowe was responsible for the phrase that now we had "to compel our future masters to learn their letters", often misquoted as, "we must educate our masters". He was not only concerned with making the new voters literate but he also believed that a drastically reformed type of education was necessary for the middle classes, if they were to maintain their political influence. This would not be possible as long as its younger members were restricted to an education consisting only of the classics and pure mathematics.

Lowe's own upbringing and inclinations were in favour of the time-honoured curriculum but he was sufficient of a realist to perceive that that day had passed, and his great concern was that the mass of the wage-earning voters should be guided by those who had greater knowledge and experience. This explains his criticism of the traditional forms of education. "Learning the language," he wrote, "is a joke compared with learning the grammar. The grammar is one thing, and the language another. I agree with the

German wit, Heine, who said—'How fortunate the Romans were that they had not to learn the Latin grammar, because if they had done so they never would have had time to conquer the world'".

He spoke of the new science of "ponderation" which had for its object the weighing of the merits of the different subjects of the curriculum. The priorities he assigned were as follows: because we live in a world of things rather than words, the knowledge of things is more essential than the knowledge of words. We ought to attach a greater value to what is true than to what is false. Hence it is more important to teach the history of England than stories about Roman and Greek mythology. Because our time is limited, we should teach what is practical in preference to what is theoretical. Finally, we should bear in mind that the present is of more value to us than the past.

In the light of these principles, Lowe criticised the existing classical curriculum. He urged that language is not valuable in itself but rather for the thought of which it is the vehicle. He believed that the pupil should study his own language before going on to learn Latin and Greek. Also there are other languages such as French which have a strong claim for inclusion in the curriculum. The same applies to modern history and geography. The root of the matter was that society had altered its balance and that now we had to decide upon an education suitable for a democratic and not an aristocratic community. The schools, therefore, should make provision for instruction in English and modern European literature, modern history, and the recent developments in physical and natural science. Lowe brought the address to a conclusion with the words: "I am most anxious to educate the lower classes of this country in order to qualify them for the power that has passed, and perhaps will pass in a still greater degree into their hands. I am also anxious to educate, in a manner very different from the present, the higher classes of this country, and also for a political reason".

The next year he gave two addresses to the Liverpool Philo-mathic Society on Middle-Class and Primary Education. He lamented the apathy of the middle classes, who, although he was fighting their own battle, gave him little sympathy or support. The reason lay in their own imperfect education. They either sent their children to "commercial academies" to learn reading, writing, arithmetic, and bookkeeping, or to establishments which copied the public schools in the hope that they would obtain a smattering of classical knowledge. He stressed the value of learning both French and German, but above all, he advocated the study of physical science.

The following extract shows the point of view adopted by Lowe. "First, I recommend to your notice a subject generally overlooked in our public schools, and that is—what do you think?—the English language; the language of Bacon and of Shakespeare; the language of Pitt and Charles Fox; the language of Byron and of Shelley—a language richer, probably, and containing more varied treasures than the treasures contained in any other language—which began to be formed and fashioned sooner than any other in Europe, except the Italian, which it surpasses in everything, except mere sound, that constitutes the beauty of a language. Is it not time that we who speak that language, read that language, so much of whose success in life depends on how we can mould that language; we who make our bargains in that language, who make love in it, should know something about it; that our care should not be limited to the reading of penny, threepenny, or even sixpenny newspapers; but that we should, at least in our boyhood, be called on to remember what sort of writers England produced in the sixteenth and seventeenth centuries; that we should know our own tongue theoretically as well as practically? I can only speak from my own experience. During the last two years that I was at school I was, if not actually idle, at least not wholly devoted to Latin and Greek, and I had some qualms of conscience on the subject. But there was a certain bookcase in the corner of the study which was full of standard and sterling English books; I spent my time in reading those English books, and I felt like a truant and ashamed of myself when I did so, because I was stealing those hours from the study of Latin and Greek. I can only say that I owe my success in life to those stolen hours—that the power of being able to write and speak my native language with some precision and force has been more valuable to me than all the rest I have learned."[1]

Thus with other motives in mind, Lowe fell into line with the views of the contributors to *Essays on a Liberal Education*.

The most influential advocate for the inclusion of science in the curriculum was T. H. Huxley (1825-95). Professor Huxley was an eminent scientist, a distinguished lecturer, and a man who took an active part in all forms of education from the London Board Schools to the Working Men's Colleges. He was quite as enthusiastic as

[1] A. Patchett Martin, *Life and Letters of Viscount Sherbrooke*, vol. 2, p. 335, Longmans, Green, 1893.

Spencer for the advancement of scientific and technical education, but his broad and liberal outlook would not permit him to restrict education to these studies only. Thus in an "after-dinner" speech to the Liverpool Philomathic Society in 1869, he told his audience that while it was his belief that no boy should leave school without possessing a grasp of the general character of science, he was not a supporter of a purely scientific education. "To furnish a boy with such an education, it is by no means necessary that he should devote his whole school existence to physical science: in fact, no one would lament so one-sided a proceeding more than I. Nay more, it is not necessary for him to give up more than a moderate share of his time to such studies, if they be properly selected and arranged, and if he be trained in them in a fitting manner."[1]

When Josiah Mason opened in 1880 a college which was destined to be one of the institutions which gave rise to the University of Birmingham, Huxley delivered a lecture on Science and Culture. After emphasising that science as well as the classics can be an instrument of culture, he went on to say: "Nevertheless, I am the last person to question the importance of genuine literary education, or to suppose that intellectual culture can be complete without it. An exclusively scientific training will bring about a mental twist as surely as an exclusively literary training. The value of the cargo does not compensate for a ship's being out of trim; and I should be very sorry to think that the Scientific College would turn out none but lop-sided men, . . . every Englishman has, in his native tongue, an almost perfect instrument of literary expression; and, in his own literature, models of every kind of literary excellence. If an Englishman cannot get literary culture out of his Bible, his Shakespeare, his Milton, neither, in my belief, will the profoundest study of Homer and Sophocles, Virgil and Horace, give it to him".[2]

Huxley's most important contribution to ideas about the nature of the curriculum is contained in his address to the South London Working Men's College, entitled, *A Liberal Education; and Where to Find it* (1868). He compared education to a game which is infinitely more difficult and complicated than chess. "It is a game which has been played for untold ages, every man and woman of us being one of the two players in a game of his or her own. The chess-board is the world, the pieces are the phenomena of the universe, the rules of the game are what we call the laws of Nature.

---

[1] *Science and Education* (vol. 3 of *Collected Essays*), p. 123, Macmillan, 1895.
[2] *ibid.*, pp. 153-4.

The player on the other side is hidden from us. We know that his play is always fair, just, and patient. But also we know to our cost, that he never overlooks a mistake, or makes the smallest allowance for ignorance. To the man who plays well, the highest stakes are paid, with that sort of overflowing generosity with which the strong shows delight in strength. And one who plays ill is checkmated—without haste, but without remorse; . . . what I mean by Education is learning the rules of this mighty game. In other words, education is the instruction of the intellect in the laws of Nature, under which name I include not merely things and their forces, but men and their ways; and the fashioning of the affections and of the will into an earnest and loving desire to move in harmony with those laws."[1]

He was scathing in his denunciation of the narrow and arid teaching in the secondary schools, but he made it quite clear that he was not so much attacking the classics as the methods by which they were taught. "Do not expect me," he said, "to depreciate the earnest and enlightened pursuit of classical learning. I have not the least desire to speak ill of such occupations, nor any sympathy with those who run them down. On the contrary, if my opportunities had lain in that direction, there is no investigation into which I could have thrown myself with greater delight than that of antiquity".[2]

The chief fault of the classical teaching in the grammar schools was that "it means turning Latin and Greek into English, for the mere sake of being able to do it, and without the smallest regard to the worth or worthlessness of the author read . . . And it means, finally, that after a dozen years spent at this kind of work, the sufferer shall be incompetent to interpret a passage in an author he has not already got up; that he shall never open, or think of, a classical author again, until wonderful to relate, he insists upon submitting his sons to the same process".[3]

Huxley defined his own conception of a liberal education in the memorable passage beginning: "That man, I think, has had a liberal education who has been so trained in youth that his body is the ready servant of his will, and does with ease and pleasure all the work that, as a mechanism, it is capable of; whose intellect is a clear, cold, logic engine, with all its parts of equal strength,

[1] *Science and Education* (vol. 3 of *Collected Essays*), pp. 82-3, Macmillan, 1895.
[2] *ibid.*, p. 97.   [3] *ibid.*, pp. 100-1.

and in smooth working order; ready, like a steam engine, to be turned to any kind of work, and spin the gossamers as well as forge the anchors of the mind; whose mind is stored with a knowledge of the great and fundamental truths of Nature and the laws of her operations; one who, no stunted ascetic, is full of life and fire, but whose passions are trained to come to heel by a vigorous will, the servant of a tender conscience; who has learned to love all beauty, whether of Nature or of art, to hate all vileness, and to respect others as himself".[1]

Such are the effects of a truly liberal education in the individual but what should be its content and where can one find a liberal education? Huxley's own plan for the curriculum envisaged natural science, the study of morals and political and social life, history and geography with emphasis on the pupils' own country, English language and literature, English composition, the study in translations of the world's greatest writers, both ancient and modern, drawing and either music or fine art. In regard to the last question, Huxley confessed that as a result of a survey of all our educational institutions from the elementary school to the university, he was forced to conclude that a liberal education was not provided by any educational agency which existed at that time. Hence the need to examine our ideas about education afresh. Huxley's lectures exercised a profound influence on public opinion, and many of the improvements in the curriculum and methods of teaching in the latter years of the century were in no small measure due to him. It should be noted that for Huxley a liberal curriculum meant a harmonious, well-balanced one.

Huxley was not only a distinguished scientist and a well-known lecturer and writer but he was also a busy man of affairs. He served on the first London School Board, at the College of Science, as a Governor of Eton College, and as a member of several Royal Commissions. All this public work helped in the spread of his ideas. He was responsible for the syllabus of instruction adopted by the London Board Schools and for the decision of the London School Board on religious instruction which was followed by the majority of School boards in the country. He also envisaged the establishment of an educational ladder from the elementary school to the university, an ideal which became realised as a result of the Education Act of 1902.

Science and Education (vol. 3 of *Collected Essays*), p. 86, Macmillan 1895.

The last writer selected to represent English educational ideas in the latter part of the nineteenth century is Matthew Arnold (1822-1888). He was the eldest son of Dr Thomas Arnold of Rugby, and brother-in-law of Mr W. E. Forster, the architect of the Elementary Education Act of 1870. After securing a second class in classics at Oxford, Arnold had a brief experience in teaching at Rugby and then returned to Oxford as a Fellow of Oriel College. He relinquished his Fellowship after a year to become private secretary to Lord Lansdowne in 1847. The latter was Lord President of the Privy Council and thus titular head of the Committee of Council on Education. This appointment was responsible for bringing Arnold into touch with public education. In 1851 Arnold was contemplating marriage but he wished to secure a post which would bring him a sufficient salary to meet his expenses. Lord Lansdowne offered him the post of Inspector of Schools, which he held until his retirement from public life in 1886. As an Inspector it must be confessed that Arnold was not ideal. In reality he was too big a man for this job, and it must have been a considerable relief to him when on three separate occasions he was released from his immediate duties to undertake special inquiries into the state of education in Continental countries. On two occasions he held the post of Professor of Poetry at Oxford and in 1883 he undertook a lecture tour in America.

The appointment of Matthew Arnold to the inspectorate marks one of the occasions when the Education Department took into its employment a man of real genius and it must be admitted that at times he was a thorn in the flesh of his official superiors. When he entered the inspectorate, the system which Sir James Kay-Shuttleworth had originated was still in operation. In 1833 Parliament had voted the sum of £20,000 a year to assist voluntary effort in the building of schools. The money was divided between the National and British and Foreign School Societies (£11,000 to the National Society and the remainder to the British and Foreign School Society). The Government was not at first anxious to introduce inspection although one member, Mr Wyse, had suggested the idea. When the Committee of the Privy Council on Education was established in 1839, Dr Kay was appointed its secretary. He insisted upon the right of inspection as one of the conditions for the receipt of the Parliamentary grant. The Church opposed this demand because it saw in it a threat to its claim to control education but in the following year a compromise agreement was reached.

The details of the Concordat do not concern us here but the net result was the appointment of separate inspectors for Church, Nonconformist, and Roman Catholic schools.

As a layman, Arnold was not able to inspect Church of England and Roman Catholic schools and, therefore, he was only concerned with those supported by the British and Foreign School Society and by religious bodies outside the Church of England. This fact is important because it goes a good deal of the way towards explaining the attitude he adopted in *Culture and Anarchy*.

Sir Joshua Fitch suggested that Arnold tended to regard his inspectorial duties as a drudgery. He wrote: "Another limitation less pleasant to dwell upon, becomes very manifest as the reader makes the personal acquaintance of the writer of these familiar and charming letters. He speaks constantly of his official work in terms that show it was distasteful to him, and that he regarded it as drudgery".[1] In support of this, Fitch quotes from the following letter. "It is a long, tedious business this week, hearing the students give specimen lessons at the training schools. There is little utility in it, and a great deal of clap-trap, and that makes the expenditure of time the more disagreeable to me. However, I get a good many notes written, and odds and ends of things done."[2]

One can readily sympathise with Arnold's dislike of routine. What man of genius would not feel the same? It should, however, be said in his favour that he always carried out his duties conscientiously. The fact is that Arnold was a man of vision, a prophet, an individual of far-reaching ideals who was intensely interested in educational ideas but who found the day by day administration interfere with what he regarded as the vital things in education. Dr W. F. Connell realised this when he wrote: "Arnold seldom commented on specific pedagogical methods in use, to him they were 'machinery' just as pupil teachers; managerial details, and even the subjects of the curriculum were 'machinery', subordinate to the leading purpose of the schools. They were all of value but they were not the matters upon which he thought it essential to insist".[3] Hence the welcome relief from routine duties

---

[1] *Thomas and Matthew Arnold* (Great Educator series), p. 163, William Heinemann, 1897.
[2] G. W. E. Russell, *Letters of Matthew Arnold* (1848-88), vol. 2, p. 44, Macmillan, 1895.
[3] *The Educational Thought and Influence of Matthew Arnold*, pp. 239-40, Routledge and Kegan Paul, 1950.

when he was sent by the Newcastle Commission to the Continent to study popular education in France, Holland, and Switzerland.

Arnold's out-spoken criticisms of the demoralising effects of the Revised Code are well known. Some writers, such as Patchett Martin, thought that his attitude was disgraceful, a stab in the back for his seniors, and that his correct procedure would have been to have tendered his resignation. Arnold could not afford to do this because his reputation as an author was not yet fully established in 1862. It is probable that he rendered greater services to education in this country by remaining where he was and doing his utmost to bring about a change of policy. He told the Cross Commission: "I have never had any great sympathy from the other inspectors, I think, in my disapprobation of the code". His criticisms could not have been welcome to Lowe and Lingen and this may have been a reason why he did not obtain a much more influential post. It was not until 1870 that he was promoted to the newly established rank of Senior Inspector. But it should be said that he was given a fairly free hand by his seniors. After all, it was a difficult matter to rebuke a man of his ability and reputation.[1]

In 1865 the Taunton Commission sent Arnold once more to the Continent as Assistant-Commissioner to report on middle and upper class education in France, Germany, Switzerland, and Italy. The results of his work were published in *Schools and Universities on the Continent*, 1868. He had already written *A French Eton or Middle-Class Education and the State*, 1864. These books established his reputation as the foremost English authority on

[1] Arnold's habit of riding rough-shod over official red tape is illustrated by a story related by Sneyd-Kynnersley. (*H.M.I.*, p. 158, Macmillan, 1908). When he was responsible for the districts of Westminster and Edmonton, he was expected to stay the night at the latter place if his inspections there occupied more than a day. His claim for the journey home and back was not admissible. "Being a poet, of course, he returned home, and charged his fare every day. 'The Knight of the Blue Pencil', as he called his enemy, sharpened his blue pencil, and wrote—'Mr M. Arnold, H.M.I. Why not stay at Edmonton?' and the great man plaintively replied: 'How can you expect me to stay at Edmonton, when John Gilpin couldn't?'" The account was passed.

The writer knew a retired inspector who when a beginner was attached to Arnold to be taught his job. It was the junior's business to see that his senior observed his timetable and did not stay over his time in any one school. This was frequently a difficult task for Arnold would often linger longer than he should when something caught his interest. On one occasion they were inspecting students of a women's training college who were giving a gymnastic display. Arnold fell into a pensive mood and resisted all efforts to drag him away. When the junior insisted, Arnold replied: "How unfeeling you are! These girls have such magnificent legs that they provide me with more aesthetic pleasure than has come my way for many weeks".

Continental education. With considerable justification one may regard him as the founder of comparative education.

He was much impressed by what he saw on the Continent, and he was led to compare, what seemed to him well organised systems of education there, with the almost total lack of organisation in this country. Hence his message: "Organise your secondary education". When he had visited French and German universities, he recast his slogan to "Organise your secondary and your superior education". His advocacy for the creation of a well organised system of secondary schools in England were also a consequence of his burning desire to see a transformation of the English middle classes which he thought could only be brought about through education. He was acutely aware of the inadequacies and shortcomings of the middle class and his remedy was in an organised system of education administered by the State through an effective local government. Although State intervention in elementary education had been an accepted principle for many years, the idea of its extension to public and secondary schools was generally distasteful. The Revised Code was partly responsible for this. Arnold had found both in France and Prussia, State systems of secondary and higher education and he believed that they were far superior to the haphazard set up in this country. His ideal was a planned civil organisation which should at the same time preserve the principle of freedom. In urging this he was to some extent foreshadowing the views of modern thinkers like Karl Mannheim and Sir Fred Clarke.

Speaking of the countries he had visited, he said: ". . . these countries have a civil organisation which has been framed with forethought and design to meet the wants of modern society; while our civil organisation in England still remains what time and chance have made it".[1] He then added: "Modern States cannot either do without free institutions, or do without a rationally planned and effective civil organisation".

He believed that the lack of an adequate educational organisation in England was having unfortunate economic consequences. "Our engineers have no real scientific instruction, and we let them learn their business at our expense by rule of thumb; but it is a ruinous system of blunder and plunder. A man without the requisite scientific knowledge undertakes to build a difficult bridge; he builds three which tumble down, and so learns how to build a fourth which

[1] *Higher Schools and Universities in Germany*, p. 181, Macmillan, 1892.

stands; but somebody pays for the three failures. In France or Switzerland he would not have been suffered to build his first bridge until he had satisfied competent persons that he knew how to build it, because abroad they cannot afford our extravagances. The scientific training of the foreign engineers is therefore perfectly right. Take the present cost per mile of the construction of an English railway, and the cost per mile as it was twenty years ago; and the comparison will give you a correct notion of what rule-of-thumb engineering, without special schools and without scientific instruction, has cost the country."[1]

Arnold's own scheme is prophetic in the sense that so many of its main points have been fulfilled within the last fifty years. He showed that if the State were to take responsibility for education, a Minister of Education would become a necessity. He would also need a body which corresponded to the High Council of Education which actually existed in France and Italy. He wrote: ". . . comprising without regard to politics and personages most proper to be heard on questions of public education, a consultative body only, but whose opinion the minister should be obliged to take on all important measures not purely administrative, would be an invaluable aid to an English Education Minister, an invaluable institution in our too political country".[2]

He thought that the functions of the council should be similar to those recommended by the Bryce Commission in 1895. One modern writer, emphasising the prophetic character of Arnold's ideas, says: "Just as in local affairs Arnold foreshadowed developments the end of which we have not yet seen, so in his suggestion for one public department with a Minister of Education responsible for the whole service did he anticipate the Board of Education Act of 1899 and the Education Act of 1944. Even the idea of a Consultative Committee is clearly expressed in his report—an unpaid council to supervise examinations, school books, and the broad questions of curriculum".[3]

He also advocated the setting up of eight or ten Provincial School Boards to function as local education authorities. All secondary schools, including the public schools on which the Clarendon Commission had reported, ought to be inspected. The universities also, should be brought into the organisation. In

[1] *Higher Schools and Universities in Germany*, pp. 197-8, Macmillan, 1892.
[2] *ibid.*, p. 201.
[3] J. Leese, *Personalities and Power in English Education*, p. 198, E. J. Arnold, 1950.

addition to the ancient universities, he looked forward to the foundation of provincial universities in about ten of our largest cities and he urged that the University of London should be overhauled to make a real teaching university of it instead of a mere examining body. Moreover, he believed that university professors ought to be appointed by the Minister of Education. Arnold did not foresee the consequences of such a step since the totalitarian countries of modern times were something which he never envisaged. The nineteenth century firmly believed in the virtues of a democratic and constitutional government and thought it would only be a matter of time before it was realised in all civilised countries.

Arnold's own comment on his scheme was as follows: "The reorganisation proposed will to many people in England appear chimerical. Yet I have a profound conviction that if our country is destined, as I trust it is destined, still to live and prosper, the next quarter of a century will see a reconstruction of English education as entire as that which I have recommended in these remarks, however impossible such a reconstruction may to many now seem".[1] One can imagine his immense disappointment when the report of the Taunton Commission was set aside by the Government, and its only consequence was the Endowed Schools Act of 1869 which was far from realising his ideal. Unfortunately he did not live to see his advice repeated by the Bryce Commission of 1895 and acted upon by the Board of Education Act of 1899 and the Education Act of 1902.

Before leaving Arnold's ideas about the reorganisation of English education, there is one important point that should be mentioned. Arnold was mainly responsible for popularising the term "secondary" to describe education which was beyond elementary but below that given in institutions of university rank. The word seems first to have been employed in a report on the organisation of public instruction which was presented by Condorçet to the French Legislative Assembly in 1792. In 1802 the French Government recognised the distinction between the *école primaire* and the *école secondaire*. R. L. Edgeworth, who was conversant with educational developments in France, used the term "secondary" in his *Professional Education*, 1809. It was on one occasion used by Dr Thomas Arnold in a letter to the Press. Matthew Arnold found it in common use in France and thought that it was an apt term to describe the education which was suitable for the middle class

[1] *Higher Schools and Universities in Germany*, p. 227, Macmillan, 1892.

children. Thus he commended the use of the term by Mr Grant Duff who introduced it in a parliamentary resolution. " I am glad," he wrote, "you have employed and given official stamp to that useful word secondary".[1] The term was later used in the reports of the Taunton Commission and the Bryce Commission was officially described as the Royal Commission on Secondary Education. Arnold also referred to the three parts of education as primary, secondary, and superior. The latter included the further education of the Education Act of 1944. One should, however, be careful not to read into Arnold's use of these terms the idea that education should be organised into three progressive stages. In agreement with the thought of his day, he conceived secondary and higher education as suitable for quite a different social class from those for whom the elementary schools were intended.

Arnold also recognised the technical school as a type of secondary school. "Technical schools are needed, and in elementary schools manual training should be given; yet it is undesirable to bestow in the elementary school too much prominence on this training, to turn the elementary school itself too much into a technical school. The technical school is in fact, a secondary school, to follow the elementary school, after some manual training has there been acquired."[2] This view is allied to that expressed by Mr (later, Sir) Michael Sadler in the report of the Bryce Commission.[3]

Arnold's most important contributions to English educational ideas are contained in *Friendship's Garland* and *Culture and Anarchy*. The former consisted originally in two series of letters written in the *Pall Mall Gazette* between July 1866 and April 1867, and June 1869 and November 1870, respectively. They purport to be an account of the visit to England of a very forthright young Prussian whom Arnold uses as a mouthpiece for his own ironical criticism of the English middle class. *Culture and Anarchy* consisted of six articles written during the years 1867-8 which were combined in one volume in 1869. Both *Friendship's Garland* and *Culture and Anarchy* had the same aim, namely, by means of a mixture of light irony and superficial levity which partly disguised their underlying seriousness, to shake the English middle class out of its complacency. As Dover Wilson puts it: "Disposed as it were on the flanks of the attacking force, the two letter-series in the

---

[1] G. W. E. Russell, *Letters of Matthew Arnold*, vol. 1, p. 233, Macmillan, 1895.
[2] Quoted in footnote, *Report of the Consultative Committee on Secondary Education*, p. 54, H.M.S.O., 1938 (Spens Report).
[3] Vol. 1, pp. 135-6.

Pall Mall were like light cavalry sent forward to harass the enemy with the shafts of ridicule while the main onslaught was launched from the centre".[1]

In the preface to *Culture and Anarchy*, Arnold as an introduction to the theory of culture, describes what he conceives to be the function of culture. "The whole scope of the essay is to recommend culture as the great help out of our present difficulties; culture being a pursuit of our total perfection by means of getting to know, on all the matters which most concern us, the best which has been thought and said in the world; and through this knowledge, turning a stream of fresh and free thought upon our stock notions and habits, which we now follow staunchly but mechanically, vainly imagining that there is a virtue in following them staunchly which makes up for the mischief of following them mechanically. This, and this alone, is the scope of the following essay."[2]

Arnold was very careful to explain exactly what meaning the term culture held for him. He did not agree with the sense in which the word was ordinarily used. "The culture which is supposed to plume itself on a smattering of Greek and Latin is a culture which is begotten by nothing so intellectual as curiosity; it is valued either out of sheer vanity and ignorance, or else as an engine of social and class distinction, separating its holder, like a badge or title, from other people who have not got it. No serious man would call this culture, or attach any value to it, as culture, at all."[3] Since culture aims at our total perfection, it must be wider than mere knowledge. Certainly, knowledge is connected with culture but, in fact: "If a man without books or reading, or reading nothing but his letters and the newspapers, gets nevertheless a fresh and free play of the best thoughts upon his stock notions and habits, he has got culture. He has got that for which we prize and recommend culture; he has got that which at the present moment we seek culture that it may give us. This inward operation is the very life and essence of culture, as we conceive it".[4]

Culture, then, for Arnold, consists "in a study of perfection". One of its motives is curiosity, "a desire after the things of the mind simply for their own sakes and for the pleasure of seeing them as they are", or in the words of Montesquieu, its aim is "to render

---

[1] *Culture and Anarchy*, edited by J. Dover Wilson, Editor's Introduction, p. xxii, C.U.P., 1932.

[2] *Culture and Anarchy*, p. 6. All page references are to Dover Wilson's edition.　　　　[3] *ibid.*, p 43.　　　　[4] *ibid.*, pp. 6-7.

an intelligent being yet more intelligent". There is, however, another motive which is eminently social. It is "the noble aspiration to leave the world better and happier than we found it", or as Thomas Wilson (Bishop of Sodor and Man, 1663-1755) phrased it, "To make reason and the will of God prevail". Because it aims at perfection, there is a similarity between culture and religion; both aim at seeing and learning the will of God and both seek to make the will of God prevail. Religion proclaims: "The kingdom of God is within you". In like fashion, culture "places human perfection in an *internal* condition, in the growth and predominance of our humanity proper, as distinguished from our animality. It places it in the ever-increasing efficacy and in the general harmonious expansion of those gifts of thought and feeling which make the peculiar dignity, wealth, and happiness of human nature".[1]

In spite of this measure of agreement, Arnold allotted to culture a wider aim than religion. The latter emphasises the moral element in human nature, but culture goes beyond this. It is "a harmonious expansion of *all* the powers which make the beauty and worth of human nature, and is not consistent with the over-development of any one power at the expense of the rest".[2] Hence culture is not the frivolous and useless thing that some have imagined; it has a vital function to perform, one more necessary in our mechanical civilisation than in the civilisations of Greece and Rome. Arnold felt more strongly that the mechanistic and materialistic tendencies of his age were opposed to the growth of culture. He wrote: "Our coal, thousands of people were saying, is the real basis of our national greatness; if our coal runs short, there is an end of the greatness of England. But what *is* greatness?—culture makes us ask. Greatness is a spiritual condition worthy to excite love, interest, and admiration; and the outward proof of possessing greatness is that we excite love, interest, and admiration. If England were swallowed up in the sea to-morrow, which of the two, a hundred years hence, would most excite the love, interest, and admiration of mankind—would most, therefore, show the evidence of having possessed greatness—the England of the last twenty years, or the England of Elizabeth, of a time of splendid spiritual effort, but when our coal, and our industrial operations depending on coal were very little developed?"[3]

These thoughts led Arnold to attempt an analysis of contemporary society. In fact, he might have anticipated Karl Mannheim

[1] *Culture and Anarchy*, p. 47.   [2] *ibid.*, p. 48.   [3] *ibid.*, p. 51.

and have selected as his sub-title for *Culture and Anarchy*, "Diagnosis of My Own Time". He divided English society into three classes whom he named Barbarians, Philistines, and Populace. The Barbarians represented the aristocracy, who were in name, still the rulers of England. If culture in achieving perfection begot sweetness and light, it must be said that the Barbarians lacked culture because, although to some extent they possessed sweetness, they were without light. They were deficient in ideas and in the flexibility of mind which would enable them to adjust themselves to changing situations and become intelligent leaders of the nation.

The middle class, the Philistines, had neither sweetness nor light. They were those who believed that England's greatness consisted in her material wealth. In the essay entitled *My Countrymen*, the following words are put into the mouths of Arnold's foreign friends: "What brings about, or rather tends to bring about, a natural, rational life, satisfying the modern spirit? This: the growth of a love of industry, trade, and wealth; the growth of the love of the things of the mind; and the growth of a love of beautiful things. There are body, intelligence, and soul all taken care of. Of these three factors of modern life, your middle class has no notion of any but one, the first . . . But what notion have they of anything else? Do but look at them, look at their lives . . . Your middle class is educated to begin with, in the worst schools of your country, and our middle class is educated in the best of ours. What becomes of them after that? . . . Drugged with business, your middle class seems to have its sense blunted for any stimulus besides, except religion; it has a religion, narrow, unintelligent, repulsive. All sincere religion does something for the spirit, raises a man out of the bondage of his merely bestial part, and saves him; but the religion of your middle class is the very lowest form of intelligential life which one can imagine as saving".[1]

Arnold tends to equate the middle classes with nonconformity. Certainly, Nonconformists formed the majority of the lower middle class, with whom as school managers, Arnold came into contact in his inspectorial duties. As Dover Wilson writes: "Thus Arnold's whole official career was spent in that atmosphere of 'disputes, tea-meetings, openings of chapels, sermons' which made up 'the dismal and illiberal life of the nonconformists in the 'sixties', a life so unlovely, so unattractive, so incomplete; so narrow, so far removed from a true and satisfying ideal of human perfection, 'that he found

[1] *Friendship's Garland*, pp. 136-7, Smith, Elder, 1903.

himself compelled to write *Culture and Anarchy* for its sweetening and enlightening' ".[1]

But what of the Populace? Arnold expresses both his pity and his fears in the following passage: "But that vast portion, lastly, of the working class which, raw and half-developed, has long lain half-hidden amidst its poverty and squalor, and is now issuing from its hiding-place to assert an Englishman's heaven-born privilege of doing as he likes, and is beginning to perplex us by marching where it likes, meeting where it likes, bawling what it likes, breaking what it likes—to this vast residuum we may with great propriety give the name of Populace".[2]

Arnold, through his inspection of schools in East London, had come to know something of the squalor and degradation of the poor in mid-Victorian England. Thus he describes the pupils as "children eaten up with disease, half-sized, half-fed, half-clothed, neglected by their parents, without health, without home, without hope".[3] At the same time, the Hyde Park riots of 1866 when the mob demonstrating on behalf of the Reform Bill broke down the railings, invaded the Park and insulted bystanders, raised in his mind the fear of the spiritual anarchy which was rife among the nation.

He looked ahead to a time when Barbarians, Philistines, and Populace would cease to be and would be absorbed into a unity on the basis of their common humanity, and that the nation "when in the fulness of time it has reason and beauty offered to it, and the law of things as they really are, it should at last walk by this true light with the same staunchness and zeal with which it formerly walked by its imperfect light".[4] Culture with its gifts of sweetness and light is dependent on education. Arnold believed that the Revised Code with its insistence upon a knowledge of the three R's could have little stimulus for the Populace. His experience of elementary schools taught him the immense value of literature. He wrote in his Report of 1871: "What is comprised under the word literature is in itself the greatest power available in education; of this power it is not too much to say that in our elementary schools at present no use is made at all . . . the whole use that the Government, now that its connection with religious instruction is abandoned, makes of the mighty engine of literature in the education of

[1] Introduction to *Culture and Anarchy*, p. xv.
[2] *Culture and Anarchy*, p. 105.   [3] *ibid.*, p. 194.   [4] *ibid.*, pp. 206-7.

the working classes amounts to little more, even when most successful, than the giving them the power to read the newspaper".[1]

The education of both Barbarians and Philistines needed a
complete overhaul in the light of the advice to organise your
secondary and higher education. The Barbarians needed a wider
curriculum than "the grand, old, fortifying, classical curriculum",
and the select private schools patronised by the Philistines were
powerless to promote sweetness and light. Thus the self-made Mr
Bottles "was brought up at the Lycurgus House Academy, Peck-
ham. You are not to suppose from the name of Lycurgus that
any Latin and Greek was taught in the establishment; the name only
indicates the moral discipline, and the strenuous, earnest character
imparted there. As to the instruction, the thoughtful educator who
was principal of the Lycurgus House Academy, Archimedes Silverpump, Ph.D., you must have heard of him in Germany?—had
modern views. 'We must be men of our age,' he used to say.
'Useful knowledge, living languages, and the forming of the mind
through observation and experiment, these are the fundamental
articles of my educational creed.' Or, as I have heard his pupil
Bottles put it in his expansive moments after dinner—'Original
man, Silverpump! fine mind! fine system! None of your antiquated
rubbish—all practical work—latest discoveries in science—mind
constantly kept excited—lots of interesting experiments—lights of
all colours—fizz! fizz! bang! bang! That's what I call forming a
man' ".[2]

Arnold had his defects. His conception of culture was perhaps
too academic; and as Frederic Harrison pointed out, after he had
given his eulogy of culture, he omitted to furnish the details for
attaining culture. This criticism is only relevant as regards Culture
and Anarchy. The answer was supplied in his reports both on
English and Continental schools and colleges. Arnold was
necessarily a believer in the faculty psychology, and emphasised
the function of English grammar as mental training. He insisted
upon would-be teachers learning long passages of poetry by heart,
and he tended to underrate the value of science in the curriculum.
When arguing with Huxley on the subject of science and culture, he
came off second best. Nevertheless, he showed considerable insight
when he wrote: "To have the power of using, which is the thing
wished, these data of natural science, a man must, in general, have

[1] *Reports on Elementary Schools*, pp. 142-3, H.M.S.O., 1910.
[2] *Friendship's Garland*, pp. 50-1, Smith, Elder, 1903.

first been in some measure *moralised*: and for moralising him it will be found not easy, I think, to dispense with those old agents, letters, poetry, religion. So let not our teachers be led to imagine, whatever they may hear or see of the call for natural science, that their literary cultivation is unimportant. The fruitful use of natural science itself depends, in a very great degree, on having effected in the whole man, by means of letters, a rise in what the political economists call the standard of life".[1]

SUGGESTIONS FOR FURTHER READING

Newman's lectures are available in the Everyman series, J. M. Dent, under the title *On the Scope and Nature of University Education.* Ruskin's works have been published in many editions. From the point of view of his contributions to educational thought, the following are the most important: *Unto This Last, Sesame and Lilies, Time and Tide,* and *The Crown of Wild Olive.* Huxley's educational ideas will be found in vol. 3 of *Collected Essays (Science and Education),* Macmillan, 1895.

The student is recommended to begin his study of Matthew Arnold by reading the account presented by Sir Joshua Fitch in *Thomas and Matthew Arnold* (Great Educator series), William Heinemann, 1897. Fitch was a colleague who knew Arnold well and could speak with authority about his career in the inspectorate even if, at times, Arnold's attitude did not entirely meet with his approval. The weakness of Fitch's account lies in his lack of sympathy with Arnold's view of English society of that age, possibly because he did not thoroughly understand it. The student should then study Arnold's educational writings beginning with his *Reports on Elementary Schools,* H.M.S.O., 1910. Arnold's experiences of Continental educational establishments and his criticisms of English education are contained in: *Higher Schools and Universities in Germany,* Macmillan, 1892, and *A French Eton or Middle-Class Education and the State. Friendship's Garland,* Smith, Elder, 1903, forms a useful introduction to the more serious discussion of *Culture and Anarchy.* The most useful edition of the latter is that edited by J. Dover Wilson, C.U.P., 1932. It contains a valuable introduction which provides the political and social

---

[1] *Reports on Elementary Schools,* p. 148, H.M.S.O., 1910.

background necessary for understanding Arnold's views. The most complete study of Matthew Arnold as an educationist is: W. F. Connell, *The Educational Thought and Influence of Matthew Arnold*, Routledge and Kegan Paul, 1950. This work is indispensable for any serious study of the life and thought of Matthew Arnold.

In connection with his study of chapters 15 and 16, the student is recommended to read *Pioneers of English Education*, edited by Professor A. V. Judges, Faber and Faber, 1952. It is the published account of a course of lectures delivered at King's College, London. The following have a direct bearing upon English educational ideas in the nineteenth century: "The English Tradition in Education" (Sir Philip Morris); "Bentham and the Utilitarians" (Dr Hans); "John Henry Newman" (A. C. F. Beales); "Herbert Spencer and the Scientific Movement" (Professor J. A. Lauwerys); and "Matthew Arnold" (Professor B. Pattison).

CHAPTER XVII

JOHN DEWEY, 1859-1952

John Dewey, American philosopher, psychologist, and practical teacher, is the thinker *par excellence* whose beliefs have emerged, not only from his teaching experience, but also from the fundamental social and religious characteristics of his early environment. The historical situation is of paramount significance in any consideration of Dewey's theories, methods, and achievements, and it must not be underestimated in any analytical criticism.

Born in Vermont, the son of a village shopkeeper, he grew up in a rural community typical of a multitude of others in New England where matters of religion and politics maintained their traditional importance in everyday life. It is not too much to say that the experience of those early years brought John Dewey the two outstanding convictions which directed the whole course of his educational work—a conviction that traditional methods of schooling were futile and fruitless, and an even firmer conviction that the human contacts of everyday life provide unlimited natural, dynamic "learning situations". A different social environment or another era might have failed to lay such firm foundations for a new educational philosophy. The strongly Puritan communities of New England had contributed much to the moral and intellectual development of the new America by their recognition of the value of elementary education. Their children had always been taught to read because their religion demanded the individual's direct reference to the Bible in establishing his relations with his God. The strict principles of Dewey's pilgrim forefathers had grown no softer with the easing of life as the new continent prospered and the communities imposed adult standards on their young people. The ideals of Comenius had failed to penetrate far beyond the limits of the Moravian settlements and the typical New England village school was the epitome of formal desk-learning and strict discipline —probably much the same as the school the Pilgrim Fathers knew in England.

At the same time, the strong social consciousness was also due to the nature of the original settlements. The religious bond was the oldest persistent factor, but the determination to survive as individual, independent communities had generated a widespread interest in politics, not merely as a topic for intelligent conversation, but as a matter which concerned the community and which every individual had a duty to understand.   John Dewey heard the shrewd, lively comments and discussions in his father's shop, and he was able to see the strength and power of group consciousness in the varied activities and interrelations in a small society.   Another significant factor was the change being experienced by that society and many other little New England communities, a change from rural activities in an unmechanised age to manufacturing industries growing and spreading with the development of trade and science.

In 1879 Dewey graduated at the University of Vermont, and after a year's study of philosophy and a brief period of school teaching,[1] he proceeded to John Hopkins University where he sat under celebrated lecturers who exerted a profound influence on the evolution of his philosophy and educational philosophy.   An undergraduate course in physiology had introduced him to Darwinian ideas through Huxley's writings and the contrast of such ideas with the fixed concepts of his familiar world, shook him so deeply that his brilliant plunge into philosophy became a life-long effort to resolve the dualism of the moral and the material.   He read psychology under G. Stanley Hall, history under Herbert B. Adams, and philosophy under C. S. Peirce and G. S. Morris.   After two years he gained his Ph.D degree and became a lecturer in philosophy at the University of Michigan.   Then he became Professor of Philosophy, first at the University of Minnesota, and then at the University of Michigan.   In 1894, while still in his middle thirties, he became head of the Department of Philosophy at the University of Chicago,[2] and from 1902 to 1904 he was also Director of the School of Education.

The decade which followed saw the research and experiment in education which won for its initiator a world-wide reputation.   The "laboratory school", set up in connection with the university, came into existence largely through the vigour and enterprise of Dewey's young wife.   It was conducted on lines indicated by the theories evolved by philosopher-psychologist-historian Dewey, who was also by this time head of a growing family.   The varying results of this practical work enabled him to clarify and modify his concepts in his

---

[1] High School, South Oil City, Pa., 1879-81.   Village School, Charlotteville, Vt., 1881-2.
[2] Chairman of the Department of Philosophy, Psychology, and Pedagogy.

later writings. The school was opened in 1896 for the express purpose of research and experiment in new ideas and methods. Pupils between the ages of four and fourteen were accepted, and experienced primary teachers were appointed to work under Dewey's direction. Groups were kept small—eight or ten pupils to each teacher—but otherwise, curriculum and methods in the early stages differed little from those of the formal type of primary school of the day. Dewey had no "crank" scheme to impose upon the school; he only wished to create the conditions for the discovery of more natural ways of teaching and learning.

Given the space, the equipment, and the freedom from mass instruction, the teachers were required not to employ any well-defined new methods, but to be constantly on the alert to notice and discover ways of breaking down the barriers between school and community life, and also to find ways of including a richer, more varied subject matter in pupils' studies without adding to the burden of rote learning and symbol-interpretation. Moreover, the teachers were to bear in mind constantly the need to make more interesting and relevant the acquirement of basic skills dependent on rote learning and symbol-interpretation—that is, the three R's were not to be neglected, but rather developed more effectively because the pupils would work better at them when feeling them to be necessary in other studies.

The Chicago experiment was not only a great contribution to educational research, it was also the experience which gave conviction and certainty to Dewey in his philosophical views as applied to education. For him the two studies, philosophy and education, drew closer and eventually merged. Both came to signify the experimental study of man and his world—that is, the experimental study by each individual, of himself and his environment. In the nine articles which constitute the *Elementary School Record*, Dewey did his utmost to emphasise that his school did not exist for the purpose of putting into practice a preconceived educational theory, nor to demonstrate methods already developed—as did the Herbartian and Froebelian schools. The project was not without purpose, however, for Dewey aimed to seek ways of bringing the school into closer touch with the community. In as much as any set rules of planning and teaching existed, they were directed to this end. Apart from this, the teachers sought not to perfect techniques and methods but to find out how children learn.

If any one set of educational ideas was adopted it was perhaps, Froebel's—in practice, if not entirely in philosophy. Dewey acknowledges Froebel's inspiration, and describes how a visitor had remarked on the similarity of the school's activities to those of a kindergarten, although some pupils were as old as thirteen. Dewey points out that the school tried to carry into effect principles first expressed by Froebel—principles which he summarises thus:—

1. That the primary business of the school is to train children in co-operative and mutually helpful living.

2. That the primary root of all educative activity is in the instructive, impulsive attitudes and activities of the child, and not in the presentation and application of external material.

3. That these individual tendencies and activities are organised and directed through the uses made of them in keeping up the co-operative living already spoken of, taking advantage of them to reproduce on the child's plane the typical doings and occupations of the larger, maturer, society into which he is finally to go forth; and that it is through production and creative use that valuable knowledge is secured and clinched.[1]

Dewey had written several books by this time but mostly on philosophical or psychological topics;[2] now during the Chicago period he published his first works on education. The first was published in the year the school opened, and its title might well be used as a summary of Dewey's psychological principles for the new venture—*Interest and Effort as Related to Will*. Better known is the book, written after three years of experiment, which emphasises in its title the relationship Dewey strove to foster—*The School and Society*.[3] The turn of the century saw the publication of *The Elementary School Record*, and in 1902 appeared *The Child and the Curriculum*.

Although the Chicago period was somewhat short, its importance in influencing Dewey's later work—and in stimulating educational research throughout the western world—cannot be over-emphasised. In 1904 he became Professor of Philosophy at Columbia University, a position he held for the rest of his long career, during which time he not only wrote prolifically and engaged in further practical experiment, but also undertook from time to

---

[1] *The Elementary School Record*, p. 142, Chicago, 1900.
[2] *e.g.* Psychology, 1887 and 1895; Ethics, 1891 and 1894.
[3] During this period he also wrote an *Interpretation of the Culture Epoch Theory* for the Herbartian Society, 1896, and *My Pedagogic Creed*, New York, 1897.

time educational engagements and commissions abroad. It is probable that never since the days of Comenius had an educator received such universal recognition or had his books translated into so many languages.

During the first decade of the new century, Dewey's ideas became known abroad through his books and through the activities of such men as Georg Kerschensteiner in Germany, Edouard Claparède in Switzerland. Georges Bertier in France and Professor J. J. Findlay in England. In this country he was recognised as a leader in educational thought by the time of the First World War, and, according to Sir Percy Nunn, had already helped to "emancipate the professional intelligence" of the teachers of the time. After the war, even the Far East sought his guidance, and he lectured on philosophy and education at the Imperial University of Tokio in 1919, and then at the University of Pekin, spending two years in the latter centre and stirring a ferment of interest and experiment which continued long after his departure.

By this time he had reached, by a series of brilliant steps, another literary pinnacle. He had produced books on educational psychology—*How We Think* (1910) and *Interest and Effort in Education* (1913)—and one, *Schools of Tomorrow* (1915), written in collaboration with Evelyn Dewey on the results of their practical experiments.[1] Above all, however, he had published in 1916 *Democracy and Education* which may well be considered a masterpiece of strategy, timed to impinge on American political consciousness just when it was sensitised by the conflict in attitudes towards the European war. From that time onwards, in spite of many attacks on his philosophy, and criticisms of his admittedly difficult style of writing, it was clear that he had sown seeds which had taken root, if only because the social soil and political climate were ready for them. Although the dark days of the late 'twenties saw reaction against a force which threatened to sweep away the old sheet anchors which gave a semblance of stability, Deweyism was never eclipsed, and its leader gave the rest of his long life to the service of a society in whose power for good he had the utmost faith.

During the War of 1914-18 he had helped to found the first two professional unions of teachers in America—the American Association of University Professors and the New York Teachers' Union,

---

[1] These were by no means his only works. Among others were *Moral Principles in Education*, Boston, 1909, *German Philosophy and Politics*, 1915, and *Creative Intelligence*, 1917.

which later became a Guild of the American Federation of Teachers. Such unions were able to safeguard academic freedom during the inter-war period which saw the triumph of the Aristotelian state— a state which demanded that the teacher, as an officer of the state, should not work to change the *status quo* but should "teach loyalty to its institutions and obedience to its laws".[1] As a similar problem is with us to-day, we can appreciate the factors behind such a policy, but it would be folly to deny its dangers. If a teacher is "not employed to explore the controversial fields of political economy with the view of championing utopian schemes of reform or change" then he must be either very brave or very cunning to go ahead with the task of producing pupils adequately equipped to improve the state. The predominance of such an attitude entails the danger of standing still—of non-growth—which Dewey would deplore. It would also increase the possibility of further encroachment on the academic freedom of the teacher. That this actually happened in America is shown by the well-known Scopes' case created by the infringement of a Tennessee state statute prohibiting the teaching of the theory of evolution. The decision went against the offending teacher. The attitude of Dewey in the face of conservatism and reaction is indicated by his acceptance in 1929 of the presidency of the People's Lobby and the chairmanship of the League for Independent Political Action. He was a liberal, not an extremist, in all matters political and economic.

Between 1923 and 1933 Dewey influenced Soviet schools through the discipleship of Lunacharsky. In 1928, he was invited to Russia where some half a dozen of his books were published in Russian. When, in 1930, he received an honorary degree of the University of Paris—largely as a result of his championship by philosopher Emile Durkheim, he was described as "The most profound and complete expression of American genius".

Turkey was another country which welcomed Dewey's ideas, and he drew up a report on the reorganisation of Turkish schools. In Mexico, Brazil, and the Argentine his books were translated and considered with particular enthusiasm, but there were few countries in which, during the period between the wars, educators did not give a measure of attention to his writings.

He was a prolific writer but never a shallow one. What he had to say was not easily expressed in words, but his only answer to

---

[1] *Report of the Joint Legislative Committee of the State of New York Investigating Seditious Activities*, 1920.

accusations of bad style and lack of intellectual discipline was to point out that his immature writings had won commendation for style and clearness. He confessed: "Since then, thinking and writing have been hard work". He retained his deep interest in psychology, ethics, and politics,[1] and even after his official retirement—he became Emeritus Professor in 1930—he produced a series of books which show the extraordinary breadth and depths of his interests and capacities.[2] At eighty, he headed a Commission of Enquiry in Mexico on the question of Trotsky's part in the alleged plots against the Soviet Government. The Commissioner's Report showed Soviet leaders in an unfavourable light, so did no good to the declining Dewey movement of Russia. At eighty-seven, Dewey remarried and founded a second family. At ninety, in collabora- tion with Arthur T. Bentley, he produced *Knowing and the Known*[3] in 1949. When he died of pneumonia at ninety-three he was still physically vigorous, mentally active, and completely alert.

Of the man himself can be said little but good. A simple man of great integrity, he made no attempt to achieve the art of spell- binding. One feels he would have said, with Homer, "Hateful to me as the gates of Hades is the man who speaks one thing with his lips and hides another in his heart". Whatever the verdict of posterity on the right or wrong of his philosophy, on the good or evil of his influence, it will not be denied that he was of the stuff of the pioneers. He had the courage and restraint to be a rebel in thought without flamboyance in action. He had humility and per- tinacity, qualities which only the few can combine. His personal life was not free from acute problems and stresses but it was characterised by his gentleness and patience. Max Eastman, des- cribing him in his prime, writes, "In those days, John Dewey looked like portraits of Robert Louis Stevenson: the same flat hair and black moustache and the same luminous eyes, wells of dark, tender, intelligent light. He used to come into class with his tie out of contact with his collar or a trouser leg caught up on his suspender. Once he came for a whole week with a rent in his

[1] *Reconstruction in Philosophy*, Holt, 1920; *Human Nature and Conduct*, Holt, 1922; *Experience and Nature*, Open Court, 1925; *The Public and its Problems*, Holt, 1927; *Characters and Events*, Holt, 1929; *The Quest for Certainty*, Minton, Balch, 1929; *Individualism, Old and New*, Minton, Balch, 1930.

[2] *Philosophy and Civilisation*, Minton, Balch, 1931; *Art as Experience*, Minton, Balch, 1934; *A Common Faith*, Yale U.P., 1934; *Liberalism and Social Action*, Putnam, 1939; *Problems of Men*, N. York Philosophical Library, 1946.

[3] Boston, Beacon Press, 1949.

coat which caused a flap of cloth to stick out near the shoulder like a cherub's wing. His hair looked as though he had combed it with a towel". Comparison with Pestalozzi is irresistible. Describing his teaching, the writer continues, "He was thinking rather than lecturing, and taking his time about it. The process was rather unrelated to his pupils . . . until one of them asked a question. Then those glowing eyes would come down from the ceiling and shine into that student, and draw out of him and his innocent questions intellectual wonders such as the pupil never imagined had seeds in his brain".

The learned professor had a capacity for friendship and fruitful relationships with all sorts and conditions of people, especially with working men and people in humble circumstances. He remained at heart the New England countryman, enjoying nothing better than the care of his garden and smallholding. It is told in America that a lady active in public life was not a little surprised when the distinguished guest at one of her meetings turned out to be her egg man.

The Philosophy of John Dewey

In the 1880s Dewey returned to university study as a result of encouragement given by W. T. Harris, an American disciple of Hegel. This fact not only accounts, to some extent, for the attention Dewey paid to Hegelian doctrine, it also shows that very early in his career the link between philosophy and education was familiar to him, for he had already been a teacher, while Harris was destined to become U.S. Commissioner for Education. The influence of German thinkers was strong in American universities, this being the era of pilgrimage to Germany and of the development of cults such as Herbartianism. Dewey became a leading member of the Herbartian Society, but he no doubt gave his attention to a new philosophical viewpoint during the years which followed the first exposition of pragmatism by C. S. Peirce in 1879. It is clear that he was evolving his own particular brand of pragmatism by the time William James startled the philosophical world with *The Will to Believe* in 1896. There were several other major factors contributing to the development of Dewey's philosophy, not the least being the importance of contemporary controversy on the theory of evolution. James is concerned with moral and religious concepts whereas Dewey's outlook is biological and scientific. Many of his most challenging statements reflect this viewpoint. It lies behind his assertion that education has no aims. "Since there is nothing to which growth is relative save more growth", he contends, "there is nothing to which education is subordinate save more education. The educational process has no end beyond itself—it is its own end".[1]

The main principle of pragmatism is that the personal and purposive character of thought must be taken into account in the formulation of any adequate philosophic theory. As thinking is influenced by human emotions and capabilities, it is impossible to establish any absolutes of truth, reality, and those other wide concepts which have always fascinated philosophers. The pragmatist defines a concept by acquiring what practical effects it involves in the way of experience and action, and he regards these effects as constituting the concepts themselves. If faced with two rival philosophical concepts, he would ask what practical effects are involved in each case. If there is no difference in effect, then the concepts are the same. Dewey applied this argument to logic and ethics, and so formulated his "Instrumental" theory of truth—the idea that all knowledge is personal and is made by each individual for himself for the purpose of adapting himself to new situations. There can be no absolute truth because the meaning of a concept depends on its relationship to the individual; even scientific laws are but generalisations which may be modified again and again—they remain true only as long as they summarise truly the current state of human knowledge. In the application of pragmatic method in their own field, some scientists of the period adopted the term "humanism" to indicate that personal factors in thought were to be taken into account. The student of education, familiar with another interpretation of humanism, may need to bear this in mind when reading. Dewey was a thinker who strove to avoid the use of the old familiar jargon because of this very danger of misinterpretation. Meanings of significant words had been multiplied or hazed over with the passage of time and argument, therefore Dewey preferred to find new terms, and in doing so he incurred much criticism and even ridicule. Nevertheless his "warranted assertability" as a substitute for "truth" has, at least, more meaning and less dissonance than many clumsy additions to the English language of the past decade.

Dewey's emphasis on the personal, variable element in thinking leads to the assumption that although the *result* of thought is important to the individual, it is subsidiary to the *process* of thought.

[1] *Democracy and Education*, 1916, p. 60.

It is *inquiry* which matters, for through this process the adjustment between a person and his environment is brought about. Inquiry is, indeed, the same process as that which enables the growing biological organism to modify its environment and to be modified by that environment into a state allowing *more* growth, more development. Thus the truth or falsity of human inquiry depends on its success—or failure—in its results for the individual himself. Dewey claims inquiry to be "the controlled or directed transformation of an intermediate situation into one that is so determinate in its constituent distinctions and relations as to convert the elements of the original situation into a unified whole". This statement is not so involved as at first appears.

The beliefs, thoughts, efforts, which may constitute a person's inquiry, have no truth or falsity, they are either satisfactory or unsatisfactory. What is satisfactory at one time may be unsatisfactory at another, because the stage of development will be different. Thus the truth of a belief that you can swim depends on whether or not you succeed in swimming when you try. If you have not been in the water before, you may well find your belief is false because your purpose will not be achieved in spite of your careful marshalling or relevant information beforehand. No mutual adaptation between organism and environment is effected. Your mouth and limbs do not adjust themselves to the water, neither is the water displaced horizontally in its upper layer. Continued inquiry or a later effort may bring success. This elementary interpretation of instrumentalism may possibly be deemed unsound by purists, but it is offered in order to illustrate the factors of preparation and investigation as well as the personal nature of the pursuit of truth.

The control and direction of inquiry is a major factor in Dewey's educational theory. He argues that the natural method of inquiry, whether intellectual or otherwise, involves a preliminary review of the situation and the making of an estimate as a guide in inquiry. It may entail the collecting and arranging of material in intellectual activities, a process probably related to the organism's purposive strategy in physical and biological spheres. That is, developmental effort is not haphazard, the objective of each effort is decided beforehand, so that the mental or physical equipment is organised first. In the processes which involve thought, the truth or validity of that preliminary organisation of ideas is tested by inquiry—by experiment. It is in the course of putting ideas to the test of experience that education is gained, and therefore Dewey requires his pupils to be given wide opportunity for the practice of purposive inquiry.

Dewey's reference to a "unified whole" is an instance of his concern for the one-ness of the world. If it dared be said he had an aim, it was to see the world become a more organic, smoothly-functioning whole. Some writers believe that he did not succeed in shaking off completely the influence of Hegelian absolutism although he turned away from Hegel's eternal Idea. His attitude is much more akin to that of Froebel and his concept of unities, although the two educators are poles apart in that while Froebel believed that the potentialities of an organism are enfolded in the germ, Dewey sees no end to the possibilities of change, mutation, evolution—possibilities dependent not only on something innate in the organism, but arising from the interrelations and cross-modifications of organism and environment.

Dewey's determination to turn men from a preoccupation with the past to a more conscious effort on behalf of the future has called forth much protest and argument. Some say his metaphysic is faulty—that it implies we must decide whether a past event really did happen or not, on the basis of an appraisal of future events. Some disapprove of his rejection of traditional religion, although others appreciate that it was a difficult and courageous procedure in view of his upbringing, his appreciation of the past, and his own personal integrity. He threw off the old idea of God much in the same way as he avoided adherence to any social or political creed, whether old or new, which pointed to inflexibility and the danger of conflict. "Professed idealisms", he asserts, "turns out to be a narrow pragmatism".[1] His attitude to conflict owes something to his discipleship of Hegel and Herbart, for he clearly recognises the significance in individual, social, and political development, of the interaction of contrasting factors. The titles of many of his books indicate this, but always the duality holds the possibility of reconciliation, progress coming not from the triumph of one element and the submergence or destruction of the other, but through the mutual adjustment of one to the other. The function of inquiry is largely a process of the reconciliation of opposites, both in the make-up of the individual and in the make-up of the group, the community, and the larger society.

This leads to another significant aspect of Dewey's philosophy which has occasioned much criticism. The criticism is implied in

[1] *Creative Intelligence*, 1917, p. 19.

George Santayana's words: "In Dewey, as in current science and ethics, there is a pervasive, quasi-Hegelian tendency to dissolve the individual into his social functions, as well as everything substantial and actual into something relative and transitional". This, and similar comments of other writers are not always consistent, for they suggest that Dewey would have men nonentities yet all-powerful, masters of destiny yet insignificant in their impermanence. Such objections arise largely because he seeks to give new direction and cohesion to group-life and effort—a not unworthy aim, one would think, in these days when the old directives and binding forces are proving inadequate, and when there are few hermits except for an occasional scientific investigator. He poses as "the deepest problem of our times", that of "constructing a new individuality consonant with the objective conditions under which we live".[1]

Dewey sets out not to deprive the individual of his inner soul, his communion with nature and his wonderment at the universe; he wishes not to "dissolve" the individual but to help him to fill his soul with humanity, to commune with his fellows and to wonder at their achievements. The individual's environment is both natural and human; why should he not value the one as much as the other? why should he not preserve his uniqueness even though his dependence on his fellows and his interrelations with them become better understood by him than ever before? Even before Dewey, man could rarely escape from man. Alone in a picture gallery, the thoughts and impressions of fellow men impinge on him, alone with a book, their ideas dart out at him from the pages.

Dewey tries to show that the self does not grow in solitude, nor in the mere contact with nature. An essential element in the natural conditions for the growth of man is the rest of mankind. The make-up of an individual includes reflections of a multitude of men; his thoughts are their thoughts, or, at best, are a unique fabric woven from selected parts of their thoughts. Dewey argues that even as the growth of knowledge of the physical world has led to the achievement of a measure of control and modification for the benefit of man, so an increase in the understanding of social inter-relations could bring about an extension of human development. In our present primitive state it would be presumptuous to us to try to foresee the limits of that development. Humanity is divided

---

[1] *Individualism—Old and New*, p. 34.

—is held back—by innumerable barriers between individuals and groups, barriers of language, of time and distance, of caste, of nationality, of colour, of religion, of superstition, and of human prejudices great and small, which hold men to the well-worn paths of ignorance, stagnation, and sometimes retrogression.

It is not surprising, therefore, that Dewey conceives education to be a training in breaking down barriers and forging links. He is not afraid that the closer association of groups will wipe out unique and valuable differentiations, any more than he fears that association between individuals will tend to standardisation. He is willing to sacrifice uniqueness, if necessary, to ensure the interpretation of influences between groups. He writes: "To learn to be human is to develop through the give-and-take of communication an effective sense of being an individually distinctive member of a community".[1] It is clear that fruitful interchanges of ideas and influences can only take place under conditions of complete freedom and amity. There is no place for either the colour bar or the Marxist conflict in Dewey's world of interrelated communities. There would be no place for war in an integrated world, but when democracy is in danger it must be defeated—so Dewey came, with reluctance to support the First World War. Without the democratic way of life there could be no adequate "growing better" by mankind.

It will be for posterity to determine whether Dewey's idea of purposive striving for democracy—for free-growing conditions for all—is not the more hopeful message to mankind than the older philosophies. Is it any less noble a thought that *we* are helping to gain the four freedoms for all men than that *I* am living an exemplary life according to the precepts of the apostles of eternal values? The first thought carries with it the hope of success, the second carries with it the frustration of the impossibility of achieveing the end. Dewey's is not the only philosophy which measures man's significance in terms of effort rather than achievement, but few imply greater faith in the power of the individual to contribute to the upward evolution of mankind. "The time has arrived", says Dewey, "for a pragmatism which shall be emphatically idealistic, proclaiming the essential connection of intelligence with the unachieved future". Living, he believes, should be "the ever enduring process of perfecting, maturing, refining".[2]

[1] *The Public and its Problems*, 1927, p. 154.
[2] *Reconstruction in Philosophy*, N.Y., 1920, p. 177.

Dewey's Psychology

It has already been suggested that Dewey exemplifies his own theory—he was a product of his environment, and in turn he modified that environment. Moreover, he stands as an unanswerable refutation of suggestions that he denied the personal uniqueness of the individual. When he postulates that the latter is the product of society he implies that self-shaping has been part of the process, if only because the individual has been part of the society which has made him. There is nothing of the Herbartian robot about Dewey's moral man. Dewey has to recognise, if only as a biological fact, the existence of individual differences, and his concern is that each individual shall be truly educated by the fostering of individual growth through a richness of social opportunity. This last term has little to do, directly, with economics, but much to do with the extent to which the community, great or small, school or town, provides opportunity for active experiences and undertakings by its members. Dewey has faith that such opportunity for the realisation of human interdependence will encourage the will to do better, to *be* better. "The good man," says he, "is the man who no matter how morally unworthy he has been, is moving to become better".[1]

One of the main reasons for Dewey's tendency to refer to the individual as though he were a piece of mechanism or a biological organism in a controlled experiment, is related to a factor in Dewey's own environment—a factor which helped to shape his ideas. This was, of course, the development of psychology as a science—a development which was many-sided in the last quarter of the nineteenth century. By this time, Herbart's belief in the measurability of psychological data had been accepted, and the valuable work of such men as Binet and Simon in France, and Thorndike in America, on the measurement of intelligence, emphasised the new function of mentality—and, later, personality—as raw material for scientific experiment and research. Dewey could hardly avoid being somewhat influenced by this new work although he opposed strongly the assumption that all aspects of man, even potentialities, are measurable. It is worth bearing in mind that Dewey, always looking to the future, does not expect to find a technique of measuring what does not yet exist, but he would not reject scientific

[1] *Reconstruction in Philosophy*, N.Y., 1920, p. 177.

N.B.—No modern educator can be entirely impartial and unbiased in discussing pragmatism. It will be clear to the reader that the writer of this chapter leans further towards pragmatism than does her colleague.

judgment on what already exists, as it would help him to make his own estimate for the guidance of future action.

At the same time, psychology itself was splitting up into "schools" of thought differing widely from one another in their conceptions of human make-up and human learning, but all regarding man with the same coldly scientific eye. Behaviourism was too mechanistic for Dewey, but the biological basis of gestalt psychology with its provision for newness, was more in line with his philosophy. He saw the development of Freudian psychology and in so far as it, too, was biological rather than mechanistic, he was not entirely opposed to it, especially as it demanded attention for the problems and difficulties of children. At one stage, however, the experimental and theoretical exaggerations of some "progressive" educators drove him to repudiate the linking of his name with the new cult of "freedom" for the child.[1] "Some teachers", he protested, "seem to be afraid even to make suggestions to the members of a group as to what they should do. I have heard of cases in which children are surrounded with objects and materials and then left entirely to themselves, the teacher being loath to suggest even what might be done with the materials lest freedom be infringed upon. Why, then, supply materials?"[2]

The foundations of Dewey's own psychological theory were laid in his early contacts with William James and G. Stanley Hall. The former evolved a functional psychology based on a theory of many "instincts" or learning through natural reactions. The latter focused attention on the study of the child—a study which included investigation and observation of the content of the child mind. He also gave a biological interpretation to the old theory of the recapitulation of racial evolution in child life, an idea translated by Dewey into practical issues of the curriculum. Such ideas, then, contributed to the formulation of Dewey's own psychological principles which are closely allied to his philosophical concept of the instrumentality of the mind in all its aspects, thinking, willing, and feeling. In the process of evolution, man has gradually acquired mind and intelligence superior to that of other animals. It has been a process of learning through activity, through practical experience in the normal struggle for existence, for survival, which life presents. Through practising the use of the intelligence to overcome obstacles, make

---

[1] J. Dewey, *Art and Education*, Barnes Foundation Press, Pa., 1929; *Education and Experience*, Macmillan, 1938.

[2] *Experience and Education*, p. 84.

adjustments and to obtain satisfactions, man has developed and increased that aspect of his make-up, and he can only continue to develop it through practising the use of it in living situations. The acquirement and retention of knowledge is only part of man's natural activity in adjusting himself to environment. His ideas are activities of the mind—part of the whole activity of adjustment. Further adjustment—improvement—is dependent not on abstract information or knowledge but on coming to some conclusion after some new experience gained as a result of movement—action—on the part of the learner. Biologically, the action of the organism arises from inherited instincts and impulses so that in a straightforward evolutionary process innate impulses result in educational experiences, each organism gradually acquiring knowledge or learning to the level of his predecessors and eventually surpassing them.

If the philosophical argument as to the independent existence of knowledge is avoided, this interpretation of human evolution affords clear guidance for the teacher. First, the complexity of experience and relationships now achieved by man may hinder the "straightforward evolutionary process", especially as man has raised up obstacles for himself and his successors in the shape of political and economic inequalities and social and moral taboos. Therefore, the function of the teacher is to guide the young through the complexities of life and give them opportunities to learn in the natural way without encountering the severe frustrations and injury that slow down—and sometimes dam up—the outflowing of impulses towards greater and more abundant life. In the second place, man has now achieved a measure of control over his own evolution. The future function of the teacher should be not only to help children to cope adequately with contemporary conditions as their predecessors coped with less complex conditions; the new teacher should aim to produce not a set type of individual or citizen but a race of young people competent to cope with new experiences, new tasks which must come. "We live forward", says Dewey, "we live in a world where changes are going on whose issue means our weal or woe . . . every act of ours modifies these changes and hence is fraught with promise, or charged with hostile energies".[1] From this it follows that education must start by the capturing and focusing of natural impulses—by the gaining of "spontaneous attention" to problems and topics which, in offering challenge to investigate, call into play those human powers which need to be not only developed

[1] *Creative Intelligence*, p. 12.

but also controlled. This is but a beginning, however, for man has reached a stage when he can expand and grow not only through the development and control of his natural unconscious impulses; will and reason may operate in the making of deliberate conscious decisions to embark on activities. Even in childhood, then, "reflective attention" needs to be called into play, as it was in the early days of the race. The conscious impulse associated with this, however, is still part of the dynamic "outgoing" of the self—part of the great process which Dewey believes to be the driving force of life.

He regards the organism as having the capacity for active self-propulsion, for reaching out towards objects and experiences which may bring it greater life, or rather, which may serve as instruments for the achievement of its purposes. That is to say, innate impulses are not lying passive, ready to be called into play by stimuli in the environment; rather is the environment explored, as it were, selectively, by the organism itself, which has the capacity to pick out and reach towards those environmental factors offering opportunities for expression, satisfaction, growth. In the human being, this outward impulse, according to Dewey, is true interest which he defines as "a form of self-expressive activity—that is, of growth through acting upon nascent tendencies".[1]

If, therefore, an interest is an outgoing of the self towards that which "lies" in the direction of the agent's own growth and is therefore imperiously demanded, if the agent is to be himself",[2] it follows that the stronger the interest, the stronger the effort of will which can be summoned to the attack of intervening difficulties and problems. That is, learning through interest is not merely an easy or lazy way of acquiring a certain amount of knowledge; it is a way of calling into play the full powers of effort and determination of the learner.

Thinking, according to Dewey, is a capacity the human organism has acquired in the evolutionary practice of seeking and attaining these objectives. Thinking has been found useful in the process of reaching what is "imperiously demanded" for the purpose of growth; thus, it is a result of challenge of environment and not the primary cause of the human being's entry into the contest. It is here Dewey makes one of his most significant contributions to ideas

[1] *National Herbart Society Yearbook*, 1895. *Interest as Related to the Training of the Will*, p. 15.
[2] *ibid.*, p. 9.

on the nature of thought. He denies that thought can come from contemplation alone or that it results directly from sensation. Even as the ability to think developed as an aid to the full biological expansion of man, so it takes place, not when nothing much is happening to him, but when some extra effort is needed to prevent the interruption of that expansion. He starts thinking when a change in the environment affects his comfort, he starts thinking when circumstances offer a choice of routes to a desired goal, he starts thinking whenever a problem arises. This argument explains Dewey's formulation of the "problem" method of learning. He contends that thinking and reasoning are exercised in the tackling of problems. The thinking not only arises in the natural way, it is also focused on a definite objective, and as a result, "every suggested conclusion is tested by its reference to this regulating end, by its pertinence to the problem in hand".[1]

The task of the mind presented with a question to be answered is to consider the factors in the situation and to decide on a line of action which seems more likely than any other to lead to a successful conclusion. If, when pursued, the line of action leads to a goal, readjustment to environment has now been accomplished and at the same time valuable experience has been gained, which, having merged into the original activity, will render it even more effective should a similar problem arise. If the goal is not reached it is a sign that the thinking has not been good enough. Another mental analysis must be made, another course of action thought out and acted upon. The first trial will not have been entirely fruitless, for the experience gained will modify the mental activity leading to the next experiment.

In *How We Think*, Dewey discusses in some detail the implication of his theory with reference to inductive reasoning, but here his suggestions go little further than the ideas of many of his predecessors. His five logically distinct steps have sometimes been likened to Herbart's formal steps, but they are, in fact, no more than the steps of the experimental investigator of the past three centuries and more. Dewey's first stage is the consciousness of a problem or obstacle; his second, the mental survey, the analysis of the situation, and the location of the main factor; next comes the listing of possible solutions, followed by more thinking out of the implications of each so that comparison will indicate the most suitable course for experiment. The fifth stage is the actual putting

[1] *How We Think*, p. 12, Harrap, 1910; pp. 14-15, revised 1933.

into practice of the decision and the reaching of a conclusion as to its success or failure. The value of personal investigation and of testing hypotheses would be denied by few to-day, but some educators would feel that however useful the implied methods might be in purely intellectual pursuits, their function would be less easy to justify in aspects of education involving aesthetics, sentiments, and morals. Be that as it may, it will not be denied that John Dewey's psychology gives a vigorous, dynamic, realistic interpretation to the needs of the human organism in its social matrix, a surer foundation for educational method than are the psychologies of several of his contemporaries. While it is clear that Dewey would not wish the child to suffer undue mental, emotional, or physical hardship, it is equally clear that he cannot envisage the development of the integrated dynamic personality except through a life which presents constant challenges to the immature human organism.

In consequence, Dewey sees schooling as a life which toughens by requiring the surmounting of obstacles rather than their avoidance, a life which increases sensitivity and adaptability by requiring contribution to a self-controlled group rather than conformation in a regimented society. In *My Pedagogical Creed* he gives a high place to psychology as a guide to the educator in interpreting pupils' capacities, interests, and habits, which, he affirms, "must be translated into terms of what they are capable of in the way of social service".

Dewey's Pedagogy

Dewey would point out that expression of a need to formulate aims and ideas of education, is tantamount to confession that the existing order is unsatisfactory. An aim is only of value, therefore, inasmuch as it is sufficiently in touch with actuality to indicate the means by which improvement may be achieved. He would differentiate between the kind of aim conceived only for the purpose of seeking greater efficiency in producing knowledgeable and disciplined youngsters, and the aim which involves the reform and revision of the social system. The one is concerned exclusively with the transmission to posterity of what are deemed by living adult authority to be the best standards of racial or community tradition. Dewey would not hesitate to use the term "indoctrination" for this process. The other is concerned with the search for ways of educating the young so that they themselves become the regenerating force of society. Dewey holds to this—to him the child is not merely an uncontrolled ignoramus who must be raised up to the level of his predecessors and imprinted with their die-stamp, but rather a being who by reason of the adaptability and plasticity of youth, has potentialities for development beyond the stage reached by his predecessors. Plato's scheme, with its emphasis on social reorganisation is more acceptable to Dewey then Aristotle's maintenance of the best ideals of Athenian citizenship. Similarly, Rousseau's criticism of contemporary society falls into line with Dewey's attitude, while he would regard Matthew Arnold's reverence of tradition as the antithesis of progress.

Such a reorientation of the mind of the educator towards the future demands the sacrifice of preconceived ideas on the content and method of education. The handing on of past knowledge and codes can only be achieved by instruction, either direct or indirect. However pleasant and interesting the methods devised, they are still concerned with a content of known quantities and pre-estimated values, and, in addition, they still set limits to the pupils' learning. Whether the mind is regarded as the Lockian *tabula rasa*, the Herbartian arena, or the Froebelian source of creative and exploratory impulses, teaching methods must aim at either moulding the mind to a known pattern or guiding it to a known end. The teacher who can face the future with an open mind is also ready to risk the impact of new knowledge, new experiences, and new ideas on the minds of pupils. He is prepared to refrain from interfering with the natural or social situation in which education is to take place, except to make it more comprehensible to children.

The last proviso indicates Dewey's idea of the function of past knowledge and experience in education. The heritage of the past is with us, he would argue—we cannot escape it. It is the material the educator has to hand, and he must use it, not as a series of goals to be reached but as examples of knowledge, customs, and institutions, which may afford valuable practice in critical appreciation and evaluation; for the young are not likely to become willing or able to reform society unless they are aware of its defects and conscious of the height of achievement of which man is capable. "Imaginative recovery of the bygone is indispensable to successful invasion of the future, but its status is that of an instrument", he writes, ". . . to isolate the past, dwelling upon it for its own sake, and giving it the eulogistic name of knowledge, is to substitute the reminiscence of old age for effective intelligence".[1] Dewey is con-

[1] *Creative Intelligence*, p. 24.

vinced that youth—the period of maximum growth and adaptability—is the stage when it is most possible to generate the social improvement of the future. The adult is bound by existing conventions and responsibilities, and his mind has lost much of the flexibility of immaturity.

Stressing, as he does, the significance of growth, "the primary fact with which education deals", it is not surprising that Dewey claims his educational ideal to be the protection, sustenance, and direction of growth. He believes this concept to include all that is worth while in the narrower aims which have been formulated in the past. Spencer's definition of education as preparation for life is only significant, asserts Dewey, if it refers to life now and in the immediate future. Pupils are little interested in the distant future so the motive to learn is lacking—unless it has the artificial, external stimulus of rewards and punishments. The fostering of continuous healthy (*i.e.* successful) growth ensures adequate preparation for immediate life, and, moreover, arouses the will of the pupil to venture further. This idea of the constant reorganisation of powers and realisation of present possibilities is not unlike Professor Whitehead's concept of progression by *successful* cycles of learning.

Some educators have aimed at the self-realisation of the individual, which, again in Dewey's opinion, has validity only if considered as a process and not a mere aspiration. The teacher should not look into the distance at an imaginary finished product, but to the present at a pupil who *exists*—who grows, develops, and achieves realisation of his powers all the time. It is in the real, active development of the pupil that Dewey sees the place for individual education and the education of individuality. The remote aim he would deem too general and conjectural to be individualistic, whereas the inescapable fact of individual differentiation renders acceptable an immediate aim to develop each pupil's power and personality fully, not according to any absolute standards, but to the pupil's own best advantage in relation to his capacities and opportunities. His progress is thus to be measured by his own best standards, not set against those of other pupils differing in natural ability, environmental experience, and temperament. Dewey's concern for the individual also emerges in his interpretation of the old disciplinary aim of education. As a psychologist he would say that the teacher's function is to observe individual desires and behaviour, and to seek to use these tendencies to strengthen the process of growth. Similarly he would accept cultural aims so long as they allow a refining and guiding of personal taste rather than an imposition of arbitrary standards.

Although in the last few paragraphs an attempt has been made to interpret Dewey's educational theory in familiar terminology, it is not intended to suggest that he holds the ideal of growth to be directed towards some remote finality. He applies his philosophy consistently in defining his educational theory. Growth and movement are fundamentals of the universe; the human mind cannot envisage their cessation into a state of static perfection. Therefore the educator need not try to envisage an end for human growth. His task is to guide and foster growth and to find ways of studying changes and discovering what they signify.

Any school methods based on Dewey's principles must reflect the processes and interrelations of society as a whole, for Dewey sees both the school and the wider community as arenas for the development of the individual through contact and communication with his fellows. The child is to share the resources of a good society and to give back to that society, thus helping in the development of other members. It is in the give and take process that the growth of the individual and the advancement of the group is achieved, but it is not a mere matter of exchange of information but rather the availability of opportunity for richly varied experience— the more varied, the better the society, for each member can develop more fully as an individual and thus has more to give back to the group. It is his emphasis on this network of group interconnections which has earned for Dewey criticism on the grounds that he underestimates both the individual and the type of human experience not dependent on the functioning of groups. He would, no doubt, reply that it is only through the resources made available by the group that the uniqueness of a personality becomes emphasised, and it is only because the group makes such resources available that the individual is able to enjoy solitary experiences.

In emphasising the educational function of the group, Dewey gives signficance to the concept—inherited from his predecessors— of racial culture stages. He contends that the major developmental experiences of the human race have been gained in the struggle to satisfy needs essential to survival. The operation of the natural impulse of the human organism to seek food and protection has resulted in the evolution of human intelligence. Thus, these dominating impulses of the race are those through which the fullest development of the young, growing organism can be achieved. A stage in human evolution has been reached when a conscious effort can be made to accelerate the process of "civilising" by making men more competent to take part in the activities and purposes of the race. This effort is education—"the process of the reconstruction or reconstitution of experience, giving it a more socialised value through the medium of increased individual efficiency". Dewey points out that the achievement of the democratic way of life is singularly opportune for the making of this effort because the old dualisms—work and leisure, mind and body—have been proven unsound and because the significance of each man's contribution to his community is implicit in the democratic ideal.

The educator, an outstandingly important figure in the democratic society, must therefore aim constantly to see the relationship between the child's natural impulses and those great biological forces of the race. Moreover, he must try to provide comparable material and situations for the beneficial exercise of those impulses. "The child has his own instincts and tendencies," writes Dewey in *My Pedagogical Creed*, "but we do not know what these mean until we can translate them into their social equivalents. We must be able to carry them back into a social past and see them as the inheritance of previous race activities. We must also be able to project them into the future to see what their outcome and end will be". These words, particularly the last sentence, indicate clearly that Dewey does not underestimate the role of the teacher, as some critics believe. True, the pupils' impulses as expressed in their interests, are to concern the teacher more than the inculcation of knowledge, but the pupils' freedom is to be as regulated and organised as that of Emile. The teacher as a stage manager is more powerful than the teacher as a player strutting and fretting. He may lack the plasticity of immaturity in adapting his own personality to new growth, but he is, after all, well ahead of his pupils in experience and, therefore, more capable of surveying the social heritage, looking to a more distant end and purpose than his pupils, and making a reliable hypothesis as to the best course of action to pursue. According to Dewey's theory, the novice, faced with the problem of organising educative activities for pupils, may not at first fully achieve his own readjustment to the new situation. The arising of the problem makes him think, makes him marshal relevent information and ideas, makes him weigh up possibilities and finally embark on a scheme. Only trial will show whether it "works". Following up the same theory it may be assumed that the competence of teachers is to be judged by their skill in estimating what will "work". If this is so, the question arises, who is to be the judge of that skill? Is the teacher alone to be the judge of his own competence? Surely the criterion must be the evidence society has as to the quality of the product or result—as in the case of the artist, the cobbler, or the army general? Perhaps the good Deweyan teacher is he whom society, accepting the estimate of his fellow specialists, can entrust with the task of ensuring that the process of "perfecting and refining" will continue.[1] He is one who realises his own power and responsibility to guide the young to the acquirement of the skills and knowledge which have raised man in the past. Dewey suggests, "There is no point in his being more mature if, instead of using his greater insight to help organise the conditions of the experience of the immature, he throws away his insight".[2] But he needs to realise that his own superiority in experience and knowledge are but temporary, that he can set no limit to the development of pupils who ought to take civilisation a stage higher in the evolutionary scale.

For the guidance of the teacher, Dewey suggests that the main racial tendencies may be observed in the behaviour of children, particularly in their "interest in conversation or communication; in inquiry, or finding out things; in making things, or construction; and in artistic expression".[3] He believes that skill in these activities may best be achieved in pursuit of purposes akin to those pursued by our predecessors, whose main efforts through the centuries have been devoted to the sustenance and protection of the groups which constitute the human race. Whether or not the theory is accepted that the primary stage of education should be focused on the primary needs of mankind—food, clothing, and shelter—it cannot be denied that the outside world is still largely concerned with the struggle to satisfy such needs, and that the basic activities involved are more comprehensible and attractive to children than intellectual abstractions. Dewey hopes that in providing scope for such activities the school will compensate for the decreased educational opportunities of the modern home, although it is still possible for children to gain important experience and satisfaction through home activities.

He wishes to see neither the perpetuation of the dualisms of home and school nor the purposeless pursuance of adult industrial

---

[1] Dewey contends that education must be free to determine its own ends and must seek within itself criteria for judging social and individual growth.

[2] *Experience and Education*, p. 32.

[3] *The School and Society*, p. 45, C.U.P., 1915, revised edition.

activities by children. Even as he contends that education is not a preparation for life, but life itself, so he strives to make the school a family. Similarly, school is to reflect the larger society through activities selected by psychological consideration of their reality and purpose for children; society itself is to make its resources available for selected studies and experiences—it is to be an educative society. In the old days the family used to introduce children to experiences now appertaining to the wider society—as, for instance, spinning, weaving, and associated processes. Children are now gaining little of this informal education in fundamental racial activities—the loom is now in the factory, water now comes to the house from afar through tubes, fuel is only here and there obtained by the labour of wood-cutting, and most food, even potatoes, may be bought in cans.

The school must take over the task of introducing the young to fundamental processes. In doing so it will resolve other conflicts—that of informal and formal education, and that of play and work. Such dualisms need no longer divide childish activities into those enjoyed and those endured. Lest this proposed change in the function of the school should suggest that it is to be set up in opposition to other groups, it must be emphasised that Dewey sees the whole situation not as one of conflict, but as one of interrelations. The school has its unique part to play, very much in the same way as the individual person has his part to play, independent, self-determining, yet co-operating in the development of greater whole. Education, as the purposeful effort of a community, is to play an equal part with politics in the assessment and pursuit of the better life.

In view of the kindergarten characteristics of the Chicago experimental school, it was not difficult to introduce activities based on home life and basic industries in place of more formal activities such as play with the "gifts". Accustomed as we are to see cookery, sewing, and carpentry in the schools of to-day, we are likely to underestimate the significance of those modest changes made by Dewey and his colleagues. Almost the whole range of the new concepts could be tried out. The activities were fundamental to the human race; they belonged to the wider community; they demanded both material and space, so that desks and silence rules must be swept away; they offered challenges to pupils to think and experiment; they provided individual tasks in the accomplishment of group purposes; they trained the senses and allowed the incidental acquisition of "basic skills"—reading, writing, and number; they offered links with the whole realm of knowledge. Thus from the household occupations engaged in by the small people of six and seven, Dewey pointed the way to later investigation of sources and origins. Activities concerned with goods and textiles led the young workers to want to discover where they were grown or made; later they would want to know how people produced them in the past— they would relive the history of group development and rediscover for themselves elementary processes and inventions.

Even as the dependence of man upon nature and upon society has led to his development of science and history, so, in Dewey's opinion, would children feel the need to study nature and make simple experiments in order to solve problems which they encountered in familiarising themselves with their environment. The example most often quoted is the work with textiles, which leads to the real understanding of simple mechanised devices such as the spindle and the loom and the investigation of the nature of a textile —the cotton seed, its planting, the conditions for its growth, its marketing, its manufacture, and associated processes, leading, perhaps to experiments with dyes—and also, of course, the discovery of the whole story of the industry's development. It is very probable, however, that to the teacher of the modern child other examples would be more convincing. Thus the small boy's inevitable interest in mechanical devices such as the telephone, was used to lead to studies of communication—ways in which people, now and in the past have kept in touch with one another. It is clear that no teacher would have difficulty in setting the stage so that pupils choose to engage in such attractive activities. In the Elementary School, pupils were free to choose their own methods and materials for making their investigations, but, again, it is clear that the selections made must be profoundly influenced by the teacher's care in collecting material and wisdom in offering advice. Moreover, in the course of discussion the teacher may need to contribute suggestions as to the most fruitful method of group co-operation. Working together to solve a common problem is essential to the Deweyan theory, yet the school society is no more perfect than its wider equivalent in providing equal opportunities for all its members. One of the Deweyan teacher's tasks is to ensure that individual and group move in harmony, both acquiring the best and most positive habits of growth. There is time for the teacher to observe, plan, and encourage, because time is not wasted in "chalk-and-talk" instruction and in the establishment of "good discipline". Self-discipline and group-discipline develop through the will of the pupils themselves in order that their purposes shall be achieved with the minimum hindrance.

Thus the Deweyan teacher's task is not merely to follow the child wherever he leads. In rejecting the "luxury learning" based on the imitation of leisured-class intellectualism, and in substituting the intelligent *doing* of ordinary people, Dewey suggested a version of "child-centred" curriculum which gave to the teacher a heavier responsibility—and a greater opportunity—for guiding the young not only into the habit of democratic co-operation, but also towards the highest intellectual pursuits, and the fullest aesthetic experiences. He rejected the subject-based curriculum not because he denied the value of subject material, and discipline, but because he objected to its presentation to children as the logical summary of adult experience. Subjects are but summaries and recapitulations of human activities, and therefore they should be reached by children summarising their own experiences. Moreover, subjects are but adult compartments for the convenient storage of human knowledge. The compartments are not necessary to children; indeed, they are likely to be harmfully confining. If the traditional subjects figure on the time-table, how can pupils delve into economics, or astronomy, or engineering, or other important spheres in their search for solutions to their problems?

It is significant that enrichment of subject matter rather than its neglect is implied in this argument. As educators became more and more preoccupied with method, Dewey felt impelled to offer a warning reminder. "It is a ground for legitimate criticism, when the ongoing movement of progressive education fails to recognise that the problem of selection and organisation of subject matter for study and learning is fundamental." [1] In rejecting the readymade curriculum Dewey gave to the teacher the task of evolving curricula suited to the needs of different groups. The fund of past human experience is available to be drawn upon. The teacher, with his own greater experience and his own knowledge of his pupils, is to help them select from that fund. "What concerns him, as teacher," writes Dewey, "is the way in which that subject-matter may become a part of experience; what there is in the child's present that is usable with reference to it; how such elements are to be used; how his own knowledge of the subject-matter may assist in interpreting the child's needs and doings, and determine

[1] *Experience and Education*, pp. 95-6, N. Y., Macmillan Co., 1938.

the medium in which the child should be placed in order that his growth may be properly directed".[1] This indicates conclusively that the Deweyan teacher's task is to organise learning situations for pupils. It is equally clear that planning ahead by the teacher is necessary. Dewey's disciples favour the term "course of study" for the plan made by the teacher—a hypothesis, as it were, of what might give balanced and coherent experiences to each pupil and at the same time foster the growth of group consciousness. "Curriculum" is used to signify the complete range of experiences gained by pupils in school.

The good Deweyan teacher will not omit from that curriculum aspects of education traditionally termed aesthetic, moral, and religious. In fact, in a true Dewey scheme the child cannot escape such education, for, as Froebel pointed out, development is a single process, not a series of movements along parallel lines which never meet. Art education is implicit in the study of fundamental processes, for a work of art is a perfected expression of basic human activity. Dewey writes: "Viewed both psychologically and socially, the arts represent not luxuries or superfluities, but fundamental forces of development".[2] The practical attack on his problem gives the pupil wide opportunities for creative and appreciative activity in the arts and crafts, thus laying the foundations for the later development of a wider understanding of artistic quality in industrial design and imaginative significance in more abstract art.

Moral education should be similarly an integral part of basic experience. Dewey deplores its separation from the acquirement of knowledge by the use of intelligence. He pours scorn on systems which claim to have the development of character as the main aim, and yet treat the main part of school work as having nothing to do with character. This, he asserts, can only lead to attempts to give moral instruction—attempts which have been effective only in authoritarian societies. "Not the teaching as such," he writes, "but the reinforcement of it by the whole régime of which it was an incident, made it effective. To attempt to get similar results from lessons about morals in a democratic society is to rely upon sentimental magic".[3] He is convinced that the pupils' purposeful activities in a curriculum representing "standard factors of social life" will give them moral interest and insight, through the functioning of

[1] *The Child and the Curriculum*, p. 30, Chicago, 1903.
[2] P. Monroe, *Cyclopedia of Education*, vol. 1, p. 224, Macmillan, 1912.
[3] *Democracy and Education*, p. 411, Macmillan, 1916.

intelligence and will in the achievement of self-control and the appreciation of social values. The moral import of discipline comes through the free and purposive judgment of the individual.

The main achievement of Dewey's experimental school was to show that his own learning activity had been satisfactory—his hypotheses had been sound, particularly for the age-range six to twelve. Through the planning of the staff, the pupils in tackling their problems entered naturally into activities which involved not only cooking, sewing, and woodwork, but also gardening, science, music, geography, history, arithmetic, drawing, painting, reading, and writing. It was demonstrated that the need often arose naturally for group co-operation and effort, especially in the construction of apparatus not only scientific and gymnastic, but also recreational and utilitarian such as tents and bicycle stands; thus the school society functioned as "an organic union of individuals". Dewey's own considered conclusions on reviewing a range of such experiments, was that his basic theory was confirmed although the danger of fruitless repetitive activity needs to be circumvented, that is, the teacher must indicate short cuts and tempt pupils to engage in progressive activities—he must know the nature of the practical and intellectual difficulties to be encouraged, and he must know the intelligence and temperament of each pupil.

We have no equally impressive example of the Dewey method at the secondary level, but the implications of his creed point to the continuance of "psychological order" in the curriculum, the retention of the "problem method", and the extension of social opportunity. It seems reasonable to suggest that the ordinary good secondary school could achieve this without a major upheaval, even as Dewey's ordinary elementary school achieved it. Dewey agrees that there may come a stage when the psychological order becomes the logical order—when pupils will apply themselves to "subjects" with interest. If this happens at some point in the secondary school, there is still ample scope—and need—for the problem approach within the general subject framework; it is still essential to "teach not so much things as the meanings of things".[1] As to the development of social consciousness, this is clearly the most significant stage, when the majority of future citizens must bring to bear their intelligence in the shape of specific realistic thought. In societies, clubs, and general school projects they will plan co-operative efforts in the

[1] *How We Think*, p. 236.

pursuit of their own objectives. In participation in social service and in the enjoyment of civic amenities they will come to appreciate their group's relationship to the wider community.

"Democracy must begin at home," asserts Dewey, "and its home is the neighbouring community".[1] Yet little can be achieved if the elementary school fails to play its part. "I have never been able to feel much optimism regarding the possibilities of higher education," writes Dewey, "when it is built upon warped and weak foundations".[2] Nothing less than the full and effective reorientation of the school, at all stages, can ensure the reinforcement of the human organism with the qualities of resilience and adaptability needed to wipe out the "disproportion between powers and wisdom", which now exists as a result of the new growth and change of the twentieth century. Dewey suggests that we are passing through a phase of adolescence. Even as early as 1910, he saw that our mastery of the physical world was growing more quickly than our capacity to reformulate our values so that we were "at the mercy of habit, of haphazard, and hence of force". After four decades, his words have even greater significance: "With the tremendous increase in our control of nature, in our ability to utilise nature for human use and satisfaction, we find the actual realisation of ends, the enjoyment of values, growing unassured and precarious".[3]

In the struggle for stability, Dewey has no doubt that there must be aroused an awareness of individual responsibility in an enlarged and complex world. The school can contribute by training the young in specific and experimental thinking and by helping them to experience the need for democratic co-operation. He sees human progress as dependent upon the opening up of lines of communication between peoples—nations, classes, and all smaller groups. Early in the century he expressed his hope that American schools, in bringing together children of many nationalities, languages, traditions, and creeds, would demonstrate the development of social unity through the culture common to all groups. How far this has yet been achieved must be decided by the Americans themselves, for the course of American education was destined to be influenced by other conflicting philosophies.

[1] *The Public and Its Problems*, p. 213.
[2] J. Dewey, *From Absolutism to Experimentalism*, in G. P. Adams and W. P. Montague, *Contemporary American Philosophy*, vol. 2, pp. 22-3, Macmillan, 1930.
[3] J. Dewey, *The Influence of Darwin in Philosophy*, p. 71, New York, 1910.

After the Great War of 1914-18 Dewey's problem method was reinterpreted by W. H. Kilpatrick[1] as the project method, which was perhaps more acceptable and comprehensible to the ordinary teacher. The project method was not bound up with the culture-stages theme, and it offered the possibility of some direct action on the part of the teacher. In essence, however, it was methodology related to the Dewey school of thought. No other scheme was so closely akin to Deweyism, but several experiments were designed to achieve similar ends. Helen Parkhurst's "contract plan" developed at Dalton, Mass.,[2] stressed both the independence of the pupil to work at his own rate, and the consultative capacity of the teacher. Carleton Washburne's scheme at Winnetka, Ill., recognised these factors, and also the need for providing the child with measuring rods for his own progress, and giving him significant group experience during at least half of each school day Washburne's attitude is well summarised in the title of one of his books—*Adjusting the School to the Child*.

In realms of philosophy, however, the last three decades have seen many expressions of both revolt and reaction against the moderate democratic pragmatism of Dewey. Some thinkers, such as G. S. Counts have been dissatisfied with the place given to the social factor and have urged the building of a new order on collectivist lines akin to the Russian.[3] Others, such as R. M. Hutchins and M. J. Adler reverted to the Aristotelian viewpoint of happiness through morality as the ultimate aim of education. The "new realism" of F. S. Breed[4] aimed to achieve more stability in practice than pragmatism offers. W. C. Bagley the "essentialist" wished to establish clear and stable aims based on the findings of common experience. Roman Catholics were particularly emphatic in denouncing the pragmatist rejection of an ultimate aim.

Some of the most appreciative of Dewey's students and fellow educators have been among his most severe critics. Such a one was Herman H. Horne whose *Democratic Philosophy of Education*[5] was written as an exposition and commentary on *Democracy and Education*. Horne's work is a skilful exercise in criticism, but it errs in being too deliberately critical of many subsidiary ideas which

[1] W. H. Kilpatrick, *Foundations of Method*, New York, 1925.
[2] H. H. Parkhurst, *Education on the Dalton Plan*, Bell, 1922.
[3] G. S. Counts, *Dare the School Build a New Social Order?*—John Day, New York, 1932.
[4] F. S. Breed, *Education and the New Realism*, Macmillan, 1939.
[5] Macmillan, 1936.

Dewey expounded more adequately in the years between the writing of the two books. Upon one point, however, he voices the doubts of some fellow educators. They are not satisfied that it is enough to aim at continued growth; they have no confidence that without a fixed, universal aim, growth would always be in the right direction.

English thinkers have received Dewey's ideas with similar doubts. Bertrand Russell, avowed realist, confesses that he goes almost all the way with his American friend, except on the question of aims and values. That Dewey was occasionally provoked to retaliation by the shafts of his critics is illustrated by an incident related by Russell. The latter wrote in an article: "Mr Dewey has an outlook which, where it is distinctive, is in harmony with the age of industrialism and collective enterprise. It is natural that his strongest appeal should be to Americans and also that he should be almost equally appreciated by the progressive elements in countries like China and Mexico". Dewey's sharp retort was "Mr Russell's confirmed habit of connecting the pragmatic theory of knowledge with obnoxious aspects of American industrialism . . . is much as if I were to link his philosophy to the interests of the English landed gentry".[1]

In the next few years it is certain that much criticism and appreciation of Deweyism will swell educational literature. Whatever the final decision it cannot alter the fact emphasised by Jerome Nathanson in these words: "The Deweyan revolution in education, we see, has already carried us a long way".[2]

SUGGESTIONS FOR FURTHER READING

Many of Dewey's works are available in English editions, but for preliminary study it may be advisable to make a varied selection covering the main period of his educational writings, as, for instance, *The School and Society* (C.U.P., 1899, revised 1916 and 1949), *How We Think* (Harrap, 1910, revised 1933), *Schools of Tomorrow* (Dent, 1915), *Democracy and Education* (Macmillan, 1916), *Experience and Nature* (Allen and Unwin, 1929), and *Experience and Education* (Macmillan, 1938). The practical significance of these ideas is well indicated in *The Dewey School*, by K. G. Mayhew and A. C. Edwards (Appleton Century, N.Y., 1936). Students particularly interested in philosophy will find a useful selection of

[1] B. Russell, *History of Western Philosophy*, Geo. Allen and Unwin, 1946.
[2] J. Nathanson, *John Dewey, The Reconstruction of the Democratic Life*, Scribner, 1951.

extracts in *The Philosophy of John Dewey*, edited by J. Ratner (New York, 1928).[1] It is suggested that H. H. Horne's criticism, *The Democratic Philosophy of Education* (Macmillan, 1932), be read in a critical spirit after a wide reading of Dewey texts. Those who find intensive concentration on the latter exhausting will find a "reviver" in Jerome Nathanson's interpretation of Deweyism, *John Dewey, The Reconstruction of the Democratic Life* (Scribner, 1951); it is stimulating and at times brilliantly illuminating. Perhaps the most significant contribution on Deweyism in the general histories of education is the chapter in W. A. McCallister's *The Growth of Freedom in Education* (Constable, 1931).

[1] See also H. S. Thayer, *The Logic of Pragmatism: An Examination of John Dewey's Logic*, Routledge and Kegan Paul, 1952.

CHAPTER XVIII

MONTESSORI AND SOME CONTEMPORARIES

With the foregoing summary of Dewey's ideas our main task of tracing the evolution of educational theory is at an end. Few will deny that Dewey is the outstanding figure in the educational world of the past sixty years, and it only remains to emphasise that the whole period has been one of fruitful thought and experiment by a far greater number of skilled educators than any period of the past could boast. If names of major importance are omitted from this chapter and from our conclusion, it is submitted that it is neither relevant nor timely to attempt a fair evaluation of modern ideas and experiments. It is fitting, however, to consider briefly some of those educators who have striven for the liberation of both pupil and teacher from the shackles of outmoded pedagogy.

In this sphere, **Maria Montessori (1870-1952)** achieved a universal reputation hardly second to Dewey's, and in the course of a long lifetime suffered, as he did, some misinterpretation by earnest disciples developing their own lines of thought. Like Dewey she was a product of her times, born in an awakening Italy and trained as a doctor at the University of Rome. This was a more remarkable achievement than Dewey's progress to Johns Hopkins, for she was the first woman M.D. of the university. Thus, like educators of the past, she came to teaching through "physic", so that her concern for the handicapped or weakly child is a natural consequence of her early training—as, indeed, is her emphasis on the importance of healthy school conditions.

Her first experience with children was as an assistant in the psychiatric clinic of the university; later she became director of a special school for handicapped children, an experience which won her interest in the development of teaching methods, for she writes : "I felt that mental deficiency presented chiefly a pedagogical rather than mainly a medical question".[1] There is no doubt that her original sense-training apparatus owes much to the demands made on her ingenuity by the needs of her first pupils, and partly through this association, it is sometimes assumed that she underestimated the power of the normal child. More worthy of note, however, is the fact that she was almost certainly the first to attempt

---

[1] *Montessori Method*, trans. by A. E. George, p. 31, Heinemann, 1912.

to equate normally developing intelligence with subnormally developing intelligence. Although to-day there may be much glib reference to I.Q.s and mental ages, very little has been done further to ascertain whether there is any correspondence in the order of awakening powers in normal and defective children. That Montessori apparatus is now little used with normal children is not an indication of her failure to understand infantile capabilities, but rather a proof of her success in starting teachers off on fruitful lines of experiment. Her ideas were not those of a medico dabbling in education, for as a mature woman in her late twenties she embarked upon a seven years' university course in experimental psychology and anthropological pedagogy, thus gaining the qualifications which earned her the post of organiser of infant schools in Rome. Aporti's example on behalf of the alleviation of poverty through education, had not been forgotten, but Italy had not achieved stability enough to embark on State social and educational projects, so that Montessori's opportunity came through the philanthropy of a private citizen, Edwardo Talamo. From 1906 onwards the Casa dei Bambini were developed, and the reputation of their organiser was so enhanced in the process, that she was soon recognised as the leader of a movement becoming so widespread in the last four decades as to gain a permanent place in educational history. The Montessorians, under the constant guidance and inspiration of their leader, have evolved a somewhat rigid methodology which has yet to stand the test of time. They have developed these methods at both the primary and the secondary stage, but outside their own schools the whole realm of infant and junior education has felt the impact of Montessori's ideas.

Montessori was a Catholic, a democrat, and a scientist. Into this pattern it is not difficult to integrate her philosophy, her psychology, and her methodology. As a Catholic she could be neither pragmatist nor naturalist. As a democrat she upheld individual liberty and sought to foster the full and free development of children. As a scientist she aimed to educate through realities—by providing concrete material and by organising learning situations for pupils. For a time, many of her fellow Catholics looked askance at her departure from traditional practice, and especially at her postponement of orthodox religious teaching, but she demonstrated convincingly that her work was not opposed to Catholic principles. Rusk calls her philosophy "spiritual realism",[1] a term which indicates that her

[1] R. R. Rusk, *A History of Infant Education*, p. 88, U.L.P., 1933.

attention to the developmental needs of children, and her emphasis on practical experience in the real world, were not incompatible with her religious principles nor with her acceptance of the best standards of democratic discipline and individual self-control.

Like Dewey, Montessori contends that the main problem of the child is to adjust himself to his immediate environment, in which process the educator should play the part of guide and organiser. This principle is followed to-day in primary schools far more widely than earlier critics would have believed possible—it is the principle underlying the "activity methods" in which all young primary teachers in this country are now trained. Montessori stresses that the teacher's background function is not mere passivity but rather "anxious scientific curiosity . . . the teacher must understand and *feel* her position of *observer*".[1] The value of such observation by the teacher is acknowledged to-day, although opinion may vary as to the function of non-intervention, non-co-operation, and non-leadership. Montessori requires the careful organisation of the child's environment, the regulation of his liberty, and the provision of special material for his use, designed to give him practice in activities which might otherwise be encountered in the environment only fortuitously or irregularly. Through the regular, graded use of this didactic material, children are to gain skills of manipulation and judgment through the senses, physical and intellectual development thus being associated throughout. It was inevitable that during the years which followed, innumerable attractive sense-training toys should be devised, largely on the principles of the original apparatus, even as it was unavoidable that changes in fashion would obviate the need for much of it—the lacing and buttoning frames, for instance, but there is still some value and some fascination in the long and broad stairs, the weights in their sockets, and the little packets to be identified by sound or smell. Although the modern child may learn to manipulate buttons by dressing himself, and although some of his senses may be somewhat neglected, the attractions of his school life are due partly to the common sense of Montessori as well as to the wisdom of Froebel. Although the theoretical functions of the gifts and of the didactic apparatus may not be the same, their results, in application are not dissimilar.

The main characteristic of Froebelian practice not approved by Montessori—or by Dewey—is the use of fairy-tale, fable, and

---

[1] *Montessori Method*, p. 87.

fantasy for the stimulation of the child's imagination. All agree that the imagination of children is to be used and developed, but Montessori aims to achieve this through realities because "the imagination of modern men is based upon the positive researches of science".[1] Yet her philosophy will not allow her to deny that in art, music, poetry, and also in morality and religion "there is a creative work which lifts man up from earth and transports him to a higher world which every soul may attain within its individual limits".[2] The Froebelian kindergartner is a teller of stories, as well as a group leader and organiser of short-period activities. The Montessorian directress is an observer of individuals who select their own activities and decide for themselves when to change. Thus the Montessori school needs much more apparatus than the Froebelian. For instance, the latter give physical training through group work, the former through specially designed apparatus such as the climbing frame now found in many nursery schools.

Montessori's methods allow of development at an individual rate, free of the stress of rivalry and from the false incentives of rewards and punishments. They involve learning through interested activity and are thus in line with the methods evolved by psychologists—although Montessori herself was sceptical of the value of much contemporary work in the field of psychology. Finally, they do not ignore the social factor in education. The "Children's Houses" are communities which require their members to conform to standards of cleanliness and behaviour necessary for the comfort and welfare of the group. Pupils are responsible for the tidiness of the classroom and for helping with the laying of tables for meals. There is no interference with natural tendencies to group together in some activities, nor any prohibition of the guidance of one child by another. Montessori indicates that she is not unmindful of the child's social needs and of the task of improving society, when she writes : "The discipline to which the child habituates himself here is, in its character, not limited to the school environment but extends to society".[3] It is significant that Montessori's doctrine of free development was interpreted as a threat to authoritarian government. In 1935 the German Montessori Society was dissolved by the political police, and in 1936 all official Montessori schemes in Italy were abolished by decree.

[1] *Advanced Montessori Method*, trans. by F. Simmonds, p. 241, Heinemann, 1917.
[2] *ibid.*, p. 245.   [3] *Montessori Method*, p. 87.

That two dictators of large countries should be afraid of an elderly lady and her teaching of small children surely indicates that her individualism seemed likely to lead to more intelligent group cohesion. Although she was to suffer a long exile from her country in her old age she had the spirit to give personal direction to her disciples in countries as far apart as America, India, the Netherlands, and Britain.

Other European Experiments

During the infancy of Dewey and Montessori there took place two educational experiments which have rather more significance for teachers to-day than have other schemes of the period. One was but short lived; the other developed into a system of teaching and teacher-training. The brief experiment was initiated by Count Leo **Tolstoy** (1828-1910), the great Russian writer, when, after studying educational methods in Germany, Switzerland, France, and England, he took over the elementary school of his native village of Yasnâya Polŷana in 1861. This gesture, in fact, marked his rejection of current teaching practices which had become stereotyped and lifeless even though originally inspired by great teachers. The "object lesson", for instance, won his scorn, but he was equally impatient of any method which involved the maintenance of attention by discipline imposed from above. He ran his school on principles of freedom such as few others have dared to put into practice. Pupils could attend or stay away, learn or not learn, as it pleased them. He demanded no book learning, no empty repetition of barren facts. He despised the question-and-answer method, but although he emphasised experience as the basic need in education he did not deny the value of oral communication between teacher and pupil. Believing as he did that a teacher should be one who knows his subject and "communicates it in a spirit of love", he gave an important place to teaching by "infection" not only in intellectual matters but also in emotional and moral education.

Another of his methods might be called "teaching by incitement", the fostering of discussion among youngsters in real situations. Tolstoy was ahead of Dewey in his recognition of the importance to the child of the world outside school, but he was less concerned with bringing the outside world into the classroom than with capturing in school the same spirit of wonder and enterprise that youngsters show in their play-time explorations. Given this, children would learn naturally and through free choice, all that was necessary for the harmonius development of each individual. Although the experiment, with a school of forty children between seven and thirteen, lasted only about two years, there were two important results, first, that many more schools were established in Russia, ostensibly on similar lines, and second, that Tolstoy himself, in a true spirit of research, continued to study the fruits of his experience and to record his findings and opinions. On the whole, although he decided that there ought to be a fixed curriculum, he modified his views very little. He made no claim to have reached any final conclusions, but he had proved to his own satisfaction that his principles were workable. As he pointed out, the same could not be said of most other educational writers. Michael Sadler is said to have prophesied early this century that English schools of the future would resemble Tolstoy's. As yet, in spite of the wide acceptance of principles of freedom, only a few experimenters have dared to emulate him.

The second experiment mentioned above is that of **Uno Cygnaeus** (1810-1888), a Finnish disciple of Froebel. In brief, his "new" contribution to educational ideas was the introduction of domestic manual work as educative experience. Under its Scandinavian name, "Sloyd", the scheme spread not only through Europe, but also to America. This was accomplished mainly by the establishment of summer schools for foreign teachers at Otto Salomon's Training School in Sweden in 1875, by which time Sloyd had already been a compulsory school activity in Finland for eleven years. Sloyd is mainly concerned with woodwork and its various skilled crafts. Pupils make only things that are useful, but it is equally important that the process of making shall have value in training both body and mind. It is expected that the pupil will come to enjoy working with his hands and to appreciate and respect the skills necessary in manual work. He will become independent, self reliant, clean and orderly, capable of judgment by eye and touch, dexterous with tools, persevering, and painstaking. The original Sloyd scheme required the boy to make a certain number of models without a pattern, and it provided that whenever possible he should experience the fashioning of an article from the basic raw material—the log itself. Perhaps the most significant stimulus to effort was that the things made were to be used in the homes of the young craftsmen.

Although certain educational thinkers of earlier days had implied that such activities might have a part to play in education, there had never been this kind of expression of faith in the cultural value of craft. Here was a new theory of elementary education, proven by practice and eminently acceptable to those educators lacking confidence equally in traditional methods and in untried theories.

There was much misinterpretation of its principles, for in practice it was often found more possible to introduce it as an addition to the curriculum than to accept it as a basis for the whole work of the school. Moreover, many teachers refused to require their pupils to finish each article perfectly lest frustration should cause apathy and lack of self-confidence. Nevertheless, the cult of Sloyd before the modern machine age was significant in educational history.

During the three decades before the First World War, many other educators formulated opinions and conclusions on fundamental needs in education, some on a basis of general theory or observation, others through analysis following experiment. One type of contribution was that made by Francesco Ferrer, a Spanish teacher, who set a worthy example in his backward country by erecting a fine new school in Barcelona in 1901—spending on it a legacy received from a former pupil—and later by helping and advising in the setting up of other schools. His school was co-educational, the curriculum broad, the conditions pleasant and healthy, and he gave much attention to physical as well as moral development. He displayed a mental kinship with Dewey in his exclusion of direct religious teaching; both men saw religion as a hampering, restricting, confining influence in human development. In spite of Catholic doubts, his work and its results made Spaniards, especially in Catalonia, so conscious of the near-illiteracy of their country, that many more schools were set up within a few years.

Dr Ernest Meumann made a different kind of contribution to education. In many ways his work is comparable to that of Dewey, his senior by three years, but as the German thinker died in the early days of the War of 1914-18, his valuable work has been somewhat overlooked. He was a professor of philosophy who had been drawn to pedagogy during his early lecturing days at Zurich, and who gave a great deal of time and thought to the study of children's ways of learning. The titles of his main books on educational topics[1] suggest that he was moving in the same direction as Dewey. He saw the field of education as unexplored territory which could not be mapped on a basis of theory and general principles. It could only become known through a practical, experimental science of pedagogy, a science which needed not only research and systematisation, but also the increased prestige which would be ensured by the creation of university chairs in education. Meumann's own experiments were often faulty in scientific and statistical method, but few pioneers achieve perfection. More valuable was his example in collecting accounts and results of experimental work and indicating, by discussion and criticism, possibilities for future research. In the face of some opposition from psychologists he showed that their new science could be the tool of the educational research worker. His own views on co-education, on sex education, and on aesthetic and ethical education are by no means outmoded to-day.

A further contrast is the work of **Rudolf Steiner** (1861-1925), son of an Austrian railwayman and editor of Goethe's scientific works.[2] Turning to philosophy and later to the development of a new cult, "Anthroposophy", he made his impact on education through the work of teacher disciples in several countries of Western Europe and in the U.S.A. His English campaign in 1923 included a course of lectures on education at Ilkley, Margaret McMillan opening the course with a lecture on "Education through Imagination". Later, Steiner went to see her work at Deptford—a visit which may partly account for the existence of nursery classes in almost all Rudolf Steiner schools.

Steiner's revolt against the materialistic outlook on life and education is reflected in the Ilkley lectures and in a small book, *The Education of the Child in the Light of Anthroposophy*.[3] The child's development from infancy to adult life is conceived as a movement comprising three seven-year cycles. The first extends to the seventh year and is characterised by imitation and expression in active movement. Steiner considered that it is a fundamental error to introduce the learning of the three R's at this stage. The

---

[1] 1902, *Genesis of the Earliest Word-Meanings of the Child*; 1903, *The Psychology of Learning*; 1903, *The Child's Speech*; 1904, *Home and School Work, Experiments on Children of the Primary School*; 1911, *Lectures on the Introduction to Experimental Pedagogy*; 1911, *Introduction to Present-day Aesthetics*; 1913, *Intelligence and Will*; 1914, *Outlines of Experimental Pedagogy*.

[2] The world headquarters of the movement, in Switzerland, is called the Goetheanum.

[3] Anthroposophical Publishing Co., 1909.

second stage, from seven to about fourteen, is marked by the development of the imagination and feelings, and when the basic knowledge and skills are acquired. During the last cycle more formal education, because of the pupil's maturing power of thought, becomes possible. Steiner characterises the cycles according to the powers which are predominant in the child's life as the phases of will, feeling, and thinking, respectively.

During the first two periods there is no specialisation in the school and children are grouped into classes according to age and on the basis of intellectual ability. The child's great need is security, and this is achieved through a permanent class-teacher who can establish the right relations with the pupils. The need for specialised teachers appears in the last phase, and in the upper classes pupils are entered for external examinations necessary for university or professional requirements. Apart from this, Steiner regarded examinations as being of no educational value and thus internal examinations find no place in the secondary schools. There is no head of the school in the accepted sense. It is supervised by a committee or college of the teachers which works under the leadership of a chairman and to which individual members of staff are responsible.

The Steiner schools, increasing in number since the last war, are of all types—nursery, infant, primary, and secondary schools, special schools for physically and mentally handicapped pupils and for maladjusted children who need special care, adult training centres, and colleges for adult education. At all stages, much attention is given to practical and artistic activities—painting, drawing, gardening, handwork, puppetry, eurythmics, and drama. It is claimed that the education provided at each stage is derived from the study of the child himself and his physical, mental, and spiritual development, so as to produce a harmonious and well-balanced personality.

An experimenter in the field of music teaching was **Emile Jacques-Dalcrose,** a Swiss professor of harmony born in 1865. Dalcrose evolved a system of rhythmic movement which he claimed would enable participants to express themselves creatively. Appreciation of music is gained through movement, and confidence to invent rhythms and melodies is developed. "All children feel a craving to create," he writes, "and the teacher should lose no opportunity of turning this disposition to account. He should set them, from their earliest lessons, to improvise short phrases . . . or to replace a bar of melody by one of their own composition. He will find them revel in such exercises and make rapid progress in improvising".[1] This individual experience of interpreting personal feelings is even more satisfying when related to the movement of others "to group, magnify, and give style to the emotions inspired by music and poetry".[2] Dalcrose submits that the enjoyment of such "eurythmics" would "contribute to the raising of the instincts of the race and the permeation of the altruistic qualities necessary for the establishment of a healthy social order".[3] Such a sweeping contention indicates that eurythmics should not be regarded merely as dancing or physical exercises. The purpose of the Dalcrose system is to develop and exercise human intuition, even as other studies and activities train the intellect. In learning to appreciate rhythm the pupil will gain a sense of continuity and relatedness essential to his full development as a human being. "To contrive by means of a special training", writes Dalcrose, " to enable the child to sense distinctly the nature of its instinctive corporal rhythms, is to render him capable of sensing life itself in a more freely emotive spirit".[4] The Dalcrose Method was widely accepted in this country, and during the period between the world wars classes for teachers were held in most large towns and eurythmics gained a place in the curriculum of many elementary schools, particularly infant and primary schools.

British Pioneers and Experiments

In late-Victorian Britain the study of education was considerably raised in status by the work of such eminent scholars as Joseph Payne, Professor E. A. Sonnenschein, Professor J. M. D. Meiklejohn, and Sir Joshua Fitch. Moreover, the early development of the new science of psychology was closely associated with teacher education in the work of men like Dr James Ward of Cambridge, Dr Alexander Bain in Scotland, and Professor James Sully in London. It is interesting that Sully, a leading psychologist, was appointed lecturer on the theory of education at Maria Grey Training College in 1879.

In view of later developments in educational theory and psychology, Dr Ward's views are of particular interest, for he was

[1] *Rhythm, Music and Education*, 1921, p. 44.
[2] *ibid.*, p. 219.
[3] *ibid.*, p. 220.
[4] *ibid.*, p. 243.

one of the first to reject faculty psychology. He stressed the theory of "attention", the processes of conscious life springing from "a subject attending to objects and feeling pleasure and pain in so doing". This might be regarded as a step from Herbart towards Dewey, a view which is supported by Dr Ward's insistence on the need for freedom of choice for the growing youngster. In his lectures on education in the 1880's, he emphasised that moral development is more important than intellect training. He would achieve this by presenting opportunities for experience within a framework of regulated freedom. The pupil would gain self-control, initiative, and perseverance by choosing his own activity and devoting his attention to it. The power of Ward's ideas lay not in the written word but in the inspiration they afforded to practising teachers and to budding psychologists, two of whom were later to achieve distinction as Professor G. F. Stout and Professor W. McDougall.

The work of such men contributed in no small measure to the consolidation of a new educational theory in the twentieth century. In spite of wide divergencies of opinion, modern ideas on education have in common a number of broad fundamental principles which have never before operated with such power and persistence. The findings of psychology on many major issues—such as the significance of "maturation", "motivation", and other factors—are accepted by all thinkers; the place of education in human polity—civic, national, and international—is acknowledged by all thinkers; the indications of educational practice—both long-term experience and short-term experiment—are taken into account by all thinkers; knowledge of results and problems of education in many parts of the world is available to all thinkers. Consequently, it is not surprising that the tendency has been to venture further than ever before into "narrow but deep" educational investigations and experiments.

The specialist educator has always existed, no doubt, even before Bulwer's contribution to the education of the deaf and dumb in seventeenth-century England. From the nineteenth century—starting, perhaps, with the training of the "idiot boy" by Itard and Seguin in Switzerland—there has been a great extension of experimental work in specialised branches of education and re-education. Thus, although the main achievement of the McMillan sisters was to convince England that it must free its children from dirt, disease, malnutrition, and fatigue before any educational process could succeed, much of their practical work was, in fact, experimental education.

Margaret McMillan (1860-1931), born in New York and educated in the Scottish Highlands, later claimed that her schooling at an establishment for young ladies made her a rebel and a reformer. Although family resources permitted her to "finish" in Germany and Switzerland, she knew she had her living to earn, and she worked as a governess for several years. Her destiny, however, lay in social work, to which she was irresistibly attracted by her experience of life in a Bloomsbury hostel. Both sisters were already deeply interested in the new movement of Socialism and had read widely in both philosophy and social theory, from Plato to Marx, from Carlyle to Kingsley, Spencer, Ruskin, and William Morris. From 1888 to 1893, Margaret led a curious dual existence, on the one hand exploring the East End of London, trying to teach music to factory girls, distributing Socialist leaflets to men on strike and attending meetings addressed by leading rebels, and on the other hand training for the stage under the patronage of a titled woman.

Although she went to Bradford in 1893 as a Socialist, not as an actress, her stage training was of immediate value, not only in winning her success as a speaker but also guiding her in campaigning for remedial medicine. She was shaken to the core by her first exploration of Bradford, and, having gained a place on the School Board within a year of her arrival, embarked on a crusade to improve the condition of school children. From the bathing of dirty, verminous, and diseased children, from the writing of pamphlets to advise mothers on hygiene, she advanced to a campaign for school medical inspection, school clinics, and school meals. By the time she left Bradford in 1902, the town had official school baths at one school, unofficial school medical inspection, "illegal" school medical treatment, school meals for poor children—by voluntary effort—and a population of parents and teachers better educated in the need for adequate ventilation and correct breathing habits. The foundation of school clinics and the abolition of half-time employment of eleven-year-olds were objectives she did not achieve for several years, but she started the battle in Bradford and continued it until the victory was won.

During the next fifteen years she worked with Rachel in South-East London on behalf of poor children. First they planned a health centre for preventive treatment rather than remedial.

Margaret's conviction that the scheme ought to be publicly and officially supported caused her to postpone the project when the L.C.C. refused to build a clinic with £5,000 offered by soap millionaire, Joseph Fels. It was not until a medical inspection clause in the Education Administrative Act of 1907 sanctioned the foundation of clinics by local authorities that the sisters opened, in 1908, the first clinc at Bow, followed by the more successful venture at Deptford in 1910. Here dental treatment was given, minor operations were performed, remedial breathing taught, and exercises to remedy spinal curvature given. Soon a night camp for girls was established—primitive in amenities, but highly successful in improving both health and cleanliness. Then, in a nearby churchyard, camp-beds for boys were set up, and when it was possible to move the boys' camp to a waste plot near the Clinic a daytime school was also started there and flourished for many years. The girls' night camp eventually became the birthplace of an open-air nursery school, which moved, in 1914, to a new site with specially designed shelters.[1] Rachel died in 1917, but Margaret continued the work they had pursued so doggedly, always with inadequate support of authority and only spasmodic help from patrons.

Margaret had the satisfaction of seeing her example copied after the Great War, and finally she achieved the establishment of the Rachel McMillan Training College, officially opened in 1930.

Margaret started to write quite early in her career, at first political articles, but later books and pamphlets dealing with the health, education, and welfare of children. In Bradford she wrote an election manifesto on the evils of bad school ventilation, an essay on training children to breathe correctly, and a pamphlet attacking the half-time system of child labour[2]—this last after leading an unsuccessful deputation to Premier Asquith. She was so disgusted by the refusal to raise the "half-time" age from eleven to twelve that she reviewed her studies of educational thinkers more in exasperation than appreciation. "Like Ruskin, Locke pre-supposes that a child will not have to pay the rent", she writes, "Froebel wrote of children who may live in gardens . . . When you have closed your Froebel you may open your Goethe—only be sure you will not find in either any mention of child labour in mills". Seguin was one of the few educators she really respected, because

---

[1] A brief account of the nursery school is given on pp. 333-5 of S. J. Curtis's *History of Education in Great Britain*, U.T.P., 1948.

[2] M. McMillan, *Child Labour and the Half-time System*, Clarion Pamphlet, 1896.

he, too, emphasised the physical needs of the poor neglected seedling. What did the others know of hungry children? Why should a State compel to attend school starving children who could not afford an enforced "expenditure of nervous energy and living tissue"? Margaret's attitude was firm throughout on the question of State responsibility. Once it had imposed schooling on all, it must accept responsibility for making all fit to learn. Even when the State accepted its duties towards children of school age it must go still further and care for the pre-school child. Margaret's experience taught her that irreparable damage could be done to children in the five years before schooling began.

Her first book, *Early Childhood*, published during the Bradford period, puts forward the theory that "all right training is physiological and has as its aim the evolution of the ethical man or woman". Margaret has a mental kinship with Tolstoy in her faith in the power of emotion in human development. She speaks of the wonder-provoking sense impressions of early childhood as "involuntary culture". Feeling is the foundation of all education, for even the process of reasoning is "going forward upborne by emotion". The free movement of children in play, itself dependent on feeling, is Nature's way of developing the young. Teachers should study these movements and encourage their repetition in school activities.

In a pamphlet, *The Ethical End in Education*, Margaret McMillan precedes Dewey in defining the function of "spontaneous attention" in the learning process. "The successful teacher", she writes, "is one who knows what the child spontaneously attends to and endeavours . . . to build up the power of the voluntary attention from the involuntary". She condemns the teaching method of her time as " a sin against the involuntary and the subconscious, a sin against the power of emotion as the sustainer of all vigorous mental and moral life". She regards spontaneous attention as "the only possible basis of any intellectual life". Such arguments are indicative of a wide study of contemporary psychological theory and research. For her ideas on the emotional factor she was indebted to T. A. Ribot, the French psychologist who worked on the psychology of the emotions and on "creative imagination".

So deep grew her interest in the whole question of educational theory in relation to psychology and sociology that soon after leaving Bradford she prepared a series of lectures which served as the foundation of her book *Education through the Imagination,* a curious mixture of vision and reality, of theory, and down-to-earth practice. She calls upon Tolstoy, Ruskin, Herbart, Froebel, Dewey, Stanley Hall, Matthew Arnold, and even Herbert Spencer, to support her arguments, and she makes reference to a score of writers, psychologists, and doctors in developing her theme. She describes imagination as "the creative power of the mind which gives life to *all* work", and in deploring its suppression by the factory system, she looks forward to a day when there will be needed workmen possessing not only skill but also "enterprise, insight, initiative, in a word, *imagination*". She contends it is time to take this faculty into account in elementary education—to apply the findings of modern psychology to teaching method and school curriculum. Starting from a doctrine of innate endowment, she proceeds to examine the development of perception and the exercise of emotion through contact with people and things. Imagination, "a tertiary formation", depends for its full development—as an expressive and creative faculty—on freedom for the primary sensations to gain practice in association and co-ordination. This is achieved mainly in play and in activities resembling play; if these are denied, children become dreamers, "the impotent members of the creative world".

Then follows an examination of those activities characteristic of play. Such activities, freely engaged in, give the child a wealth of impressions as the foundation of a vigorous imagination and an enterprising, independent personality. Margaret's contention is that "many a child passes through his school life using only a minimum of his powers and expressing only a fraction of his personality".[1] This she attributes partly to the lack of imagination and initiative in the teacher, resulting in routine instruction and too much supervision of any activities introduced to encourage "modern methods". Another reason, however, is that many children growing up in the modern world suffer physical and psychological disabilities which prevent them from enjoying to the full those developmental play experiences—movement, emotion, colour, music, poetry, dancing, drawing, craft work, and scientific investigation. Visual perception is blunted by short sight—and here, research statistics on myopia are brought in as evidence; hearing is often dimmed by bad atmosphere and faulty breathing habits—here statistics on types of mouth-breathers are given; memory is often faint, through malnutrition; emotion is rarely felt because play-things,

[1] M. McMillan, *Education Through the Imagination*, p. 11, Swan Sonnenschein, 1904.

beautiful things and loving people have not been known. The task of society, then, is to provide remedial and preventive medicine, psychological, and social welfare services. The task of the school is to surround children with these opportunities for physical and emotional experiences and so organise and arrange these opportunities that there is a progression of appreciation, a building up of the imagination—a task by no means incompatible with the development of the intellect.

Although Margaret bravely tackles the problem of training the imagination in the commercial school, and although she discusses the importance of science, it is clear that she regards art as the basis of adequate education through the imagination. Speech is important, because without it "there could be little development of the reasoning power" and no communication of thoughts. Art, however, is essential to the development of the emotional life and the communication of feelings. "The human imagination embodies itself first in the free forms of art", she concludes, "Through art the creative power is exercised and prepared for the world of realities. So that, having found materials, not impediments, it begins at last to manifest itself in other forms, in the inventiveness of the artisan, the tradesman, the moral reformer, and the thinker".[1]

Margaret McMillan's contribution to education is selected from among many others because it is unique in its emphasis on the duty of a democratic society and the importance of the *prevention* of injury (both physical and mental) to young, growing human beings. Although history records earlier schemes for instructing the poor, and earlier theories on the relationship of State and education, only Comenius and Pestalozzi had previously given a place to fresh air, adequate food, and abounding love as requisites for the encouragement of learning. Montessori devised methods in school to "guard that spiritual fire within man, to keep his real nature unspoiled and to set it free from the oppressive and degrading yoke of society".[2] Margaret McMillan set out to transform that degrading yoke into a protective fence, and in Victorian England the task of persuading society to accept this function was so prodigious that Margaret is often neglected as an educational thinker because the work of the school, as generally understood, appears to play a minor part in her theory.

[1] M. McMillan, *Education Through the Imagination*, p. 189, Swan Sonnenschein, 1904.
[2] *The Montessori Method*, M. Montessori, Heinemann, 1917, p. 377.

Her true concern for the whole function and process of education is revealed in a broadcast talk of 1927. After describing a Nursery School day with its adventure, its movement, its food and rest, its music, dancing, and talking, Margaret continued: "You may ask, why should we give all this to the children? Because this is nurture, and without it they can never really have education. For education must grow out of nurture as the flower from its root, since nurture is organic; it is the right building up of nerve structure and brain cell . . . Much of the money we spend on education is wasted because we have not laid any real foundation for our educational system . . The educational system should grow out of the Nursery School system, not out of a neglected infancy".

Homer Tyrrell Lane (1876-1925), American pilot of an English experiment in the re-education of delinquents, was born in New England of a working-class family. He ran away at fourteen from a strict Baptist home and gained hard experience in lumber camps before settling down as a grocery clerk and marrying at twenty-two. As soon as he became a father he grew so interested in education that he decided to become a teacher even though it was necessary to take a course of training. He studied at the Sloyd Training School in Boston, where he achieved marked success not only in manual work but also in psychology. His subsequent experience included teaching boys in evening classes, convicts in a prison, and children in ordinary schools, and by the time he became superintendent of a boys' home at the age of thirty, he had also acquired an extraordinarily thorough knowledge of young people and their activities. He had given much of his spare time to club leadership among gangster boys and to observation of children in playgrounds. Moreover, he had made a study of nursing and weaning problems by watching babies and small children in hospitals.

Lane's reputation was such that he was able to gain not only the Boys' Home headship but also agreement to his insistence that the Home be moved to the country. Thus his major work started in an old farmhouse, with sixty boys who worked the farm. A disastrous fire the following year served to show that the project had won recognition, for the Ford family subsidised the building of a new Home. The colony was then named "The Ford Republic", to recognise not only its debt to benefactors but also its development as a self-governing community. Lane's determined venture in self-government was so successful that he was often asked to speak about it to interested audiences. He met with no success, however, in his aim to divide the group of boys into "families". He hoped to establish them in cottages on the estate, but he could not gain official consent to such a radical change. His frustration was one of the main reasons for his visit to England in 1911. He lectured in this country and examined a project for a school in Dorset, but it was not until the end of the following year that he received a definite invitation to take charge of such a school. During the intervening period he worked as a labourer in his own country, rising to be director of a gang of navvies from whom he won record efficiency. His methods, which freed the men from the controls represented by foremen and systems of timekeeping, gave him renewed confidence in his basic principles, so that when he started "The Little Commonwealth" on a Dorset farm in 1912, he put them into practice in no half-hearted way. The venture was not a "crank" school, nor a private experiment, but a public institution, classed as a reformatory school. The farm was provided by George Montagu, later Lord Sandwich, a loyal supporter of Lane and a true benefactor of education. The "clientèle" was provided by Boards of Guardians and by magistrates, Lane often visiting the Courts and taking delinquent youngsters straight to the Commonwealth.

The story of the Commonwealth and its untimely demise is told with sympathy and insight by Miss Bazeley,[1] who recorded its message so that forty years afterwards a magnificent failure is seen in perspective as a sure justification of the ideals which motivated Homer Lane. While it is to be regretted that after the closing of the Commonwealth in 1918, Lane had no further opportunity for practical educative work—which was his chief interest —it would be wrong to assume that his efforts were in vain and his principles faulty. The Commonwealth might have become the greatest practical experiment in education of this century. Instead, its ideals are reflected in many present-day provisions for the restoration of self-esteem in the maladjusted child. The "new" type of approved schools and the "prisons without bars" are but two results of the wide acceptance of a considerable part of Lane's humane viewpoint. It is timely that the full implications of his educational theory be examined.

His methods in the Commonwealth were developed in the belief that the main cause of delinquency is the repression of the *élan*

---

[1] E. T. Bazeley, *Homer Lane and the Little Commonwealth*, Allen and Unwin, 1928.

vital, the denial of opportunity for the full outflowing of the individual's vital energy. The citizens of the Commonwealth governed themselves and assumed responsibility for the misdemeanours and failures of individual members. They grew to understand the economic and social functioning of a community by working for a living in the houses and on the farm. They were regenerated by freedom and social responsibility.

In a lecture given in 1918, Lane described the population of the Commonwealth—five adults, forty-two boys and girls between fourteen and nineteen, and nine young children, divided by choice and mutual agreement into three "families". It is doubtful whether any previous educational experiment and theory gave the same pre-eminence to freedom, for the only rules and laws were those made by the boys and girls. Adult authority did not exist except in teaching duties and in the supervision of labour. This was an educational experiment in which formal education figured only as a privilege, an amenity, which citizens sought voluntarily as the need or desire arose. Being beyond the school-leaving age, the citizens were concerned with making a living and managing the public and private affairs of their families. "There is no direct relationship between prosperity and morality", writes Lane, "What better field could there be for the cultivation and growth of a code that is based on the spontaneous virtues of adolescent human nature? . . . The moral standards of the citizen group, as measured by its attitude towards the individual delinquent, have always been wholesome and clear and definite. This is as true of those offences that do not cause any expense to the taxpayer as of those that do".[1]

Lane points to the beginning of self-government as one of the most interesting developments of the early days of the Commonwealth. Previously, the citizens knew no order but that of authority, and had to be encouraged to accept the freedom offered them. Therefore, Lane destroyed his own authority—and at the same time spoilt the fun of abusing it—by joining the gang and inciting the citizens to mischief. His principle was always to admire them as "stout-hearted ruffians". From that time the group used its newly-realised freedom constructively, holding in check the too-unruly elements and co-operating in the work of the community. A Citizens' Court and a form of parliamentary procedure evolved from a felt need for laws and rules.

[1] *Talks to Parents and Teachers*, Allen and Unwin, 1928, p. 190.

Some hints on Lane's wider educational theory are found in the earlier chapters of *Talks to Parents and Teachers*. Taking a viewpoint of child development which is closely related to Percy Nunn's, he aims to show how the "naughty" activities of infancy are developmental. "Mind, from its earliest development, has two different needs, to possess and to create, to have and to experiment, to repeat former pleasures and to do new things for the sake of doing them", he writes. "Mind is dynamic: it must go forwards, or, if it cannot, then backwards . . . to go backwards is to regress to earlier pleasures, to have the purpose fixed at a point which should have been passed and left . . . All punishment, all fear, forces the child into deeper forms of immorality than the one we try to cure".[1] He shows how factors in the mother-child relationship, in weaning, in dealing with sex and God, may cause this regression, and he suggests how the child may be stimulated to move forward, both intellectually and emotionally, by the presentation of wider sense experiences in graded order.

Early childhood he calls the Age of Imagination (surely Whitehead's Romance Stage) when, again, there is danger of checking right development. Lying of various kinds springs from frustration of the imagination. It may be in the first place only an expression of the imagination during a period when "unrealities are added on to fact". From seven to eleven is the Age of Self-Assertion which has its origin in "violent conflict between the social spirit and the individual".[2] The adult's defence against it is to withdraw prohibitions or to remember the weapon of contra-suggestion. The cause of over-aggressiveness should be sought. Cruelty may be due to some old weaning difficulty or past punishment, and every effort must be made to restore self-love and self-confidence, and, of course, to try to find more desirable outlets for energy. The avoidance of contradictions in granting free choice of action is essential, and free play in small groups of children of similar age will give scope for the working-out of individual difficulties in the course of the games, the quarrels, the arguments, and the dramatic improvisation.

If the youngster resolves satisfactorily his inner conflict between "the love of mother's apron strings and the love of adventure",[3] he will then pass through two phases—transition and adolescence—

[1] *Talks to Parents and Teachers*, p. 19.
[2] *ibid.*, p. 80.
[3] *ibid.*, p. 101.

until "The Age of Loyalty" is reached. From eleven to fourteen he changes from an unethical being to one of high ideals. It is a period when he submerges his own interests in those of his group. Then come puberty, the age when the child whose development has not been "in step with Nature" frequently emerges as a "delinquent". Lane suggests that the problems in dealing with adolescence are similar to those at the age of weaning, "how to draw off the physical desire to wider interests . . . it must be given fields of responsibility, service, and loyalty—group activities of one kind and another—which will develop it upon the spiritual side".[1] This is the time when freedom and self-government in a truly democratic setting are essentials. But "Freedom cannot be given. It is taken by the child". That is, the teacher cannot impose authority or enforce its acceptance. He can only identify himself with the group and cast off his authority.

Lane writes briefly, but with skill and sympathy, on the problems of conscience, on ideas of God, and on punishment. His faith in the goodness of the child shines through his writings as well as in his activities, but he makes it explicit in the following words: "Human nature is innately good; the unconscious processes are in no way immoral. Faults are not corrected by, but brought about by, suppression in childhood . . . The freer a child is, the more it will be considerate and social, the more its chief interests will be progressive, and the more its fundamental instincts . . . will have valuable social outlets".[2]

It is indeed difficult to decide who shall represent in this chapter the experimenters in private "monied class" education, but few will cavil at the choice of the Bedales venture as one which was not only daring in conception but also flexible in its development and fruitful in its findings as a research project. Founded in 1893, it became the first co-educational boarding-school in England to include the whole range of education from five to eighteen (and, eventually, two to eighteen) in the one school. J. H. Badley, its first Headmaster, writing thirty years after its opening, pointed out that the traditional boarding-school adhered to an out-of-date classical curriculum, an ill-balanced, unhealthy régime, and a barrack-like social atmosphere, whereas the new school aimed to avoid the "narrow absorption in factitious intellectual exercises and in games", and to offer "a complete and wholesome school

[1] *Talks to Parents and Teachers*, p. 107.
[2] *ibid.*, p. 130.

life". He continues: "If it accomplishes its aim, the new school, like that of Vittorino da Feltre in the fifteenth century, might well be called 'La Giocosa', as being a place full of active and joyous life". Moreover, he asserts, the principles of Froebel and Montessori, far from being out of place in the Public School, are of universal application.

Mr Badley wrote more fully on co-education in *Advance in Co-education*,[1] justifying the creation of a natural society in the school. It is clear that he accepted freely the idea of woman's emancipation and her future equality with man in many fields. Thus, his pupils were "accustomed to see authority dependent not on sex but on fitness". Nevertheless, the school society, like Dewey's, was refined, undesirable elements being excluded. Competition was an element Badley distrusted. In a report[2] on moral teaching in his school, he wrote: "We are not giving a moral basis to life if our whole school system is based upon competition". Morality he contends, like all other learning, is a matter of the right kind of experience. One kind of experience at Bedales is the living together, another is "real work" and its disciplines—useful work, not only woodwork and cooking, but also gardening, dairying, and the arts and crafts. There is also the experience of managing group affairs. "The first condition of morality is freedom", he writes, "and the problem of school government is how to allow the utmost freedom possible at each stage. We don't want too much cotton-wool in education".[3]

There must have been in Badley something of Ruskin, something of Tolstoy, something of Dewey. He loathed snobbery, and even as Ruskin led students forth with spades, so Badley led out his gently-bred boys to level playing-fields and clean earth-closets. He had faith that culture could be caught, and so brought to the school many brilliant visitors—Cecil Sharp set going folk-dancing, and Arnold Dolmetsch started an orchestra. He had a belief in the educational value of the fundamental processes of civilisation, and so his pupils took part in the home production of bread, butter, bacon, and honey; they could do wood and metal work and cooking, boys and girls alike; they were encouraged to share in the household chores, bed-making, boot-cleaning. Tolstoy, learning of this domestic work, voiced his warm approval.

[1] Sidgwick and Jackson.
[2] *Moral Instruction and Training in Schools. Report of an International Enquiry*, ed. M. E. Sadler, Longman, Green, 1909, p. 236.
[3] *ibid.*, p. 241.

There was still time left to include a curriculum similar to that of a modern grammar school, but there was constant experiment in new methods of teaching, and a "laboratory method" based on individual work was developed. The library was the only room where a silence rule was enforced, but in spite of the apparent absence of a set of school rules or clear-cut system of discipline, there was, in fact, a deliberate—though pragmatic—provision for the fostering of true discipline and self-control. In describing the working of the School Parliament, Mr Badley points out, "A heavy reckoning must be paid, both to nature and society, for disregarding their laws. It is for education to anticipate this discipline of life and to enforce its lessons by using more direct and speedier means".[1]

The above examples of special educational experiments would not be complete without mention of a different kind of specialist contribution—the development of theory on the function of special bodies of knowledge as instruments of education, and the expansion of research into methods of organising learning at different ages and stages. In some spheres, both theory and research are still largely undeveloped, but in others—geography, for instance —the older, general educational theory has been outstripped both in philosophical depth and in ascertained validity. The development of geography in this country has been due almost entirely to the deep intellectual insight and unflagging practical endeavour of James Fairgrieve. Born in the same year as Montessori, this Scots teacher of mathematics turned to geography in mid-career, and led the way, not only in the establishment of geography as a university study, but also in its reform as a school study particularly significant in relation to new philosophical ideas on the function of education in society. As a colleague of Sir Percy Nunn, at the University of London, his prestige was such that he gained the unique title of "Reader in Education with special reference to Geography". His example, in showing the function of specialist interpretation and investigation, might well be heeded and imitated.

Fairgrieve's theory of education is as strongly "child-centred" as that of Nunn, as firmly "universalist"[2] as that of Dewey, and as

[1] J. H. Badley, *Bedales: A Pioneer School*, Methuen, 1923, p. 153.

[2] The clumsy word is used, for want of a better, to indicate a very real educational viewpoint which is strong enough to-day to provoke challenge and opposition. As this chapter was being written, newspapers reported that the School Board of an American town had voted five to one for the withdrawal from use in its schools of a handbook on UNESCO, on the grounds that it weakened students' patriotism in favour of "one worldism".

insistent in cyclic progression as that of Whitehead. From his wide knowledge of contemporary educational ideas and practice, he has synthesised a doctrine of his own which postulates that willing effort in seeking answers to problems, through both individual and group experiences, and through the investigation of the environment both natural and cultural. For him, the subject approach is not one which erects "barriers", but one by which pupils may conveniently gain a point of view and an understanding of fundamentals and realities.[1] He believes the study of geography should help pupils "to imagine accurately conditions of the great world-stage" so that they will be equipped as citizens, to consider social and political problems with interest, intelligence, and personal concern. He acknowledges his own personal debt to fellow world-citizens for the necessities and amenities of his daily life—a "confession of faith", which carries with it a Deweyan confidence in the civilising power of human interrelations and cultural interpenetration.

In spite of its lengthy excursions into fields of theory, this chapter is intended as a tribute to the practical experimental teacher of modern times. Almost all educators mentioned above have been teachers of children by inclination, even though the pioneer spirit drove them to become organisers, supervisors, trainers, and writers. These are the makers of modern education and their conclusions will outlast the theories of thinkers who have not enjoyed the hurly-burly of school life with ordinary children. It only remains to acknowledge the work of many teachers who have stayed in schools and have continued to collect evidence on which, in the future, a sounder educational theory may rest. Caldwell Cook wrote his classic[2] on the teaching of English during the War of 1914-18, but followed it up with many years of inspired teaching. To-day only the idiom of boyhood needs revision. John Duncan put forward his modest, practical suggestion on the nature of "concrete intelligence"[3] only after years of experience in the education of mentally handicapped children. No modern history of educational ideas can be complete without reference to the continued efforts of many teachers of similar calibre.

[1] He was among the first to give reality to classroom jargon such as "Spinninan-weavin" by giving pupils direct experience of spindle and loom. See his *Geography in School*, U.L.P., 6th edition, 1949.
[2] *The Playway*, Heineman, 1917.
[3] *The Education of The Ordinary Child*, Nelson, 1942.

SUGGESTIONS FOR FURTHER READING

In addition to the works mentioned in the text and footnotes, the following books are recommended:

C. E. Culverwell, *Montessori Principles and Practice*, Bell, 1913.

W. H. Kilpatrick, *Montessori Examined*, Constable, 1915.

O. Salomon, *Theory of Educational Sloyd*, G. Philip, 1892.

H. Holman, *Séguin and his Physiological Method of Education*, Pitman, 1914.

M. McMillan, *The Nursery School*, Dent, 1919.

W. R. George, *The Junior Republic*, Appleton and Co., 1910.

J. H. Simpson, *Adventure in Education*, Sidgwick and Jackson, 1917.

A. S. Neill, *A Dominie in Doubt*, Jenkins, 1921.

C. Burt, *The Young Delinquent*, U.L.P., 1925.

S. Isaacs, *The Children We Teach*, U.L.P., 1946.

G. Crump, *Bedales Since the War*, Chapman and Hall, 1936.

CHAPTER XIX

SOME EDUCATIONAL WRITERS OF THE PRESENT CENTURY

It is probable that the number of books written in this century on different aspects of education is much greater than the total of preceding ages. A whole volume and not a short chapter would be necessary to deal at all adequately with the views presented by modern thinkers in regard to the aims of education, the curriculum, the nature of the educand, the aims of different types of school, the various teaching techniques, and many other relevant topics. The only possible solution of the difficulty has been to select a few representative thinkers and to outline very briefly the views they held. Immediately one is faced with the invidious tasks of both selecting the individual and assessing the value of the ideas for which he has been responsible. One is living too close to these writers to put their views in clear perspective and what one may at present consider a valuable contribution to educational theory may be thought much less important by a future generation. Nevertheless, it is necessary to take the plunge in order to illustrate some of the trends in modern educational thought. One simplification is possible; that is to exclude all consideration of living writers.

H. C. Barnard has drawn attention to the gap which exists between the educational literature of the mid-Victorian period and the group of present-century thinkers that this chapter proposes to consider.[1] From 1870 to 1902, English educational effort took a practical rather than a theoretical form. This can be readily explained. The main tasks during this period were to provide a sufficient number of school places for the child population and to secure that these were occupied. It was argued that more education was needed and education is a good thing, so why ask further questions? Hence the chief interest of these years lies in the provision of legislation dealing with either national education as a whole or some significant part of it. The State which intervened in 1870 to "fill the gaps" soon found itself forced to accept greater responsibilities and to extend its activities to types of education other than elementary. After 1902, this process was accelerated by

[1] *A Short History of English Education*, chapter 23, University of London Press, 1947.

521

the Act of that year which reached a point when the principle of State supervision of national education was no longer seriously challenged. It was inevitable, therefore, that discussion should arise about the ultimate aim of public education and the kind of techniques which were suitable to achieve the end.

There was another factor which influenced the situation. More schools meant more teachers and ideas had progressed to the extent that it was becoming desirable that the new entrants to the teaching profession should receive an adequate training in the two-year training colleges. As Professor Barnard points out, this affected the educational literature of the nineteenth century which now consisted mainly of books on teaching method and general school management. The aim was to teach the young student his job and after this immediate duty was fulfilled there was little opportunity for the consideration of the philosophy and psychology of education. At this time, the educational thought of Herbart was considered to be very appropriate. It was acknowledged that his ideas presented insuperable difficulties to beginners, but if one ignored his philosophical and ethical teaching, there still remained sufficient of his psychology which could be of value in the classroom. This was the age in which numerous stodgy manuals of school management were published which took up the weary refrain of "Avoid this but stick to the following rule". Such books "tended to overlook the philosophical and ethical implications of his (Herbart's) doctrine and to concentrate rather on deducing from them a psychological justification for a technique of teaching. They therefore stressed the correlation and concentration of studies, and, in particular, they formalised five (or four) 'steps', which formed a convenient frame for the setting-out of a lesson. A theoretical basis for these methods was found in the Herbartian doctrine of apperception; but its application tended to result in what was little better than a mechanical device".[1]

As the nineteenth century drew to its close, certain developments presaged a complete change of outlook. Modern psychology was beginning to cast aside its swaddling clothes and the infant science was already showing an interest in some of the major activities of life including education. The development of educational psychology is beyond the scope of this work, but one should not neglect the mention of the impact the new science had upon the theory and practice of education. By the beginning of this present century, many teachers had become acquainted with the works of

[1] H. C. Barnard, *op. cit.*, p. 360.

William James, if not in the more academic treatises, *The Principles of Psychology* and *The Textbook of Psychology*, at least in the more popular *Talks to Teachers*. This was a definite step forward from the arid and formal treatment of the English associationist school.

A more significant event was the publication in 1908 of William McDougall's *Introduction to Social Psychology*, a book which has passed through an incredible number of editions and which for more than a quarter of a century was the most widely studied textbook in English training colleges. Another stream of ideas emanating from the psycho-analysts, Freud, Jung, and Adler, was flowing into this country in the years immediately preceding the War of 1914-18. Yet another influence was the development of experimental psychology and, in particular, the theory and practice of mental testing which sprang from the first workable intelligence tests devised by Binet in 1908, and which later became associated with such names as Cyril Burt, Godfrey Thompson, F. J. Schonell, C. Spearman, and many others.

The accumulation of psychological data with regard to the nature and measurement of general and special abilities, the theory of mental discipline and transfer of training, the methods of selecting children for different types of school and the causes of backwardness and delinquency, was bound to have repercussions on educational philosophy.

Another important influence was a consequence of the establishment of day-training departments attached to the universities and university colleges, a step which had been recommended by the Cross Commission in 1888. Education was now studied at the university level with the result that many important contributions were made by the heads and staffs of the university education departments. In a brief survey it is quite impossible to deal with the large number of distinguished scholars and writers who were members of university training departments. The writer, therefore, has restricted consideration to three; Sir John Adams, Sir Percy Nunn, and Sir Fred Clarke.

Finally, without doubt, the most influential factor in shaping recent English educational philosophy has been the complete upheaval of the whole of our national life occasioned by two world wars. This is of such importance that it will be considered later in this chapter.

Sir John Adams was a brilliant teacher and lecturer, a prolific writer on educational subjects, and a distinguished scholar who exercised a decisive influence upon educational thought during the first quarter of the present century. His earliest important work was *The Herbartian Psychology applied to Education*, first published in 1897. This book struck a new note in educational literature. Previously most books on educational theory had been dull and wearisome reading even for the trained student. Adams's *Herbartian Psychology*, because of its author's sound common sense, his delightful humour, and his gift of simple, clear expression, is still a book that appeals to present-day students.

Adams realised that one of the chief weaknesses of English education was its neglect of psychology. He thought that the Herbartian psychology was, for that time, the most profitable for teachers, and his object was to enable them to grasp those ideas of Herbart which would have most bearing upon their work in school. His method was, therefore, to abstract all that was most valuable in Herbart's educational thought and to apply it to the problems of the English school. He felt that for many years the centre of interest had been the subjects of the curriculum and the techniques of teaching them. The pupil who was required to study these different branches of knowledge had been largely neglected. Adams wished to focus attention upon the pupil. Hence the famous paragraph which heralded the view he expressed later in his books, that education should be paido-centric.

"Verbs of teaching govern two accusatives, one of the person, another of the thing; as, *Magister Johannem Latinam docuit*—the master taught John Latin."

Thus for the Latin rudiments. When the master seeks to apply the principle in real life, he finds that he can manage his double accusative only by the possession of a double knowledge; he must know Latin; and he must know John. Not so long ago it was considered enough to know Latin.[1]

Adams wrote much on the practical side of school work: *Exposition and Illustration in Teaching*, 1909; *The New Teaching*, 1918, which consisted of a series of essays on the new outlook on the teaching of school subjects written by himself and a number of distinguished teachers; *Modern Developments in Educational Practice*, 1922; and *Errors in School*, 1927. In these books, Adams made no claim to originality of thought. His aim was to introduce new ideas in educational practice to English teachers. He was very successful in this and the improvement in the standards of teaching

[1] *The Herbartian Psychology applied to Education*, p. 16, D. C. Heath.

in this country during the first thirty years of the century was largely the effect of his stimulus.   His most important work was *The Evolution of Educational Theory*, 1912.   This book undertook the analysis of educational ideas both from the historical and philosophical aspects and is undoubtedly the most brilliant work of this kind so far produced.   Adams grouped educational thought under the categories of Humanism, Naturalism, Idealism, and Materialism. At this time, Dewey's ideas and the application of the Pragmatic philosophy were only just becoming known in England.   Hence, later writers on the same subject, such as R. R. Rusk and J. S. Ross, have adopted the classification used by Adams with the addition of Pragmatism.

Sir Percy Nunn, like Sir John Adams, was a brilliant, practical teacher.   He was specially interested in the teaching of mathematics and his *Teaching of Algebra* represented a new development.   His *Education: Its Data and First Principles* is probably the outstanding book of the period.   Although presented in the form of a textbook, it is really a most important philosophical treatise.   It was first published in 1920.   A revised edition was issued in 1930, and a third edition, revised and enlarged, was published in 1945 a few months after his death.   The views expressed in this treatise had a profound influence on the generation of teachers who entered the profession in the period between the two great wars.   They were also responsible for many of the recommendations of the Hadow Reports.

From one point of view, Nunn was an eclectic.   He made use of philosophical and psychological ideas gathered from other thinkers but his book is by no means a compilation.   His originality shows itself in the way in which he absorbed such ideas and wove them into the pattern of his own thought and used them to support his own philosophical doctrine.   McDougall, when he adopted the term "Hormic" to describe his particular psychological standpoint, attributed its origin to Nunn.   He wrote: "The view that all animal and human behaviour is purposive in however vague and lowly a degree, and that purposive action is fundamentally different from mechanical process, may be conveniently called the hormic theory . . . In adopting this word I am following the suggestion of Professor T. P. Nunn in his very excellent little book, *Education: Its Data and First Principles*".[1]

---

[1] *An Outline of Psychology*, p. 72, Methuen, 1923.

Nunn's book is so well known that no useful purpose would be accomplished, even if space were available, by an analysis of its contents. What is important is the philosophical doctrine which permeates it. The book was written during the concluding phases of the 1914-18 War and is one of the best expositions of the traditional English system of individual democracy. The central theme is quite clearly stated: "We shall stand throughout on the position that nothing good enters into the human world except in and through the free activities of individual men and women, and that educational practice must be shaped to accord with that truth".[1] Although after the publication of the second edition, Nunn's philosophical views were challenged, he was not affected by the criticisms and adhered to his original position. In the Preface to the third edition, he wrote: "The central thesis of the book remains unchanged: it maintains that the primary aim of all educational effort should be to help boys and girls to achieve the highest degree of individual development of which they are capable. A widespread acceptance of this idea is a striking and, it is to be hoped, a permanent by-product of the war years; but there is still some disposition to suspect that one who embraces it too heartily may be led to undervalue the just claims of public duty and social service".

Nunn had inherited the traditional belief in the freedom and responsibility of the individual, and when he was writing his book he saw in the claims of Imperial Germany a direct threat to this way of life. He realised that the philosophy of Hegel which regarded the State as a super-personal entity which should dominate the wills of individuals, and the later developments of Nietzsche (1844-1900), which led to the worship of successful force, were largely responsible for the German outlook. In the first edition of his book, Nunn wrote: "From the idealism of Hegel more than from any other source, the Prussian mind derived its fanatical belief in the absolute value of the State, its deadly doctrine that the State can admit no moral authority greater than its own, and the corollary that the educational system, from the primary school to the university, should be used as an instrument to engrain these notions into the soul of a whole people".[2]

Nunn was by no means an extreme individualist. He rejected the egoism of Hobbes and the narrow individualism of the Utilitarians. Hence he freely admitted the claims of society upon

[1] Third edition, p. 12, Edward Arnold, 1945.
[2] ibid., p. 3.

the individual. He writes: "It is sufficiently plain that a man becomes what he becomes mainly as the result of his reactions to his social environment—the influence upon him of intercourse with parents and brethren, of school-fellows and schoolmasters, companions and rivals, friends and enemies, employers and employees. It is, moreover, easy to recognise the deep influence which the 'social heritage'—the whole body of traditions and institutions of a people—has upon the growth and structure of the individual mind. To deny or to seek to minimize these patent facts would be to exhibit a strange blindness to reality".[1] Later, he adds, "This view does not deny or minimize the responsibilities of a man to his fellows; for the individual life can develop only in terms of its own nature, and that is social as truly as it is 'self-regarding'. Nor does it deny the value of tradition and discipline or exclude the influence of religion".[2]

If individuality is the ideal of life, it would follow that our educational efforts should be organised for its accomplishment. Nunn's treatise is really the unfolding of this cardinal principle with regard to the problems which face the educator. Some critics have placed him amongst the followers of Naturalism on the ground that he appeals to biology to show that the rule of nature is that all living creatures strive towards their own greater perfection. This constitutes a misunderstanding of his purpose. It is significant that in his opening chapter, he outlines a philosophy of life and applies it to enunciate an aim for the educative process. He follows this discussion by utilising the principles of biology to illustrate the truth of his deductions. In reality, he is an idealist. He regards perfect individuality as a goal which has not yet been realised in human experience but towards which it is the nature of every person to strive. In other words, because the moral aspect is always prominent in his thought, his ideal is that of self-realisation rather than self-expression.

The problem of the priority of the claims of the individual and those of society has been with man ever since he began to philosophise. Throughout the course of history, first the one and then the other alternative has predominated, and since the Reformation, the Western democratic communities have tended to stress the claims of the individual. Nunn has endeavoured to effect a compromise between the two extremes, but in striking his balance it has seemed

[1] Third edition, p. 11, Edward Arnold, 1945.
[2] *ibid.*, p. 12.

to some that he has leaned too far in the direction of individualism and has thereby neglected the claims of society. Thus, as early as 1922-3, Campagnac in *Society and Solitude* and Sir Fred Clarke in *The Politics of Education*, challenged Nunn's central thesis.

Meanwhile, in America, a similar movement of thought had been developing. Dewey had popularised the idea that the school is essentially an institution which aims at socialising the individual child. In *Democracy and Education* he wrote: "Since education is a social process and there are many kinds of societies, a criterion for educational criticism and construction implies a particular social ideal. The two points selected by which to measure the worth of a form of social life are the extent in which the interests of a group are shared by all its members, and the fullness and freedom with which it interacts with other groups . . . A society which makes provision for participation in its good of all its members on equal terms and which secures flexible readjustment of its institutions through interaction of the different forms of associated life is in so far democratic. Such a society must have a type of education which gives individuals a personal interest in social relationships and control, and the habits of mind which secure social changes without introducing disorder".[1]

Other American writers, especially those interested in economics and social philosophy, stressed the social implications of education and developed a new field of study which passed under the name of educational sociology, or the sociology of education. It was not long before a similar tendency developed in this country. So far the new science is in the stage where data is being collected and tentative hypotheses are being suggested. At first sight, the sociology of education appears as a mixture of facts gathered from history, geography, social psychology, economics, anthropology, and other sources. This should not prejudice one to its future. In its present state it is in the position that geography found itself at the beginning of the century.

The impacts of the war which broke out in 1939 are far too numerous to mention in detail. A few may be selected on account of their bearing on educational ideas. At the beginning of the war the immediate need was to emphasise the British way of life as a counterblast to the doctrines of Nazism and Facism. The vital concern was to win the war, and quite early it was realised that the maintenance of national morale was equally important with the

[1] *op. cit.*, p. 115, Macmillan, 1916.

provision of fighting forces and armaments.   Our enemies knew exactly what they were fighting for, but in the mind of the average Englishman, the statement that we had been forced into the conflict in the defence of freedom and democracy was too vague and shadowy to arouse any adequate measure of enthusiasm.   Hence it was imperative to make clear to soldier and civilian alike the essentials which were at stake and to furnish them with a reasoned faith which would fortify them against the insidious propaganda put out by the Germans.   This was the idea behind the A.B.C.A. pamphlets issued to instructors in H.M. Forces and the broadcasts to different types of school.

Many developments had to be postponed on account of the war and, in particular, the provision of the Education Act of 1936 which, with certain qualifications, raised the school-leaving age to fifteen, became inoperative.   As usual, frustrated action gave rise to active thinking, and discussion soon revealed the desire for changes of a much wider nature, in fact, a complete overhaul of the English educational system.   Ideas about reconstruction were being discussed at every level of society, and one of the first legislative acts was to present to Parliament the proposals which became law through the Education Act of 1944.   Probably at no time in our history had educational issues awakened so much public interest, but the burning question was about the nature of the educational change.   The idea of planning to win the war was quite familiar. Ought not a similar planning to win the peace to be considered? One of the most enthusiastic planners was Karl Mannheim, who undertook to show how post-war society could be planned but at the same time, as much as possible of the freedom of the individual could be preserved.   The democratic planning of education was, in his view, an essential part of the social and economic planning that he advocated.   It is unfortunate that this theory like the issue between the multilateral school and the tripartite system of secondary education has become bound up with the fundamental views of opposing political parties.[1]

From the practical standpoint, the very fact that the planners have stressed that their planning is for freedom is a confession that

[1] The writer has long held the view that certain things, education being one, ought to be outside the control of the political parties.   If it be objected that this is not possible, one can point to the B.B.C. as an example of a public corporation which is responsible to Parliament but which is non-political.   Can we not work out a scheme on similar lines whereby the Minister of Education holds office for a stated period irrespective of the political party in power?

they fear that it could result in a bureaucratic interference with the private life of the individual. For a moment, the writer feels impelled to leave the position of impartiality which he has endeavoured to preserve up to this point and to state quite categorically that he feels strongly that a planned society is an idea which raises all kinds of dangers, and before he would agree with any extension of planning, he would require to be satisfied that it is really necessary in the interests of the nation at large. Mannheim anticipated the kinds of criticism that were likely to be directed against his theory of a planned society. In reply to the query about who should plan those who are to do the planning, he says: "The planners can recruit themselves only from already existing groups. Everything will, therefore, depend on which of those groups with their existing outlooks will produce the energy, the decisiveness, and the capacity to master the vast social machinery of modern life. Is it to be those human groups in which traces of primitiveness—the 'old Adam'—operate without restraint or those which have, through gradual education, developed their rational and moral capacities so far that they can act, not only for a limited group, but also for the whole of society, and bear the responsibility for it? It is true that such groups are only small minorities to-day. But this conflict, too, like all the conflicts of history, will be decided by a small minority, for the masses always take the form which the creative minorities controlling societies choose to give them".[1]

Putting aside the emotional tinge attached to certain phrases in the above passage, its meaning seems quite clear. The planning will be carried out by a minority, evidently a group which considers itself the cultured élite, the people whom Aristotle described as not only being able to recognise the right principles but who have progressed to the stage at which they can develop their own principles of action. The assumption is that planning is inevitable. No doubt there are aspects of our national life which would benefit from a more close supervision. The behaviour of certain road-users is an example where selfishness has reached the point that some members of the community seem to be able to threaten the life and security of others. Planning in particular cases may be necessary but a policy of planning in the abstract may lead direct to the totalitarian state as exemplified by Russia.

Intensive and extensive planning may be the only way in which it is possible to win a modern war, but nearly everybody in this

[1] *Man and Society*, pp. 74-5, Kegan, Paul, Trench, Trubner, 1940.

country will be relieved when the restrictions of the war period are finally abolished. The idea of planning in the abstract seems akin to the saying that the man from Whitehall knows what is best for you. The average British citizen wants to live his own life. He is open to be convinced about the kind of life it is best for him to live, but whether he earns his living in an office, a shop, or a factory, he claims, within reason, the right to try out his own ways of life and is willing to abide by his own mistakes.

Mannheim believed that a planned society depends upon a transformation of man and that education is the chief means of bringing this about. In a series of essays entitled, *Diagnosis of Our Time*, 1943, he devoted considerable space to the consideration of educational problems. He pleaded for sociological integration in education and contrasted his views with those like Nunn who emphasised the self-realisation of the individual as the supreme aim of education. He asserted: "In its theory, liberal education insisted upon the statement that the basic values and the aims of education were eternal, and the final and exclusive purpose of education was the fostering of the free development of personality through the unhampered unfolding of innate qualities. The integral theory of education, in its sociological aspects, does not object to that theory as such . . . What it objects to is that this theory is too aloof from history to be really helpful in concrete situations. Whoever tries to state such eternal values very soon realises that they are bound to be too abstract to lend concrete shape to education at a given moment. In the same way, if the final core of the self is something that is eternal and beyond environmental influence, we still have to consider that more empirical and historical attire in which we meet our fellow-beings as citizens of a given state, as workers in factories, as clerks in an office, as human beings striving for such satisfactions as are available in a given social order".[1]

It is because the writer believes in eternal values and is convinced that the Christian religion has shown the way to bring them down to the concrete situations of everyday life, that he disagrees entirely with Mannheim, and wholeheartedly supports the views of Sir Percy Nunn.

Sir Fred Clarke accepted a point of view that on the surface seems similar to the teaching of Mannheim. In *Education and Social Change*, 1940, he declared that "we propose to accept unreservedly what may be called the sociological standpoint and to

[1] *Diagnosis of Our Time*, pp. 56-7, Kegan, Paul, Trench, Trubner, 1943.

exhibit as well as we can its concrete application to the field of English education". Clarke brought to the discussion of educational problems a very thorough knowledge of the historical development of education in England, and an experience of educational institutions in the Dominions gained while he occupied the Chairs of education at Cape Town and at McGill University, Montreal. He was also a very devoted member of the Church of England. Hence all his writing on the subject of education is permeated by a strong religious conviction. Clarke was no revolutionist. He possessed too living a sense of the history of the English people to be inclined that way. Hence, *Education and Social Change* begins with a shrewd analysis of the historical determinants of English education and passes on to an equally able examination of the situation in this country in 1940. Like most people, Clarke knew that change was inevitable but he wished it to be an evolution of the past. He believed that English institutions including the educational system were sufficiently flexible to be adapted to the new conditions. This belief led him to examine the past and the present to discover the degree to which the existing social order could be modified to meet "the demands of a regime consciously planned and directed towards the guaranteeing of freedom for diversity of personality in a social order much more thoroughly collectivist in its working than any of which we have yet had experience".

Though he was opposed to the central theme of Nunn, Clarke had a warm regard for the ancient culture of the English people and valued greatly the English traditions and folklore. This furnishes the reason why he so constantly deplored the banishment of our ancient popular culture from the schools in favour of useful knowledge and skills and why he stated that "the mass of the English people have never yet evolved genuine schools of their own. Schools have always been provided for them from above, in a form and with a content of studies that suited the ruling interests".[1]

In considering the lines of readaptation, Clarke asserted that it is the habit "of thinking about education in terms of class which has made our educational categories and terminology the chaotic thing they are".[2] He advocates the unification of the system over the whole range, but he is at pains to emphasise that this should be subject to "the freedom of individual schools to use and develop their resources in accordance with their own expert judgment of the

[1] *Education and Social Change*, p. 30, Sheldon Press, 1940.
[2] *ibid.*, p. 48.

needs to be met, and the freedom of parents within reasonable limits to select the schools to which they will send their children".[1] There is no need to examine in detail the proposals for reconstruction he suggested for many of them were accepted in the Education Act of 1944, and when Mr R. A. Butler selected him as the first Chairman of the English Advisory Council established by the Act, it was a tribute to Clarke's knowledge of educational problems.

Clarke's last book, *Freedom in the Educative Society*, 1947, is a continuation of the theme of the earlier work. In the Preface he states: "This book is about freedom and the strains and demands that 'planning for freedom' in contemporary Britain must impose upon the agencies that educate, whether children or adults". The educative society and its functions was described by Plato in the *Republic* and the *Laws*. Sir Fred thinks that after a long exile it is once more in being. "We say 'returned' advisedly, since the idea has been in temporary abeyance only during the brief interlude of *laissez-faire* through which we have passed. Then we heard much more of the free development of the individual. What is novel is the idea of the free development of the individual as a practical possibility within the life of an organised industrial society."[2] He suggests that the urgent problem of the present is to apply the idea of the educative society in a form which will be compatible with individual freedom.

Perhaps the most important of Clarke's observations are those which relate to the idea of culture. He takes up the discussion at the point where Matthew Arnold had left it and stresses that culture is not an addition or a background but is the medium in which individual development takes place. He both accepts and enlarges Arnold's idea of culture. As a working definition he suggests that it is the adequate expression of what it feels like to human beings to live in a certain way. With the English school pupil in mind, he argues in terms with which Nunn would surely have agreed, that the development of the child's powers can only take place in terms of the common culture. "He has potentialities of speech, and these take the form, in England, of the English language. He can learn to reckon, and this he does in the decimal system until he comes to British coinage and weights and measures. At that point, it becomes a condition of his development that his mathematical powers should function amid a maze of queer deposits from

---

[1] *Education and Social Change*, p. 49, Sheldon Press, 1940.
[2] *Freedom in the Educative Society*, p. 15, University of London Press, 1947.

mercantile history from which he can hope to be partially emancipated when he comes to 'do science'. He has religious propensities, and these are 'developed' into the elements of Christianity rather than of Buddhism or Islam. The very table manners that he acquires with so much difficulty are those which are approved as proper by the society in which he is brought up. Politeness is a local technique as well as a universal virtue."[1] All this is very true and merely confirms what Nunn had to say in his chapter on *Routine and Ritual*. It seems that Clarke's role has been to make more explicit what Nunn had taken for granted.

Clarke has performed good service in calling attention to the relation between the culture of a given community and its basic vocations. In past ages there was a tendency to identify culture with the standards which obtained amongst the upper classes. One cannot deny that a great deal of the culture we now enjoy came from this source, if only for the reason that this minority, freed from the necessity of daily toil to earn a living, had time and opportunity to develop the refinements of life. In fact, there were two cultures; one typified by the court of Louis XIV or the elegant gentleman of eighteenth-century England, and that which belonged to the people which Clarke calls the old folk-culture of rural England.

One of the results of the Industrial Revolution was to make it difficult for the people to obtain any real culture. What little was accessible was allowed to reach them through the elementary school. Clarke is on sound ground when he contends that a living culture must be intrinsically related to vocation. In these days of mass production and machine minders, the connection is not so easy to find, and it is the duty of the educator to ensure that the "cultural lag", the failure of habits, ideas, institutions, and aptitudes to keep level with technological changes, is reduced to the minimum.

It is often assumed that human activities fall into two fairly well marked categories which are entitled work and leisure. The tendency has been to think of them as mutually opposed and this has received support from books and syllabuses which profess to deal with education for leisure. Clarke deplores the gulf set between the two types of activity. His criticism of the modern outlook is that work is regarded as something servile from which the individual escapes during certain hours of the day. Leisure is then conceived as something entirely divorced from work. His remedy lies in what has been called the Christian doctrine of work which takes its ideal

[1] *Freedom in the Educative Society*, pp. 34-5, University of London Press, 1947.

from God as a worker who found satisfaction with His work. Clarke asks that if the citizen is given the rights of full employment and social security, what are his duties, since every right carries with it a corresponding duty. "The answer surely is, 'To be responsible'. That responsibility he will discharge, first and foremost, by honest and faithful *work*. The primacy of work as a citizen duty is one good reason why, in education, we should correct the over-emphasis that has been placed upon leisure."[1] In theory, Clarke is right, but there are a number of practical problems which have to be settled before such a happy state of affairs becomes universal. The chief problem concerns those thousands of workers engaged on repetition processes whose activity is drudgery rather than work, and because they have never felt the satisfaction of having produced something themselves, they regard their work as merely a means of gaining a livelihood and feel that they only really live in their period of leisure. It is essential that practical ways of humanising and socialising this kind of work shall be found and one looks to education to assist in making this discovery.

To many readers of his book, Clarke's appendix, *Note on Original Sin*, may come as a surprise. As a Christian, Clarke had not only accepted the view that man is a free and responsible agent, but also that he is sinful. St Paul expressed the experience of every thoughtful person when he wrote: "The thing that I would, I do not. The thing that I would not, that I do". Speaking about the thought of Martin Buber, Clarke comments: "Buber, like Rousseau, is facing the task of showing that the exercise of formative influence is not only compatible with freedom, it is more, it is essential. If this can be shown, then discipline is vindicated as a central conception of the philosophy of education".[2] Discipline, not in the old and bad sense of repression, but in the meaning of setting right one's inner feelings and motives, is vital to education and is a corollary of the fact of original sin. Some time ago, the writer was discussing educational theory with Sir Fred Clarke who made the remark that all educational philosophies fell into two classes which could be typified by St Augustine and Rousseau, respectively. He added that the difference was that St Augustine believed in original sin and Rousseau did not.

Thinkers who were not members of the teaching profession or of university training departments have made some valuable

---

[1] *Freedom in the Educative Society*, p. 59, University of London Press, 1947.
[2] *ibid.*, p. 67.

contributions to educational theory. Amongst them are Bertrand Russell, Sir Richard Livingstone, and A. N. Whitehead. The latter raised a number of questions which are extremely pertinent at the present time. Whitehead's chief interest was in the intellectual aspects of education. Earlier reformers from Locke and Rousseau to Pestalozzi, recognising that teaching in the schools was losing touch with reality, thought that the fault consisted in the use of words which intervened between the pupil and the ideas and things which the words signified. Whitehead went a stage further and insisted that very often the ideas to which the words referred had lost all liveliness and value. Such ideas he characterised by the epithet "inert". Thus in his Preface to the series of essays entitled *The Aims of Education* he tells us: "The students are alive, and the purpose of education is to stimulate and guide their self-development. It follows as a corollary from this premiss, that the teachers also should be alive with living thoughts. The whole book is a protest against dead knowledge, that is to say, against inert ideas". In another of his books, he criticises modern education as being too academic in the worst sense of the term. He said: "At present our education combines a thorough study of a few abstractions, with a slighter study of a larger number of abstractions. We are too exclusively bookish in our scholastic routine. The general training should aim at eliciting our concrete apprehensions, and should satisfy the itch of youth to be doing something. There should be some analysis even here, but only just enough to illustrate the ways of thinking in diverse spheres. In the Garden of Eden, Adam saw the animals before he named them: in the traditional system, children named the animals before they saw them".[1]

Whitehead's position has some likenesses to that of the Mills. He was opposed to the idea that the accumulation of facts is power. The facts are only valuable when they function in a way in which they are of use. The ideal is to produce a student who has specialised in one subject but who has at the same time a more generalised knowledge which brings culture to him. He opens his discussion of the aims of education by saying: "Culture is activity of thought, and receptiveness to beauty and humane feeling. Scraps of information have nothing to do with it. A merely well-informed man is the most useless bore on God's earth. What we should aim at producing is men who possess both culture and expert knowledge in some special direction. Their expert knowledge will give

[1] *Science and the Modern World*, p. 247, C.U.P., 1927.

them the ground to start from, and their culture will lead them as deep as philosophy and as high as art".[1] He believed that any scheme of education must be judged by the extent to which it stimulates the child to think. Note that he is mainly, though not exclusively, concerned with the child in the stage of secondary education and with the student at the university. His warning to all teachers is: "In training a child to activity of thought, above all things we must beware of what I will call 'inert ideas'—that is to say, ideas that are merely received into the mind without being utilised, or tested, or thrown into fresh combinations".[2]

Whitehead's advice to teachers is first not to teach too many subjects and, secondly, to teach thoroughly whatever you have decided the pupils ought to learn. What is important is not so much the number of ideas to which the child is introduced, but the number of combinations into which those ideas are thrown. Whatever ideas the child receives it is essential that he should make them his own and should realise how they apply to the situations of his own life. He writes: "From the very beginning of his education, the child should experience the joy of discovery. The discovery which he has to make, is that general ideas give an understanding of that stream of events which pours through his life, which is his life . . . Pedants sneer at an education which is useful. But if education is not useful, what is it? Is it a talent to be hidden away in a napkin? Of course, education should be useful, whatever your aim in life".[3]

So far, Whitehead's thought has close similarities to that of Dewey. Another likeness consists in his view of the past as a subject for the pupil. Dewey once wrote: "The past just as past is no longer our affair. If it were wholly gone and done with, there would be only one reasonable attitude towards it. Let the dead bury their dead. But knowledge of the past is the key to understanding the present".[4] Whitehead is no less emphatic. He says: "I would only remark that the understanding we want is an understanding of an insistent present. The only use of a knowledge of the past is to equip us for the present. No more deadly harm can be done to young minds than by depreciation of the present".[5]

Whitehead defines education as the acquisition of the art of the utilisation of knowledge. This is difficult to impart. He does not

[1] *The Aims of Education*, p. 1, Williams and Norgate, 1929.
[2] *ibid.*, pp. 1, 2.
[3] *ibid.*, p. 3.
[4] *Democracy and Education*, pp. 250-1, Macmillan, 1923.
[5] *The Aims of Education*, pp. 3-4.

believe in spoon-feeding pupils. "Whenever a textbook is written of real educational worth, you will be quite certain that some reviewer will say that it will be difficult to teach from it. If it were easy, the book ought to be burned: for it cannot be educational. In education, as elsewhere, the broad primrose path leads to a nasty place."[1] He regards the central problem of education to be that of preventing knowledge from degenerating into a mass of inert ideas. The remedy is easy to prescribe but difficult to follow. It means that every idea taught must find an important application within the curriculum of the pupil. The old idea that certain topics are to be taught because of their disciplinary value as sharpeners of the mind, must be discarded. This is one of the most dangerous doctrines ever introduced into education. "The mind is never passive; it is a perpetual activity, delicate, receptive, responsive to stimulus. You cannot postpone its life until you have sharpened it. Whatever interest attaches to your subject-matter must be evoked here and now; whatever powers you are strengthening in the pupil, must be exercised here and now; whatever possibilities of mental life your teaching should impart, must be exhibited here and now. There is the golden rule of education, and a very difficult rule to follow."[2]

Throughout the nineteenth century, educational thinkers had argued the relative merits of a classical and a scientific education, of a useful and a liberal education, and of a general and a technical training. Nineteenth-century thought culminated in the view expressed by Sadler in the memorable passage of the Bryce Commission's Report in which he said that no definition of technical instruction is possible which does not bring it under the head of secondary education, and that the latter cannot be defined so as to exclude absolutely the idea of technical instruction. Sir Robert Morant's view of the curriculum of the secondary school ignored the advice offered by Sadler, and when the new types of post-primary school and the continuation school developed after the First World War, the old argument reappeared in a modified form. The value of technical and vocational instruction was now beyond dispute but there still remained the problem about their relation to the humanities. That this problem was seriously considered is evidenced by the publication of the Board of Education pamphlet written by Dover Wilson and entitled, *Humanism in the Continuation School.*

[1] *The Aims of Education*, p. 7.
[2] *Ibid.*, p. 9.

Whitehead took up the discussion at this point. He agreed that the ideal condition would be that which was described in Shaw's *John Bull's Other Island*, namely a commonwealth in which work is play and play is life. Whitehead was convinced (and in this respect his thought approaches that of Sir Fred Clarke) "that work should be transfused with intellectual and moral vision and thereby turned into a joy, triumphing over its weariness and pain".[1] The nation's immediate need was a supply of skilled workmen and individuals with inventive genius and also employers who would be eager to accept and use new ideas. This state of affairs can only be brought about by workmen, scientists, and employers who enjoy their work.

His conclusion is that a technical or technological education ought to be conceived in a liberal spirit. If we take Plato and St Benedict as representing the two types in education, then the two ideals must be brought together. Apart, they only express an incomplete truth. In words almost parallel to those of Sadler, he declares: "The antithesis between a technical and a liberal education is fallacious. There can be no adequate technical education which is not liberal, and no liberal education which is not technical: that is, no education which does not impart both technique and intellectual vision. In simpler language, education should turn out the pupil with something he knows well and something he can do well . . . There are three main methods which are required in a national system of education, namely, the literary curriculum, the scientific curriculum, the technical curriculum. But each of these curricula should include the other two".[2]

During the last century there had been a considerable amount of discussion about the planning of the curriculum and the general principles which ought to form the basis of teaching method. Thus Herbart, starting from the doctrine of apperception, had enunciated his Formal Steps, and Spencer had formulated his maxims, one of which, namely, that of education of the child should accord both in mode and arrangement with the education of mankind, considered historically, was considerably developed by later educators. Pestalozzi and Froebel had drawn attention to the unfolding nature of the child and insisted that educational method should have regard to this fact. In the present century, Sir John Adams and others had stressed the idea of paido-centric education.

[1] *The Aims of Education*, p. 67.
[2] *ibid.*, pp. 74-5.

Whitehead put forward an idea which seems to do justice to the truth contained in all the theories mentioned above. He describes his principle as the Rhythm of Education and bases it upon the broad principle "that different subjects and modes of study should be undertaken by pupils at fitting times when they have reached the proper stage of mental development".[1]

He objected to certain widely accepted ideas, one of which was the belief that the progress of the pupil was at a steady uniform rate. This was assumed by the Revised Code which sought to prescribe the standards in reading, writing, and arithmetic which pupils should attain at different ages. It was also responsible for the common practice of assigning ages at which new studies should be introduced, *e.g.* French at ten, Latin at eleven years of age. Whitehead was impressed by the periodic nature of life: alternating periods of activity and rest, work and play as well as the seasonal periods which are marked by school terms and holidays. Life is rhythmic throughout and this rule must therefore apply to mental development. Many of the failures in education, he thought, were a consequence of the neglect of this truth. Hegel in his consideration of the development of thought had called attention to the three stages of Thesis, Antithesis, and Synthesis. These terms do not express exactly what is required by educational theory and Whitehead suggests in their place, Romance, Precision, and Generalisation. The general meaning of rhythmic is "the conveyance of difference within a framework of repetition".[2]

Younger pupils are in the stage where their contacts with reality stir their minds into a ferment which produces the emotional state of wonder. The child is caught by the romance, the novelty, the feeling of the riches of the unexplored world which the curriculum offers to him. Knowledge is not yet determined by systematic procedure. The motive force behind the child's intellectual activity is that of curiosity, the desire to ask questions, seek answers, and enjoy new experiences. About the age of thirteen with the beginning of adolescence, there comes a change. The pupil evinces a desire to learn facts and to master skills. It is the stage of the grammar of language and the grammar of science, but the factual stage of formulation and precision would have no meaning unless it had been preceded by the period of romance. The pupil neither desires nor has the power to generalise about facts. The fault of the traditional

---

[1] *The Aims of Education*, p. 24,
[2] *ibid.*, p. 27.

education was that this was the only stage of learning seriously considered by the schools.

With later adolescence comes a period of generalisation. In a sense, it represents a return to romance but with a vital difference. "Something definite is now known: aptitudes have been acquired; and general rules and laws are clearly apprehended both in their formulation and their detailed exemplification. The pupil now wants to use his new weapons. He is an effective individual, and it is effects that he wants to produce. He relapses into the discursive adventures of the romantic stage, with the advantage that his mind is now a disciplined regiment instead of a rabble. In this sense, education should begin in research and end in research."[1]

Whitehead makes some important provisos in regard to this theory. There is a danger of drawing too hard and fast a line between the stages. For instance, the experienced teacher will know how, during the stage of precision, he can keep alive the spirit of romance. He will also realise that in language studies the pupil will have reached the stage of precision, whilst in science he will still be in the period of romance. Moreover, the rhythmic principle which governs the pupil's progress as a whole, holds good in regard to the separate parts of it, whether in a lesson sequence or in relation to individual topics within the sequence.

Quite independently, Nunn developed a similar theory of periodicity.[2] He used the formula: "wonder-utility-system" but these terms do not differ greatly in meaning from those employed by Whitehead. Nunn illustrated the principle by reference both to the historical development of knowledge and to the psychology of school learning. For example, the early investigators of the phenomena of magnetism and electricity were stimulated by the characteristics of mystery and wonder; but as knowledge in this field grew, they became attracted by its practical application. The result was the discovery of the telegraph, telephone, the dynamo and electric motor, and the applications of magnetism and electricity to a multitude of other purposes. The final stage was the attempt to discover a comprehensive theory to provide an explanation of the whole series of electro-magnetic phenomena.

Nunn also claimed that a parallel rhythm could be observed in pupils' reactions to their studies. At first, the driving force is their

[1] *The Aims of Education*, pp. 57-8.
[2] *Education: Its Data and First Principles*, pp. 268-71, Edward Arnold, 1945.

interest in the strange and wonderful, but it is not long before the practical value of their studies makes its appeal. In later adolescence, there appears the quest for a comprehensive formula which will provide an explanation of all the varied phenomena they have studied. Nunn pointed out that the "project method" is well adapted to the utility stage in the pupil's development and that a premature presentation of systematic theory may account for the boredom of pupils when they are studying the subjects of the grammar school curriculum. Whitehead and Nunn have initiated a theory which might be applied with interesting and useful results to the teaching of the main subjects of the school curriculum.

Three Continental philosophers, Giovanni Gentile, Benedetto Croce, and Henri Bergson have made important contributions, directly or indirectly, to educational theory. In the Introduction to Gentile's *Reform of Education*, Croce asserted that in conjunction with himself, Gentile aimed at shaking Italy "out of the doze of naturalism and positivism back to idealistic philosophy, or, as it would be better to say, to philosophy pure and simple, if, indeed, philosophy is always Idealism". Croce and Gentile were writing during the disturbed condition of Italy which followed the conclusion of the First World War. In their general philosophical outlook, the two thinkers developed similar theories although on some points they differed materially. For example, in their political theory there was an important difference, for Croce was imbued with the spirit of Liberalism whilst Gentile gave wholehearted support to the Fascist movement.

Gentile had some experience in secondary school teaching before he was offered a university appointment. Eventually he became Professor of the History of Philosophy in the University of Rome. In 1913, the first edition of his *Outline of Pedagogy as Philosophic Science* was published, and this was revised and augmented in 1923. He contributed a large number of articles on philosophy, education, and politics to various journals, and his major philosophical work, *Theory of Mind as Pure Act*, appeared in 1922. His educational work best known to English readers is *The Reform of Education* (English translation, 1923). Croce was a supporter of Gentile's views on education, and when he was appointed Minister of Education in 1920, he attempted to put these theories into practice, but the confused state of affairs in Italy rendered his efforts unsuccessful. From 1922 to 1924, Gentile was Mussolini's Minister of Education, and during this short period he completely refashioned

Italian primary, secondary, and university education. The Gentile reform of education had two aspects. The first, as the quotation from Croce indicates, was a movement away from naturalism and positivism towards idealism. The second consisted in a complete reorganisation of the schools and the curriculum. The system he inaugurated was carried on by his successors at the Ministry.

One may ask why a wholesale reform of the educational system was necessary. During the latter part of the nineteenth century, the Italian schools and universities had been losing their liberal outlook, and in becoming institutions dominated by a materialistic philosophy of life, had degenerated into places which prepared their pupils for the different certificates and diplomas required for professional life. Secondary and higher education became completely bookish in the worst sense of the word, and learning developed into pure memory drill, the effort to master a large number of subjects in the shortest possible time. Both Croce and Gentile realised that the schools needed to be revitalised, and in their efforts to bridge the gap between school and life outside the school, they showed a similarity with the aims of a philosopher of a very different type of thought, John Dewey.

In their opposition to materialism, Croce and Gentile sought inspiration from the great idealists of the past, Kant, Fichte, Schelling, but above all, from Hegel. Gentile, however, was not satisfied with Hegel's conception of philosophy as a particular form of the spirit. Using the Hegelian dialectic; the thesis: art, and the antithesis: religion, are resolved in the higher synthesis of philosophy. Thus, philosophy represents the most complete manifestation of the spirit. Gentile defined spirit as the pure act of self-conscious thinking. He emphasised that reality is spiritual, and, hence, it is not surprising to find that he denied the view that the basis of human activity is to be discovered in man's instinctive tendencies. "But here, as in every other manifestation of his spiritual activity", he wrote, "man does not behave in sole conformity with instinct : he does not teach by abandoning himself, so to speak, to the force of natural determinism. He is fully aware of his own doings, He keeps his eyes open on his own function, so that he may attain the end by the shortest course, that he may, without wasting his energies, derive from them the best possible results. For man reflects".[1]

[1] *The Reform of Education*, pp. 33-4, Benn, 1923.

We shall not attempt to examine in detail the educational philosophy of Gentile, but there are certain features which should receive notice. In agreement with his adherence to absolute idealism, Gentile adopts the view that all truth is to be found within man himself. In the opening chapter of the *Outline of Pedagogy as Philosophic Science*, he states that all truth, not only spiritual truth, is to be found within man, and that knowing is a spiritual process which moves through infinite steps of perfection without ever reaching the most perfect. "The master, as St Augustine long ago warned us, is within us."

The same idea applies to culture. The realist thinks of culture as something existing externally to which the individual is admitted; something awaiting to be revealed to us. Gentile calls this abstract culture. "It slumbers in the libraries, in the sepulchres of those who lived, who passed away and created it once for all. It belongs to the past, to the things that have died".[1] His use of the terms abstract and concrete is apt to puzzle the reader who has become accustomed to think of a concrete object as being material. Gentile and Croce use the word concrete to designate that which is whole and complete. That which is partial and not fully integrated to the whole is abstract. The idealist does not conceive culture as abstract. Idealistic culture is the only culture which really exists. "It is not in books, nor in the brains of others. It exists in our own souls as it is gradually being formed there. It cannot, therefore, be an antecedent to the activity of the spirit, since it consists in this very activity." [2]

Gentile emphasised this view of culture because he was opposed to the bookish nature of the education prevalent in the Italian schools. He wrote: "A textbook is a textbook: when it was written, and if the author was capable of thinking and living in his thought, it too, was a living thing; and a living thing, that is, *spirit*, it will continue to be for the instructor who does not through indolence allow himself to believe that all the thinking demanded by the subject was done once for all by the author of the manual. For the manual, is a book intended for the teacher, meant to be constantly awakened by teachers to an ever-quickened life, the life of the spirit, can only be what the instructor makes it. He, therefore, must have culture enough to read it as *his* book; he must be able to restore it to life, to re-create it by the living process of his

[1] *Reform of Education*, p. 83.
[2] *ibid.*, p. 84.

personal thought . . . the teacher re-creates the book when he revives it in the mind of the one for whom the book was written : when author, teacher, and pupil constitute but one single spirit, whose life animates and inwardly vivifies the manual, which, therefore, ought not to be called, as it is, a *hand*-book, but a spiritual guide for the mind. Unfortunately the oft-deplored indolence which freezes and stiffens spiritual life, fastens the books to the hands of the teacher first, and then to those of the pupils".[1]

Gentile would agree with Dewey, who wrote: "Philosophy may even be defined as the general theory of education".[2] Gentile and Dewey are the only two modern philosophers who have identified philosophy and education. Many of the thinkers mentioned in this book, *e.g.* Plato, Aristotle, Locke, and Kant, have discussed education in their works as subsidiary to their main purpose. Gentile in the *Outline of Pedagogy as Philosophic Science*, tells us that in all times philosophy has been found to hold the problem of education in its bosom. The problem of education is really twofold. It is concerned with both the actual, man as he is, and the ideal, man as he ought to be. The resolution of the dualism is to be found in philosophy, and it is in bringing together these two aspects of human nature, that philosophy and education become identified.

Gentile's view of the relation between teacher and pupil is important. The activity of education is spiritual, in which two spirits are indissolubly linked. The ideal is reached when teacher and pupil are so absorbed in the same spiritual process that the distinction between the two vanishes. It is not sufficient for the teacher to study the pupil, as it were, from outside. He must penetrate the mind of the pupil, and by losing his life in that of the pupil, he actually finds it. The pedant is the teacher who pins his faith to repetition and memorising. The true teacher learns as well as the pupil; he renews himself perennially in the spirit of the pupil. This ideal state of affairs is only possible in the atmosphere of freedom. "A school without freedom is a lifeless institution."

How, then, are we to solve the antinomy of the freedom of the pupil and the authority of the teacher? Gentile answers that the antinomy disappears when we replace "the abstract idea of the

---

[1] *Reform of Education*, pp. 156-7.
[2] *Democracy and Education*, p. 383, Macmillan, New York, 1923.

18

dualism of teacher and pupil, by the idea of their intrinsic, profound, unseverable unity as it gradually works out and is actualised in the process of education . . . the real teacher is within the soul of the pupil, or, better still, the teacher is the pupil himself in the dynamism of his development. So that, far from limiting the autonomy of the disciple, the master, as the propulsive element of the pupil's spontaneity, penetrates his personality, not to suppress it, but to help its impulses and facilitate its infinite development".[1] Hence, in the *Outline of Pedagogy as Philosophic Science*, Gentile describes the true teacher as the spiritual parent of the pupil. As through his parents the child has been inserted into the creative process of the world, so in the life of the teacher, the pupil advances to self-creation, a part of the universal and eternal process of culture. Teaching is not a profession; the true teacher regards it as a vocation, a mission.

Possibly the most interesting and important contribution of Croce, as regards education, lies in his theory of beauty. His view has been called the expressionist theory of art and beauty, for he identifies these two terms. He considers that there are two forms of knowledge: "either *intuitive* knowledge or *logical* knowledge; knowledge obtained through the *imagination* or knowledge obtained through the *intellect*; knowledge of the *individual* or knowledge of the *universal*; of *individual* things or of the *relations* between them; it is, in fact, productive either of *images* or of *concepts*".[2]

Art and beauty must be distinguished from what are commonly called works of art. Croce denies that beauty is a quality of the objects which are considered beautiful. It comes as the result of a spiritual activity. Its essential nature is expression. Croce attaches a special meaning to this term. He would deny that the essence of art is dependent upon the translation of the artist's intuition through a physical medium. The work of art lies in the soul of the artist. Imagine Robert Burns singing a lyrical poem as he trudged behind the plough. Suppose he had suddenly died before he had the opportunity of communicating his intuition to others, he would have been none the less an artist. As E. F. Carritt explains: "This spiritual activity is the aesthetic experience of the man who finds beauty in a cathedral or a tragedy, a sunset

[1] *Reform of Education*, p. 63.
[2] *Aesthetic*, p. 1, Macmillan, 1922.

or a tune . . . My work and my satisfaction *as an artist* are completed when I have made a melody or a poem, and when I have seen or imagined, in the perfection of every detail, a landscape; and nothing artistic will be added then by my putting pen to paper or paper to the press".[1]

Nevertheless, the true artist feels an urge to communicate his intuition, and will do so unless he is prevented by circumstances outside his control. He will communicate his intuition through poetry, painting, music, or some other appropriate means, but the real work of art lies in his own experience. Croce wrote: "One often hears people say that they have many great thoughts in their minds, but that they are not able to express them. But if they really had them, they would have coined them into just so many beautiful, sounding words, and thus have expressed them. If these thoughts seem to vanish or to become few and meagre in the act of expressing them, the reason is that they did not exist or really were few and meagre".[2]

It is not our purpose to decide whether Croce's belief in the identity of intuition and expression, or that whilst the beautiful does not admit of a more or less beautiful, it is possible to discover degrees of ugliness, are views which can be justified. What is important for the teacher is the assertion that the artistic form in the soul of the artist is the essence of the work of art. It is the translation of that form and its communication through a physical medium which we commonly refer to as a work of art.

Now comes a significant point. Croce insists that whenever an individual appreciates a beautiful landscape, a picture, a sonnet, or a symphony, he becomes, to a certain extent, an artist himself. He has recaptured, in so far as his powers permit, the original intuition the artist possessed. In other words, through appreciation we become, to some degree, artists ourselves, even though we have not the technical skill to translate the intuition born within us into a visible or audible form. The teacher will immediately realise that this is a theoretical justification of training in aesthetic appreciation, which in modern times is a feature of the curriculum of most schools.

Croce wrote: "Each of us, as a matter of fact, has in him a little of the poet, of the sculptor, of the musician, of the painter, of the prose writer: but how little, as compared with those who

---

[1] *The Theory of Beauty*, p. 180, revised edition, Methuen, 1928.
[2] *Aesthetic*, p. 9.

bear those names, just because they possess the most universal dispositions and energies of human nature in so lofty a degree".[1]

Carritt sums this up as follows: "But we have maintained throughout that the man who appreciates a picture or a mountain aesthetically is, in his degree, an artist. None of these things is beautiful to him unless he expresses in it his feeling, or, which once more is the same thing, it expresses, that is, reveals them to him. The writer of a poem expresses his passion in it. It expresses the passion to me, but only on condition that I have some such passion to express. The truth is that in reading a poem I express myself in it. I find words for what I have already been, and so first come fully to know it. It is true, that for good or evil, we are not all Romeos, or Macbeths, or Shakespeares; but unless, for good or evil, we have all something of Romeo and Macbeth and Shakespeare in us, unless we have had moments when our experience has been what theirs perhaps constantly was,—though theirs was also so much more,—all their talking must be for us, words. We should not know what they mean, for to us they would mean nothing. Language only has a meaning for me when in hearing it I express myself in it".[2]

Bergson was quite a different type of thinker from those we have been considering. He was not primarily concerned with education, but his doctrines have an important bearing on the problems of the educator. He was born in 1859, the same year as Dewey, and even in his school days he showed anticipation of his brilliant intellectual powers. After some years of teaching in provincial lycées, he returned to Paris and accepted a teaching appointment at the Lycée Henri-Quatre. In 1900 he was given the Chair of Greek Philosophy at the College de France, and in 1904 he was appointed Professor of Modern Philosophy. The writer will always remember, just before the Second World War, attending a philosophical conference at Paris at which Henri Bergson was one of the chief speakers.

Bergson was a prolific writer. His principal works are: *Time and Free Will*, 1889; *Matter and Memory*, 1896; and *Creative Evolution*, 1907.

Dr H. Wildon Carr quite justly described the thought of Bergson as the "Philosophy of Change", and chose this title for two

[1] *Aesthetic*, p. 11.
[2] *The Theory of Beauty*, pp. 182-3.

books which he wrote about the philosophy of Bergson.[1]   Quite apart from the classic dispute between realists and idealists, philosophies may be divided into two types.   Commencing with the Greek thinker, Parmenides (c. 470 B.C.), who regarded change as illusory, many thinkers from Plato and Aristotle onwards have been impressed with the idea that only the permanent can change, and that the task of the philosopher is to account for change.   In contrast, Heraclitus (c. 536-470 B.C.), taught that all is change and becoming, and thinkers who have agreed with this line of thought have insisted that change and movement are fundamental and it is the apparent immobility and permanency of things that requires explanation.   Bergson belongs to this school of thought.

He emphasised that not only do we live in a world which is constantly changing, but, at the same time, we are constantly changing ourselves.   Change is the essence of reality.   In a lecture delivered at the University of London in 1911, he said: "Change, then, is simple, while the 'state of things' as we call it, is composite. Every stable state is the result of the co-existence between that change and the change of the person who perceives it".   For many purposes, physical scientists consider the universe as static, and investigate the successive states which occur.   This involves an abstraction by the intellect which views reality as consisting of solid, stable objects, and is a necessary point of view for many purposes.   The intellect is an instrument of the mind forged for the purposes of life, and the knowledge obtained through intellectual activity is for life and not life for knowledge.

Bergson likens the activity of the intellect to the taking of a cinematograph film of a moving scene.   The camera records a series of static views, but when the film is run through the projector, the movement is restored.   The scientist is interested in the static view and regards change as consisting in a succession of states. The philosopher when he conceives reality as continuous change is like the person who sees the film projected on the screen.   Movement is continuous and indivisible, and the neglect of this truth was responsible for the famous paradoxes of the Greek philosopher, Zeno of Elea (c. 490-430 B.C.).   Zeno's best-known paradox is the race between Achilles and the tortoise.   The latter is given a start, but Achilles can never pass the tortoise because he has first to reach

[1] *The Philosophy of Change*, Macmillan, 1914.   Wildon Carr also wrote a briefer sketch of Bergson's philosophy under the same title.   (Jack and Nelson, second revised edition, 1919.)

the spot where the tortoise is now and by that time, the tortoise has moved forward. This is repeated so that whilst Achilles draws ever nearer to the tortoise he never actually overtakes him.

Movement involves the conception of time, and Bergson draws a distinction between true and false time. The latter is clock time and is spatial in character. True time is *la durée*. The nearest English equivalent, duration, is inadequate. The common conception of time is that of a homogeneous medium in which events succeed one another just as space is a homogeneous medium in which objects co-exist. Bergson believed that, like space and movement, time is an indivisible flow. One moment does not cease and is followed by another. It flows into the next moment and that in turn flows into another. Time is not the same for everybody; in fact, to call it a flow is really misleading, for it is bound up with the individual's conscious states, that is, with his life. Hence, real time cannot be measured mathematically. The few minutes during which a man is drowning are only a few minutes when viewed externally, but may seem years to the person himself when the whole of his past is reviewed by his mind.

Intelligence is not the only means by which knowledge is acquired. Instinct and intelligence exist side by side in our consciousness, and the former is akin to direct insight, which Bergson terms, intuition. His teaching in this respect approaches that of Croce and Gentile. The two powers of intuition and intelligence are not necessarily opposed, for each has its particular functions. It is through intuition that we grasp the reality of change and true time, and it is through the same power that the philosopher can come to see all things *sub specie durationis*.

Bergson also distinguished between memory as a habit and pure memory. Both co-exist in our experience, but they are essentially different. The child who learns the multiplication table by heart, so that it trips easily off his tongue, is making use of habit memory. On the other hand, the person who is recalling a past experience is primarily employing pure memory. Bergson explained the difference as follows: "I study a lesson, and in order to learn it by heart I read it a first time, accentuating every line; I then repeat it a certain number of times. At each repetition there is progress; the words are more and more linked together, and at last make a continuous whole. When that moment comes, it is said that I know my lesson by heart, that it is imprinted on my memory. I consider now how the lesson has been learnt, and picture to myself the successive phases of the process. Each several reading then recurs to me with its own individuality. It is distinguished from those which preceded or followed it, by the place which it occupied in time; in short, each reading stands out before my mind as a definite event in my history. Again, it will be said that these images are recollections, that they are imprinted on my memory. The same words are then used in both cases. Do they mean the same thing? The memory of the lesson which is remembered, in the sense of learned by heart, has *all* the marks of a habit. Like a habit, it is acquired by the repetition of the same effort. Like every habitual bodily exercise, it is stored up in mechanism which is set in motion as a whole by an initial impulse, in a closed system of automatic movements, which succeed each other in the same order and together take the same length of time. The memory of each several reading, on the contrary, has none of the marks of a habit, it is like an event in my life; it is a case of spontaneous recollection as distinct from mere learnt recollection".[1]

Bergson was convinced that any explanation of life which rested solely on physical and chemical factors was doomed to failure. Thus, he was opposed to the naturalism of Herbert Spencer, but at the same time he upheld a principle of evolution. The true view of evolution is that it is creative. Space forbids a discussion of this, one of the central points in Bergson's philosophy. All that can be said is that Bergson conceived life as an original impulse, (*une poussée formidable*). In this drive, instinct and intelligence represent two important termini. One is not so much higher as different from the other. The reality of our life is pure duration. The past as memory exists in the present and pushes forward into the future. Matter and spirit are not independent; the former is the product of the latter, but flows in an opposite direction. Spirit is the initial *élan vital* and characterised by creativeness. Matter is determined, but spirit is free. One should notice that, from a widely different starting point, Bergson is at one with Italian idealists in so far as he is antagonistic to a materialist interpretation of reality. Such English thinkers as MacDougall, and Nunn, although differing from him in many details, include him in the hormic school. On its negative side, Bergson's thought shares with that of William James the characteristic of a revolt against an exaggerated intellectualism.

[1] *Matter and Memory*, pp. 89-90, George Allen and Unwin, 1911.

Dr Olive Wheeler, in *Bergson and Education*, has worked out the relations of Bergson's philosophy to the problems of modern education.[1] She emphasises that Bergson provides the theoretical background to the revolt against the narrow academic outlook so long associated with the grammar school tradition. This revolt was also expressed in the desire to provide a practical and realistic bias for the central and senior school of pre-war days and in the curriculum of the present secondary modern schools. The modern emphasis on creative and constructive activities is in line with the philosophy of Bergson. The same applies to his views about the nature of intuition. In spite of this, it may seem to some that even now, with the recognition of the value of practical and creative work in school and the opportunities for developing appreciation, the modern age puts a premium on intelligence and academic attainments. The latter are valuable, but by no means the only valuable things in life.

SUGGESTIONS FOR FURTHER READING

The following books to which reference has been made in the chapter are recommended: —

Sir John Adams, *The Herbartian Psychology applied to Education*, D. C. Heath (various editions).

Modern Developments in Educational Practice, University of London Press, 1929.

The Evolution of Educational Theory, Macmillan, 1912.

Sir Fred Clarke, *Education and Social Change*, Sheldon Press, 1940.

Freedom in the Educative Society, University of London Press, 1947.

Karl Mannheim, *Man and Society*, Kegan Paul, Trench, Trubner, 1940.

Diagnosis of Our Time, Paul, Trench, Trubner, 1943.

The case against economic and social planning is well argued by F. A. Hayek, *The Road to Serfdom* (abridged edition), Routledge, 1946.

Sir Percy Nunn, *Education: Its Data and First Principles*, 3rd edition, Edward Arnold, 1945.

A. N. Whitehead, *The Aims of Education*, Williams and Norgate, 1929.

[1] Manchester University Press, 1922.

In addition to the works of Gentile, Croce, and Bergson mentioned in the text, L. Minio-Paluello, *Education in Fascist Italy*, O.U.P., 1946, contains a full account of Gentile's educational reforms.

CHAPTER XX

EMINENT AMERICAN EDUCATORS

During the seventeenth and eighteenth centuries the development of American education was closely related to the political and religious convictions of the various communities of the eastern seaboard. It is clear that new ideas of educational thinkers were known—at least in New England and the middle colonies. It is possible that the methods of Comenius and the theories of William Penn may have been used in some schools, but, on the whole, the educational process was not vastly different from that which had been left behind in Europe. In the North, communities taxed themselves to pay for universal education—the nearest approach to a Comenian system—but the schools and universities were like those in England. In Pennsylvania and New Jersey the many different churches controlled education, and schools were either charity schools for very poor children or private schools for those who could pay fees. In the South there was no general system of education; the European tradition of home education was accepted by the landowning classes.

With the creation of the United States of America in 1776, it is understandable that the political motivation in education grew even more predominant, but this did not prohibit the appreciation of more specifically educational theories by those outstanding men who were to guide the early steps of the infant Republic. Indeed, the impact of such theories was almost inescapable in any part of the western world inhabited by literate people, for this was the era of Rousseau, whose brilliant and dramatic revelation of the relationships between the free individual and the democratic society shattered the Old Order in Europe. British political scientists of the period contributed in some measure to new theories of government, and most of these men—Adam Smith, Tom Paine, William Godwin, and others—gave consideration to education as a relevant side issue, but at this time French ideas played a predominant part in United States affairs, especially in education. Many Frenchmen settled in America to work in some field of education. The American counterpart of the Royal Society was founded by a Frenchman and another wrote one of the first surveys of American education.

During the first fifty years of the Republic the most outstanding native-born thinkers on education were Benjamin Franklin and Thomas Jefferson. Both were statesmen, and both, like many other statesmen of the period, strove mightily in word and deed to justify their own individual ideas on education.

Benjamin Franklin (1706-90), although a New Englander, opposed the establishment of free universal education. His reasons were neither political nor religious, but were truly educational. Admitting to the social need for the public education of very poor children, he maintained that a general public system would prove enervating and harmful in that it would remove the challenge to individual effort in self-education. He was a magnificent self-made scholar, and not only did he feel that similar efforts to his own would be of inestimable value to future leaders, he also considered that the typical school of his day gave a useless education, especially the grammar school with its firmly entrenched Latin and Greek.

Franklin started his own private academy to show a type of education more suitable for a new age. The curriculum was wide and included practical and vocational activities. Great emphasis was laid on the teaching and use of the English language. Franklin's ideas are often reminiscent of Locke, but his belief in frequent rewards and prizes denies any complete discipleship. The plans for this academy are contained in a pamphlet, *Proposals Relating to the Education of Youth in Pennsylvania* (1749), in which he quotes from Locke and other realist writers. Franklin proposed to have a pleasantly built and located school equipped with practical teaching aids and materials, including maps for geography. There was to be a garden and land for the study of agriculture and natural history. There was to be a space for physical training—exercises, wrestling, jumping, running, and games. In addition to the teaching of English language and literature there would be the teaching of handwriting and drawing. Modern history and geography and useful mathematics and astronomy would be included. Religious education was to proceed by the historical approach and should induce "benignity of mind".

Franklin hoped his academy would be a boarding establishment, but the trustees did not implement this proposal. Moreover, they insisted on the inclusion of the classics, which soon became predominant and so frustrated the intention of the designer. Yet this school was for little boys of eight to fourteen years of age.

Nevertheless, Franklin gave two great ideas to a people who were soon to achieve nationhood—the idea of self-education and the idea that mastery of the English language was the key to all the rest of education for the New World.

In the plan for his academy he wrote: "As to their studies, it would be well if they could be taught everything that is useful and everything that is ornamental. But art is long, and their time is short. It is therefore proposed that they learn those things that are likely to be most useful and most ornamental; regard being had to the several professions for which they are intended". Many other commentators on education favoured the broadening of education. Some would have included the useful arts and vocational training. Others advocated the introduction of various sciences, including practical and applied sciences. This movement is often considered to be a purely American trend, whereas, in fact, similar ideas were equally widespread in Britain.

Noah Webster (1758-1843), the American lexicographer, was even more extreme in his rejection of the concept of liberal education. His idea of education was "to keep young persons from childhood busy in some employment of use and reputation",[1] preferably activities related to their future occupation. Here spoke the schoolmaster, for he held several teaching posts during his varied career, and he wrote several school grammar, reading, and spelling books. In fact, Webster Americanised the school textbook, not only setting standards of spelling and pronunciation somewhat different from those in England, but also providing general knowledge relevant to the interests and needs of Americans. He explained to Franklin that he had added to his *American Selection of Lessons in Reading and Speaking* "some American pieces under the discovery, history, wars, geography, economy, commerce, government, etc., of this country in order to call the minds of our youth from ancient fables and foreign events and fix them upon objects immediately interesting in this country".[2]

Thomas Jefferson (1743-1826) was at no time a professional educator and he belonged to that group of states least interested in education. Yet he is regarded as the chief architect of democratic education in the U.S.A., although he did not see the fruition of his proposals. Moreover, his concept of democratic education is still one of vital interest and concern to American educators,

---

[1] N. Webster, *The Importance of Accommodating the Mode of Education to the Form of Government*, 1788.
[2] E. E. F. Skeel, *Notes on the Life of Noah Webster*, vol. 2. p. 454, 1912.

and many would now wish to see it interpreted in its entirety in order to remedy what they consider to be weaknesses in the present system.

Although he was a member of a Virginian land-owning family, and although his entry into politics and public life was in accordance with the gentlemanly tradition, Jefferson did not reflect the indifference of his fellows towards questions of national education. His *Bill for the More General Diffusion of Knowledge*, which he put before the Virginia legislature in 1779, proposed the development of a state system of free universal education. Many Northern communities had tax-supported schools, but there was no such state-wide system in any state, so it is hardly surprising that Jefferson's scheme was not accepted for Virginia. His advanced views on this subject arose from his profound conviction that the common man must be given the tools by which democratic government could be made to work.

Jefferson envisaged the division of the country into districts, each five or six miles square and each containing a school, so that no child should be out of reach of elementary education. The masters were to be paid by local taxation, and one of their tasks was to be the selection of the best pupils who should proceed to the secondary schools where Greek, Latin, geography, and higher arithmetic were taught. As one secondary school would serve a group of elementary schools it is probable that Jefferson had boarding schools in mind. At this level, there was to be further selection after a year's trial, the poorest brains being expelled. At the end of the course half the pupils were to be kept as masters and the rest sent to college. By this process, asserted Jefferson, "the best geniuses will be raked from the rubbish". He believed that public officials needed university education, but this view was not widely held at a time when appointments were governed by politics.

Although all states were destined to put into practice the main principle of Jefferson's scheme—even Virginia adopted a system of free public schools in 1860—the working out of the general plan of American education has not been strictly according to the Jeffersonian ideal, although much of the detail of the Virginia scheme has been incorporated. The school districts of to-day are comparable to the hundredths of counties of Jefferson's schemes. These districts provide their own schools and run their educational administration on a democratic basis. Both boys and girls are educated, as Jefferson wished. The present system, however, provides complete primary and secondary education free for all children, whereas Jefferson suggested that the extent of free universal education should be three years only, but that further elementary education should be available on the payment of fees. It is at the next stage, however, that the greatest divergence has come about. Jefferson envisaged public secondary education as the further education of a carefully selected intellectual élite who would be worth the expenditure of public money by virtue of the services they would eventually perform for state and community. The essential concept appears to be that of the modern English grammar school. One high school would serve several elementary school districts, and the best pupils of each would be able to obtain higher education free—in Virginia at the College of William and Mary. There is no equivalent of the secondary modern school in Jefferson's scheme. Comprehensive education as provided in the modern American high school is a negation of Jefferson's theory of education for democratic leadership, and some American educationists would prefer to see a measure of selection for specially accelerated secondary education. Two features of Jefferson's scheme do not appear entirely in accord with his principles, but he probably regarded them as necessary expedients—first, the restriction of elementary education, and second, the admission of fee payers to high schools irrespective of ability. The present universal system is much more in line with his basic assumptions, except that it does not sufficiently foster the maturation of the intellectually gifted. Jefferson urged the secularisation of schools and universities; he advocated the widening of curricula at all levels; he led the way in the movement towards state universities. Although private and non-secular education exists in America, the Jeffersonian ideals have, in a very large measure, been achieved. Even his contention that citizenship should be withheld from those who do not learn to read English is reflected to-day in the country's immigration laws.

Nineteenth-Century Educators

The first part of the nineteenth century was a time of action rather than of contemplation and theorising. There was so much to be done, both to escape from the trammels of European tradition and to provide for the expansion and extension of the real American education. Great strides were made towards the ideal of a common school—open to all, tax-supported, and without the stigma of the English charity school. The abolition of the last vestiges of fees in public schools came more slowly, and the elimination of sectarianism more slowly still. State universities came into being as funds from taxation became available. Improvements in girls' education came as the shadow of Europe receded and the new American woman undertook pioneering in a variety of fields. Even the public high school became a *fait accompli* soon after the passing of the half-century, and this in spite of the powerful rivalry of Latin grammar schools and the private academies. In an age of action the educational thinkers and theorists were men and women of action. Pre-eminent are Horace Mann and Henry Barnard among the men, and Emma Willard, Catherine Beecher, and Mary Lyon among the women.

Horace Mann (1796-1859) was an eminent young lawyer and a rising politician at the time he secured the passage of a law setting up a state board of education for Massachusetts. So deeply were his interests engaged by that time that he sacrificed his career and his political opportunities to serve the state as secretary of the new board. There was much work to be done in welding the public schools of the various communities into a complete and efficient state system. It was necessary to find more money, better buildings, adequate equipment, and adequately-prepared teachers. All of these were scarce. There were not even enough schools to ensure that all children had schooling. During the twelve years he spent as secretary, he remedied these weaknesses and also founded the first normal school (or teacher-training college) in the States—the beginning of a nation-wide movement with which his name is always associated.

Later, after serving on the Congress of the United States, Mann brought about the founding of Antioch College, Ohio, a co-educational, non-sectarian liberal arts college, of which he became the first president. This was a new venture in higher education, but one which was destined to be imitated frequently as time went by.

Henry Barnard (1811-1900) also moved from law to legislature and thence to the secretaryship he had helped to create. Until his appointment as secretary of the board of education in Connecticut, his story had followed closely that of Mann, except that he had spent two years in Europe studying Pestalozzian education in Switzerland and Germany. Thenceforward, however, he experienced more vicissitudes than Mann and attained greater eminence. Although he achieved much for the schools during his three years as secretary, it did not meet with the approval of the legislature, so he moved to Rhode Island, where he was instrumental in getting an education bill through the legislature. He became the state commissioner for education, and in this capacity achieved much success. Among the important offices he held later were the presidency of a normal school, the presidency of a university, and the position of United States Commissioner of Education.

The school reform work of both Mann and Barnard was accomplished in the first half of the century. Mann's main writings, in the form of annual reports, also belong to this period, but Barnard's writings were later. To many students of education his name suggests not the builder of school systems but the founder and editor of the *American Journal of Education*, a publication of great influence on the educational thought of the period and of considerable interest to the educator of to-day. It must be emphasised that in the earlier task of establishing state school systems, many states had their Manns and Barnards who merit recognition as pioneer educators.

Space will not permit the full story to be told of the women pioneers in American education. **Emma Willard (1787-1870)** spent many years of her life teaching in private academies for girls, including her own boarding school, but she did not consider the general standard of girls' school education—whether public or private—to be adequate in either quantity or quality. Her remedy was state-supported higher education for women, and towards this end she put forward a scheme to the New York legislature. This body passed an act granting Mrs Willard a charter to enable her to start a school, but as she could not obtain the necessary money, the scheme remained on paper. Eventually, however, the town of Troy, N.Y., raised enough money to establish the "Female Seminary" which was successful from the first under Mrs Willard's guidance, setting new standards of scholarship for girls and preparing them for teaching and other community service. In the 1850s Mrs Willard was an associate of Mann and Barnard in their campaign for the foundation of normal schools.

Catherine Beecher (1800-78) was a teacher who founded a famous girls' school at Hartford, Conn., and who was anxious to see improvements in the nature and standards of female education. She did not aim to educate girls to compete with men, but rather to carry out more effectively and efficiently those activities and occupations belonging to womanhood, not only in professions such as nursing and teaching but also in housecraft and in the social graces. Mrs Beecher worked in many ways for the advancement of women's education, and many new schools and educational organisations in New England and in the Middle West owed their origin to her efforts.

Mary Lyon (1797-1849) concentrated her attention on the higher education of women at a time when school education was still largely undeveloped. She founded the first institution of higher education for women in 1836 at Mount Holyoke after an arduous money-raising campaign. The following year, girls over the age of sixteen were admitted on the passing of a minimum attainment test. The establishment of other colleges for women followed remarkably soon afterwards.

Thus it is seen that the main American educators of the first half of the century were essentially pioneers in action. There were many other pioneers—among them the Pestalozzians mentioned in another chapter, the teachers of physically and mentally handicapped children, and the experimenters in scientific and technical education. The literature of education for this period is indicative of a widespread lively concern for education. Although outstanding treatises were extremely rare, there were a number of books on down-to-earth topics, such as *Lectures on School Keeping* (1829) by Samuel R. Hall, and *Theory and Practice of Teaching* (1847) by David P. Page. A more notable feature, in that it has no counterpart in England, is the number of educational journals which flourished—although for short periods only—between 1818 and 1852. Many of these served individual states or even single school districts; others were published by education societies.

The most eminent writer on education outside the circle of professional educators was **Ralph Waldo Emerson (1801-82)**, who approached the subject as a philosopher. Like Rousseau—whose basic concepts he reinterpreted from his own viewpoint—he was an onlooker, free from the pedestrian detail of school teaching and administration. As a result, his ideas on education flow upward and forward away from the limitations of the immediate situation. His social theory provides the link between Rousseau and Dewey in emphasising that the process of becoming civilised is all-important. In rejecting the concept of the noble savage he is restating Rousseau's fundamental conviction that the increasing richness of man's social experience and his growing command of knowledge ought to lead to the gradual perfecting of mankind. He believed, with Rousseau, that education was the chief instrument through which the individual gained the freedom to use and evaluate these experiences and this knowledge. In emphasising the uniqueness of the individual, Emerson is the precursor of Dewey, for both men conceived the free, mature human being as one whose beliefs and attitudes were truly his own, although reconciled to the limitations and demands of human society. This optimistic belief in the Social Contract was a highly civilised viewpoint as well as an expedient attitude in a democracy of mixed peoples. It was the failure of education to produce generations of *more* civilised people that later instigated, first, Dewey's reminder of its social function, and then Bertrand Russell's contention that social adjustment is more dispensable than individual uniqueness—in fact, that nonconformism is more fruitful in terms of human progress than is the mass mind.

Nevertheless, the ideal of Emerson may yet prove right. It led him to envisage an unlimited range of educational opportunities for all citizens—provided by the State and available to any person on demand. This was a reversion to the Comenian concept of universal education as a human right and was a rejection of the Jeffersonian viewpoint that the State—or the smaller governmental body—should decide on the amount of education to be given to each member on the basis of natural ability. This is a powerful argument for the freedom of the individual human will—an argument which has prevailed in the development of modern American education.

It was inevitable that Emerson should be a critic of prevalent traditional methods of education. He reiterated Rousseau's scorn of mere book learning and oral instruction, and advocated education by experience, experiment, and activity. To him, as to Dewey, education was essentially a process of growth—moreover, of increasing individual consciousness of growth. Thus the kinship of Emerson's philosophy to that of the German idealists is manifest, although his inspiration was rather the English school of transcendentalists—including Coleridge and Carlyle. His view of human growth as an *unfolding* is very similar to that of his European contemporary, Froebel. The following might have been written by either: "Man is endogenous and education is his unfolding. . . . The aid we have from others is mechanical compared with the discoveries of nature in us. What is thus learned is delightful in the doing, and the effect remains. Right ethics are central and go from the soul outwards".[1]

This reinterpretation of Platonism is at the same time an augury of later experimentalism which, in its rejection of absolutes, contends that there is nothing by which growth—or education—can be measured except *more* growth. To Emerson the individual self sets its own standards and grows by transcending itself in a *natural* order of unfolding. Formal instruction could only stunt this growth and prohibit the achievement of self-consciousness. Each mind must be free to follow its own structure and seek for itself those experiences which would bring about growth for that particular, unique mind. Emerson was not unmindful of the achievements and progress of the human race as a group of minds, but, like Dewey, he denied that instruction in this could substitute for the achievement and progress of each individual human being. "The two points in a boy's training", he writes, "are to keep his *naturel* and to train off all but that: to keep his *naturel*, but to stop off his uproar, fooling, and horse-play; keep his nature and arm it with knowledge in the very direction in which it points. Here are the two capital facts, Genius and Drill. The first is the inspiration in the well-born, healthy child, the new perception he has of nature. Somewhat he sees in forms or hears in music, or apprehends in mathematics, or believes practicable in mechanics or possible in political society, which no one else sees or hears or believes." [2]

Emerson, son of a New England minister, tasted several kinds of schooling—a dame school at the age of three, a private elementary school, the famous Boston Latin School, and, after only a year, a brief spell at a village school. In addition, he had writing tuition for a time, and also for many years was informally educated by a brilliant and forceful aunt. After working his way through Harvard he spent four years teaching at a school for young ladies before returning to Harvard to enter the Divinity School. Many years later, after travelling in Europe—where he met his idols, Coleridge, Carlyle, and Wordsworth—he lectured at the Boston Mechanics' Institute on a wide variety of topics.

It was after such experience that he matured his theory of education in the light of his transcendentalist philosophy. "Why should we not enjoy an original relation to the universe?" he enquired in his first book, *Nature* (1836). "There are new lands,

---

[1] R. W. Emerson, *Works*, IV, p. 8, Boston, 1903.
[2] R. W. Emerson, *Works*, X, p. 144.

new men, new thoughts." The following year, in an oration at Harvard on *The American Scholar*, he appealed for the rejection of old cultures and for the intellectual exploration of the American world. At the same time he warned the scholar to preserve his intellectual integrity and his independence of vision. The following year he attacked the Church as an influence hampering true scholarship in its failure to explore new spiritual resources and in its insistence on communicating only the old. This was indeed an augury of Dewey, but not many teachers, whether at the school or college level, were ready and able to foster independent and original thought in their students.

Emerson was always deeply interested in early education and he loved children. He often visited the school of his friend Bronson Alcott,[1] one of the most radical experimenters of his day, and was delighted with the pleasant rooms, the school library, the absence of corporal punishment, and the activity-methods of teaching. Alcott's misjudged efforts to stimulate in young children rational thinking on moral and ethical matters were too advanced to please contemporary society, but his writings on education[2] were approved by his eminent contemporaries and friends—Emerson, Hawthorne, and Thoreau—and were greatly appreciated by later educators, such as W. T. Harris.

Few eminent writers and philosophers of the period remained outside the arena of verbal contest on matters educational. Some of these men wrote from personal observation or practical experience. Such a one was **Walt Whitman (1819-92)**, who, although always curiously silent about his own primary education in a Brooklyn school run on Lancastrian lines, was unremitting in his efforts to reform public opinion on the nature and method of public education. Whitman became a schoolmaster at seventeen, and although he taught for only four years he gained valuable experience not only in several schools but also in a variety of lodgings in the homes of pupils. After he became a writer he visited many schools, wrote newspaper articles, and gave lectures on education.

It is understandable that much of his educational theory should be embodied in criticism of education as he saw it. His greatest and longest campaign for children was against corporal punishment, which he had, no doubt, experienced as a boy and which

---

[1] Father of the author of *Little Women*.
[2] *Observations on the Principles and Methods of Infant Instruction*, 1830.

he knew to be the normal way of achieving discipline. It is said that he used no corporal punishment even when he had charge of eighty-five children between five and fifteen. His manner with his pupils was easy and friendly, and he used methods which were outside the normal inculcation of book learning—mental arithmetic, poetry, and games such as "Twenty Questions". In 1841 he contributed to the *United States Magazine and Democratic Review* a dramatic story entitled *Death in the School Room—A Fact*, telling of the death of a child under corporal punishment. This created a stir, but no public measure against such punishment was taken for many years. Whitman reiterated his views in many forms. "To teach a good school it is not at all necessary for a man to be inflexible in rules and severe in discipline", he wrote in 1846. "Order and obedience we would always have and yet two of the best schools we ever knew appeared always to the casual spectator to be complete upoar, confusion, and chaos."[1] There is a world of significance in this comment. Whitman must have been extremely sympathetic towards experiments in education, and was obviously influenced by the writings of Rousseau.[2]

A second major criticism of education made by Whitman concerned the quality of the teachers—a criticism which evolved into a warm support of teacher training and a plea for the employment of more women. He pointed out a twofold evil—that as genuine teachers were not available, many schools were open for only a few months each year, and as schools were open only for these few months, only "chance teachers" were available. The supply of teachers was one of the main problems which held up progress. "The monotonous *old* still resists the fresh philosophical *new*. Form and precedent are more thought of than reality",[3] Whitman complained. Better salaries, improved social status, and adequate training would bring into the schools a type of teacher who could dispense with corporal punishment and who would be enterprising in teaching method. His own "tips" to teachers are still acceptable: "In connection with every lesson have something to tell your scholars that is not in the book they study. . . . Never make a contemptuous remark concerning a scholar. . . . Teach children to govern themselves".[4]

[1] *Brooklyn Evening Star.*
[2] He is said to have denied ever reading Rousseau, yet some translations of the latter were found among Whitman's papers.
[3] *The Gathering of Forces*, I, p. 138, Putnam, N.Y., 1920.
[4] *Brooklyn Daily Eagle*, 17 July 1846.

In his concept of the function of education, Whitman is surely a precursor of Dewey; it is not to make the mind "a storehouse of the exploded theories of past generations", but rather to awaken and develop, though not to perfect, the natural abilities of the individual. This could only be accomplished by providing space and stimuli for a wide range of activities[1] and by ensuring that dull and stupid children were encouraged and understood. Believing that nurture rather than nature developed the character of children, he urged that more and better schools, both day and evening, were the only sound measures against crime and delinquency. There is much of Comenius in his views on health, his desire for pleasant school buildings, and his belief in teaching "things before words".

As he matured from journalist to poet, Whitman expanded his ideas on education from the criticism of practice and the examination of examples to a broader theory—a vision of an American system of schools preparing a new people who would create an indigenous art and literature. In such a system the environment would set standards of beauty and harmony, the methods would foster creative ability, and the spirit would engender understanding and love of democracy.

Emerson, Whitman, and their kin held in common a concept that has been strong throughout American life, one which has survived many attacks and vicissitudes, especially in the realm of education. Emerson said in his Harvard address: "Everything that tends to insulate the individual—to surround him with barriers of natural respect, so that each man shall feel the world is his, and man shall treat with man as a sovereign state with a sovereign state—tends to true union as well as greatness". Whitman echoed this conviction in *Democratic Vistas* when he wrote: "For to democracy, the leveler, the unyielding principle of the average, is surely join'd another principle . . . individuality, the pride and centripetal isolation of a human being in himself, identity, personalism".[2]

From Civil War to First World War

The first half of the century had seen a great battle for public education. Had not the suspicion of federal power and the opposition to centralisation been so deep-rooted and permanent in the

[1] He suggested music, drawing, botany, chemistry, astronomy, American history, shorthand, in addition to the three R's.
[2] Walt Whitman, *Complete Writings*, vol. II, p. 94, Putnam, 1902.

new Republic, the task might have been easier, for, from the beginning, the Federal Government had made financial aid available for the maintenance of public schools. In the new territories this enabled the building up of district systems of education to proceed, but in the east, tradition, politics, and the differing interests of urban and rural areas, set up many obstacles and hazards to be overcome. Perhaps the most important achievement of men like Horace Mann was the educating of public opinion in favour of free public education for all.

The extent to which the battle for education had been won during the half-century is shown by such events as the Morrill Act of 1862, subsidising by land grants the establishment of state colleges of agriculture and industrial arts, and the Act of Congress of 1867, setting up the United States Bureau of Education,[1] with its secretary a member of the President's Cabinet. The nature of the first of these events indicates the trend of American education towards a much wider curriculum than hitherto accepted in any country. Even college presidents, such as Wayland of Brown University, campaigned for the inclusion of science, modern languages, and practical subjects. Wayland pointed the way to the present elective system in asserting that a boy should study what he chose and nothing else. Many leading educators believed that boys should be able to specialise in studies related to their future vocations as farmers, mechanics, and other craftsmen, rather than be limited to the old classical education for aristocracy.

With the acceptance of the doctrine of equality of status in the new democracy, came provision for equality of opportunity by the rapid increase of secondary and higher education. It was established by the Kalamazoo case (1874) that taxes could be levied to develop high schools. The increase in land grant colleges and specialist courses in universities led to a "degree-mad" phase and, incidentally, to the growth of many abuses. By 1905 one third of elementary school children went to high school; 9 per cent. stayed there to eighteen and 4 per cent. went on to college. These were very high proportions indeed to have been achieved in so short a time, but in the twenty years which followed, these figures were to be increased threefold. During the two decades preceding the First World War the whole scope and purpose of American education was examined and defined, and the pattern emerged clearly for the new century to follow. The main architects were the members

[1] The Bureau published Circulars of Information from 1889 onwards.

of three national committees—the Committee of Ten on Secondary School Studies,[1] the Committee of Fifteen on Elementary Education, and the Committee on College Entrance Requirements, appointed in 1891, 1893, and 1895 respectively. The reports of these committees aroused much controversy, but they served to focus attention upon weaknesses to be eliminated and goals to be striven for. They also contributed to the eventual liberating of American education from the domination of European ideas.

Although Horace Mann had displeased the people of Massachusetts by his praise of Prussian education, German influence had grown during the century—the methods of Froebel and Herbart, the philosophy of Hegel, and even the university pattern linking philosophy with pedagogy. Yet even when this influence appeared to be at its strongest, a refining process was going on—the rejection of the outmoded, the sterile, and the misused, and a welding of the acceptable elements into truly American instruments. Pestalozzi and Froebel survived in Parker and Dewey, and the Herbartian Society became the National Society for Scientific Study of Education in 1902. Pedagogy in the university remained and developed, giving us eminent educators who were also philosophers and psychologists. But the academic had no love for the educationist. G. Stanley Hall relates how, when he was president of Clark University, his interest in the National Education Society[2] was frowned upon by his colleagues. The leaders of educational thought were now professors of education, trainers of teachers, and superintendents of school districts. These last, a truly American genus, the only highly placed educators who even now can never achieve security of tenure of their positions, were challenged by circumstances to initiate new ideas and experiments into the small groups of schools which they controlled. Their success in these innovations frequently determined their translation to college, university, or higher administration. Two outstanding educationists of the post Civil War period developed their theories as superintendents. One was **Edward Austin Sheldon (1823-97)**, the pioneer of the "Oswego Movement" for Pestalozzian education. As a young citizen of Oswego, New York, he had organised an Orphan and Free School Association and had eventually become a superintendent, organising and developing school systems, classifying and

---

[1] Chairman, Charles W. Eliot, President of Harvard, the designer of the elective system in American high schools.
[2] Founded in 1889.

grading the pupils, and establishing school libraries and evening classes. After the Civil War he was instrumental in bringing about the establishment of Oswego Primary Teachers' Training School, the first city training college in U.S.A. From 1862 until his death, Sheldon was principal of this college, which soon became the Oswego and State Normal and Training College, receiving financial aid from the State of New York. The college was the main centre of Pestalozzian training, and as both staff and students moved out to the later training centres, so Pestalozzian methods —at least in modified form—played a great part in the teacher training movement of the whole country. In 1862 Sheldon published a *Manual of Elementary Instruction*, in which the theory and methods of Pestalozzi were interpreted and exemplified.

In contrast to Sheldon, both in philosophy and in the nature of his contribution to education, is **William Torrey Harris (1835-1909)** who, after a patchy school education and a broken university career, rose in his early thirties to be a superintendent of the schools of St Louis, where he established the first public kindergarten in U.S.A. The intense but varied enthusiasms of his youth had, by this time, become concentrated in a lasting obsession with Hegelian philosophy. He aimed to show how Hegel's principles could be applied to all branches of human knowledge, but especially to education. His extraordinarily powerful influence on American thought was exerted mainly through a journal on speculative philosophy which he ran from 1867 to 1893, and through the annual reports he wrote as a school superintendent between 1868 and 1880. These latter gained much attention, even outside the United States.

From 1880 to 1889 he helped to establish and conduct the Concord School of Philosophy, which was held as a summer session. From 1889 to 1906 he was U.S. Commissioner for Education, exerting considerable influence through his lectures, reports, and articles. In 1898 he published *The Psychological Foundations of Education*, in which he expounded the concept of a rational correlation of studies—a Herbartian touch, which, however, did not conflict with his basic Hegelian concepts.

While the impact of Harris on educational thought was considerable, he was less successful as a philosopher. He had hoped to take Emerson's place in the revival of idealism, but he lacked the genius. His main philosophic points were probably more challenging to the educator than to the philosopher, especially in his emphasis on the importance of the State and the indivisibility of individual and society. He interpreted the concept of natural causation as implying self-activity—especially in the development of will—in the educational process. Such ideas were obviously of significance to younger thinkers, such as John Dewey. His theistic version of Hegel's Absolute was doubtless acceptable to more orthodox minds. One of his greatest contributions to education is his work in the drive to gain recognition and respect for psychology. Another was the service he rendered to the National Committees of the 1890s.

Of the same generation as Harris, and with a somewhat parallel career, **Colonel Francis Wayland Parker (1837-1902)** is an equally great figure in the history of the period. After a limited schooling, Parker started teaching at sixteen, fought in the Civil War at twenty-two, returned to teaching and rose quickly to be principal of a normal school in Dayton, Ohio, where he followed Sheldon's methods of training teachers. From 1872 to 1875 he studied at Berlin and toured Europe, visiting Herbartian and Froebelian schools and seeing Ritter's new methods of teaching geography— which had been derived from Pestalozzi.

When he returned to a superintendency in Quincy, Massachusetts, he was eager to put into practice his newly-found ideas, but in New England such innovations were not always welcomed. In 1883 he again became head of a normal school, this time in Cook County, Illinois. He was resolute in the pursuance of his ideals and the application of his principles, and the school became famous in spite of the continuous opposition of the conservative elements in the school and in the community. During this period he published *How to Study Geography* (1889) and *Talks on Pedagogics* (1894).

In 1899 Parker was offered the principalship of the Chicago Academic and Pedagogic Institute, a new independent normal school. In 1901 the Institute became part of the University of Chicago, where John Dewey was Professor of Education. The two men were good friends and colleagues, and Parker became the Director of the School of Education—a position he held for all too brief a period until his death in 1902.

Through Parker's work in producing teachers and trainers of teachers, the recommendations of the National Committees were made at a time when a proportion of the nation's teachers were fitted to put them into practice. The widening of the curriculum

—the introduction of science, geographical studies of the home area, and arts and crafts—had already been advocated by Parker for many years. He had shown how arithmetic and English could be taught through common interests and experiences and how learning could be made more meaningful by interrelating studies around centres of interest. Moreover, he had already shown the uselessness of the old regimentation and harsh discipline, and he always insisted that in the classroom children should be allowed to "work with all the whispering and noise compatible with the best results".[1]

His methods, especially as accepted and adapted by Dewey, became the foundation of the progressive movement of the twentieth century, and many have permanent value. That language should grow with thought itself is now accepted by all teachers of reading. That the best in education is unconsciously acquired is a maxim heeded to-day, especially at the primary level, where the spontaneous activities of children are encouraged and followed. Parker might indeed be regarded as the father of "child-centred" education.

A generation younger than Sheldon, Parker, and Harris were a group of noted teachers who also turned to Europe for their inspiration, although they looked not to Pestalozzi or Froebel, nor to Hegel, but to Herbart as reinterpreted by Professor Rein at the University of Jena. **Charles De Garmo (1849-1934)** and the McMurry brothers, Frank and Charles, had all studied at Jena before starting a vigorous Herbartian movement in the last decade of the century. They initiated the National Herbart Society which exercised considerable influence and stimulated fruitful debate and writing,[2] and they wrote a number of books on Herbartian methods of education.[3] De Garmo described Charles McMurry's work as "the best extended exposition of the results of Herbartian thought in elementary education as amended and developed by American experience and common sense".[4] De Garmo became Professor of the Science and Art of Education at Cornell University, and proved himself a widely-read, adaptable thinker, but, like Sir John Adams,

---

[1] F. W. Parker, *The Quincy Method*, *American Journal of Sociology*, vol. 6, p. 118, 1900.

[2] Dewey wrote several important articles for the Journal.

[3] *e.g.*, C. A. McMurry, *General Method*, 1892; C. A. and F. M. McMurry, *The Method of Recitation*, 1897; C. De Garmo, *Herbart and the Herbartians*, Heinemann, 1895.

[4] C. De Garmo, *Principles of Secondary Education*, vol. 1, p. 181, Macmillan, 1907.

his British contemporary, he retained his realist convictions and a marked leaning towards Herbartian concepts. His *Principles of Secondary Education*, published in two volumes in 1907 and 1908, was a landmark in American educational literature in that it surveyed curricula and methods on a comparative, critical basis, deliberately stimulating discussion and wider thinking by a method of layout which is familiar to-day in American textbooks. "That the use of the book may not invite a violation of the very principles it insists upon," he writes in the Preface, "topics for discussion are placed at the close of the various sections." These frequent insertions often include guidance on further reading: "Discussion: Modern attempts to formulate a simple aim for education: 'Complete living,' 'Character,' etc. See Bagley, *The Educative Process*, pp. 40-65". Discussion always presupposes the examination of relevant facts and ideas: "Discussion: Which shall be the ideal of the American high school; a complete general education fitting directly for all higher professional institutions, or as at present an incomplete general education, to be finished by a few years in college or university?".[1]

Volume II is an excellent example of how a good teacher grades his problems in difficulty. De Garmo intends his students to learn by experience "the few but vital mental processes that alone lead to enduring results".[2] Thus in examining the meaning of facts, attention is given to "Analogy as a Guide to Discovery", and students are required to discuss "Limits to the validity of argument by analogy: Is the state an organism? Is electricity a fluid? Does history 'repeat' itself? Are the experiences of our people 'like' those of another? Should American secondary education be patterned after that of German? Do the motives that are found active in one pupil indicate with certainty that the same motives will be equally powerful with another?".[3]

This characteristic of De Garmo's work is perhaps more interesting and significant than any other, for it shows how the denial that the teacher could do the student's thinking for him was being made in actual practice by leading educators years before Whitehead voiced his distrust of "inert ideas". De Garmo's teaching was at university level and thus, legitimately, could be basically oral, but he began with the personal experience and simple knowledge of his students and showed them how to make new knowledge for themselves. The content of the work, however, is also extremely

[1] Vol. I, p. 214.   [2] P.V. Preface, vol. II.   [3] Vol. I, p. 42.

interesting, for in attempting to present his data impartially, De Garmo reveals not only his own bias but also the main trends in American education at the turn of the century. For instance, considerable attention is given to the spread of manual and vocational education. It is clear that applied science was gaining ground in the schools and that there was a tendency to assume that all subjects should be treated scientifically—even English literature. The nature of the educational theory learnt by De Garmo's students is suggested by this discussion topic on the social function of education: "Contrast between the social and psychological aspects of the educational theories of: (1) Pestalozzi; (2) Herbart; (3) Froebel; (4) Huxley; (5) Harris; (6) Hall; (7) Dewey". Here is the essence of the American viewpoint in the period before the First World War—a recognition of the debt owed to European teachers, scientists, and philosophers, and a confirmation that thenceforward Americans would make their own theories, philosophies, and ways of doing things.

Thus the time was ripe for the emergence of great native products of native education and culture. Towering above all as an educator, and equal to the best as a philosopher, is John Dewey, whose powers matured during the two decades before the First World War and whose work is discussed in another chapter. The great breadth of Dewey's knowledge and interests reminds us that many great minds of the period had a dual or triple function. Thus William James (1842-1910), the precursor of Dewey in the philosophy of pragmatism,[1] wrote not only on philosophy and psychology but also on education. In 1899 he published *Talks to Teachers on Psychology and to Students on Some of Life's Ideals.* G. Stanley Hall (1844-1924), the great pioneer psychologist who started the child study movement, wrote much that was invaluable for teachers and influenced the whole trend of educational theory.[2] Charles W. Eliot (1834-1926), the teacher of chemistry who became president of Harvard, wrought lasting changes in the content of school and college education by his opposition to uniformity in curricula. "Flexible and diversified school programmes will give all the children their most favourable chance", he said in 1888, with reference to the public elementary school. Nicholas Murray Butler (1862-1947), the philosopher who became President of Columbia University, was the first Professor of Education of the

[1] See p. 470.
[2] *e.g.*, G. S. Hall, *Adolescence*, Appleton, 1904. Hall was also editor of *The Pedagogical Seminary.*

Teachers' College created by his efforts from the Industrial Education Association. He believed education could bring about world peace, and he shared the Nobel Peace Prize in 1931. He did much to raise the status of teacher-training by maintaining firmly that the university was the right place for the study of education to be pursued.[1] Edward Thorndike (1874-1949) earned world-wide fame as a psychologist, but his work was closely allied to education. He started the first scientifically-based child study at the beginning of the century, and it was as a professor of Teachers' College, Columbia, that he achieved his great work in educational measurement. Finally, there was the work of those literary men whose sensitivity to humanity and to their own early experience made them particularly effective vehicles for the conveyance of the true meaning of education—writers such as Mark Twain, who in *Huckleberry Finn* (1885) interprets so exquisitely the explorations and emotions of childhood.

During this period the population of the United States had increased enormously through successive waves of immigration, each of which brought its own problems—social, economic, and educational. Change and flux made it difficult to test fairly any policy in any sphere of life, and education in particular had the immense task of welding together a new generation of Americans and of handing on the most valued ideals of democracy and right human behaviour. The conflict of ideas—individual versus society, liberal education versus general, discipline versus freedom, pragmatism versus "essentialism"—all these issues, and many more, were already in embryo at the turn of the century, although the worst of the conflict did not come until after the First World War. In U.S.A. the idealist rearguard was stronger than in Britain, probably owing to the influence of Harris in education and Royce in philosophy. Two of the most powerful post-war opponents of the "progressive" movement in education had already earned recognition as writers during the first decade of the century. William C. Bagley published his *Educative Process* in 1905, and Herman H. Horne produced *Philosophy of Education* in 1904, *Idealism in Education* in 1910, and *Free Will and Human Responsibility* in 1912.

On the other side were the flourishing camps of naturalism —the group of eminent psychologists, Hall, Thorndike, Terman,

---

[1] *The Meaning of Education*, revised edition, Macmillan, 1915; *Scholarship and Service*, Scribner, 1921.

and others, developing it as a science—and pragmatism as introduced by James's *Will to Believe* in 1896, and expanded in his *Pragmatism* in 1907—an intriguing creed with a brilliant and influential leader, winning several eminent disciples. In between was the Herbartian camp, basically realist in temper but destined to be broken up before the later conflict in which a school of New Realists identified their interests with those of the opponents of pragmatism and progressivism.

Modern American Theories and Controversies

It has already been indicated that universal free education in the States was not brought into being by a stroke of the pen nor by the passing of half a dozen laws. It did not proceed state by state, for the initiative was in the hands of the many districts of each state. To-day there as as many American educational systems as there are states, but even this is a situation of recent development, for by the end of the First World War only thirty-nine states had set up State Boards of Education. Of these, six were not in existence before the twentieth century. Moreover, there is not necessarily any similarity in the composition of these boards nor uniformity in methods of working.

These facts are mentioned to emphasise that the leaders of education, whether innovators or diehards, whether theorists or practitioners, had an extraordinarily difficult task in seeking the desiderata of a good American education. Another most important complicating factor was the variation in financial resources between states. There still exist economic extremes which can hardly be envisaged without first-hand observation.[1] The existence of the Mason-Dixon line was a further great hindrance to the peaceful ebb and flow of educational theory. The constitution of the American population, even though immigration was reduced to a comparative trickle in 1914, compelled all American educators to weld social and national factors into their theories and practices. That is, ideas and methods which might have developed from abstract educational theories in countries free from immigration and colour problems, were here modified or even metamorphosed by the impact of these problems. It is not intended to deprecate this development, for it focused attention on the real needs and

---

[1] *e.g.*, see C. M. Olson and N. D. Fletcher, *Learn and Live*, Sloan Foundation, 1946. Account of Project in Applied Economics in poor areas of Kentucky, Florida, and Vermont.

characteristics of citizens of the United States in the twentieth century. However exaggerated, however coloured by emotion educational thought may have been during this century, it has, in ample compensation, been vital, meaningful, and exciting.

The conflict which has ensued, however, over the past three or four decades has had unfortunate repercussions, particularly on the professional educationist. Psychology, as a subject, gained status during the early years of the century, and although its contributions to education played a great part in the conflict, it has not suffered in prestige to the same extent as "education" as a field of higher study. The educationist may possibly have been rather too assiduous in building up his subject with ramifications of jargon and methods or in maintaining that knowledge of academic subject-matter is of minor importance in teaching. Whatever the cause, it is certain that until very recent years the rest of the learned world looked askance at the educationist. Happily, there are now many signs of reconciliation and of the acceptance of the educationist as an expert. Hitherto, as in other countries, the critics of education have often been the classicist, the scientist, the university teacher of English or history, or others of limited experience in and around schools but with deep concern for their own fields of human knowledge.

In order to appreciate fully the extremes of contrast between modern American theories and philosophies of education, the reader may find it helpful at this point to re-examine John Dewey's ideas as discussed in a previous chapter. In Britain the rivalry of the philosophies of Arnold and Spencer, the partial rise of Herbartianism, and the triumph of neo-realism in Nunn's individualistic concepts, were evolutionary rather than revolutionary changes, and their coming and passing caused only mild storms. Many Americans feel that pragmatism in its various educational forms was also an inevitable product of evolution—that Dewey was a product of his times—but although Deweyan ideas seem to have suited the general temper of the country, at least until the depression of the 'thirties, strong opposition was never lacking. The conflict was aggravated by developments in psychology similar to those in Britain after the First World War, leading to innovations in child treatment and classroom procedure. These pressures for a breaking down of traditional ideas and methods of education were held by many to be responsible for the intensification of social ills and economic stress.

Among the many wartime developments and events which affected the general attitude to education were the publication of *Democracy and Education* in 1916, and the Smith Hughes Act by which in 1917 the federal government granted aid to vocational education. Moreover, between 1913 and 1921, the National Educational Association produced a series of reports, the most important of which was that of the Commission on the Reorganisation of Secondary Education. In 1918 this body issued its Cardinal Principles of Secondary Education, a document which was, in many ways, a charter of triumph for the professional educationist, and in particular of the group of innovators whose natural leader and spokesman was John Dewey. The report claimed that reorganisation was needed because theory and practice must change according to the changing needs of society and the varying characteristics of pupils. The Committee of Ten had proposed the widening of the curriculum, but only to include other academic subjects and it was to be the same for all pupils. It was now pointed out that secondary education for all must be of a different kind. Apart from changes in the general social, economic, and international situation, there were also changes in conditions of employment. There was much less in-service training than formerly—the apprenticeship system had broken down, there was little domestic service, and many more young people worked in factories.

Seven cardinal principles were laid down; the school should aim to give the pupil health, a command of fundamental knowledge, skills and right attitude for his home life, skills for vocation, citizenship training, leisure interests, and a well-developed ethical character. Thus, education for living in a democracy was to include not only the learning of civics and national history, but also group participation in the investigation of society and its institutions. This in itself was a challenge to classroom instruction in "subjects". The provision of vocational courses of many kinds, calling on many qualities and abilities, emphasised that equality of status between occupations was part of this particular democracy. The present pattern of American high schools follows the Seven Cardinal Principles, and it is in this way that Deweyism has had its most lasting effect. The report recommended that all pupils should be admitted to secondary education without examination, that all should be promoted according to age, and that there should be a differentiated curriculum on broad vocational lines so that those not interested in traditional subjects should not be excluded. Finally, it laid on the schools the task of unifying all the peoples of the United States in a true democracy.

Thus were summarised, modified, and to some extent "potted", the philosophy, the aspirations, and the convictions of Deweyan thinkers—Kilpatrick, Bode, Childs, Counts, and Rugg—whose individual theories were more radical and different one from another.

The progressive movement, initiated officially in 1918 by the founding of the Progressive Education Association, resulted in a division of educational opinion rather different from that in Britain, where the individualism of realist theories of education[1] and of educational psychology opposed successfully for many years the social aims of idealist thinkers[2], and where educational philosophy resolved itself into a relatively simple division between a scientific realism of the Russell type and a Platonism of the Livingstone type. In Britain there was little pragmatic theory of education. In U.S.A., the pragmatists were ranged side by side with the "freedom" psychologists,[3] at least in the eyes of both realist and idealist thinkers, many of whom submerged their own differences in a union of "Essentialists" whose purpose it was to stem the tide of "Progressivism". It is hardly surprising that the heated controversies of the inter-war period were often confused in both aim and conduct, and were sometimes the result of individual and group emotion rather than of rational consideration and intellectual understanding.

In practical application the controversies appear to be based mainly on insistence by the Essentialists on systematic training in public schools in traditional subjects and discipline, and pleas by the Progressives for activity methods, informal learning, and the encouragement of self-discipline and initiative. In the sphere of ideas, however, the conflict was more complex, reflecting serious differences in attitude towards the great social, ethical, and political problems which were part of the American heritage.

The six representatives of Progressivism mentioned above, all paid tribute to Dewey as leader, and, in spite of their difference, held in common a great basic concept—that of the supreme social purpose of education. In their placing of the group before the

---

[1] e.g., Adams Nunn, Bertrand Russell.
[2] e.g., Campagnac, Jacks, Clarke.
[3] Here again, more than one group is covered—the rearguard of the Pestalozzians and Froebelians, the Freudians and others, but not scientists such as Judd and Thorndike.

individual they differed from their fellow progressives, the psychologists of the period. Moreover, they differed from their precursor, William James, who shared the individualism of his age. Nevertheless, he had given them a lead before his death by his proposal that young people should be organised to undertake tasks for their community and country "in forests, in fields, on roads and in mines, on ships . . .",[1] not only to provide much needed labour for conservation measures, but also to preserve for peace those virtues of wartime—co-operation, unselfishness, loyalty, discipline, and toughness. That James's idea was eventually adopted was partly due to the impact of the great economic depression which started in 1929, but it was also partly due to the work of those educationists who influenced public opinion towards the view that education for society would not harm individuality in the long run. Their conviction that education could promote the evolutionary uplifting of social groups was combined with a belief in intellectual freedom and the need to foster the expansion of intellect to enjoy that freedom. In their complex and diversified civilisation, such beliefs, even in the twentieth century, were intolerable to some of their fellow citizens. In a country where teachers might be forbidden to teach Darwinism or prevented from teaching history lest they sow seeds of Communism, opposition to any kind of progress was likely to make itself felt. These men, however, achieved a commendable measure of success in their various fields of endeavour.

William H. Kilpatrick (b. 1871), a Southerner, taught mathematics in schools and university before turning to the study of education and eventually joining the faculty of Teachers' College, Columbia University, in 1909. He maintains that Parker's account of his "Quincy Method" was an early inspiration, and he regards Parker as "the greatest man we had to introduce better practices into the country's schools". His strict upbringing as a minister's son, and the narrow intellectual horizons of his first university were factors in his later fervid acceptance of pragmatism, but he confesses that he was not at first particularly impressed by Dewey's lectures. A man of intellectual stature, Kilpatrick turned his critical powers on theology and mathematics as well as on education, but he is best known for his development of the "experimentalist" version of pragmatism as applied to education. Among

[1] Essay. *The Moral Equivalent of War*, 1910.

his many books on education, the titles of the following reveal something of the nature of his convictions: *Education for a Changing Civilisation* (1926), *Education and the Social Crisis* (1932), *Remaking the Curriculum* (1936), *The Teacher and Society* (1937), and *Self-hood and Civilisation* (1941).

He is the most faithful of all the Deweyans and did much to make clear the philosophy, methods, and psychology of pragmatism. He rejected current psychology, even that of the eminent Thorndike, because it sought to depersonalise humanity and assess it by standardised tests. "It tried to make education mechanical," he wrote, "partly to have it more easily controlled from within and above."[1] Instead he would substitute a conception of learning and thinking that is "essentially creative and dynamic as befits a plastic and changing world".[2] He deplored the prevalence of the old instructional methods in school because pupils gain nothing from mechanical repetition, drill, and recitation unless they have first felt a personal need for them. Of the upholders of traditional methods he writes: "When people have interests they wish to hold undisturbed, they fall naturally into this older Platonic logic. . . . These people in their hearts reject freedom of speech and freedom of study because they themselves already have the truth and these freedoms might, if followed, 'subvert' their 'truth' ".[3] The teacher's task, according to Kilpatrick, is to guide rather than to compel, to stimulate rather than to indoctrinate. Like Dewey, he points out the interdependence of peoples in the modern world, and suggests that the adults of a community might well co-operate with their young people in the planning and carrying out of community activities. The whole idea of the Project—which was Kilpatrick's rather than Dewey's—was directly in line with James's proposal of 1910 and won considerable public support in the inter-war period. Not only were large-scale projects on such topics as "Conservation" and "Pan-Americanism" undertaken by many schools—often all the schools of an area—as part of the curriculum, but, in addition, community service by school children became common—planting and caring for trees, regulating traffic, campaigning for pest exterminations, organising fire drills, farming and canning activities, local history groups, orchestras, and many other

---

[1] W. H. Kilpatrick, *Remaking the Curriculum*, p. 17, Newson, 1936.
[2] *ibid.*, p. 22.
[3] W. H. Kilpatrick, *The Teacher and Society*, p. 36, Appleton Century, 1937.

efforts which are within the capacities of children, but which do not enter into the normal curriculum.

Kilpatrick repeats his faith in the educative value of these activities in his essay on *The Experimentalist Outlook* in the Yearbook of Education for 1942. "We need now to build social intelligence to enable man to grapple more effectively with these resistant social problems", he writes; "One thing the school can do is to lay a foundation of social knowledge by having the pupils and students study their communities and undertake socially useful work along with others in the community. A more directly intellectual attack on the building of actual social intelligence is to have the pupils and students, especially as they advance in years, study social problems, trying to understand our society and its strengths and its weaknesses."[1]

Boyd H. Bode (1878-1953) became a university lecturer in philosophy early in his career, and was appointed to a professorship in education at Ohio State University soon after the end of the First World War. He wrote several books on educational psychology before publishing his *Progressive Education at the Crossroads* in 1938. He contributed many articles and essays to educational publications, and as an eminent university philosopher exerted considerable influence in educational spheres.

He joined Dewey and Rugg in a critical analysis of progressive education in 1938, a date which marked the final withdrawal of the pragmatist group from identification with progressivism. Bode's book published that year claimed that "child centred" methods had become a cult, setting up false "absolutes". "To interpret the doctrine of interest as meaning that all activity must be motivated by immediate and spontaneous interests," he writes, "is to misrepresent it."[2] He goes so far as to contend, "The purpose of sound education is to emancipate the pupil from dependence on immediate interest".[3] He maintains that a superstitious reverence for childhood had led to the abandonment of the planning and organising which ought to be done in a school to ensure the intellectual development of pupils. He speaks of "indiscriminate tirades against 'subjects' ",[4] a comment that supports the assumption that

---

[1] National Society for the Study of Education, Forty-first Yearbook, Part I, pp. 83-4, University of Chicago Press.
[2] B. H. Bode, *Progressive Education at the Crossroads*, p. 53, Newson, 1938.
[3] *ibid.*, p. 58.   [4] *ibid.*, p. 70.

Dewey had no quarrel with the subject-based curriculum at the secondary stage.

Bode echoes Kilpatrick's plea for the better use of the intelligence of the people of a community. He believes that schools should train young people to think by enabling them to study and discuss contemporary problems, institutions, and beliefs. It is hardly surprising that he is particularly interested in education at university level and that he warmly approves of the state universities with their wide provision for the needs, interests, and abilities of all citizens. Of the old type of university which sought absolute standards and gave liberal education he comments, "the common man is always told that his little affairs do not count in comparison with these august absolutes".[1] Therefore, he has no regrets that the content of new courses for degrees might range "all the way from stable manure to multi-dimensional space".[2]

John L. Childs (b. 1889) was a colleague of Dewey, Kilpatrick, Counts, and Rugg at Teachers' College, Columbia University. Among his books expounding the philosophy and methods of his group—and his own particular version of pragmatism—are *Education and the Philosophy of Experimentalism* (1931), *Education and Morals* (1950), and *American Pragmatism and Education* (1956).

Childs, together with Bode, is a true disciple of Dewey. He speaks of "experimental naturalism" as Dewey's viewpoint, and he has given one of the best expositions of how that viewpoint was gained by an American and accepted by many Americans while remaining unappreciated by the rest of the world. His arguments are used frequently to explain this phenomenon—that America has no "rigidly fixed system of ancient traditions, customs, and institutions, such as tend to orient the life of a people towards the past rather than towards the future"[3]; that men had learned to improvise in "frontier" conditions of uncertainty, and that abundant natural resources and the need to use machines as substitutes for manual labour had "put scientific processes into the ordinary affairs of everyday life".[4]

---

[1] B. H. Bode, *Progressive Education at the Crossroads*, p. 23, Newson, 1938.
[2] *ibid.*, p. 28.
[3] J. L. Childs, *Education and the Philosophy of Experimentalism*, p. 16, Appleton Century, 1931.
[4] *ibid.*, p. 16.

In discussing the development of the mind he extends this argument: "Had our environment been different, our experiences would have been different. Had our experiences been different, our minds also would have been different. In short, to live differently is to think differently".[1]

In a period when the pendulum was swinging towards social considerations in education, Childs performed a valuable service by defining the pragmatist attitude to personality. He declares that the denial of absolutes of goodness establishes the experimentalist respect for human individuality, and he urges that a true democratic society must preserve individual differences and not seek to obliterate them "in the interest of some static social arrangement".[2]

He traces the progress of individuality from the learning of responsibility and "intelligent self-direction" in school to the exercise of critical thought in adult civic life. Conditioning and indoctrination he condemns as immoral, for "any response which is so fixed that it cannot be modified in the light of consequences is a dangerous response to acquire".[3] As a good experimentalist he believes that much of the experience which develops responsibility and critical thought must be gained in society itself. Here his comment on project work answers many criticisms of that method: "As children grow older, artificial school projects are too superficial to call out whole-hearted responses. This is as it should be, for maturing individuals cannot be expected to derive nourishment from significant development apart from contacts with actual life situations".[4] Dr Childs became Emeritus Professor at Columbia in 1954, and thus his influence in favour of the experimentalist viewpoint has continued until the present day.

George S. Counts (b. 1889) was head of a college department of education at the age of twenty-seven. At twenty-nine he was a professor of sociology in a teachers' college, and in 1927 he was appointed to Teachers' College, Columbia University. Much of his writing has been on sociological and administrative topics, but several of his books have been provocative in their discussion of social philosophy: *The American Road to Culture* (1930), *Dare the School Build a New Social Order?* (1932), *The School Can Teach Democracy* (1939), *The Education of Free Men in American*

---

[1] J. L. Childs, *Education and the Philosophy of Experimentalism*, p. 9, Appleton Century, 1931.
[2] *ibid.*, p. 227.
[3] *ibid.*, p. 161.
[4] *ibid.*, p. 164.

Democracy (1941), *Education and the Promise of America* (1945), and *Education and American Civilisation* (1952).

The ideas of Counts are closely allied to those of Kilpatrick and Bode. Of the social function of education, he writes: "The meeting of a social situation involves the making of decisions and the working out of adjustments. . . . Society requires great numbers of persons who, while capable of gathering and digesting facts, are at the same time able to think in terms of life, make decisions, and act".[1] Like Kilpatrick, he deplores developments which render schooling more mechanistic, whether in psychological measurement or in the large-scale organisation of masses of children, for he believes American democracy to be "a way of life in which human personality is judged of supreme, of measureless worth".[2]

He feels that teachers should be more decisive in their opinions and methods, and should "seek power and then strive to use that power fully and wisely and in the interests of the great masses of the people".[3] By their efforts, education can help America to achieve a synthesis of democracy and industrialism, while at the same time preserving the integrity of the individual. As a sociologist he is so insistent that the schools must teach democracy that he is sometimes more in favour of indoctrination than is consistent with his general creed.

In his post-war book, Dr Counts reiterates these points, emphasising even more strongly that education should strive for individual excellence, physical, intellectual, and moral. He sees the school as a place for the strengthening of principles of equality and for the learning of world-citizenship. "The stakes in this issue involve the whole future of mankind",[4] he urges in condemning the isolationist attitude.

Harold O. Rugg (1886-1960) reached the faculty of Columbia University in 1915 as an educational statistician. His early publications were textbooks on statistical method and school books on social science, but in 1928, at the height of the progressive movement, he and Ann Shumaker published *The Child Centered School*, a provocative and widely-read book putting forward "new articles of faith"—freedom, child-initiative, self-activity, child interests, self-expression, and personality adjustment. Among Rugg's other

[1] G. S. Counts, *Dare the School Build a New Social Order?*, p. 22, Day, 1932.
[2] G. S. Counts, *The Prospects of American Democracy*, p. 20, Day, 1938.
[3] G. S. Counts, *Dare the School Build a New Social Order?*, p. 30, Day, 1932.
[4] G. S. Counts, *Education and American Civilisation*, p. 422, Columbia University, 1952.

influential works are *Culture and Education in America* (1931), *The Great Technology* (1933), *Foundations for American Education* (1947), and (with B. M. Brooks) *The Teacher in School and Society* (1950).

His social science textbooks were widely used in American schools, although his directing of attention to problems—not only in history and geography, but also in politics and economics—and his frank discussion of them, earned the opposition of many groups of people—associations of manufacturers and advertisers, exclusive women's organisations, and people who disliked his approach to religion and politics.

In *The Child Centered School* he criticised the education of the previous generation for aiming merely at the addition of socially useful subjects to the traditional curriculum—reorganisation rather than reconstruction. It was not long, however, before he began to doubt that he could go all the way with the new process of curriculum reconstruction. In *Culture and Education in America* he contends that there are many human experiences in which the experimentalists' "problem solving" has no part, however useful it may be in dealing with external needs. He feels that in creative activities there is no recognising of a "felt difficulty" and no decision on action in a "forked road situation", but only "the constantly changing, indefinite character of the artist's subjective vision".[1]

As Dewey in *Art as Experience* did not refute this contention, it is clear that there were no major deviations from pragmatism in Rugg's general principles. He has exercised influence mainly in the field of social and economic planning related to education, and he has been particularly eager to see an extension of adult education. He believes that the techniques of the high-powered salesman should be used to make the people "production-in-terms-of-consumption-needs-conscious, economic-government-conscious, scientific-technology-conscious".[2]

Carleton W. Washburne (b. 1889) is an exception among this galaxy of professors, for although he eventually joined their ranks, his main life-work was accomplished during twenty-six years as a school superintendent. Prior to his appointment in 1919 to Winnetka, a pleasant suburb of Chicago, he had taught in Californian

---

[1] H. O. Rugg, *Culture and Education in America*, p. 369, Harcourt Brace, 1931.
[2] H. O. Rugg, *The Great Technology*, p. 202, Day, 1933.

schools, acted as a director of playgrounds, and conducted the science department of a teachers' college. As a superintendent he was able to introduce throughout his district many Deweyan principles without lowering the academic records of the schools. He won the co-operation of teachers and parents, and the "Winnetka Plan" was established as a lasting proof that progressive education could be good education. He wrote *What is Progressive Education?* a few years ago, but his personal aims and ideas are more fully discussed in *A Living Philosophy of Education* (1940).

The high schools of Winnetka became particularly well known for their curricula based on individual work in academic subjects and co-operative work in enterprises similar to those in the outside world—bank, insurance society, trade union, retail store, livestock corporation, conservation authority, school journal, and many other activities. The pupils progressed in academic work at their own rate, testing themselves at the end of each assignment.

By the time he left Winnetka in 1945 Washburne had become an eminent educationist and had influenced many teachers through his work at university summer schools. After the war he worked in Italy for the United States Information Service and for UNESCO in the task of educational reconstruction,[1] before accepting the chairmanship of the department of education at Brooklyn College in 1949. Several of his books have been translated into other languages: *Remakers of Mankind*, *Adjusting the School to the Child*, and *Better Schools*—the last written with M. Stearns.

Although it is clear that he accepts much of Dewey's teaching, Washburne did not gain his reputation in verbal encounter with the protagonists of the 'thirties. He went on resolutely with the task of showing that generalisations could not be made about progressive education. While the Essentialists were condemning Kilpatrick and Counts (although usually exonerating Dewey), Dewey, Bode, and Rugg were condemning the adherents of child-centred education. Meanwhile, Washburne was organising efficient child-centred education which gave attention to individual needs and opportunity for social adjustment. While Bagley calmed Essentialists' fears that experimentalism aimed to bring about social and political change, Washburne was proving that Bagley's

[1]*The World's Good* (Day, 1954) deals with the work of UN, UNICEF, and UNESCO.

arguments were faulty. Bagley suggested that the social and political significance of pragmatic schools would be negligible because most of them were private schools for the well-to-do. Washburne showed that new methods, new curricula, and new attitudes were being developed in the public school system.

If the origins of Washburne's ideas are sought outside his own studies of current thought, they surely may be found in Francis Parker, whose school he attended, and in his mother, a writer on Froebel and child study. At one time, Mrs Washburne worked with Parker and she was a friend of Harris and Dewey. Professor Washburne pays warm tribute to Parker, but he also feels that his own teaching experiences—in rural multi-racial schools, in classes of "misfits" and handicapped children, and in work with "bad" boys—helped him to formulate his philosophy. His ideas are not mere theory, his philosophy is a consideration of *what* he is doing, *how* he is doing it, and *why*.[1] His methods lack neither standards nor purpose, and his aims are definite. Thus in discussing the question of indoctrination he writes: "It is the function of education in controversial fields to give children a powerful motive for action through showing them vividly the commonly desired goals; then to train them in the scientific exploration of the various paths which have been suggested as a means of reaching these goals".[2]

Washburne was not the only progressive of the public schools who achieved success and recognition. One of the best known of his contemporaries is **Miss Helen Parkhurst (b. 1892)** who, in 1919, when Washburne went to Winnetka, started her first experiment in individual learning by "the laboratory plan" with a class of crippled boys. The following year it was introduced into the public high school of Dalton, Massachusetts.

Miss Parkhurst claims kinship with Madame Montessori—with whom she worked for a time—rather than with Dewey, although she quotes him in her book, *Education on the Dalton Plan* (1922). It is interesting that both Washburne and Miss Parkhurst mention appreciatively Dr Frederick Burk, of San Francisco State College. Washburne was a teacher at that college from 1914 to 1919, and Helen Parkhurst was there in 1915: "I enjoyed, through the courtesy of Dr Frederick Burk and his interest in my work, the

[1] Preface. *A Living Philosophy of Education*, Harper, 1940.
[2] *ibid*., p. 466.

satisfaction of making a practical test of my laboratory plan upon a selected group of one hundred children".[1]

Miss Parkhurst gives as the two principles of her plan, freedom and co-operation—freedom from interruptions, from bells, from pressures of teacher and companions—and co-operation, the interaction of group life. The second principle is often lost sight of in modern discussions of the Dalton Plan, and in view of the history of the progressive movement it ought to be borne in mind that Miss Parkhurst did not envisage undue extremes of individual freedom.

"The Dalton Plan lays emphasis upon the importance of the child's living while he does his work," she writes, "and the manner in which he acts as a member of society rather than upon the subjects of his curriculum. It is the sum total of these twin experiences which determine his character and his knowledge." [2]

Experiments in methods more closely related to Dewey's were also flourishing in the 'twenties, and in 1927 J. A. Stevenson, of the Carnegie Institute, Pittsburgh, was able to summarise much of this work and define its characteristics under the name Project Method.[3]

The best of the new methods and experiments were approved by many of those leading educationists who could not accept the new philosophy. Of the older generation, Charles McMurry wrote a book on teaching by projects, but he interpreted the project as a Herbartian centre of interest involving a great deal of classroom teaching rather than creative group activity. W. C. Bagley, a realist and educational psychologist of McMurry's generation, wrote a somewhat unenthusiastic preface to Stevenson's book, suggesting that the method was by no means new. He quotes from Thoreau's[4] Walden: "Which would have advanced most at the end of the month—the boy who had made his own jack-knife from ore which he had dug and smelted, reading as much as would be necessary for this, or the boy who had attended lectures on metallurgy at the Institute?".

Professor W. C. Bagley was sixty years old when he published, in 1934, his most powerful refutation of pragmatism, Education and Emergent Man. He had been a professor at Teachers' College,

[1] H. Parkhurst, The Dalton Plan, p. 12, Bell, 1922.
[2] ibid., pp. 24-5.
[3] J. A. Stevenson, The Project Method of Teaching, Macmillan, 1927.
[4] Contemporary of Emerson.

Columbia University, since 1917, and was instrumental in establishing the Essentialist Committee for the Advancement of American Education in 1938. Bagley's philosophy is more akin to that of the Neo-realists than to the idealism of some of his Essentialist colleagues, but he shared their views on the value of knowledge for its own sake, not merely as an instrument. He was as opposed to the mechanistic attitude as firmly as the experimentalists; in fact, he was one of the first to question the ultimate validity of intelligence testing. He respected John Dewey, his colleague, but he believed not only in "systematic and sequential" effort in learning, but also in the cherishing of permanent values in a time of change.

Among his many eminent Essentialist associates were his colleague Dr Kandel, Dr Eby of Texas, and Dr Breed and Dr Morrison of Chicago. They saw in the extension of the progressive movement the abandonment of standards of scholastic achievement, the neglect of system and sequence, indiscriminate use of activity methods, an over-emphasis on social studies, irresponsibility in curriculum revision, and the use of elementary schools to establish a new social order. Bagley spoke for many who were not opposed to better schools, better teaching, and better methods when he wrote: "It is true that the world of to-day is a different world from the world of 1913 and from the world of 1929—but that does not mean that everything has changed . . . the winds that blow still follow the laws of storms; *Huckleberry Finn* and *Treasure Island* still delight youth; and the Sistine Madonna is just as beautiful as of yore".[1]

F. S. Breed (*b.* 1876) continued the campaign at the philosophical level in his *Education and the New Realism* (1939) and in *The Realist Outlook*, a contribution to the Yearbook of Education for 1942. He was a trained philosopher who joined the School of Education of the University of Chicago in 1917. His early work had been in the field of psychology and teaching method, but he now emerged as a defender of the scientific viewpoint against both pragmatist and idealist. It is somewhat curious to find that he accuses Dewey's disciples of "unrestricted emphasis on individualism". He expounds a "bipolar view" as a guide to education: "It begins with respect for individual demands, but it includes respect

[1] W. C. Bagley, *Education and Emergent Man*, p. 151, Ronald Press, 1934.

for social demands . . . it asserts that liberty should be supplemented by authority in both school and state".[1]

In the years preceding the outbreak of the Second World War when the doctrine of education for society was making headway in Britain, a new school of opposition to current pragmatic trends was strengthening in the United States. One of the early leaders was Herman H. Horne (1874-1946), a trained linguist and philosopher who joined the faculty of New York University in 1909. His early writings established his idealist viewpoint, and he then concentrated on theological topics until his commentary on Dewey's *Democracy and Education*. This was published in 1932 under the title *The Democratic Philosophy of Education*. It purports to be an exposition and appreciation, but it is, in fact, a refutation of Dewey's views. Horne's summary of his own wordy thesis is that Dewey's thinking is not theistic, he has no theory of feeling, he ignores health education, he neglects home education and education for leisure, he is not clear whether education should aim at individual growth or social efficiency, he does not appreciate the significance of personality, and his naturalistic view of intelligence is unsound. This book is one of the most complete expositions of the idealist viewpoint.

Following Horne, a younger philosopher, Mortimer J. Adler (*b.* 1902), a professor of law at the University of Chicago, took up the cudgels for the restoration of an Aristotelian viewpoint. Maintaining that there are unchanging verities he sought a return to an education fixed in content and aim. He wrote *In Defense of the Philosophy of Education* for the Yearbook of Education (1942), an edition which reflects the trend in current opinion by including essays by three idealists—Horne, Adler, and the Roman Catholic W. McGucken, against one representative of realism and one of pragmatism. Adler claims to prove by philosophical inquiry that "education is the process by which those powers (abilities, capacities) of men that are susceptible to habituation, are perfected by *good* habits, through means artistically contrived, and employed by any man to help another or himself achieve the end in view (*i.e.* good habits)".[2] Adler was an editor of *The Great Books of the Western World*,[3] a venture which played a

---

[1] F. S. Breed, *The Realist Outlook*, Forty-first Yearbook of Education, p. 137, University of Chicago Press, 1942.

[2] Forty-first Yearbook of Education, p. 246, 1942.

[3] There are about a hundred "Great Books", including *The Bible*, *The Odyssey*, *Canterbury Tales*, Grosseteste's *On Light*. John Erskine first put forward the idea in 1919 as a means of educating war veterans for citizenship.

great part in the extension of idealist methods of education, especially in colleges and adult education organisations.

Contemporary with Adler, and well known for his activities and publications on behalf of liberal education, is **Robert M. Hutchins** (*b.* 1899), who was also professor of law before he became President of the University of Chicago at the early age of thirty. He remained in this office until 1945, after which he was Chancellor for six years and then served as a director of the Ford Foundation for several years. His practical endeavours and his writings have always been in the field of higher education, but it was inevitable that there should be repercussions in the high schools which feed the universities. His main publications are: *No Friendly Voice* (1936), *The Higher Learning in America* (1936), *Education for Freedom* (1943), *Morals, Religion and Higher Education* (1950), and *The Conflict in Education in a Democratic Society* (1953).

His solution to the ills of the world is a return to Platonic concepts. His theory is democratic to the extent that all young people between sixteen and twenty, unless subnormal in intelligence, should have the same intellectual training—a balanced, all-round introduction to the knowledge and ideas man has accumulated. The curriculum, therefore, should be fixed. "The liberally educated man must know how to read, write, and figure", he writes; "He must know and understand the ideas that have animated mankind. He must comprehend the tradition in which he lives. He must be able to communicate with his fellow men. Through familiarity with the best models he must have constantly before him that habitual vision of greatness. . . ."[1]

Hutchins's campaign is against two features of American education that had come into being without any help from the progressives—the elevation of vocational and practical subjects and the acceptance of the elective system in high schools. Subjects of little intellectual significance were taught in universities —games, advertising, housecraft, stenography, and even cosmetology. In the high school not only could pupils choose to study subjects for one year only, they could also select a heavy proportion of subjects with little intellectual content.

These practices were too well established to be seriously affected by the visionary idealism of Hutchins. Two liberal arts colleges[2]

[1] *The Conflict in Education*, p. 95. Harper, 1953.
[2] An appraisal of St John's College scheme may be found in S. Hook, *Education for Modern Man*, Dial Press, 1946.

put his ideas into practice, but in his own university many of his colleagues were opposed to any thorough experimentation in liberal curricula and to the abolition of vocational courses. In perspective, however, it will probably be found that Hutchins's earnest and persevering work in expounding his doctrine was of considerable value, not only in drawing public attention to the things of the mind but also in reminding Americans that education must be continually watched, criticised, and refined.

His attitude to specialisation is frequently expressed in his post-war writings: "When I was on the faculty of Yale we taught Engineering English in the Engineering School. This meant, of course, that an engineer was taught to talk only to another engineer. Since 50 per cent. of the graduates of the Engineering School did not become engineers, I can only assume that they went through life cut off from communication with their fellow men".[1]

He is equally antipathetic to social aims for education: "I believe that it is dangerous as well as futile to regard the educational system as a means of getting a program of social reform adopted",[2] he argues. It may be remembered that in Britain Sir Fred Clarke a few years earlier had denied that the school could bring about changes in society. For Hutchins, education is not only intellectual and liberal, it is also individual and verbal: "The process of such education should be dialectic", he submits. "The Socratic dialogue is the great mirror of pedagogy whether the student is a child or an adult".[3]

Hutchins stimulated discussion and criticism of American higher education, and philosophers as well as educationists published their views.[4] Of Hutchins's contribution, Professor Feibleman, a philosopher, writes in the Yearbook of Education (1955): "Hutchins deserves credit for having advertised in this country the fundamental question of what a university ought to be. His answer and Adler's, of course, are wrong, but American education owes him this: Any other answer will have to be made at high level of the questions he has asked".[5]

[1] R. M. Hutchins, *The Conflict in Education*, p. 37.
[2] *ibid.*, p. 52.   [3] *ibid.*, pp. 95-6.
[4] *e.g.*, Mark van Doren, *Liberal Education*, Holt, 1943; Theodore Greene, *Liberal Education Reconsidered*, Harvard, 1953; Thomas Woody, *Liberal Education for Free Men*, University of Pennsylvania, 1957; H. Mumford Jones, *One Great Society; Humane Learning in the United States*, Harcourt, 1959. There had been experiments before Hutchins's time, *e.g.* Alexander Meiklejohn's work at Amherst and Wisconsin.
[5] *Modern Philosophies of Education*, National Society for the Study of Education, pp. 638-9, University of Chicago Press, 1955.

Mid-Century Views of American Education

Although the time is hardly ripe to identify the most influential thinkers on education of the era after the Second World War, there is little doubt that the inevitable process of stocktaking gave a measure of victory to the Essentialists, the conservatives, the anti-Deweyans, and the anti-Progressives. Schools were criticised for failing to discipline their pupils and for not exacting adequate standards of scholarship. Colleges and universities were criticised for not providing true education. Many of the failings and weaknesses of education that were laid at the door of Dewey and the Progressives were due less to the influence of any educational theories than to the accumulation of results of the rapid changes that had come about in all aspects of the life of this immense country. An example of a "weakness" that surely cannot be laid at Dewey's door is the survival of the abuses associated with the lightning growth of universities at the end of the last century. It has been necessary recently to investigate the trade, which still persists, in bogus degrees.

It is a significant fact, however, that the American Education Fellowship—which changed its name from the Progressive Education Association in 1938—ceased to exist in 1955. Two years later the journal *Progressive Education* was discontinued. The change of name had involved a change of objectives from "child development" to "reconstruction of society". It might seem that after 1955 there was no great enthusiasm for the reconstruction of American society. Dr Kandel, one of the original Essentialists, recently gave his view that progressivism was not widespread because "the schools have in fact been protected by a certain conservatism on the part of the teacher".[1] This view of American teachers is not shared by other educators, however. Some feel that "current fads" spread all to quickly. A high school principal, D. M. Miles, contends that the newest is that of the gifted child: "Schools all over the country are jumping on the band-wagon of this new fad, with advanced placement programs, the introduction of special seminars for the gifted, honours classes, and even an adaptation of Mortimer Adler's Great Books Program".[2] If this is true, then the second reaction of post-war thought on education appears to be bearing fruit.

Briefly, the first reaction after 1945 appears to have been to wish to build a better world, and, in particular, a better United

[1] *Yearbook of Education*, p. 465, 1958.　　　　[2] *ibid.*, p. 469.

States. For the first four years of peace, only the heavy spending of money and resources to help other peoples—the Marshall Plan, the Atlantic Pact, UNESCO activities—limited the process of improvement and development in education. The social function of education was recognised, and the acceptance of the obligation to educate for internationalism was growing. The federal authorities were prepared to play a greater part in improving education. In 1948 the Federation of Teachers issued the report of its Commission on Educational Reconstruction, and in 1949 the National Citizens' Commission was formed with the object of furthering the improvement of education by co-operative action in local communities. Unfortunately, however, the cold war with Russia was followed by the Korean War, and these disturbing events had their repercussions on American education. The year 1950 saw not only the outbreak of the Korean War but also the culmination of a wave of bitter criticism of the nation's schools.[1]

During the past decade American educators have wrestled with problems generated by the urgently felt need to build a strong, united America—the wave of McCarthyism in 1953, the desegregation measures in the South, and recently the Sputnik set-back which has brought to the fore the neo-Jeffersonian doctrine of educating an élite. Here and now, it is temporarily—and therefore pragmatically—the education of the potential scientist that is at issue.

It is indeed a difficult task to select from the many eminent American writers on education those who best represent current trends of thought. However, few will quarrel with the suggestion that posterity will pay tribute to three men who represent three different viewpoints—Theodore Brameld, Robert Ulich, and James Conant.

In many ways **Professor Brameld (b. 1904)**, of New York University, represents the rearguard of the Deweyan pragmatists. One of the most debatable points in pragmatic educational theory was the question of education for change. Professor Kandel called it the Cult of Uncertainty,[2] and many critics rejected the pragmatic viewpoint on the ground that change would not necessarily be for the better. This argument ignores Dewey's firmly held faith that the path of human endeavour must be upwards. Brameld

---

[1] e.g., M. Smith, *And Madly Teach*, 1949; B. E. Bell, *Crisis in Education*, 1949; A. Lynd, *Quackery in the Public Schools*, 1950; A. Bestor, *Educational Wastelands*, 1953.
[2] I. L. Kandel, *The Cult of Uncertainty*, Macmillan, 1943.

feels he has found the answer to the criticism, and he is clearly the subject of Hutchins's comment: "One of Mr Dewey's followers, who has invented an educational policy called reconstructionalism, wants to use the schools to reconstruct society, and, in particular, to bring about a world government . . . but I do not see how the schools can preach world government unless the American people are willing to have this aim promoted in the schools".[1]

Among the books in which Professor Brameld discusses this new philosophy are *Ends and Means in Education* (1949), *Philosophies of Education in Cultural Perspective* (1955), and *Towards a Reconstructed Philosophy of Education* (1956). Most of his detailed proposals apply to education from seventeen to twenty, which he envisages will be a period of compulsory education. In the elementary schools he would be satisfied with good Deweyan schemes, and at the secondary level subject-based learning should lead to "high standards of literacy and mastery of vital contents . . . because these are the necessary tools of social power for people struggling to obtain the dominant goals demanded by our age".[2]

Although this education from seventeen is to include continued subject study and training in skills and vocational knowledge, these are to be alternated with group discussions and investigations. In the first year, contemporary cultures would be studied; in the second, the problems, methods, needs, and goals of science and art; in the third, education and human relations; in the fourth, a review of the courses would be made in order to determine the means by which the desired goals might be reached.

The purpose of this process would be to ensure that majority opinion—which must decide what goals and values are valid here and now—is capable of arriving at that decision by discussion and scientific enquiry. This implies, of course, that the goals and values of a democratic community will be likely to undergo change and modification, as the process of coming to majority decision is a continuous one. Minority opinion is free to express itself, but not to impose its decisions on the majority—as happened so often in the past.

Professor Brameld is a champion of freedom, but he would welcome the extension of federal influence in education. He

[1] R. M. Hutchins, *The Conflict in Education*, p. 50, Harper, 1953.
[2] T. Brameld, *Towards a Reconstructed Philosophy of Education*, p. 253, Dryden Press, 1956.

ridicules the widespread fear of the "bugaboo" of federal control, and suggests that the Tennessee Valley Authority has proved it to be "completely practical to combine centralised authority and decentralised administration in a working synthesis".[1] He is equally contemptuous of the opposition to progressive education. He believes that in spite of smear campaigns by those whose individual power depends on the ignorance and meekness of the common man, and in spite of stubborn resistance by the "perennialists" in education, progressivism is still very much alive and active. With the passage of time we can still ask Brameld's question—Will progressive education "successfully engage in a counter-offensive before mortal damage has been done"?[2]

Dr Robert Ulich (b. 1890), professor of education at Harvard, did not go to U.S.A. from Germany until 1934, and as his writings in English belong to the past twenty years he is a true representative of mid-century views on education. Appreciative of the great virtues of American education, he is, at the same time, eager to see it improved in intellectual quality. Basically, he has much in common with Hutchins, perhaps because of his own European training, but he is an idealist who has learned that it is wiser to resolve the conflicts of the contemporary situation than to seek isolation from them. "We can no longer maintain the old separation of the theoretical studies which mould the 'educated man' and the applied studies . . . which have not a large liberalising element in themselves",[3] he acknowledges, but at the same time he deplores the disintegration of the liberal tradition. This he attributes partly to the utilitarian attitude he feels American parents and children have towards education. In particular, in this era, "The interests of talented youth have become more and more absorbed by the applied sciences which promise a more spectacular career than the older humanities".[4]

His suggestions for the improvement of American high schools are reminiscent of early ideas of multilateral schools in Britain. He would have many provisions for communal activities—a chapel, halls for music and drama, library and art gallery, gymnasia and playing fields—but, for study, the pupils would be divided into houses—humanists, scientists, executives, artisans, and workers.

---

[1] T. Brameld, *Ends and Means in Education*, p. 79, Harper, 1950.
[2] *ibid.*, p. 37.
[3] R. Ulich, *Fundamentals of Democratic Education*, p. 241.
[4] *Crisis and Hope in American Education*, p. 38, Beacon Press, 1951.

The vocational slant of such an education renders these suggestions somewhat inconsistent in a theory of liberal education, but on examination it is thoroughly Platonic.

Of the curriculum, Ulich contends it must have "organic structure, where subjects lead up to a certain end and height, and where the relations between various parts of knowledge are pointed out."[1] Although his proposals for the grouping of pupils—comparable to the English process of streaming—appear to favour specialisation, he envisages that all should receive an education "to a degree general, but primarily liberal".[2] Yet he voices the eternal problem of the teacher when he comments: "There is something insoluble in the problems of educating the unskilled worker, because there is something insoluble in his human situation".[3]

Ulich's main dilemma is the education of the teacher, for while he deplores the decline of some of the older disciplines—particularly languages, both classical and modern—he is torn between a conviction that specialisation in one subject is essential at college level, and the realisation that "the more specialisation progresses on higher levels, the greater will be the difficulty for the prospective teacher to find his particular need of professional preparation adequately satisfied".[4] He feels that "general education" at the teacher educational level can only aid the development of a well-rounded intellect if the different courses are interrelated. Moreover—and here he voices a major difficulty that is rarely acknowledged—"Courses in general education can fufil their purpose only if they are given by the most mature and comprehensive minds of the university".[5]

In spite of his criticisms, Ulich has a high regard for American education. He points out its advantages over other systems, and claims that modern American children learn not less but more than their fathers and grandfathers. He is anxious that undue emphasis on democratic principles should not lead to mediocrity. Democracy does not mean uniformity. On the other hand, he does not advocate that the education of the gifted should be only intellectual and academic. He points out that Plato's guardians were "men who had shown their worth through a continued interaction between an active or vocational, and a contemplative life".[6]

---

[1] *Crisis and Hope in American Education*, p. 43, Beacon Press, 1951.
[2] *ibid.*, p. 118.   [3] *ibid.*, p. 83.
[4] R. Ulich, *Professional Education as a Humane Study*, p. 104. Macmillan, 1956.
[5] *ibid.*, p. 106.   [6] *ibid.*, p. 75.

We need to foster the qualities of the guardians—balance, maturity, humanity, and altruism.

The name of **James Bryant Conant** (*b*. 1893) is to most people that of a High Commissioner and Ambassador rather than that of an educator. That he embarked upon a field investigation of his country's schools immediately after his resignation in 1957 is a fact which not only lifts education to a "first priority" in the nation's affairs, but is also evidence of his deep and selfless concern for the betterment of his countrymen.

Dr Conant won recognition as a brilliant chemist early in his career. After working with the Chemical Warfare Department during the First World War he taught chemistry at Harvard from 1919 to 1933—for the last two years as head of department. In the Second World War he was advisor to the project which produced the first atom bomb, and after the war he was a member of the General Advisory Committee of the Atomic Energy Commission. A scientist of this calibre might be expected to hold strong views on the education of potential scientists, but Dr Conant has an "over-view" which enables him to appreciate the other essentials for educating a democracy.

The termination of his chemistry teaching in 1933 was due to his elevation to the presidency of Harvard, a position he filled with distinction for twenty years. It was inevitable that his attention should be focused on the problem of the content of university education, and in 1943 he appointed a committee of Harvard professors to investigate "The Objectives of a General Education in a Free Society". The celebrated Harvard Report was published in 1945, and it was one of the first post-war American books on education to be widely read in Britain. Dr Conant emphasises in his preface that the Committee had examined "the entire problem of providing adequate education for all American youth". The findings of the Committee of twelve—with their multitude of advisors and witnesses—were that although there could be no uniform general education owing to the absence of a centralised system, there could at least be fixity of aim in schools and colleges. It was agreed that general education, representing "the common knowledge and common values on which a free society depends",[1] was essential in the cultivation of the power to think effectively, to communicate thought, to make relevant judgments,

[1] *General Education in a Free Society*, p. 58, University of Harvard Press, 1945.

and to discriminate among values. For the meaning of "general education", however, we must turn to Dr Conant: "For the use of the current phrase 'general education' instead of 'liberal education' the writer is ready to take his share of blame. . . . The heart of the problem of a general education is the continuance of the liberal and humane tradition. Neither the mere acquisition of information nor the development of special skills and talents can give the broad basis of understanding which is essential if our civilisation is to be preserved . . . even a good grounding in mathematics and the physical and biological sciences, combined with an ability to read and write several foreign languages, does not provide a sufficient educational background for the citizens of a free nation. . . . It includes no history, no art, no literature, no philosophy. Unless the educational process includes *at each level of maturity* some continuing contact with those fields in which value judgments are of prime importance, it must fall far short of the ideal".[1]

It was suggested that at both school and college all students should study "the physical world, man's corporate life, his inner visions and standards". In school, at least half the time should be devoted to this "core" which should be a planned, continuing whole rather than a haphazard series of courses. There should be courses of differing difficulty for pupils of differing ability, but the purpose must always be the same, and pupils must be persuaded of the importance of these courses which lack vocational bias or final diploma.

A few years later, Dr Conant wrote *Education in a Divided World*, in which he admitted to a growing consciousness of the immense difficulty of ensuring that the "common core" meant the same, in terms of insights and values, to all children, whatever their social or economic environment. The great diversity of American schools—from the private schools for the rich to the public schools on the wrong side of the railroad track—meant that there was a diversity of needs: "Our schools and colleges neither operate in empty space nor serve identical communities. Before you judge a school analyse the families from which it draws its students and the opportunities presented to its graduates. What may be a satisfactory curriculum for one group of pupils may be highly unsuitable for another, and the difference

---

[1] *General Education in a Free Society*, p. 8, University of Harvard Press, 1945.

due not to discrepancies in intellectual capacities of the student but to the social situation in which the boys and girls are placed. This in turn depends on the nature of the local community of which the pupils and their parents are part".[1]

Realising that these problems were likely to be aggravated by the rise in the birth-rate, he undertook the task of finding ways of providing better education for the twelves to twenties. In *Education and Liberty* (1953) he first compares American education with British, then considers the influence of the university on secondary education, and, finally, suggests possible solutions of the main current problems of education.

Conant is Jeffersonian in his outlook. He does not believe that equality necessarily means uniformity. He would prefer to see the abler students being challenged more in school,[2] and he would limit entrance to four-year college and university courses to young people of intellectual calibre, thus preserving those institutions as centres of true scholarship. For the less able he suggests the provision of other colleges working at more modest levels, but, if necessary, granting degrees. Thus he conceives of a universal system of higher education which would reconcile the British and the American viewpoints—the training of an intellectual élite and the provision of higher education for all.

If Conant's philosophy were to be sought, it would appear to be akin to the humanistic realism of A. N. Whitehead. He has no impractical revolutionary or revivalist schemes. He accepts that American education is egalitarian and that it includes a wide range of non-intellectual activities. His main concern is that it shall become more efficient. "I am convinced American secondary education can be made satisfactory without any radical changes in the basic pattern", he wrote recently. "This can only be done, however, if the citizens in many localities are willing to support them. The improvements must come school by school and be made with due regard for the nature of the community."[3]

The improvements he hopes to see include not only the overhaul of curricula to ensure an adequate general education for all, but also, in the high school in particular, the inculcation of habits of study and the identification of able pupils. Of working habits, he maintains: "Intellectual interest must be keenly stimulated

---

[1] *Education in a Divided World*, p. 48, University of Harvard Press, 1949.
[2] M. J. Adler condemns Conant's proposals as "unashamedly undemocratic, or worse, anti-democratic" (*Life*, 12 May 1958).
[3] *The American High School To-day*, p. 96, McGraw Hill, 1959.

during the entire last four years. There must be a zest for intellectual adventure. There must be an inculcation of belief in the relevance of formal study and book learning to the problems of to-day. There must be the ability to knuckle down to hard intellectual work".[1]

The gifted child must not be lost to the nation either through his parents' inability to pay for his higher education or through over-anxiety to give all people the same education. Equality of opportunity does not mean that all should be educated in the same way, suggests Conant, and at present the intelligent child is not discovered early enough nor is he guided properly or educated adequately.

In 1957 Dr Conant embarked on a two-year study of the American public high school—a project which he reports in *The American High School Today* (1959). On the completion of this he started immediately upon an investigation of elementary schools. The methods of the scientist may well discover how far the fruits of educational research and philosophy have influenced the nature and quality of teaching and learning. Conant does not rail at the philosophers and psychologists. He looks at facts, and he contends that schools must "continue to experiment with general education at every level for the future manual worker, the future salesman or executive, and the most highly specialised university graduate".[2]

He does not challenge the inevitability of change in the affairs of men, for change is "the birthright of a free people seeking new insight and anxious to apply new knowledge . . . with interest in demonstrating the neighbourly spirit".[3]

Conclusion

Many other distinguished educators not mentioned in this chapter have influenced the course of American educational development. The measure of disagreement has been formidable. Not all have approved of the upward extension of universal education, not all have welcomed the widening of curricula, but these characteristics have appeared as manifestations of the spirit of a great democratic multi-racial society. We have tried to show how educational thinkers have endeavoured to guide teachers, parents,

[1] *Education in a Divided World*, p. 143, University of Harvard Press, 1949.
[2] *Education and Liberty*, p. 58, University of Harvard Press, 1953.
[3] *Education in a Divided World*, p. 98, University of Harvard Press, 1949.

and administrators to wise interpretations of their great national concepts.

SUGGESTIONS FOR FURTHER READING

BIOGRAPHICAL

T. Woody, *Benjamin Franklin*, McGraw Hill, 1931.

C. T. Arrowood, *Thomas Jefferson*, McGraw Hill, 1930.

B. A. Hinsdale, *Horace Mann*, Heinemann, 1898.

J. S. Brubacher, *Henry Barnard*, McGraw Hill, 1931.

M. Knight, *William James*, Pelican, 1950.

S. Tanenbaum, *William Heard Kilpatrick*, Harper, 1951.

G. M. Geiger, *John Dewey in Perspective*, Oxford, 1958.

R. Ulich on Franklin, Jefferson, Emerson, and Dewey in *History of Educational Thought*, American Book Co., 1945.

EARLY TWENTIETH CENTURY

Thorstein Veblen, *The Higher Learning in America*, Sagamore (Reprint), 1957.

N. Murray Butler (Ed.), *Education in the United States*, American Book Co., 1910.

INTER-WAR EXPERIMENTS

M. Johnson, *Youth in a World of Men*, J. Day, 1929.

L. S. Mitchell, *Our Children and Our Schools*, Simon and Schuster, 1951.

INTER-WAR CONTROVERSIES

Upton Sinclair, *The Goslings. A Study of the American Schools*, Laurie, 1930.

H. D. Gideonse, *The Higher Learning in a Democracy* (a reply to Hutchins), Farrar and Reinhart, 1937.

C. H. Judd, *Problems of Education in the United States*, McGraw Hill, 1933.

BACKGROUND HISTORY

E. W. Knight and C. L. Hall, *Readings in American Educational History*, Appleton, 1951.

R. F. Butts and L. A. Cremin, *A History of Education in American Culture*, Holt, 1953.

RECENT TRENDS

W. L. Warner, R. J. Havighurst, and M. L. Loeb, *Who Shall be Educated? The Challenge of Unequal Opportunity*, Harper, 1944, Routledge, 1946.

H. Mumford Jones, *Education and World Tragedy*, O.U.P., 1946.

C. A. Arndt and S. Everett, *Education for a World Society*, Harper, 1951.

P. Woodring, *Let's Talk Sense about our Schools*, McGraw Hill, 1953.

B. Hollinshead, *Who Should Go to College?*, Columbia, 1953.

R. Ulich, *The Human Career*, Harper, 1955.

P. F. Brandweis, *The Gifted Student as a Future Scientist*, Harcourt, 1955.

Fifty-Fourth Yearbook of Education (N.S.S.E.), Chicago U.P., 1955.

R. M. Hutchins, *Some Observations on American Education*, O.U.P., 1956.

J. L. Childs, *American Pragmatism and Education*, Holt, 1956.

J. B. Conant, *The Citadel of Learning*, Yale U.P., 1956.

P. Woodring, *A Fourth of a Nation*, McGraw Hill, 1957.

M. J. Adler and M. Meyer, *The Revolution in Education*, Chicago U.P., 1958.

H. M. Jones, *One Great Society* (Humane Learning in the United States), Harcourt, 1959.

H. C. Rickover, *Education and Freedom*, Dutton, 1959.

CHAPTER XXI

EXISTENTIALISM, LOGICAL POSITIVISM, EDUCATION IN SOVIET RUSSIA

Among post-War ideas concerning education, the Logical Positivists, the Existentialists, and the views of Soviet educators have drawn considerable interest. The Logical Positivists and the Existentialists including the Personalists represent two opposite types of thought. Both groups of thinkers, however, do not claim that their views are entirely new, but were foreshadowed by philosophers some centuries earlier.

One would be in error to suppose that the Existentialists constitute a definite system of philosophy. They consist of individual thinkers who to some extent have some important ideas in common but they represent a variety of standpoints. They can be grouped roughly into two sections. One of these include such men as Heidegger and Jean Paul Sartre who represent a kind of thought which can be described as agnostic or atheist. Although Karl Jaspers was influenced in some respects in religion, he can be regarded as a member of this section.

If one uses the term "existentialist" at all, it really belongs to this group. Thinkers of the second group have been strongly influenced by Christianity but are members of different religious bodies. Typical thinkers are Sören Kierkegaard (Danish Lutheran), Nicolas Berdyaev (Russian Orthodox), Gabriel Marcel (Roman Catholic), and Leslie Paul (Anglican). When the writer wants to distinguish them from the former group, he will refer to them as Personalists.

Marcel, possibly because of Papal censures of the views of the former group, repudiated the title "existentialist" as a description of his philosophy. The term "personalist" would allow us to include in this group the Jewish thinker, Martin Buber, and the Roman Catholic, Jacques Maritain, who is a Neo-Thomist. On the whole the thought of this second group is the more valuable for the philosophy of education.

Even this group contains different types but there is sufficient likenesses in their individual thought which links them together.

For example, they are all in opposition to the objective and systematising tendencies which began with Descartes and reached their apex in the system of Hegel. They have, therefore, not worked out a complete philosophy but would claim that they aim at replacing concentration on the objective world by considering the human person as the centre of their thought and have developed an outlook based on the individual. This is quite at variance with Logical Positivism which would reject the tendency of Kierkegaard and Berdyaev towards mysticism. The writer does not intend to give a detailed exposition of Existentialism, but confines himself to those features of their thought which have most relevance to education. Some of these philosophers claim that their ideas can be traced back as far as Socrates, the Stoics, St Augustine, St Bernard, and Pascal. There is no doubt that each of the above had expressed ideas similar to those of the Personalists, but for practical purposes the Personalist standpoint began with the Danish theologian and philosopher, Sören Kierkegaard. The works of Kierkegaard were published over a century ago but on the whole they were not well known by most of his own countrymen.

He was born in 1813, the youngest of seven children. His father was a dour melancholy person who was constantly concerned with the sense of his sins and exaggerated the harsher concepts of Christianity. In his early years he was dominated by his father but in later adolescence he revolted and concentrated on his studies. A break between father and son occurred but after three years they came together again and the father left him the house and sufficient money to make him independent. Kierkegaard for a short time attended a lecture course on the philosophy of Hegel which was given by Schelling at Berlin. He quickly found that he could not accept the Hegelian system. In his student days he rejected Christianity but returned to it when he discovered that Hegel's system was a philosophy of pure thought which ignored the fact of individual existence. From this time he consistently opposed any kind of system whether in philosophy or religion.

Kierkegaard was unfortunate in the possession of poor health and suffered morbid depression. He was a hunchback and had to cope with vicious attacks which were a kind of persecution. Among his many publications, *Philosophical Fragments* (1844) and *Concluding Unscientific Postscript* (1846) are the most important for his thought. In both these works he criticised and ridiculed the Hegelian system. For him, religion was a matter for the individual and in the concluding years of his life he bitterly criticised the State Church of Denmark which he described as being neither Christian nor honest. He believed that religion should be separate from the State and the world. Most Christian philosophers such as St Anselm and St Thomas Aquinas sought to show the connection between faith and reason.

Kierkegaard spent his last years in defending himself against unfair criticism and in his attack upon the Established Church of Denmark. Whilst engaged in these he collapsed and died in hospital in 1855. There is little point in giving a lengthy exposition of his philosophy because he had little to say concerning education. One writer of the present day has described him as "the man from whom, either directly or indirectly, every major stream of so-called Existential thought is derived".[1] Emmanuel Mounier writes as follows, "Kierkegaard seems to be the titular father of the school. What a curious fate this has been for the original Existential philosophers! In their own day, they were remarkably modest about success. Success has amply repaid them for it. I don't know how the Danes got on for a hundred years with a prophet so unattractive to anyone in his right senses as Sören Kierkegaard. In any case, he had to wait until the beginning of this century before he was translated in Germany and until the troublous inter-War years before his works got to France".[2]

Mounier's remark was quite true. The War of 1914-18 was frequently described as a war to end war but the inhabitants of most of the countries involved in it were quickly a prey to disillusionment. They had experienced a disastrous war and during the uneasy peace events seemed to show that their sacrifices had been in vain. The world was moving towards another war during which most of them were exposed to invasion and enemy occupation, and when this ended in 1945 they lived under the threat of the atom and hydrogen bomb. The world they once knew had gone for ever. They were living in a broken world in which life seemed to have lost its meaning.

Professor W. R. Niblett wrote, "Sören Kierkegaard lived from 1813-55 and all that he wrote might have been buried till now in its obscurity but for the sufferings and experiences which our century has brought to men, making audible some of the things he

---

[1] C. D. Kean, *The Meaning of Existence*, p. xi in the Preface. Latimer House, 1947.

[2] *Existentialist Philosophies, An Introduction*, translated by Eric Blow, p. 4, second reprint, Rockcliff, London, 1951.

poured forth amid the incomprehensible nothingness by which he felt himself enveloped".[1] Some existentialist thinkers like Jean Paul Sartre were overcome by the sense of nothingness and could find no meaning nor direction in life. The personalist philosophers, on the other hand, rebuilded their hopes for the future by turning away from the objective world to the inmost being of man.

The personalist thinkers from Kierkegaard to the present day began to emphasise the gulf between scientific and philosophical thought which are based on the subject and object distinction and envisaged another path to knowledge which is open to man. It is not so much that they rejected the former, for they had a great respect for intellectual thought but they opposed what they believed was a wrong use of reason. Mounier points out that their way of thinking is one in which "the man who has acquired knowledge doesn't *stand off from* the world, doesn't *stand up* in front of the world in order to survey the world as a spectacle and to describe it from a distance".[2]

They objected to the purely intellectual and lifeless theories of knowledge which began with Descartes and reached their apex in the system of Hegel. They followed Kierkegaard in his belief that the system thrives by neglecting the individual. Martin Buber expresses his opposition to the system when he describes Hegelianism as a philosophy "which has exercised a decisive influence not merely on an age's way of thought but also on its social and political action—an influence which can be characterised as the dispossessing of the concrete human person and the concrete human community in favour of universal reason, its dialectical processes and its objective structure. This influence, as is well known, has also operated on thinkers, who, though deriving from Hegel, have travelled far from him, such as Kierkegaard on the one hand, the critic of modern Christianity, who certainly grasped like no other thinker of our time the significance of the person, but still saw the life of the person entirely in the forms of the Hegelian dialectic as a movement from the aesthetic to the ethical and from there to the religious, and Marx on the other hand, who entered with an unexampled earnestness on the actuality of human society, but considered its development in forms of Hegelian dialectic

---

[1] *On Existentialism and Education* in the *British Journal of Educational Studies*, Vol. II. No. 2, May, 1954, Faber and Faber.
[2] *op cit*. p. 13.

as a movement from primitive communal economy to private property and from these to socialism".[1]

Personalist thinkers see a further threat to the individual in the developments of our modern technological civilisation. Denmark in the lifetime of Kierkegaard had scarcely been touched by the industrial revolution, but he expressed anxiety at the growing tendency to lose sight of the individual in the masses. He had not experienced the tyranny of the dictator but he saw how the individual members of a democratic state were being crushed by the institutions which were moulding public opinion. Since his time we could add to newspapers and the political parties the cinema, radio, and television and other kinds of organised propaganda.

Those who had experienced Fascist tyranny and the Soviet police state were more emphatic. Buber wrote, "Machines which were invented in order to serve men in their work, impressed them into their service. They were no longer, like tools, an extension of man's arm, but man became that extension, an adjunct on their periphery, doing their bidding".[2] Jaspers speaking of our technological society stated that "our era has altered the course of history more radically than any other era known to us". He considered that the tendency of the technological age is to transform the nations into masses, seemingly able to understand and participate in developments, but actually transformed into slaves to be made use of. He summed up: "if we listen to the words that are uttered amid this tumult, they seem like a veiled preparation for death. Mass education has made men blind and thoughtless, capable of everything in their drunkenness, until finally they accept death and killing, mass death in mechanical warfare as a matter of course".[3]

We have seen this tendency in America and Africa in the discrimination between white and coloured citizens, leading to racial riots and murders. Are we moving in the same direction in Britain? One everyday example suggests this. When an individual acquires a motor vehicle, at first he is the master of the machine and drives with consideration for other users of the road, but sooner or later, the machine can influence him. His vehicle is as much an instrument of death and mutilation as a gun. He feels he must make full use of its speed and consideration for others begins to decline. Even the law, as far as he is concerned, becomes

[1] "What is man?" in *Between Man and Man*, pp. 137-8, Kegan Paul, 1947.
[2] *op cit.*, p. 158.
[3] *The Perennial Scope of Philosophy*, p. 154, Routledge and Kegan Paul, 1950.

something to be broken. He wants to use the full speed of his vehicle on every occasion. The writer does not condemn speed when the circumstances make it safe, but the urge to pass all other vehicles which are driven at a more moderate speed, leads the driver to drive at fifty or sixty miles an hour in a thirty mile limit, to cross continuous white lines to overtake, or to pass others before he has reached the brow of a hill. His own experience is that an increasing number of motorists ignore the Highway Code completely. Hence the mounting number of serious accidents at weekends and holiday periods.

Nicolas Berdyaev took a position similar to that of Martin Buber. He was born in Kiev in 1874 and in his youth he broke away from his aristocratic and military family to embrace socialism. As a result he was expelled from the university and, later, the Imperial Government exiled him to the north of Russia. After the Revolution of 1917 he was appointed Professor of Philosophy in the University of Moscow, but after two spells of imprisonment, he was expelled by the Soviet Government. He sought refuge in Berlin and then in Paris but was once more imprisoned at the time of the Nazi occupation. Thus he suffered from both the Marxists and the Nazis. Originally he was a Marxist but later he became an Idealist and finally a Christian. He regarded himself as a loyal member of the Orthodox Church but this did not deter him from criticising conventional Christianity.

Like Kierkegaard, he was an opponent of systems and of modern Humanism, which, unlike the Christian Humanists of the Renaissance, has turned away from religion. He felt that human personality and freedom were being crushed by a technological age. In his *Slavery and Freedom* (Paris 1940. Reprint by the Centenary Press, 1944), he stated that men desire freedom and are capable of it, but they are also afraid of the responsibility which freedom involves, and as a result they choose slavery but do not realise they have done so. He described how the heart of man gradually is wasted away from the hard blows dealt by the machines. Technicisation, mechanisation, and materialism inevitably end in the death of life.

Gabriel Marcel also put the idea in a different form when he wrote: "Travelling on the Underground, I often wonder with a kind of dread what can be the onward reality of the life of this or that man employed on the railway—the man who opens the doors, for instance, or the one who punches the tickets. Surely everything both within him and outside him conspires to identify this man with his functions—meaning not only with his functions as a worker, as a trade union member, or as a voter, but with his vital functions as well. The rather horrible expression 'time table' perfectly describes his life. So many hours for each function".[1]

The existentialists and personalists point out that the error in our theories of knowledge is that they ignore existential thinking. They are ready to accept the objective thinking of the scientist if it is confined to its own proper sphere. Jaspers wrote: "Science, it is true, shows us remarkable and highly surprising things about man, but as it attains greater clarity, the more evident it becomes that man as a whole can never be the object of scientific investigation. Man is always more than he knows about himself. This is true both of man in general and of the individual man. We can never draw up a balance sheet and know the answer, either concerning man in general, or concerning any individual man".[2]

Jaspers was a pupil of Wilhelm Dilthey (1833-1911), who was not himself an existentialist but in one way he stressed a very important point which was elaborated in Buber's *I and THOU*. Dilthey realised that the type of thought which is suitable to the human studies differs greatly from that employed in the physical sciences. The latter are concerned with the objective world but in the former the thinker is dealing with mental and spiritual life; we get to know physical objects from the outside but the only way of understanding a person is from the inside. We relive another's experience; we project ourselves into another's being. Our knowledge of physical objects is through appearance but in understanding a person a real meeting takes place. Dilthey used the words: "Understanding is a rediscovery of the *I* in the *Thou*".[3]

Buber's *I and Thou* is not an easy book to understand fully in one reading. It takes the form of a philosophical poem. Buber begins his exposition as follows: "To man the world is twofold, in accordance with his twofold attitude. The attitude of man is twofold in accordance with the twofold nature of the primary words which he speaks. The primary words are not isolated words, but combined words.

The one primary word is the combination *I-Thou*.

[1] *The Philosophy of Existence*, p. 2, Harvill Press, 1948.
[2] *The Perennial Scope of Philosophy*, pp. 61-2, Routledge and Kegan Paul, 1950.
[3] H. A. Hodges, *Wilhelm Dilthey—An Introduction*, p. 114, Routledge and Kegan Paul, 1944.

The other primary word is the combination *I-It*; wherein, without a change in the primary word, one of the words *He* and *She* can replace the *It*.
Hence the *I* of man is also twofold.
For the *I* of the primary word *I-Thou* is a different *I* from that of the primary word *I-It*".[1]

Buber means that the world of man is not only the world of objects but is also the world of relations such as man to nature, man to man, and man to God. The first relation is expressed by the primary word *I-It*. Physical objects for him are instruments for carrying out his purposes. Unfortunately, man at times considers other human beings as things. In Kantian terms he is behaving to them as means and not as rational beings who are ends in themselves. Such a relation is a wrong one and it has been a major cause of many of the problems that arise in modern life. Men have failed to form the right relations with their fellow-men.

M. V. C. Jeffreys illustrates the twofold ways of knowing as follows. "An astronomer 'knows' how far it is to the nearest star. An exiled Irishman 'knows' how far he is from Tipperary or Eileen Mavourneen. The distance in the first case is mathematical; in the second case it is primarily emotional.

"Again, we can 'know' a human being in what may be called *dossier* terms; we can measure his I.Q. and record his height, weight, colour of hair and eyes, and other particulars by which he could be identified. And we can 'know' our best friend in a different and intimate way though we probably are ignorant of his I.Q., or even eye-colour, and such other data as the police would require if he were missing."[2]

Buber believes that the primary problem for each individual is how to re-discover the *I-Thou* relationship. This relation is a direct one in the sense that "No system of ideas, no foreknowledge, and no fancy intervene between *I* and *Thou*. The memory itself is transformed, as it plunges out of its isolation into the unity of the whole. No aim, no lust, and no anticipation intervene between *I* and *Thou*. Desire itself is transformed as it plunges out of its dream into the appearance. Every means is an obstacle. Only when every means has collapsed does the meeting come about".[3] There are no true relationships in the world of *It*. "The man

---

[1] *I and Thou*, trans. by R. G. Smith, p. 3, T. T. Clark, 1937.
[2] From *Existentialism*, in *Education and the Philosophic Mind*, pp. 66-7, ed. by A. V. Judges, George G. Harrap, 1957.
[3] *I and Thou*, pp. 11-12.

who experiences has no part in the world. For it is 'in him' and not between him and the world that the experience arises.

"The world has no part in the experience. It permits itself to be experienced, but has no concern in the matter. For it does nothing to the experience, and the experience does nothing to it."[1]

Buber describes three possible true relations. The first is our relations with nature. We can examine a tree from a purely scientific point of view or we can experience it as something which is beautiful. In the latter case the tree ceases to be an *It*. "It can, however, also come about, if I have both will and grace, that in considering the tree I become bound up in relation to it. The tree is no longer *It*. I have been seized by the power of Exclusiveness."[2]

The second sphere is that of the intelligible form. "This is the eternal source of art: a man is faced by a form which desires to be made through him into a work. This form is no offspring of his soul, but is an appearance which steps up to it and demands of it the effective power. The man is concerned with an act of his being. If he carries it through, if he speaks the primary word out of his being to the form which appears, then the effective power streams out and the work arises."[3]

The reader who is interested in aesthetic theory will notice some affinity between the view of Buber and that of St Thomas Aquinas and Benedetto Croce. Beauty exists in the intelligible form which is received by the soul of the artist. The latter is unable to give a perfect description of the form but in the work of art, he tries to reproduce it, to body it forth as far as is possible but the form does not lend itself to scientific analysis. When the form is embodied in a work of art it has entered the world of common experience and becomes an *It*. The receptive beholder rediscovers the intelligible form through meeting it in his aesthetic contemplation.

The most important relationship is that which exists between persons. It is not merely a relationship of feeling but is one of love, sympathy, mutual respect, and understanding, in which feeling plays a necessary but subordinate part. Buber tells us that the *I-Thou* relationship cannot last for ever even between two most devoted friends. "But this is the exalted melancholy of our fate, that every *Thou* in our world must become an *It*."[4] But on the other hand, "Without *It* a man cannot live. But he who lives with *It* alone is not a man".[5]

[1] *I and Thou*, p. 5.
[2] *ibid*. p. 7.
[3] *ibid*, pp. 9-10.
[4] *ibid*., p. 16.
[5] *ibid*., p. 34.

Buber is emphasising that a man is obliged to pass his life in an environment of objects but it is in the world of relations he discovers the meaning of life. In so far as a man develops his ability to experience and to use, to that extent his power to enter into genuine relationships is diminished. Man can only truly live through the spirit which is to be found in the relationship of *I* and *Thou*. This is in complete agreement with the view of Berdyaev.

When man lives in the world of *It*, he has to obey its laws; he is living as a part of Nature and everything he does is governed by cause and effect, but when he lives in the world of *I-Thou*, his actions are free and he escapes from the determination of Nature. Like Berdyaev, Buber believes that institutions, however necessary they may be, lay a dead hand on the life of spirit and tend to enslave man. All the personalist thinkers utter a call to a more comprehensive and deeper sense of living.

Buber states that the opposite of freedom is shown in a life which is governed by arbitrary self-will. Man's true destiny is to become a person. He is already an individual because he is other from other individuals but something more is needed before he can be regarded as a person. "He must sacrifice his puny, unfree will, that is controlled by things and instincts, to his grand will."[1] This involves a complete change from his former attitude towards life. Like the cave dwellers in the Platonic myth, he must be converted, turned to another direction. The self-willed man is always emphasising his difference from others. A person seeks to share with others. Sharing is never selfish. It belongs to the person with whom I share just as much as it belongs to me.

There is one *Thou* which can never be an *It*. God is the eternal *Thou*. God cannot be reached through a process of conceptual thinking such as we find in the different arguments for the existence of God. "God cannot be inferred in anything—in nature, say, as its author, or in history as its master, or in the subject as the self that is thought in it. Something else is not 'given' and God elicited from it; but God is the Being that is directly, most nearly, and lastingly, over against us, that may properly only be addressed, not expressed."[2] Man comes to know God as the result of establishing a relationship with Him, meeting Him in our inward being. "You know always in your heart that you need God more than everything; but do not know too that God needs you—in the fulness

[1] *I and Thou*, p. 34.   [2] *ibid.*, p. 80-1.

of His eternity needs you. You need God in order to be—and God needs you, for the very meaning of your life."[1]

The thought of Buber, like that of Berdyaev, is tinged with mysticism. Both philosophers distinguish true from false mysticism. Berdyaev condemns the type of mysticism which insists upon a complete withdrawal from the world, the desire to avoid sin by mortification of the flesh and severe ascetic practices. Man is obliged to live in the world of *It* but this need not hinder him from developing his creative and spiritual powers. Complete withdrawal from the world and concentration on the inward self leads to the destruction of personality. Berdyaev teaches that true mysticism strives for union with God with the consequence it turns the self to other selves. Buber speaks in the same vein, emphasising the importance of community as opposed to mere organisation. The modern religious personalists are communal in their outlook and differ from Kierkegaard who saw nothing but corruption in the external world and, therefore, centred his thoughts on the subjective.

One of the chief characteristics of the existentialists and personalists is the importance attached to choice. There comes a time in his life when a man has to make a choice in regard to a mate or a career. The supreme instant is when he has to choose between a life which is governed by no universal principles and that which conforms to the demands of morality and religion. The supreme choice is the choice of God. Man cannot evade choosing, for as William James declared, to delay choosing is really to make a choice.

The two thinkers who have contributed most to the philosophy of education are Martin Buber and Gabriel Marcel. The early life of the latter was by no means a happy one. His father had been a Catholic and after ceasing to practise his religion, he accepted the views of the late nineteenth century agnostics. Marcel's mother died when he was a small child and he was brought up by an aunt who had been converted to Protestantism but "showed by her choice of a pastor that her reason rejected its dogmatic beliefs and that she could accept it only in its most liberal form".[2]

He was also unhappy at school mainly because of the anxiety of his aunt and grandmother for his success. "I was racked by a kind of tension which at times reached an almost intolerable degree.

[1] *I and Thou*, p. 82.
[2] *An Essay in Autobiography*, in *The Philosophy of Existence*, p. 81, second impression, the Harvill Press, London, 1949.

Consciously, I suffered from the exaggerated attention devoted to me as an only child. . . . I felt watched, spied upon; I guessed that, after I had gone to bed, the conversation in the drawing-room turned on my inadequacies and on what could be expected of me. Our school system, if it is not to do positive harm, should be balanced by a goodly dose of scepticism and indifference on the part of the family. . . . My parents had been brilliant pupils and they gave too much importance to my marks and to my places in class. Thus, every composition became a drama. I felt each time that it was a test of my whole being, since no distinction seemed to be made between my scholastic output and myself."

As one might expect, Marcel's attitude to the education of the earlier days of this century was that of criticism and condemnation. His references to education in the *Mystery of Being,* the Gifford Lectures of 1949 and 1950, show that he had not forgotten his early experiences of school. He wrote: "Teaching, or rather certain traditional inadequate ways of conceiving the teacher's function, have encouraged the general acceptance of such gross images of truth. In Dickens's novel, *Hard Times,* there is a character called Mr Gradgrind, for whom anybody and everybody can be treated as a vessel capable of containing truths (such as, 'The horse is a graminivorous quadruped') extracted from the crude ore of experience, divided, and evenly dealt out. Mr Gradgrind is aware, certainly, that one vessel is not so sound as another; some are leaky, some are fragile and so on. . . . I believe I am not exaggerating when I say that the educational system, even in countries that think of themselves as rather advanced, has still something in common with the coarseness and absurdity of Dickens's satirical picture of it. The interesting question is, under what conditions does this illusory image of truth as a physical substance, even as the stuff contained in a vessel, present itself naturally to the mind? It is obvious that the use of fixed forms of words in teaching plays a prominent part in fostering the illusion. A history teacher, for instance, has to din dates into his pupils. They have to give back just what they have been given, unchanged by any mental process, and they have to memorise the dates in a quite mechanical way. It is very natural in this case to think of the pupil as a vessel, into which a certain measure of liquid is poured, so that it may be poured out again; an even apter metaphor would be that of the gramophone record. Such metaphors, however, cease to apply in the case where, having explained some idea to a pupil, I ask him to explain it back to me in his own words and if possible with his own illustrations; the idea certainly may still be thought of as a content, but it is a content that has to be grasped by the intelligence; it cannot be reduced, like the history master's dates, to some exact, particular formula. It is this irreducibility that we must keep a grip on if we want to get beyond the illusory image of truth as a physical object, a substance, the contents of a vessel, a mere thing, and to recognise the impossibility of adequately representing by material images those processes by which I can both conceive a true proposition and affirm it to be true."[1]

Later, in the same lecture, he said: "I have often said that if one were rash enough to ask what will remain, under any form at all, in the minds of children, of all that has been painfully taught them, what will be the final positive result of the effort that is demanded from them, the whole system would fall to bits, for it is absolutely certain that regards most of the subjects taught this responsible result will be precisely nothing. Those who are responsible for our educational programmes have not the elementary shrewdness of the industrialist who, before undertaking a new enterprise, ascertains what will be the initial outlay, what are the probable yearly profits, and whether the proportion between these two figures makes the whole thing worth his while. One is careful not to ask such a question of educational experts; one would not be insulting a noble profession. Yet fine words butter no parsnips. They are simply taking advantage of the fact that in teaching the outlay is less visible, less easily definable than in the case of an industrial enterprise; hence a waste of time and strength whose remoter consequences are beyond all calculation".[2]

In his criticisms, Marcel does hint how education can be brought to life but Buber in *Between Man and Man* gives the text of two addresses he gave in 1925 and 1939, *Education* and *The Education of Character* which express in more detail the personalists' ideas concerning the aims of education and the relations which should obtain between teacher and pupils. He contrasted the traditional and the modern ideas as follows: "Let us take an example from the narrower sphere of the originative instinct—from the drawing-class. The teacher of the 'compulsory' school of thought began with rules and current patterns. Now you knew what beauty was, and you had to copy it; and it was copied either in apathy or in despair.

---

[1] *The Mystery of Being*, Vol. i, pp. 19-20, Harvill Press, 1950-1.
[2] *ibid.*, pp. 37-8.

The teacher of the 'free' school places on the table a twig of broom, say, in an earthenware jug, and makes the pupils draw it. Or he places it on the table, tells the pupils to look at it, removes it, and then makes them draw it. If the pupils are quite unsophisticated soon not a single drawing will look like another. Now the delicate, almost imperceptible and yet important influence begins— that of criticism and instruction. The children encounter a scale of values that, however unacademic it may be, is quite constant, a knowledge of good and evil that, however individualistic it may be, is quite unambiguous. The more unacademic this scale of values, and the more individualistic this knowledge, the more deeply do the children experience the encounter. In the former instance the preliminary declaration of what alone was right made for resignation or rebellion; but in the latter, where the pupil gains the realisation only after he has ventured far out on the way to his achievement, his heart is drawn to reverence for the form, and educated".[1]

Buber agrees that the influence of the teacher must not be too obvious to the pupil. In medieval society journeymen and apprentices lived with the master. They learned through being allowed to live with him and to receive instruction from him. We cannot return in our technological age, to this simple relationship in its purity, but the master craftsman has still a lesson for the modern teacher. The apprentice scarcely noticed that he was being taught by the master. The modern educator, although he has a definite objective before him, must act as though he had not. He must never allow the pupil to think that he is interfering. Interference breeds dissension in the soul whereas the educator must be an integrating force. The reader will note that Buber's view approaches that of Adamson in his tri-polar theory of teacher and pupil relationship.

"It is usual to contrast the principle of the 'new' education as 'Eros' with that of the 'old' education as the 'will to power'. In fact the one is as little a principle of education as the other. A principle of education, in a sense still to be clarified, can only be a basic relation which is fulfilled in education. . . . Eros is choice, choice made from an inclination. This is precisely what education is not. The man who is loving in Eros chooses the beloved, the modern educator finds his pupil there before him. . . . He enters the schoolroom for the first time, he sees them crouching at the desks,

[1] *op. cit.*, pp. 88-9.

indiscriminately flung together, the misshapen and the well-proportioned, animal faces, empty faces, and noble faces in indiscriminate confusion, like the presence of the created universe; the glance of the educator accepts and receives them all ... If this educator should ever believe that for the sake of education he has to practise selection and arrangement, then he will be guided by another criterion than that of inclination, however legitimate this may be in its own sphere; he will be guided by the recognition of values which is in his glance as an educator."[1]

Buber believed that the real process of education involves a dialogical relation between teacher and pupil similar to that to be found in genuine conversation. "Its elements are, first, a relation of no matter what kind, between two persons, second, an event experienced by them in common, in which at least one of them actively participates, and, third, the fact that this one person, without forfeiting anything of the felt reality of his activity, at the same time lives through the common event from the standpoint of the other."[2]

Friendship is the highest form of the dialogical relation because it is based on a concrete and mutual experience of inclusion. Without friendship, the relation of teacher and pupil, however much give and take enter into it, is always one-sided. The teacher experiences the pupil being educated but the pupil does not perceive the educating of the educator. "The educator stands at both ends of the common situation, the pupil only at one end. In the moment when the pupil is able to throw himself across and experience from over there, the educative relation would be burst asunder, or changed into friendship."[3] Buber, in common with other members of the personalist group, regards the essence of education as the meeting of two persons. Education is a personal relation not merely one of words.

Buber emphasises the importance of character in any scheme of education. He wrote: "Education worthy of the name is essentially education of character. For the genuine educator does not merely consider individual functions of his pupil, as one intending to teach him only to know or be capable of certain definite things; but his concern is always the person as a whole, both in the actuality in which he lives before you now and in his possibilities, what he can become".[4] Although the formation of character is significant

---

[1] *Between Man and Man,* pp. 94-5.   [2] *ibid.,* p. 97.
[3] *ibid.,* pp. 100-1.   [4] *ibid.,* p. 104.

in education, Buber warns the educator not to over-estimate what he can do in the development of character.

He wrote: "If I have to teach algebra I can expect to succeed in giving my pupils an idea of quadratic equations with two unknown quantities. Even the slowest-witted child will understand it so well that he will amuse himself by solving equations at night when he cannot fall asleep. And even one with the most sluggish memory will not forget, in his old age, how to play with x and y. But if I am concerned with the education of character, everything becomes problematic. I try to explain to my pupils that envy is despicable, and at once I feel the secret resistance of those who are poorer than their comrades. I try to explain that it is wicked to bully the weak, and at once I see a suppressed smile on the lips of the strong. I try to explain that lying destroys life, and something frightful happens: the worst habitual liar of the class produces a brilliant essay on the destructive power of lying. I have made the fatal mistake of giving instruction in ethics, and what I said is accepted as current coin of knowledge; nothing of it is transformed into character-building substance".[1]

Buber believes that the education of character is not a class subject such as mathematics or history and that direct moral teaching is of little value. There is only one approach to the education of character. "Only in his whole being, in all his spontaneity can the educator truly affect the whole being of his pupil. For educating characters you do not need a moral genius, but you do need a man who is wholly alive and able to communicate himself directly to his fellow beings. His aliveness streams out to them and affects them most strongly and purely when he has no thought of affecting them."[2]

Character is formed by a great number of opposing influences and the teacher must realise that he is only one of the influences which affect the pupil's character. He must gain the confidence of the pupil so that the latter feels he can trust the teacher. One of the problems which face the educator is the behaviour and attitude to life of many young people who have lost the sense of responsibility. Buber strongly stresses that genuine education of character is genuine education for community; a great and full relation between man and man can only exist between unified and responsible persons.

[1] *Between Man and Man*, pp. 104-5.
[2] *ibid.*, p. 105.

M. V. C. Jeffreys writes: ". . . it is the teacher's obligation to combat everything that disintegrates human personality, undermines the value set upon persons as such, or reduces human life to abstractions. He must vigilantly reckon with all those influences in modern society which numb the sense of responsibility, including those interpretations of human behaviour which sanction, or appear to sanction, the view that we cannot help being what we are".[1]

The standpoint of Logical Positivism is quite opposite to that of the personalist philosophers. In its strict form, Logical Positivism originated with a group of thinkers in the Vienna of the 1920's in which Wittgenstein was a prominent member. When the original members of the group died, according to W. F. Barnes, Logical Positivism also died but it has strongly influenced philosophical ideas in England and America. Barnes writes: "What exist now are philosophical movements related in various ways to that original movement but consisting of philosophical groups whose members would not call themselves, nor wish to be called by others, Logical Positivists".[2] Professor A. J. Ayer is an example which bears out this statement in disclaiming the label of Logical Positivist.

Like Existentialism and Pragmatism, one can find some foreshadowing of Logical Positivism in some trends of Greek philosophy and in the Middle Ages. The writer remembers that when he was introduced to Professor Ayer he asked with what branch of philosophy I was concerned in the University of Leeds. I replied that my course in the History of Medieval Philosophy would not interest him. Ayer answered that he was interested in William of Ockham because of his ideas about the function of language. He was quite correct in this statement for as S. C. Tornay wrote: "The following two chapters (i.e. of Ockham's Logic) constitute Ockham's doctrine of supposition, an intimate understanding of which will throw a great light on problems related to the philosophy of language, the symbolism of the mind, logical positivism, and to the unification of the sciences".[3] The more modern forerunners who rejected the Absolute Idealism of Hegel were G. E. Moore and Bertrand Russell. Ayer in his Preface to the first edition of *Language, Truth and Logic*, Victor Gollancz Ltd, 1936, declared that his views

[1] *Existentialism*, in *Education and the Philosophic Mind*, George G. Harrap, 1957.
[2] In *Education and the Philosophic Mind*, ed. A. V. Judges, p. 122, George G. Harrap, 1957.
[3] *Ockham, Studies and Selections*, p. 113, The Open Court Publishing Company, 1938.

derive from Bertrand Russell and Wittgenstein whose doctrines were the logical outcome of the empiricism of Berkely and Hume.

One should not confuse Ayer's views with the Positivism of Auguste Comte (1798-1857). Space forbids an exposition of Ayer's standpoint and will only allow a brief mention of some of his prominent doctrines. The second edition of Ayer's treatise was revised and reset in 1946. Thus he modified the principle of verification. Briefly, one can describe his standpoint as a rejection of the view of traditional philosophy which claimed that metaphysics gave a knowledge of transcendent realities such as the existence of God, the freedom of the will, the relations of mind and body, and the existence of an external world. He believes that metaphysics is a waste of time and thought, and that philosophy is not a search for first principles but is really an activity of analysis. "In other words, the propositions of philosophy are not factual, but linguistic in character—that is, they do not describe the behaviour of physical, or even mental, objects; they express definitions. Accordingly, we may say that philosophy is a department of logic. For we shall see that the characteristic mark of a purely logical enquiry is that it is concerned with the formal consequences of our definitions and not with questions of empirical fact."[1]

The conclusion of this line of thought is that philosophy does not compete with science, for the difference between scientific and philosophical propositions is so great that they cannot be in contradiction. Hence philosophical analysis does not depend on empirical assumptions, and, of course, is absolutely independent of metaphysical assumptions. Ayer points out: "What has contributed as much as anything to the prevalent misunderstanding of the nature of philosophical analysis is the fact that propositions and questions which are really linguistic are often expressed in such a way that they appear to be factual".[2]

Space again prevents a discussion of Ayer's views on the verification principle and the modifications he added in the second edition of his work. Whether one agrees or not with Ayer, one can be grateful to him for his emphasis on the use of language. As Professor W. H. F. Barnes wrote: "Philosophy in the past has often suffered from a certain woolliness of language and thought; and educational philosophy has not escaped infection. Logical Positivism, with its search for clarity and its bringing every proposition

[1] A. J. Ayer, *Language, Truth and Logic*, second edition, p. 57.
[2] *ibid.*, pp. 57-8.

before the bar of meaning, makes short work of edifying platitudes masquerading as novel theories. . . . it is always salutory to inquire of any proposition with which one is called upon to deal such questions as: How could one put it to the test? What would confirm it? What sort of things happening would incline me to give it up? If there are some things we believe and are determined to go on believing, no matter what happens, this is a fact worth knowing whether or not what we agree with the positive contention that they are thereby rendered meaningless. In another respect the positivist attitude is helpful. Children, and even many adults, will discuss almost anything. Part of the educational progress must consist in learning that there are matters which can only be settled by conducting experiments or by establishing facts with the aid of documents. Where this is so, discussion is misplaced".[1]

The positivist treatment of valuation has aroused most opposition. Ayer holds the view that "in so far as statements of value are significant, they are ordinary 'scientific' statements; and that in so far they are not scientific, they are not in the literal sense significant, but are simply expression of emotion which can be neither true nor false".[2] He adds that the same conclusion applies to aesthetic judgments. This view is generally termed the Emotive Theory of Values, and is strongly criticised by Professor Barnes and C. E. M. Joad. The latter wrote, "It is, Ayer thinks, an implication of the emotive theory that ethical and aesthetic judgments provide us with information about our feelings which is of interest to the psychologist. I am not sure whether this statement is wholly consistent with the 'nonsense' conclusion previously reached. If aesthetic and moral judgments do provide such information it can only be because to say 'this action is right', or, 'this picture is beautiful', is to throw light upon our feelings, upon those feelings, namely, which the judgment expresses. If this is the case, it is hard to see how the propositions in which the judgments are expressed can be 'nonsensical', since nonsense is a meaningless set of noises which cannot, one would suppose, give us any information about anything".[3]

As regards methods of teaching, the positivists have little to say. Some of them, like D. J. O'Connor, would find no place in the school curriculum for moral and religious training. We now turn to another system of education which like the positivists has little use for religious instruction, namely communist education.

[1] *Logical Positivism*, in *Education and the Philosophic Mind*, pp. 132-3.
[2] *Language, Truth and Logic*, p. 103.
[3] *A Critique of Logical Positivism*, p. 117, Victor Gollancz, 1950.

Education in Soviet Russia has made great progress especially since the death of Stalin. Its outlook is based upon the Marxist philosophy. To understand what is involved in the Marxist system, it is useful to give a short account of the views of the founders of the Marxist philosophy: Karl Marx (1818-83), Friedrich Engels (1820-95), and Vladimir Lenin (1870-1924). This philosophy known as Dialectic Materialism, a title which shows its derivation from the Hegelian Dialectic but which in the well-known statement, claimed to have turned Hegelianism the right side up.

Hegel was mainly concerned with the development of ideas through which we reach the truth of things. Marx gave prominence to the material world. As Engels taught, the real causes of social change and revolutions are not the result of men's thought but of production and exchange. This is the doctrine of Economic Determinism, the belief that the course of history, including the birth and development of institutions, depends on the influence that the economic environment has over man's economic needs. Economic Determinism develops on the dialectic principle.

Marx and his collaborators in their thought did not accept the mechanical materialism which influenced some of the Victorian scientists. They did not entirely discard human freedom. Marx believed that man makes his own history, but his freedom is limited by his environment which is not the consequence of his choice. Material conditions form the framework in which his freedom operates. Like Hegel, Marx applied his dialectic theory towards an explanation of history, which is a record of class struggles which will not cease as long as the State and productivity are dependent on class. As we survey history two opposing tendencies can be seen. Thus the medieval world was based on feudalism but as soon as this system was established, it generated a number of tendencies which led to its ultimate destruction. It suffered the rise of the *bourgeoisie* who gradually obtained control over the means of production, and by the wealth derived from trade, brought about the downfall of feudalism. This led to capitalism which in turn brought forth its opposite, the proletariat. Opposing tendencies in a society eventually lead to a synthesis which transcends them and brings into existence a new type of social organisation. A given state of society, when firmly established, produces a more violent conflict which gives rise to its successor.

The change from the slave-owning society of ancient Greece and Rome to feudalism produced a less violent reaction than that of feudalism to capitalism. The latter is most firmly established, so that the advent of a socialist society will produce a violent revolution. The capitalists own the means of production and control the armed forces with the result that the conflict will be long and bitter. A stop has to take place at some stage. Will the socialist society lead to another form of social organisation? The Marxists reply that the socialistic stage will eventually give way to a classless society. Logically the latter would in time generate a new type of organisation but the Marxists believe that the final stage has then been reached. When the capitalist opposition has been overcome and the classless society firmly established, the State will wither away. The official title of Communist Russia is at present the Union of Soviet Socialist Republics which suggest that the classless society has yet to come. The State showed no indication of its decease and under the tyranny of Stalin its power increased.

Under Khruschev some significant changes appeared. One important factor since the last World War is the beginning of a nationalist outlook in Russia which may bring closer unity among the fifteen different states which constitute the U.S.S.R. The recent ill-feeling between Russia and China seems to have softened the harsh relations between Russia and the non-Communist countries. The U.S.S.R. appears to admit the possibility of peaceful co-existence. But Russia still remains a communist state and this explains the ideas which still control Soviet education.

One has to remember that under the Tsarist regime the government permitted the existence of a considerable number of schools organised by voluntary bodies but there was a strict control over the State schools. This contrasted with the British educational system in which the State is only one of the partners, although the most powerful. This centralisation of authority has become more rigid under Soviet rule.

The dialectic materialist firmly believes in the possibility of establishing the perfect society on earth. Most Christians have in mind the saying of Christ: "My kingdom is not of this world", but at the same time they would not deny that our aim should be to improve our present society. In a communist state the individual is entirely subordinate to the collective, that is the community. It is obvious that the community consists of individuals so that it follows that each individual should develop to the highest degree that is possible for him.

The most serious problem which faced Soviet leaders after the revolution was that of illiteracy. They realised that in European Russia, especially in the large towns, the people were not so backward as regards education as the eastern parts of the Union where in some communities the illiterates formed the greater part of the populace. The civil strife which followed the revolution and more recently the German invasion of 1941 slowed down progress but the Russians made a wonderful come-back. The developments both in primary, secondary, technical, and university education are spectacular.

One cardinal fact must be in our minds. All education takes place within the framework of the Marxist philosophy, which means absolute conformity with the principles laid down by Marx, Engels, and Lenin. A former President of the Soviet Union, M. I. Kalinin, wrote: "Communist principles, taken in their elementary form, are the principles of highly educated, honest, advanced people; they are love for one's socialist motherland, friendship, humanity, honesty, love for socialist labour, and a great many other universally understood lofty qualities; the nurturing, the cultivation of these attributes, of these lofty qualities is the most important component part of communist education".[1] This was written during the Stalin regime but the same ideas continue at the present.

Side by side with his general and technical education the Russian pupil is constantly reminded of the Marxist principles. Only the very young children because they would not be able to understand such ideas are exempt for a year or two. Thus Kalinin wrote: "To learn Marxism means to know after mastering the Marxist method how to approach all the other problems connected with your work. If, let us say, the sphere of your future work is agriculture, will it be of advantage to employ the Marxist method? Of course it will. But to employ the Marxist method, you have to study agriculture, too, you have to be an agricultural expert. Otherwise nothing will come of your attempt to apply Marxism to agriculture. This should not be forgotten if you wish to be men of action and not textmongers of Marxism. But what does being a Marxist mean? It means being able to adopt the correct line. But to be able to adopt the correct, Marxist line, you also need to be a first-rate expert in your particular sphere of activity".[2]

[1] *On Communist Education*, Foreign Languages Publishing House, Moscow, 1950.
[2] *ibid.*, p. 16.

Yesipov and Goncharov take the same line. They emphasise that pupils must be educated as Soviet patriots and explain it thus: "Soviet patriotism is expressed in devotion to the Communist Party and supreme readiness to serve the cause of Lenin and Stalin".[1]

Russian writers often use the word "democracy" but it means something different than the view of the western nations. The Soviet Union is a totalitarian state and in education, as in other activities, curricula and methods are closely supervised by the authorities. In the early years of Soviet rule the schools experimented with more up-to-date ideas derived from the western democracies. Thus the Dalton Plan of individual studies was tried out and there was a great interest in the project and activity ideas of Dewey and Kilpatrick. When Stalin rose to power he clamped down on such experiments and returned to the traditional formal teaching of the pre-revolutionary period. Although Khrushchev introduced many reforms in Soviet society he did little in regard to education and Soviet educational practice corresponds with the traditional outlook which we saw was condemned by Marcel.

No religious instruction is given in Soviet schools and colleges. The Marxist philosophy has no use for religion which was described as the opiate for the people. The Orthodox Church has several million devout members, and in some parts of Russia the Baptists have a considerable number of adherents. The leaders of the Orthodox Church, at the time of the 1917 revolution, opposed the Soviet government and this resulted in persecution which was extended in some of the satellite states like Poland, to the imprisonment and ill-treatment of the higher clergy of the Roman Catholic Church. During the war of 1941-5 when the armies of Hitler invaded Russia, the Churches supported the government against the invaders and secured greater toleration. As Kalinin wrote in 1950: "Among our men, particularly the older ones, there are religious people who wear crosses and say their prayers, and the younger ones make fun of them. It should be remembered that we do not persecute anybody for his religion. We consider it a delusion and fight it by educational means".[2]

Even now, as Nigel Grant records: "Freedom of pro-religious propaganda is not mentioned, and though religious observances take place quite freely, at least in the major cities, there are still many indirect pressures, and adherence to any church is likely to be a considerable drawback to the ambitious. From time to time,

---

[1] *I Want to be like Stalin*, p. 41.   [2] *op. cit.*, p. 215.

if church-going appears to be on the increase, anti-religious propaganda is stepped up in the Press and the schools. As far as religious education is concerned, this is completely divorced from the classroom; apart from a few church-run seminaries for the training of priests, education and religion never come together. . . . Religious instruction is therefore not given in the schools at all, and parents who want it must make their own individual arrangements through their own churches in their own time".[1]

SUGGESTIONS FOR FURTHER READING

EXISTENTIALISM AND PERSONALISTS

T. H. Croxall, *Kierkegaard Studies,* Lutterworth Press, 1948.

C. D. Kean, *The Meaning of Existence,* Latimer House Ltd, 1947.

Leslie Paul, *The Meaning of Human Existence,* Faber & Faber, 1949.

Emmanuel Mounier, *Existentialist Philosophies, An Introduction,* second impression, Rockcliff, 1951.

J. B. Coates, *The Crisis of the Human Person: Some Personalist Interpretations,* Longmans, Green & Co., 1949.

Gabriel Marcel, *The Philosophy of Existence,* Harvill Press, second impression, 1949.
The Mystery of Being, Gifford Lectures of 1949-50. Vol. I, *Reflection and Mystery.* Vol. II, *Faith and Reality.* Harvill Press, 1949-50.

H. J. Blackham, *Six Existentialist Thinkers,* Routledge & Kegan Paul, 1961.

Martin Buber, *I and Thou,* trans. R. G. Smith, T. & T. Clark, reprint, 1947.
Between Man and Man, trans. R. G. Smith, Kegan Paul, 1947.

W. R. Niblett, *On Existentialism and Education,* in *British Journal of Educational Studies,* vol. ii, No. 2, 1954.

M. V. C. Jeffreys, *Existentialism* in *Education and the Philosophic Mind,* ed. A. V. Judges, George G. Harrap, 1957.

LOGICAL POSITIVISM

A. J. Ayer, *Language, Truth and Logic,* second edition, tenth impression, Victor Gollancz, Ltd, 1954.

C. E. M. Joad, *A Critique of Logical Positivism,* Victor Gollancz, 1950.

[1] *Soviet Education,* pp. 28-9, Penguin Books, 1964.

W. H. F. Barnes, *The Philosophical Predicament*, A. & C. Black, 1950.

Logical Positivism in *Education and the Philosophic Mind*, ed. A. V. Judges, George G. Harrap, 1957.

G. J. Warnock, *English Philosophy since 1900*, O.U.P., 1958.

SOVIET EDUCATION

Books on education by Soviet authors may be difficult to obtain. The following books by English authors are recommended:

H. B. Acton, *Dialectical Materialism*, in *Education and the Philosophic Mind*, ed. A. V. Judges, George G. Harrap, 1957.

Nigel Grant, *Soviet Education*, Penguin Books, 1964. This is a full and critical account of Soviet education at the present time.

Olaf Stapledon, *Philosophy and Living*, 2 vols. Pelican Books, 1939. This work contains a review of Dialectic Materialism and Logical Positivism.

INDEX

INDEX OF NAMES AND TITLES MENTIONED IN THE TEXT

(Major references are shown by numerals in heavy type)

PRINTED IN GREAT BRITAIN BY UNIVERSITY TUTORIAL PRESS LTD. FOXTON
NEAR CAMBRIDGE